When God Made Hell

WHEN GOD MADE HELL

The British Invasion of Mesopotamia
and the Creation of Iraq
1914–1921

CHARLES TOWNSHEND

faber and faber

First published in 2010
by Faber and Faber Ltd
Bloomsbury House
74–77 Great Russell Street
London WC1B 3DA

Typeset by Donald Sommerville
Printed in England by CPI Mackays, Chatham

A CIP record for this book
is available from the British Library

ISBN 978–0–571–23719–7

10 9 8 7 6 5 4 3 2 1

For Kate, Leo and Max

Contents

Plates

View up the River Tigris from Qurna *courtesy of the Council of the National Army Museum (NAM), London*
British troops enter Baghdad, March 1917
  Mary Evans Picture Library / AISA Media
Turkish infantry launching a counter-attack
  Imperial War Museum (IWM), London, HU 94153
A Gurkha manning a Lewis gun, 1916 *IWM Q 79438*
Colonel Heawood's map of the defences at Kut
Major-General Sir George Gorringe *IWM Q 70423*
Lord Hardinge of Penshurst
Townshend and Halil Pasha after the surrender at Kut *NAM*
'P Boats' on the River Tigris *IWM Q 71329*
The boat bridge across the Euphrates at Nasiriya
  IWM Q 34379
British soldiers buying eggs from Arab women *IWM Q 24588*
General Maude with British and Russian officers
  IWM Q 25732
Men of the King's Own bathing near Basra *IWM HU 94155*
Turkish prisoners from the Battle of Ramadi *IWM Q 24294*
Percy Cox and Gertrude Bell with Ibn Saud and the Sheikh of Kuwait in Basra *Illustrated London News Ltd / Mary Evans Picture Library*
Emir Abdallah and Winston Churchill in Cairo, 1921
  IWM Q 60172

Abbreviations

ADC	Aide-de-Camp
AFC	Australian Flying Corps
AG	Adjutant-General
APO	Assistant Political Officer
APOC	Anglo-Persian Oil Company
AQMG	Assistant Quartermaster-General
BO	British Officer
C-in-C	Commander in Chief [also GOC-in-C]
CC	Civil Commissioner
CGS	Chief of the General Staff
CIGS	Chief of the Imperial General Staff
CRA	Commander Royal Artillery
DAAG	Deputy Assistant Adjutant-General
DAQMG	Deputy Assistant Quartermaster-General
DMI	Director of Military Intelligence
DMO	Director of Military Operations
DMS	Director of Medical Services
GHQ	General Headquarters
GOC	General Officer Commanding
[GOC-in-C	General Officer Commanding-in-Chief]
GSO	General Staff Officer
IEF	Indian Expeditionary Force
IMS	Indian Medical Service
IO	Indian Officer
HLI	Highland Light Infantry
HMG	His Majesty's Government

Abbreviations

LI	Light Infantry
LofC	Line of Communications
MAC	Mesopotamia Administration Committee
MED	Middle East Department
MEF	Mesopotamia Expeditionary Force
MO	Medical Officer
OC	Officer Commanding
OP	Observation Post
PO	Political Officer
QMG	Quartermaster-General
RAF	Royal Air Force
RE	Royal Engineers
RFA	Royal Field Artillery
RFC	Royal Flying Corps
RNAS	Royal Naval Air Service
SNO	Senior Naval Officer
WO	War Office

Author's Note

When I set out to write this book, I was conscious of the pioneering work done by A. J. Barker in his book *The Neglected War*, published by Faber in 1967. That book was strong on military detail, but less so on the political dimensions of the Mesopotamia campaign. I hoped to adjust this balance. In the course of writing, my respect for Colonel Barker's achievement increased, and I hope my debt to his work is clear even where it is not explicitly acknowledged. I am most grateful to a number of very helpful keepers of archives, especially at the Imperial War Museum, the National Army Museum, and the Middle East Centre at St Antony's College, Oxford. The National Archives, despite abandoning their hallowed and globally recognised title of Public Record Office, now provide a wonderfully improved service, fast and accessible, a world away from that in which I started research forty years ago.

My editors at Faber, Neil Belton and Kate Murray-Browne, both ploughed through drafts of the book with admirable tenacity, and produced careful and helpful critiques, as also did Roy Foster. Richard Holmes gave me the benefit of his unparalleled expertise on many occasions. Neil first put the idea of the book to me, and came up with the title. The book itself may, I fear, perhaps not quite match his original vision, but I hope it goes some way towards it.

It has been an odd experience to write a book with a key character bearing the same name as me. I first read Charles Townshend's book many years ago, and once pulled up his personal file from the War Office records – a bulging folio of hard-done-by grumbles. I am not related to him, as far as I know, and I felt no need to defend his reputation, but in working on this book I came to the conclusion that he was in some ways hard done by. I hope that in assessing the many criticisms of him I have not strayed too far from the path of critical detachment.

Maps

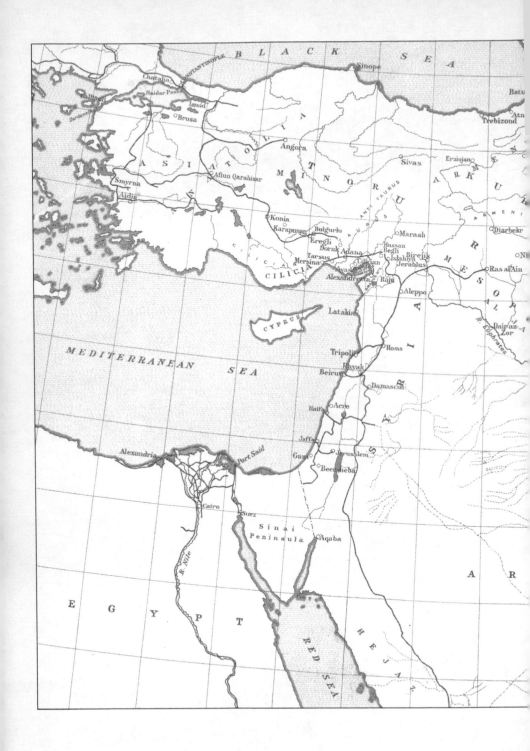

THE MIDDLE EAST.

Scale of Miles.

100   50   0   100   200   300

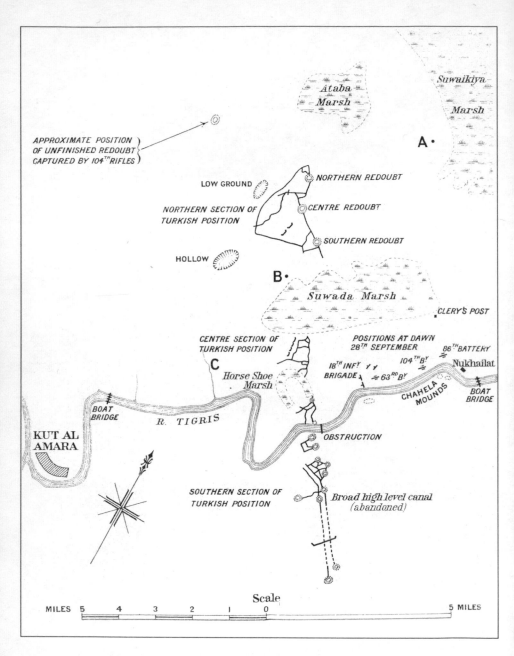

APPROXIMATE POSITION
OF UNFINISHED REDOUBT
CAPTURED BY 104TH RIFLES

*Ataba
Marsh*

*Suwaikiya
Marsh*

A ·

LOW GROUND

NORTHERN REDOUBT

NORTHERN SECTION OF
TURKISH POSITION

CENTRE REDOUBT

SOUTHERN REDOUBT

HOLLOW

B ·

Suwada Marsh

CLERY'S POST

CENTRE SECTION OF
TURKISH POSITION

POSITIONS AT DAWN
28TH SEPTEMBER

86TH BATTERY

C

104TH BY

*Horse Shoe
Marsh*

18TH INFY
BRIGADE

63RD BY

Nukhailat

CHAHELA
MOUNDS

BOAT
BRIDGE

BOAT
BRIDGE

R. TIGRIS

OBSTRUCTION

KUT AL
AMARA

SOUTHERN SECTION OF
TURKISH POSITION

*Broad high level canal
(abandoned)*

Scale

MILES 5   4   3   2   1   0   5 MILES

The Battle of Kut (Sheikh Saad), September 1915

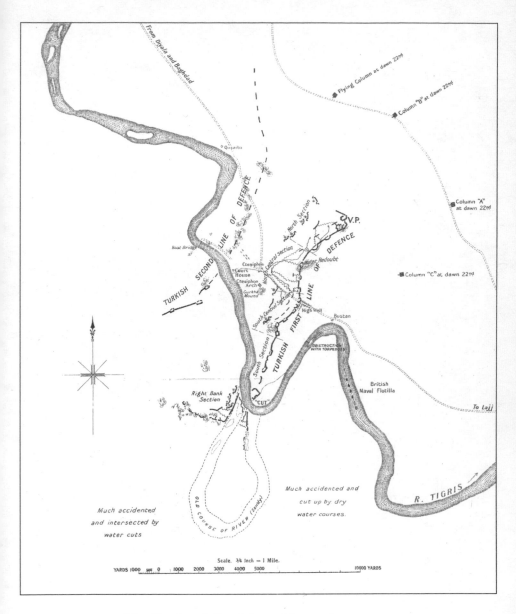

The Battle of Ctesiphon, November 1915

Introduction

Since the Coalition conquest of Iraq in 2003, British people have come to know more about that country than at any time since Iraq became a state after the First World War. How well they understand Britain's role in creating that state is harder to say. But it is no exaggeration to say that modern Iraq was created, deliberately and unilaterally, by the British over the seven years following their first invasion in 1914. Recent history contains few examples of such dramatic and fateful intervention.

Creating a new state was certainly not one of the objectives of the British military expedition which entered the country known in the West as Mesopotamia in 1914. That move began a sequence of unintended consequences. This will not surprise students of history, though it should probably be emphasised for the makers of national policy. Iraq was a 'geographic expression' rather than a political entity – the provinces of Basra and Baghdad. It was a remote and rebellious corner of the Ottoman Empire. The rebelliousness of its Arab people stemmed not from nationalist objection to Turkish rule, but from the resistance of traditional tribal groups to Ottoman government; in part this was Shia resistance to Sunni control. There were few Arab nationalists, and fewer Iraqi nationalists, to point the way to the political future.

The expedition's aims were primarily strategic. The Ottoman Empire was the world's only remaining Muslim state, and if Britain went to war with it – as seemed almost inevitable in September 1914 – a wider Islamic movement, perhaps even a religious war, could spread through Persia and threaten the security of the British Raj in India. The display of British military power was aimed at impressing the Arabs, and supporting Britain's key allies in the Persian Gulf region, the Sheikhs of Kuwait and Mohammerah (now Khorramshahr). Oil was also an issue, but a secondary one in 1914. Britain had part ownership of the Anglo-Persian Oil Company, which had begun to pump oil in 1912. The company's oilfields in southern Persia, and the pipeline to its refinery at Abadan on the Shatt-al-Arab, the border between Persia and the Ottoman empire, were strategically important. But Britain did not use its own military forces to guarantee their security: this was done economically by arrangement with a local potentate, the Sheikh of Mohammerah. The oil in Mesopotamia itself did not loom large in British strategic calculations when the war broke out. But by the time it ended, this was changing. The potential oil resources of Mosul province were beginning to exert an influence on the developing idea of establishing an Arab state in the conquered territory.

An Arab state was a remote prospect in 1914. The Mesopotamia expedition was sent by the British Government of India; and the rulers of India had a low opinion of Arab political capacity. More importantly, they had no wish to see an Arab state emerge in an area of British paramountcy. Some actually foresaw the transformation of Mesopotamia into an Indian colony, where the colonists might outnumber the natives ten to one. The people responsible for administering the territory occupied by the expeditionary force pursued a policy that diverged from the British government's policy. During the war, a new world order emerged based on the principle of national self-determination. By 1918 Britain was committed to this principle, but the men who governed Iraq in its name believed that self-determination was a sham.

It was the local administrators who made sure that the three former provinces of Basra, Baghdad and Mosul should be turned into a single political entity. The British government, from the moment of the invasion onwards, found itself adjusting to the effects of actions it had not expected, or even wanted. The result was an extraordinary transformation of Britain's traditional stance in the Middle East.

Before the outbreak of the war in 1914, Britain had been one of the most cautious of imperial powers. Given the vast global scale of its empire, on which, famously, 'the sun never set', this may seem surprising. But though British power stretched far and wide, it was exerted at comparatively trivial financial cost. The key instruments of global power – armies and navies – were, of course, not cheap. Though the Army was kept as small as possible for a great power – far too small in the view of many – the Navy was becoming ruinously expensive. Yet while the naval building race against Germany had global significance, it was essentially part of a European power struggle which had to be won at almost any cost. Overseas territories, by contrast, were maintained on a minimalist principle: they should pay their own way and not be a burden on the British taxpayer. This meant that power was habitually exercised indirectly, and Britain was often content with mere 'influence', as long as it had more than its competitors. In the Middle East, especially, this principle shaped its policy.

At the end of the war, though, something strange happened. Suddenly abandoning its traditional caution, Britain grasped at an imperial expansion on a dizzying scale. The surge of British imperialism in the Middle East was, as one leading historian has observed, just as astonishing and unpredictable as the earlier sudden acquisition of the Indian and African empires in the eighteenth and nineteenth centuries. For generations, Britain had been vitally concerned to secure the route to India, around the Suez Canal and in the Persian Gulf, but it had not dared to accept more than a limited liability. Now it committed itself to dominating the whole region between Suez and India. This was not only a big area, it presented exceptionally difficult problems to any power aiming to control it. 'The middle east was no remote protectorate to be governed on a shoestring and garrisoned with a corporal's guard of local levies.'[1] The kind of commitments Britain entered into were shockingly expensive; yet they were taken on at the end of a world war that had eviscerated Britain's financial power.

The conquest of Mesopotamia and the creation of Iraq represented the central act in this dramatic bid for supremacy. The aims of the expeditionary force expanded as it went. By seizing Basra, it secured the oilfields against any likely threat. But impressing the Arabs seemed to call for continuous demonstrations of military strength. Within a year the British were lunging at Baghdad, and by the end of the war they were envisaging a vast Middle-Eastern zone of power exercised through Arab puppet states. This was 'mission creep' on a grand scale. It unfolded in an exceptionally hostile environment, and passed by way of one of Britain's worst military disasters to a military success which itself raised searching questions about Britain's global power. This book tries to explain why.

I: BASRA

1. Into Mesopotamia

Things are going on very bad here.
WILLIAM BIRD

On 16 October 1914, a British convoy sailed from Bombay, heading for Egypt. The Great War between the Western Allies and the Central Powers was nearly three months old, and troops of the Indian Army were making the long journey, via the Suez Canal, to join Britain's battle against the German invasion of France. At this point, although Japan had attacked the German colony of Tsingtao (modern Qingdao), and small colonial armies were skirmishing in Africa, the war was still essentially a European clash. After the dramatic moves of August and September, it was heading towards stalemate. Russia's invasion of Germany had been brought to a halt, as had Germany's invasion of France. Austria-Hungary's attempt to crush Serbia – the original cause of the war – had stalled. The Ottoman Empire, the bridge between Europe and Asia, was hovering on the brink of taking the German side. But for now it was still at peace with Britain, the power which for over a century had defended it against Russia's ambition to seize the Ottoman capital, Constantinople, and the straits that linked the Black Sea to the Mediterranean.

Once the convoy was out of Bombay, there was an unexpected development. Four of its ships contained the 16th Indian Brigade, belonging to the 6th (Poona) Division of the Indian Army, and ostensibly part of Indian Expeditionary Force A, on its way to the trenches in Flanders. As they steamed slowly across the Indian Ocean, the brigade commander, Brigadier-General Walter Delamain, opened sealed orders he had been handed on embarkation. His brigade was to divert into the Persian Gulf, becoming part of a new expeditionary force, whose mission was to protect British interests at the head of the Gulf. He was instructed that, if war broke out with Turkey, the rest of the division would join him as quickly as possible; until then he should avoid hostilities with the Turks and 'friction with the Arabs', but prepare not only to support Britain's ally in Persia, the Sheikh of Mohammerah – who guaranteed the security of the Anglo-Persian Oil Company's oilfields, pipeline, and refinery on Abadan Island – but also to occupy Basra: in other words to invade 'Turkish Mesopotamia'.[1] Britain's global policy was on the brink of a dramatic shift.

On 23 October, under the protective guns of the battleship *Ocean*, Delamain's force of 5,000 men arrived at Bahrain. This, he was informed by Sir Percy Cox, the British political representative in the Gulf, was 'a quasi British protectorate' (a deft way of describing a long and complicated relationship). It was also very hot. With no hint of a breeze, and drinking water soon running short, the troops were told they could not disembark. For day after day they, and still more their 1,200 animals – cavalry and artillery horses, and pack mules – sweltered in their iron hulls. 'Things are going on very bad here,' Private William Bird of the Dorset Regiment wrote in his pocket diary on the 26th, 'the food is disgracefull – we are packed together like sardines.' His brigadier reported that 'our meat in hand will be finished on the 30th'; supplies of fuel on shore would last seven days. 'No more cattle and no further wood procurable.'[2]

The brigade was trapped in its ships because Bahrain, although a 'quasi protectorate', where Britain had been patiently nurturing its influence for the last century, did not react well to the arrival of a British army. While the local people were used to British warships, which cruised the Persian Gulf in search of the pirates infesting the Arabian coast, troop transports were a different matter. Soon after they arrived, several deputations urged their sheikh to forbid the troops to land. The women seemed especially alarmed, and though the ladies of the American Mission did their best to calm them, as the days passed 'the uneasiness of the people and their objection to the presence of the troops increased to a very considerable extent'. So much so that the British consul at Bahrain, Captain Keyes, also began to feel 'some uneasiness'. The large Persian community there was strongly pro-German, and there was a general suspicion that Britain intended to occupy the islands permanently.[3]

Three days later, Private Bird, living on tinned pineapple and German mixed biscuits (confiscated from the warehouse of the Hamburg merchants Wonckhaus), was 'beginning to wonder why we came this route'. After a week, some relief came in the form of boat drill to prepare for eventual landing – carefully avoiding the shore itself. For some it was comic relief: Pathans from the trans-frontier region and Sikh farmers were 'not usually adepts at aquatic sports', and many had never seen an oar. 'The oars had a way of taking command', and at least one man had a close encounter with a shark after being knocked out of his boat.[4] But at last something happened. At the end of October shots were exchanged between Ottoman and Russian ships in the Black Sea – a staged 'provocation' signalling that Turkey intended to enter the war. Delamain's force was ordered to move 300 miles northwards to the Shatt-al-Arab, at the head of the Gulf. Bird was elated: 'Now understand everything,' he wrote next day. 'Just told war is declared on Turkey & we are going to Turkistan to fight them. All excitement & cheers galore.' For him as for most soldiers, the dangers of combat were better than the boredom of idleness – especially on ships. ('What's the use of lectures?' he had asked his diary: 'Roll on the real thing.')

Bird's information was slightly premature. War was actually declared on 5 November, and Delamain put 500 men ashore at Fao, at the mouth of the Shatt-al-Arab, next day. A short bombardment by the 4-inch guns of their escorting sloop HMS *Odin* silenced the artillery in the old Turkish fort, and its defenders hastily abandoned it – luckily, since the carefully rehearsed landing operations did not work out well. The tide turned just as the landing began, 'the boats swung around at anchor, the men lost what little skill they had'. Some boats landed, some were carried out to sea, some driven on to the Persian shore. The rest of the brigade reached Abadan next day, and on the 8th it finally disembarked on enemy soil. Now Bird not only shared the Dorsets' eagerly anticipated 'baptism of fire', but he also had a glimpse of a different side of war. When a captured enemy scout refused to give any information, the interrogating officer 'called up three men & made pretend that they would shoot him'. Bird seems to have found this an eminently sensible proceeding: 'he soon came round.'[5]

Bird was not, in fact, in Turkistan, as he quickly discovered: he was in Mesopotamia. This Greek name, the land 'between two rivers' – Tigris and Euphrates – resonated deeply with all literate Europeans. And the Greek framed their take on it. It was the land of ancient history, the cradle of civilisation, the site of Ur and Babylon, the place where Alexander the Great died. Later religious myth located in it the Garden of Eden, and Noah's flood. In 1914 few Westerners would know the Arabic name for the area, al-Iraq (the *iraq* being the long ridge in the desert that separated it from Syria). Since the Mongol conquest it had become a byword for decay and ruin. In ancient times it had supported the densest population on earth, and some thought it should still be able to support thirty million people.[6] But it was now seriously underpopulated, with barely two million inhabitants. (The exact number could only be guessed, since the Ottomans did not attempt a census outside their Anatolian heartland.) The majority were Arabs, but there were big communities of Kurds, Christians and Jews in the north – in Baghdad itself, one of the world's biggest urban Jewish communities, these minorities outnumbered Arabs. It had no political or even administrative unity; the Ottoman government had actually separated the three *vilayets* (provincial governorships) of Baghdad, Basra and Mosul in the mid-nineteenth century. Baghdad's pre-eminence remained indisputable. But even this fabled city was remote to the Turks themselves, who had a proverb: 'a rumour will come back even from Baghdad'. For Ottoman bureaucrats, a posting to Basra or Baghdad was a dreaded form of exile. Outside those cities, governmental power was constantly disputed by turbulent tribal groups.

Like the rest of 'Turkish Arabia', as the British called the Arab lands of the Ottoman Empire, Mesopotamia was lamented as a sad shadow of the land of plenty that had once been the Fertile Crescent, arching from the Levant to the rivers Tigris and Euphrates. Its legendary fertility, due to once-magnificent irrigation systems, had died when they were destroyed by the Mongol ruler Hulagu in the fourteenth century. Disorder, depopulation, and the 'silting and scouring of the rivers once let loose', made restoration of control 'the remote, perhaps hopeless problem today still unsolved', as Stephen Longrigg wrote in the 1920s. The land was now alternately a desert and a swamp, a vast flat plain lying below the level of the great rivers, and regularly inundated as the embankments that contained them were ruptured by the spring floods of meltwater from the northern mountains. Between the awesome mountains of Kurdistan in the north, and the Gulf coast in the south, the plain hardly varied a hundred feet in height. When it flooded, swamps formed in low-lying areas far from the river, and could move around visibly in high winds. In the heat of summer, the friable soil turned from mud to dust, and could be so hard that even the detonation of artillery shells hardly scratched it. From May to September, the average daytime temperatures in Baghdad ranged from 110 to 120 degrees Fahrenheit. Paralysing humidity was accompanied by sandstorms and locust plagues, with flies in stupendous numbers. Cholera was endemic, and typhus often broke out, along with less deadly but debilitating conditions like 'sandfly fever'. It had become, in Western eyes, one of the most repellent parts of the whole world – a quintessential 'white man's graveyard'.

Robert Byron, crossing the land twenty years later on his 'Road to Oxiana', evoked its character pungently: 'Mesopotamia has remained a land of mud deprived of mud's only possible advantage, vegetable fertility. It is a mud plain, so flat that a single heron, reposing on one leg beside some rare trickle of water in a ditch, looks as tall as a wireless aerial. From this plain rise villages of mud and cities of mud. The rivers flow with liquid mud. The air is composed of mud refined into a gas. The people are mud-coloured; they wear mud-coloured clothes, and their national hat is nothing more than a formalised mud-pie. Baghdad ... lurks in a mud fog, and when the temperature drops below 110, the people complain of the chill and get out their furs.' Byron could afford wry humour, but the heat and the mud – which Napoleon once called the 'fifth element' – would create a grim and deadly environment for the military campaign which followed the landing at Fao.

Mesopotamia's communications were legendarily primitive. When the junior diplomat Reader Bullard, then acting consul at Trebizond, took up the acting consulship at Basra in the spring of 1914, he was attracted by 'not only the post itself, but the journey'. To get from the north to the south of the Ottoman Empire involved a two-week horseback ride to Diyarbakr, a six-day journey from there to Mosul and then on to Baghdad by raft, and then a three-day trip to Basra by river steamer. It was the raft journey that spoke most eloquently of Ottoman communications. The *kelek* transported Westerners, almost literally, back to a pre-biblical world. Another traveller described it in detail. 'Two hundred inflated goatskins arranged in the form ten by twenty, are bound to a few thin transverse poplar trunks above them. Over these again seven or eight more tree-trunks not more than 7 inches thick, are placed crosswise, and upon these, to form a deck, is placed a layer of bales. Between two pairs of these bales a basket-work affair is fixed, which, with a stake, forms a rough thole-pin.' The craft was steered by 'a pair of enormous sweeps' swinging on these, turning it into the right currents and away from rocks in mid-stream. On the upper Tigris, the *kelek*s with their shallow draft (only three inches) were vulnerable to side-currents 'sweeping round the rocky banks at the velocity of a galloping horse', and to wind, often 'too much for oars to fight against'.[7] On arrival at Mosul the raft was dismantled, the poles sold and the deflated skins taken back to the starting point by donkey-back. Travelling in April involved a good deal of rain, but because the river was running high – from the melting snows in the mountains, not from the rain – the passage was quicker and 'there would be no bursting of skins against rocks in the river bed'. Bullard found it 'a pleasant way to travel. The raft turned round slowly so that one saw the whole landscape without having to move. Catering was easy. I carried yogurt in a calico bag: it got quite dry but revived when mixed with water; and I had a roll of apricot paste, which looked like linoleum but tasted very good. Flapjack, walnuts, and, when we tied up for the night, eggs and an occasional chicken, made up an excellent diet.' South of Mosul, though 'the nights were exquisite, the days were getting hot, and the last two, when hundreds of locusts settled on the raft, were not comfortable'.[8]

Hubert Young of the Mahratta Horse, who would later become Bullard's deputy, made the same journey with similar sensations. 'Never was there a more idyllic way of travelling'. Diyarbakr to Mosul took him nine days, as the river was low. 'Furious rapids were succeeded by long, still reaches of beautifully clear water, down which the raft moved so slowly that I could easily swim to the shore, run along the warm sand, and swim out to meet it again before the rapids came once more . . . Every now and then we tied up at some village, where I bought supplies while the raft-men mended and blew up any goatskin that had given way. This happened many times in the shallow reaches, where skins scraped along the bottom with an indescribable rustling and whispering.' Young found that the British flag he took with him was surprisingly effective in scaring off the bands of armed men who occasionally 'ran alongside and threatened to shoot us'. Some fifty miles below Mosul, on his second raft, he ran into the oily discharge from the bitumen springs of Qaiyara – traces of the oil that would later be commercially exploited, but for now presenting merely an extraordinarily beautiful vision. 'The entire river was coated with an iridescent film which looked like a contoured map on which the highest peaks were jet black and the lower levels were shown by concentric rings of every colour of the rainbow.'[9]

As he finally approached Baghdad, the ever-slowing current and the extravagantly expansive meanderings of the river reduced his speed to the point at which, realising he was likely to be late, Young found it quicker to go ashore and walk. This laborious journey, romantic as it might be to the tourist, told its own story about Mesopotamia's remoteness and backwardness. Bullard and Young's route would now become the supply line for the Ottoman Sixth Army, the garrison which would have to try to repel the British invasion. But why were the British – and more precisely, the Indians – there?

2. 'An unexpected stroke'

The political effect in the Persian Gulf and in India of leaving the head of the Gulf derelict will be disastrous.

SIR ARTHUR HIRTZEL

We must give the signal *before* war breaks out and the best way of doing so is to send a force from India to the Shatt-al-Arab *at once*.

SIR EDMUND BARROW

The invasion of Mesopotamia was a dramatic reversal of traditional British policy towards the Ottoman state. The slow decline of Turkish power over the last two hundred years had become one of the great international issues of its time – the 'Eastern Question'. If Turkey collapsed, how should it be divided up? Swathes of its territory in south-eastern Europe were already being gobbled up by fierce new Balkan states – Greece, Serbia, Bulgaria. Two destructive Balkan wars in 1912 and 1913 had reduced the Ottoman lands, which once reached as far as Hungary, to a small strip around Istanbul (still known to the world as Constantinople). But Britain had set itself to stop Russia gaining access to the Mediterranean via the Straits: in the words of Jingoism's defining anthem, 'the Russians shall not have Constantinople'. So British policy had been to uphold the territorial integrity of the Ottoman Empire, intervening not only to choke off Russian ambitions (as in the Crimean War), but also to neutralise internal threats such as that posed by overmighty governors like Muhammad Ali of Egypt.

Since any conceivable post-Ottoman structure seemed likely to be worse for Britain than the status quo, Britain opposed 'partition', while trying to maximise British political and commercial influence in Turkey. Even this was problematic. A case in point was the river transport business on the Tigris, where a British firm played a major role. Surveying the situation in 1904, the War Office lamented that 'between Basra and Baghdad the arbitrary restrictions of the Turkish Government reduce traffic to a minimum. The English firm of Lynch Brothers are allowed to employ only two steamers at a time, a third being kept laid up at Basra in case of accidents. These steamers draw 4 feet of water, and are not allowed to ascend above Baghdad.'[1] Noting, too, that the current steaming time from Basra to Baghdad was between 78 and 100 hours up – against the current – and around 47 hours back, it observed that 'owing to neglect of dredging operations, the navigation is becoming increasingly difficult'.

So Mesopotamia had been militarily off limits for the British. This hands-off policy had recently survived the temptation to intervene in a spate of tribal rebellions in 'Turkish Arabia' in 1910. The Viceroy of India, Lord Hardinge of Penshurst, a former top Foreign Office official, believed that 'the Turks are in a tight place in Mesopotamia and unable to assert their authority', and wanted to 'show the Turks we mean business' by sending a strong force to the head of the Gulf. Contingency plans were prepared for a Mesopotamian expedition. But these showed that such action would require more naval support than was likely to be available, and also carried the prophetic warning that a local operation might escalate into a major campaign.[2] The Director of Military Operations at the War Office tartly minuted that 'if we wanted to fight Turkey, we should not do so up the valley of the Euphrates'. When Hubert Young made his journey via Mosul and Baghdad to Basra in 1913, he was firmly told that military intelligence needed 'no special information' about the area he would pass through; and Captain William Shakespear, the political agent at Kuwait, had great difficulty in getting official permission to make his epic crossing of Arabia via Riyadh to Suez early in 1914.[3]

But if Britain had steered clear of Mesopotamia, it had always been acutely interested in Persia and the Persian Gulf, the shallow waterway (no more than 50 fathoms deep) running 500 miles from the Strait of Hormuz to the Shatt-al-Arab, where the 'two rivers' meet. Long before oil was discovered, strategic conflict along the distant borders of the Indian Empire – the 'Great Game' – led Britain and Russia to divide Persia into rival 'spheres of influence'. The British sphere in the south did not include the future oil-fields. British concerns were with freedom of navigation in the Gulf, menaced by piracy. The 'Residency' at Bushire (Bushehr), occupied by Percy Cox for a decade before 1914, was the centre of elaborate British arrangements aimed at crushing piracy; a series of military 'truces' with the so-called 'Trucial States' such as Oman, Bahrain and Kuwait established a 'Pax Britannica' backed by a naval presence. This presence was limited – a handful of gunboats – but Britain was deadly serious about its 'paramountcy' in the area, insisting that no rivals interfered with its cultivation of allies amongst the tribal leaders of Turkish Arabia. In 1903 the Foreign Secretary, Lord Lansdowne, warned that Britain would 'regard the establishment of a naval base or fortified post in the Persian Gulf by any other Power as a very grave menace to British interests, and we should certainly resist it by all the means at our disposal'.

Casting its gaze back over a century of Gulf history in 1922, a Cabinet committee pithily expressed Britain's sense of proprietorship. 'It is due entirely to our efforts that this important maritime highway has been kept open for the commerce of the world. We have policed the waters; built lighthouses; laid down buoys; suppressed piracy; put an end to the slave trade; and controlled the traffic in arms. We have compelled the restless Arab chieftains on the shores of the Gulf to maintain a maritime peace. We have been in treaty relations with them for many years past.' Maintaining predominance here was 'an axiom of British Indian policy'. The 'obvious corollary' was that 'the head of the Persian Gulf must be preserved from influences potentially hostile to Great Britain'.[4]

For a hundred years before 1914, the stakes had been steadily raised in Eastern Arabia. Control of the Gulf was not, for

Britain – at least until oil became a major concern – primarily a commercial issue. Rather commerce was a means of securing influence over the Arabs. Britain believed that Arab resentment of corrupt, incompetent Ottoman Turkish rule would eventually turn into open conflict. Its two key allies at the head of the Gulf, the Sheikhs of Kuwait and of Mohammerah, positioned Britain to benefit from an eventual showdown between Arabs and Turks. In 1914 Britain was also cultivating the leader of the Wahhabi movement, Abdul Aziz ibn Saud, Amir of Najd and future founder of Saudi Arabia, who was fighting a long-drawn-out struggle against the pro-Turkish Amir of Hail for control of central Arabia. But the British had no wish to provoke an Arab–Turkish conflict. Experience of tribal revolts had shown that they could damage British as well as Turkish interests. The possible fall-out in terms of wider Muslim reactions, above all in the subcontinent, was seriously alarming. ('The effect on our own Mussulmans [sic] in India would be disastrous.') As late as May 1914 the Foreign Office reasserted the cardinal need 'to prevent, or at least postpone, anything which might lead to a general Arab outbreak, and so endanger the integrity of the Turkish dominions in Asia'.[5] Sir Edward Grey, the Foreign Secretary, had noted that 'amongst other things, it would give great offence to Moslem opinion in British territory if we took part in a policy of destroying the Turkish government and dividing its territory'.[6]

Britain did not shake off its fear of a Muslim jihad, but its established policy of propping up the Ottomans was weakening by 1914. An increasingly influential group of political intelligence officers sent by the Government of India to the Gulf area was strongly pro-Arab, and correspondingly anti-Turk. Experts like Arnold Talbot Wilson and Gertrude Bell had become convinced that removal of Turkish power – capricious, incompetent and violent – from the Arab lands would be a humanitarian blessing. The most prominent of these was Captain William Shakespear, the consul at Kuwait. Shakespear pressed enthusiastically for a British alliance with his friend, Ibn Saud, head of the fundamentalist

Wahhabi movement, and an increasingly formidable opponent of Turkish power.[7]

The Arabists' moral take on the future was bolstered by a growing worry, by now amounting to obsession, with the threat posed by Germany to Britain's paramountcy. Not the least of Turkey's faults, in the British view, was its decision to turn to Germany for advice on modernising its army in the 1880s, and to lean closer to Germany as time went on. The Ottoman government's effort to exert more effective control of 'Turkish Arabia' from Baghdad was seen as paving the way for a *Drang nach Osten*, a drive to the east in which Germany's commercial muscle might threaten to overpower Britain's. The iconic project at the heart of this was the Berlin to Baghdad railway, and Britain watched the painfully slow process of building this line with mounting alarm. In reality, the Ottoman state's railway system was seriously underdeveloped – barely more than 3,500 miles of track for an area of 680,000 square miles in 1914 – and the line to Baghdad was vital for any real economic development of the 'empire'. But although 580 miles had been laid, there were still three gaps in which movement was as slow as it had been since biblical times. Two of them were in the mountains of Cilicia, and the third was the long stretch from Ras-el-Ain through Mosul to Samarra.

Growing German–Turkish intimacy had a critical impact in 1914. In the weeks after the outbreak of the war in Europe, British strategic priorities became clearer. Oil was certainly an issue. The first military action taken at the head of the Gulf, in mid-September, was the despatch of the sloops HMS *Odin*, *Espiègle* and *Lawrence* to cruise the Shatt-al-Arab between Abadan and Mohammerah. The *Odin* arrived at Mohammerah on the 16th. Though the little warship could hardly hope to protect the oil pipeline and installations alone, its power was magnified in a region where the Ottoman Navy had just a single gunboat and a handful of Thornycroft launches. This was a classic piece of 'gunboat diplomacy', showing Britain's determination to assert its position in the Gulf, and support its ally Sheikh Kaza'al of Mohammerah. It was Kaza'al's military strength (he was thought able to raise an army of 20,000) that could provide the muscle to secure the oil.[8] But it was significant that only the Admiralty was ready to take any direct action, and even it was less concerned about oil than about the threat of German warships operating from Basra, menacing the vital Indian Ocean route to Suez.

The *Odin* was vindicating an 'international' custom – established by Britain over many years against dogged Ottoman resistance – as it steamed up the Persian side of the Shatt-al-Arab to Mohammerah, where the Karun river flowed into the Shatt. Arguing that territorial waters extended only three miles from the coast, Britain had induced the Ottomans to accept that British ships could do this at will, without securing official permission. This right had recently been recognised in the 1913 Anglo-Turkish conventions, and part of the flotilla's mission was to reassert the British legal position, which Percy Cox worried was 'a weak one'. But this time the Turks rebelled against it. The Resident at Bushire reported that '<u>Vali</u> [governor] of Basra has raised formal protest against *Odin* entering Turkish waters without giving formal notification of leaving within twenty-four hours and without having W/T [wireless] sealed.'[9] The Ottomans, who had been flourishing their lone gunboat, the *Marmariss*, around Basra since August, declared the whole of the Shatt and the sea to six miles from their frontier to be territorial waters closed to warships. 'Guns at Fao will fire on any man-of-war disregarding prohibition.'[10] Britain replied by insisting that its flotilla would remain in the Shatt until the Ottoman government fulfilled its neutral obligation to intern the crews of the German battle squadron (the battle-cruiser *Goeben* and the cruiser *Breslau*) that had run into Constantinople at the start of the war in August 1914. The Turks in turn announced that they would mine the Shatt. The Foreign Secretary said Britain would be 'forced to regard any attempt to lay mines in the river as an act of open hostility'.[11] When the *Odin* was withdrawn, it was only to be replaced (on 29 September) by the *Espiègle*. With Ottoman troop movements also becoming more demonstrative, war looked more and more likely.

But who was provoking whom? The British official view was simple. Even before war broke out, the Foreign Office was preparing its 'blue book' listing Ottoman provocations (amongst which the affair of the German warships figured prominently). This charge sheet has convinced some historians of Turkish guilt.[12] From the Ottoman viewpoint, though, the British stance looked just as aggressive. The British decision to commandeer two battleships (the *Sultan Osman* and the *Reshadieh*) under construction for the Ottoman Navy in British shipyards, which had been paid for by a public subscription, may have been inevitable in the circumstances. But the way it was handled was revealing. Britain knew how provocative the seizure would be. As Winston Churchill, the First Lord of the Admiralty, wrote to Enver Pasha on 19 August, 'I knew the patriotism with which the money had been raised all over Turkey.' (Women had sold their hair to subscribe.) He proposed a complicated scheme of compensation, which the Turks rejected. Some say the Turks were not really interested in compensation, and argue that the British had 'unwittingly called the Ottoman bluff'. But this hardly fits with Churchill's brutal remark (over a week before his letter to Enver) that there was 'no hurry' to recompense the Turks. 'They may join the Germans, in which case we shall save our money. Negotiate and temporise.'[13] His 19 August letter was 'temporising' of the most calculated sort.

By this time, British officialdom was mentally girding itself for war with Turkey. The war in Europe was taking the unexpected form that was to become so grimly familiar over the following years. At the end of August, the German Army had crushed the advancing Russians in the battle of Tannenberg, but in France its commanders had lost their nerve at the knife-edge battle of the Marne and fallen back. Yet any hope of Anglo-French victory was soon buried on the River Aisne, where the retreating

Germans halted and dug in. The trench warfare that would create the 'Western Front' had begun, and by the end of September the fighting line had extended all the way to the Channel coast. Months and years of attritional battle would follow.

General Sir Edmund Barrow, the Military Secretary at the India Office, and his minister, Lord Crewe, were sure 'from the very outbreak of the war that Turkey sooner or later would be involved'. In that case, Barrow wrote, 'the great danger of pan-Islamic combination against us in India would become both imminent and vital'. This ominous argument would echo throughout the war. The Army had long worried that the Ottoman Sultan's role as Caliph of Islam might give 'a religious character' to wars between him and Christian powers. This invoked deep-seated Western fears of the possible upsurge of Muslim fanaticism, jihad, which could prove disastrous for British power. Some years before the war, the military authorities had warned that 'hostility to the head of the Mahomedan religion cannot fail to have very far-reaching military consequences for an empire which contains so many of the Sultan's co-religionists'. Even success in such a war might be risky, while failure 'would be followed by a general uprising against British authority throughout the East'.[14]

When Winston Churchill proposed to send a flotilla of destroyers up through the Dardanelles to torpedo the German ships (and encourage the neutral Balkan states to join the Allies), he raised a chorus of alarm in Egypt as well as India. The Prime Minister thought that Turkey 'ought to be compelled to strike the first blow'. At the same time, official attitudes were hardening. At the Foreign Office, Sir Eyre Crowe had decided (two days before Churchill wrote to Enver) that 'the Turks are, and have been, playing with us'. A week later he fumed that 'our representations on the subject of British grievances are treated by the Turkish Govt. with undisguised contempt', and another week on he had abandoned belief in 'the prospect of Turkey remaining neutral'. So Britain should begin 'precautionary measures'; and at this point Mesopotamia began to come into the frame. At the end of August the Admiralty, in the shape of Admiral Slade, former commander of the East Indies station, started nagging General Barrow about the area's strategic importance, the need to protect the Anglo-Persian Oil Company oilfields and refineries, and the advantage of encouraging friendly Arabs. Slade was himself a director of the APOC.

The India Office agreed that 'leaving the head of the Gulf derelict' would have a disastrous effect not just in that area, but in India as well. Arthur Hirtzel, the Political Secretary at the India Office, thought that Britain could not afford to wait while the main issues were being settled elsewhere, and in particular 'we cannot begin by sacrificing the Sheikh of Kuwait'. Sheikh Mubarak was Britain's firmest ally in the Gulf, a venerable potentate with genuine pro-British sentiments. (Sheikh Kaza'al of Mohammerah, by contrast, was judged by Cox to be 'more of a politician', if equally sound and statesmanlike as an ally.) Barrow took up Hirtzel's line with alacrity. Warning that if the two sheikhs were attacked or 'seduced', 'all our prestige and our labours of years will vanish in air', he suggested that Indian Expeditionary Force B – slated to be sent to East Africa – should immediately occupy Abadan and Mohammerah. At first the Secretary of State was 'obdurate' against the idea, but Barrow kept up the pressure as a series of reports of Turko-German preparations came in. These reports were mere unsubstantiated rumours, but their message was instinctively believed. On 24 September even the reluctant Crewe accepted (on the basis of further unsubstantiated reports from agents in Baghdad and Basra) that the Turks were 'now trying to win over the Arabs to a Jehad against us'. He suggested that Barrow 'talk it over with Shakespear – the Arab explorer'. This was the opening Barrow needed. The ground was prepared for the dramatic proposal he presented to Crewe two days later, shortly before the *Espiègle* arrived at Abadan.

Barrow, a former divisional commander in India (who had been passed over for the chief command there – some said because his wife was indiscreet), did more than any other individual to launch the Mesopotamia campaign.[15] His policy paper, 'the Role of India in a Turkish War', started from the arresting assertion that 'all the omens point to war with Turkey within a few weeks or even days', and weighed its implications. It would not necessarily worry India, he said – unless the Turks succeeded in getting the Arabs on their side. That would open up India's nightmare scenario: the Turks would 'proclaim a Jehad and endeavour to raise Afghanistan and the Frontier tribes against us'. So the aim must be above all to 'avert a Turko-Arab coalition'. Barrow noted that 'Turkey has been intriguing right and left to win over the Arabs', and if it were true that, as had been reported, 'even Bin Saood [ibn Saud], the leading Arab chief, has been induced to join the Turks, we may expect serious trouble both in Mesopotamia and in Egypt'.

Barrow actually doubted this particular report – according to Major Shakespear, Ibn Saud's hatred of the Turks was 'too pronounced to admit of an easy surrender to their blandishments'. Shakespear, one of the select band of British political agents who had explored Arabia in the years before the war, had become a close friend of the Amir. He was 'convinced that we have only to give him some sure sign of our intention to support him and the Arabs generally against the Turks'. But how could Britain give such a sign, and when? Barrow thought 'we must give the signal <u>before</u> war breaks out', and the best way to do it was 'to send a force from India to the Shatt-el-Arab <u>at once</u>'. Since troops and ships were already prepared in Bombay, this could be done 'without arousing any suspicion'. The expedition could arrive at the mouth of the Shatt-al-Arab 'without a soul knowing anything about its despatch for this purpose'. This 'unexpected stroke' would have a 'startling effect'. Quite a small force – a single infantry brigade bolstered by two mountain artillery batteries and two sapper companies – would be enough, at least until war broke out. (Then it would have to be reinforced, because it would be 'necessary to occupy Basra at once'.) It could land either on Persian territory at Mohammerah, or on Abadan island – 'ostensibly to protect the oil installations, but in reality to notify to the Turks that we meant business and to the Arabs that we were ready to support them'.[16] Britain's priorities were clear.

Barrow did not just send his paper up to the Secretary of State, Lord Crewe; he took the idea over to Maurice Hankey at the Committee of Imperial Defence, where it was immediately approved.[17] Crewe telegraphed to the Viceroy of India, Lord Hardinge, that because 'the situation as regards Turkey is most menacing, it may be necessary to demonstrate at the head of the Persian Gulf'. Assuming the Cabinet accepted this, a brigade should be shipped at once 'as if they were urgently required for Egypt, but with sealed orders to proceed to the Shatt-al-Arab'. The Cabinet hesitated for a couple of days when the situation seemed to be improving, but then agreed. The die was cast.

The only resistance to Barrow's 'startling effect' came from the Viceroy himself, and it signalled a difference of view between Britain and India that would soon become wider. Hardinge was still worried that worsening relations with Turkey would upset wider Muslim opinion. Turkish violations of neutrality, as with the German battle squadron, were 'too technical to be understood by the Mahomedan masses', but the presence of British ships and the landing of British troops in Turkish waters were facts whose 'provocative character' would be very obvious to them. He accepted that if it was really vital to protect the oil works, then nothing short of an occupation of Abadan would do. But he not only pooh-poohed the likelihood of an attack on them, he even doubted whether they were valuable enough to 'outweigh consequences of an apparent attack by us on Turkey'. If, on the other hand, the real aim was 'to demonstrate at the head of the Gulf', there were less provocative and equally effective places – such as Bahrain – to do this.[18]

Charles Hardinge was a career diplomat of vast experience – he had come to the viceroyalty from four years at the top of the Foreign Office, as Permanent Undersecretary. Though he had backed intervention in Arabia in 1911, he was against military action in Mesopotamia. He had sharply disagreed with Sir Douglas Haig over this, when Haig as Chief of the Indian General Staff in 1911 called for the creation of a suitably equipped expeditionary force in case of war against Turkey. Hardinge thought that such a force could not be afforded, and in any case his confidence in the Indian Army's effectiveness was limited: it had too many 'opera-bouffe' soldiers like the sentry he once saw outside Government House in Calcutta, who had taken his shoes off and left his rifle leaning against the gate before sitting down to smoke a cigarette.[19]

London made light of Hardinge's objections. Hirtzel insisted that, since the Sheikh of Mohammerah – who was responsible for 'policing' the oil pipeline – could not protect it against attack by Turkey, 'public opinion should surely recognise our right to protect our own property'. Even if the pipeline was destroyed, the worst effect would be not so much the loss of oil as 'the loss of prestige with the Arabs'. His minister, Lord Crewe, feared that the Arabs would be 'agitated by reports that Turks will spread of our retirement at their dictation from the Shatt-al-Arab'. They must be reassured. Once again, though, the Viceroy argued that the pipeline was not under threat, and even if it was, the APOC should pay for its security. A small force at Bahrain should be a perfectly effective 'reply to any boastings of the Turks and should reassure completely the Arabs'.[20] London accepted this caution reluctantly; but the vital step had been taken. British troops would go to the Gulf, and the fate of the Middle East would be changed forever.

3. Turks and Indians

An army of Asiatics, such as we maintain in India, is a faithful servant but a treacherous master.

LORD ROBERTS

The commander of 16th Brigade had the kind of global experience typical of the British Army in the imperial age. Walter Delamain had invaded Egypt with Sir Garnet Wolseley in 1882, served in Burma, with the Zaila Field Force, fought on the North-West Frontier, and in the international intervention against the Boxer Rebellion in China in 1900. In 1911 he had directed military operations in an expedition to expel Afghan gun-runners from the British 'sphere of influence' in southern Persia, as close to Mesopotamia as the British had come. His brigade, for its part, was typical of the Indian Army. Private Bird's Dorset battalion was its 'European' quarter; the other three battalions were 'sepoys' – the 20th Duke of Cambridge's Own Infantry (also known as 'Brownlow's Punjabis'), the 104th Wellesley's Rifles, and the 117th Mahratta Infantry.[1] This brigading was a legacy of the Great Mutiny, and extended down into the structure of many of the Indian battalions themselves. The 20th Infantry, for instance, included Pathans, Sikhs and Dogras. (Dogras, mainly orthodox Hindus from the Kagra Hills, were enlisting in increasing numbers at this time because they generally refused to work on the land.)[2] Force D was a kind of Raj in miniature.

'India', as the British Government of India was casually called in official circles, had sent this force reluctantly, and its reluctance was soon to become more obvious. The 'Indian Army' – properly the Army in India – was there to guarantee the security of India. Many people thought it barely adequate for that in 1914, without sending precious soldiers overseas. For half a century it had countered the menace of Russian advances in Central Asia, the turbulence of the Afghans on the North-West Frontier, and the threat of internal upheaval amongst the 400 million subjects of the Raj. The memory of the Mutiny, when the old Indian armies had rebelled, could never be entirely erased. The 20th Infantry, like most Indian regiments, was a 'class company' unit: each of its companies was recruited from one of the so-called 'martial classes', whose rules of life, beliefs, and often diet, were different. The idea was to stimulate competition between the communities. This it did, but since men of one community could not be put in command of men of another, there could not be a single system of promotion within such a regiment. This built-in inefficiency was the price of the deliberate decision, in the late nineteenth century, to foster the 'race and caste animosities' that had tended to be eroded by the previous system of 'general mixture'. This erosion might be admirable in principle, but not for the British rulers who relied on such divisions to prevent their subjects from uniting against them.

'An army of Asiatics, such as we maintain in India, is a faithful servant, but a treacherous master', the most famous of British soldiers in India, Field Marshal Lord Roberts, wrote. 'Powerfully influenced by social and religious prejudices with which we are imperfectly acquainted, it requires the most careful handling.' Above all, 'it must never be allowed to lose faith in the supremacy of the governing race'. British officers – thirteen for each battalion, alongside seventeen 'Indian Officers' (IOs) – secured the reliability of their sepoys by winning their absolute personal loyalty and affection. And to make quite sure, there were the British infantry battalions alongside them.

So an Indian infantry brigade was a variegated ethnic mix – and an Indian division still more so. The 6th contained, along with its three British and nine Indian battalions, an Indian cavalry regiment (Queen Victoria's Own), two Indian mountain batteries – the elite corps of the Indian artillery, and the only native troops allowed to have cannon – as well as units of the field engineers developed for the special needs of the Indian forces operating in remote roadless territories: two companies of the 3rd Sappers and Miners, and the 48th Pioneers. These were engineers who doubled as infantry when necessary. All Indian units also brought along a vast contingent of 'followers', both official and unofficial. They performed the most menial tasks – looking after tents, latrines and waste disposal. They were noncombatants, but one of their most important functions, water-carrying, routinely brought many followers right into the firing line.

The picturesque complexity of the Indian Army survived the most serious effort to reorganise the force in the years before 1914. Lord Kitchener, as Commander-in-Chief, set about redefining the army's basic mission, shifting from internal security to external defence. This meant that it had to become much more effective militarily, so that it could credibly fight modern 'European' military forces of the kind deployed by Russia. The old territorial division of the army into three (Bengal, Madras and Bombay, of which the Bombay Army had been seen as the most 'martial', the Madras Army as the least) was replaced by a unitary structure. The division of power between the C-in-C and the Military Department of the Government of India was wound up in favour of a single source of authority, the C-in-C: Kitchener himself. Kitchener only achieved this at the price of a fierce clash with the Viceroy, Lord Curzon, who eventually resigned in protest against such 'militarism'. After Kitchener's reforms, the Indian Army could muster just over seven divisions fit for active service. But it was still short of trained staff officers, and levels of equipment were notoriously low. (The field army units were the only ones equipped with the current British service rifle, the short Lee-Enfield, and there was not enough clothing and boots even for all the seven divisions.) India's undeveloped economy meant that it could not fully equip, from its own resources, even a single infantryman.

This was not an army that was prepared for a war like that of
1914. As the British official history pointed out, the possibility
that Britain and its empire would be involved in a world war at
the same time that India would need British help to make good
its shortages 'had not been allowed for'. The kind of manpower
expansion that such a war would require was simply beyond the
capacity of the Indian recruitment system. Compulsory military
service was not an option, even *in extremis*. The idea of a short-
service system with a large active reserve – conscription on the
European model – had been dismissed as 'unsuitable to the
country and to some extent politically undesirable'.[3] But the size
of the army was ultimately limited not by recruitment but by the
fixed belief that Indian soldiers could only reach a 'European'
level of effectiveness if commanded by British officers who knew
and understood them. Such officers, who had to know several
languages and spend a long time with their men, could not just
be multiplied at will.

The Ottoman troops who fell back as the 16th Brigade advanced
were not much better prepared for modern war. Though the
head of the Persian Gulf was obviously a point of major strategic
importance, it lay at the far end of a very thinly stretched military
structure. The Ottoman Army had been shaken up in the years
before 1914. The bloodless coup of the Committee of Union
and Progress, a group of modernising military officers, in 1908
was quickly followed by a reactionary uprising in favour of the
restoration of Islam and the *Seriat* (*sharia*). This left an indelible
scar on the minds of the modernisers when they recovered power
through the occupation of Istanbul by the 'Action Army' in April
1909. From then on, the Army would have a special role in the
struggle to modernise – and to 'Turkify' – the creaky Ottoman
administrative system. (This role would outlast the Ottoman
state, and is still crucial in debates about Turkish identity.)

At that point, the question whether the state would represent
a multi-ethnic 'Ottoman' (*Osmanli*) identity – incorporating
Arabs and others as well as Turks – or Turkish nationality, was

still being resolved. After the war, the tension between Turkish and Islamic identities would become crucial for the state's future. For now, though, the military reformers focused on the slow process of bringing the Army up to modern European standards; the disaster of the Balkan Wars of 1912–13 showed how much was still to be done.[4] The officer corps was drastically purged, so that by 1914 most commanders even at the highest level were in their thirties – like Enver Pasha himself, only thirty-two years old when he became Minister of War in 1914. An ever-increasing contingent of German advisers helped to energise the command system, though it could never entirely overcome its inbuilt limitations. The sharp hostility of Britain and Russia to the arrival of Liman von Sanders and his staff confirmed nationalists like Enver in their determination to push military reform ahead.

The Ottoman Army's manpower problems were less acute than India's, but they were serious enough. The empire's population was estimated at some 19 million in Anatolia, and perhaps 25 million altogether – including the outlying areas of Arabia, where the census was erratic or non-existent. Ethnic Turks, who, as one Turkish historian said, 'must be held to be the only willing bearers of the military burden', may have numbered barely 10 million.[5] (Among the rest were some 6 million Arabs, 1.5 million Kurds, the same number of Greeks, and a million Armenians.) Military service was theoretically compulsory and universal, but most non-Muslims (Jews and Christians made up a fifth of the population) paid an exemption tax instead of serving. Many Muslims – Arabs and Kurds – were also exempt from compulsory service, so the core of the army was Turkish. About 100,000 men were called up each year, but only three-quarters of them actually turned up. The Army's peacetime strength of around 150,000 – two annual classes – could be raised to nearer 800,000 on full mobilisation, including all reserves. But this amounted to barely four per cent of the total population. Modern conscript systems like the French, by contrast, mobilised ten per cent.[6]

The garrison at Fao was part of the Fourth Army Inspection area, centred in Baghdad. This would be redesignated the Iraq Area Command (Irak ve Havalisi Komutanligi), and eventually the Sixth Army, when war broke out. Its two army corps, the XII and XIII, each contained two infantry divisions. These, though, were noticeably different from British divisions. Made up of three regiments of three battalions each, they had a nominal strength of 8,000–9,000 'rifles' – barely half that of a British division. Mesopotamia was 'the backwater of the Ottoman Army'; units there were starved of support services, and especially of experienced officers. (The training effort launched by the reformers in 1913–14 had not reached Mesopotamia.) Most of their soldiers were local Arab levies rather than regulars. A Turkish staff officer, Bimbashi (Major) Mehmet Emin, later wrote a withering critique of these forces. The 38th Division was weak (with only six infantry battalions rather than the normal nine) and virtually untrained in large-scale operations, having been distributed in frontier posts. It was 'permeated by the same disloyal ideas as the surrounding Arabs', and suffered a 'huge' desertion rate. Its equipment was sadly deficient: few or no uniforms, only a quarter of the tents required, almost no entrenching tools – the Qurna detachment 'had eight picks and ten shovels' altogether – 'no water gear except what they could buy themselves', 'bayonets tied on with string instead of belts'.

Mehmet Emin sharply criticised the strategic thinking of the Ottoman high command as 'impossible dreams'. In their 'grandiose ideas of sweeping east with hordes of Arab and Tartar horsemen and armies from Austria, etc, and no idea of defence', Iraq could look after itself. The Fourth Army Inspectorate, he said, had protested that its orders were unrealistic, but General Headquarters 'could not be bothered even to answer'. Still, he reserved his fiercest criticism for the local command, which failed to appreciate the vital need to oppose any hostile landing, and left its forces fatally divided. There were 4,700 infantry (with eighteen artillery pieces, and only three machine guns) in the

Basra area when the British landed, as against the 13,000 who might have been concentrated there. And of these, fewer than 400 were actually at Fao, with a mere three artillery guns. So the potentially decisive advantage of contesting the enemy landing was sacrificed.[7] The British had been handed success on a plate.

4. Basra

I find it difficult to see how we can well avoid taking over
Baghdad.
SIR PERCY COX

The invaders were lucky, because they hardly knew where
they were going. Lieutenant-General Sir Arthur Barrett, the
divisional commander, arrived at Saniyah with Major-General
Charles Fry's 18th Brigade on 14 November. 'We steamed
quietly up [the Shatt] behind the *Elephanta* [with Barrett's HQ],'
recorded one regimental medical officer; 'we drink river water
but it gives about half an inch of mud per tumbler'. (At least it
'adds body to soup', he wryly noted.) As Fry's and Delamain's
brigades pushed forward, and the defenders at last made a stand,
the invaders began to grasp the difficulty of movement on the
Tigris banks. They advanced on the enemy position at 'Sahil'
– a name meaning 'shore' which may have been derived from
a British misunderstanding of an Arab informant – early on 17
November. The troops carried minimum equipment, but as Fry's
brigade paced forward 'a very heavy rainstorm came on which
turned the surface of the ground into a quagmire'. An hour later,
more torrential rain brought down an impenetrable mist, and
the ground turned to ankle-deep mud. Men, guns and horses
were reduced to a glutinous walk, and the handcarts used to
carry forward the HQ telephone cable stuck so fast that for the
rest of the day orders could only be sent by courier.

The battle of 'Sahil' gave a hint of what more serious actions
would be like. The ground was broken by a mass of mounds
and cuttings big enough to make movement hard, but not to
provide the infantrymen with cover. As they rushed forward,

30

their artillery support suddenly stopped: mirages around the palm groves made it impossible for the gunners to see any targets. Delamain's immobilised troops were saved not by the cavalry but by the naval flotilla, which closed in and peppered the Turkish trenches with gunfire. The defenders made off, handing the British a victory, but one with a warning for the future. Barrett had already grasped how sharply his options were restricted by the shortage of river transport. The available steamboats and lighters could barely keep his force supplied; landing heavy equipment was risky. And his force had the first hint of what it could expect from the Mesopotamian weather: on 10 November they were hit by a storm that delivered the biggest hailstones Private Bird had ever seen. 'Our kit gave up the ghost & floated away, leaving us soaking wet & no change. We cannot move about for mud, & hungry.' The rainstorm during the battle was even more destructive. Barrett telegraphed, 'Sorry to report that in violent storm evening 17th November 3 dhows sunk, one containing supplies, one bedding of 7th Rajputs, column Mule Corps and 120th Infantry, and one containing RFA waggons and one limber with 350 rounds shells . . . 10 sepoys and 2 sailors drowned.' For the medical officer of the 48th Pioneers, the loss was personal: 'I lost my sleeping bag of camel's wool, two blankets, my toilet things, much of my khaki including my great coat, and all available underclothes and pyjamas. It all went to the bottom of the muddy river.'[1] Losses like these were all the more serious because the shortage of transport made replacement a slow process.

The assaulting troops had, as Private Bird grumbled, been forced to go in across bare ground with little support. The Dorsets were the spearhead of the 16th Brigade: 'We fought them out of their position advancing over a mile without the least bit of cover. At 400 yards we charged their trenches shouting & cussing & they ran for their lives.'[2] Too many of the assaults that followed would rely on this infantry spirit to overcome the deadly terrain. They would rely, too, on the defenders' reluctance to face a bayonet charge; a feature of the early fighting that would change once Anatolian infantry began to arrive later in 1915. And 'Sahil' was only the first of many actions where, with too little transport, the victors could not exploit the rout of their enemies, and allowed them to escape. Then there would, always, be the phenomenon of the mirage. Advancing on Basra, Major Spackman, medical officer of the 48th Pioneers, had to screw up his eyes against 'a blur of mirages as the morning sun got higher and hotter. We distinctly saw the masts of steamers on the horizon, but after going four miles they disappeared again. Any slight hollow in the desert ahead looked like a pool of water with the leading troops wading into it.' Edmund Candler, a military journalist who arrived a little later as the 'Official Eye-Witness' to the expedition, tried to give his readers some sense of the delusions the mirage could generate. 'Everything is magnified. A low-lying mud village becomes a fort with walls twenty feet high, a group of donkeys a palm-grove . . . The first row of duck I saw, I took for a battalion of infantry.' Cavalry on reconnaissance often had to get within 600 yards before they could tell whether an enemy force was mounted or on foot.

But however difficult conditions were, the troops were happy to be in action at last. Spackman and his unit, 'all agog for our first battle', was delighted with the fierce fighting at Sahil, and 'the thrill of seeing a battery of our own RFA (the old 18-pounders) galloping across the plain to swing their guns into position and open fire upon the hostile battery in the far distance by the palm groves . . . Such a sight is never to be forgotten.'[3] 'The most wonderful week of my life', another officer wrote to his parents, undismayed by the deluge. ('In a few minutes we were drenched to the skin. The ground was nothing but a marsh, with mud inches deep, in which we could hardly walk. That was how we started our attack!') Another feature of war that peacetime training did not prepare men for was harder to take: the ordeal of the wounded. 'It was awful to see' the Turkish casualties, and 'awful to have to leave them alone in their agony, with a

sandstorm coming up! I can still hear their groans and cries.'⁴
Ottoman medical services were rudimentary. As yet, though,
the small numbers engaged, and the relatively low casualty rate
on the British side, obscured the fact that their own would be
unable to cope with the campaign to come.

Basra itself was not so much captured by the British as
abandoned by the Turks. The Cabinet designated it as Force
D's 'immediate objective' on 16 November, but Lord Crewe
suggested that Barrett should only advance 'if military situation
renders immediate advance both practicable and advisable' with
the force at his disposal. Otherwise he should wait until his third
brigade arrived before attacking the town. And indeed Barrett
found himself unable to advance. Though he reported on the
20th that he was strong enough, and 'anxious . . . to attack
enemy's position at Baljaniya', he told the naval commander
that the difficulties of landing horses, guns, ammunition and
stores meant that he probably could not. In the evening, though,
he heard that the Ottoman forces were falling back towards
Amara. Once again, the defenders had not only let themselves
be outnumbered, but after ordering his southern detachment to
hold Baljaniya the commander of the 38th Division had simply
cleared out without waiting to be attacked. Mehmet Emin
alleged that he had panicked, and thus the retirement turned
into a chaotic retreat. But things would only get worse for the
incompetently led Ottoman force with the appointment of a new
commander, Suleiman Askeri, who (in Emin's view) posed as an
expert on Mesopotamia on the basis of very short experience.
Since the War Ministry knew almost nothing about the area (the
Army had no local maps, for instance), this 'cocksure' junior
colonel was given the command of the theatre.

Next day, as British ships were looking for a way through the
obstructions laid in the river channel between Shamshamiya and
Dabba islands, a group of Basra notables and British residents –
representing the substantial commercial community in the port
– came out in a steam launch and hailed them. They were in a

33

panic. As soon as the Ottoman garrison had left, the inhabitants of Basra had begun enthusiastically looting their stores. The British moved into the town that day less for strategic reasons than simply to protect property. But even getting troops into an undefended town proved far from easy. The obstruction hastily improvised by the retreating Turks was very effective, and if the blocking operation had not gone slightly wrong (the string of boats being sunk in the channel broke apart, to leave a narrow gap) it might have proved impassable. In the event, the sloop *Espiègle* cautiously made its way through 'Satan's Gap' in the early afternoon of 21 November, and the other sloops followed, anchoring by the Turkish battery at Baljaniya and landing a party to dismantle the four field guns abandoned there. Hours later the occupying troops had still not appeared, and with fires starting in Basra, two of the sloops moved on into the town and sent landing parties to clear the looters from the Custom House area. Fry's troops, held up at Sahil by the now familiar embarkation snarl-up, only arrived next morning, by which time looting had started again in earnest.

Barrett's main force had set out for Basra the previous evening, and reached the southern outskirts around midday; after a 28-mile march that was, for Bird, 'the hardest march I have ever done'. Endless banks and old irrigation channels had to be levelled or bridged by the sappers before the troops could cross, and when they arrived the town's few bridges had to be repaired or strengthened before they could be used. The 'indescribably filthy condition of the town' meant that Barrett's tired and hungry troops could not be billeted, but had to bivouac near the Khora creek. 'We were so hungry', wrote Bird, 'that my chum Rusty & myself went & bought 1 rupee of Arab chappattis & 8 annas of dates, & we sat down & ate the lot, & they seemed beautifull to us.'[5]

The fall of Basra was formalised in a ceremonial march on 23 November, ending with the Union flag being raised over a building near the Ashar bridge to a salute of naval gunfire. This was undoubtedly a dramatic coup. 'Another Red Patch on the Map', as the *Daily Mail* exulted. Basra, the fabled home of Sinbad the Sailor, was, if not 'the key of Mesopotamia' as General Barrow said, by far the most important place in southern Mesopotamia, a major commercial centre of some 60,000 inhabitants. Ethnically the town was a fascinating mix of Arabs, Indians, Armenians, Jews, Assyrians, Chaldeans, Persians – and others besides. 'Very cosmopolitan', Spackman noted, 'from very fair Armenians to black Ethiopians and Somalis, and talk is in Arabic, Persian, Turkish, French, English or Italian in about that order.' Barrett himself was less enchanted, writing to a friend that the town was 'full of Jews, Armenians and non-descripts of all sorts, including a few English merchants, American missionaries and so on'. It had, in fact, a significant European merchant community, a number of substantial buildings, notably the Custom House, the British, German and US consulates, and the Ottoman commodore's residence. Much of the urban area was 'comparatively well built and double storied', but it was all effectively uninhabitable: 'a maze of tortuous lanes whose centres were ankle-deep in filth, offal and litter', with a 'total absence of any sanitary system or method, and the presence of numerous disease-ridden brothels'.

Seen in the right light, Basra could exude Eastern promise. Mrs Stevens, visiting just after the war, saw it 'by night, when the palms in their lofty beauty lay, plumed and black, against the milky spaces of the Eastern night, and the great full moon barred the many waterways with shining ivory silver. The houses, with their overhanging lattice windows, propped up by wooden struts, looked like illustrations to tales of Oriental adventure.' Noting that, 'like Venice' Basra was 'wedded to the sea', she was 'stirred by the gondola-like boats and high-prowed mahailas which lay moored to the dark banks. Here and there little fires kindled on shore or vessel sent ribbons of red across the water, here and there lamps shone in house or coffeeshop. The frogs kept up a loud, perpetual chorus on marshy bank or hidden creek, but except for their discordant music all was magic and silence.' But she soon discovered that silence was a rarity in the Basra night – at high tide especially, 'tumult begins – shouting, curses, tornadoes of speech, yells, demoniac cries'. And the charm of the vast groves of date palms soon paled. They were, in the end, 'a weary vegetable to live with', with 'an uncanny habit of throwing shadows, but never shade, and in the long days of heat, when green means so much, they are grey with dust, as is everything else'.[6] Dust and heat would define the Mesopotamia experience for hundreds of thousands of troops.

The capture of Basra was more than a military event. At the policy level it raised big issues. One emerged in the speech that General Barrett delivered as the British flag was being hoisted over the town. After declaring that Britain had not wanted to fight against 'Turkey', and had no 'enmity or ill-will against' the local population, he announced that 'No remnant of Turkish administration now remains in this region.' In its place 'the British flag has been established – under which you will enjoy the benefits of liberty and justice'. But just what was meant by the phrase 'the British flag has been established'? And did liberty mean 'liberation'? Interestingly, in reporting the event to Lord Crewe, Barrett used a rather different phrase. The 'proclamation prepared by Cox read in Arabic announcing annexation', he wrote, had been 'very well received by inhabitants'.[7] Annexation was another thing altogether. It raised issues that resonated far beyond Mesopotamia.

Percy Cox was convinced that Britain would not get Arab support without a definite statement that the Turks would never be allowed to return. The upsurge of Arab national, or merely anti-Turk feeling, promised by so many pre-war experts, was not materialising. The Arabs in and around Basra were sympathetic, and outwardly friendly for the most part, but the local officers believed that only a declaration of British annexation would remove the fear of Turkish reprisals. As long as this fear persisted, Arabs were not likely to give active assistance. Shortly after the proclamation, Cox advised the Government of India that 'it would be convenient if we could make a public announcement that our occupation is permanent'. When the Viceroy forwarded this telegram to London, he added, 'we assume that administration will be under Government of India whose interests in the Gulf are intimately involved'.

Now alarm bells began to ring at the London end. The Foreign Office was worried that 'Indian ambitions' could 'get out of hand'.[8] Lord Crewe insisted that no declaration of permanent annexation should be made. Since the Allies had agreed that any occupation of conquered enemy territory would be provisional until the final postwar settlement, such a declaration would 'arouse French and Russian suspicions'. And he told Hardinge sharply that 'no attempt should be made at present to transform vilayet into an Indian district'.[9] Existing structures of government 'and local agency should be retained as far as possible', and 'leniency' observed in revenue collection. The Viceroy tried again three days later, 'strongly urging' that Cox might at least be authorised 'to let it be understood, in conversation but not in writing, in respect of places where we assume control with the cooperation of the inhabitants, that whether we remain permanently or not, they will in any case not be handed back to mercies of Turks'.[10] But even this compromise was ruled out.

In this situation, the ambiguity of Force D's mission became more problematic. For all the care taken by Barrow in his original proposal to limit the scope of the operation, and so the commitment of manpower, the apparently limited objectives set out for Force D proved to be unattainable. If, as Delamain's sealed orders suggested, and most subsequent writers have held, securing the Abadan oil terminal was the paramount objective, then it was already achieved. Barrett's lone division needed to, and – as Barrow's appreciation had suggested – could, do no more than occupy and hold Basra. In fact, though, protecting the APOC installations was clearly a formal justification for invasion rather than a final objective. Oil was a secondary issue, even for the Admiralty, whatever Admiral Slade might think. Churchill had opposed the expedition as a diversion from the effort to deal with the Turks 'at the centre' where it counted, brusquely saying that if Abadan was lost Britain would simply 'buy our oil from elsewhere'. The real objective was the one that lurked at the end of Delamain's instructions, 'to show Arabs that we intend to support them'. Arab opposition would render Force D, and any force that India was likely to be able to field, pointless.

This logic was felt as soon as Basra was occupied. As early as 23 November, Cox began to raise 'the question of an advance to Bagdad [sic]'. On the evidence of the early fighting he suggested that Turkish troops were 'very unlikely to oppose us again', and thought that 'we should be received in Bagdad with the same cordiality as we have been here'. He was less confident of the attitude of the tribes between Basra and Baghdad, though he hoped that their neutrality could be secured, if not perhaps their active cooperation. But immediate action was vital: 'effect of recent defeat has been very great, and if advance is made before it wears off and while cool season lasts Bagdad will in all probability fall into our hands very easily.' In fact, he concluded that it was 'difficult to see how we can well avoid taking over Bagdad'.[11]

Percy Zachariah Cox, a protégé of Lord Curzon, who had been British resident at Bushire – in charge of the whole Gulf region – for ten years before the war, was already well on the way to achieving legendary status in the Middle East. Fifty years old in 1914, 'Kokkus' was famous for his tact and his command of Arabic – a patient negotiator who achieved results not only by words but also by his 'commanding presence' and conspicuous silences, which enhanced his gravitas in Arab eyes. Like so many political officers he was a 'soldier consul', beginning his career with a short stint in the Army before transferring to the Indian political service. Knighted in 1911, he now became an honorary colonel, and eventually a major-general. 'A quick, efficient, and tireless worker', shrewd and incorruptible, he was no doubt more socially adept than his wife, the daughter of an

Indian Army Surgeon-General, a 'forbidding, austere woman', not above ticking off ordinary soldiers for failing to address her as 'your ladyship'.[12]

Still, he had got used to seeing his advice ignored. 'I have given up making suggestions,' he once wrote, 'the result of continual snubs from home.' But he had always persisted in spite of the 'mortification'.[13] True to form, his proposal to take Baghdad did not at first attract either India or London. Though the Viceroy was (like Curzon) an admirer of Cox, and had sent him with the expeditionary force 'to control all political matters', he asked his military chief, Sir Beauchamp Duff, to assess its military feasibility, and his verdict was negative. Though Duff estimated the available Ottoman forces at 15,000, of which only 4,000 were properly armed – so that a single brigade might conceivably seize Baghdad if sent promptly – any such advance would depend on Arab support. The river transport shortage would mean that the force would have to maintain itself unsupported at Baghdad for a fortnight while reinforcements were brought up. A division might be enough to hold Baghdad, but only if Russia kept up its pressure on the Turks in Armenia. If not, the situation would be acutely dangerous. Reinforcements – even if available – could not be got there quickly, so 'we should have either to withdraw or run the risk of a considerable disaster'. Could such a risk be justified? This was partly a political question, but in military terms Duff rated Baghdad as of little strategic value. 'However desirable politically the seizure of Baghdad may be, the military considerations indicate that even success would result in our general strategical position being weakened rather than strengthened.'[14]

The India Office was also less than enthusiastic. Although Hirtzel thought that it was 'so desirable as to be practically essential' to occupy Baghdad eventually, he accepted that it could not be done straight away. Barrow was sceptical, and Crewe was solidly against it. Yet even the cautious Barrow felt that sitting tight in Basra was not an option: 'a policy of passive inactivity is to be deprecated if we are to continue to impress the Arab and Indian world with our ability to defeat all designs against us.' But who could now tell what it would take to impress the Arabs? Barrow thought an advance as far as Qurna, at the junction of the Tigris and Euphrates some thirty miles north of Basra, would make military sense, and besides its moral effect on 'the Arabs', it would 'completely cover Persian Arabistan and safeguard it from Turkish intrigues or incursions'. Once there, he somewhat hesitantly suggested, we could consider whether we should go further. 'But whatever we do, let us not stand still.'[15]

5. 'Conciliating the Arabs'

The task of controlling the tribes of the desert should not be one
of the most difficult problems of Mesopotamian administration.
GERTRUDE BELL

Before Basra fell, Lord Crewe instructed the Viceroy to 'impress
on Barrett the necessity of conciliating the Arabs in every
possible way'. Barrett should do his best to treat Basra 'as a
friendly and not an enemy town'. Governments often fail to give
their military commanders such clear political guidance, so in
principle this was helpful. In practice it was more complicated.
It was easy enough, for instance, to comply with Cox's wish that
Basra trade should be exempted from the usual naval harassment
– stopping and searching, and sometimes impounding – applied
to neutral commerce in wartime. It was less easy to treat the
Arabs on the ground as friends. Many of them were, in fact,
suspicious or even hostile. At Bahrain, where as we have seen
the inhabitants immediately feared a British takeover, the consul
reported with regret that Britain's declaration of war had 'not
made a favourable impression on the mass of the people'. They
asked why the British, 'who have taken Egypt, Cyprus and Aden,
and have joined Russia, pose as friends of Turkey. The feeling
against us', he thought, 'is strong and almost universal.'[1] And
this was in a place quite familiar with British power. At Basra,
with its long commercial tradition, the British were welcomed
enthusiastically by its notables – who actually wanted to become
part of the British Empire. But the countryside of the Basra
vilayet was different. This was a famously ungovernable region,
where Ottoman power had barely extended outside the main
urban areas.

But the resistance of tribes like the Bani Lam or the Muntafik was not a manifestation of Arab nationalism.[2] Outside the towns there were few if any Arab nationalists in Iraq, and indeed few who saw Iraq itself as a distinct political unit which might want British support. Authority rested with the religious leaders of the Shia holy cities and the heads of the tribal confederations. There was no reason for such groups to welcome a new, alien ruler. Even for the Shia of Basra and Baghdad provinces, with a deep-rooted and consistent antagonism to their Sunni Turkish rulers, the British were less likely to appear as liberators than as intruders. There was a serious risk that the *mujtahids* of Najaf, Karbala and Khadimain, the leading Shia clerics, would echo the Ottoman government's call for a jihad against the infidel invaders. The British did have some leverage with them: the so-called Oudh Bequest, a fund (worth 120,000 rupees a year) bequeathed by the Rajah of Oudh for the benefit of the Shia in Najaf and Karbala, was distributed by the British Resident. The British expected that the income would, as the Ambassador in Constantinople rather crudely put it when war threatened, 'teach them on which side their bread is buttered'. (After toying with the idea of making payments conditional on cooperation, the Indian government eventually decided in March 1915 to guarantee them regardless of political attitudes.) Even so, the call for jihad spread to a disturbing extent.

Many of the Shia *mujtahids* in the holy cities preached jihad and sent emissaries to the Euphrates tribes urging them to fight the British in the name of Islam. By January 1915, jihad had supposedly been preached in every mosque in Mesopotamia.[3] The most important tribal leader to respond was Sheikh Ajaimi al-Mansur of the Muntafik confederation, and the failure to get him on Britain's side would prove to be an enduring problem. He corresponded cautiously with Cox for a few weeks before eventually raising his flag in open resistance. Unusually amongst local Iraqi leaders he made a public declaration of his position. Replying to an appeal from Britain's ally Ibn Saud in 1916, Ajaimi asserted 'it is known to me and beyond doubt that my attitude is the one which is necessary to earn the approval of the Most High God and the elevation of the name of the Arabs . . . what greater loyalty is there than this, that I should carry out faithfully what God ordered me in regard to Jihad against non-believers, the enemies of God and our religion. The "blame of the blamer" cannot apply to me, who walk in the love of God and of his Prophet and of our country, and in the protection thereof from the pollution of the infidel.' He accused Ibn Saud of betraying Islam by supporting the enemy of the Turkish government, 'a protection to the purity of Islam', and so 'my helper and the helper of my tribes'.[4]

Ajaimi's striking fusion of religion and local patriotism manifested the traditional view of 'the Arab race' as distinguished by its special position in the Islamic world. In this view the Arabic language was important primarily because it was the language of the Prophet and the Quran. This was not nationalism in any modern sense. Though it was not entirely incompatible with it, it was ideologically quite distinct from the nationalist idea that ethnicity should be the basis of political independence. Gertrude Bell, who called Ajaimi 'the most virile member' of the Sa'dun family, pointing out that he was 'a bitter foe of Sayyid Talib' (who had decoyed his father into the hands of the Turks), implied that his loyalty to Islam was a cloak for his personal ambition, and that nothing Britain could have done would have brought him round. 'Proud as Lucifer, like all the Sa'dun, and with an overweening estimate of his own importance, his ambition must always have overstepped any favours which could have been accorded him.'[5] Such aspersions tended, inevitably, to be cast on all those unenlightened enough to oppose Britain.

While some tribesmen joined a new Ottoman auxiliary force, known as the *Mujahidin*, designed to overcome their traditional resistance to military service, more sat on the fence and watched the clash of arms as neutrals. Cox's deputy, Arnold Wilson, argued that this was not surprising. The Arabs were quite ready to accept the British, he believed, but unless it was officially declared that 'we should eventually be prepared to stand by them, a policy of whole-hearted cooperation was impossible'. Britain could expect at best 'friendly neutrality', paid for by subsidies or indirectly by employing labour and transport at fair rates. 'We could not frankly appeal to the leaders to abandon their ancient, if half-hearted, loyalties, and to cast in their lot with the new order of things.'[6] Britain's only weapon was, in effect, bribery. Cox reported that he had 'expended freely to encourage members of the clergy and other individuals inclined to be friendly and render service', but 'as long as a large proportion of the Arab public were convinced that the Turks were in superior strength, conciliation expenditure was useless'.[7]

The fact was that the British belief in Arab hatred of the Turks was not entirely wrong, but misread a more complex relationship. Muslim consciousness was sensitive. Anti-Christian activists played on deep-seated fears of Christian crusading; two of them deported by the British early in 1915 had been urging people 'to carry jihad against them before they wage it against you'.[8] (Even for those unmoved by religious enthusiasm, there was a real culture clash; witness the 'peculiar surprise and indeed resentment' of the Arabs at the bare knees of the British troops.) Wilson experienced the uneasiness of the situation directly in April 1915, when he found himself 'amongst the crowd who watched the arrival at the Zubair gate of the first batch of Turkish prisoners' after the battle of Shaiba. 'Their numbers were so disproportionate to the escort of British troops, themselves scarcely less haggard in appearance and ragged in dress than their captives, that at first the rumour spread that the Turks were re-entering the town in triumph, and a shrill cry of joy arose.' It was silenced by the reproachful shout of a Turkish sergeant (who had misunderstood the crowd's meaning), but the silence was broken again by 'the cry of one of a group of Arab women on a housetop: "Lord how long shall the ungodly, how long shall the ungodly triumph?" A hundred faces were turned to her, and a wail went up that was echoed for a moment from housetop to housetop: then silence again, and discretion.'⁹

In any case, the primary British aim at this stage was not to secure Arab help but to turn Basra into a workable base. Even this limited objective carried wider implications, however. Occupied territory had to be administered, and the situation at Basra was an administrator's nightmare. International law required that Britain maintain, as far as possible, the status quo, yet as Wilson – soon to be a key figure in the running of the country – noted, 'no remnant of the Turkish administration remained'. Ottoman officials high and low had all decamped, taking masses of essential records with them, and most of the remaining papers had been either looted by locals, or thrown out by British troops desperately trying to find some habitable space. The result was a dangerous vacuum. The old government might have been inefficient, but it had been comprehensive, and long established: 'it had governed the lives and transactions of the Arab population for three centuries'. It could not be reconstructed – and in any case the British would not have dreamed of doing such a thing.

The British liked to think of themselves as immune to ideological enthusiasm, but they were enthusiasts for administration. Efficient, honest administration was, in effect, the British ideology. Confronted with the wreckage of a system they despised, their natural impulse was to reshape it to meet British standards. Pragmatically, too, they assumed that good government would be the most effective way of bringing the people to their side. The Ottoman system was 'radically bad', a series of separate departments without any coherent relationship. Five of these 'excrescences' independently raised revenues and sent them to Istanbul. They all demonstrated the Turkish determination to maximise revenue by neglecting public services. Typical of Turkish abuses, in the British view, was the parlous state of the Awqaf department, which managed the *waqf* properties – the traditionally independent religious endowments that formed a keystone of Muslim society. Since they had been taken over by the Ottoman state, their funds had been stripped bare to supply revenue.[10]

All the British administration could do at this stage was to 'set the whole of a strange and complicated system on its legs as quickly as possible' – and as cheaply. But even minimal measures initiated structural changes. To keep the army healthy, it had to launch urgent improvements in public sanitation. Law and order presented another challenge. Efforts to recruit police locally failed, and police had to be drafted in from the Punjab and Aden, with a handful of British ex-policemen who were serving as soldiers. A new Commissioner of Police set about instructing the local community in British ideas of law-abidingness. Wilson claimed this as a 'remarkably successful' experiment: 'The good temper, common sense, and impassive dignity of the metropolitan or county policeman endeared him from the beginning to all classes.' Other elements of civil society were added: a 'modest news service' was established, with an English–Arabic news sheet edited by 'an able & energetic officer', which Colonel F. I. Bowker of the Hampshire Regiment thought an 'excellent idea & I really believe widely read by the native population with good results'. Several banks – including the Imperial Bank of Persia – opened branches in Basra.

Education would also be targeted. Here the same radical defects could be seen: Iraq had not been exposed to the 'wholesome influence' of Western ideas in the way that Syria had. Most education took place in the mosques, where little was taught except Arabic language and close study of the Quran. The few government schools (a single secondary school in Basra, and a few primary schools) were staffed by 'men of bad moral character, highly paid and incompetent', who taught only in Turkish. British policy was to open new schools only when they could find enough 'good' teachers, so the process was slow; in the meantime they provided grants for the existing American Mission School and the Christian and Jewish community schools at Basra. The education programme would develop as the occupation lengthened, but it would never become the kind of determined cultural offensive that would have happened under French control.[11]

Nothing much about the day-to-day reality of Anglo-Arab relations appears in the official reports. Wilson (with a vagueness that was surely deliberate) admitted that 'bitter experience of Arab hostility, Arab thefts, and Arab rapacity occasionally tempted departmental chiefs to embark without full consideration upon policies the repercussions of which might well endanger a delicate political structure'. Stephen Longrigg, one of his political officers, later wrote that British soldiers were repelled by the 'low standards of life and, as they judged it, low types of humanity' who confronted them. Common tasks or interests which could produce friendly cooperation were 'too rare', while 'mutual non-comprehension and inhibition between "the Army" and the population were to prove sadly permanent'. The turbulence of 'tribal communities unused to the new tranquillity or eager for loot' was a constant problem, and 'many punitive columns sought to chastise offenders', not always successfully.[12]

The Arabs' comprehensive skills in larceny drew exasperated admiration. This had a funny side. At Camp Tigris in January 1915, Arabs 'approached in close and took off a latrine flag' from Captain Shakeshaft's unit (the Norfolks). 'We wondered if this would be hung up in the military museum at Constantinople.'[13] Usually, though, the target was more difficult to take and more valuable: boots, equipment, and above all else rifles. 'Soldiers had to sleep with their rifles beneath them, and various forms of booby traps and alarms were installed on the barbed wire entanglements surrounding the bivouacs. Sentries were told to shoot marauders on sight, but despite all these precautions various items – even at times the blanket one was sleeping on – were spirited away.'[14] Their inexhaustible determination and ability to get through even the tightest defences was a constant nuisance with ultimately serious security implications. ('From first to last', wrote the padre of the Leicestershire battalion,

Edward Thompson, 'nothing moved deeper anger than their constant exhumation of our dead, and murder, for robbery's sake, of the wounded or isolated.'[15])

Private records show how far from amiable relations were, especially at ground level between the troops and the 'Buddoos' – the derogatory sobriquet did not bode well. Philip Graves, a journalist specialising in Turkish affairs, who later became Cox's biographer, held that 'it is no exaggeration to say that the Arabs were loathed by the greater part of the army, whether British, Indian-Moslems or Hindus'. Cox would struggle for years 'to prevent indiscriminate reprisals and induce military commanders to punish treachery within measure'.[16] One of the longest entries in Private Bird's usually laconic diary (a full two pages of his little notebook) recounts his experience of military raid-and-search operations after the occupation of Basra, in surrounding Arab villages that had been judged to be less than friendly. The troops would approach the village by night, on foot or by boat, 'then silently surround it & wait for daybreak'. At dawn several companies of infantry 'fix bayonets & rush the houses, any house that refused to open when we first knock, we immediately break down the door, & make prisoners of all the male occupants, we then search everything & everywhere for arms'. Even if conducted with the utmost punctiliousness and politeness – which was, experience suggests, rare – such total searches were (and were usually intended to be) inevitably intimidating. Since virtually none of the officers or men spoke any Arabic, assessing the attitudes of the inhabitants was a rough-and-ready business. 'Those who attempt to run away', Bird noted, 'are caught by our ring of men outside the village. They are treated as combatants & meet their end on the scaffold. And of course', he added, 'those who shoot at us are either shot or captured & hung in the market square.'[17]

J. W. Barnett of the Indian Medical Service thought the Arabs 'swine' and treated them with aggressive contempt. They had 'no modesty . . . strip naked at any moment'. When an Arab brought eggs into camp and refused to accept money, he 'kept eggs and kicked Arab out'. It was 'very difficult to get eggs from the women as they scratch the sepoys' faces'. He disliked the 'Arab practice of trying to kiss hand and arm'. An Arab woman 'kissed my arm four times in vain attempt to save her favourite ram, but as ram was very fat I was unable to see my way to giving it back'. Eventually, the Arabs were 'no longer offering chickens and eggs' to troops on the march; 'I wonder why?' When he saw Arabs being flogged, he savagely noted in his diary, 'most pleasing sight'.[18] In this he was certainly not unusual.

How much did the British understand of the Arab people they now hoped to rally to their side? They relied on the knowledge of the handful of 'Arabists' like Shakespear who had travelled through the Hejaz, the Najd and the Fertile Crescent before the war. (As Britain was officially uninterested in these areas, their journeys had been unofficial or demi-official.) In 1914 their expertise became a major national asset: the war was 'the Arabists' moment in history'.[19] But most of their travels had been in Syria, Palestine and Arabia; in fact only two, Captain Gerard Leachman and Gertrude Bell, could really claim anything like extensive knowledge of Mesopotamia. (Coming from Damascus, Bell had got as far as Baghdad.) And 'even allowing for their formidable talents it was thin coverage', as Elizabeth Monroe pointed out.[20] These travellers were genuinely fascinated by the Arabs, but they also had an interest in enhancing their mystery. For T. E. Lawrence, who would become the most celebrated of them, the Arabs were a 'riddle', which could be solved only by 'going far into their society'. They were 'a people of primary colours, especially of black and white, who see the world always in line'. It was hard for Westerners to grasp 'the clear hardness of their belief, a limitation almost mathematical, which repels us by its unsympathetic form'. They were 'a certain people, despising doubt, our modern crown of thorns. They do not understand our metaphysical difficulties, our self-questionings. They know only truth and untruth.'[21]

Those who understood them had absolute confidence in their own judgement. Lawrence could encapsulate in a terse paragraph the essence of the desert Arabs. 'They are a limited narrow-minded people whose inert intellects lie incuriously fallow. Their imaginations are keen but not creative. There is so little Arab art today in Asia that they can nearly be said to have no art ... They show no longing for great industry, no organisations of mind or body anywhere. They invent no systems of philosophy or mythologies. They are the least morbid of peoples, who take the gift of life unquestioning, as an axiom. To them it is a thing inevitable, beyond our control.' Inertia, lack of formal organisation, fatalism – these were key components of the 'Orientalist' understanding of the Arab mind.

It was above all the structure and culture of tribal society that fascinated Arabists. Their vision focused on a set of key features of Arab society. They tended to see a sharp distinction, if not outright conflict, between urban and rural communities. Echoing the widespread Western view (launched by the French in their conquest of Algeria) of an opposition between the pure, tribal, egalitarian 'noble savages' of the desert and the corrupt, despotic Arabs of the towns, they saw the tribes as elemental social groups. A volume of Gertrude Bell's essays issued by the Government Press at Basra in 1916 under the title *The Arab of Mesopotamia*, a kind of primer for new British arrivals, pointed to sharp social distinctions between tribes: the settled Arabs who had migrated northwards had, by turning to agriculture, 'lost caste with the true Badawin' (though they remained 'of the same blood and tradition, and not infrequently fragments of very famous Arabian tribes are present among the cultivators upon the outer limits of the Arabian migration'). Thus the Albu Muhammad, rice growers on the Tigris who bred immense herds of buffalo for export to Syria, were 'a socially inferior and possibly non-Arab people'. The sheikhs of the Bani Lam, who had occupied the country above Amara for the last four or five hundred years, claimed descent from a 'famous pre-Mohammedan tribe of East

Arabia', but in spite of their pretensions 'none of the Badawin of the inner desert would regard them as equals or intermarry with them'. Tribes could be confidently characterised. The Bani Lam were 'good shots, especially from the saddle'. The Bani Rabi'ah were 'a turbulent people, well-known robbers and disturbers of traffic along the river'. The Shammar, by contrast, were 'a proud and valiant people, possessors of their full share of desert virtues, and obedient to their old ideals of desert conduct'. In southern Mesopotamia, 'from the head of the Persian Gulf up to Qurnah tribal organisation has almost died out', but the country to the north was occupied by such groups as the Muntafik, 'a large and loose confederation of tribes of different origin, all of whom acknowledge, to a less degree or greater, the over-lordship of the Sa'dun clan'.

The need to make administrative sense of the country impelled the British to identify tribes with definite geographical boundaries, and 'the shaikh, as the personification of his tribe, became the pivotal indispensable figure in British conceptions'.[22] Bell believed that the power of the sheikh or headman remained 'deeply rooted in the daily life of the people'. The essential homogeneity of the tribe could be preserved even in the large-scale 'regroupings' common in Mesopotamia, since 'homogeneous tribes will readily admit a stranger group', which would subsequently 'lose all touch with their own people'; so that 'the amalgamation of divergent elements under a common Shaikh falls well within tribal custom'.

The Arabists tend now to be dismissed for romanticising tribal life and misreading tribal structure.[23] As against their 'essentialist' conception of tribes as primordial, essentially changeless units, and of tribal society as resolutely anti-modern, modern studies see Iraqi tribes as much looser entities, closely integrated into the wider economy. The differences between them stemmed not so much from fixed tribal rules as from their varied economic activities.[24] Yet, though Bell was certainly a determined system-atiser, she tried harder than is often acknowledged to understand the tribes from within, as Lawrence urged. She was also aware that tribal structures were not unchanging, and that the urban–rural divide was no more fixed than it had been in developing Western societies.

The Arabists' confident grasp of tribal society made them remarkably optimistic about the ease with which Mesopotamia could be governed. For them, it was the vicious incompetence of the Turks – 'their colossal ignorance of the temperament of the alien races whom they ruled, and their blind impulse to draw all authority into a single net' – that explained the turbulent state of the country. The Ottoman system had failed to understand the 'delegation of power' through local structures, which of course was a British speciality. 'The task of controlling the tribes of the desert should not be one of the most difficult problems of Mesopotamian administration.' A close study of one tribe, the Albu Muhammad, concluded that 'notwithstanding the turbulence under Ottoman rule, the task of the administrator would not seem to present overwhelming difficulties once the tribal character of the Albu Muhammad country is admitted and used to advantage'. Even the lowly Marsh Arabs might progress, 'far down in the scale of civilization as these amphibious dwellers in swamp and reed bed would seem to be'. The reason was 'the amazing quickness of the Arab in adapting himself to new conditions and profiting by unexpected opportunities'.[25]

The British were not entirely unaware of potential complications. Bell's essay on 'The Pax Britannica in the Occupied Territories' recognised the impact of Ottoman reforms in land tenure, reducing the tribes to the status of tenants, and generating 'acute agrarian discontent [that] has kept the Muntafik district in constant rebellion'. But it seemed to miss the point that the impact of these reforms, part of the wider Ottoman governmental reform programme – the Tanzimat – went far beyond mere turbulence. They dramatically altered relationships within Arab society. The irony was that these land tenure reforms had not stemmed from the 'blind impulse' of the Turks to centralisation, but from Western – and above all British – pressure on the Ottoman state to bring its administrative system into line with liberal ideas.[26] The reform programme, most energetically advanced by Midhat Pasha as Governor of Baghdad in the late 1860s, was designed to create a peasantry more directly linked to the state than to the traditional ruling class. Land was to be allocated to the peasants, the *fallahin*, who would receive title deeds giving legal security of tenure, while ultimate ownership rested with the state.

But such far-reaching change had to be steered consistently over more than one generation if it was to produce the results intended by the reformers. Unfortunately, Midhat's visionary energy was the exception rather than the rule; and he himself was in power at Baghdad for only a few years. His successors were all replaced before they could develop long-term policies. In social terms, the land reforms failed disastrously. The rural population as a whole resisted them, refusing to register titles which they believed were hereditary. The new paper titles, the *tapu*, were scooped up instead by the existing landowners and urban notables. Hence the social role of the sheikhs 'shifted perceptibly from that of champion of their tribesmen to that of landlords'.[27] So while, as the nineteenth century ended, 'the decline of the political and military power of the shaikhs, agas and begs was unmistakable', the process of 'granting or leasing to them or the registering in their name, through fraud or bribery, of vast estates supporting many tribes, in utter disregard of the prescriptive right of rank and file tribesmen', was simultaneously turning them into the possessors of overwhelming economic power.[28]

There were, as Bell's analysis indicated, significant ethnic as well as religious differences amongst Mesopotamia's 'Arabs'. The Ma'dan or 'Marsh Arabs' of the lower Euphrates area, such as the Albu Muhammad and Bani Lam tribes, claimed descent from Arab invaders from the western deserts – and persisted in calling themselves 'settled nomads' well into the twentieth century. But their lifestyle and customs showed an eclectic mix of influences, in which some ethnographers found traces of descent from the ancient Sumerian people of Mesopotamia. The Ma'dan were certainly despised by the tribes of the mid-Euphrates, partly because of their ethnicity (they were held to be Persians) and partly because of their customs. Their irregular marriage practice – the Persian custom of permitting temporary marriage by sheikhs and *sayyids* (locally recognised holy men) – and the belief that their sheikhs took more wives than the Quran permitted, were particularly offensive. Even amongst the Shia, the Marsh Arabs were unconventional in their religious observance. For them the Prophet's son-in-law Ali and his descendants seemed to have almost divine status. They had discarded many fundamental tenets of Islam in favour of devotion to their imams. Religious practice was largely private, as there were no mosques in the marshlands. They rarely practised the Ramadan fast, for instance, but were devoted to pilgrimage (to Najaf and Karbala) and mourning the murder of Hussein. For them, the key to salvation was above all to be buried at Najaf.[29]

The area held by the British was particularly unusual. The vast marshes surrounding Basra formed a unique environment, with a distinctive way of life – 'a whole world under the water', as Gertrude Bell put it. Some 4,000 square miles were flooded by meltwater from the Persian mountains from March to July, and became almost a single sheet of water. After the floods subsided, the shallower marshes became dry islands, surrounded by water four or five feet deep, thickly covered with reeds, bulrushes and floating water-plants. The Marsh Arabs' reed houses, built on stilts to survive the floods, or set on artificial islands of layered reeds and mud, formed 'villages built on floating piles of reed mats anchored to palm trees, linked only by boat'. At the heart of the village was the substantial barrel-vaulted reception hall, the *mudhif*, of the sheikh – 'a perfectly regular, exquisitely constructed yellow tunnel, fifty yards long' – built on one of the permanent islands. Some tribal branches were semi-nomadic, moving herds of buffalo around the marshes as the water level shifted. Others were settled, breeding buffalo or growing barley, wheat and especially rice. Everyone fished, naturally, although the use of nets was regarded as demeaning – poisoned spears were the only socially acceptable weapon. Strict lines of social demarcation and tribal relations would inevitably limit the Arab communities' potential for political engagement.

The Arab of Mesopotamia took a strikingly relaxed view of sectarian divisions. Sunni contempt for Shias was portrayed as a curiosity rather than a potential political problem. The fact that the Sunni Sa'dun elite ruled over several Shia tribes of the Lower Euphrates seemed to show that tensions could be resolved. (Indeed, 'because of the unquestioned nature of the Sunni ascendancy, there has been little jealousy or bitterness between the two branches of Islam in the Iraq'.[30]) This was at the very least a blinkered view. It would soon become clear that the conversion of the masses of the southern Iraqi tribes, of both marsh and desert, to Shia Islam had massive political implications. It was a fairly recent phenomenon; such groups as the Shammar and the Bani Tammim, who had arrived in Iraq during the eighteenth century, and also the older confederations such as the Muntafik, the Zubayd and the Albu Muhammad, had only converted in the nineteenth century. They may have been influenced by the increasing threat to the Shia holy cities from the Wahhabi of central Arabia, or even by shifting flow patterns of the Euphrates itself, but the main cause seems to have been the impact of Ottoman tribal policy. As governmental action undermined traditional tribal structures, the social influence of the Shia *sayyids*, recognised descendants of the Prophet, strengthened. In the nineteenth century, the number of *sayyids* in the Euphrates area multiplied dramatically. It was they who formed the transmission network for the calls to jihad from Najaf, Karbala and Khadimain. In the British Army they faced a would-be ruler far more formidable than the old Ottoman provincial governors. They would accommodate to it where it was determined enough, but their accommodation would be guarded at best.

The lack of any real British effort to mobilise the Arabs of Mesopotamia may still seem baffling. Cox and Wilson's insistence on the need for a declaration of virtual British annexation shows that they saw the Arabs as, at best, potential allies rather than protagonists in a war of liberation. Cox urged an advance to Baghdad because he believed that only this would sway powerful Arab leaders like Sheikh Ajaimi. He did think in terms of a wider Arab movement, but he envisaged a kind of loose confederation owing allegiance to Ibn Saud – an idea that would persist for many years – rather than a national state as the objective. Neither he nor Wilson thought that there was either the will or the capacity to generate a true national movement.

But the real point was that they did not want to see such a movement. The perspective of the 'Indian' administrators in Mesopotamia was very different from that of the British officials in Egypt who were, from the very start of the war, looking for signs of an Arab nationalist organisation capable of leading an effective revolt against the Turks. Such signs could certainly be found. In August 1914 Aziz Ali al-Masri, a former Ottoman Army colonel who had founded al-Ahd al-Iraqi, a secret group of Iraqi officers dedicated to the liberation of Arabia, arrived in Egypt. He told the British authorities that his organisation planned to use the Arab divisions in the Ottoman Army in Mesopotamia as the basis for a national revolt, raising some 15,000 men. He asked Britain to provide funding and arms. The British were impressed by his enthusiasm, but though he seems to have tried not to exaggerate his organisation's ability to act on its own, they found his scheme too 'vague'. As the head of intelligence in Egypt, Captain Gilbert Clayton, put it, 'the details do not seem to have been thought out'.[31]

Still, al-Ahd was potentially the most promising local ally for Britain. The Iraqi 'military class' was unusually well educated, in Western terms. Since the creation of the first military intermediate school in Baghdad by Midhat Pasha in 1870, two more military schools had been set up. They were the first to teach modern subjects like mathematics, physics and history, and they offered a path to higher education at government expense in Constantinople. By 1914 they had 1,338 students – at least 10 per cent of the male school population. Mainly drawn from the urban middle classes, and alert to Western ideas of progress, the military officers certainly formed 'an important segment of the Iraqi intelligentsia'.[32] Many of the officers who joined al-Ahd had spent several years in secret anti-government organisations, moving in political terms from a programme of devolution and Arab autonomy towards separatism. Paradoxically, perhaps, the nationalist officers, mostly Sunnis, became far more hostile to Turkish rule than the Shia religious establishment and tribal leaders with their long history of resistance to Ottoman government. Unsurprisingly, though, they were equally hostile to the idea of a British invasion: al-Masri specifically asked for British aid to be confined to money and guns, not troops.

London welcomed the news about al-Ahd – the Foreign Secretary urged that 'the Arab movement should be encouraged in every way possible'. But in Mesopotamia the reaction was strikingly different. Shortly after Basra was occupied, while Cox was developing his argument about the uselessness of conciliation, he had an interview with an officer whom al-Masri called 'by far the most important' member of al-Ahd in Iraq. This was Nuri al-Said, who would become a major figure in the government of Iraq under the monarchy over the next thirty years. Cox reported that Nuri, 'a delicate Arab youth of about twenty-five years of age, suffering from some affection of the chest, and highly Europeanised', was 'primarily a visionary socialist'. These were obviously negative qualities. Cox was scathing about Nuri's 'visionary and impracticable' proposal to 'help by converting and detaching from the army some of Djavid Pasha's officers', and winning over some of the tribal sheikhs to his ideals. He was sure that 'the "young Arabs" and their propaganda would not have the slightest effect' on the 'backward tribes and Sheikhs with whom they would have to deal'. And even if they did, 'they might do more harm than good and would be of no immediate use to us'.[33]

Nuri had unwittingly sabotaged his own case by telling Cox that his group had 'entered into relations with Sayyid Talib'. This formidable political figure, the son of the Naqib of Basra, had achieved such a grip on Basra province before the war that he could effectively defy the Ottoman government. He was a sophisticated operator, with a grasp of modern nationalist rhetoric, who had moved from supporting the all-Ottoman Liberty and Accord Party to establishing his own Basra Reform Society in 1913, eventually demanding local autonomy in 1914. He was also not averse to strong-arm methods – blackmail and violent intimidation. He was keen to work with the British: he had met Kitchener in Egypt, and talked to officials in India before the war. When the war began, he offered to facilitate a British capture of Basra, if he was recognised as its ruler. The British might easily have seen him as a 'strongman' they could do business with. But they chose to brand him a self-seeking rogue, violent and corrupt, and so an unacceptable collaborator. ('Definite arrangements with a man of Sayyid Talib's calibre are better avoided.') They rejected his bid for personal power, even when he adjusted it to a proposal to be appointed governor under British authority. They dismissed his nationalist rhetoric as a sham. Cox does not seem to have stopped to ask why, if the people were as backward and unreceptive to nationalist ideas as he maintained, Sayyid Talib thought it worth employing such language. Not long after Cox's meeting with Nuri, Talib was deported to India – as was Nuri. So 'almost the only person who could have acted as the leader of the slowly-growing political movements among the city dwellers' was removed.[34] Without such leaders, the chance of any spontaneous upsurge of political activity was fatally reduced.

Cox would amplify his view decisively later in 1915. 'The formation of an autonomous state in Iraq appears to be both impossible and unnecessary.' (The message was sent by the

military commander, Sir John Nixon, but the words were plainly
Cox's.) 'Here in Iraq there is no sign of the slightest ambition
of the kind among the people, who expect and seem to be quite
ready to accept our administration . . . It is highly inexpedient
and unnecessary to put into the heads of the backward people
of the country what seems to us the visionary and premature
notions of the creation of an Arab state.' Such notions would
'only tend to make endless difficulties for Great Britain' and
'serve no present purpose but to stimulate a small section of
ambitious men to turn their activities to a direction from which
it is highly desirable to keep them for many years to come'.[35]
Here indeed was the authentic voice of Indian administration.

There was to be no Arab mobilisation against the Turks in
Mesopotamia. 'In contrast to the many revolt attempts in the
Levant [during the war] in Iraq hardly any such ideas arose.'[36]
The most plausible British candidate to promote such resistance,
Gerard Leachman of the Sussex Regiment, a desert explorer
with a reputation second only to Shakespear's, was left cooling
his heels in India until March 1915. When he was finally sent
to Basra in the spring, he was only tasked with setting up an
intelligence network amongst the tribes behind enemy lines. In
April he was still in the British camp at Shaiba, fuming as he
watched the irregular Arab cavalry 'careering impertinently'
around. His attitude to the local population was based on a belief
that 'in tribal war you either dominate or submit to treachery
and almost certain death'. Short-tempered and physically
aggressive, Leachman was Orientalism red in tooth and claw.
He made some early progress in establishing his network, but in
May 1915 was reined in to act as a political officer with the force
advancing up the Tigris. This limited him to tasks like foraging for
supplies and animals, and punishing Marsh Arabs who cut field
telegraph cables. Later, his influence with the extensive Anaiza
confederation led him to be nominated 'O.C. Desert', with the
aim of organising a blockade of Turkish communications with
Amir Ibn Rashid of Hail in central Arabia.[37] Whether or not

Leachman had the right approach to mobilising Arab forces, or indeed much interest in doing so, he was not given the remit or the resources to do it. The British in Mesopotamia shied away from the political implications of any direct Arab involvement in the campaign.

In the end, the only systematic enrolment of Arab fighters was in local police or *shabana* units under close British control. Harold Dickson, who left the 33rd Cavalry in mid-1915 to become political officer at Suk-es-Shuyukh, managed to put together a forty-strong force. 'Arabs all and my own creation, but not nearly enough. They are good fellows, and all fought against us at the battle of Shaiba. They would turn against us tomorrow if the tide turned.' (Dickson, who was born in Beirut and grew up in Jerusalem, claimed a special insight into the 'Arab mind'. He took a dim view of the allegiance of his local sheikhs – 'not sure what is happening, they prefer to sit on the fence. A more treacherous lot of "blighters" I've never met.')[38] When the issue of raising Arab auxiliary forces was aired later in the war, the commander in Mesopotamia would reject the idea with barely concealed contempt. We do not know if the issue was ever aired with his predecessors; they may also have rejected it, but if so they helped to ensure that their army would campaign amongst a largely hostile population. For a long time to come, the Arabs fighting for the Turks would vastly outnumber those fighting against them.

6. Qurna

We may be permitted to indulge a very confident assurance that henceforth a more benign administration will bring back to Iraq that prosperity to which her rich potentialities give her so clear a title.

LORD HARDINGE

The British may have thought they knew something of Mesopotamia's people, but they could not deny their ignorance of its physical geography. The expedition was woefully unprepared – no pre-war staff exercises had ever involved a landing at the head of the Gulf. The result was all too clear as Barrett cautiously sent a 'reconnaissance in force' towards Qurna early in December 1914. Beset by mirages and hampered by lack of cover – as well as, more avoidably, by lack of cavalry reconnaissance – this force fought its way through the Turkish forward defences at Muzairaa but came to a halt at the river. The difficulty of crossing the Tigris – two to three hundred yards wide at this point – seems to have come as a surprise. Lieutenant-Commander Wilfrid Nunn, captain of the *Espiègle*, noted that when the flotilla pushed up towards Qurna 'we had only an old rough sketch-map of the river, showing no soundings, and affording very little information'.[1]

Arnold Wilson witheringly pointed out that the summary of elementary facts about Mesopotamia that forms the opening chapter of the Official History of the Mesopotamia campaign concludes with the remark that much of this information 'was only obtained by our forces after months of actual experience'. But why were months needed? For over a century the Government of India had maintained a representative at Baghdad, and members of the Indian Political Department on the consular staff at Basra

– 'men well accustomed to furnish reliable reports on every conceivable subject', as Wilson said – and themselves usually soldiers. There was simply no excuse for knowing so little; and the fault was compounded once the expeditionary force was there, in Wilson's view, by the incomprehensible 'marked reluctance' of the divisional intelligence staff to exploit what expertise existed on the ground, in the form of the local British and European residents. They apparently preferred 'to proceed by method of trial and error'. Wilson acidly added, 'the trials were those of the troops; the errors those of a shortsighted and complacent hierarchy'.[2]

Fortunately, the Ottoman Army was if anything worse informed than the British.[3] They knew little more about the country beyond the riverbanks, and considerably less about navigating the River Tigris, whose channels were surveyed and buoyed by the British. But the British had another problem. The lack of maps would be rectified – albeit slowly and painfully – once aircraft arrived, but assessing enemy strength remained an intractable challenge. British intelligence was baffled by what it saw as the quirky organisational structure of the Ottoman Army. 'The Turks rarely stopped tinkering with their organization for more than a month together,' one British intelligence officer wrote. Sometimes they merged battle-weakened units, but other changes seemed arbitrary, as when the V Army Corps in the Caucasus was renamed the 5th Caucasus Division, when a 5th Division was already operating on the same front. The effective strength of nominally similar units varied dramatically.[4]

Luckily for Barrett, ignorance did not prove fatal at this stage. As his troops trudged forward again after the thwarted 'reconnaissance in force', and stuck once again on the riverbank, some of them 'persuaded' two local *mahelas* (the sailboats favoured by Gulf pirates, able to carry 30–50 tons of freight) to ferry them across. Laborious preparations were being made to bridge the river, but the surprise crossing convinced the defenders once again that they had been outmanoeuvred. Just before midnight on 6 December, 'a small steamer with all its lights burning brightly was sighted coming slowly down the river, blowing her syren [*sic*] as she approached to attract our attention'. Commander Nunn took three Turkish officers on board the *Espiègle*, where they asked to be allowed to march the garrison out and leave the town to the British. Nunn, who could not get in touch with Fry, refused. After 'an angry scene' the Turks eventually agreed to surrender unconditionally.⁵ Qurna, and its garrison of 45 officers and 989 troops, were formally surrendered by the Vali of Basra, Subhi Bey, to Fry and Cox at 1.30 p.m. on 9 December. For the commander of a sloop to negotiate the surrender of a town was a rare event, though it was only the first of a series of *Boy's Own Paper*-style adventures that were shortly to follow. Nunn was rewarded by being made Senior Naval Officer for Force D a few days later.

Qurna was, admittedly, not much of a town. It found even fewer admirers amongst its conquerors than Basra had. As the supposed location of the Garden of Eden, it drew a predictable chorus of mockery – 'no need for an angel with a flamin' sword to drive me out of 'ere!' and so on. It was a strategic key point, but perhaps as Barrow had said a little too far from Basra to be ideal for such a small expeditionary force. Disagreeable enough in itself – 'a collection of filthy lanes and mud and reed hovels, with a few brick houses, barracks and a custom house' – it was surrounded by vast marshes. The plain of the Tigris to the north was totally inundated during the spring flood, and the town itself was only kept dry by major earthworks. The new garrison, when not 'strafing' ('punishing' – a usage imported from the Western Front) Arab villages, found themselves fully occupied for the next two months in constructing both military and flood defences. In mid-January Captain A. S. Cane, a medical officer in the artillery, found 'the trenches and defensive works a marvel of ingenuity and labour'.⁶ Cane's generally sanguine view of the situation in other respects was widely shared at all levels in Force D. Though 'the water here is awful, liquid mud', he himself was 'well and happy, as fit as a fiddle and thoroughly enjoying it all'. Especially the fighting: 'I love to see a bit of fighting and be where the bullets are', he wrote in his diary, 'or rather' – he added, in case this seemed odd in a doctor – 'to have been near them and to enjoy the nice comfy feeling when they stop singing.' ('Of course we see the sad and uncomfortable side', he added, 'but it is war.')

In the aftermath of the Qurna engagement he saw no problems at Basra base hospital, where the staff 'seemed very pleased at the rapidity with which the sick were collected to the hospital boat and cleared to the base after the recent fighting'. In Camp Tigris he thought that 'sickness is very scarce and the mosquitoes, though numerous, don't bite much'. Christmas brought a real treat: early on Christmas Day 'some thousands of pounds of plum pudding arrived', a gift from the Women of Bombay War Fund. This provided a pound of pudding for every officer and soldier.[7] There were other goodies too – Spackman noted that though he now had no pyjamas at all, 'I have been given as loot two Turkish Mannlicher rifles with bayonets, in first class order, .450 bore', which would 'do very well for big game shooting in India'. He had acquired (for £5) 'a charming little milch cow with a gay little calf that went quite mad after its feed'. The cow was taken on his battalion's strength disguised 'as a mule for ration purposes': 'the sepoys took to her with delight'.[8]

The icing on the cake for Captain Cane came early in the New Year, when he returned to Qurna from a trip to Basra by river 'just as the Arabs, backed by the Turks, were advancing to attack the camp from the north along the right bank of the Tigris'. 'The field guns from the camp had just come into action when our boat, the *Mejidieh*, drew alongside with her guns facing the attack . . . Our guns', he noted in the grim artillerymen's phrase, 'made magnificent practice . . . Being on the bridge of the ship myself immediately behind the guns, I could see every shot . . . shell after shell burst all among them and laid them out right and left . . . all the camp were standing on the trench parapets watching the fun.'⁹ Here was war as it was supposed to be. But this was one of the few moments when the Arab sniping and harassment of the British position crystallised into something resembling a determined assault. For the most part it was confined to noisy demonstrations that the troops called 'Salvation Army meetings': tiresome but seemingly no more than a loud nuisance.

The boat Cane stood on to admire the gunnery was one of two river steamers attached to the force as transports (the other was the Lynch Bros. flagship, the *Blosse Lynch*), each armed with two 18-pounder field guns strapped to its decks. The *Mejidieh* itself was an especially interesting case. Its owner and captain, Charles Cowley, had volunteered his services (though the official history rather slightingly recorded his ship as having been 'requisitioned'). As he had been born in Baghdad and spent his working life on the Tigris, he was regarded as an Ottoman citizen and hence a traitor in Turkish eyes. He and his ship were to play a part as central as any of the naval flotilla in the coming campaign, right up until the climax of the drama at Kut in the spring of 1916 when he paid for his patriotism with his life.

Force D's total dependence on water transport had already sparked calls for more boats able to navigate the shallow and unpredictable waters of the Tigris–Euphrates. As the waters rose in January, troop movements by land came to a halt, and every battalion had to organise a 'bellum squadron' for reconnaissance and minor amphibious operations, as well as 'a mobile bridge train for crossing small waterways'. Beyond the main waterways which larger boats (*mashufs*) could navigate, *bellums* were the universal mode of transport in the Basra marshes – reminding the romantically minded of gondolas, others of Canadian dugout canoes. In mid-January, the troops began to get systematic training in handling them – 'the men look upon it as great sport', Bird said – and every battalion had to equip a squadron of four *bellums*, each crewed by eight men. Each was supposed to be 'a self-contained unit carrying the necessary kit, rations and supply for its crew'.¹⁰

Enjoyment of this quiet period of consolidation around Basra was crowned by a Viceregal visit in early February. ('It was so nice of him,' thought Major Dickson: 'I fancy he thought of the King's example.') Hardinge arrived at Basra on the 4th, and sallied forth to tour the front-line defences over the next three days. Escorted by a squadron of cavalry, he rode over to the position at Shaiba Fort, across the lake west of Basra, on the 5th, and then went upriver to Qurna. The visit was intended to send a signal, reassuring the wavering Arabs that Britain was serious about driving the Turks from Arabia. It also demonstrated India's ownership of the Mesopotamia expedition, and maybe of Mesopotamia too. In Basra Hardinge stressed that, while Britain's obligations to its allies prohibited it from unilaterally 'laying down plans for the future', 'we may be permitted to indulge a very confident assurance that henceforth a more benign administration will bring back to Iraq that prosperity to which her rich potentialities give her so clear a title'. Quite what this heavily coded message meant would remain to be seen. Hardinge's sanguine view extended to the local medical facilities, which, like Captain Cane, he found good. He also reversed his previous agreement that IEF D should be reinforced to two divisions, and cancelled the despatch of an infantry brigade being held in readiness in India. 'To these optimistic views he clung', said Wilson, 'long after any sort of justification had ceased to exist.' Still, Hardinge had at least been to the front, and in this he was unusual. Regrettably, 'his example was not followed by the Commander-in-Chief in India or any of his principal staff officers for more than two years'.[11]

It would quickly become clear that the expanding theatre of operations was overstretching the expeditionary force. Intelligence reports now warned that more Arabs were cooperating with the Turks, and that a reinforced Ottoman division was assembling upriver at Ezra's Tomb. And there were growing signs of how nasty the country could become. William Bird of the Dorsets, who was in the force sent to Shaiba, found the march across the inundated land from Basra the 'hardest imaginable. We had to march waist deep in water for 10 miles with thick mud below our feet, it was simply killing.' Even in January the weather was 'getting murderous hot the theometre [*sic*] "registring" 127 degrees in the shade. Many men are falling down with heat stroke & malaria fever.' Bird thought the sandstorms 'the worst thing to get caught in, than any other thing in the world'.

The political situation was also worrying. Even before Hardinge's visit to Mesopotamia, a torrent of reports warned of German intrigues in Persia aimed at arousing a jihad. In late January Cox heard that a Turkish force, supported by the Bani Turuf and Bani Lam tribes in the area between the Tigris and the Karun, was moving across the Persian frontier in spite of Persian protests. Shortly after that the Vice-Consul in Ahwaz reported that a 'large section of the population will undoubtedly join Jihad when it reaches Karun'. He had been told by the town's Persian governor that 'he cannot rely on local tribesmen or answer for safety of Europeans' at Ahwaz. Such alarms were not easy to evaluate. Cox accepted that the Qurna position was 'very strong', and believed that the Arab 'tribal contingents are not pulling together and are short of ammunition'. But he warned that it was 'not safe to under-rate their fighting value when their fanaticism is roused'. Lord Crewe worried that 'considering spread of Jehad' it might be 'too late to protect pipe line and oil fields as without visible support friendly Arabs and Bakhtiaris may lose confidence in our power'. He asked whether some troops could be sent 'from Basra forthwith by river to Ahwaz'. To this the Viceroy rather airily replied that the 12th Brigade was already on its way to Mohammerah, and even if it was too late to protect the pipeline and oilfields, 'in our opinion their protection should not be regarded as our principal object'. That was 'to crush any attacks on Kurna or Basra', and Barrett should only send troops to Ahwaz if he felt confident that he could safely spare them. This he doubted.[12]

Crewe, clearly nettled, urged once more that 'prompt support now' for the Sheikh of Mohammerah 'may obviate larger military efforts later'. By the time Hardinge arrived at Basra, 'the Jahad was having apparently increasing effect in the region of the lower Euphrates, in Arabistan, and even in Basra itself'. Then it was reported that the powerful Bawi tribe had 'risen against' the Sheikh, who was 'sending about a thousand of his own particular tribesmen whom [sic] he hopes will be against jehad', but he was clearly not sure. He, too, 'expressed inability to guarantee security of Europeans'. At last, on 11 February, Barrett decided that he could spare some troops to reinforce Ahwaz. But he sent an odd force – thirty cavalry, two Indian battalions, thirty men of the Dorsets, and a handful of guns – under the division's artillery chief, Brigadier-General C. T. Robinson. They arrived too late to prevent an Arab attack on the pipeline, which was cut in several places. This was exactly the kind of reverse that Crewe had been warning of, as he testily pointed out. Reiterating 'the necessity for prompt action', he wanted to know 'how in case of emergency you propose to provide the troops necessary to make position in Mesopotamia secure, as I am strongly of opinion that some such emergency is more than possible'. His warning was soon followed by a potentially serious defeat on the Karun.

Robinson's position, encamped just across the Karun river from Ahwaz, was awkward, with Ottoman troops and Arab irregulars massing in large numbers around Ghadir to his north. On 3 March he decided to lead a dawn strike on Ghadir, seemingly 'convinced that if he could get his guns in effective range of the hostile camp without alarming them, he could do so much damage with his quick-firing artillery that the enemy would retire or disperse'.[13] If this was his thinking, it went badly awry. The enemy came forward, and Robinson was soon in full retreat, facing the possible destruction of his force. The official line is that 'the accounts of what followed are not at all clear',[14] but Lieutenant Staples of the 11th Rajputs sent his parents an exceptionally vivid one. 'Well', he began, 'at 2am on 3rd March we were marched out, a force of less than 1,000 men all told, to make "reconnaissance in force" (father knows all

the meanings of that mysterious phrase). We had two field guns
& two mountain guns. About 6am we got to a place about 3
miles from the Arab camps & it got light, so we wished them
good morning by pumping shells into the camps. We watched
the Arabs with our glasses come buzzing out like a disturbed
wasps nest & thought they were going to run away. We all felt
sorry for them – however they didn't run away but produced
green, red & white banners exactly the same shape as those
used in May processions at Greenwich (I remember that thought
occurring to me).' Mounted Arabs with these banners 'galloped
round both our flanks & some got on to hills between us & our
camp'. Pressed hard on all sides, the force 'drifted back the eight
miles or so to camp. We had to make the rearguard retire at a
walk, to steady the sepoys, as we dared not let them double.
Personally I never expected to get back to camp as we were being
pelted with bullets from never less than three sides all the time &
were cruelly outnumbered.' The force survived for two reasons:
'One (& the most important) was the surprising inaccuracy of
the Arabs' fire. The second was that they never had the pluck
to push us & cut us all down, as I am sure they could have
done. They used to make spasmodic efforts to do so, but only
about 50 men would start & gallop on us, shouting – & as soon
as a dozen or so were shot, they used to reel off.' So although
the Arabs 'exposed themselves very recklessly to get hold of any
loot, such as a loose horse', they would not close in en masse. 'If
the whole lot of them had really made a determined charge upon
us, they <u>must</u> have got in & finished us. As it was, little lots of
50 or so had no chance.'

Staples, who was wounded in the foot, eventually fell in with
the British infantry platoon for the last couple of miles to the
camp, in extended order with bayonets fixed, 'because we were
being followed at about 300 yds by swarms of their mounted
men . . . We used to halt & face about and & start firing when
they had got to about 200 yds & when they had got to 100 yds
from us, they always had about 12 empty saddles & the rest

would invariably wheel round & gallop off . . . I never saw anything so steady as those few men of the Dorsets. It really was a joy to see them.' He was also full of admiration for the force's three medical officers, and the medical staff. ('When I got into Camp I had to be lifted off the horse. The boot being an ordinary Tommy's boot, it took off easily enough. "Saves a lot of trouble that", said the hospital orderly Tommy, when he saw that the bootlace was cut through by the bullet.') But Staples was less impressed with the Indian troops. As we have seen, the officers 'dared not' let the sepoys double-march for fear they would run for it; and Staples found amongst the platoon of Dorsets 'at least five other British officers of the 7th and 4th. Tell father to ponder that over', as he put it in terms that would pass the censor.

Similar suspicions were already affecting ideas about the kind of reinforcements that could be sent to Mesopotamia. Lord Crewe, 'aware that we are very deficient in Indian Infantry', suggested that 'this may not be altogether a disadvantage in present circumstances'. Considering how anxious he was about manpower, this was a striking remark. He worried that the enemy would 'every day get stronger', and hoped that their advanced forces would be 'smashed' as soon as possible. Hardinge, agreeing that Force D needed another division, insisted that it could not be taken from India: 'we are strongly of opinion that we have reached the limit of risk which can justifiably be imposed on the people of India who pay for the Indian Army.' The War Office would have to take it from the Indian forces in Egypt and East Africa. Thus baulked, the India Office began casting about for alternative manpower sources. Barrow wrote to the Admiralty politely asking whether, 'considering the very important Naval interests involved', they might not be disposed to 'send one or more battalions of Marines' to Basra. (He received a predictably frosty reply.)

When Kitchener did eventually agree to transfer the 30th Brigade from Egypt, Hardinge pointed out that it was 'not desirable to send' one of its regiments, the 136th, to Mesopotamia.

'It contains not merely 2 Hazara Companies who are Shias', but also a 'strong trans-frontier element' – and Barrett had 'twice reported that he does not trust the 4 trans-frontier companies of the 20th and has asked me to recall them to India'. (Though he had refused to do this.) To cope with this problem, Barrow was forced to devise some complicated arrangements, involving dropping 'a selected half battalion at Muscat where they would be amongst a Sunni population', while the other half battalion 'with no Shias could be suitably located at Bushire'. Alternatively the 136th could be dropped at Aden where the Arab population was 'Sunni and anti-Turk'. Either way the brigade would be one battalion short, but 'you may be able to complete it eventually with a British regiment'.[15] The official story to cover this awkward reduction of the brigade was that the Baluchis had 'been stopped at Bushire to deal with local disturbances engineered by the German Consul'.[16] Which was true, up to a point: there were disturbances, but they had more to do with Persian exasperation at endless British interference than with German machinations. In the British view, Persia was a failing state whose governmental weakness represented a threat to regional stability. But Britain's self-appointed task of bringing Persia up to scratch was perceived, rather ungratefully, by many Persians as an insulting licence to imperial manipulation. Its 'sphere of influence' in south Persia looked little different from the chain of protectorates and client states that it had methodically built up in the region over the last century. Like the people of Bahrain, the Persians had a strong suspicion that the next stage would be even more disagreeable.

7. 'Morally responsible to humanity and to civilization'

Taking Mesopotamia, for instance, means spending millions
in irrigation and development with no immediate or early
return. Keeping up quite a large army in an unfamiliar country,
tackling every kind of tangled administrative question worse
than anything we had ever had in India, with a hornet's nest of
Arab tribes, and even if that were all set right having a perpetual
menace on our flank in Kurdistan.

H. H. ASQUITH

The arrival of the (ethnically adjusted) 30th Brigade under Major-General Charles Mellis signalled the end of Sir Arthur Barrett's campaign in Mesopotamia. On 18 March Simla announced that 'we have decided to organise the force as an Army Corps under the command of a suitable General Officer'. The officer deemed 'suitable' was Lieutenant-General Sir John Nixon. The precise basis of his suitability would be much debated later. The Indian General Staff maintained that it was simply a question of seniority. At any rate Barrett was clearly judged unsuitable. Some say that he was invalided out, while others suggest that he 'had not proved to be a particularly inspiring leader'.[1] In fact he left because, offered command of the 6th Division under the new corps commander, he rejected this as a virtual demotion. He was clearly piqued that Hardinge had said nothing to him about the change during his visit, and complained to Cox that he had been given no hint of dissatisfaction with his conduct of the campaign. Cox himself later suggested that Barrett was 'probably better fitted to solve the Mesopotamian military problem than his dashing successor', and so it seems did Lord Crewe, who would tell the Mesopotamia Inquiry that he was 'sorry the change had been made'. Crewe had indeed specifically protested to Hardinge that it was 'quite unnecessary to constitute an Army Corps of two Divisions under present conditions in Mesopotamia'. All that was needed was for Barrett to be given a proper staff to support him.[2] He was 'against advancing, at least in a hurry', and was 'a little nervous of developments' under Nixon, who was known as 'a fighting pushing kind of general'. Mellis, whose arrival began the redefinition of Force D, thought the official reasoning unconvincing, and took a dusty view of Nixon's appointment: 'it seems a shabby bit of jobbing.'

Nixon was an infantry officer who had morphed into a cavalryman in mid-career. He had been given command of a cavalry column during the Boer War – his only operational command – and gone on to become Inspector-General of Indian Cavalry. In 1912 he became commander of India's four-division Southern Army. Mellis's charge of jobbing has a ring of truth, but if no other senior commander seems to have been considered for the job, it is clear that Nixon was no bland administrator. (Which, as Crewe and Cox thought, was just what IEF D needed.) Though he was not without staff experience, he evidently cultivated the image of a 'thruster', and those who appointed him were undoubtedly aware of it. Whatever Barrett's own feeling, his generalship had certainly come in for some criticism. The Viceroy's view that he had been 'dissipating strength by sending driblets to various places' was perhaps harsh, but he was given to 'reconnaissances in force' that had several times led to unnecessary setbacks and, as in the Ahwaz case, required larger forces to rectify the damage.

Underlying his caution, though, lay a strong awareness of the difficulties of operating in Mesopotamia. He had virtually abandoned the idea of movement by land, but could not get the extra river transport he wanted. He immediately grasped the potential of aircraft, but his requests for more of them had stuck in the system. In both cases he was the victim of not just the limitations of India's military resources, but also a deliberate penny-pinching administration whose ingrained parsimonious methods would eventually become a public scandal. The crucial issue may have been his demand that a light railway be built to take supplies forward from Basra to Qurna. With hindsight, this was absolutely vital for any operations further up the rivers. But India saw the cost as prohibitive unless the railway could be assured of long-term postwar profitability. Barrett would probably have refused to go forward from Qurna until he had an adequate logistic structure. Cox grumbled to Lord Curzon, 'I did all I could to get the force pushed to Amara.' He was convinced that the Turks were 'thoroughly on the run' and had practically no reserves at that time: if Amara and Nasiriyeh had been taken quickly, the powerful local tribes like the Bani Lam could have been won over. But Barrett had not felt strong enough, and 'we had to stand fast at Gurna'.[3] In Nixon, India found a general who would not be troubled by the logistical problem. And it seems that India was now looking for a general who would take things forward.

Hardinge, who had originally been cautious about the Mesopotamia commitment, became noticeably more enthusiastic after his February visit. The Indian officials expected Britain to take control of Mesopotamia after the war. Arnold Wilson went further. His argument for annexation went beyond the contention that it would reassure the Arabs, and his vision of the future nearly cost him his job even before he could start to implement it. In November 1914, 'in an idle half hour in a P&O saloon' (aboard the SS *Multan* bound for Basra) he wrote a letter to an MP, Colonel Charles Yate, suggesting that 'in the annexation of Mesopotamia may be found the solution of some of the most difficult questions that must arise in India after the war'. It should become an Indian colony and absorb some of India's surplus population. By constructing the irrigation scheme worked out before the war by the irrigation expert Sir William Willcocks, Britain could 'gradually bring under cultivation its vast unpopulated desert plains, peopling them with martial races from the Punjab'. This would mean, Wilson argued (he was already alert to the need for economy), that the colonists could 'defend themselves without the aid of a larger garrison than the Turks previously kept' – around 8,000. There would be room for 25 million people if the country were properly developed. A distinguished 'Indian Shiah' could be made governor, to keep the administration 'wholly Mohammedan'. All in all, it would offer 'Mohammedan India . . . a quid pro quo for its action in this war'.[4]

Wilson thought there would be 'no trouble from the Arabs' faced with this staggering scheme (in which the Indian colonists would outnumber the natives by ten to one): they would 'gladly accept British rule as they have done at Basrah'. Yate soon went public with the idea. Urging the Foreign Secretary that Baghdad was 'the plum', he declared that lower Mesopotamia 'under Willcocks' irrigation scheme will become one of the granaries of the world'. Because its climate rendered it 'unfit for European colonization', India was 'the only country that can properly develop it'. When the government found that the idea had come from Wilson, he was forced to write a grovelling letter blaming Yate for his 'gross breach of confidence'. (Unthinkable, Wilson implied, in a former Indian political official.) He protested that his letter had been no more than 'enthusiastic vapourings', and entirely private.[5] He never mentioned it in his extensive memoirs, and nor did his biographer. But his claim that he did not expect Yate to do anything with his plan seems disingenuous – the tone of the letter, and the fact that it was sent to an MP, suggests that he took the plan seriously. At this point the government should surely have taken Wilson out of Mesopotamia, but it left him in place; the colonisation idea also survived. When he arrived in Mesopotamia early in 1916, Amar Singh heard 'there is a scheme to build a big dam and collect all the waters of the rivers and flood all the desert and thus bring it under cultivation'. The land was to be given 'in grants to the Indian soldiers as rewards – the idea being to found a colony for India and to give them an outlet'. He thought it 'not a bad scheme' (though he had also heard that German East Africa was to be reserved for Indian colonists, and thought that a better idea).

But if London remained dead set against annexation or colonisation, its commitment to keeping the Ottoman Empire intact was at last being abandoned. Early in March 1915 Britain agreed that Russia would receive Constantinople as part of the postwar settlement. Russia demanded this in reaction to the Dardanelles expedition, the Allied attempt to seize the passage between the Mediterranean and the Black Sea, to open up a warm-water supply line to Russia. Conceived as a naval rush through the Straits, it began with an ineffective naval bombardment of the Turkish forts in February. After an attack by sixteen battleships in mid-March also failed, 30,000 troops were landed on the Gallipoli peninsula in April – dramatically raising the stakes in the war against Turkey. The whole operation was ill-conceived, and probably doomed, but that would not become clear for several months. At the start, the Russians had to consider what would happen if it succeeded. Gratitude for the Allies' efforts to provide them with supplies was mixed with a suspicion that if the British actually captured Constantinople, they would never leave. Russia demanded a guarantee that it would have the city. France was dismayed – fearing a formidable new Mediterranean rival, it stuck to the old British Jingoist line, 'the Russians shall not have Constantinople'. It wanted to give a non-committal reply, but Asquith was happy 'to see the Turkish Empire disappear from Europe' and believed that Constantinople should rightly be Russian. Grey feared that without the guarantee Russia might pull out of the war. This was, as he reminded the Russians, 'a complete reversal of the traditional policy of His Majesty's Government . . . in direct opposition to the opinions and sentiments at one time universally held in England'.

The concession was an historic shift, with historic implications. Partition was back on the international agenda at last. As soon as the Cabinet accepted Russia's demand for the Straits, Lord

Kitchener argued that Britain must respond with its own Middle Eastern project. He urged his colleagues to think ahead to the postwar world, where 'old enmities and jealousies may revive'. Britain must assume that it could find itself again confronting Russia or France, or both. There could be a serious threat to Egypt. The answer was to establish 'an Arab kingdom under the auspices of England', reaching as far north as the Tigris and containing 'the chief Mahommedan Holy Places, Mecca, Medina and Kerbela'. Baghdad and lower Mesopotamia, though, should be incorporated in the Empire – not just because 'this region only stands in need of irrigation and of scientific development to become again one of the most fertile and highly productive areas in the world'. An even stronger argument was that this 'at present thinly populated tract provides an almost ideal field of colonisation for the surplus population of India'. Echoing Wilson and Yate, he suggested that possession of Mesopotamia 'would help to solve one of the most serious problems with which the Government of India is confronted'. It would also 'secure all the approaches to the Mahommedan Holy Places', and establish the British Empire as 'the greatest of Moslem States'. If Britain held Alexandretta, strategically placed between the Levant and Anatolia, it would form the key point in a structure arching from Cyprus to Persia and guaranteeing the security of the Persian Gulf oil resources as well as Egypt, and of course India itself.[6]

The implications of this project were obvious. As the Foreign Secretary asked his Cabinet colleagues, 'if we acquire fresh territory shall we make ourselves weaker or stronger?' (The order he chose for his adjectives indicated his view.) Grey thought there was a 'very strong feeling in the Mohammedan world that Mohammedanism ought to have a political as well as a religious existence'. Britain needed to be able to say to its Muslim subjects that 'as Turkey had handed itself over to the Germans, we had set up a new and independent Moslem State'.[7] But how big should this state be? And was it the same as an Arab state? Grey was well aware not just of India's objection to the whole idea of an Arab state, and its proprietorial attitude to Mesopotamia, but also of French suspicions about British expansion. When the French got wind of Kitchener's ideas, he played for time by telling them that while the centre of any future Muslim state would 'naturally be the Moslem Holy Places', Britain had not yet 'come to a definite opinion whether Mesopotamia should be included', or 'whether we should put forward a claim for ourselves in that region'.[8]

The India Office was now staking out the British claim to control of Mesopotamia in a more muscular way than before. Hirtzel (an Oxford don as well as a mandarin) produced a magisterial assessment making two central arguments. First, that in spite of previous administrative divisions the former Abbasid provinces of 'Jezireh and Irak Arabi' remained fundamentally 'a geographical unit', and must be treated as a whole. Second, there was a moral justification for 'detaching' this unit from the Ottoman Empire – 'the misrule of the Turk, who has reduced one of the most fertile regions in the world to a wilderness', and 'throughout his history has shown no sign of the administrative honesty and capacity necessary to reclaim it'.[9]

Hirtzel insisted on the economic potential not only of the 'exuberantly fertile' northern plain – 'where in the spring the rider is almost overpowered by the scent of the flowers which his horse treads underfoot' – but even of the wasted alluvial plain of the south. Sir William Willcocks, whose pre-war reports had alerted many to Mesopotamia's potential, had argued that reclamation of the central belt would be 'very easy as compared with Egypt' because of the lime in its soil. (Some, admittedly, held that much of the land away from the two rivers would always be uncultivable because of the high proportion of gypsum.) For Hirtzel the 'essential unity' of this great 100,000-square-mile area was emphasised by the homogeneity of its almost exclusively Arab population. The people were superficially disunited, admittedly: on one count they were divided into over a hundred tribes. But Hirtzel argued that their appearance of ungovernability was illusory. Their wildness was not due to any natural objection to settling down as farmers, but because 'their ruling passion is acquisitiveness, and where cultivation can be demonstrated to be more profitable than robbery they show no objection to applying themselves to it'. Patronising though it was, this was meant as a compliment. The future administration would 'complete the process of transformation and pacification to which the Turks have never addressed themselves'. The Turkish practice of playing off one tribe against another had made the situation look hopeless; but their occasional efforts to impose order 'with a fairly efficient gendarmerie' had been effective. Hirtzel concluded that the policing of the area should be 'comparatively easy': all in all, 'the Arabs are easily governed'.[10]

Hirtzel skilfully interwove power-political with moral arguments. The power that detached lands from Ottoman rule would become 'morally responsible to humanity and to civilization for their reclamation and development'. Britain could not simply drive the Turkish Army out of Mesopotamia: it must take on the future government of the region. The only question was, what region exactly? With an almost breathtaking sense of freedom in the exercise of power, Hirtzel set forth various possible options. Britain might 'detach from Turkey the three vilayets of Mosul, Baghdad and Basra'; or it might take Basra alone. Either course, he demonstrated, had drawbacks. The first would, amongst other things, 'raise the Kurd question in its acutest form'. If it were possible to set up Kurdistan as an independent whole, under the rule of a Kurd family, 'the problem would be comparatively simple'. But there was no suitable family available, so it might actually be better to consign the Kurds to Russian control.[11] Then Britain would have to carve up the Mosul *vilayet*, detaching the eastern part, as well as ('for administrative convenience') the fertile tract north of the Jebel Sinjar where the Kurds had joint rights. As he mulled over various lines that might be drawn, he noted that 'in the absence of natural features, the frontier, wherever it is, can be nothing but a line' – no line that could be drawn seemed to be better than any other.

As for the minimalist option of merely detaching the town of Basra and the Shatt-al-Arab below it, Hirtzel deployed Force D's experience to demonstrate that Basra was strategically untenable by itself. It would always depend on controlling the river further north, at least as far as Amara and probably as far as Baghdad. 'Whoever holds Baghdad commands not only our trade with Mesopotamia but also that with North-West Persia.' So Britain could not avoid annexing most of Mesopotamia. Only thus could Indian colonisation be possible. Like Wilson, Hirtzel said that 'an Indian, and especially a Punjabi, colony would help to provide the army necessary for its own defence'. It would give India 'a tangible reward for her services in the War', and would also mean that (in a revealing phrase) 'the excuse for emigration to the white man's colonies would be removed'. Beyond the annexed territory, in the north and west where no better frontiers could be found than 'shadowy lines across the wilderness', British control should take the form of a protectorate. The answer to the tricky question of where that control should stop was that 'it should not stop until the points are reached at which the control of other civilized Powers begins'.

Hirtzel was aware that British annexation might not go down well with either international or Arab opinion, but he dismissed out of hand the idea of an independent Arab state. 'The Arabs have never shown any cohesive power', and the few leading individuals such as Ibn Saud and the Sharif of Mecca were 'too far away' to have an impact in Mesopotamia. Because the Arabs 'have not so far shown any administrative capacity', to hand the country over to them would be to betray Britain's responsibility to civilisation. Hirtzel played with the idea of a 'puppet ruler with an effective British administration', but thought that Egyptian experience showed that it was unsatisfactory, and anyway 'as a political device it is worn somewhat thin'. He even mooted the bizarre possibility that Mesopotamia be placed under Persian sovereignty, but leased in perpetuity to Britain. In the end, though, he concluded that 'there is no practicable alternative to annexation and direct administration by Great Britain'. The Arabs would not object, he argued: they were 'accustomed to abrupt changes and easily adapt themselves to a new order if it is equitable'.

Hirtzel was an influential adviser, but he did not make government policy. Even within the India Office there was a clash of views. General Barrow urged caution, invoking 'the lesson of the decline and fall of Rome' to teach 'the necessity of avoiding over extension'. Turkey-in-Asia should be preserved as a 'buffer state', and Baghdad *vilayet* become 'an autonomous province administered in the name of the Sultan by a British administrator, under British protection on the same lines as Egypt'. But even the cautious Barrow's aims were pretty ambitious. 'Let us restrict our aspirations and our energies to obtaining a controlling influence over the Arab world, and thus becoming in fact as well as in theory the leading Islamic Power, the one on which all Islamic races will lean.'[12] Hirtzel, though, brusquely dismissing the idea of preserving Turkey, held that the 'very nature' of the Turk was ingratitude and intrigue. Turkish war policy meant that no compromise was possible now: 'It has become necessary for us to choose finally between Turk and Arab.'[13]

The Cabinet was still not yet ready for this. The Prime Minister and the Foreign Secretary, at least, refused to accept the logical implications of their support for Russian annexation of Constantinople, and resisted the idea that Britain might itself grab some Ottoman territory. But Asquith now feared that 'Grey and I are the <u>only</u> two men who doubt and distrust any such settlement', as he told his confidante Venetia Stanley on 25 March. Their belief in a peace without annexations had a moral basis, but it was also pragmatic. 'Taking on Mesopotamia, for instance,' Asquith said, 'means spending millions in irrigation & development with no immediate or early return; keeping up quite a large army white & coloured in an unfamiliar country;

tackling every kind of tangled administrative question, worse than we have ever had in India, with a hornet's nest of Arab tribes, and even if all that were set right having a perpetual menace to our flank in Kurdistan.'[14] All this was prescient; but the Prime Minister would not bring the issue to a head. Characteristically he accepted that the immediate demands of the war took priority over long-term concerns: 'the great thing for the moment' was 'to bring in Italy, voracious as she is'.

As the policy debate stalled, policy drifted – and drifted towards expansion. Insisting on remaining in 'permanent occupation of the Basra vilayet', the Viceroy argued that any political problems in setting up an administration would ease 'if and when we get to Baghdad'. Getting to Baghdad was edging on to the agenda. Though Hardinge still claimed to favour the minimum necessary military commitment, he warned that 'with an unfriendly government at Baghdad our political, military and commercial position at Basra might become very difficult'.[15] It is in this light that we must read the orders issued to Sir John Nixon as he headed out to Mesopotamia. He was asked, after assessing the situation, to submit 'a plan for the effective occupation of the Basra <u>Vilayet</u>'; and 'a plan for the subsequent advance on Baghdad'.

8. 'One of the decisive battles of the world'

> It looks as if the assault of the 2nd Dorsets decided great issues,
> and in fact averted a disaster, the possible consequences of which
> have never been realised.
> H. BIRCH REYNARDSON

By the time the 30th Brigade reached Basra, Major-General
Mellis was already in a bad mood. Sailing across the Red Sea
in late March, and suffering from eye trouble that stopped him
reading to pass the time, he found his ship (the SS *Chilka*) 'rather
a beastly one & the food is vile. I wander about the deck trying
to kill time,' he wrote to his wife. The first day of April found
him 'sitting in my cabin rather melting', with a 'strong wind
blowing which seems to suit my eyes, although it seems to melt
one morally & physically, there are some winds that absolutely
depress both mind & body'. It was hot, and he reflected that
it was 'curious how the old fellows dread the heat' (Mellis
was fifty-two) – 'we hate the idea of it, the young fellows of
course don't feel it'. His initial impression of 'Busrah or Busra'
on 9 April was not wholly unfavourable – 'a queer spot very
picturesque in its way'. That was, of course, 'its dirty eastern
way quite untouched by western improvements'. The town was
mostly Arab, and 'the Arab headdress as you see in pictures
prevails everywhere', with hardly any sign of the red fez of the
Turks and Egyptians. This benign touristic view would not last.
In mid-April he was writing that 'it is getting very warm & the
flies are terrible', and asking his wife to 'send some more covers
with weights to put over things'. Towards the end of the month
he was fuming – 'a more God forsaken spot would be hard to
imagine, an absolute level plain of scrub & sand as far as you

can see devoid of life. I seem to strike all the ghastly holes on the earth.'[1]

But by that time Mellis had transformed Britain's military position in Mesopotamia, and potentially his career too. Within a few days of reaching Basra he and his brigade were sent to reinforce Fry's brigade at Shaiba. He took the 6th Division staff with him: with Barrett gone, Mellis as senior brigadier was in temporary command of the division. Typically, Barrett had taken his time in reinforcing Shaiba. With the town now encircled by floods, he had chosen to send supplies rather than troops (transport shortages prohibited sending both). The newly arrived Nixon was sceptical of the Shaiba position, since it did not cover its communications with Basra and could be cut off by a determined enemy advance. But he decided to send Mellis out, and planned to visit the position himself. Just before he did, the Turks launched their first serious offensive effort.

The Ottoman commander Suleiman Askeri Bey had put together about 4,000 regulars, including the only reinforcements so far sent to Mesopotamia, the Istanbul Fire Brigade Regiment (regarded as an elite unit), with a large irregular Arab–Kurdish contingent of maybe 18,000. This was not the strongest force he could have assembled. Most of his regular units remained dispersed – many covering Qurna in irrelevant positions – and the fighting value of the irregulars was doubtful. The newly formed *Mujahidin* were expected to carry out regular tactical manoeuvres, but these were a big step from traditional Arab fighting methods. Arab warfare was based on the raid, in which mobility and surprise were crucial, and spoils – rather than strategic victory – were the main objective. For Arab raiders, retreat – indeed flight – was an instinctive recourse 'once defeat had become certain'. It had nothing of the stigma that regular armies attach to it. The kind of military discipline that induces regular troops to hold on against the odds was not part of their tradition.[2]

The battle fought at Shaiba in mid-April underlined the big differences between the armies facing each other. The British position there, 'a charming oasis where the saltpetre gleams like snow through the sparse and airy green of the tamarisks', had a perimeter of over 3½ miles, lying slightly above the flood waters. Its western front rested on a walled *serai* called Shaiba fort, half a mile north of which was a 60-foot-high brick kiln. Covered only by erratic bursts of artillery fire – their gunners had the same problems of visibility as the British – the Turkish infantry ambled out of Barisiya wood, about four miles from the entrenched camp. 'Advancing in happy-go-lucky fashion and deceived by the British silence into thinking Shaiba deserted, they hurled themselves on the wire.' Attacks on the fort, the brick kiln and southern salient were put in repeatedly, with grievous casualties.[3] Arab irregulars on the hillock known as North Mound 'made several half-hearted attempts to advance'. After three hours of this inconclusive fighting, Mellis set off towards the ruins of Old Basra, presumably with the intention of taking the Turkish attackers in the flank. Wading knee-deep through the flood waters, he had got about a third of the way when a message from Nixon suggested he should head directly to Shaiba to reinforce Fry. As the water proved too deep for him to do this, Nixon told him to go back to Basra and then take one battalion out to Shaiba by boat.

Mellis wrote a dramatic account of what followed. 'You should have seen my fleet!' he told his wife – 'the men poling & of course awkwardly being new to it. It was very scattered . . . quite dark incessant firing going on all around for the enemy were attacking. We were afraid of being shot by our own side or by the Turks, however we got inside the defences alright, my canoe man being shot in the arm. Bullets were flying all over the camp, maxims going, star shell rising in the air & falling in blue green lights to show up the enemy. It was picturesque but unpleasant . . . ' He was a long way from Fry's position, and 'felt much at sea trying to get the hang of things in this huge camp & try to grasp the situation'. Now his luck turned. He went to a section of the perimeter where firing had been especially heavy to see what was going on, and found an old friend, Colonel Chitty, commanding the 119th Infantry there. 'He took me to the top of what must have been an old Babylonish tower which stood near his part of the defences. That tower proved my good friend & was the cause of my good fortune.' From it he could see the whole situation, 'thousands of Turks & Arab riflemen on all 3 sides of us at a distance of ¾ mile & nearer in some places, behind trenches in houses & holding sandy ridges they simply swarmed'.

And there, Mellis declared, 'was the cavalry brigade just moving out! It was too late I could not stop them.' In fact the cavalry move against the Arab riflemen on North Mound can hardly have been a surprise to him, as he had directly confirmed Fry's order for it. The real problem was that only a small force – a single squadron of the 7th Hariana Lancers – actually put in the attack. The result was gruesome, as the squadron dissolved under rifle fire, with only its commander, Major George Wheeler, with his senior Indian Officer getting on to the mound. Only after an under-strength infantry assault also failed did Mellis order a full-scale attack. 'I sent for General Delamain & ordered him out with 3 battalions ... to attack the mound & the house etc in its vicinity & I got my CRA (an old friend Colonel Cleeve) on to the mound [the Kiln Post] where we overlooked everything & told him to support the infantry with all the guns. From there we switched them on to whatever point we wished ... we just pounded them with shells & under cover of it the infantry advanced & captured the enemy's position with little loss. The houses were blown up & over 90 dead were found on one mound called the north mound.' This was a rout, but it was not exploited. The cavalry brigade were watering their horses, as so often, and there was no pursuit. (So at least said the official history; Mellis himself was less charitable to the cavalry brigade commander. 'I can't stick Kennedy,' he told his wife, 'a most incompetent person or gives grudging cooperation, I don't know which, but he is useless.')

The Dorsets were first into the enemy position, around 11 a.m. It was a bad day for William Bird, whose best friend Rusty was shot by a sniper before the attack began. 'He died without a chance of defending himself,' Bird lamented in his diary, '& it has upset me more than I can write here.' He also recorded a grim feature of fighting with the Arabs that was to become all too familiar. 'When we were on this mound, we found one European Major of our cavalry dead, & stripped naked, he was also mutilated beyond recognition, & also a native cavalry officer all alight, & practically burned to a cinder.'[4] Mellis left the Dorsets to hold the mound, and redirected the rest of Delamain's force towards the west to seize two abandoned mountain guns (which Mellis could see from the kiln, but which Delamain could not). Eventually it ran on 'a strong body of Turks, in successive lines of trenches' – not the last such nasty surprise – and had a stiff fight before driving them back. Delamain offered to push on to the South Mound, where more enemy forces were assembling, but his troops were exhausted and Mellis decided to call it a day. It was a victory of sorts, though Mellis noted that 'the enemy who I had driven off were chiefly Arabs, & there still remained the regular Turkish troops in the background'.[5]

Mellis planned to wait for the other two battalions of the 30th Brigade to arrive from Basra before going forward again, 'but when I went out next morning to look out from my tower I thought I could see through my glasses some movement in the direction of Barjisiyeh woods as if a retirement was commencing back to Nakheilah'. (Once again, reconnaissance was non-existent.) 'These woods were a long belt of trees edging a sandy plain very difficult to define owing to the mirage.' He 'thought I might miss an opportunity of hitting him again if I waited', so ordered his whole force forward at 9 a.m. He led the advance personally. 'I first came on the out posts & drove them back easily but as I advanced against the woods I found the enemy entrenched along a front of nearly 4 miles & the rifle fire began to get very hot & the shells to fall amongst us.' His CRA was killed, and so, almost immediately, was Cleeve's successor. 'The fight lasted from 10.30 to 5pm. I never want to go through the anxiety of some of that time, reports came in to me of heavy losses on all sides & doubt if further advance was possible. I had thrown my last man into the fight – still it hung very doubtful.' In fact, his position was critical. Losses were severe, ammunition was short, and water had run out. When the artillery ammunition ran low, he decided he would have to retreat. 'Can you imagine my feelings!' – no doubt his wife could – but then 'to my joy a report came to me that the Dorsets and others had carried the enemy's first line of trenches & they were on the run. Can you imagine how thankful I felt.' But because of his troops' physical (and maybe his own mental) exhaustion he decided not to follow the retreating enemy, who 'would probably have prepared a 2nd position'. Daylight was fading, and his men 'had suffered great thirst & heavy casualties'. Instead Mellis retired to Shaiba (unmolested) and spent a bad night worrying 'if I had been rash & foolish & had thrown away good brave fellows in vain'.

Next morning it was clear that the enemy had abandoned all their defensive works and fled, 'leaving camp standing, arms, ammunition, gun & rifle 70000 rounds of the latter, clothing, even their cooked food untouched'. Some were mystified: 'We did not know what had prompted the Turks to retire', Lieutenant A. J. Shakeshaft wrote, 'when our men were absolutely exhausted and incapable of further effort.'[6] Still, it was, as Mellis said, 'a complete victory'. He knew just how lucky he had been. Lucky not least that Nixon had called him back from his initial advance against Old Basra – 'I saw the position afterwards which I should have had to attack after my men were tired out with wading through mud for 3 miles: I think we might have been destroyed.' Nixon delighted him by giving him a pat on the back after the battle, but both generals knew who had really won it. Nixon noted that at Barisiya the Turkish troops had been 'well disciplined, well trained, brave, their machine guns have been well concealed and used with great effect, and their trenches have been admirably sited'. The Turks refused to be 'shot out of' their trenches, and had to be turned out by a charge of the whole line. If the 'pluck and determination of our troops had not been of the sternest', the battle would have been lost.[7] At the other end of the scale of ranks, a machine-gun officer in the 120th Infantry called it 'the stiffest fight we are likely to see, it was touch and go'.[8]

Shaiba was a classic 'soldiers' battle', fought by the footsoldiers' instinct. It was the Dorsets, above all, who won it by their decisive bayonet charge at the end of a gruelling day's fighting. 'From 12 – 4.30 we laid 400 yds from them firing thousands of rounds & without a blade of grass for cover the heat & the dust being simply terrific. Men wounded & dying were crying out for water. Some drank their own <u>urine</u>', Bird disapprovingly observed, '& of course made themselves worse.' Where the impetus for their final charge came from was a mystery – perhaps, as the official history suggests, the sudden cessation of Turkish artillery fire created a sense of opportunity. But that was the destiny of the regular infantryman: survival meant that anything, even a rush across a bare no-man's-land, was better than a retreat under fire. 'Victory' meant a lot, but it was also an empty formula. Bird had lost his best friend, and 'it was awfull to walk across the field & see such havoc, men, rifles, helmets & equipment lying everywhere. Our red cross are out picking up their wounded, the sights are awfull, some of them are starving & I am afraid more dirtier & lousy than we are.'[9] To a medical officer, the situation was still worse. 'Can you imagine', Spackman asked, 'having broken limbs and coming in with other wounded in a springless cart for miles across a rough desert under a burning sun?' In the evening of the 15th, 'cartloads of dead and wounded Turks were brought in all mixed up. It was horrible beyond description.'[10] Shakeshaft declared he would 'never forget the hideous sight of that blood-soaked field'.

The British conceded that the Turkish defenders had 'every reason to be proud of the fight in which, in spite of their inferior artillery and the failure of their Arab allies, they nearly succeeded in beating off the British attack'. In fact, though, Suleiman Askeri was so ashamed of the rout of his troops that he shot himself in front of his assembled officers.[11] Shakeshaft later, as a prisoner, was told by a German who had been with Suleiman that he had killed himself after the reserves he ordered to counter-attack had simply refused to move except in the direction of Nakhailat. Mehmet Emin was less charitable, and put a different perspective on the clash. 'The accursed mirage-ridden battle of Shaiba was a contest between knowledge and ignorance' – on one side medieval methods, on the other 'the skill and experience of forty years' soldiering possessed by Fry, Mellis and Delamain'. He maintained that, although Suleiman Askeri was commander in name, the conduct of the battle had fallen to Bimbashi Ali Bey of the Fire Brigade. 'What an unkind fate put at the head of this little army a commander with hardly the knowledge of a major!' No one was capable of organising a new position at Barisiya to save the force from yet another chaotic retreat. 'Soon the British shrapnel began to fall on the disorganised mass and a panic began. Had not the British attack been overcautious, terrible would have been the fate of our force.'[12]

Certainly the British were in no position to exploit their victory – the cavalry once again failing to pursue. Even so the defenders kept running 'in wild confusion, harassed and robbed by the Arabs', until they reached Khamisiya, nearly a hundred miles up the river. The four hours in front of Barisiya wood were a turning point in the Mesopotamia campaign, as Captain Reynardson of the Oxfordshire and Buckinghamshire Light Infantry insisted. 'It looks as if the assault of the 2nd Dorsets decided great issues, and in fact averted a disaster, the possible consequences of which have never been realised.'[13] Sir George MacMunn, later a senior officer in Mesopotamia, judged Shaiba 'one of the decisive battles of the War, if not the world'.[14] It had a marked effect on Arab attitudes. The tribesmen who took part in the battle had either left the field or turned on the Turkish troops with terrible effect once defeat seemed clear. A number of tribal leaders, as well as the Shia *mujtahids*, began to distance themselves from their Ottoman allegiance: indeed Najaf broke out in open revolt in April, to be followed in June by Karbala. The battle 'shattered all hopes for a massive and organised Jihad campaign'.[15]

As Mellis digested the scale of his success, he found new reasons for annoyance. His temporary command of the 6th Division ended, but he thought that if news of his victory had reached Simla in time, he would probably have got the division permanently. Instead his brigade became part of the 12th Division under Major-General George Gorringe – 'rather rough luck on me as he is only just my senior'. The new commander of 6th Division was Major-General Charles Townshend ('2 British service generals commanding 2 Indian divisions', as Mellis acidly noted). Even more annoying was that Reuters news agency published nothing but a brief report of the battle 'as if it had been a skirmish! Not even a mention of the general who commanded!' he grumbled to his wife – '& yet it was a real battle & our losses were over a fifth of our force. They don't get hotter fighting than that with the Germans.' All in all, it was 'a rotten country', 'a hideous country', 'an awful country', getting ever hotter. 'We all hate it & feel no interest in the operations, neither want to fight the Turks or do they want to fight us. We pray for the fall of Constantinople.' The only consolation, he wrote in late April, and again early in May, was that soon 'any operations will be impossible from the great heat'.

Probably most of Force D felt as Mellis did. Soaring daytime temperatures were accompanied by the arrival of 'millions of flies', to which the only official remedy was the supply of Japanese clockwork flytraps, 'fascinating to watch but hardly touching the problem'. If the days were bad, the nights were perhaps still worse. For Colonel Bowker 'night is made hideous by the pariah dog'. He had 'heard canine noises in different cities of the world more or less hideous, but nothing to touch this place'.[16] Amidst the general tedium, the so-called 'Euphrates Blockade' seems to have been as useful in providing recreation as it was in preventing enemy movements. (Some thought it was designed to screen Basra from a possible Turkish advance from Syria, others that it was stopping Turkish supplies from reaching Ibn Saud's enemy Rashid.) 'Those who took part in it', Captain Reynardson recalled, 'would disappear from our midst for a week or ten days, during which they seemed to wander about on the Hammar Lake without the slightest idea as to where or what exactly they were expected to do, beyond getting out and pushing the steamer whenever it stuck in the mud. However, they always found their way back in the end, and appeared to have had a pleasant and mildly adventurous outing.'[17]

The force's new commander, however, was upbeat. Presented as an arrival gift with a decisive victory, another man might have taken the view (as did the Mesopotamia inquiry later) that the expedition's key objectives had now been achieved. 'Basra and Muhammerah were saved and our oil interests secured', as General Barrow noted. But Nixon's instructions from Simla spoke more ambiguously of securing the 'effective occupation' of the whole Basra *vilayet*, and even mentioned the possibility of an advance on Baghdad. One contemporary military writer thought it 'not unnatural' for Nixon to 'read into these instructions an intended change of policy'.[18] This, of course, is exactly what Crewe and Barrow feared. From the seizure of Qurna onwards 'the initiative and the direction of events passed from the India Office to the Government of India'.[19]

The rift between London and Simla over Nixon's appointment would be concealed from the parliamentary inquiry, but it was quite serious. The India Office protested against the decision to turn Force D into an army corps no less than three times (on 10 and 19 March, and on 5 April), and Crewe privately told Barrow that he was 'on the merits entirely unconvinced of the need for this "Napoleonic" staff'. ('I grudge the expense as well as the locking-up of officers who might be wanted elsewhere.') To Barrow it was 'subversive of all discipline for "India" to ignore so completely the wishes & views of the Secretary of

State'. Shocked by 'this lapse in official decorum', he went so far as to refer the issue to another senior official, Sir Charles Egerton. Egerton agreed that Barrett had been 'shown scant consideration', and that the proposed corps staff was excessive, but warned that 'India might resent our interference' if it was pressed too hard. Crewe eventually accepted that he must 'give them as much of a free hand with their private war as I can', as otherwise 'they will believe that either we or the WO are perpetually nagging them, and relations will become difficult'.[20]

This spat was the symptom of a real policy change: as Nixon later testified, 'the orders given to me when I was appointed to command were to take the offensive rather than remain on the defensive'. The India Office clearly did not accept this. When he heard of Nixon's request for a further brigade, to include a British cavalry regiment and also 'a pioneer battalion to work on river obstructions etc.', Lord Crewe objected that it implied offensive operations, and 'the Government will not sanction such action at this moment'. Even if such units had been available, with the hot weather approaching it was a bad idea to send more troops – especially British – to Mesopotamia. 'During the hot season Nixon must clearly understand that he is to confine himself to the defence of oil interests in Arabistan and of the Basra Vilayet.' Britain's position was now sound, and 'a cautious policy in Mesopotamia is the correct one'. Yet by talking again of the 'Basra Vilayet' (which included Amara, 87 miles north of Basra) Crewe fatally undermined his instruction. Equally perilously, he offered Hardinge the option that 'if after smashing enemy in Karun direction it is possible to advance to Amara . . . I should be disposed to agree to such an operation if proposed by Nixon and supported by you'. A successful Karun operation would bring the Arab tribes between Karun and Amara under control and so protect the pipeline.[21]

For Nixon the Karun situation offered the chance to demonstrate what could be done with the force he already had. Following Robinson's defeat, he sent a much larger force there in late April. Its commander, General Gorringe, got the job done, at the price of 'a heavy sick-list', in a seven-week campaign in immense heat. In doing it he cultivated a fire-eating hard-man image that did not appeal to everyone. Captain Cane, who was running the officers' hospital housed in the sheikh's house at Ahwaz, called him a 'selfish beast' for issuing 'most peremptory orders' to make six rooms in the building available for him and his staff. 'The way Gorringe has treated the medical staff and sick is disgraceful and there is great disgust throughout the camp about it.'[22] Then he found that Gorringe was only occupying one of the six rooms, while eight sick officers were crowded into two rooms, and more were in tents outside. To compound the offence Gorringe lectured the medical staff on how to treat various endemic illnesses suffered by their patients, speaking 'like an advertisement for patent medicines, how he had cured when many doctors had failed . . . ' Captain Ubsdell of the 66th Punjabis was equally forthright – in private: 'Really I can't stand being with this man much longer . . . He is the most unspeakable cad.' He noted that when the Bishop of Lahore visited on 3 September, it was 'amusing to see Gorringe with him, trying to be pleasant for once. He even graciously smiles & makes remarks to us in the Bishop's presence, but it is a sore trial to him . . . as soon as the Bishop retired to his tent G bursts in full flood again & bites everyone with rage.'[23]

The important point was that while London saw the Karun operations as an end in themselves, 'Sir John Nixon would appear' (as Barrow disapprovingly remarked) 'to have regarded them as subsidiary to the main advance along the Tigris.' Crewe had tried to veto 'any scheme involving further demands for reinforcements and undue extension of operations'. Nixon simply pushed on from Qurna without waiting for reinforcements, maybe assuming that an advance would force London's hand. In any case it would soon become clear that troop numbers were only part of the problem. Even if reinforcements were sent, there was just not enough river transport to deploy them.

9. Townshend's Regatta

> I must have the gift of making men (I mean the soldier men) love
> me and follow me. I have only known the 6th Division for six
> months, and they'd storm the gates of hell if I told them to.
> CHARLES TOWNSHEND

The new commander of 6th Division would have the task of leading the advance. Charles Vere Ferrers Townshend had enjoyed brief fame as commander of the garrison during the siege of Chitral fort on the North-West Frontier in 1895. Lord Curzon had visited Townshend's post at Fort Gupis the previous year, and found his host 'somewhat unusual'. Impressed by Townshend's 'absorbing interest in military science' and familiarity with the work of writers like Clausewitz and Hamley, the Viceroy had evidently been somewhat bemused by his equal interest 'in the gayer side of existence of which Paris was for him the hub and symbol'. The walls of his mud house were decorated with 'daring' illustrations from *La Vie Parisienne*, and 'he regaled us through a long evening with French songs to the accompaniment of a banjo'.[1] (The stress on the word 'long' can be sensed here.) Since then, Townshend had acquired a French wife – daughter of the Comtesse Cahen d'Anvers – and become the heir presumptive to the family marquisate in Norfolk. He had fought at the battle of Omdurman and in the Boer War. His love of the banjo and French music-hall songs endured (his troops would call him 'Charlie', but his officers nicknamed him 'Alphonse'). He believed he was destined to be a great commander, and his ambition had already given him a potentially damaging reputation as a 'stickler for his rights'. Even his admiring biographer admitted that he was 'one of the most restless individuals in the whole of the army. As soon

95

as he obtained one appointment by the incessant wire-pulling among his influential friends, he thirsted for a change.' His 'ineradicable habit of grumbling' – notable even in a profession famous for it – several times threatened to derail his career.

Within hours of Townshend's arrival at Basra on 23 April, Nixon instructed him to 'drive the Turks away from their position north of Kurna, push northward and occupy Amarah, a very important town which, he said, was part of the Basra province'.[2] Townshend went up in a steam launch to reconnoitre the situation at Qurna, and did not much like what he found. Brigadier Dobbie of the 17th Brigade told him that the Turkish position outside Qurna was 'one of great strength, owing to the deep creeks that ran across the front, with a veritable sea of flood water, and thick reeds in addition'. Going up the rickety 100-ft high observation tower he saw the floodwaters, which 'gave the landscape the air of Lakes Superior or Michigan', dotted with sandhill islands which housed the half-dozen Turkish redoubts. The centre of the enemy position was at Bahran, held (intelligence believed) by some six battalions with ten guns, supported by the gunboat *Marmariss*, 600 Arab riflemen and 1,200 Marsh Arabs. It was an unpromising prospect. 'The swamps around Kurna were entirely overgrown with tall reeds and rushes, intersected by channels of deeper water in which direction could easily be lost, and where lurking Arabs in their mobile mashoofs could fire on any troops advancing in their heavy bullams at almost point blank range from safe cover.'[3]

Townshend, an avid student of strategic theory, was driven to a disagreeable conclusion. 'I should have to deliver a frontal attack, methodically undertaken in successive phases as in siege warfare.' Nothing could have been more foreign to his belief in the classic Napoleonic manoeuvre *sur les derrières* than this, 'the most unsatisfactory and costly manner of attack', which in these circumstances could not produce decisive results if the enemy 'stood to his guns'. He went straight back to report to Nixon in Basra. Nixon had not yet been upriver to look at the Qurna position, and if Townshend had judged an offensive impossible, would have had to accept his view. Townshend was obviously sceptical, and suggested a larger strategic plan in which his own frontal assault on the Turks at Qurna would become the holding action, while Gorringe's 12th Division carried out a wide turning movement to the east. 'I thought it would be possible to find a route or track [from Ahwaz] by which he could attain the Tigris about Khalat Salih.' Nixon wanted to avoid violating Persian territory, but thought that if the 12th Division 'had a fight and beat the enemy they might follow them up in pursuit all the way to Amara'. Townshend noted in his diary that 'this amounts to the same as my project', though it clearly did not. He seems to have been doing his best to persuade himself that it was feasible.

Gorringe would in fact return to Basra after completing his mission on the Karun. His demonstration towards Bisaitin had 'had the desired effect of preventing reinforcements from joining the Turkish forces on the Tigris in time to oppose General Townshend's advance', in Barrow's opinion. Mehmet Emin took a different view: Gorringe's failure to pursue and destroy the Ottoman 'left wing detachment' was incomprehensible. It was 'so ill disciplined and disorganised that a vigorous pursuit would have destroyed it', if the British had not delayed crossing the Kharka river. Even so, the Ottoman detachment suffered a grim fate as it fell back on Amara. 'The Amara Arabs, who at the beginning had greeted the left wing advance with cheers, now set on the detachment, stripped, looted and murdered them.'[4] Part of Gorringe's force also eventually made the gruelling hundred-mile march from Ahwaz to Amara, though the unexpected speed of the 6th Division's advance up the Tigris would render it irrelevant.

Nixon himself seems to have been impervious to the Mesopotamian climate, and unconcerned about his troops' capacity to function in the hot season; he was certainly keen to press forward as soon as possible. But the offensive was held up for over a month by the need to wait for Gorringe's force to become free, assemble enough boats for Townshend's force, and train the troops to use them. As 'that ass Lord Crewe' (Mellis contemptuously snorted) told the House of Lords, the operations around Qurna would have to be 'of an amphibious nature'. Mellis – whose brigade was attached to the 6th Division for the attack – reported to his wife that 'numerous small boats are being collected to carry men, & others defended with iron plates for guns & maxims'. A large number of cannon were being assembled, 'some quite big ones, we ought to be able to blow them out of the water'. Mellis's optimism was not fully shared by the 6th Division commander. The small boats involved were indeed numerous: eventually 372 *bellums* were assembled, of which 296 were allotted to carry forward 2,560 men of the 17th Brigade. Of these, 96 were 'shielded' with light armour plate in the way Mellis described. (Reynardson found the fixing of long strips of boiler-plating, projecting some three feet each side of the boats 'a dismal failure' which had to be persisted in because the idea 'came from high quarters at Basra'. The idea was that if they were held up by frontal fire, the men could push the boat forward wading behind the wings of armour; but the boats became unmanageably heavy, and the armour got snagged in the reeds.[5]) The other 75-odd *bellums* were to carry the various supporting forces – the mountain artillery battery, sappers, signals and field ambulance (a medical unit, not a single vehicle). Five heavy guns were mounted on barges, and four extra machine guns on specially constructed rafts.

Townshend went on fretting over the risks of amphibious frontal assault, and the apparent strength of the enemy's position. He might rather have been encouraged by its precariousness. It had once been well integrated, but the floods had broken it apart. Mehmet Emin did not much exaggerate in saying that 'dotted about on islets in groups from a section to a battalion, without any means of communication or supply but Arab mashufs, the position was hopeless'. The real problem, yet again, was the commander, Nureddin Bey – an old classmate of Mehmet Emin's, 'now a very ordinary Bimbashi of Gendarmes'. He would be effectively a spectator, who would do nothing 'but watch the piecemeal destruction of his Division through his glasses and send wires to Baghdad Headquarters'.[6]

Townshend was more justified in grumbling about his shortage of artillery, and the removal of his divisional cavalry for 'detached duty'. He was not pleased to be told to 'remember that we have no line of communication troops and your division has to find the necessary troops for that duty'. One of his brigades, the 18th, was doing garrison duty at Dirhamiyeh, covering Basra from the south-west, where there was no discernible enemy threat. Townshend characteristically fumed that 'all the errors of our maritime operations during the 18th and early part of the 19th centuries were here repeated with interest'; and tried to argue 'on the Economy of Force principle' that a battalion was more than enough to hold Dirhamiyeh. He got nowhere; instead he found that even the military police in Basra, and the clerks in the GHQ offices, were taken from the fighting ranks of the 6th Division.[7] He had more success in dealing with the mines laid by the enemy in the ever-deepening floodwaters his force would have to cross: the device of offering 400 rupees for every mine found by the Arabs reduced the mine danger as well as diverting energies that were normally applied to the harassment and robbery of the British forces.

Nixon and Townshend went on discussing operational details, especially the number of boats available, over the next fortnight. Nixon's close involvement in detail planning was unusual, and it would not stop with the planning stage: he eventually decided to join his divisional commander for the battle. The Senior Naval Officer, who witnessed many of these meetings, later wondered why Nixon did not take over 'the direct control of the whole affair'. Since 'the arrangements of the military high command in this and other parts of the campaign were a puzzle to me', he could only speculate that Nixon, 'having confided this operation to General Townshend's division, would be – or thought he would be – committing some military discourtesy if he took over'.[8]

The ultimate breach of official etiquette, though, was committed by the Government of India, which failed to inform the India Office until 23 May that the advance on Amara was planned to start the following day. Was this some kind of oversight, or deliberate deception? Nixon later told the Mesopotamia inquiry that he made a note at the time 'that it looked as if India were trying to lay down a policy behind the back of the Secretary of State and the Cabinet'. The C-in-C India was outraged by this allegation – 'so utterly incorrect that it is really difficult to say it was not knowingly incorrect'. But did Duff really believe that Nixon was lying – and if so, why? London was certainly taken aback when the news eventually arrived. Barrow accepted that capturing Amara might be strategically useful, but warned that there was 'a certain risk in holding so advanced a post during the summer months before we have our light draught gun boats to secure the line of communication'. It would also disperse the available force, whereas the previous position had been 'absolutely impregnable'. But 'we have to make the best of it' – 'Gen. Nixon has rather forced your hand,' he suggested. Crewe was outraged. 'Arrangements for this move must have been made some time back', he objected to Hardinge, 'and General Nixon should have submitted his proposals before the last moment.' But his instruction that 'questions of high military policy should under present circumstances only be decided by the Cabinet' was too late.

Crewe left the India Office before the advance began. The new coalition Cabinet formed by Asquith in May brought in Austen Chamberlain, perhaps the weightiest of the leading Conservatives, as Secretary of State for India. He tried to get a grip on the Mesopotamia campaign straight away: in his first telegram to Hardinge he insisted that the generals there must grasp 'their proper place in the perspective of the whole scheme of the war'.[9] He asked for a report on how Nixon planned to distribute his forces 'if the occupation of Amara is contemplated'. Hardinge waited nearly a week before replying that 'while military operations are actually in progress' (the attack was launched two days before) 'it would be undesirable and even dangerous to tie him down with precise orders which might not fit in with the local situation'.[10] The Cabinet's hand had certainly been forced by somebody.

The unique battle that would be christened 'Townshend's Regatta' was launched at 5 a.m. on 31 May. The divisional commander had spent an apprehensive night. 'Supposing the attack of the 17th Brigade were repulsed! It would be a veritable disaster, for it would be almost impossible for it to retreat. The labour of pushing and pulling the bellums through the thick reeds was immense, and progress painfully slow. All the wounded would be drowned ... ' Townshend's thoughts 'returned repeatedly to the advance of the infantry in their flimsy *bellums*, struggling through deep water thick with reeds, to close with redoubts pumping shrapnel on them ... ' Waiting in one of those *bellums*, Henry Reynardson of the Ox and Bucks LI had, as ever, an eye for the view. 'An extraordinary stillness brooded over this scene of water and sky. High overhead flew a flock of pelicans, their white plumage tinged with pink, very like some huge blossoms drifting through the air; looking down the lane of boats one could see figures sitting motionless, helmet and puggaree silhouetted in black against the golden background of the sky. Now and then came the sound of half-whispered orders, or the rattle of a pole against a boat. Then suddenly the sun shot up above the level horizon. The magic colours faded from the sky and the marsh turned to a hard metallic blue, splashed with blatant green.'[11] Just as suddenly the silence was broken by four booms from the howitzer battery that opened the forty-gun artillery bombardment – something 'we had never seen in Mesopotamia before'.

In the event, everything went remarkably well. As the armed tug *Shaitan* and the launch *Sumana* forged ahead of the force with a chain between them to sweep up mines, Townshend 'expected to see them blown up at any moment – but nothing happened'. Townshend himself was in Nunn's flagship, the *Espiègle*, keeping pace with the *bellums*, and shelling the Turkish redoubts. Nunn also found the situation worrying, as his ships were not armoured, and were under continuous artillery fire. 'It was mighty unpleasant to contemplate the effect of an enemy shell bursting in our unprotected magazines!' *Espiègle* and *Odin* were both hit, but not seriously damaged. Under cover of their guns the troops got to the foot of the Tower Hill redoubt, giving Nunn a view 'such as, I suppose, had never been seen before from the decks of a man-of-war'. The first redoubt to fall was One Tree Hill, on which the 22nd Punjabis (the 'turning attack') had advanced from Muzairaa; then one by one the rest were taken. But Townshend was under no illusions about the reason for the smooth – if 'maddeningly slow' – progress of the advance. The artillery bombardment, especially the naval guns, produced an instant flurry of white flags. 'It was fortunate for us that these people were so ready to surrender.'[12] Captain Reynardson was also puzzled (as well as relieved) by the comparatively light casualties the attacking infantry had suffered. On Gun Hill, 'the mystery was solved as to why the boats had never come under artillery fire during their slow approach across the marsh – we found the guns were so deeply dug in that they could not depress sufficiently to fire at anything much nearer than Fort Snipe'. He thought the defenders 'had never imagined we should attack'.[13]

When the attacking infantry hit the main Turkish positions around Bahran on 1 June, there was only token resistance; 'the enemy's guns were strangely silent.' But the laborious struggle of the *bellums* across the shallow reedbeds gave the defenders time to leave unscathed: the attackers could only fire a few shots at the last boat-load of Turks as they shoved off. Previously, pursuits had failed because of the exhaustion of the troops, but now the question was whether the British forces could go fast enough to keep up with the retreating enemy. The advance became a naval as much as a military operation. The decision to push ahead seems to have been taken by Nixon himself, who had rushed up in a launch from Qurna after watching the attack from the observation tower there. He was 'insistent on the advisability of taking advantage of our success', Nunn wrote, and it was Nixon's 'energy in urging this course which decided Townshend after a little hesitation'.[14] After Nunn had scouted a way through the obstruction formed by two sunken lighters in the river at Rotah, his flotilla took up the chase.

The pursuit was not easy. Nunn's sloops were the biggest ships that had ever gone so far up the Tigris, which narrowed from 270 yards in width at Qurna to some 70 yards at Ezra's Tomb. His river maps were sketchy and outdated. 'It was necessary to keep the ship stemming the river current in its convolutions round the bends.' If the stem slid to either side of the current the ship 'could not easily be straightened up by helm or screws before she took the bank'. As the river narrowed, manoeuvre became virtually impossible. 'The only way to turn round was by letting the stern ground in the mud, while the stream swung the bow round like a top, the stern acting as a pivot.' The *Espiègle*-class sloops were, unfortunately, particularly ill-fitted for this delicate navigation, since the quartermaster had no view ahead, and 'great exertion and constant movement of the wheel was necessary to keep the ship on her course in the rapid current, and relays of men relieved each other, being soon exhausted in the intense heat'.

Ezra's Tomb was the aesthetic high-point of the lower Tigris, and the evaporation of enemy resistance allowed the pursuers to enjoy, as Reynardson did, 'the dome in perfect curves, a blend of every shade from sea-green, through lilac and mauve and blue, to a deep iridescent purple – the whole an indefinable ever-changing colour, a mirror to the blue sky above, to the swaying green tops of the palms, to the tawny flood of the river below'. Nunn persuaded Townshend to drop off his staff there to organise the pursuing infantry. (The novelty of hearing the soldiers' boots clumping around the crowded deck, and the officers clinking up and down ladders with spurs, had worn off.) In the 'dim, steely light' of the early hours of 2 June they went on up the steadily shrinking river. Around 4 a.m., as the *Espiègle* was practically grinding to a halt on the river bottom, near Garbi, they found the Ottoman Navy's one gunboat, the *Marmariss*, and opened fire on it. It turned out to be aground and abandoned, and was soon 'burning fiercely, her hull showing signs of having been hit in many places by 4-inch shells'. (Mehmet Emin contemptuously noted that the gunboat had 'led the retreat instead of covering it'.) A little further up the river they captured the river steamer *Mosul*, but could only go on by transferring from the *Espiègle* to the *Shaitan*. Nunn 'decided to push on in the lighter draught vessels to keep the Turks on the run'. The three sloops had to go astern down the river. He and Townshend transferred ship again to the *Comet*, which had come up with the remaining light vessels, while the *Shaitan* went on to reconnoitre ahead.

But this was uncharted territory in every sense. The GOC was far ahead of his division, and the ship's officers had difficulty in working out precisely where they were from their crude sketch map. Townshend was clearly apprehensive, as well he might be, and though he agreed with Nunn that they should not halt to wait for the following troops until they were 'just beyond the range of the Amara batteries', he insisted on stopping at one point to look for signs of enemy forces. 'He kept saying that we were very much "*en l'air*" and seemed rather doubtful as to what Napoleon – who had never apparently been in a similar position – would have done in the circumstances.' It seems to have taken Nunn's belief that they were as safe going forward as staying where they were to persuade Townshend to agree to go on. At last it became clear from the absence of enemy fire that the *Shaitan* had actually reached Amara safely.

So this major town, a key strategic point, was captured by a small flat-bottomed tugboat armed with a 12-pounder quick-firing gun, and with a crew of nine. When it reached Amara the town was full of Ottoman troops, including over a thousand

Turks, but none attempted to engage it, and its captain, Lieutenant Mark Singleton, took the surrender of several hundred. Nunn was following cautiously with the rest of the flotilla, but when he saw no sign of the *Shaitan*, which had been ordered to drop back for support if it ran into any opposition, he kept on; and around 2 p.m. 'we found ourselves entering Amara without having fired a shot'. It was an amazing scene. 'Crowds of people were thronging the river front, but none of them appeared to be actively hostile. Several steam craft – lighters etc – abandoned by the enemy were lying alongside in different places, and here and there a timid white flag hung limp in the heat.' Amara was 'quite a decent-looking town', with a fine river frontage, a long row of well-proportioned and well-built houses looking across towards groves of feathery crested palm trees and scattered dots of houses on the western bank – 'the whole effect, under a blue sky, in brilliant sunshine, being very picturesque'.[15] After training his guns on the town, Nunn sent a small party ashore to raise the Union flag over the Custom House. Shortly afterwards, the *Comet*'s jolly-boat, manned by three sailors, brought 'an imposing procession of officers, many of them glittering in full-dress uniform', out to be received by Townshend, who 'was most affable, talked French volubly, and gave stringent orders to the civil Governor to arrange at once for the collection of supplies for 15,000 men'.

The surrender of Amara was even more extraordinary than that of Qurna. The commander of the victorious force was at least on the spot; but his force was not – and he had only a vague idea where it was. Nunn had a small battery of naval artillery, and the three 4.7-inch guns on horse-barges which had clearly made a big impression on the Turks, and even more on the Arabs, during the fighting. Otherwise, there were only about fifty officers and men with the advance flotilla. The Ottoman force, though, had fallen apart. Once again the still-formidable Fire Brigade Regiment had been mishandled. 'Having wasted the whole night in useless reconnaissance and not entrenched at all, the regiment was ordered back to Amara. Just as they finished a disorderly embarkation the enemy opened fire on them. The towing steamer of the 4th Battalion immediately cut loose from the two barges and fled. One barge bumped ashore on the left bank and some of its occupants made for Amara, the other drifted down and was taken without resistance by the enemy.' The 2nd Battalion got back to Amara, and took refuge in a palm grove: 'threatened by Arabs and the British fire, like a flock of sheep they surrendered.'[16]

The men of the 6th Division had spent the day of 1 June at Bahran. They 'grilled upon the shadeless sand and suffered exceedingly'; only to be crammed next day, still covered in the mud of the marshes, into some of the new 'P' type paddle-steamers – 'on iron decks under a single awning' in a temperature of 114 degrees. 'What a howling wilderness we are in,' a cavalry officer wrote as he marched towards Amara. 'Heat is fearful and we have no tents whatsoever. Not a particle of shade in the shape of trees or bushes.' When the 17th Brigade reached Ezra's Tomb, they stayed in insect-infested billets for 'three grilling days and nights'. Work and excitement had kept men going for a week, but now a reaction set in – many succumbed to fever, 'and they were the lucky ones, for sunstroke and heatstroke were also common and far more serious, for most who went down with those complaints never got up again'.[17] The 16th Brigade passed them early on 3 June, on their way to provide (in the shape of the Norfolks) the first troops to join Townshend next day.

Strategically, as well as tactically, the capture of Amara was a brilliant success, but once again it highlit the question of the logic of the whole British position in Mesopotamia. Every mile the expeditionary force advanced made its logistical situation more precarious. The India Office took a predictably conservative line, hoping that the troops 'will now be able to settle down for the hot season and obtain much needed rest'. The Indian General Staff on the other hand suggested that an immediate advance would keep the enemy off balance and probably make the capture of

Baghdad itself quite easy. To the now familiar argument that this would impress Arab opinion they cannily added an even more resonant one: the need to occupy Baghdad 'before the Russians arrive anywhere near it'. The C-in-C India asked Nixon to define the boundaries of the Basra *vilayet*, and Nixon, rather surprised by this request – since he assumed that when his original orders were drawn up, these were already known – replied that Amara and Nasiriyeh (on the Euphrates) were the northern limits of the *vilayet*. He planned to seize the latter, but added that to control the local population it would be necessary – in the short term at least – to go on beyond the northern boundary and occupy Kut-al-Amara.

Nixon's strategic view won out. He secured permission to advance up the Euphrates by roughly the same method he had used for the advance up the Tigris: 'India informed London what Nixon was going to do and stated their concurrence, and then waited to see if the Secretary of State would overrule them.'[18] Hardinge told Chamberlain that as the Euphrates tribes were more hostile than those on the Tigris, he would authorise an advance to Nasiriyeh to establish control over them. When Gorringe arrived back at Basra on 16 June, he was ordered to take his division up the Euphrates as soon as possible. This forward policy was driven by several impulses. The international dimension was a worry; Russian successes were two-edged – easing the immediate pressure on British forces, yet at the same time threatening to overturn the delicate balance between the two powers in their contest for control of Central Asia. There were local worries too, like the persistent fear that the latent hostility of the tribes of southern Mesopotamia would become open. A. T. Wilson, who was co-opted by Gorringe as political officer to his division, typically dismissed this by arguing that the 'nightmare of Ajaimi and his thousands of Arabs' rising against the British should have been dispelled by the feeble Arab performance at Shaiba. But the myth of Arab military potential was still strong, and conventional 'Orientalist' logic decreed that they could only be impressed by consistent displays of British strength. ('The ease with which Orientals misinterpret any retrograde movement as a sign of weakness must not be forgotten,' the General Staff pointed out.)

By contrast, the collapse of the Turkish defenders after Qurna confirmed a deep-set belief in the inferiority of Turkish military forces and the imminent collapse of Ottoman power. The dismissive estimate of Turkish fighting capacity after the seizure of Basra may, by a sad irony, have played a part in the decision to launch the Gallipoli operation. At Gallipoli, the effectiveness of well-led Anatolian infantry was already becoming awkwardly clear. But in Mesopotamia the British had so far encountered only second-rate Turkish divisions and Arab levies; the temptation to repeat these easy successes was too strong to resist.

10. Up the Euphrates

Neither Turk nor Europeans have been allowed to set foot on the
Euphrates before we came here.
>   HAROLD DICKSON

I know you hate expansion, and so do I, but I see no way out
of it.
>   LORD HARDINGE

Stuck at Basra in June, Mellis was at his grumpiest. 'I wish to
goodness we could go to the Dardanelles. This is such a blasted
country.' He took a cynical view of British motives, too. 'It seems
a wicked waste of good men keeping us here at all. It looks as
if we're merely land grabbing . . . To me all those poor fellows
who fell at Shaiba seem to have died for nothing . . . No doubt
Mesopotamia will be added to the empire, but we have enough
already.' Towards the end of the month he wrote that Qurna
was 'simply a sweltering swamp swarming with mosquitoes of
the malarial species at night', adding sardonically that 'our noble
Indian Govt haven't provided the men with proper mosquito
curtains'. At least he was certain that they could not 'go up to
Baghdad' – 'the force is not strong enough to do so (especially
with all this sickness) & hold 500 miles of lines of communication
to the sea as well'.[1]

The launching of the 12th Division's advance towards
Nasiriyeh did not immediately improve Mellis's mood. 'This
is a rotten show, I wish you could see the situation as I write.
Imagine a large flat bottomed river steam boat with a large
iron barge on either side, all crammed with men . . . packed
like sardines. Now imagine a dozen of this sort of river steamer
each towing two iron barges, all crammed with men. This is

Gorringe's show to capture Nasiriyeh.' They had been 'lying one behind the other for four days now, while our Sappers and Pioneers try to dynamite & otherwise destroy the obstruction that the Turks have made'. 'It is neither fun nor excitement nor war,' Mellis complained. 'Some twopenny-halfpenny Turkish gunboats came down from Nasiriyeh & fired pom poms at us, but we replied with 4.7 guns & gave them more than they liked ... But we are weary of it.' And the assault had not yet begun. 'Gorringe's show' turned into one of the grimmest battles of the whole campaign. The first problem was getting across the vast Hammar Lake, a quintessentially Mesopotamian water feature with 'too much water for the army, too little for the navy'. In late June, ships with a five-foot draught could get through the passage, but in July it was reduced to a three-foot maximum. Following the 'tortuous and often unmarked channel' through the lake was not easy, and boats frequently grounded. Then the obstruction caused by a solid barrage across the Akaika channel (built on a core of sunken *mahelas*) finally halted the advance up the Euphrates on the afternoon of 27 June.

The SNO, Wilfrid Nunn, had brought his flotilla from the Tigris, but as his sloops could not get up the Euphrates beyond Kabaish he transferred to a small stern-wheeler, the *Shushan*. This and two other boats, the *Muzaffri* and the *Massoudieh*, were armed with 12-pounder, 3-pounder and Maxim guns taken from the rest of the flotilla. The armed tug *Sumana* also went along, with the two horse-barge mounted 4.7-inch guns. The stern-wheelers, 'curious old craft' Nunn thought – antiques in fact, as they had been built for the Gordon Relief Expedition on the Nile in 1884 – were given some armour, but it had to be limited to avoid deepening their draught. Gorringe travelled with some of his troops in the *Blosse Lynch*, and the rest of the force was in the river steamers *Mejidieh* and *Malamir* with their barges roped to each side.

When Gorringe and Nunn went up in a motorboat to inspect the barrage, they found it 'a very solid affair, about thirty feet thick at the top'. It would have to be blasted. Gorringe was a sapper, and Nunn saw his eyes 'glistening with pleasure' as he calculated what was the largest quantity of explosive that could be demanded from Basra. Over the next forty-eight hours, the general personally supervised the arduous blasting operations in temperatures over 110 degrees F (sometimes dragging a rather reluctant Nunn along to watch). Once a shallow gap was finally opened in it on the afternoon of 29 June, the river poured through it in a torrent so fierce that none of the boats could power their way against it, and all had to be hauled over by main force. Only after this exhausting process could the advance begin in earnest.[2]

'Not since the Mutiny have British troops carried out operations in such heat,' thought Colonel Bowker. His Hampshires had their 'baptism of fire' on 5 July: 'our cover was none too good', but 'their shooting was by no means very accurate otherwise we must have suffered very heavily'.[3] Lieutenant Fothergill Cooke of the 24th Punjabis concurred: 'the enemy had strong concealed positions and if he had had many regular troops we should have had a bad time ... We hardly expected them to put up a fight but the country is much in their favour, nothing but swamps trees towers and creeks – very difficult intersected country.' But, as he told his wife, his colonel (Climo) 'did well and is likely to get early promotion'. Suk-es-Shuyukh was occupied by Nunn and Sir Percy Cox on 6 July, Cox in his launch, and Nunn in the *Shushan*, with the *Massoudieh* 'with a barge carrying a 4.7 gun in it lashed on each side of her, looking like a curious sort of miniature battleship'.[4] (Sir Mark Sykes later compared this rig less flatteringly to 'a sardine between two cigarette boxes'.) As the division pushed up to establish a base by the Assani anchorage, the scale of the Turkish defensive position on the bend of the river christened 'Thornycroft Point' by the British became clear. (One of the Ottoman Navy's 'twopenny-halfpenny' Thornycroft launches was engaged there.)

The defences stretched around the Majinina and Maiyadiya creeks on the right and left banks of the Euphrates, and to close with them the infantry had to 'creep forward yard by yard, from sodden trench to sodden trench, in a shade temperature of 120F – a moist swampy heat – eaten alive with insects'.[5] At least Mellis got some excitement. 'We had a stiffer fight than we expected,' he admitted. 'It is devilish strong something like this,' he told his wife elatedly. 'Well this is war again no reason to grouse' – though he did. 'Wish it were in a less enervating climate, falling into deep swamps up to your neck in hot mud as I did several times the other day does not help one to command.' The situation he faced was uninviting: 'they have a dreadful open field of fire in front of both their positions on the right & left banks & across their front on the right is a water channel 5 to 6 feet deep at a distance of 200 yds from their rifles.' Mellis was assigned to an attack on the enemy right flank, while the other brigade pinned the enemy on the left. His target was 'a sort of island' (actually a small group of sandhills) 'from which we could take the Turkish position in rear'. Once again he was involved in an amphibious attack using *bellums*. 'I don't like my job the men crowded up in boats offer a beastly easy target & if their guns get on to us we shan't like it & we shall like it even less if our guns don't succeed in knocking the Turks out of some dry ground in the middle of the marshes which guard their right flank.' Owing to casualties and sickness his brigade was already 'only a skeleton of one', just 1,500 men.

Though he hoped it would 'all pan out well', the 14 July assault did not. One problem was that 'our guns although greatly superior in numbers are badly handled' (he blamed this on Gorringe 'trying to do everything himself'). Mellis thought that with more than double the enemy's strength in artillery 'we ought to be able to silence them', but 'as it is they seem to be able to do as they like'.[6] Then Gorringe changed Mellis's plan of attack, reducing the attacking force to a single battalion (the 24th Punjabis), under the command of Lieutenant-Colonel Climo. Gorringe detailed Wilson to guide the assault force: Wilson – 'convinced that the attack could not succeed' – refused.[7]

He was proved right. Things went well enough until the 24th got within 200 yards of the island, when, Mellis wrote, 'their attack was blasted by hot fire from the Turks, our poor fellows were shot down right & left trying to charge the position'. After Mellis's old friend Colonel Climo had made repeated efforts to renew the advance he had to admit defeat, but as always the retreat under fire was a desperate business. Lieutenant Cooke did not survive: as Climo wrote to his widow, they had tried to bring back the bodies of the dead as they retreated through the water – but 'then the closing in of the Arabs on us compelled us to abandon the bodies in deep water: it was a terrible experience'.[8] Over 120 out of some 400 men engaged became casualties. 'All those good fellows we have known in Suez all gone,' Mellis lamented. 'How I wish now Gorringe had not altered his plans.'

Though others thought better of Gorringe – Colonel Bowker of the Hampshires thought he was 'indefatigable and doesn't spare himself' – Mellis's relationship with his divisional commander would not improve. Gorringe seems to have agreed to transfer him to take command on the left bank – though even this proved hard, as Mellis and his staff had to find their way at night 'through about a ¼ mile of palm grove in pitch darkness'. (The only light source being a little torch his wife had given him, 'which has been such a god send, you don't know how often I have blessed you for it'. Sadly its battery died immediately afterwards, and he had left the spare at Port Said.) In fact Gorringe was in something of a fix. Outnumbered, facing strong positions, at the end of a tenuous communication line that was losing capacity daily as the water level dropped, his situation was (as Nunn said) 'most unenviable'. If he failed to get forward, he might be cut off. To renew the assault he needed reinforcements, and these painfully seeped up through the second and third weeks of July. As the Hammar Lake steadily drained away, 'much man-handling and toil was required before all the barges and boats had been punted, dragged or pushed through the mud and water of the main channel'. At long last his repeated requests for aircraft were answered by the arrival of two up-to-date BE2s, and a makeshift reserve force of 350 men 'sick but able to bear arms' was carried on the *Mejidieh*.

Nunn, who liked to spend the night before a big battle at GHQ, stayed at Gorringe's advanced bivouac on the night of 23 July. It was not a restful one; he was woken by a Turkish attack on the advanced trenches not far away. 'The date palms near us were being constantly hit by flying bullets; big branches were ripped off and hurled to the ground.' He carefully moved his camp bed away from a large hole in one side of the wall, and 'altogether was not sorry when the time came to get up and prepare for the bombardment' scheduled to begin at 4.30 a.m.[9] Crucially, the weather on the 24th, the day of the final attack, proved bearable, thanks to a cool breeze. But the defenders remained tenacious. The 12th Brigade advancing from their trenches just north of Atabiya creek had to cross several hundred yards of bare ground, and once again it took an inspirational charge by a British battalion, this time the West Kents, to get into the Thornycroft Point position. But the advance still met with 'stout opposition' until the last reserves had been committed; then gradually the defenders fell back, abandoning six guns at the Maiyadiya creek position.

The battle turned on a piece of pure luck. As soon as he could see the attacking troops on the left bank getting into the forward trenches at Thornycroft Point, Mellis's brigade began to advance. Ahead was the Majinina canal. To get across, bridging equipment and engineers were taken up the river in an armoured barge towed by the *Sumana* – a hazardous operation, in which the *Sumana* was almost crippled by rifle fire. The idea was to run the barge ashore on the northern bank of the canal, so a bridge could be thrown across for Mellis's advancing troops. The steep bank gave enough cover from enemy fire for the engineers to work, but after an hour's labour, the 'bridges proved too difficult to use'.[10] This could have been it. But the barge, partly blocking the mouth of the canal, 'had the unexpected effect of lowering the water level' in it, so that the attackers could actually walk across. So, at least, the official story went; Arnold Wilson, who reconnoitred the crossing before the fight – and got a DSO for his exploit – did not think so.

Wilson (whose role as Gorringe's political officer evidently allowed him to play soldiers as well) left a vivid account of his three attempts to assess the depth of the Majinina canal. On the second, he crawled up and lay for 'what seemed an hour' on the bank, watching a mound fifty or a hundred yards away. 'Was there a sentry there? I could hear the noise of pick and shovel in the Turkish lines, and snatches of Arab conversation. I plucked up my courage and, slipping into the canal, reached the middle. It was about 4ft 6in deep. As I did so up jumped two figures from the mound and rushed at me, firing wildly: I scrambled out and ran like a hare . . . My flight brought me near the bank of the river, and I walked cautiously up it to near the Majinina canal, reaching it some 200 yards from its mouth. No one seemed near, so I slipped in and allowed the current to carry me down the canal, letting my feet drag on the bottom to get some idea of the depth. For some time I could not touch the bottom, and dared not dive for fear of splashing and attracting notice: I closed my eyes, lest even they should attract notice, and covered my face and head with mud.' Eventually he got out again, and had to make a two-mile trek through deep mud back to the British lines. Then he went out again the next night in a boat with 'two Eton wet-bobs' from the Hampshires. 'It was an eerie experience: we had nothing but the stars to guide us; the water was shallow, with patches of reeds here and there; in the darkness all perspective was lost and a line of low reeds looked like an embankment. Again and again we stuck, and had to push our craft: if we were to be any use, it was essential that we should be able to see the low mounds on which the enemy's right flank appeared to rest, and from which their position could be invaded . . . We sat and hoped for dawn; when it began to break we could see figures moving about on the mound, some 400 to 600 yards away. That was enough for us . . . '[11]

When the final assault went in, Mellis thought it 'a gallant sight to see the Hampshires & Gurkhas rush across the creek in face of the entrenchments, bridges having to be made in face of hot fire. The Turks stood until they saw our fellows coming at them with the bayonet, then they bolted. We pushed them all the day giving them no time to rally in their many alternative positions some of which were very nasty ones.' Mellis could enjoy another victory. But 'why on earth Gorringe did not push on with the reserve brigade in ships straight into Nasiriyeh no one can say. He might have got the whole Turkish force to surrender.' As it was, they got clean away. 'He is a rotten general,' Mellis concluded, '& we all felt a great lack of confidence in him.' He was 'one of those fellows who have got on making railways in Egypt', and the last three weeks had been 'a veritable nightmare – he owes it to my advice that he did not have a reverse. He never had a connected plan of action & was always wanting to throw his troops headlong at the trenches.' Mellis thought that Gorringe was guilty of the deadliest sin in a soldier. 'He gave me the impression that he was always thinking of making a name for himself & never of the troops.'[12]

Colonel Bowker of the Hampshires had a different explanation of the failure to pursue: 'our guns kept on shelling when the Turks were bolting, so we couldn't get into them with the bayonet.' But he concluded that it made little odds, 'as they were on the run and were of course fresher than we were, besides having chucked their equipment'.[13] At the end of the day's fighting, Mellis drily noted, Gorringe 'went back to a good dinner & his bed'. Next day, 'for some unaccountable reason he did not turn up till 10am', but at 7 a.m. the ever-energetic Captain Nunn 'who had pushed on to reconnoitre in his little gun boat' came to Mellis's bivouac and reported that Nasiriyeh had been abandoned and was being looted by Arabs. In fact, Nunn had earlier got right into the town, which was a riot of white flags, before a burst of serious gunfire from the Ottoman barracks revealed that 'they had not been informed that we had won!' With his elementary armour plates clanging with bullets, Nunn had spun his boat about and retired. Mellis 'put 100 Gurkhas & 2 maxims on his boat' (Nunn's recollection was that 'we managed to pack about fifty of them on board the <u>Shushan</u> and the <u>Massoudieh</u>') and went with him into the town, where they saw off the looters, 'hoisted the Union Jack & took possession'. Gorringe, predictably, sent him 'a snorter saying my action was subversive to discipline etc.'. The main force, 'now suffering greatly from the heat', reached the town later. Nunn remembered 'during the intense heat of the afternoon watching the long-drawn-out tail of exhausted soldiers staggering through the driving sandstorm as they crossed the square opposite the ship'.[14] All ranks were no doubt much gratified to hear King George's message to Nixon – 'the splendid achievements of General Gorringe's column in spite of many hardships and intense heat fills me with admiration'.

With Nasiriyeh captured, Nixon had conclusively achieved his main objective, to secure the whole Basra *vilayet*. Britain now controlled key points on both the Tigris and the Euphrates. Though the India Office still wanted Force D to sit tight, the situation was developing its own dynamic. As the 6th Division reconnoitred up the Tigris towards Ali Gharbi, Chamberlain watched 'the gradual extension of the sphere of our military operations, with its resultant attenuation of strength . . . with some anxiety'. But Nixon had the bit between his teeth, and Kut in his sights, and so did Hardinge now. On 27 July he announced, 'Now that Nasiriyeh has been occupied the occupation of Kut-al-Amarah is considered by us to be a strategic necessity.' Kut was, he explained to Chamberlain, 'only four miles' beyond the limit of the Basra *vilayet*. It commanded the lower reaches of the Tigris and also the Euphrates by way of Shatt-al-Hai (the semi-waterway connecting Kut and Nasiriyeh). Occupying Kut would 'facilitate the re-enforcement [*sic*] of our position on either river and also enable us to control the powerful Bani Lam tribe and effectively safeguard the oil fields against aggression from the Tigris'. Once 'securely in possession of Kut', he temptingly suggested, 'we could probably reduce materially our garrisons at Nasiriyeh and Amara and thus economise our troops'.

Skewered on these strategic arguments, Chamberlain still tried to cut back Force D's mission, urging that all the troops could be removed from 'so unhealthy an outpost as Nasiriyeh, with which communications are difficult', and concentrated on the Tigris. The Viceroy again demurred. Nasiriyeh was 'too important' to be evacuated. It must be made 'a centre of civil government to control the powerful Arab tribes by which it is surrounded' and so 'effectively to occupy this vilayet'. Any withdrawal would do 'incalculable' political harm. Ajaimi would reappear with a few Turks to re-establish Turkish authority, and all the tribes 'would get out of hand'. Where troops could be economised was on the Karun. As before, he belittled 'the supposed necessity to guard the pipeline with troops', arguing that their presence abetted the Anglo-Persian Oil Company's refusal to pay the local Arabs to do the job. His view was that there was no justification for having British troops there unless hostility was expected from the Persian government, in which case a vastly bigger force would be needed.

Hardinge's imperial project was firming up now. When he protested to the former Secretary of State for India, Lord Morley, 'I know you hate expansion, and so do I, but I see no way out of it', he was not being entirely honest. He may have been equally economical with the truth when he protested, 'I have no intention of making any dash on Kut.' The move on Kut was delayed until September, but one reason was that Townshend himself fell ill in June. So did an alarming proportion of his troops. In summer 1915 Amara, believed in London to be a healthier place than Basra, was 'one long chronicle of hot days and breathless nights, of sickness and boredom, and shortage of most things that make hot weather bearable'. An ice-making machine laboriously brought up from Basra broke down after 'a fortnight's spasmodic activity' and was never fixed. Sickness multiplied, mental as well as physical. 'It affected people in various ways – worries over trifles, restlessness, anxiety, and often enough shortness of temper; but the worst and commonest form was a sort of hopeless depression, when everything and everybody (including oneself) was utterly bad, and life unbearable. Terrors were in the way and the grasshopper had become a burden.'[15]

Others seemed more cheerful; Spackman noted in July that Amara had 'improved heaps in the two months we have had it. A band plays some evenings and the river fronts are prettier than ever.' He too lamented the fate of the ice machine, but added 'we get soda' (and whisky at 2s 6d a bottle). But 1,200 men of the 6th Division were on the sick list within ten days of the occupation of Amara, and Townshend himself collapsed with fever and diarrhoea after 'a long reconnaissance all day along the road to Baghdad' on 6 June. ('No one looked after me to see that I had any food,' he complained to his wife, 'and I was too much taken up with my work to think of food, so I went empty all day under a blazing sun. When I got back my head was on fire and I vomited everything I touched.'[16]) He was sent back to India to recuperate. (Townshend 'didn't stick this climate long!' Colonel Bowker tartly observed, noting that Nixon and Gorringe 'keep pretty fit, they are hardish nuts!')

11. To Kut

Where are we going to stop in Mesopotamia?
CHARLES TOWNSHEND

It is necessary to gain strength by eating <u>now</u>, even if it involves indigestion later on.
SIR EDWARD GREY

A striking fact about Nixon's offensive commitment was how doubtful his most successful commander was about it. Though credited with a brilliant victory in capturing Amara, Townshend's main concern was 'where are we going to stop in Mesopotamia?' This was, as ever, the big question hanging over the entire invasion. He put it to the Viceroy while he was convalescing in India, but could get no answer. Just before returning to Mesopotamia he lunched with the C-in-C, Sir Beauchamp Duff, and raised the issue again. Duff told him that he would probably be ordered to advance to Kut, but said 'not one inch shall you go beyond Kut unless I make you up to adequate strength'.[1] Townshend got a similar response from the senior officials of the Indian Foreign Department, but he remained worried. He understood that his troops on the Tigris were not simply a military force. 'You may afford to have reverses and retreat in France, perhaps,' he told his wife, 'but not in the East and keep any prestige.' The risks Britain was playing with were alarming. 'Imagine a retreat from Baghdad and the consequent instant rising of the Arabs of the whole country behind us, to say nothing of the Persians and Afghans.'

Even going to Kut raised the question of the 'adequacy' of the British expeditionary force. Kut was 120 miles upriver; the faltering supply line from Basra would effectively be doubled in length. And compared to Kut, Amara was a pleasant place to maintain a garrison. Townshend thought that as long as the Gallipoli operation hung in the balance, 'we should hold what we have got' in Mesopotamia. As he repeatedly complained, Nixon did not even have two complete divisions. 'Mine is complete,' he told his wife, 'but Gorringe's has no guns or divisional troops, and whenever Nixon wants them for himself he takes them from me if Gorringe has to go anywhere!' He grumbled to Curzon (keeping up his show-business image), 'this is what they call in New York running the show at "scalp rates".'[2] And it was not simply a question of overall troop numbers, but the tight logistical limits on the numbers that could actually be deployed. Nixon's own chief of staff, Major-General Kemball, laid the issue out starkly. Since 'river transport will continue to be the governing factor in any future operations', it was vital to get plenty of more powerful light-draught steamers, with ample personnel and maintenance material. Kemball warned 'that if steps are not taken in good time to meet these requirements, we are running grave risks of a breakdown at possibly a serious moment'.

This was about as close as staff language got to hoisting an alarm signal. Because shipping was so short, 'at the present time we cannot make the most effective use of the troops available, and in any crisis insufficiency of river transport would limit the scope of reinforcements, while a breakdown of shipping might have still more serious consequences'. Sir George Buchanan, a port expert sent out later from India, was surely justified in suggesting that 'these words of wisdom should have caused any army commander to pause and think'.[3] Nixon clearly believed (as he later testified to the commission of inquiry) that he was doing enough to deal with Kemball's concerns. He could not yet know how the Indian authorities would rewrite his shopping list for extra river transport. In the end, though, it was Nixon's personality that set the course of the campaign. He was an optimist. His actions and communications breathed a 'can-do' spirit that was as attractive to the Viceroy as it was worrying to the Secretary of State. If he paused and thought, the pause was over by the time Townshend returned to Basra.

However much Townshend might fret about the situation, his troops were keen to do something after months of stifling heat in camp, and some took the appearance of clouds on the day Townshend rejoined his division (28 August) as a good omen. But moving upriver was hard work – much of the force had to do the 100 river miles up to Sheikh Saad on foot. Henry Reynardson's brigade reached Sheikh Saad early on 13 September: 'a memorable morning, for, instead of being able to pitch camp as soon as we got in, we found that the parent ships had all run aground, so that there were no tents and no food; the sun was blistering and a tremendous wind sandstorm was blowing. There was no vestige of shade or shelter, and sun and dust had to be endured all day.' Inevitably, 'a lot of men went down'.[4] When Nixon urged Townshend to speed up, he replied that troops could only be taken up by boat in 'homeopathic doses'. Concentrating in the face of a superior enemy, and in temperatures of 110–116 degrees F, he noted that if Nureddin Pasha, their new commander, had even 30 guns (he had 12 at the front, 38 in all), 'we should have a tabasco time'. At least he had, thanks to air reconnaissance, an accurate view of the defensive position that the Ottoman commander had established at Es Sinn. (The first flight of modern aircraft, three temperamental Martinsydes, had arrived on 28 August.)[5] Not that this brought him much cheer. The enemy's position, he reported on 17 September, was 'a very formidable one'.

Though the defenders had started the summer in poor shape, pulling themselves together after the rout from Qurna, Nureddin 'worked tirelessly to rally the battered infantry' of the 35th and 38th Divisions, while a slow but steady trickle of reinforcements (most importantly the 51st Division) arrived. A new division, the 45th, was formed in Baghdad around a core of 5,000 *Jandarma* (gendarmerie) and a number of frontier-guard battalions. Nureddin's position straddled the river on a ten-mile front between Es Sinn on the right (southern) bank and the Ataba marsh some eight miles north of the river. Its northern section, between the Ataba and Suweida marshes, rested on three substantial mud redoubts connected by trenches, and the central section between Suweida marsh and the river was a three-line trench system skirting what the British called the 'Horseshoe Marsh'. Townshend spoke (with typical history-mindedness) of 'a Torres-Vedras-like line of earthworks, entrenchments and redoubts of the most modern type'. The central section, 'well covered by a zone of barbed wire and other obstacles' with a sprinkling of mines in front of it, 'was by far the strongest'.

A British officer who walked around the defences after the battle was full of admiration for their strength and siting. 'Except where there was wire, the works were quite indistinguishable at 100 yards distance, the 9 inch command of the parapets being so gradually sloped, and the trenches so cleverly sited that they were impossible to spot.' Though Turkish barbed wire was poor stuff, and the defenders had been forced to use some white and too-visible concrete to face the head-cover of the redoubts, 'all trenches were beautifully dug, deep and narrow, the fire trenches solidly traversed'. Huge jars of water were placed in recesses every fifty yards, and the 10–12 feet deep communication trenches ran back a mile from the redoubts. The redoubts themselves were provided with overhead cover of poles, brushwood and earth. Some had, between the mines and wire, a course of 'most grisly pits, about 9 feet deep and 4 feet across, tapering to 2 feet at the bottom, which was decorated with a 3-foot sharpened stake: not at all nice'.[6] The southern section ran from the river to an old high-level canal running southwards from Es Sinn. The river was blocked by sunken boats, and there was a boat bridge six miles upriver, though it was 'in the last stages of disrepair, so wobbly that it was impossible to bring a field-gun across, and an attempt to pass a mule cart over ended in the untimely death of one mule'.

There was, though, one weak point: a gap was opening up in the northern section, between the two marshes. Air reconnaissance and local intelligence indicated that the Ataba marsh was drying out and shrinking rapidly. The dry ground between it and the northernmost redoubt was expanding by the day – faster than the Turks could entrench it. Although this gap was only 300 yards wide on 24 September, Townshend decided to strike there. He would throw his 'principal mass' through the gap, while pinning the front between the river and the Suweida marsh with his 'minimum force'. In line with the Napoleonic–Clausewitzian ideas which Townshend shared with the German General Staff (though not, as he noted, with the French of his day), his aim was a *Vernichtungsschlacht* – a battle of annihilation – getting across the Turkish line of retreat and cutting off all their troops north of the river. ('All the great decisive battles have been gained by the turning or enveloping manoeuvre.') Nureddin's force was divided by the Tigris, and Townshend needed to keep it that way. Unable to spare enough troops to pin down the right-bank force during the battle, he decided to launch a feint against it before rapidly transferring all his forces over a boat bridge to the left bank.

Captain Reynardson judged this 'decidedly a daring plan', calling for a high degree of mobility. But the transport shortage meant that if the 'principal mass' was to be able to move round the enemy line the 'minimum force' under Fry had to be stripped of its wagons. 'Here was one of my three infantry brigades tied, as it were, to the river bank,' Townshend reflected, adding characteristically, 'it reminded me of Wellington's letter of protest to Lord Castlereagh in 1808'.[7] His division had 330 transport carts and 740 animals. He asked GHQ to buy camels to make the flanking march possible, but those they found were 'wild as hawks and could not be trained for loading'. Reynardson watched the arrival of several hundred of them at camp at Ali Gharbi on 10 August. 'A more mixed assortment was never seen. They were not baggage camels at all, and most of them had never carried a load before, so that the Transport Sections spent a gay and giddy time trying to induce them to accept loads of blankets. To add to the difficulties there was only one driver to every twenty camels – ragged, shrivelled Bedouin, who alone could persuade the beasts to do anything but gurgle and bite, and they spoke a strange lingo which no one could interpret.' Reinforced by 'droves of tiny donkeys', and 'several cows, which obliged by carrying entrenching tools and anything else which the camels particularly objected to', the division's land transport – 'this comic cavalcade' – was finally ready to move up towards Sannaiyat.

Although Townshend took a gloomy view of the strategic situation – 'In short, all the elements demanded by the strategic offensive were lacking' – the battle he now directed outside Kut would, even more than the 'Regatta', mark him as one of the 'two generals' produced, in Edmund Candler's estimation, by the Mesopotamia campaign. By 24 September his force had been assembled near Sannaiyat, and inched forward on the south side of the river to the Chahela mounds to prepare for the feint against Es Sinn early on the 26th. This manoeuvre – the first time any such deception had been tried during the campaign – worked like a charm. 'As soon as we arrived at 7 a.m., camp was pitched – every available tent was put up, so as to make a big show and persuade the enemy that we had really "come to stay" on the right bank.' The Turkish artillery soon opened up on them, but 'there were plenty of ditches and little damage was done'; though the naval flotilla was forced to retreat downstream.

Before dawn on the 27th, 'a cloudless morning with a certain amount of mist over the river and the most extraordinary mirage effects', the feinting force moved up towards the Es Sinn canal. 'The banks of the canal showed up like lofty cliffs, broken and crumbling, and apparently miles away, while beneath them shimmered a boundless sea strangely dotted here and there with huge trees and crossed at intervals by squads of men with immensely long legs, who appeared to be walking on water.' There were no trees or water, naturally, and the men were doubtful as well. It was impossible to see the Turkish trenches or gun positions, but their artillery refused to respond to the feinting force's provocation – even though, as Reynardson recalled, one officer 'sat on an ant-heap' in full view, 'reading the *Times* most obtrusively'.[8] The Turks concentrated instead on Fry's 18th Brigade, pushing forward under cover of the barge-mounted heavy guns to within 3,000 yards of the central position round Saddleback Hill. Meanwhile working parties were building roads and cutting a ramp down to the river, where the pontoon bridge was swung across at nightfall, covered with mud and camel-thorn to deaden the sound of marching across it.

The troops of the 'principal mass' now 'shuffled off through the darkness, down the ramp and on to the bridge'. The ramps were almost too steep for the transport carts, and there were some hitches during the crossing, which in spite of all orders to maintain absolute silence, must have made a fair bit of noise. Still, there seems to have been no enemy response, beyond a sporadic bombardment of the abandoned camp on the right bank. The critical point was when the main force had to traverse the strongest part of the Turkish front at an uncomfortably close range. 'There seemed to be a terrible amount of noise: every wheel in the transport seemed to screech and scream, while the "drabis" [native drivers] were of course seized with a fit of coughing.' (And a driver's cough was a thorough business – 'he has a good rake round and suppresses nothing!') At one point, some of the transport veered left 'and bumped along between the column and the Turkish line, while the drivers carried out frenzied arguments with their friends 100 yards away'. Knowing the way sound carried over desert at night, 'this was simply agonizing' for the worried officers of the column.[9]

The column reached 'Clery's Post' on the edge of the Suweida marsh in the late evening, and after forming squares for a short rest, moved on at 1 a.m. on 28 September. Water, being conserved for the next day, was already running short. For four hours the force 'plugged on in suffocating dust through the darkness'. The atmosphere was 'damp and heavy, like clammy cotton-wool', and at every halt the men, overcome by the closeness of the air, 'would fall asleep at once, some of them as they stood'. They were not yet fully fit after the stultifying summer, and the forward march had already drained them. Finally, when the sun rose at 6 a.m., they found that there was marsh as far as they could see: there was no sign of the expected gap to the south-west.

Up to this point, the deception plan had worked remarkably well. While the main force was crossing the pontoon bridge, Nureddin was transferring his reserves the other way. Now the main part of the 'principal mass', a group of six battalions led by General Hoghton (his brigade reinforced by two battalions from Delamain's), were supposed to hook round the northern end of the Turkish line, through the gap beside the shrinking Ataba marsh. Delamain's remaining half-brigade was to attack the redoubts, while between him and the river, Fry's 'minimum force' pinned the central section of the enemy line. Marching by compass bearing alone, since he still had no accurate maps, Hoghton had found the right way between the Suwada and Suwaikiya marshes, but then strayed too far northwards between the Suwaikiya and Ataba marshes. By the time he realised this, he decided it was too late to turn back, and pressed on all the way round the Ataba marsh to take the defenders in the rear. This might have been a brilliant improvisation – the defenders were taken completely by surprise, and it turned out that the supposed gap had in any case been plugged by a new redoubt. But Hoghton's new line of march was so long that he ran out of heavy telephone cable (his force carried seven miles of it, Delamain's carried four – this being the sum total available to the entire expedition).

The 6th Division faced a communications crisis. It had only two wireless sets. Townshend, trying to direct the battle from his scaffolding observation tower – the last expedient of the pre-aircraft era – had one of them. But the other was not with the attacking force; it was on the army commander's ship *Malamir*. Nixon had once again come up to watch the battle, protesting to Townshend that he had no intention of interfering, but wanted to be on the spot 'in case questions of general policy had to be decided as a result of the battle'.[10] (This could only mean the question of going on to Baghdad – though Townshend had already said that he would pursue the enemy into the city if circumstances were favourable.) So while that vital wireless lay idle – Nixon in fact left it behind and went to join Townshend at his command post – the front-line units, once the heavy telephone cable ran out, had nothing but their fragile light telephone cable and heliograph, which was crippled by mirages. Inevitably they lost contact, and Townshend effectively lost control of the battle.

For several hours he did not know where Delamain's force was. An aircraft sent at 3.30 to find out did not return for two hours, and the key stage of the battle was organised by spasmodic communication between the three brigadiers themselves. First Delamain, thinking that Hoghton could not get round the northern flank in time to cut off the enemy retreat, decided to attack the northern redoubts to pin the defenders there. As his weakened brigade struggled towards the redoubts, Hoghton in turn detached two battalions to help him (though not, oddly, the two that had been transferred from Delamain's brigade for the battle). This cancelled out Townshend's deliberate overweighting of the encircling force, and began to turn the battle into a simple frontal attack. Delamain himself pressed his own attack harder than planned in response to calls for aid from Fry, whose brigade had become mired in the formidable defences around Saddleback Hill.

By the early afternoon, as Hoghton's attack at last developed, the British had fought their way into the northern defences, but then were hit by Turkish counter-attacks from the south-west. Delamain fell back to the western edge of the Suweida marsh, and by late afternoon the situation was worrying. The troops, with little wheeled transport, had marched and fought all through a day of fierce sunshine, tormented by a dusty wind, with scarcely more water than they carried in their own bottles. Thirst-crazed mules bolted towards the marshes in search of water. Cavalry reconnaissance had reported the water in the Suweida marsh as 'brackish, but drinkable' in an emergency, but it was impossibly saline. All the advances gradually ground to a halt. Townshend had hoped that the naval flotilla would be able to break through the obstruction and unhinge the enemy position at its centre, but in spite of heroic efforts by the commander of the gunboat *Comet*, they failed. It became clear that the dreamed-of encirclement had evaporated; and in fact the division might have faced defeat if the enemy had been more energetic. Delamain's force, which had marched and fought for eighteen miles, was 'pretty well beat, and most horribly thirsty'. The call to go forward to support Fry's brigade somehow produced a sudden 'new lease of life' in Reynardson's exhausted men. Still without water, they 'swept on in an attack at a pace which in the peaceful days of manoeuvres would assuredly have been criticised as "impossible under real conditions"'. But when night fell – 'suddenly like a black curtain' – and a bank they hoped was the river turned out to be a dry wadi, a reaction set in. 'The men were so dead-beat that they literally could not understand an order: thirst and exhaustion had produced a stupefying effect.'[11]

Now an unwelcome light began to shine on the limitations of the medical services. Wounded men could not be picked up, and lay out all night – with the temperature dropping by 50 degrees F. Not only was Delamain's force stuck, it had no idea where. Luckily, the defenders again decided to decamp in the night – 'how they managed it is rather a mystery,' Captain Reynardson thought. 'If only we had known our whereabouts and been able to push on that night, we should have been across their line of retreat and might have caught the lot.'[12] Spackman saw 'the infantry on the verge of collapse, and all they could do was to make direct to the river (our perverse but essential companion), and let a large Turkish column with all its guns march off and escape our net'. Although fourteen guns were eventually captured, eight were ancient brass muzzle-loaders – dating back as far as 1802 – and the rest semi-obsolete Krupp cannon. All the modern quick-firing German guns were got away.

Strategically, it still looked like a brilliant victory. Nureddin's force had lost some 4,000 men (1,153 of them captured) and 14 guns. Only 94 men of Townshend's division had been killed. The pursuit soon reached Aziziyeh, 102 river miles (60 land miles) above Kut and less than 60 from Baghdad. But once again, the main Ottoman force had got away. Once again the British cavalry had done little to stop them. The official historian suggested by way of excuse that they were 'to some extent tied to the steamers for lack of land transport'. They did catch up with the retreating enemy on 1 October 40 miles upriver from Kut, but since the Turks did not appear to be in disorder they decided to halt and wait until the river column arrived. This was not the first Turkish escape, nor the last, but it may have been the most fateful for the 6th Division. As Arnold Wilson suggested, 'the failure to capture the whole Turkish force was a turning-point, perhaps decisive, in the course of the campaign'.[13]

II: KUT

1. To Baghdad?

> Baghdad, like Jerusalem, stood out enticingly in the perfect map
> of the imagination.
> A. T. WILSON

> I still hope to be the Pasha of Baghdad before I leave India!
> LORD HARDINGE

When Kut fell, the British campaign in Mesopotamia reached a crossroads. The enticing possibilities that opened up were matched by alarming risks. The real question at this crucial point was whether the government was capable of assessing the issues and controlling the direction of the campaign. So far, the prospect of cheap military successes had been gratefully accepted, without any careful thought about its inevitable consequences. General Barrow, the initiator of the expedition, was afraid that this would go on. The victory at Kut, he warned shortly after the battle, was 'of so complete a nature that the idea of pushing on to Baghdad will certainly be revived'. Pressure would be brought, either directly, by Nixon and Cox who, as the men on the spot, would be seen to be in the best position to judge the feasibility of a further advance, or indirectly, 'by an agitation in the press or in commercial circles'.

Barrow was right to worry. Hardinge had already written privately to Sir Arthur Nicolson at the Foreign Office that 'if we are unable, for a long time to come, to force the Dardanelles, it becomes a question whether we should not strike a blow somewhere'. That could be done 'quite easily by taking Baghdad'. The contrast between the striking advances in Mesopotamia and the deadly paralysis at Gallipoli would naturally drive many others to the same conclusion. It was not just a matter of being unable 'for a long time' to force the Dardanelles: the Gallipoli operation was threatening to become a major disaster. August had seen the failure of an attempted major offensive at Anzac Cove, and the further landings at Suvla Bay also became bogged down after early success. The situation was set to get worse still: the Central Powers were overrunning Serbia at last, and could soon release heavy artillery for use at Gallipoli, making the cramped Allied beachheads untenable.

Though the government had repeatedly ranked Mesopotamia as a marginal theatre, Barrow knew that the 'world-wide prestige which the occupation of Baghdad would confer' would make the idea of taking it hard to resist. 'The very glamour attaching to so historic a city is in itself a temptation.' Caution would be unpopular, and not easy to justify 'in the minds of those who are not intimate with the intricacies of the problem'. But he was absolutely sure that Force D should not go forward. Its two 'very mediocre' divisions now occupied a huge area, and since the attitude of the population was at best 'doubtful' – if not actively hostile – the force could not be concentrated; too much of it had to be used to defend its own lines of communication. This, in military terms, was crucial, because it was not only, or even primarily, a question of capturing Baghdad. The city would have to be held. Simply controlling it would need at least a brigade; the 6th Division would be left with only two weak brigades to deal with any Ottoman counter-move. Barrow's conclusion was forceful: it would be an unjustifiable risk to take Baghdad 'unless we increase the force by a whole division of Infantry and one or two Cavalry regiments'.[1]

Unless all the Indian troops were taken out of France, this could not be done. But could the advance on Baghdad now be prevented? Barrow pointed out that even though the level of the Tigris was dropping fast, making it unlikely that the enemy could be overtaken, the pursuit was continuing. 'If we do not stop him, General Nixon will soon be in Baghdad regardless of orders, and we shall be faced with the grave alternative of having to withdraw again or make our occupation effective.' Barrow was almost pleading with Chamberlain to issue a definite instruction: 'everything points to our hand being forced, unless we can arrest the present trend of events by a prompt and imperative decision.' Instead, the India Secretary chose to issue a query. 'I shall be glad to learn what Nixon's intentions are,' he wired. 'Kindly send me by telegram an estimate of what you consider to be the present strength of the enemy.' Though he added that since there seemed to be 'now no chance of overtaking and breaking up the retreating Turks, there is no object in pursuing them any further', this was unlikely to be read as an imperative decision by anybody who was not looking for one.

Nixon's intentions could, in fact, have been deduced fairly easily from an assessment his staff drew up in August, while the attack on Kut was being planned. It argued that the occupation of Baghdad would be strategically decisive, since it would swing the logistical balance against the Ottoman forces. 'The Turks would have to draw their resources from a great distance, and it would be no easy task for them to eject a British force, established in Baghdad, and drawing its supplies by river from the sea.' Effectively reversing Barrow's perspective, the Force D staff argued that holding Baghdad might be easier than capturing it: 'to advance against Baghdad when it is directly covered by a prepared enemy will certainly entail another severe engagement or series of engagements.' But they held out a more attractive possibility: 'if the enemy is beaten 100 miles in advance of Baghdad, the 6th Division might be able in certain circumstances to enter that City practically unopposed provided that the pursuit is carried out vigorously.'[2]

Did these circumstances now exist? Townshend's negative opinion was clear from his very unusual instruction to Nixon's chief of staff on 3 October not to send him reinforcements – 'I do not want you to send these troops up here because I do not approve of holding on at Aziziyah.' Assuming (as he believed Duff had assured him) that 'we are not to go beyond

Kut, we ought to come back; we are too far ahead'. But Nixon was less impressed by military rules than by psychological possibilities. 'In my opinion a pursuit even though it has been slow owing to circumstances which could not be avoided, will have a demoralising effect on the Turks and a corresponding good effect on the political situation in this portion of Asia.' He sidestepped the possibility that these unavoidable circumstances might further degrade the 6th Division's military capability. Townshend, predictably, was much more concerned about this. He noted in his diary that the army commander did not 'seem to realise the weakness and danger of his line of communications'. So he decided to give him his opinion 'whether he likes it or not'.

This was 'that on military grounds we should consolidate our position at Kut'. The original hope of entering Baghdad on the heels of the Turks while they were retreating in disorder, Townshend wrote, had been denied them by the sudden fall of the river which had 'made our advance difficult, slow and toilsome'. There was now a 'possibility of our small forces being driven out by stronger forces from Anatolia which would compel us to retire down a long line of communications teeming with Arabs whose hostility would become active on hearing of our retreat'. If the government wanted Baghdad to be taken, then, 'unless great risk is to be run, it is absolutely necessary that the advance from Kut should be carried out methodically by two Divisions'.

Nixon would certainly not have liked this opinion, had he seen it (he would later deny having received it). As if in answer to its final sentence ('It is now quite impossible for laden ships to go up'), his own opinion started from the reassuring assertion that the falling river level was not a problem: 'navigation difficulties have been overcome by lightening ships and utilising them for towing laden barges and by marching troops with land transport.' Nixon held that Nureddin's force, which had stopped retreating and taken up a position at Ctesiphon, 'thereby constitutes a threat to us'. He believed that the enemy troops, especially local forces, had been 'much demoralised by defeat at Kut al-Amara, a position which they considered impregnable'. Because they were so close to Baghdad and keen to desert, Nixon suggested, Nureddin would have difficulty making a determined stand. As soon as the 6th Division had fully concentrated at Aziziyeh, and been reinforced by drafts of cavalry on their way from Basra, there was 'every probability of catching and smashing the enemy at Ctesiphon'. The British had in front of them 'a shaken enemy who has taken refuge in a position where we can manoeuvre and I hope destroy him'. If, on the other hand, the British retired to Kut 'the enemy and the whole of the tribes will place their own construction on such a move'.

As Barrow had feared, Nixon could 'see nothing which would justify letting slip such an opportunity'. But in London the opportunity looked less irresistible. At the War Office, the General Staff saw real problems with Baghdad as a strategic position. It seemed quite possible for the Turks to assemble 'a very superior force, whose arrival would lead to active operations by the Arabs against our long and difficult line of communication'. (Exactly the point Townshend was trying to make.) There were no good defensive positions around the city, and – contrary to Nixon's staff's view – there was no reason why the Turks should not be able to concentrate a large force at Baghdad. 'In fact, it seems easier for them to concentrate against us there than it would be at Kut and Amara.' The following week, the War Office spelled out that a move to Baghdad with the forces currently at Nixon's disposal would be 'a dangerous operation'.[3] This crushing military verdict, however, failed to halt Nixon's progress. Hardinge accepted that while Nixon could 'without much difficulty capture Baghdad' with the forces now at his disposal, he could not stay there without an extra division. When the Cabinet considered this on 8 October it was 'greatly impressed', Chamberlain told him. Attractive options were in short supply at that stage in the war. The Foreign Secretary passed him a note agreeing that it would make more sense to send a division to Mesopotamia 'where we can score a notable success', than 'to merge it in <u>hopeless failure</u> elsewhere'.[4]

Cabinet ministers might cheerfully commit another division, but India was less happy to. The Chief of the Indian General Staff, Sir Percy Lake, complained that they were being asked to accept a binding obligation 'practically in the dark'. His language was revealing; India felt exploited. It simply could not find the extra division. Lake said he would be prepared to run the risk of reducing the garrison still further in order to capture Baghdad – but only if they could be sure of getting the Indian divisions back from France within a reasonable time; and only if they were 'complete divisions of recognised composition, and not merely a selection of the Indian units which have had the most severe handling in France'. Even then, the most India could find for Mesopotamia would be two brigades, with two cavalry regiments and three batteries of artillery. This would hardly be enough to make Baghdad safe 'except very temporarily'. In India itself, on the other hand, 'our position would be dangerously weak should anything serious occur'. The real problem was, as Lake's phraseology made painfully obvious, that India's trust in the War Office had been undermined. 'No confidence is felt by the Chief [Lake] that these divisions will be sent to us even should they reach Egypt, and it is his belief that should we offer any guarantee that in the given circumstances more troops would be spared by us from India for Mesopotamia, it would be eagerly snatched at, and the non-return of the divisions would be practically certain.'[5]

Lake drew a conclusion that exposed a truly dangerous rift between Britain and India. Because Nixon might be 'compelled to advance whether reinforcements are sent him or not', the Chief of Staff suggested assembling this quasi-division for training. It should be 'held in readiness'; but since it was 'only a precautionary measure, the Home Government should not be informed of this'. Once again he spelled out the suspicion that underpinned his 'amazing minute' (as an angry member of the

Mesopotamia commission of inquiry would call it; the official history tactfully omitted to mention it). 'The Home Government are very anxious that Baghdad should be taken, and they will send us the required force if we hold out, but they will give us nothing if the least sign of willingness to find reinforcements is shown by us.'[6]

Happily unaware of this breach between the two halves of the Empire, the Cabinet began to focus serious attention on Mesopotamia in October. Not just the glamour of Baghdad, but the apparent brilliance of the 'invincible' 6th Division's campaign, marked it out from the increasingly depressing situation on the Western Front, where the massive and bloody 1915 offensives had failed to break the trench stalemate, and still more from the Dardanelles. By October, the prospect of being forced to evacuate Gallipoli was beginning to loom, with all the damage to British prestige that would involve. It is hardly surprising that Grey was excited by the prospect of a 'notable success' in Mesopotamia. The lure of spectacular success was reinforced by fear of the effects of inaction. In mid-October Sir Percy Cox wired to Gerard Leachman, the political officer with the 6th Division, that because the force at Aziziyeh was doing nothing, the attitude of the Arabs on the Tigris was becoming 'uncertain'.[7] Coded though it was, this cast a light into the official mind.

But the government was still getting discouraging advice on the prospects for an advance on Baghdad. The Committee of Imperial Defence stated once again that Baghdad itself was not a good defensive position, even if occupying the surrounding area could be strategically advantageous, and denying it to the Turks would certainly hamper their operations. The Dardanelles Committee, the nearest thing Britain had to a 'war cabinet' at that point, called for yet another assessment from the naval and military chiefs of staff. This should have been decisive, but once again it was inconclusive: the two service chiefs stuck to the line that the problem was not whether Baghdad could be taken, but how it could be held; and that the key issue was the weakness of communications. Though Nixon was now facing only 9,000 Turkish troops 'and some irregulars', these forces might be 'somewhat increased' by the end of the year, and might 'conceivably' reach a total of as much as 60,000 by the end of January. If the Ottoman railways were improved, there could be still more later in the year.

On the basis of this gloomy projection, they came down – confusingly – in favour of a 'raid' on Baghdad. Even though they accepted that political experts predicted dire effects for British prestige in the East if the city was lost, they still held that 'it would be unwise to occupy Baghdad with the intention of staying there until the end of the war'. A raiding force might stay there for a while, but it should not be in a position where it was obliged to stay for political reasons: the military authorities had to have the power 'to withdraw the troops at will'. The chiefs of staff found a strong argument in favour of temporarily occupying Baghdad in 'the probability that a failure to push on now might create nearly, if not quite, as bad an impression in the East as would withdrawal after occupation'. But if there were 'such strong political objections to a withdrawal from Baghdad – after having once gone there – as to make it in the least doubtful whether the military authorities would be permitted to withdraw the troops at their discretion', they would oppose either occupation or a raid.[8]

Two days after this unhelpful advice, on 21 October, Mesopotamia finally reached the top of the Dardanelles Committee's political agenda. Heavyweight ministers backed all three of the divergent options available. Lord Curzon (a former Viceroy) favoured consolidation at Kut, because the risk to Britain's prestige of a possible withdrawal from Baghdad was unacceptable. Lords Kitchener and Crewe favoured the 'raid', holding that a rapid attack would cripple the Turks without threatening British prestige. Grey, Balfour and Churchill favoured a full occupation of Baghdad. Grey believed that the whole Arab world was on the brink of commitment to either the Allies or the Central Powers, and the capture of Baghdad might decide the issue. Once again, this proved to be the key argument, trumping the issue of oil. When Churchill suggested that if they did not take Baghdad, Persia would take the Ottoman side, and Curzon noted that Nixon would then have to weaken his force to protect the oilfields, Balfour simply said that the oilfields were not vital. 'The Navy had other sources of supply,' Churchill confirmed.

The deciding voice might well have been Kitchener's. He 'did not altogether concur' (as the official historian tactfully put it) in the 21 October line. In fact, being reluctant to take the two Indian divisions from France, and ever-anxious about the security of Egypt, he was not in favour of any move except a raid on Baghdad. He was still convinced that if Gallipoli had to be abandoned, Alexandretta would become the key strategic point. 'If Baghdad is occupied and Gallipoli evacuated, a force of 60–70,000 Turks might be sent' to recover Baghdad, and since Egypt would also be threatened (something like 200,000 Turkish troops would be released in all), no reinforcements would be available for Mesopotamia. But even Kitchener delivered an ambiguous verdict, since he admitted that if Gallipoli could hold out, the Turks could not send any 'considerable expedition' to Mesopotamia.[9]

The eventual advance on Baghdad was, in the end, a classic result of multiple-agency control. The Dardanelles Committee remained, like the advice it had received, inconclusive. (Curzon typically grumbled that 'anyone who knows any particular subject connected with the war is sure to be overruled when the subject is discussed'.[10]) Now the drift of events became, in effect, the decision. Just before the Cabinet's final discussion the Viceroy suggested that 'our hands will probably be forced by Nixon advancing on Baghdad before we know where we are. He is a great thruster, and all his Generals are the same, and a very good lot they are too.' Hardinge did not, of course, know of Townshend's views, and presumably would not have liked them.

If he sounded happy to have his hand forced, the same seems true of the Cabinet.

Ministers later had to defend themselves against charges that they had authorised the advance on Baghdad to divert attention from the Dardanelles disaster. Asquith himself then insisted that he could not 'recall any step taken in this War which was more completely warranted by every relevant consideration of policy and strategy', and fortified by an 'absolute concurrence of expert authority'. He denounced the suggestion that the Cabinet 'were anxious for what is called a "political success" and therefore subordinated military to political considerations' as 'a calumny ... a vile calumny'. But his declaration that expert opinion was unanimous was hardly tenable; and the implication that a definite decision was taken was surely misleading.

Curzon's most recent biographer has alleged that 'the wrong decision was taken against the advice of the best informed minister'.[11] The real accusation, though, is that the Cabinet took no decision. While the Dardanelles Committee was in session, Hardinge sent another telegram weighing the three possible lines of action, and dismissing the idea of staying put at Kut. That would show weakness, 'and may force our hands into advancing after all. It does not therefore appeal to us.' He did not directly oppose the idea of a raid, but he strongly favoured the occupation of Baghdad. Chamberlain replied by telling him that the Cabinet would agree to an advance 'unless you consider that the possibility of eventual withdrawal is decisively against the advance'. Hardinge's certainty now trumped the government's hesitancy: whatever the future might bring, 'I am confident that the right policy at the present time is to take the risk.' Chamberlain gave way: 'Nixon may march on Baghdad' – as long as he was sure his force was strong enough. Two divisions would be sent as soon as possible, but they could not get there quickly.[12] Chamberlain implied that this consent had been endorsed by the Cabinet, but Lord Crewe thought it more likely that 'he felt justified from the general trend of the discussion in sending this'. Asquith bullishly assured the Commons that he did not think 'that in the whole War there has been a series of operations more carefully contrived, more brilliantly conducted, and with a better prospect of final success' than in Mesopotamia. But Grey perhaps gave the game away when he remarked to the Cabinet Secretary that 'it was necessary to gain strength by eating <u>now</u>, even if it involved indigestion later on'.[13]

2. To Salman Pak

I do not know any portion of the theatre of war in which a single division could achieve such great results.
AUSTEN CHAMBERLAIN

Early in November Lord Hardinge received a somewhat disquieting telegram from General Townshend. After describing the strength of the enemy position facing him, he went on to assess the morale of his men. 'These troops of mine are <u>tired</u> and their tails are <u>not</u> up, but slightly down.'[1] Townshend's moods could shift from confidence to caution, but his opinion of his Indian sepoys was now on a steady downward curve. He dwelt on the fact that he had only three British infantry battalions, and they were now barely at half strength. In mid-October he noted in his diary, 'the British troops can be relied on as before, but the Indians are now shaken and unreliable'. This was also the more stolid Delamain's view. Tiredness had undermined their efficiency; they were 'worn out', and maybe worse. Delamain reported that when he had assaulted the northern positions at Es Sinn, he found some of his Indian troops 'without spirit'. Although one battalion had done well (losing 45 per cent of its strength), he was now worried that if his troops had to assault solidly held trenches again, 'they would not succeed'. As they stood at Aziziyeh looking towards Baghdad, an older anxiety resurfaced. Amongst the Muslim sepoys the generals detected 'a widespread unwillingness to advance against the Holy Place of Salman Pak' at Ctesiphon. This was right at the heart of the Turkish defensive positions.

Morale is an elusive quality, and though some may (as Townshend worried) have dwelt on the uncomfortable fact that 'the distance from Azizieh to the sea is over 300 miles', the division's unbroken run of dramatic successes had certainly generated plenty of confidence. As Spackman said, 'it is not surprising that we came to think we were invincible, and that, led by our General, nothing could stop us'. Townshend's ADC, Captain Bastow, believed that the troops would do for Townshend 'what they could not be asked to do by anybody else'. Would it be enough? As he would tell the Mesopotamia inquiry, 'We backed Townshend's luck, and our own luck; that was all.' Luck, as Napoleon often said, was an essential attribute for generals. But numbers were needed too, and the 6th Division was well below strength. The three British battalions which formed its backbone (or so most senior officers thought) were particularly weakened: the Dorsets were down to 297 fit men. Even such replacements as were now arriving were – in Townshend's view – the most 'wretched class of recruits' he had seen; his battalion commanders seemed equally unhappy.

The shortage of transport was worse than ever. Nixon's requests for 'some powerful light draft tugs or stern-wheelers' that could navigate above Kut – where the falling level of the river meant that the new 'P' class steamers were 'useless' – became more urgent in October. But urgency was not in the Indian government's lexicon. Working at peacetime speed, the Royal Indian Marine at long last drew up a list of all available river craft and invited Nixon to pick any – ideally ones which might hope to make it across the sea from India to Mesopotamia without sinking. This would be the fate of many; but even those that reached Basra safely arrived long after the fate of the advance was decided.

One recent arrival highlit the makeshift quality of the Tigris river fleet. The *Aerial*, skippered by T. A. Chalmers, may have been the oddest vessel to serve in any theatre of the war. 'A queer boat propelled by air like an aeroplane', Colonel Bowker of the Hampshires described it. 'It is an old native-built Brahmaputra boat converted into a launch by Mr Chalmers, an engineer in

Assam. He built up a deckhouse of teak with four berths and bathroom, installed the engine himself & the air propellor (well aft and working very much like that on an aeroplane). It makes a similar noise too & there is a good deal of vibration.' It was 60 feet long and 10 feet wide, and displaced 15 tons; its 50 bhp engine could drive it at 9 mph. Spackman noted that 'except in strong wind or current it could get along at a good speed in spite of its odd appearance, and could go right alongside owing to its shallow draft' – it drew only 18 inches, as compared with the 'P' boats' 4 ft 6 in or more. Chalmers had offered it for service as a hospital boat in Mesopotamia and brought it a thousand miles down the Brahmaputra river to Bombay, whence it was shipped to Basra in late July 1915. He first saw action ferrying casualties from the riverbank to the hospitals during the battle of Kut. Chalmers went up to Aziziyeh in the last week of October, and received a visit from Townshend, who told him with grim jocosity that 'he hoped to give me plenty to do in the near future'.[2]

Townshend's forward concentration at Aziziyeh showed all too clearly the problems of movement and supply that made the prospect of an advance to Baghdad such a gamble. On 7 October the 16th Brigade left Kut to join the 18th at Aziziyeh. Next day, apparently to its surprise, the 17th Brigade was also sent forward (leaving only the understrength 30th Brigade to hold Kut). The 17th's march north was ominous. 'The hot weather, to which we thought we had said goodbye, gave a last kick to assert itself,' Reynardson wrote. On the first day, they followed the riverbank, and made only 12 miles before halting at 1 p.m., by which time the sun was 'a good deal too hot for comfort'. At this point, though, they received orders to press on with all haste. Assuming that the Aziziyeh position was under threat, they stopped following the increasingly tortuous path of the river and struck out across a loop – a march of 20 miles without water. 'This does not sound much,' Reynardson wrote, 'but it must be remembered that the sun was still horribly hot in the open from ten to four, and there was a hot, dust-laden wind.' Moreover, and more worryingly, the men were basically unfit and tired more easily than ever before as they set out at 5.30 next morning. Worryingly, too, the column lost its direction as it marched on after taking a break from 10 a.m. until 1 p.m. (with 'the sun even hotter than we expected as we lay out in the desert'), and instead of linking up with the river at the next bend it got into increasingly desperate straits. 'At 6 pm we were still marching, looking in vain for the river and getting extraordinarily thirsty.' They 'plugged on, occasionally cheered for a moment by a glimmer in the distance', but these turned out to be not water but salt deposits shining in the moonlight. Water bottles were empty, and by 7 p.m. an increasing number were falling out of the column, with 'a terrible stiffness and numbness in their legs'. With almost no wheeled transport, the brigade was compelled – unprecedentedly – to leave these men behind.

'Those who could sit were put on any ponies and mules available, while those who were too bad were collected as far as possible into groups with one or two sound men as guards, and instructed to light flares of camel-thorns at intervals to show their position.' So, 'leaving an ever-increasing trail of cripples', the brigade staggered on and finally found the river again at 9 p.m. Its 'parent ship', however, was not there – it had run aground – and the troops got no food or blankets until it eventually joined them two hours later. At least, by this time most of the stragglers had managed to crawl in: a dozen or so were out all night, but luckily were left unharmed.[3]

Almost incredibly, the brigade went through the same experience next day. Having apparently been told that the Turks were approaching Aziziyeh, they struck out overland again – this time on a 25-mile march – and again lost their way. This time, however, a convoy of water carts was sent out to meet them, 'so that the last six miles were bearable, though again a lot of men were obliged to fall out'. What was harder to take was the news, when they eagerly asked if they were in time for the fighting, that the story had been a staff officer's bright idea to spur them on their way. The debilitating extra effort had been completely unnecessary. Further exertions followed: Captain Read of the Norfolks recorded how, even though there was a mass of wood stacked on the quay, the troops were not allowed to touch it. Instead they 'took it in turns of Companies to cut brushwood from the other bank for the kitchen. A very mean and fatiguing job for unfit men, such as ours were, in the heat of the day . . . Such is the grasping close fisted character of the Indian Government we served!'

The very night that the 17th Brigade arrived at Aziziyeh, there was another sign that the balance of force was shifting. 'Frazer's Post', a redoubt on the right bank held by the 110th Mahrattas (commanded by Colonel George Frazer), was attacked by thirty or forty Arabs who cut through the barbed-wire perimeter and got into the trenches, killing several of the defenders. At this point some of the sepoys panicked, and only Colonel Frazer's personal action rallied a counter-attacking force and expelled the raiders, who made off with 'a good many rifles'. Unlike most of the Arab attackers the British had encountered so far, these had shown 'considerable determination' under quite heavy fire. Townshend decided that retaliation was necessary, and sent yet another 'reconnaissance in force' towards Zeur. This would provide practice for the night operations needed for the next, crucial battle. But it may also have been a response to the 'snorter' he had got from Nixon ten days earlier, accusing him of defensive-mindedness – his engineers had used 30 miles of barbed wire in the defences at Aziziyeh and were asking for more – and alleging that 'going to ground was the fungus destroying the spirit of the offensive in the 6th Division'. (Townshend argued that the defences were the only way to release the bulk of his force by paring down the troops guarding his rear lines; he eventually dismantled most of them to reduce the camp 'to the dimensions of a small fortified post' which could be held by the 'bed-rock minimum' garrison left there.)

At this stage the problems added to the supply chain by the extra stretch of river above Kut, vastly disproportionate to its length, should have become obvious even to the most optimistic. Townshend's force totalled 7,179 'effective rifles and sabres' on 24 October, with 483 infantry and 574 cavalry drafts and replacements in Kut. (The cavalry simply could not go forward until a big enough stock of fodder had been taken up to Aziziyeh.) Even without supply restrictions, this was none too large a force to confront a well-prepared position, even if it was held by no more than the 11,000 infantry Nixon's staff thought were there. That figure, at least, was the one Townshend said he had been given. One of Nixon's staff would tell the Mesopotamia commission that he had estimated the enemy strength at between 13,500 and 23,000, and told Townshend 13,000. Townshend himself preferred a figure of 20,000, and remained convinced that an assault with less than two divisions would be reckless.

His critics usually point out that, in addition, such a corps command would have ensured him promotion to lieutenant-general. Townshend was undoubtedly ambitious, but his worries about the strength of his force, and the pressure being put on him, are not hard to understand. He had enough political awareness to know how easily he could be hung out to dry if things went wrong. Governmental gratitude is notoriously inconstant. He spelt the issue out in his diary for 19 October: 'I must get orders to advance since I am not in command of Force "D" and Sir John Nixon is. I think it is his duty to give such an order and not make me advance on my own and so take all responsibility before Government for so doing.'[4] This was just what seemed to be happening when Nixon's chief of staff, Kemball, flew up to Townshend's HQ in mid-October to suggest that he might attack the Turkish covering force at El Kutuniya, 12 miles upriver from Aziziyeh. Nixon seems to have been hoping that this would turn into a quick move on Baghdad itself. His determination to push such a move took him as far as to conceal the imminent despatch of two new divisions to Mesopotamia from Townshend as well as from the enemy – for fear that if the Turks heard of this, they would refuse to give battle in front of Baghdad. Not until the evening before the decisive battle did he send Kemball to tell Townshend about the reinforcements. ('Make it public now, and it will hearten them up.'⁵) If they had waited for one of these divisions, or even a single brigade, the whole history of the war might have been very different.

The 6th Division had a few weeks' rest while supplies and replacements trickled painfully slowly up to Aziziyeh. Some officers were able to hop on a returning boat downriver to Basra, and got a sense of the changes in train. Looking for the scene of the 'regatta' at Qurna, Reynardson found 'a different country . . . in place of the miles of water and little sand-hills, was one vast expanse of waving crops. On either bank rose the level ranks of a wonderful crop of "jowari" quite 12 feet high, where only four months before there had been nothing but water and reeds . . . A proof, if one were needed, of what the soil will do.' At Basra, though the port was not greatly changed, connecting roads had been built, and all public buildings, stores, hospital and messes were lit by electric light – 'and ice could be had for the asking'. But some things had deteriorated – notably, and ominously, the manners of the Basra Arabs. 'They thought nothing of shouldering one into the gutter and jostling one at the shops.' He was certain that this was not casual, as 'in such things the Oriental had a very meticulous code of manners'. The Arabs 'know it, and intend it, to be an insult'. And for an Arab to be able to push a British soldier into the gutter was 'not good for our prestige'.

On 26 October Nixon formally ordered the advance on Baghdad to begin by 14 November, promising Townshend that transport would continue to be 'pushed up from Basra by every available means'. It was 'impossible to meet your full demands without incurring too great delay', but Nixon did not say how much delay was acceptable, or why. At the end of the month, in response to Townshend's continued protests about his shortages,

Kemball flew up again to Aziziyeh to explain why he could have no more – and to also to propose 'an alternative plan for the advance suggested by General Nixon'. (The details of this remain obscure.) Townshend was still bridling. He had found that Nixon's staff were issuing orders direct to his force, and was stung into asking Kemball, 'Will you kindly inform me if the Army Commander is commanding this operation in person, or if he intends me to command it as I did in the Kut operations.' The reply – 'You will of course command the VIth Div as before' – was perhaps not exactly what he wanted to hear. It meant that, as at Kut, Nixon with his 'Napoleonic staff' would come upriver to sit, metaphorically, on Townshend's shoulder during the make-or-break battle to be fought for Baghdad.

The Ottoman position defending Baghdad, called Salman Pak (after the Prophet Muhammad's barber, believed to be buried there), lay near the site of the victorious battle fought by one of Townshend's heroes, Belisarius, against the Persians in AD 530. At its heart was one of the ancient world's most extraordinary monuments, the arch of Ctesiphon. The barrel-vaulted hall of the ruined palace of the Sassanian King Chosroes was still visible for miles across the empty desert. 'One of the most imposing ruins in the world', as Gertrude Bell said in her second travel book *Amurath to Amurath*. 'The great curtain wall rises stark and gaunt out of the desert ... The gigantic vault, built over empty space without the use of centring beams, is one of the most stupendous creations of any age.' It spanned eighty-five feet, more than six feet wider than the barrel vaults of the basilica of Maxentius in the Forum in Rome. The surviving walls were decorated with shallow niches and columns which she saw as 'the final word in the Asiatic treatment of wall-spaces'. Though the defenders actually cut a fire-step in the ancient mud-brick city wall, the arch itself lay midway between the two defensive lines. The front trenches ran along a peninsula formed by a long bend in the river, crossed by several sizeable canals, and dotted with hillocks ten to thirty feet high. 'These hillocks and ruined canals are the confused traces of towns and great cities which endured here for centuries and which the storms of adversity turned into this historical graveyard', as Mehmet Emin reflected. In the middle of the defences was the feature the British called 'High Wall', a relic of a fortified city (possibly Seleucia) with a base 200 feet thick, running at a height of over forty feet along the road from Bustan to Ctesiphon, and forming a right angle along the south-central part of the front. North of it the ground in front of the Ottoman trenches was flat desert covered in low scrub; south of it, a sandbank over 1,000 yards wide ran between the trenches and the river. This sand was effectively impassable, so the key section lay north of High Wall.

Mehmet Emin was characteristically critical of the positions chosen by the 'Defence Committee' – a group of old officers 'full of the partiality for placing defences on high and commanding ground, ignorant of the new experience which demands that such should be placed in low ground, invisible from a distance'. More seriously, he judged, the position was unsound because its line of retreat ran northwards, into the area that was most vulnerable to an outflanking movement. The backbone of the position was a series of redoubts along the front. Two of these were particularly strong – those the British labelled 'Water Redoubt' and 'Vital Point' – but the supporting trench system for the line of redoubts was still incomplete. 'The zigzags connecting [redoubts] 5, 6, 7, 8 and 9 to the local and group reserves had been excavated, but were not connected in one continuous line.' Communication trenches from the reserve areas had not been dug, not for lack of time but because they were not thought necessary.[6] British air reconnaissance suggested that the Turkish front line was much better prepared than the second line, about two miles behind it.

Townshend's plan of attack was once again ambitious and complicated. 'I hoped to paralyse a great part of the forces of the enemy, entrenched along a large extent of front, by the use of an inferior fraction of my troops, disguising its weakness by boldness of action and ruse, while I hit the hammer blow on the enemy's flank and rear with my Principal Mass.' He divided his force into four groups, only one of which (Column C) was to pin the enemy frontally while Column A would attack 'Vital Point' (VP) with Column B to its right to roll up the Turkish line, and the 'Flying Column' was to sweep round into the enemy rear. The plan had to be ambitious because it aimed not just to get to Baghdad, but to exploit the weakness Mehmet Emin saw in the position, and prevent the defenders from getting away. To be at all secure at Baghdad, Townshend's small force really needed to achieve what it had failed to do at Kut – the 'battle of annihilation' beloved of the post-Clausewitzian German military theorists. This probably accounts for the unusual mixed composition of the Flying Column – mainly a cavalry force, but including an infantry battalion (76th Punjabis), which would have been necessary if the column was actually to cut off, rather than merely harass, any Turkish retreat. But the column's composition also allowed Townshend to give command of it to a man he trusted, Mellis, instead of the Cavalry Brigade commander, Roberts. (He was plainly sceptical of the explanation offered by Roberts for the failure – yet again – of the cavalry to cut off the retreating enemy after the action at El Kutuniya.[7]) With the two divisions he thought necessary, Townshend's plan was quite feasible. As it was, facing 'an enemy at least as strong as myself, on the defensive in a very strong position', it was frankly a gamble. Its all or nothing quality was starkly evident in the instruction that battle casualties were to be taken forward into Baghdad. However optimistic, this would, as it proved, have been their only hope.

Although the defensive position was certainly vulnerable to a flanking move, Townshend can hardly have been cheered when he finally saw it. It was not an attractive prospect for the attackers. The landscape facing them was dead flat, 'featureless, dreary and bare, blue sky above and plain brown beneath', with 'only the yellow, turbid river two to three hundred yards wide to vary the monotony, as it hurried round or over innumerable sandspits between high steep banks of earth, which were not broken except where the ancient canals had taken off from its bed'. The ground was 'scarred and furrowed by a network of shallow disused irrigation channels', its flatness only varied by 'scattered mounds of earth, and the banks of ruined canals great and small'. There were no trees, and the only vegetation was 'a scrubby growth of liquorice two to three feet high, thick near the river, sparse in the dry areas away from its banks'.[8]

At El Kutuniya as the advance began, the commander of the bridging train, Major Sandes, had an instructive encounter with Nixon. On the morning of 17 November, while Sandes was engaged in 'improving and beautifying' the bridge he had made the previous evening, 'the Army Commander strolled on to the bridge with some of his staff' and was introduced to him. Nixon 'asked if my danacks [small boats used as pontoons] were satisfactory, to which I replied that they were not'. He asked why, in that case, there were no pontoons: Sandes replied that only eighteen had been authorised. Nixon told him 'to wire at once to India for more', and asked how many he wanted. 'Now', Sandes recalled, 'pontoons cost from £100 to £120 each, so I debated whether I should say perhaps another twenty.' While he was pondering this, Nixon immediately said 'A hundred?' Sandes was 'so knocked over by this that I did not quite know what to say, and he then followed up his query with the question, "Two hundred?" This encouraged me to give my candid opinion, which was that another fifty pontoons (worth a cool £6,000, by the way, even in India) would do very nicely.' Nixon instantly sent a wire off, but as Sandes ruefully noted, 'perhaps my successor as a builder of bridges in Mesopotamia derived some benefit from these new boats. But they could not arrive in time to be of any use to the luckless 6th Division.'[9] Why, we must ask, did Nixon leave his intervention in this vital issue until four days before the most crucial battle of the campaign? The day before they marched out, Nixon inspected his troops, and pointedly 'remarked on the fitness of the men'. Captain Shakeshaft found the army commander's remark 'rather curious'; he remembered how when they were at Amara, Surgeon-General Hathaway had recommended that a large percentage be sent back to India – 'which of course had not been done'.[10]

When he reached Zeur, Townshend had to abandon his planned movement up the right bank. A boat-bridge was again hastily thrown across the river, and the reunited force continued up the left bank. At Lajj, he got apparently reliable information about the arrival of significant Turkish reinforcements in Baghdad. Asking Nixon about this produced the unsurprising reaction, 'Tell Charles I do not believe a word of it.' Four days later, though, Nixon's staff officially passed on to Townshend the estimate made by the Imperial General Staff the previous month that 60,000 Ottoman troops might concentrate at Baghdad. It is clear that Nixon had already seen this, and simply chosen not to pass it on to his subordinate. As the final advance began, Nixon sent a long telegram to India examining the possibility that a new Ottoman army command (the Sixth Army) was being organised under the famous German military theorist General Colmar von der Goltz. The 51st Division had in fact arrived at Baghdad, and seven of its nine battalions had reached Ctesiphon by 17 November, bringing the strength of the defenders up to 18,000 Turkish infantry – without counting regular cavalry, or Arab irregulars. And Nixon was not only wrong about enemy numbers; he also failed to factor in the fighting capacity – far greater than the battered 35th and 38th Divisions – of the 45th, and still more the 51st Division. The ranks of these units were filled with the rugged Anatolian peasantry whose tenacity the British had come to respect at Gallipoli.

On 21 November Townshend called for two air reconnaissance missions, the first long-range missions since Nixon's order of the 13th: one of the Ctesiphon position, and the other of the Baghdad area. The first returned with no report of any change. The second, flown by Major Reilly, the most experienced pilot with the force, in the afternoon, never returned. Reilly noted 'a distinct alteration in the enemy's dispositions' at Ctesiphon as he approached, and decided to take a closer look. It seemed 'obvious that considerable reinforcements had arrived at the northerly camp' (i.e. the second line), but as he flew over it his engine failed, and though he managed to glide away and set down in the desert to the east, he was captured by the ubiquitous Arab irregulars. Mehmet Emin saw the prisoner angrily refusing to answer demands for information: 'he took no notice of our questions and with his eyes flashing with the excess of his rage, he remained staring at his machine which had failed him in his hour of need.' This setback seems to have had a dramatic effect amongst the Ottoman soldiery: 'this little event was taken as a happy omen that the luck of the enemy was about to change, and it caused a deeply felt improvement in the general morale.' Reilly was carrying a map of the Tigris which was equally important in the eyes of the Ottoman command. 'For at HQ and with the troops there was no such thing as a map.'[11]

3. Ctesiphon

The conclusion of the battle of Suleiman Pak in such a
mysterious fashion was predestined by fate.
MEHMET EMIN

Would Townshend still have gone into battle if Reilly had
brought back his report? The two armies were so close that
withdrawal might well have been impossible 'even if it had
been deemed politic', as the official history said. But Nixon and
Townshend would surely not have gone ahead with assaulting
'an entrenched position held by a force now so obviously
superior in numbers'. Unfortunately, their chance of discovering
this was further reduced soon afterwards, when two more of
the remaining six aircraft were lost; only two of the rest were
still serviceable when the final advance began. Townshend's
radio communications remained problematic, too. His wireless
officer (Captain Cardew, commanding No. 34 Signal Company)
'had learnt my lesson at Essein [Es Sinn] & demanded a pack
set both for the Flying Column & Column B, & also if possible
with Column A. However there were no wireless sets available
for this column & it was with the greatest difficulty that I got
the other sets & even then each set was terribly under-manned.
Horses could only be found for the pack set proceeding with the
Flying Column.' Column B's wireless had to be sent out on two
mule carts: 'jolting over the desert in carts was hardly good for
such delicate instruments & the dust played havoc with it.'

At last, in the early afternoon of 21 November, Hoghton's
Column C moved off towards Bustan on a widely extended
front. Townshend and his divisional HQ went along with it for
a few miles. So, to the bafflement of some, did the Army HQ.

Nixon 'considered his presence necessary in view of possible developments', but decided (as he later told the Mesopotamia Commission) that his health was not up to taking over operational command. When Column C halted for water around 5 p.m. about two miles south-east of Bustan, an epic scene presented itself – across the level sands the astonishing arch of Ctesiphon 'was seen standing out against the blood red sky'. Reynardson recalled that 'owing to some atmospheric trick' the mighty ruin 'appeared quite suddenly where a minute before nothing had been visible but flat, bare desert'. Though only eight miles away, it seemed far off and immensely high – 'like some huge mass of mountains, blue and shimmering in the haze above the glaring desert, and it seemed almost incredible that it could be a mere ruin'.

After dark, the other three columns headed west in echelon, moving in silence with muffled wheels, and with a ban on all lights (including smoking). They reached their jumping-off points in the middle of the night. After four hours' rest in the bitter cold they saw the naval flotilla, ahead of them on the Tigris, open the bombardment of the area between Bustan and the Turkish front line. Hoghton inched forward cautiously – too cautiously for the commander of Column B, who, when he still could not hear the guns of Column C at 7.45 a.m., asked for permission to take his column forward. As he did so, the main Turkish front, which had been so quiet that Hoghton feared a trap, erupted with a torrent of fire. Now, for Townshend, 'events began to succeed each other in a kaleidoscopic manner and with flash-light kodak speed'. Delamain also asked to launch his attack on VP, which was agreed around 9 a.m. His column, the strongest of the four, fought its way into the redoubt by hundred-yard dashes across the bare ground, and had occupied it by 10 o'clock. But then part of his force was drawn towards the enemy second line, trying to reach eight Ottoman field guns which had been abandoned in the retreat. It soon became stuck, and the whole offensive movement ground to a halt. Townshend (who had galloped across with his staff to hold a conference in the shelter of a sand dune) made a fateful decision – to order Hoghton to 'bring up his left shoulders' and move to support Delamain's assault. Without a tactical reserve, he risked being unable to secure the decisive breakthrough. As he would always insist, a single extra brigade at this critical moment would have swung the battle.

Crucially, too, his naval artillery support was – for the first time in the campaign – missing. Nunn's flotilla had tried to fight its way through the loop in the river at Bustan, but came under intense fire from heavy artillery on the right bank. 'Throughout the ensuing three days' battle the Naval 4.7 inch guns and the Army 5 inch guns remained approximately in the same position.'[1] The dead flat terrain confined them to indirect fire – 'a considerable handicap'. The four gunboats occasionally managed to get round the bend into the southward reach, but it was 'rather an unhealthy place, for the Turks had apparently got all the ranges marked off, and they made some very good shooting'. If a force had pushed up the right bank, as first planned, these artillery batteries would certainly have been withdrawn, but as it was the lie of the land left them secure.

Townshend never admitted that ordering Hoghton's column, which had been weakened in favour of the main striking force, to move across the enemy front – 'over absolutely flat desert without a blade of cover' – broke an elementary tactical rule. 'We got heavily enfiladed by having to pass for nearly a mile at a distance of a few hundred yards in front of the Turkish trenches.' The result was inevitable: 'we lost very heavily . . . Only the lucky got through.' Worse still, the loss was pointless, since the battered and exhausted units that reached VP had no effect on the fight. Part of Delamain's column (the 30th Brigade – with the Dorsets as ever in the lead) had already broken into the second line at bayonet point. The British were, indeed, very lucky that the Turks did not seize the opportunity to counter-attack the skimpy force in front of their main position. (Reynardson thought this 'would have been rather a mystery, had not the enemy been the Turk'.)

When Nixon decided to help out by bringing his 'large staff' up to join the other two headquarter staffs at VP, Townshend was able to tell him that things were going well.

But not for much longer. As the 16th and 30th Brigades, joined by the remnant of the 17th – which had lost half its strength crossing the Turkish front – fought grimly to hold their position in the second line against increasingly fierce counter-attacks, there could be no doubt that the assault had failed. 'It was about 3 o'clock in the afternoon that the Turks counter-attacked so strongly,' one artillery officer wrote in his diary. 'The 82nd and ourselves were sent forward to try and stop it. I think we managed to do so, for a time anyway, but it was a very <u>warm</u> time. They then attacked from another quarter and drove our infantry in and we had to limber up and get out as quickly as we could under a most beastly hot fire. We retired to another position and started again and kept them off for some time . . . I was very thankful when we got orders to limber up and retire for the night to the captured Turkish position.'[2] The attempted turning movement had also ground to a halt; and after the captured Turkish artillery had changed hands several times, the exhausted British troops began to fall back to the first line. 'Now the plain became dotted with hundreds of our troops walking slowly back towards "V.P.",' Townshend ruefully recalled. 'It soon became apparent that a retirement was taking place, though no orders had been given for one.' He blamed this on the crushing losses of officers – 'there were hundreds of Indian soldiers streaming towards the rear, because there were not enough white officers to keep them in hand'. To avert a rout, the divisional staff at last took a direct part in the battle by wading in and rallying the shaken men (cajoling, berating and – of course – threatening).

At first, Townshend hoped to hang on around VP overnight and renew the assault next morning. He ordered the naval flotilla to come up to support his left, so that he could 'remain here on the field of battle', as he told Nixon. 'It will have a much better political effect not to retire.' But then he surveyed the actual state of his force. Hoghton's brigade was down to 700 men, all their units jumbled up; Delamain had 1,000, and Hamilton about 800. Though Townshend and Nixon agreed that the Turks must have suffered even more, what they saw as the night went on made such comparisons pointless. The chaos after the battle for Kut was repeated, on a vaster scale: 'walking wounded wandered about looking in vain for collecting stations; the more severely hit lay where they fell and waited.' One group of some fifty wounded men found the ditch they were sheltering in flooded with icy water by the Turks. Only after many hours in the cold were most of the wounded got back to a station south of VP, though 'the trenches were still full of badly wounded men who could not move'. All who could walk were told to make for Lajj (ten miles away) as best they could. The rest just lay around waiting for attention from the exiguous medical staff. 'If I live a hundred years,' Townshend wrote, 'I shall not forget that night bivouac at V.P. amongst hundreds of wounded.'

For two days the battle hung agonisingly in the balance. The Turks had indeed suffered even more. The defensive line, fifty days' labour, 'was entirely in the enemy's hands'. This was an 'irreparable loss . . . to think that after all this work and self-sacrifice it might be impossible to defend Iraq and retain Baghdad, its very heart!' The C-in-C was 'depressed and anxious' – not least because of the Ottoman tradition of blaming all failures on commanders, not the troops. Some units had collapsed – the hapless 38th Division had 'broken and run in a disgraceful panic before the attack of a handful of men'. Mehmet Emin denounced the 35th and 38th Divisions – Arab units – as 'more like human rubbish heaps' than 'strategic entities'. 'They were a living disaster always dragging their commander into shame and misfortune.' In this extremity, Nureddin and his staff decided to disband the 38th Division and merge what was left of it into the 35th. This dramatic step, recasting the force's organisation in mid-battle, was taken in the early hours of 23 November. Twelve hours later, Nureddin ordered a full-scale counter-attack. While the 45th Division attacked redoubts 11 and 12, the 51st Division was to turn the open left flank. Unsurprisingly this ambitious stroke was delayed for hours as the staff struggled with lack of information about the situation of the troops, due to the destruction of the telephone lines, aggravated by the difficulty (shared by both sides) of using runners and orderlies in terrain 'mirage-ridden by day and obscure by night'. As Emin said, 'it was an extraordinary piece of luck if a man succeeded in going and returning a few kilometres, or sometimes a few hundred metres, without losing his way'.

But the British were effectively now on the defensive and at a disadvantage, in positions facing the wrong way, and with half their wounded still in the line, as the counter-attack developed. An artillery officer, Lieutenant Gallup, saw 'very large bodies of Turks approaching all deployed for the attack' around 5 p.m on 23 November. 'They had apparently been reinforcing. From then onwards until this morning [24 November] we have been attacked. A very noisy night, heavy rifle fire and things humming over us and most beastly close.'[3] Ammunition was running low, and an emergency convoy was rushed back to Lajj, only returning to the battle around 3 a.m. on the 24th. This was the fiercest counter-attack yet experienced – indeed, the first serious attempt to retake a lost position. Mercifully for the defenders, the best Turkish formation, the 51st Division, took the wrong direction in the dark and failed to engage. Its orders were to move round the 'Dariyye Group' at a distance of one kilometre, but it 'not only knew nothing of Dariyye Group, but were ignorant of the very direction in which it lay'. The 45th was torn apart in the mass attacks; all its field officers had been killed or wounded, and companies were being commanded by NCOs. 'We may thus say the 45th Division does not exist,' the corps commander reported. He ordered the survivors and the 51st Division back to the second line. The Army HQ was again 'in the depths of despair and despondency'; it had little hope of even making a sustained defence of the second line, much of which was incomplete. While Nureddin fell into an exhausted sleep on the ground, those who could stay awake drafted orders for a retirement to the Diala river.[4]

'On the morning of the 24th, the remnants were to be seen withdrawing towards Baghdad, leaving us in possession of the battlefield,' Townshend wrote. 'It seemed that Ctesiphon was a great victory.' It was true that the 6th Division had fought its opponents to a standstill. But if this was victory, it was Pyrrhic indeed. The evacuation of casualties had to be organised on a scale that dwarfed the projected total of 500, and of course the original idea of a forward evacuation was now impossible. Perhaps the grimmest message sent from the battlefield at Ctesiphon was Townshend's terse warning to the medical staff in Kut (where the hospital capacity was 600 at most) – 'Have evacuated 3,500.' The only way of getting the wounded men back to the nearest ships was by cart. Early on 24 November they began to be loaded up: the start of what Reynardson (without exaggeration) called the 'Via Dolorosa'. As he noted, the 'A.T. [Army Transport]' cart was merely a framework of iron on two iron-rimmed wheels: 'there is not a spring in its entire make-up.' On these agonising platforms the wounded had to be taken across ten miles of ground that was either rough desert or sun-baked ploughland, all intersected by a mass of ditches and several deep nullahs.

'The wounded were heaped into these carts, three or four in each – there was no other way – clinging on as best they could: they were all serious cases, fractured limbs, abdominal wounds, head wounds – there was no cushioning or padding available. In some cases dead bodies were used as cushions. Then the journey began. The carts bumped and clattered over the rough soil: the ponies were nervous and now and again broke into a jinking trot: the nullahs had to be rushed to get the carts up the farther edge. Before long a chorus of groans went up from that convoy of carts, which changed to yells as the carts bumped and crashed into ditches; here and there men threw themselves off, unable to bear the torture any longer.'⁵ The convoy lost its way and wandered over the desert, frequently stopping to pick up other survivors who were crawling towards it. It reached Lajj in the late afternoon. But this was only the beginning of the medical horror-story.

Aboard the *Aerial* at Lajj, Chalmers had, as Townshend had promised him, plenty to do. 'Imagine', he wrote, 'a level sand bank about 800 yards long lying about 15 feet below the high bank of the Tigris and about three feet above the present level of the river. 100–200 yards wide, the north (wide) end used as a landing-ground by the aviators, the narrow end choked with S&T [Supply & Transport] stores, tents, A.T. carts full of wounded, and thousands of wounded lying all over the ground so that one had to pick one's way among them. Most have been wounded on the 22nd – moved from point to point on the battle field and finally brought to camp and dumped down on this sand bank.' It took hours of hard labour simply to get the men off the carts. No food or medical attention was available. Embarking them from the riverbank and getting them back to Kut was agonising enough, but the halting progress downriver to Basra in overcrowded boats and barges was truly the stuff of nightmare. In some cases the journey took fourteen days. The 'sickening horror' of the condition in which the wounded arrived at Basra made the commission of inquiry reluctant to describe it in detail; but anger at the way the authorities had 'glossed over' the suffering drove them to quote one witness's experience. Major Carter of the IMS, in charge of the hospital ship *Varela* at Basra, 'was standing on the bridge in the evening when the *Mejidieh* arrived. She had two steel barges, without any protection against the rain. I saw that she was absolutely packed, and the barges too, with men. The barges were slipped, and she was brought alongside. When she was about 300 or 400 yards off it looked as if she was festooned with ropes. The stench when she was close was quite definite, and I found that what I mistook for ropes were dried stalactites of human faeces

. . . A certain number of men were standing and kneeling on the immediate perimeter of the ship. There we found a mass of men huddled up anyhow . . . lying in a pool of dysentery some 30 feet square. They were covered with dysentery from head to foot.' One man Carter found with a fractured thigh, with his thigh perforated in five or six places, had been writhing about on the deck with his trousers 'filled almost to the waist with something warm and slimy', which Carter took at first to be a blood clot, but was excrement.[6]

At Ctesiphon, Townshend probably felt relieved about one thing at least: Nixon had left the 6th Division HQ on the 23rd during the Turkish counter-attacks (Captain Read of the Norfolks bitterly wrote, 'the shells seem to have at last roused the Army Commander, who sat with his staff arranged about him behind V.P. He drove off in his motor car and this was the last we ever saw of him.'[7]) Indeed he had left Lajj in his ship the *Malamir*, arriving at Aziziyeh at 7 p.m. He decided to move on downstream again 'to expedite the despatch of reinforcements', and it was not until 7.40 p.m. that he received Townshend's message announcing that he was going to withdraw. 'Politically speaking' it would be best to stay at Ctesiphon, Townshend said, but it was 'always fatal in history if political reasons are allowed to interfere with military reasons'. 'Strategical and tactical reasons insist on Lajj as our advanced point on which I hope you will direct ships, stores and reinforcements.' So his force was moving there 'as formerly arranged'. This suggests that Nixon had already agreed to the retreat, but he now made clear that he did not. Two hours later, after the move had begun, he telegraphed, 'I do not like your proposed retirement on Lajj.' He suggested that the enemy had not yet grasped how weak Townshend's force was – 'your resolute attitude impresses them'. Retreat would bring them on, 'and turn all Arabs on us everywhere'. He sympathised with the sacrifices of the troops, but insisted that it was 'absolutely necessary to keep their spirits up'. Reinforcements were on their way, and 'our game is to play for time'. He artfully countered Townshend's invocation of 'history' by quoting one of Napoleon's famous aphorisms – 'remember the moral is to the physical as five to one'.[8]

Next morning Townshend persuaded Nixon that to have stayed at Ctesiphon would have been 'madness and nothing else'. He would simply have been cut off – 'You must know what the result would have been.' Nixon agreed that the reported Turkish troop movements made the Ctesiphon position untenable.[9] But was it? Things looked different from the other side. Nureddin's army had lost over 6,000 battle casualties, and probably another 3,000 or more had deserted or disappeared. The 45th Division had lost 45 per cent of its strength. Bimbashi Emin, who rated Townshend's ability highly, thought that his decision to retire was the moment when 'that great power called by us Qadr, and by others Chance', shifted from the British to his own side. He thought that Nureddin's HQ was 'plunged in the depths of despair and despondency'; it 'had lost hope of even making a persistent defence of the second line'. Townshend's staff, wrongly believing that their opponents had already fallen back from the second line on the morning of the 23rd, interpreted the preparations for the counter-attack there that afternoon as a 'reoccupation' by a fresh force of three divisions. 'The conclusion of the battle of Suleiman Pak in such a mysterious fashion was predestined by fate.'[10]

4. Retreat

> General Townshend's force has suffered such severe losses and its units are so depleted of officers that it cannot be counted on for future operations as an effective Division for some time.
>
> SIR JOHN NIXON

With quite small reinforcements, the 6th Division might have held on at Lajj. As things were, if Ctesiphon was untenable, the same would prove true of Lajj as well – it was, as Townshend said, too close to the enemy. It was abandoned and the remaining stores burned: 'the scene of confusion this afternoon when Sepoys and Tommies were looting kits, stores, jams etc, was like a riot.' One of the crew of the motor car squadron 'went to the store to find the staff heaving stores into the river'; but when he 'explained the dire need for provisions for the wounded we were caring for, and picked up a parcel of biscuits', the quartermaster sergeant 'threatened to crime me for stealing, so I reluctantly replaced the parcel'.[1] Aziziyeh (where Townshend was 'disagreeably surprised to find only six days' supplies, instead of the twenty days' British and seven days' Indian I had reckoned on') was no better.

Knowing that no reinforcements could reach him until late December, Townshend 'began to see that there was no halting on the Baghdad side of Kut al Amara'. His division had been forced into the most perilous of all military actions, a full-scale retreat in the face of the enemy. Moreover, his rear communications were in danger as well, and Mellis's brigade had to be sent back downriver to ward off an Arab force threatening Kut. (Nixon's HQ ship had been forced to retreat after coming under fire near Sannaiyat on its way from Kut, and needed a naval escort.) On 30 November – 'rather an awful day', Captain Cardew mildly observed – the divisional HQ was hurriedly evacuated from Aziziyeh, 'the bridge being hastily dismantled, the barbed wire defences being torn down & thrown into the river to prevent if possible the Turks getting the wire which they were in great need of'. Unidentifiable bodies of men – or maybe camels – seen moving in the mirage caused alarm amongst the divisional staff on top of the Telegraph Office, and all equipment (transport wagons included) that could not be taken was destroyed. On the river, the ships struggled in the shallow water and fell behind the retreating troops, and the damaged *Shaitan* had to be abandoned when it sank within sight of the Turkish advance guard.

In military terms, the fighting retreat from Ctesiphon represented Townshend's – sadly brief – finest hour. It highpoint was the moment when he turned on his pursuers at dawn on 1 December, at Umm at Tubul, forty miles upriver from Kut. Nureddin – possibly misled by Mellis's dash back to Kut – seems to have thought that the British were retreating even faster than they were, and pushed his men on. Townshend called Nunn to his HQ in the middle of the night to say that he had heard gun-wheels and seen camp fires, which convinced him that the reinforced Turkish main force was nearby. He planned to attack it frontally at dawn, and also throw the cavalry at its northern flank. 'As dawn broke, an amazing sight greeted us.' Spackman saw 'a very large and complicated Turkish camp on the horizon, with lines of white tents in perfect order, horses and mules being groomed or led off to the river for water, in fact a busy camp at its morning chores, at 2,500–3,000 yards range. A gunner's dream! . . . Our soldiers rubbed their eyes, for the thing seemed too mad to be true.' Townshend (whose recollection was that the enemy were first seen 'advancing in long lines in extended order') noted with relief, 'What a splendid gun is our 18-pounder field gun!'[2] As the British artillery opened up, Spackman recalled, 'the confusion in that camp is a sight I shall never forget'.

Mehmet Emin, fast asleep in one of those tents (captured at Ctesiphon), was reluctant to respond to the patter of debris falling on it, dismissing it as 'the commencement of an unseasonable rain shower'. But the growing uproar outside, 'the bitter groans and wailings telling of some sudden disaster', drew him out to a shocking scene. 'The shrapnel bursting with deafening reports above our crowded camp, filling the air with dust and smoke like a death-dealing whirlwind of fire and iron, were turning everything upside down. Jammed together amid the storm of shells were the camps of General Headquarters, the two divisional headquarters of 13th Corps, troops, baggage, ammunition columns and the rear units of 18th Corps in inextricable confusion. Animals running loose, dashing wildly about, some dragging their carts, upsetting tents and trampling on everything alive or dead as they went. The troops of the 13th Corps were streaming towards Aziziya like frightened sheep.'

Pepped up by this sight, the tired British troops surged forward in a charge which might have led to another enemy rout. ('Had we but had the reliefs we should have had at our back, we could have completely annihilated them.') As the fight got hotter, Edward Mousley of the 76th RFA battery found himself watching his divisional commander with 'the keenest admiration' – 'so steady, collected, and determined in action, so kind, quick and confident. There, totally indifferent to the shell fire, he stood watching the issue, receiving reports from the various orderly officers and giving every attention to the progress of the transport' (as it loaded up to continue the retreat). 'Some shells pitched just over us, not fifteen yards away, killing a horse and wounding some drivers . . . I caught a humorous smile on the General's face.'[3] Major G. L. Heawood (in the 17th Brigade) found himself admiring the Turkish artillery with the company commander on his right: 'Their shrapnel was bursting beautifully, now to the right, now to the left, now in front, now behind . . . We said to each other how very accurate the dimensions were (according to the books) of each burst.'[4]

Emin believed that 'had not the enemy's cavalry come up against the 7th Regiment and been forced to withdraw, they could have ridden over and taken prisoner all three Ottoman divisions before they reached Aziziya'. The Cavalry Brigade's charge was its first really successful action of the campaign, enabling Townshend to break off the action and resume the retreat 'by echelons of brigades from the right'. This was a truly perilous movement, under heavy pressure as the 51st Division recovered from its confusion, until the return of Mellis's column brought the pursuers to a halt around 11 a.m. Now Townshend tried to put the greatest possible distance between his force and the enemy – which meant that after their dawn battle his troops faced a march of twenty-six miles to Qala Shadi. 'It became more and more difficult to keep men going,' Major Heawood wrote, 'in spite of the knowledge that nothing was left for those who dropped out – except Arabs.' [5]

Captain Mousley had just arrived from India in time for the retreat from Ctesiphon. Snatched immediately from his unit to act as Townshend's orderly officer, he spent his first days in action digging hasty shelters for his general and running messages on his increasingly exhausted horse Don Juan. At 'Monkey Village' he was repeatedly held up at the tiny stone bridge across the nullah: 'the scene was of the wildest confusion. Camels were being thrashed across, kicking mules hauled across, troops trying to cross at the same time. Several overturned vehicles complicated matters. The whole force had to go over that tiny bridge.' Everyone was hungry and, even when allowed time for rest, unable to sleep because of the bitter cold. But Mousley was assured by 'senior officers of much service' that he had 'witnessed one of the most brilliant episodes possible in war, where perfect judgment and first-rate discipline alone enables us to smash the sting of the pursuit and to continue the retreat exactly as done at manoeuvres'.[6]

The river flotilla struggled on behind the division, constantly grounding, and harassed by Arabs. 'The Arabs would crawl up to the edge of the bank and fire on the boats, but when the *Sumana* sent a shell into them they would lie low till she passed.

The sepoys on the bridge train made a great fight standing right on their boats in the open', though as Chalmers noted, Arab marksmanship even at less than forty yards' range was fortunately 'rather poor'. As darkness fell on 1 December, 'the confusion every time we stopped was great. The L boats towing a string of light bridge boats had a tail about 100 to 150 feet long and each had to turn round in the narrow channel in the dark. Sometimes you would see one tail of boats turning a circle within the circle formed by another string of boats amid much shouting and bad language.'[7] (Since Sandes's unit had been required to build and dismantle their bridge across a fast-flowing section of the river at Lajj no fewer than three times during the battle of Ctesiphon, without its being used once, their exasperation was forgivable.[8])

Chalmers was 'repeatedly asked to sound the channel for the *Sumana*, which drew 4 ft 6 in, and did so by sailing round her and shouting out the depth, having of course to stop the propeller each time we shouted'. The soundings were done with a bamboo by the invaluable Reverend Spooner 'shouting the result at the top of his voice'. 'The Padre' was one of the division's stars – 'very brave and greatly respected by the troops as he was always seen to be running to the wounded under heavy fire'.[9] In spite of these efforts, the warship stuck in midstream. Sandes watched her 'churning up the water into a great area of whirling mud'. His launch, *L9*, tried to haul the ship off, but the hawser broke at the first attempt. Eventually 'with a final lurch and a heave' she 'slid off the sandbank and, followed by the roaring *Ariel* [*sic*], shot away downstream'.[10] Then, at 8 p.m., Chalmers had the unusual experience for a civilian of being invited aboard Nunn's flagship for a council of war.

'Capt. Nunn told us how he had been called at 5am by General Townshend who had decided to continue the retreat at all costs. He explained how the *Comet* and the *Firefly* had most effectually returned the Turkish fire until the *Firefly* was hit. The army had retreated rapidly, which he thought right, and left him to do the best he could. With the *Comet* he got alongside the *Firefly* and tried to tow her away but as he drew 5ft he grounded, and the *Firefly* bumped him further on. The Turks poured in a heavy fire, which grew hotter every minute; he signalled the *Sumana* to cast her barges adrift and try to pull him off; she failed. The Turks brought a battery up and the *Sumana* was in danger. He saw it was no use taking any further risks as the *Sumana* was the only gunboat left and if she was sunk our communication by river would be in great danger.' He decided to abandon the *Comet*, 'leaving behind all our property except the clothes we were wearing'. He destroyed her with gunfire as he withdrew, while the crippled *Firefly* drifted out of control down river. He was also forced to leave behind the *Shuhrur* and the *T2*. His problem was geographical: 'The river makes a great bend covering some 60 or 70 miles whereas the road across the neck was not more than 25 or 30. There were two or three bad crossings, where if he stuck he might take twelve hours getting off again, and meanwhile the Turks would have a battery at the point and cut him off.' What, Nunn asked, was the best thing to do? Should they make a run for it in the dark, with the increased risk of getting stuck, or wait until daylight and risk getting cut off? Chalmers assured him that he would stick with the *Sumana* and take him and his crew on board if she was sunk, 'and run through taking our chance'. But her crew had to be reduced to twenty-five, with all the rest going ahead in the *Salimi*. (A 150-foot boat, drawing 3 ft 6 in, captained by 'an Arab who knows the river like a book and if the Turks catch him he will most probably be hung'.) The informal war council resolved to try to get as far as the worst crossing below Bughaila, three-quarters of the way from Lajj to Kut. Finally, after midnight, they passed Bughaila, and Chalmers was relieved to see that the lights of the town were still burning – 'they had evidently not turned against us'.[11]

The loss of the two gunboats was serious: the Turks might well be able to repair them and dramatically magnify their naval power on the river. The barges the *Sumana* had been forced to cast adrift were also a heavy loss: one was crammed with wounded troops, the other with aircraft spares that would be impossible to replace for a long time. The fact that the shellfire came from the 51st Division, pressing hard on the heels of Townshend's rearguard, showed just how dangerous the situation was. The 6th Division, promised a rest and water at Qala Shadi, was once again driven on without a halt. At last, 'on the evening of 2nd December, after a 36-mile march, dead-beat and parched with thirst, the column was in sight of Kut'.[12] They finally re-entered the camp next day. They had been fighting, marching or digging for twelve days; for three of those days, during the Ctesiphon battle, most had not eaten.

Townshend stood at the perimeter and watched his men stagger in. W. D. Lee, a gunner in the 86th Heavy Battery, noted in his diary that they were 'almost exhausted', but 'in high praise of their leader . . . To all it seemed a marvel how he had extricated them.' Lee thought that 'he was a very highly esteemed and clever leader, and there was not a murmur amongst the British troops against any order given by him. In his well fitting uniform and his F.S. [field service] cap set at the "Beatty" angle he looked the ideal General that he was.'[13] The morale of a number of units was immediately lifted as the Turkish artillery began to shell the supply park, and the barrels of draught beer stacked there were hastily distributed on a first-come basis. The tired men 'started digging at once, as we knew a siege was certain'.[14] They spent the next two days 'digging "funk pits" and what were called dugouts for officers'. These, though, 'were lightly roofed with corrugated sheet iron, covered with about six inches of earth. They were of course only splinter-proof, and many of the Kut dugouts were only roofed with canvas. No one expected them to be occupied for long.'[15]

The most fateful of all the decisions of the campaign was now made. The 6th Division would stand at Kut and wait for the reinforcements to come up to join it. Townshend announced to Nixon on 4 December that he would turn Kut into 'as strong an entrenched camp as possible' ('in the given time', as he carefully added). He was sure Nureddin would invest the town, so the relieving force might have to fight 'a second battle of Es Sinn'. But he assumed that the arrival of substantial relieving forces from Basra was a certainty. The reasons for standing at Kut were both strategic – further retreat would run the risk of allowing the whole of Mesopotamia to be 'overrun' – and practical. 'The state of extreme weariness and exhaustion of my men demands instant rest.'

This reasoning, so apparently commonsensical, has been disputed ever since. The fiercest attack on it was mounted by Russell Braddon in his 1967 book *The Siege* – a history of the campaign from the viewpoint of the lower ranks. Braddon, who interviewed many Kut survivors, reversed Townshend's perspective. It was not the troops who were 'exhausted', but Townshend himself. His decision to hold Kut was 'probably premeditated'.[16] This suggestion seems to be based on the fact that the lines-of-communication commander in Kut, Brigadier Rimington, who rode out to meet Townshend at the overnight halt on 2 December, argued that it would be 'very difficult to make an entrenched defensive position covering Kut which cannot be turned'. The enemy would invest the 'very confined' position with a small force, and reoccupy the strong Es Sinn position to hold off the relieving force. Rimington proposed that retreating to Es Sinn could avoid this risk, and said that if they did this, they had available 'about thirty mahelas on which we can place wounded and supplies'.[17]

In fact, it is clear that Rimington's project for removing the material downriver was much more comprehensive than this suggests, and that the LofC staff had a fully worked-up plan for such an operation. After Rimington returned from his meeting with Townshend, he and his deputy, Captain Julius, met Cox to discuss the issue, and agreed that although from a political point of view 'the further ahead our front was the better, from a purely military point of view Kut bend was a death trap'.[18] But, oddly, Rimington delegated the task of persuading

Townshend to Julius, whose attempts to explain 'the means I possessed of moving the Advanced Base, and to explain the real and exact situation of the 3rd and 7th Divisions and of General Younghusband's Brigade' – the forces on which the possibility of early relief depended – were brusquely dismissed by Townshend's staff. Townshend himself would say only, 'I don't go a yard beyond Kut.'[19] (An echo maybe of Duff's promise to him, 'not one inch shall you go beyond Kut unless I make you up to adequate strength'.)

Braddon suggested that Rimington 'might well have retorted' to Townshend's statement that if his force was 'too exhausted to move a yard further' (Braddon misquoted this as 'even an inch'), 'then how will they manage to dig six miles of trenches and fight off the Turks?' He even speculated about the reasons why Rimington did not make this reply. But even if he did not agree that 'it was an impossibility to move all the supplies and ammunition in time', Rimington will have known as well as Townshend that there is no comparison between the effort required to dig in and that called for by forced marches under enemy pressure. Just how close that pressure was is hard to say – as Major Walker of the 1st Indian Field Ambulance said, 'we had no idea how close the pursuing enemy might be but hoped the knocks we had given him and the 13 hours continuous marching would be enough to keep him off'. But again, as he added, 'some enterprise on the part of the Turks would have done the trick' for them on 1 December, since 'the transport was badly parked and the cavalry and artillery jammed up with them'.[20] Braddon implied that Townshend's troops could, if he had wished, have gone further. But none of the survivors he interviewed seem to have said this directly, and it does not quite fit with the language he uses to describe them as they reached Kut – 'grotesque columns of sleeping men . . . excruciatingly . . . dazed and aching, they plodded on', and finally 'stumbled' into Kut. Certainly all the accounts by men of the 6th Division stress their exhaustion, often pointing out (as did Major Walker) the achievement of marching fifty-one miles in thirty-six hours 'in addition to fighting a battle of 5½ hours, beating off a pursuing enemy more than double our strength'.

Some of the doubts about the division's ability to continue the retreat were linked with the worries already expressed about its Indian sepoys. A fighting retirement was always difficult, as Major Walker said, but 'especially so with oriental troops in face of a numerically superior enemy'. And while he had thought that they seemed 'very steady' after Umm at Tubul, 'General Hamilton has told me it was a very nervy business, 110th especially were inclined to run, he had to make the whole regiment lie down several times.'[21] (Before Ctesiphon, the 110th had nearly broken in the fight at 'Frazer's Post'.) For many, the nightmare vision of the division simply disintegrating loomed.

Braddon had personal experience of the failure of British military leadership as a soldier in the army that surrendered at Singapore in 1942, and then in a Japanese prisoner-of-war camp. In his account, Townshend stands out as the villain of the piece; Nixon has only a walk-on part. Braddon's Townshend has barely a trace of the man described by others. In place of the amiable – if incongruous – banjo-playing music-hall performer *manqué*, or the obsessive student of military history, we see a monster of self-absorption, abusing his manservant, Boggis, and thrashing his pet dog for preferring to sleep by Boggis's side. (Sadly, there is nothing to confirm or refute this account in the fragmentary papers Boggis left behind.[22]) Others may speak, but Townshend 'grunts' or (more often) 'snarls'. His situation reports are a series of 'exaggerations', 'peevish and imprecise' assessments, 'crying wolf'. At the height of the battle of Ctesiphon, in Braddon's account, Townshend sends Boggis out to run a mile through the Turkish shellfire to fetch the general's fresh uniform for his daily change of clothing. 'Deliberately, Townshend stripped and stood naked among his dead troops and his living officers: then slipped on a silk vest, silk underpants, a khaki shirt, his breeches, boots and sun-helmet', before resuming his inspection of the battle while 'eating a piece of plum cake passed to him by a junior staff officer'.[23]

Townshend was certainly not an entirely likeable character, or by any means a flawless commander. After the war it would be possible to get good marks in staff colleges by concluding (as did the future Lord Ismay in 1922) that Townshend had succumbed to – quoting Lord French on the retreat from Mons – 'the terrible temptation which a fortress offers to an army seeking shelter against heavy odds'. (This skirted the fact that, as many of Townshend's critics stressed, Kut was far from being a fortress.[24]) Townshend's actions – or failures to act – were also to be criticised at high level during the siege. The C-in-C India noted that he would have much to explain after he was relieved, though he insisted that as a field commander he had 'displayed a gift of imagination, of putting himself in the enemy's place and acting in unexpected ways which I have found none too common'.[25] Maybe some of these gifts now turned against him.

Even those writers – such as Ronald Millar – who take a more charitable view of Townshend's personal qualities, have seen the decision to stand at Kut as his own.[26] But whatever his faults or qualities, he cannot be held directly responsible for it. This was what Nixon clearly wanted, and it is equally clear that, though the Indian General Staff dissented, both Indian and British governments supported him in this. (The Mesopotamia Commission would note that 'after full consideration, Sir John Nixon and General Townshend agreed that Kut should be held. This decision received the assent of both Simla and Whitehall.'[27]) The agreement was not one between equals. Captain Julius, on the LofC staff, was convinced that Townshend's refusal to listen to plans for further retreat followed the arrival of a message from Nixon: 'Trust you will see your way to holding Kut.' ('Such words', as Julius later insisted, 'are not forgotten by a trained staff officer.'[28]) Nixon confirmed on 11 December that 'I fully considered the question of abandoning Kut [but] decided from every point of view, military and political, that it was not advisable.' He added that 'it looked at one time as if the whole division would lie down and not be able to move'. In London, General Barrow accepted that the Kut position was 'a strong and important one to hold', and that if it were abandoned 'our communications would have been everywhere threatened', and an even more disastrous situation would have arisen in December than eventually followed next April.[29]

Unsurprisingly, 6th Division's officers would also debate the decision at length over the following days and weeks. They tended to agree with it. Captain Read of the Norfolks, a fierce critic of the Indian government's handling of the campaign, filled a page of his diary with a list of the pros and cons of the decision. In favour of it were the 'state of exhaustion of the troops', and the fact that Kut's position in a big loop of the river made it defensible. Reinforcements 'would presumably be able to relieve us', and in any case there was not enough river or land transport to evacuate the sick and wounded. Abandoning Kut would expose Nasiriyeh to an enemy advance, involve the loss of large quantities of stores and ammunition to the enemy, and further reduce British prestige ('already lowered by retirement'). Against it, the 'shutting up of a force greatly reduces the morale and initiative of the troops'. River floods were to be expected in the spring – though the relief force would have 'a clear 3½ months' before that time. And in principle, a division of forces was not ideal: 'the sum of the fighting strengths of two forces is less then their concentrated strength.' Read concluded, nonetheless, that 'there was, in the humble opinion of many of us, no other reasonable course open to our Commander, than to hold Kut'.[30] The most judicious modern assessment has followed the same line.[31]

The key issue, of course, was that relieving forces should arrive soon. Here Nixon's inveterate optimism once again skewed his assessment of the situation. He had already, in the middle of the battle at Ctesiphon, implied that reinforcements would arrive in time to enable Townshend to hold on there. Making his way back downriver on 26 November, he sent India the grim news that 'General Townshend's force has suffered such severe losses and its units are so depleted of officers that it cannot be counted on for future operations as an effective Division for some time.' But in spite of this, he said he would be 'in a position to capture and hold Baghdad by the middle of March 1916 without any additional troops. As I feel confident of capturing Baghdad, I do not propose to discuss the alternative of taking up a defensive line in rear.' At the India Office, Barrow was taken aback that Ctesiphon had done nothing to bring Nixon to a sense of reality.[32] But in India some doubts were creeping in. The Viceroy still held that taking Baghdad was 'our best means of countering the German intrigues in Persia and Von der Goltz's plans for organising Persia and Afghanistan against India'. But now he thought that Nixon would need five divisions – and also that 'as a matter of vital urgency' he 'should receive a large accession of river craft without delay'. Townshend was reported to have six weeks' supplies, so that he would need to be relieved within two months: and 'the distances in Mesopotamia are so great that two months is a very short period in which to relieve Kut'.[33] This was to prove all too realistic.

5. Under Siege

Every kind of trial, every kind of obstacle is to be met in this accursed country of Mesopotamia.
CHARLES TOWNSHEND

At this point, of course, the huge significance that the siege of Kut would assume could not be even dimly perceived. Townshend was naturally aware that being besieged was, in principle, bad: 'I knew well the fate which in history is generally reserved for the force which deliberately shuts itself up.' He could reel off lists of disasters, and it seems unlikely that his own experience of brilliant success in defending the little post at Chitral on the North-West Frontier gave him much encouragement in the vastly different circumstances of Mesopotamia. But he could expect, after all the recent demonstrations by his opponents of the strength of entrenched positions, that even his hastily constructed defences could withstand Turkish assault for a while. He thought that Kut offered the possibility of defence 'by manoeuvre on a central position'.[1] And he definitely expected that a relief force would get through, as Nixon promised, within two months at the outside. So did his troops. 'Everyone reasoned that up till the end of December was the very best time of year for an advancing column, being cold and not yet wet; that the 6th Division had managed to advance even in September over this bit of country, and that we would surely occupy such a considerable part of the enemy forces as to give material help to the relief force, even before we were able to sally out and join hand with them by an attack on the Turkish line of retreat.'[2]

For the first two weeks after Townshend's force returned to Kut it was at work day and night to improve the rudimentary defences that had been put up to deal with artilleryless Arab irregulars. 'It found', as Major Sandes disapprovingly noted, 'no complete defensive position outside the town ready for its occupation.' A line of four blockhouses had been built (by contractors Lynch Brothers) in November, running across the neck of the Kut peninsula, with a more substantial fort at the eastern end. A single barbed-wire fence ran across the front. The design, Sandes noted, was 'eminently suited for defence against savages, but useless against artillery'. Townshend ordered the blockhouses to be demolished and replaced by low redoubts, and three lines of trenches were dug. He thought the first line lay too far north, but could neither abandon the fort (which was stuffed with supplies) or demolish it quickly enough, so kept it as the eastern anchor of the line. It would quickly prove its worth. But on the other hand, to keep the line as short as possible, it ran south of a group of sandhills which would later offer the besiegers a disagreeable advantage.

Another crucial decision was taken before the Ottoman forces closed the ring around Kut. Townshend was well aware that, in principle, the civil population of the town should be evacuated. But it was not. His own account blames this on Percy Cox, who argued that it would be inhumane to expel the Arab citizenry in the middle of winter – an odd argument, perhaps, in that the alternative was to expose them to direct artillery bombardment and possibly worse. Townshend said this 'intercession' was Cox's initiative, but Cox held that it was Townshend who raised the issue and asked for political advice. (He did not, though, deny that his advice was more or less as Townshend recorded it.) In his memoirs Townshend wrote that expulsion would have had 'a disastrous political effect among the Arab population, whom we had engaged to protect against the Turk'. Arnold Wilson gave this short shrift: the general was 'not competent to judge' the first point, and the second was simply untrue.[3] Whatever the truth of the matter, the ordeal of the people of Kut over the next five months would be severe.

Townshend's political competence was not aided by his refusal of Cox's offer to stay in Kut. This was probably the right decision for the wider campaign; but it is less easy to see why Leachman, with greater local knowledge than any other political officer with the force, also left. He 'came out of Kut with a crowd of cavalry to nurse them down to Ali al Gharbi', he wrote, 'and then could not get back again owing to the enemy on the road'. This is rather hard to believe.[4] The decision to send the most seriously wounded downriver was more straightforward (500 were sent on; 2,000 who were expected to be fit for duty soon were kept at Kut). So was the despatch of the cavalry brigade – though this was oddly protracted. It might have been expected immediately the decision to stand at Kut was taken (not just because of its irrelevance in static fighting, but because of its huge fodder requirements), but it was not until 6 December that the cavalry left.

The reason was partly the problems faced by Sandes's long-suffering bridging unit. Throughout the day on the 5th they battled the current to link up their battered danack rafts, which had to be supplemented here by three 'gissaras' stiffened with huge 40-foot beams (9 inches square) lashed across them. 'After about eight hours' hard work, we found ourselves within ten yards of a large sandbank near the right bank, with not another danack available.' (Sandes's last three successful bridging operations had taken only seven hours each.) A bitter cold night had fallen, but his men had to stand in four feet of water to finish the span with trestles and a transom. The cavalry commander, Roberts, had already decided not to try crossing that evening, and there was some doubt about the viability of the twenty-yard stretch of three-foot deep river between the sandbank and the right bank. Sandes's men had to spend the night trying to keep their leaky bridge rafts afloat. When the cavalry began to cross next morning, the sandbank turned into 'a heaving and oozing mass', and once again Sandes had to rush across enough trestles and planks to link the sandbank to the shore, another one-and-a-half-hour job. Eventually the cavalry, and even 'a heavy RFC motor car of whose safe crossing I had the gravest doubts', got across and away. But if any hostile forces had appeared, the crossing could have been a disaster.[5]

Inevitably, the long-suffering Sandes was ordered to demolish his bridge immediately. His next order was more surprising: he was to build yet another one just over a mile upstream. His men detached the last danack at 3.30 a.m. on 7 December. They were 'very weary', and Sandes himself was 'so sleepy that I could hardly stand', but had to start work at dawn. 'It appeared that the early completion of the bridge at this new site was a matter of great importance.' Why, he was never told, but he speculated that it was to allow Townshend to retire on the right bank to Ali Gharbi 'if he decided, even at this eleventh hour, to abandon Kut'. It seems more likely that Townshend was trying to give himself the option of transferring his force to the other bank in battle. As he later explained, 'I intended to use my entrenched camp as a pivot of manoeuvre, when, by improvising a bridge and a fortified bridge-head, I should be able to throw the principal mass of my force on to either bank in an offensive against an isolated fraction of the enemy.' Either way, the bridge proved a wasted effort for Sandes's exhausted men. After working all day on the 8th – without any infantry cover – they were visited by the GOC in the late afternoon. To Sandes the bridge was 'like the curate's egg, excellent in parts though doubtful in other places', but Townshend seemed happy with it.

Then, after the usual hours spent 'repairing leaks, adjusting planks, tightening lashings, and the thousand and one small jobs inseparable from bridge work' on the morning of 9 December, the bridging unit found itself under attack by waves of Turkish infantry led by an officer waving his sword. An 'exciting' fight ensued, with General Mellis dashing over from Kut to take personal command of the counter-attacking troops across the bridge. Now, inevitably again, the bridge had to be demolished – and under enemy fire. This meant using explosives, since the usual gradual dismantling was out of the question. And the bridge would have to be blown at the far end, so that it would not drift into enemy hands. An engineer officer, Lieutenant Matthews, volunteered to take a small party across with two 50-pound gun-cotton charges. 'Two deafening explosions rent the air,' as Sandes sadly recalled: 'the work of so many months destroyed thus in a moment ... My men as well as I took great pride in the bridge, which was of our own design and manufacture, and it was with heavy hearts that we turned away from the river.'[6]

Sandes soon cheered up, though, when his unit was given a new task – housebreaking. Kut, like most Arab towns, had few viable roads, and none of them ran east–west, so Townshend ordered the cutting of a series of 'emergency roads' between the river front and the brick kilns zone where the artillery and services were placed. Sandes found it 'rather amusing work' knocking these 'rabbit runs' through the houses. The inhabitants were less amused – indeed they were seriously distressed as their privacy was destroyed – but only the most influential could get the 'avenues' diverted around rather than through their houses. 'There was always a pleasing uncertainty', Sandes recalled, 'as to where one was going to come out when a hole in the wall was started.' This 'added to the undoubted fascination of knocking things down which is felt by most male human beings'. The unfortunate inhabitants were given 'sheets of matting for use as screens', and 'compensated liberally'. As 'the shining rupees began to trickle into their palms,' Sandes thought, 'they quickly recovered from any injury to their feelings'.[7] After finishing and signposting the avenues, he went on to erect screens to shield the north–south roads from observation by snipers on the southern bank of the river. Using the same 'large sheets of matting', these worked as well as walls, until they were all stolen by townspeople, after which Sandes had to build real walls with mud bricks.

The bridgehead to the east, in the direction of the relieving force, had been lost, but the Kut garrison retained a bridgehead to the west at 'Woolpress Village', Yakasum, which the Turks called the Liquorice Factory position. It contained large stores of grain, and thirty-three days' fuel supply, and would withstand several assaults during the siege. But whether it justified the effort required to hold and supply it, as Townshend believed, has been questioned. (His biographer thought it an 'odd conclusion' from so gifted a tactician.) He might have thought that it would increase his chances of a successful break-out at some stage, though this seems doubtful.

Kut was an unbeguiling place to be stuck in. Set in the southern corner of a big flat sandy loop of the Tigris, the town lacked the charm that Amara's waterfront was reckoned to have. Apart from the Ottoman military headquarters building, the *serai*, and the turquoise-domed mosque behind it, the town was a featureless block of mud-walled houses, mostly roofed with rush matting, in streets running along parallel to the river's north bank for about half a mile. With a population of about 6,000, almost all Arabs though with small Jewish and Nestorian Christian communities, it was essentially a market town for the surrounding grain-producing area. Its granaries were largely empty by the time the 6th Division descended on it, and one of the first British actions was to buy up and stockpile all available grain. The officer responsible for securing food supplies, the Local Produce Officer, was convinced that much of it remained concealed. A systematic stocktaking and search was not carried out until late January 1916, by which time the Arab inhabitants were suffering the same shortages as the troops. Their homes were not directly bombarded, but their water supply had become hazardous. Soon after the siege began the British military engineers installed two pumps to feed river water into two 7,500-gallon canvas tanks concealed in the palm groves north of the town, but the possibility of distributing water to the civilian population does not seem to have been entertained. Arabs were kept away from the tanks for security reasons, and as a result there was a daily troop of women to the riverbank at dusk, sometimes with deadly results.

Townshend's 'entrenched camp' stretched, as he explained to Lord Kitchener, about 3,200 yards northwards from the town, and was about a mile wide. Kitchener demanded to know whether the Turks had 'heavy guns superior to ours', what barges had been lost, and how long Townshend supposed he could hold out. To this key question the general returned a somewhat imprecise reply. For some reason not mentioning that he had food supplies for sixty days, and 800 rounds of ammunition per rifle, he said he was 'very anxious to be relieved in say, ten to fifteen days', because he was worried about the declining fighting value of his troops since Ctesiphon. Though 'discipline maintains', they were being 'constantly shelled all day', and he believed too many men were going sick ('I have 800 and am convinced there should not be more than 300 at the outside'). As a result he was 'very anxious as to result if enemy makes a determined assault with very superior numbers'.

Others, though, assumed that the Ottoman forces would have little to gain from a direct assault, and would prefer to wait the defenders out. Such indeed seems to have been the view of the newly arrived German commander of the Baghdad front, Colmar von der Goltz. But Nureddin had other ideas. His strategic options were either to contain Kut and try to hit the relief force before it could fully concentrate, or to 'wipe out the Kut obstacle' immediately. He decided that he did not have enough transport for the first. (The available land transport was 'scarcely sufficient to supply stages on the riverbank four or five miles from Divisional HQ'.[8]) He called on Townshend to surrender on the grounds that occupying Kut was against the laws of war – an argument that was meat and drink to Townshend, who relished refuting the 'curious and extraordinary error' with a barrage of historical examples. After this, two serious assaults were launched, in early and late December. The first began two days after the ring around Kut had been closed on 7 December. The Turkish infantry pushed their forward trenches disturbingly close to the British front, and after a heavy artillery bombardment on the 9th, they attacked the north-western section of the line. But they still had to cross flat, open ground, in the teeth of heavy fire; and despite repeated efforts over the next three days they never reached the British line.[9] British casualties were fairly light (199 on the 9th), but even so the limited hospital facilities were stretched. Ten days of 'comparative quietude' followed, though artillery and sniper fire still caused worrying losses, and Townshend was still concerned about the morale of some of his Indian units. (He told Nixon on the 10th that one had been withdrawn from the trenches the previous night, as the brigade commander 'said he could not guarantee the safety of his sector unless it was taken away at once'.[10]) Ammunition supplies, especially for the artillery, would also become doubtful 'if the enemy in greatly superior numbers makes a determined assault'.

The second assault was more determined, and dangerous. It began, with a nice sense of timing, on Christmas Eve. For a week the garrison in the fort had watched the Turkish saps edging ever closer, and on the 18th a sortie under artillery fire cleared the first two trench lines, 'filled in a good part of them', and brought back eleven prisoners. It established that the Turks were not trying to tunnel under the fort, but beyond that, as Captain Robert Anderson of the Volunteer Artillery battery there reflected, 'of course it could have little real effect'. All the defenders could do was to wait, until on the morning of the 24th 'a very heavy bombardment' began, with twenty-two guns targeting the fort alone. Anderson was glad of his ear protectors, though 'the observation post was a most unpleasant spot, but shells coming from so many directions, no cover anywhere was safe'. The telephone line from the OP to the field and heavy batteries was cut and could not be repaired that day; a shell burst in the mess dugout destroyed treasured whisky supplies; and even more seriously, 'the walls on the N, NE, and SE including the NE bastion were gradually crumbling and along big stretches were practically demolished, as also the barbed wire outside'. (The defenders could see right through to the enemy trenches.)

Bimbashi Emin, with the HQ staff of the Sixth Army, stood on the walls of Bashara Fort as day broke, anxiously waiting for the mist to clear. 'Gradually the light and heat of the risen sun dispersed the mist . . . The sight of our guns, which were situated in a semi-circle around the fort, offered a brilliant spectacle.' The British line was 'soon enveloped in clouds of smoke and bursting shrapnel'. The walls of the fort disappeared in clouds of dust, which were occasionally blown aside by the light morning breeze, revealing a glimpse of the mounting destruction. The Ottoman staff were puzzled by the 'very slight reply' of the defenders' artillery – were they trying to conserve ammunition? But their own artillery itself began to run short, and the heavy guns soon ran out entirely when the ammunition column failed to reappear.

Then the infantry of the newly arrived 52nd Division went forward, led by the 43rd Regiment. 'The first line approached right up to the walls of the fort without any opposition whatsoever, when it suddenly came under heavy fire from the front, left and right flanks.' Some of them got through gaps in the outer wall, but then came on 'an intricate part of the defence consisting of other walls and loopholes'.[11] Inside the fort, Anderson set out as arranged to take his gunners forward to the party of Oxfords manning the barricade at the NE bastion. Finding that the communication trench 'was completely blocked by men of the Indian regiment [the 119th] from the NE wall, I realised that something was wrong. I could find none of their officers, so on looking over the parapet and finding that the Turks were already appearing on the debris of the wall and learning that the intervening trenches were denuded of any troops, I did all I could to organise a firing line out of the men who were blocking the trench.' Eventually he found some officers, and went to join his own men at the NE bastion, where the enemy assault was successfully fought off. He then got together a force to go forward and reoccupy the NE wall and river corner, where only the Rajput company of the 119th had held on.

The failure of this first attack 'filled everyone with despair' at the Ottoman HQ. 'Nobody could understand how the fort, which was defended by only one battalion, could not be captured by three whole battalions after an artillery bombardment of 2,000 rounds.' Nureddin ordered a renewal of the assault, but without (Emin thought) grasping the reasons for the first failure. The attacking troops had 'not made adequate plans for cooperation, and instead of pushing forward relentlessly they halted between the wire and the walls, where they had become demoralised, blocking the path of reinforcements . . . the pressure on the enemy was not kept up'. But in any case, the operation was ill-conceived: 'military science which seeks out the weakest point in the enemy's line could not possibly have accepted the fort as a suitable objective.' (Mehmet Emin believed that the assault should have hit the other end of the British line, nearest to Kut itself.) The renewed attack already seemed doomed to the officers as they assembled in the darkness, before the moon rose. As they rushed on the walls again, they were 'met by a devastating fire. From loopholes and from the right and left of the broken walls poured a rain of projectiles, and the ground between our own trenches and the fort was filled with dead and wounded.' Although a few reached the wall, those who were in the open when the moon rose found movement impossible.

In a kind of medieval siege action in the NE bastion, the defenders under Goldfrap of the 103rd Mahrattas and Anderson had planned to fall back into the side galleries of the bastion and so trap the attackers as they came up to the barricade. The fighting was fierce, and 'the din was appalling, as in addition to the enormous volume of rifle and machine gun fire at such close quarters, and constant bursting of bombs [grenades], our own heavy and howitzer batteries were keeping up a strong fire of lyddite on the enemy trenches outside the Fort'. It was touch and go, but the handful of men at the barricade held on, and the Turks came to a halt. Finally, around 11 p.m., 200 men of the 48th Pioneers who had been digging a second line of defence behind the fort, advanced and pushed the attackers out. They held the line against the final Turkish attack in the early hours of Christmas Day. The fort had proved, in Anderson's view, 'the key to our front line because as long as we held it, it prevented anything but a frontal attack'. In the end, the commander of the 52nd Division had to report that nine company commanders in his two leading regiments had been killed; 'there is nobody left to command the men'.

Though the Turkish assault concentrated on the fort, the town was under bombardment all day. At divisional HQ, Captain Cardew saw several of his comrades killed before he went to help a medical officer tend the wounded. One of these was a sergeant who had been with him on the *Espiègle* during the Qurna battle 'when the one and only shell of the, I might say hundreds fired at the *Espiègle* hit here and laid us both out. It was very hard luck on him getting badly smashed up a second time.' (He died some five weeks later from blood poisoning and exhaustion: 'I think he worried himself too much & hastened his end.')

'Daylight on Christmas morning showed masses of dead lying round the walls,' Anderson recalled. 'A number of their badly wounded lay outside and all our attempts to bring them in were stopped by rifle fire, so all that could be done was to throw over water bottles and bread to them. Several attempts were made to get them in at night but owing to casualties we had to stop this.' The few who were brought in 'were so bad with gangrene that nothing could save them'. The Turks eventually attempted to negotiate a truce to bring in the dead, but Townshend – determined to prevent any troop movements under cover of the truce – refused to negotiate with anyone but the 'Turkish supreme commander'. His assessment of the Christmas assault was crushing: the commander 'should not have been pardoned for his failure'. The 52nd Division was fresh and at full strength. The attack should have been continually reinforced and pushed home: 'the reserves should be crammed on the heels of the storming parties. It is only by piling in your masses that you can succeed.'[12] And the preliminary bombardment had alerted the defenders to the coming attack without sufficiently destroying the defences. The artillery bombardment of Woolpress Village in the morning may have been intended as a diversion, but it was not followed up as it should have been to make it effective. Bimbashi Emin endorsed Townshend's critique, both of the artillery preparation and the 'hesitant' infantry assault – indeed he pointed to 'a whole chain of inexcusable mistakes', including failure by both corps and divisional commanders to get close enough to the fighting to grasp what was going wrong.

All in all, there were signs that Turkish military effectiveness was still below par – hopeful signs, perhaps, for the success of the impending relief effort. But there had been a truly desperate moment for the garrison. All but one company of the 119th Infantry had broken, and the defences had been breached; the trenches 'denuded of troops', as Anderson had put it. If the attackers had been properly backed up, the front might well have dissolved. Townshend's own account did not mention the collapse, and later writers have mostly followed him.[13] But the official history's remark, that the under-strength British battalion (the Oxfords) had to be thrown in from the brigade reserve to hold the gap, made it clear enough what had happened. It might be portrayed as a minor setback, successfully restored, but it had a longer-term significance. Its psychological effect on commanders already anxious about the reliability of their Indian troops would have an enduring influence on the conduct of the siege.

6. To the Rescue

It is so English this way two men and a boy have been expected
to conquer Mesopotamia. At last what ought to have arrived
a year ago is arriving. But it is a question whether the Turks
haven't arrived also.
   HAROLD DICKSON

Everyone agrees that we had more real fighting this month than
the regiment had in their whole year in France.
   HUGH NORTHCOTE

London and Delhi were now trying to get a sense of the whole
strategic situation in the Middle East. On the day that Kut was
invested, the Cabinet took the decision to evacuate the army
pinned down at Gallipoli. The evacuation, potentially hazardous,
was a success – a specially British kind of success, it might be
thought. The problem was that it released Ottoman forces that
might be transferred to Mesopotamia. Did the Turks share
the British view, reiterated yet again in December 1915, that
Mesopotamia was a subsidiary theatre? Just as importantly, did
Nixon accept this? On 14 December he made a formal request
for 'another two divisions to be sent to me as soon as possible'
if he were not to have to fight without any reserves. This was
approved, though Chamberlain was as apprehensive as ever
about Nixon's thinking. He complained to the Viceroy that the
General's reports 'leave us in some uncertainty as to his plans'.
His top priority was presumably the relief of Townshend, and
his second should be the protection of the oil production area,
but Chamberlain was puzzled by reports that he was moving
troops to Nasiriyeh.[1] It turned out that India was also unable to
understand Nixon's worry about a possible Ottoman operation

to threaten Basra via the Euphrates. There was no sign of any strong Turkish movement there, and Nixon himself had argued that while Kut was held the Turks could not use the Shatt-al-Hai to approach Basra. His suggestion that by reinforcing Nasiriyeh he might 'deceive enemy as to real direction of my own concentration' seemed dubious.[2]

Crucially, though, nobody doubted that relieving Kut would be a straightforward matter. General Barrow at the India Office drew up two strategic assessments in late December. The first, reflecting his primary concern for the security of the oilfields, suggested that von der Goltz might be planning to contain Kut while operating elsewhere. There had been no reports of troop levels in the Kut area being increased, but there might be a real danger in the Karun direction. A week later he focused on the situation at Kut itself. Assuming that after the failure of the Christmas assault there would be a lull, and Townshend had at least three or four weeks' supplies in hand, Nixon should begin the relief operation by 7 January. By then he should be strong enough to succeed. The Kut position would prevent the Ottomans from sending a large force very far beyond it, since they could not use the river there, and they would not have enough time to prepare strong defensive positions. In any case the nature of the terrain on the left bank should enable the relieving force to manoeuvre them out of any position they might take up.[3]

As Townshend and his officers saw it, the relieving force had only to do what they themselves had already done with weaker forces – turn the Turks out of the Es Sinn position. Sadly, things proved less simple. Two massive problems complicated the issue: supplies and the weather. The supply problem was all too familiar in Mesopotamia, though it was a shock to the man brought in to solve it. On New Year's Eve Sir George Buchanan, an expert on port management, arrived at Basra from India. Originally instructed to 'advise General Sir John Nixon in regard to dredging work in the theatre of operations', Buchanan had helpfully proposed that his 'very considerable experience in port management and organisation might be utilised at Basra, where it seemed obvious that someone with expert knowledge was required'.[4] This idea seemed to attract Sir Percy Lake, as indeed it should have. But he did not tell Nixon. When Buchanan called on Captain Huddlestone, the Principal Marine Transport Officer at Basra, he found him 'under the impression that I had come up as one of his subordinates to advise him on questions of dredging'. He went on to see the DAQMG at force HQ, Major-General Maitland Cowper. 'This officer was very busy and preoccupied, and unable to talk consecutively on any one subject.' Cowper seemed puzzled and surprised by the terms (particularly 'river conservancy') used in Buchanan's letter of instructions from the Government of India. He went off to consult Nixon, who eventually agreed to see Buchanan three days later. When they met, Nixon blandly professed himself unable to understand what was meant by the title 'Director-General of Port Administration', since there was no port to administer. He thought Buchanan could see what improvements might be effected on the rivers to assist military operations, and launched into a complaint about the uselessness of the dredgers that had been sent out from India. Finally he read out 'a long list' of duties which Buchanan was *not* to carry out – 'making it clear that I was to have nothing whatever to do with the port'.[5]

The evidently miffed Buchanan 'explained the meaning of Port Administration and pointed out that a military port required management of traffic and execution of works as much as a purely commercial port'. Nixon flatly disagreed. 'All he wanted me for was to improve, if possible, navigation conditions on the Tigris and across the Hammar Lake.' Buchanan grumbled that he might as well go back to Bombay. Cowper persuaded him to stay on, but Nixon confirmed a few days later that while the idea of port administration might be considered after the war, 'no such question meanwhile could be allowed to impinge on the military necessities of the present situation'.

Nixon's view of port administration as a hindrance rather than a help was obscure, but its effects were clear, even to the inexpert eye. 'All arrangements give the impression of a very recent landing rather than an occupation of over a year,' thought an officer who arrived at Basra in January. Until recently there had not even been any ramps to disembark animals.[6] To Buchanan, 'the chaos was pitiable'. The steady expansion of the expeditionary force had simply led the various separate organisations – Supply and Transport, Ordnance, Engineer Field Park, and various others – 'who had originally dumped themselves on any dry spot', to form a ribbon nearly two miles long on the riverbank. A few additional jetties, adequate for emergency use, 'should have been replaced long ago by proper floating pontoon landing stages'. Storage sheds of inflammable matting had not been replaced by corrugated iron. When it rained, 'the whole of the camp area was a huge quagmire, with rotting stores dumped here, there, and everywhere'. The situation at Ma'qil, with its amateurish attempts at jetties, was even more farcical – or tragic. This, it appeared, was the military system that Buchanan's idea of 'administration' threatened to disrupt. Buchanan watched some of the reinforcements for the relief of Kut arrive. Fourteen transport ships carrying General Keary's 3rd Division were waiting in the stream to be unloaded. The troops for the front were usually landed at Ma'qil, but all their stores sat and waited – a month to six weeks – to be unloaded via *mahelas*. 'A *mahaila* carrying twenty to seventy tons was loaded by the ship's gear and then taken to a small jetty and unloaded by hand.' Incredibly, there was not a single crane in the port.

Nor, just as incredibly, had adequate river transport been provided to supply Force D. It was not until the campaign was eight months old that a formal request for purpose-built river boats was made. General Kemball's July report had contained a request for six paddle steamers of the *Mejidieh* class, three stern-wheelers of lighter draught, eight tugs of the *Sumana* class, and forty-three barges of special specification. The request reached

London on 4 August, but it was not until it was repeated on 9 September that any action was taken. Orders for the first three groups of vessels were placed on 3 November. The very first delivery of new boats – the tugs – reached Abadan in April 1916, the first paddlers and stern-wheelers in June. The barges arrived between late March and December. Even then, there was a sting in the tail: all except the paddle steamers were shipped either in sections or in plate form. Assembly in the primitive facilities at Basra was painfully slow. Some were not ready until January 1917. To top it all, even when assembled the barges did not match the strict specifications issued by Force D. It turned out that the India Office had ignored the requirement that they be 150 feet long, with pointed bows (on Lynch's model), and had them built 170 feet long with square or punt-shaped ends. Presumably it felt it was doing Force D a favour by giving it bigger craft, but (as the Mesopotamia Inquiry would note) 'while these square-ended barges may be suitable for other parts of the world, they were fatally unsuitable for the navigation of the Tigris'. The India Office stuck to its idea even when the GOC in Mesopotamia protested (as early as 27 March, when the error became clear) that any further barges must follow the Lynch pattern. It maintained that its design was 'suitable for the Tigris, and in many respects superior to anything there'. The GOC was 'driven to something approaching desperation' by the extraordinary refusal to accept 'the idiosyncrasies of the Tigris'. In the end, thirty-five of the barges, having been bought, shipped, and assembled, were 'condemned as totally unsuitable for navigation on the river'.[7]

The transport system had been at full stretch in – barely – maintaining the 6th Division. Now, after a number of boats had been lost in the Ctesiphon operations, it would have to supply a significantly larger force for operations against the deadline of the Kut garrison's survival time. The single-track railway that both Barrett and Nixon had called for might just have made the difference, but India had turned it down as too expensive. So the enlargement of the relief force to three divisions was part of the problem rather than the solution. 'Three divisions were scattered for 250 miles up the banks of the Tigris, marching by detachments along the banks, drinking its foul water, struggling through mud and swamp, or clinging to the decks of crowded steamers and barges . . . dropping along the way all formations and components save bayonets and a portion of the guns.'

The second big problem, the weather, was also depressingly familiar: Mesopotamia's climate combined with its topography to create a military nightmare at certain times of the year. January, however, was not usually one of the worst months. It was cold – more tolerable than the summer heat – but not as wet as the spring. Unfortunately, January 1916 was different. Soon after he arrived, Buchanan saw the entire Basra base area ploughed up by men, animals, and vehicles into 'liquid mud fifteen inches deep'. This was bad enough in a camp, but on a battlefield it would be deadly. At Kut, Anderson noted in early January, 'unfortunately the weather which had been threatening for some days had now broken and the rain came down in torrents. No one who has not experienced Mesopotamia can have any conception of what it is like.' The resulting mud 'sticks to your feet and makes them as heavy as lead, and is slippery like ice to walk on, so that it takes your utmost care to avoid falling, and you feel glued to the spot you are on'. This was, as he glumly recognised, 'bound to affect our operations seriously as guns become practically immobile in such conditions'.[8]

The new commander of the relief force, Lieutenant-General Sir Fenton Aylmer, 13th baronet, was a man of undoubted physical courage. Like Mellis he had won a VC – storming a fort on the North-West Frontier with a gun-cotton charge, which he placed and ignited himself and, though severely wounded, killing several of the defenders with his revolver before fainting from loss of blood. He had known Townshend since the Chitral relief expedition. Was he qualified for the demanding task of rescuing him a second time? Senior command needed a different kind of nerve. 'The more I see him', Gertrude Bell later wrote, 'the more colourless, indecisive and nervous I think him. How he got to be a Lt. General is a mystery to me.' This was after the war, but even in 1916 there seem to have been few who found him inspiring. (Chalmers thought him 'a thorough gentleman', but as a general having lost 'that personal touch so necessary', through 'years of office work'. An intelligence officer on his staff also found him 'a charming man' – but could not 'picture him as a great commander'.) He arrived in mid-December, while his new corps, now known as the Tigris Corps, consisting of two Indian divisions, Hugh d'Urban Keary's 3rd and George Younghusband's 7th, was assembling at Amara and Ali Gharbi. He fired off cheery messages to the Kut garrison about imminent relief, but was already worried by the limitations on his force. The assembly of the relief force was as chaotic as Buchanan's observations would have implied. Battalions were sent straight up the river in the order they arrived at Basra. Troops went up first, then equipment, then 'first-line' transport, and finally medical facilities. Sickness rates mounted as the climate took its toll. Many units lacked even the simplest provision – the blankets and other kit left behind in Basra with the second-line transport – against the bitter winter nights. Aylmer was as short of land transport as Townshend had been. There were plenty of wagons in Basra but they could not be taken up to the front, because not enough fodder could be taken up to maintain draught animals. There were more troops at Basra on 21 January than at the front.

The Tigris Corps mustered 19,000 men by early January, with 42 guns; the naval flotilla had been reinforced by four new *Fly*-class mini-monitors. ('Weird looking craft', as one officer described them, 'armed with a 4-inch gun forward, a couple of six-pounders and two maxims.' Their draught was so shallow – only about three feet – that they could be impossible to manage in high winds.) The Ottoman Sixth Army was thought to have 22,500 men with 72 guns, distributed – exactly how was not known – between Kut and their forward positions from Es Sinn to Sheikh Saad. Aylmer, reasonably enough, expected to be able to factor the strength of the Kut garrison (reported on 22 December at 9,185, of whom 7,211 were infantry) into his final battle plans, and sounded Townshend out about the kind of sortie he could undertake. Townshend, equally reasonably, argued that the prime necessity was to hold the Kut position. But his implication that a sortie might endanger it was more questionable. His division's offensive capacity had certainly been reduced, but Townshend harped on its weakness, and the urgent need for relief. Immediately Aylmer arrived at Amara, Townshend told him he was worried about his ammunition stocks, and hoped to be relieved within ten to fifteen days. (The timescale airily proposed by Nixon at the start, but already looking far too optimistic.)

On 30 December Aylmer sent Townshend a long message weighing his options. A single division might start out as early as 1 January, but the best option would be a 'methodical' advance by the whole corps. Pointing out that 'it is essential to postpone our actual methodical advance as long as possible, as hurry means inevitable want of organisation, and consequently decreased efficiency', he assured Townshend that 'everything possible will be done to hurry relief to utmost if your circumstances really demand it'. Townshend agreed, and promised that he would only appeal for immediate help in 'the direst necessity, which I do not think will arise now, because my adversary is clearly worried and anxious as to your advance now, and is turning his siege into a blockade'.[9]

To Nixon, though, Aylmer pointed out that 'the enemy will not allow me to join Kut garrison without most serious struggle at some place below Kut'. The truth of this became clear as soon as Younghusband's division began to move forward on 6 January. The idea was to lever the defenders out of their position at Sheikh Saad by forcing back their line on the right bank into the loop of the river and thus enfilading the left-bank trenches. But the natural aptitude of the Anatolian infantrymen for defensive fighting immediately became apparent again. Their trenches were mysteriously difficult to spot in the level desert. (Younghusband optimistically told Aylmer he could 'hear of no regular entrenchments, which looks to me as if enemy means falling back'.) British artillery fire was hampered by poor visibility. The advancing troops of the 28th Brigade were brought to a halt by heavy fire and it became clear that the Turkish line was much more extensive than had been thought. In adjusting their line to the front, the assaulting battalions lost formation, while the cavalry ordered to outflank the enemy right found movement across the mass of irrigation ditches painful: soon they were pinned down by rifle fire and threatened by a large Arab cavalry force. The main force on the left bank suffered the same problems, and they stuck there until they were forced to dig in and try to hold on overnight – an exhausting and destructive process, especially as the rain began and became steadily heavier. Casualties were already heavy when the attackers pushed on again in the late morning of the 7th. It took another display of old-fashioned heroics on the part of regiments like the Black Watch and the Buffs to get within 500 yards of the Turkish line. And once again it was an inspired spontaneous charge, led by the Leicesters and the 51st Sikhs, that gained the only significant foothold in the enemy line on the right bank – but at a cost of 300 casualties to the Leicesters alone.

The Black Watch lost 18 officers and 375 men, then 'marched thro the night, & had to dig in when we halted, & struck the hardest ground in the desert I should think', wrote Lieutenant Thorburn. 'At 3.30 am we lay down for a couple of hours' rest & a more miserable time I never remember. You have no idea of the cold just lying in the desert with a coat on.' The regiment's CO, Colonel Arthur Wauchope, had a shrapnel wound in the shoulder. When he was being treated at Basra he spoke bitterly of his orders 'to make a frontal attack on a plain as bare and flat as a billiard table without any artillery support'. After a 25-mile march on 6 January and another five miles on the day of the battle, his men were lying down without packs or equipment when the order to advance arrived. 'No time was given for the issue of orders, no frontage or direction was given, no signal communication arranged, and to all inquiries the one answer was "Advance where the bullets are thickest."'[10]

In the end, after three days of combat in increasingly glutinous mud, the Turks fell back. Lieutenant Hugh Northcote, the machine-gun officer of the 41st Dogras, came into the front line on the 10th. 'The scene that morning was very strange as we were holding a line over which one of the British regiments had had to retire the day before, and the ground was strewn with dead men and animals, and kit, rifles and ammunition were lying about the place.' Then around 10 a.m., 'we were watching the enemy's line through glasses when we suddenly saw them put their rifles in the air'. Northcote's unit went forward and captured some fifty Turks with two officers – 'we found we had gained a complete victory, and all our troops advanced at once'.[11]

But pursuit was impossible – the British forces were exhausted and movement was agonising. Northcote, surveying the sea of mud, noted that 'old Noah's Mount Ararat means any high ground, & I can quite understand the story of the Flood now'. Chalmers on his makeshift hospital boat had the familiar melancholy impression. 'The staff did not think it possible that the Turks would put up a serious fight here and therefore only expected some 300 casualties. No definite plan seems to have been made and we simply marched right up and made a frontal attack expecting them to retire.' Inevitably, 'the wounded are dying of exposure and some even of hunger'.[12] And still it rained. 'Rain, rain, rain!' reads the laconic diary entry for 17 January by Brigadier Theodore Fraser, on the 3rd Division staff. Thorburn grimly noted, 'Last night was a record. It simply came down in buckets, thunder & lightning. Three of us had a tarpaulin, but that could not keep it out. I tell you, this is a campaign. The men are like what they were when they had been in the trenches for a week in France in winter, & there are no billets to go to get cleaned up.' He thought they must have had four inches of rain in the last three days, as against three inches expected for the whole year, 'so there can't be much more to come'.[13]

Nureddin pulled his force back as far as Hanna. He had belatedly, and it seems accidentally, discovered the defensive strength of the area between the Tigris and the Suwaikiya marsh. On an inspection tour, when he and his staff approached the defile at Falahiyeh, they were 'astonished to see a small camp of white tents'. This turned out to be yet another mirage – the 'encampment' was actually a flock of geese. But 'by this extraordinary bit of luck', as Bimbashi Emin, who was riding with the army commander, wrote, 'we were able to discover a short line of 1,200 metres between the marsh and the river. The existence of this defile was completely unknown to the army – a serious reflection on our military methods.' Then, perhaps under orders from von der Goltz, who was in the process of replacing him by Halil Pasha, a cousin of Enver Pasha, Nureddin went forward again to the Wadi river. (According to Mehmet Emin there was a four-day delay between Halil's appointment and his taking over, to allow the movement to the Wadi to be completed.)

Aylmer was happy enough with this, as the Wadi was a more exposed position, offering some chance of turning its open flank. But in the event, the attack there on 13 January was just as sticky as Sheikh Saad: a stumbling encounter in which units were pushed off their intended lines of advance, and attempts at outflanking movement stalled. 'Our men were sent across 1000 yards of flat open plain without a vestige of cover & over ground that was sodden with rain to the condition of a bog. They had been out in the rain without blankets or cover & the cold chilled one to the bone ... The enemy were much further off than we expected,' Northcote reported to his father, 'so we had a long march across perfectly flat and in some cases marshy country before getting into touch.' Then came the storm of steel: returning from a long trek back to bring up his guns and more ammunition, Northcote 'found the C.O. had been killed, and the three other BOs wounded, though in the confusion we could not make out much of what was happening . . . The last 200 yards to the firing line was rather nasty . . . We then tried another advance but we had not enough BOs to lead the men.'[14] Major T. C. Catty of the 69th Punjabis, acting as DAAG at 3rd Division HQ, 'talked to various Regt officers who were on the show & they all say that the turning movement wasn't nearly wide enough'. Catty heard that 'the Corps staff seem to have lost its nerve at the critical moment' and redirected the outflanking force.[15] At all events, the fight was another costly stalemate, with huge efforts needed merely to secure a hold on the enemy front line. The Turks again withdrew unmolested during the night.

Catty, like so many Indian Army officers, raged continually at the crippling effects of governmental parsimony – 'the usual cheap & nasty Indian way'. (His divisional commander reflected with bitter cynicism that 'the Indian Government are rather given to trying to acquire country in the cheapest possible way and they stint and screw in every way to save pennies and thereby sacrifice lives which is cheaper to them'.[16]) In the case of the battle at the Wadi, it was the miserable inadequacy of the boats available to build the bridge by which forces were to be shifted to the other bank in another attempt to enfilade the Turkish line. (Chalmers recorded that a bridge was begun on 17 January, 'but as the men are new to the job it takes some 40 hours to throw a bridge across, whereas Sandes of the 6th Division can do it in 8'.)

But in human, rather than simply military terms, there was worse. 'The tales of the wounded at Shaikh Sa'ad and Wadi are really awful,' Catty noted in his diary. 'If one wasn't on the spot they would be unbelievable. There were no MOs to dress them properly & not 20 per cent of the proper number of stretcher bearers. Men were left out for 2–3 days before being picked up – some poor devils with fractured legs crawled in 4 or 5 miles.' There were still no hospital ships as such: sick and wounded were 'shoved on board' the ordinary transports, without beds or bedding, sanitary or cooking facilities. 'Men with fractured thighs are shoved alongside dysentery cases & there they lie till they get to Basra.' Catty charitably allowed that the reason might be 'perhaps they thought that there wouldn't be so many casualties or that time was so important that they couldn't wait any longer for the hospitals' – but this in itself was hardly encouraging. Chalmers was horrified that wounded men were 'dying of exposure and some even of hunger', fuming that it was 'a perfect scandal to embark on a campaign without sufficient ships to convey the wounded and with a totally inadequate medical personnel'. For Major Crowdy of the corps intelligence staff, 'the sight of so much avoidable suffering' induced alarmingly radical thoughts. It 'makes one wonder whether our system of government is as good as our governors make out'. Might there not after all 'be a good deal to be said for the point of view of the Indian we dub "sedition monger"?'[17]

Aylmer's first full-scale offensive effort followed a few days later. He was already gloomy enough to pronounce the enemy position at Hanna virtually impregnable: 'the position of affairs must be frankly faced,' he urged Nixon. 'It is impossible in my opinion to take the first position by a coup de main from this side alone [the left bank] without losing half the force.'[18] He wanted to push the 3rd Division forward on the right bank to enfilade the strong Turkish position at Hanna while Townshend broke out of Kut to join it. Nixon's response was crushing: 'I do not in any way agree with your appreciation of the situation.' The only justification for such an extreme step would be 'a demoralisation of your force which I have no reason to suspect'. He vehemently insisted that 'the course you now propose for Townshend would be disastrous from every point of view – to Townshend's force to your force to the whole of the forces in Mesopotamia and to the Empire and I can NOT sanction it'.[19] Once again Aylmer was forced into a frontal assault against a formidable defensive position. On 21 January, 'against an enemy securely entrenched in this ideal defensive position', one of his staff officers wrote, 'Aylmer launched the remnants of the

7th Division in a purely frontal attack totally unsupported from the other bank.'

This time the slaughter was the worst yet – only 120 of 300 in the already battered Black Watch survived. Northcote's Dogras had pushed up to within 100 yards of the enemy line on the 20th and 'stayed there all day while our artillery bombarded the Turkish trenches. We kept saying to each other that the enemy were bound to bolt under the bombardment. We had been told that their morale was bad.' At first light, however, 'we saw that the enemy's trenches were still strongly held . . . Then came the charge – I was carrying a rifle and bayonet, and was about 20 yards in front of our line. The men advanced splendidly, but we were mown down by frantic fire.' Fifty yards from the enemy, Northcote 'felt a blow like a hammer in my left arm, which knocked me down'. He crawled away under fire – 'it was pelting with rain and I was soaked and frozen' – and after dark he 'luckily struck a hospital ship'.

Catty was increasingly critical. 'The attack started at 8am and at first it seemed as if all was to be well.' The Black Watch and the 6th Jats on the right got into the Turkish trenches, 'but the supporting Brigade was too far back, so after a bit – it's impossible to say how long as accounts vary from 15 minutes to 3 hours – the men were bombed out and forced to retire'. Catty heard from the Black Watch that 'another reason for giving up the trench was on account of the bad bombs we had': only one out of ten had exploded. 'They all say that given decent bombs they would be there now.' Major Crowdy soberly judged 'the whole scheme of operations' to have been 'extraordinarily ill advised and indifferently executed'. It was 'a hopeless and depressing show'.

The sequel was even more depressing. 'Notwithstanding our heavy losses Hd Qrs (who hadn't left their comfortable ship) ordered another assault at 2pm. By this time everyone was knee deep in mud so the attack never had a chance. So the troops dug in where they were.' It rained hard all night, and 'by morning a more miserable dispirited force could not be imagined. Everyone was numbed with cold and hadn't a kick left in them.' Once again, as the AT carts could not move in the mud, the wounded had to lie out all night untended. 'Many a poor devil with only slight wounds, died of exposure.'[20] Even those who got to the medical tents found a miserable situation. At the start of the attack the field ambulances had been ordered to move up in the hope of a breakthrough, so had struck their tents. By the time they were ordered to pitch them again, the heavy tents were soaked with rain, and the ground had turned into mud.

For Lieutenant Thorburn of the Black Watch this was the culmination of a series of grim experiences. 'Difficult you will understand it is to attack an intrenched position over dead flat ground in broad daylight . . . Those who have experienced war in France only do not know what war is.' During the preliminary bombardment, 'The noise & shrieking are indescribable. The shooting seems good, so I don't see how any man can live under it. But they keep on sniping in their wonderfully plucky way.' Indeed the snipers were so active that he could not get out of his trench for duties. Finally, during the battle he was bayoneted in 'the leg and bow-hind', but when he came to, 'the pipes were playing beside me so I knew we had the trench!' But then, 'we had to come back, which was the awful part'. Chalmers sadly recorded that 'the Hampshires, who I dined with on Christmas day at Amara, went in 240 strong & came out with 60 men and 2 officers out of 11'. Among the dead was its CO, Colonel Bowker himself.

7. Marking Time

Aylmer has made a pretty good mess of his relief operations so
far, I'm afraid.

ARTHUR MONEY

For a month, Tigris Corps licked its wounds. It had become
seriously disorganised. Units had been attached to the nearest
formation as they arrived at the front, and now had to be
redistributed. Most had been shredded, and rebuilding them,
and distributing the replacements who had arrived for units of
the Kut garrison, was a slow process. Aylmer was well on the
way to being awarded the nickname 'Faylmer'. Major Crowdy
thought 'the troops have been so battered during the last few
days that they have lost all confidence in the Corps Commander
and his staff'. The corps staff (he was one of them) were 'most
hopelessly out of touch with the troops'. None of the senior staff
ever left their offices on the *Mejidieh*; Aylmer himself only took
a ride on fine days. 'How can they expect to know what the
troops are good for unless they paddle around in the mud and
see them?' Major-General Arthur Money, Nixon's Chief of Staff,
told his wife, 'Aylmer has made a pretty good mess of his relief
operations so far, I'm afraid.' Whilst all the previous fighting
had been 'fairly expensive in casualties' as it was bound to be
in 'attacking over open ground without any cover', it had so
far had generally decisive results. Aylmer's operations, however,
'have been more expensive & less decisive'. In adding that 'the
weather has been pretty appalling too', Money suggested that
it was only a subordinate factor; though he admitted that the
Tigris was as high as it had been at the height of the flood season
the previous year, and that 'we have 10,000 troops on the march

up absolutely stuck in various places, some columns surrounded entirely by water'. They would, he said, 'just have to wait there until the floods subside'.[1]

While they waited, significant changes were made at the command level. Nixon, who had at last succumbed to the climate and asked to be relieved, was replaced on 19 January by General Sir Percy Lake, formerly the Indian Chief of Staff. Hardly a new broom: as Arnold Wilson remarked, he had controlled the scale and equipment of the expeditionary force from the outset, and 'was rightly regarded as having been constitutionally responsible for some at least of its deficiencies, and for past errors of strategy'. He had directly appointed all the senior officers. He had not yet visited Mesopotamia, and was horrified by the situation when he finally arrived to take command. To his credit, he did then go on to do something to improve it; on the whole, though, Wilson judged that his appointment as C-in-C was 'in all the circumstances unfortunate'.[2] At the Imperial level, the change was more far-reaching: on 10 February the War Office took over control of the campaign from the Indian government. This was a belated recognition that the scale and significance of the Mesopotamia campaign was far beyond India's human and material capacity. Indian Expeditionary Force D was no more; now it was the Mesopotamia Expeditionary Force.

Officially, no serious effort to break the siege was made between the stalling of the Hanna offensive and the start of the fateful battle of Dujaila on 8 March. Most accounts have treated this as a period of inactivity.[3] Those on the ground had a different impression. Aylmer decided in the middle of February to make what the official history called 'a surprise demonstration against the rear of the Turkish position at Hanna'. This 'demonstration in force' – yet another instance of the attraction of this tactic – was intended to inflict damage on the enemy and force them to 'disclose their dispositions'. But Aylmer told Townshend that it might persuade the enemy to retire, and if so he would press on and Townshend might have an opportunity to attack. If this was the true rationale of the operation, it underlines the tentative approach that marked so many of Aylmer's efforts.[4]

The result seems to have been a real missed opportunity for a decisive stroke. In mid-February the weather seemed to be favourable. Aylmer's ADC (who had noted in late January that though the trenches were 'wonderfully dry', the country was 'more and more appalling', and in early February 'going underfoot awful – mud indescribable') registered the 19th as a 'quiet day and delightfully warm'; 'Anyway things look hopeful.'[5] Catty thought the Hanna position was 'now so strong that a dart across country seems to be the only solution', and Crowdy on the corps staff certainly agreed. It seemed obvious to him that there was no room for manoeuvre on the northern bank, while the southern bank was much more open, with the ground quite passable in dry weather. He covered several pages of his diary-letters with evaluations of the best ways to get across the twenty-five waterless miles between Sheikh Saad and the Shatt-al-Hai. If the British could reach that, they would find water and relieve Kut.

On the night of 21 February, while the 21st Brigade made a feint at crossing the Suwaikiya marsh and the 7th Division 'demonstrated' in front of the Hanna trenches, the 3rd Division, reinforced with the 36th Brigade and most of the Cavalry Brigade, moved up the right bank towards the Falahiyeh bend. Aylmer took the odd decision to give command of the 3rd Division for the operation to General Gorringe, who had come up with his divisional staff from the Euphrates to Amara on 22 January to organise the forward despatch of reinforcements, and then been appointed Aylmer's Chief of Staff.[6] That arrangement was odd in itself: Gorringe had his own staff chief (GSO1) who refused to work with Aylmer's. And Gorringe was actually junior to the commander of 3rd Division, Keary, who had also spent much longer 'on the ground'. Keary was not the only one to think this a bad idea – 'the place of a Chief of Staff is at his commander's side', Crowdy grumbled, 'and not in executive command of a senior officer's division'.

At daybreak Gorringe's artillery bombarded the Ottoman camps north of the Falahiyeh bend, while his column pushed on up as far as Sannaiyat. On this stretch of the river, as the maps laboriously drawn by Crowdy clearly show, the left bank was commanded by the right. At the Sannaiyat bend, in particular, command was 'extensive'. The ground from there to the Dujaila depression, only four miles from Kut, was 'level – good going'. Catty noted that 'unless it rains, the road to Kut across country is quite feasible'. Gorringe had options: he could strike out across country or, if he had had a bridging train, he could have crossed the river and taken the Hanna position in rear. But he did not. Instead, his troops were lugging twenty dummy pontoons designed to suggest that a crossing would be attempted. These were 'ostentatiously launched' at nightfall. ('Damned nonsense on the part of our Senile Commanders,' Catty fulminated.)

Harry MacDonald at Aylmer's HQ heard that 'bombardment of Turkish trenches and camps at dawn caught him on the hop and inflicted severe damage'. The artillery 'had magnificent target, clear morning, mounds to observe from, everything favourable'. About 5.30 a.m., Catty recorded, '9th Brigade reached Mason's Mounds and surprised a Cavalry patrol who fled like hares'. Amar Singh of the 9th Brigade (one of very few Indian officers whose diary has survived) 'saw a sight that very few men have seen. We had got in rear of the Turkish camp and started shelling it and very soon caused tremendous confusion. Horses, mules and donkeys together with camels, cattle and men started stampeding . . . Our losses were practically nothing.'[7] Catty believed that 'We were now absolute masters of the situation and if only we had had material a bridge could have been made and our Division put across under cover of the artillery bombardment.' As it was, 'it seems to have been a wasted opportunity'. So felt the cavalry, who had joined the 3rd Division in the advance. They moved out having been 'rather led to believe that this was to be the big push', as Edgar Bridges told his father, 'we went to bed wondering whether we might find ourselves on the Shatt el Hai the next evening, and possibly in Kut the next'.

The Turks had indeed been completely surprised – Crowdy noted that they made no attempt for thirty-six hours to guard the northern bank against a possible crossing. In spite of the 'ostentatious' launching of the dummy pontoons, no sign of a fire trench appeared on the other side until the morning of the 24th. 'We all thought that this threat would frighten the Turks out of their lines at Hanna – at least those of us who had not been in France thought so,' Crowdy admitted. Unfortunately, as he added, this 'included practically the whole of the Corps staff'. So 'no arrangements were made to take advantage of the surprise', and 'the whole operation fizzled out ingloriously'.[8]

Gorringe himself was shot in the backside ('evidently by an Arab rifle') on the 23rd, a gratifyingly symbolic end to the operation. 'This general has the reputation of being a pusher & an able man tho extremely selfish & indifferent about the wounded,' Chalmers noted. 'Now he is wounded himself he wired for the X-ray apparatus to be sent from Amara so he could have the bullet extracted at once.' Only when that proved impossible did he go down to Amara, 'very sick at being knocked over & wants to get back again so as to win all the honour & glory as he is practically cock of the walk over here'. He was taken down in Leachman's launch the *Lewis Pelly*, then brought back on the 27th after attempts to remove the bullet had failed. 'As he cannot walk he will have to direct operations from camp.'[9] Keary resumed command of the 3rd Division. Crowdy heard that the men of the division had taken to calling the little depression near Mason's Mounds where the general had been wounded 'Gorringe's Bottom', but sadly he was refused permission to add this place-name to the corps maps.

Aylmer unsurprisingly took a different view of the 22 February operation from Catty, seeing it as 'very successful'. Keary's forward troops pushed further up the right bank on the 24th, shelling some Ottoman cavalry at Beit Isa. But the hope that the Turks would pull back from the Hanna position once they were enfiladed was not fulfilled. Worse, they had now been alerted to their potential vulnerability on the right bank, and began strengthening and extending their trenchworks southwards from Es Sinn towards Dujaila, which Aylmer had identified as the key point in his make-or-break effort to relieve Kut. Still, as the official historian charitably observed, Keary's forward position gave Aylmer 'the nearer starting point he required for his coming attack'. Whatever advantage this provided, though, was to be squandered in the event by the mismanagement of that crucial offensive.

8. Flood and Famine

Then suddenly, in a spot we had never suspected, in burst the water in a torrent which nothing on earth would stop.

G. L. HEAWOOD

The 22 February operation caused real excitement amongst the Kut garrison. 'All garrison prepared for momentous events,' Captain W. A. Phillips of the 24th Punjabis noted in his diary. 'The GOC's intention, according to rumour, is to force a great battle, provided the show downstream goes decently well.'[1] Townshend's diary recorded 'heavy gunfire about 7am to the eastward. We could clearly see the shells bursting over Hanna, and the smoke, though the distance must be fully twenty miles. Apparently some confusion was caused in the enemy's main camp, but they did not retreat. As is the Turkish custom when defending earthworks, they held on like grim death, their officers, revolver in hand, shooting if any man tried to get up and go. Aylmer wired me that a certain amount of movement from east to west could be seen at Hanna. But nothing more came of this.'[2] Townshend had, finally, detailed a force of sufficiently able-bodied troops – some 2,500 – for a possible sortie to the right bank, leaving a pared-down garrison of 4,000. The sappers received 'secret orders' on the 21st to prepare for the sortie – 22 Company was 'to make two trench bridges for artillery between A and B Redoubts'.[3] Lieutenant H. S. D. McNeal of the Royal Artillery had to prepare his battery (the 63rd) to accompany the 66th and 76th Punjabis, 2/7th Gurkhas, Norfolks and West Kents, 'to cross a swinging bridge and hold up the retirement of the Turks until the relieving force could cope with them'. They stayed awake while 'the whole night long the guns of the relieving force were both seen and heard pounding away at the enemy's positions'.[4]

With the West Kents themselves, Major Heawood had received 'very confidential instructions as to what should be done (in details) in case of certain other orders being received'. At 6 a.m. 'a tremendous cannonading began downstream and we were all on the tip top of expectation, imagined how they had assaulted at 8, exactly what the present phase of sound and sight meant, and exactly what time we would be able to sally out'. Mousley's unit was 'all ready and waiting for immediate debouch. I am "booted and spurred" and feeling very important.' They had to content themselves with this imagined battle. By the 24th, they were 'to remain in a state of diminishing expectancy and increasing disappointment'.[5]

McNeal had been 'hard put to it to get horses sufficiently strong to pull the guns', and could only make up his teams by taking the best horses from the first line of wagons. This was a problem that could only get worse as the 6th Division approached the end of its third month under siege. The horses were being steadily slaughtered, and the process would accelerate – not primarily because of the need for food. But when the first ration of horsemeat was issued on 28 January, the Muslim troops refused to eat it. Their *atta* ration was increased in lieu of meat, which in turn reduced the feed available for the division's transport animals. (To the point where a thousand had to be destroyed, McNeal recorded.) The officers' own chargers survived longest, but in the end all had to go. Mousley lost his beloved Don Juan on 10 April: 'his companions stood by him trembling as the quick shot despatched one after another. Not so he! Now and then he stamped, but otherwise stood perfectly still. I asked the NCO to be careful that his first bullet was effective, and kissed Don on the cheek "goodbye".' (He ate his heart and kidneys for dinner, 'as they are now reserved for the owners'.[6])

How long could the Kut garrison survive? Considering how vital this question was, it is surprisingly hard to answer with any precision. Townshend's initial estimate, that he had sixty days' supplies for his British and Indian troops – though meat for only thirty – and thirty days' fodder for his animals, was not based on a systematic investigation of the town's food resources. The division stayed on full rations (except for potatoes and vegetables) until 21 January, when rations were halved. At that point a thorough search of the town uncovered over 900 tons of barley, 100 tons of wheat and 19 tons of ghee. On 24 January Townshend sent the surprising news that, while he had twenty-two days' food left now, 'by collecting all the *atta* in town and eating up the horses, we can last out much longer'. After elaborating next day on the extra supplies he had found, he produced the almost startling estimate that he could now hold out for eighty-four more days as long as the Turks did not mount a determined assault. (His anxiety about this had now subsided.) This produced a mixture of relief and annoyance at corps HQ, which, like some later writers, found it hard to see why the 24 January search had not been made at the outset.

Townshend blamed the delay on the 'distinctly hostile' and pro-Turkish attitude of the inhabitants. Such numbers of 'virtual enemies' in the midst of his position represented a 'positive danger', he told Aylmer – 'I have to keep a considerable force of military police to watch them day and night.' He had searched houses for arms, but 'did not want to search for food until obliged, as will be easily understood'. In case this was not quite so easy for others to understand, he added that he 'knew there was much food in the town, but not as much as we discovered'.

Townshend's ration policy has been indicted by later writers, most angrily in Norman Dixon's assertion that 'his first move towards hastening his rescue was so to manipulate his would-be rescuers that they felt compelled to try and relieve the siege before they were ready'. This allegation does not entirely make sense: Townshend knew as well as his later critics that to make a premature effort was to risk the failure of the relief effort. He had to balance the need to survive against the need to maintain fighting effectiveness. Most commanders – following Napoleon's imperishable maxim about the army's stomach – would err on the side of over- rather than under-feeding their troops. In Kut, it is clear that worries about the force's morale outweighed other issues.[7] The charge against Townshend has been buttressed by psychological arguments: for Braddon, it was his 'relentless pursuit of promotion' that was the key. Unless he was relieved within two months, the command of the second corps that would be assembled in Mesopotamia would almost certainly go to his junior, Gorringe, who would get a lieutenant-generalcy for it – and would also command the force that would eventually take Baghdad. For Townshend this would be the 'end of his career'.

Seen in this light, Braddon suggested, 'his lavish allocation of rations, his failure to unearth hidden grain, and his demand for an impossibly early relief, all make sense'.[8] Dixon (who got his information from Braddon, but injected a psychoanalytical take) called the general's arguments for holding Kut 'nonsense'. 'For a man of Townshend's temperament', he wrote, the memory of being besieged at Chitral was 'a wish fulfilment not easily forgotten in time of stress', and Kut was merely 'the nearest thing to Chitral'. (Why Kut rather than any of the other places he could have stood, Dixon does not say.) Townshend's behaviour during the 147 days of the siege was 'that of a man who, while sliding inexorably towards a precipice of his own making, assumes that someone will not only step forward to break his fall but hand him a prize for having done so'.[9] These authors attribute Aylmer's failures entirely to the pressure placed on him by Townshend's 'lies'. This conclusion would have suited Tigris Corps HQ, but as usual Major Catty was rather sharper in his judgement. When he heard in mid-February that 'Corps HQ are now blaming Townshend for the heavy losses and failure to get through, as after saying he had to be relieved by the 15th Jan or so, he now says he can hold out till the end of March', he drily commented, 'but they cannot blame him for their faulty strategy or the continued frontal attacks.'[10]

By far the gravest charge levelled at Townshend is that he deliberately falsified intelligence information. When Aylmer suggested that he faced 30,000 combatants with 83 guns between Sheikh Saad and Kut, Townshend 'retorted, more like 20,000 and 32 guns'. Noting that these figures were, 'for him, quite unusually precise', Braddon adds 'that they were false no one knew better than he'. Braddon recognises that such a deception, which was so likely to guarantee the failure of the relief effort, needs some explanation. What conceivable advantage could Townshend gain from it? Whether Braddon's answer – 'that such an advantage could have existed only in the mind of a man no longer completely stable' – is convincing, is an open question. What seems certain is that Townshend's estimate, far from being false, was about as close to the facts as it could reasonably have been.

Even the most detailed study of the Ottoman Army has not produced clear figures for the Sixth Army's infantry or artillery strength throughout the siege of Kut. But at the end of 1915 the Sixth Army ('in some ways an "army" in name only') mustered five infantry divisions, each of nine battalions. Like the British units, these were all seriously under-strength – operating at between 30 and 40 per cent of normal strength. The Ottoman replacement system had broken down in Mesopotamia. (The entire infantry strength of the 52nd Division when the assault on Kut was launched in December 1915 was 3,678.) The Sixth Army then had 20,018 combat troops and 11,656 support troops. At Ctesiphon it had disposed 38 guns, and may have acquired a few more. Its logistical situation was much worse than that of the Tigris Corps: during the whole of 1915, no more than 5,000 rifles, 10 guns, 16,000 artillery shells, 8 machine guns and 40,000 hand grenades were shipped to the Iraq Area Command.[11] All this material could only be transported by train as far as the Pozanti Gap, where it had to be laboriously lugged by pack animals over the Taurus Mountains, reloaded on trains and taken to the Osmaniye Gap, where once again animals carried it over to the Euphrates valley; there it went by train to the river and was then loaded on barges or animals to be taken to Baghdad. And since two of Sixth Army's divisions were besieging Kut, it seems possible that even Townshend's figure of 20,000 exaggerated the effective strength of the forces directly facing Aylmer.

A further charge against the Kut garrison's commander rests on the series of communiqués he issued to his force, usually following a failed relief attempt. These were of an unusually direct emotional nature, and surprisingly indiscreet as to operational specifics. (On 8 December, for instance, he announced that 'our relief force will be concentrated at Shaikh Saad within the next week'.) The most often quoted, on 26 January, running to two pages, ended with open criticism of his superiors. 'I want to tell you that, when I was ordered to advance on Ctesiphon, I officially demanded an army corps, or at least two divisions, to perform the task successfully. Having pointed out the grave danger of attempting to do this with one division only, I had done my duty. You know the result . . . ' He added, 'Perhaps by right I should not have told you of the above, but I feel I owe it to all of you to speak straightly and openly and to take you into my confidence. God knows I felt our heavy losses, and the sufferings of my poor brave wounded, and I shall remember it as long as I live. I may truly say that no General I know of has been more loyally served than I have been in command of the Sixth Division. These words are long, but I speak straight from the heart, and you see I have thrown all officialdom overboard. We will succeed; mark my words.' After the failure of the 8 March assault, emotion brimmed over. He told his force that it had 'passed three months of cruel uncertainty, and to all men and to all people uncertainty is intolerable . . . I ask you to give a little sympathy to me, who, having come to the Division as a stranger, now love my command with a depth of feeling I have never known in my life before. I am speaking to you as I did before, straight from the heart, and as I say I ask your sympathy for my feelings, having promised you relief on certain dates on the promise of those ordered to relieve us.'

The communiqués demonstrate, Dixon suggests, 'a flagrant disloyalty towards his superiors, a thinly veiled contempt for the valiant but unsuccessful relief force, and a total absence of gratitude towards those who were losing their lives in trying to rescue him'. (To add to his persistent lying to Aylmer about his supplies, his deliberate falsification of estimates of enemy strength, and his hypocrisy towards his own troops.) Yet Townshend had immediately added that the failure was 'not their fault – do not think that I blame them! They are giving their lives freely, and deserve our gratitude and admiration.' His communiqués are certainly open to the polite criticism offered by the official historian – 'it is always difficult to judge how much information it is advisable to publish to troops, especially in a case like this, when the Turks were in constant communication with the Arabs in the town'. Townshend 'decided to run the risk, both to keep up the spirits of his men and to prevent the dissemination of groundless rumours', and it was hard to say 'whether by his action he did any harm'.[12] Though he was, evidently, also relieving his own feelings, he did indeed achieve some of these objectives. Gunner William Lee, for instance, carefully transcribed parts of the communiqués in his diary, and noted, 'I must say these communiqués had a way of bucking one up.' They 'always inspired us to make a further effort' or 'have a little more patience'.[13]

What does seem clear is that these messages formed pretty much the only contact Townshend had with most of his troops. Private Harold Wheeler of the 1st/4th Hampshires was typical in noting that 'as far as I was concerned, he was an aloof figure at his HQ in the town, and never at any time during the siege did I set eyes on him'. (Though he added that 'there is no doubt whatsoever that he enjoyed the confidence and esteem of his command'.) The only general he saw was Mellis, who materialised one day (Wheeler noted it precisely – 21 January

1916) at the firing line 'splashing his way knee-deep through the waterlogged trench, with a cheerful "Good morning sentry!"'.[14] For the 6th Division's officers, the situation was much the same, though some had a stronger sense of their general's personality. When 18th Brigade sent him Christmas greetings, the brigade major thought his reply 'very characteristic': 'Many thanks for your kind message which I heartily return – as James Pigge of immortal memory said, "Keep the tambourine a-rollin"'!' (Major Dunn vowed, 'We will.')[15]

The Kut garrison needed all the patience that men like Gunner Lee could muster. Life was monotonous and uncomfortable, 'a mole and frog-like existence', Private Wheeler thought, living 'underground in open trenches and dugouts for a total of 145 consecutive days and nights'. Trench digging, for many of his Territorial comrades, was unfamiliar manual work. Fatigues, 'plague of duty-men on call at all hours and subject to an arbitrary method of selection by NCOs, were wearisome and at time exceedingly dangerous'. Going into the firing line after the Christmas Eve attack, 'I shall never forget the grotesque scene of battered defence works, dead bodies fast decomposing under the hot sun of Turks hanging on the wire, immediately below the parapet where unfortunate sentries had to do duty for two hours at a stretch'.[16] (The duty period was later halved.) Anderson recorded that after the new year, 'there are only occasional days on which anything outstanding occurred'. The besiegers kept up constant sniping – 'a wonderfully wasteful way of using ammunition' – as Anderson disapprovingly (or enviously) observed, though he admitted that 'such bullets found victims'. The Ottoman artillery operated sporadically: 'very few days passed without a "hate"' (as the troops from the Western Front called German nuisance barrages), 'though they varied greatly in intensity'. Real bombardments were rare. The excitement of seeing the first enemy aircraft early in January was tempered by the fact that it kept well away from the defences. 'It evidently had no intention of bombing us, and we soon ceased to take any interest in it, as we had no anti-aircraft guns.' British aircraft occasionally appeared to drop parcels (of money or other desiderata) – but 'the seaplanes were extraordinarily unsuccessful in this, as they frequently managed to drop their parcels either into the river or on the far side of it'.

The real drama was the weather. The unseasonal deluges of early January had already driven the garrison from their trenches temporarily. (The Turks had suffered even more, and never reoccupied many of their forward trenches.) But by the middle of the month the bad weather was 'gaining strength . . . The wind would get up from the S. with rain, and turning to a gale would veer round to the N. becoming bitterly cold – then would follow a day or two with brighter weather and frost, only to give way again to the next depression. The trenches were miserable and the river rising rapidly.'[17] This soon became alarming, since much of the Kut area was below river level. After 21/22 January ('about the worst days of the lot – a howling northerly gale with torrents of rain') the front-line trenches became untenable.

While floods could be caused by heavy rain, this was episodic: the really serious flood threat came from the melting of the snows at the head of the Tigris and Euphrates valleys, and these floods came even after the weather had improved in early spring. So January was merely a prelude, no less arduous for that. Heawood fought a long battle to save Redoubt B: 'At first we could only drain out with old tins (a very doubtful proceeding, as the redoubt was very low-lying, and we sometimes got our own back somewhere else), or else throw down more or less dry earth for the water to soak up, and then heave that up, which took twice the time, and was very heavy work. Then we had to do all our end of the echelon trenches which was a most despairing task though by this time we had got hold of a pump from the sappers, so we threw down whole traverses to make complete barricades, and then drained it by sections, and redug those bits afterwards. But we got it done somehow at last.' But the river kept rising, 'and we began to have very restless nights'. The big trouble was a combination of 'percolation for immense distances both by old rat holes [and] the extraordinarily porous kind of soil ... All the proper bunds on the river had to be made not only of great thickness and most thoroughly rammed, but with a core of heavy damp mud, besides being well keyed into the earth; of course we could do no more than key our temporary trench bunds ... After several dry but anxious days, the main flood water started advancing at about the rate of a yard an hour. I watched it on and off one night from about 11 till about three in the morning.' When it was about to pass the barbed wire, it changed direction towards a previously unthreatened sector; then, suddenly, when 'we thought we were safe for the present', the water burst through 'in a spot we had never suspected, in a torrent which nothing on earth would stop'.[18]

Heawood took care to add that, 'Tho this reads like a chapter of gloom it was not so in the very least. There was plenty of work digging and repairing banks in and around the fort by day and night. Then there was counting the days to the exact hour when we each had severally decided that the relief force would make their appearance.' (In the hospital, after the 22 February operation 'a sweep was got up for the day on which we should actually be relieved'; Anderson drew a blank, 'but the feelings of all those in the same position was that we were no worse off than those who had drawn dates in April!') Back in Heawood's trenches, 'we were plagued with frogs, so we cut earthen staircases in the sides and especially across the corners of the Mess dugout and it really was most laughable sight in the world to see the frogs (particularly after a heavy meal of flies) trying to climb up just to show us that fine weather was really coming, and generally falling down from the top step.'

Gunner Lee paid oblique tribute to the enemy's contribution: 'The Turkish quick-firers were excellent and the shells were upon you before you heard the report of the gun, and gave you those thrills when running to take cover that made life worth living – even in Kut.' (Several officers made the point that the 'enemy

artillery, though destructive, was nothing to what it might have
been had they had high explosives'.[19]) After mid-February, when
the Ottomans brought up an ancient bronze mortar which the
troops christened 'Flatulent Flossie', the search for fragments
of its bombs – 'in great demand as ash trays etc' – helped to
pass the time.[20] When not under fire, 'The troops would pass the
days by making out lists of food they would require when they
were relieved. The lists were generally written on the backs of
the School Certificates that most soldiers carried in their Small-
Books.' They organised talks on cooking – a fatal obsession.
Lee 'learned a lot about cooking, especially about chickens and
other dishes I have never yet tasted. It is very funny how men in
these circumstances always pick on the best of foods.' For Lee,
who eventually 'found that I could not stand for any length of
time', thinking about bully beef 'made me feel faint, and I would
tighten my belt making new holes to do so'.[21]

9. Dujaila: The Second Battle for Kut

It seemed that all those lives were being devoted as an
extenuation of a blunder in command.
EDMUND CANDLER

Morale in the Tigris Corps was also fragile. Edgar Bridges
told his father, 'I never knew how poisonous things could be.
I am not grousing, and I don't wish to be anywhere else,' he
added, but people from France were saying 'that for hardship,
unpleasantness, and discomfort generally, they simply didn't
know what it meant before they arrived here'.[1] He later reported
that 'there have been some slight regrettable incidents among
the troops'. After the battle of 22–23 February, Catty thought
that 'a bad feature about it was that 48 per cent of the wounded
are in the hand or foot, which looks very suspicious'. The level
of losses meant that 'Brigades now cease to exist as such for
fighting purposes', as Catty noted on 22 February. The 6th Jats,
who had been 800 strong when they arrived a month before,
'can now muster 30–40 rifles! Isn't it wicked?' It was not simply
a question of absolute levels; such replacements as arrived were
distributed randomly, undermining the careful internal balance
of the Indian regiments.

At the level of high command, War Office control seems to
have done little more than add another voice to the critical chorus
already in place. The Chief of the Imperial General Staff, General
Sir William Robertson, grumbled to the C-in-C India in February
that Lake's statement that Aylmer's plan offered 'a fair chance of
success' was not good enough. 'To my mind, after considering
the relative rate of arrival of our reinforcements and those of the
enemy, and also the conditions at Kut', they should select a time

which offered 'the most favourable prospect of success'. Told of this, Lake protested that 'the CIGS should be fully informed of the situation in this country, and how evenly balanced the chances are' of relieving Kut. River transport was still barely sufficient to supply the relief force, without adding reinforcements. When the CIGS went on to urge that 'what is required is to get every possible man and gun right up to the front' (in particular the 13th Division, which was in much better condition than many of the battalions at the front), Lake protested, 'I cannot hope to convey to the front in time for Aylmer's advance more than a few individual units.' The 13th Division was not due at Basra before 28 February in any case. Once again Robertson advised Force D to find 'a middle course . . . there are occasions, and this appears to be one, when a less number of fresh and good troops are more valuable than a greater number of tired and second class troops'. If Lake could not enlarge Aylmer's force, he should increase its quality – 'and particularly increase his guns' – by 'any possible means' before he struck.[2] Duff suggested that there was no need to strike before 15 March.

In spite of this, Aylmer made what turned out to be his final effort to relieve Kut at the end of the first week of March. His plan, building on the 'successful' reconnaissance-in-force of 22 February, was to push forward on the southern side of the river. The key objective was the redoubt at Dujaila, which commanded the defensive lines running south from Es Sinn; it was the last major defence before Kut. The advancing forces would strike out south-westwards towards the Dujaila Depression, splitting into two columns (under Generals Kemball and Keary) to assault the redoubt from the south and then break into the main position. This was an ambitious plan, but much more promising than the head-on assaults along the narrow corridor north of the river. Surprise would be vital, and to achieve it the columns needed to advance by night to their jumping-off positions. Night marches were inevitably complicated, and the ground between the assembly area three miles south of the Hanna position and the enemy lines was, as usual, broken by mounds and dry channels, but otherwise featureless. To navigate by night, elaborate direction-finding methods were used by the lead unit under sapper Captain Mason, whose staff 'checked the dead reckoning with a bicycle wheel, three pedometers and an improvised pace-stick'. Though the need for improvisation at this stage may appear worrying, these worked well enough. Despite delays caused by late arrivals at the assembly point, congestion owing to the decision to take the transport along amidst the marching infantry, and Kemball's hesitation over whether to leave his field ambulance behind, the march has been called 'probably unique in British military history'. The columns whose task was to get round to the south of the Dujaila redoubt did not quite manage to deploy for the assault under cover of darkness as the plan required, but they did achieve surprise.

It might have been decisive. As dawn broke just before 6 a.m., the Dujaila redoubt could be clearly seen some 4,000 yards north-west of the leading troops of the 36th Brigade. The Turks seemed to have no idea they were there. Colonel Leachman had got into the redoubt during the night and found it empty. Colonel Watson took his 26th Punjabis forward; but his column commander had other ideas. Kemball laboured under two disadvantages. His force was made up of units from three different divisions, brought together at the last moment for the operation; he and his scratch staff did not know their subordinate commanders. They were also saddled with extremely detailed instructions from Aylmer. Kemball had been tricked too often by Turkish trenches and their hidden occupants to allow his troops to go forward across a bare plain in daylight. He pulled Watson back, and shortly afterwards, at 7 a.m., Aylmer himself decided that the enemy 'could hardly have failed to discern from their commanding redoubts' the British forces to their east. He assumed that surprise must already have been lost, and the assaulting infantry must wait while the planned artillery preparation went ahead. ('Stick to programme', was his terse instruction to Kemball.) This caution was understandable, but fatal. The artillery preparation took three hours. As before, it stampeded the Arab cavalry and transport behind the Ottoman lines. Edmund Candler found it 'comforting to watch this black line streaming across the plain towards their bridgehead on the Shatt-el-Hai. But there was that other stream less comforting to witness, the stream of infantry which poured in from all points of the position to reinforce the redoubt.' Amir Singh drily observed that 'our officers ought to have known from our experience in France that guns do not do much harm to troops that are well dug in'.[3]

When Kemball's attack finally began, three hours later, Halil had been able to shift forces to his right flank. His position was still dangerous, but as before it would be saved by the tenacity of his infantry. The realisation of failure dawned on Aylmer painfully slowly. At 11 a.m. Kemball sent him a message indicating that he was making satisfactory progress; and it was not until Aylmer directly asked him to push his troops in to seize the Dujaila redoubt – so that Keary's column could go forward, according to plan – that he realised that his leading troops were still 2,000 yards away from it. By early afternoon it was clear that the artillery bombardment had been ineffective, and the infantry were stuck. The attackers now faced an almost impossible task, but Aylmer decided to press on all the same: he ordered Keary's column forward across two miles of open ground. Candler, who had just ridden over to Keary's HQ when the advance began, was aghast at the decision. 'It is hard to speak of the order for the assault in dispassionate terms. It did not seem possible that the position could be carried after the earlier repulses. Nothing had changed except that our troops were exhausted – theirs, encouraged and reinforced . . . it seemed that all those lives were being devoted as an extenuation of a blunder in command.'[4]

In the end 8th Brigade actually got a foothold in the redoubt, and two lines of trenches were taken, but at crushing cost. The brigade would lose half its strength. 'Two Brigades before ours had already attacked the Redoubt in the early afternoon and failed to get near it,' wrote Captain C. D. Noyes of the 2nd Rajputs. 'At 4.30pm we were sent to take it at all costs. The Manchesters and 59th were put in the front attacking line – we were in support and the 47th in Brigade Reserve. The ground was a perfect billiard table with no cover at all for 2 miles . . . After advancing 100 yards we deployed into line – the men working just like clockwork. We never halted or fired a round during the advance and the men were being knocked over like ninepins from shrapnel, maxims and rifle fire. When we got to within 800 yards of the position we started a steady double – the men cheering like blazes though they were sadly depleted in numbers. We were soon all mixed up with the Manchesters and by the time the Redoubt was reached I don't think there were more than 100 of them and 50 of ours who got into the Turkish trenches.'[5]

A desperate struggle for those trenches went on for hours, but after the attackers ran out of grenades the outcome was inevitable. Column A never reached the southern line of Turkish trenches. And the cavalry brigade was once again missing. This time it may have been the vagueness of their orders – to 'operate' on the left flank – that was partly to blame, but without definite objectives the powerful (and expensive, in precious supply tonnage) cavalry force achieved 'little more than their usual swan round the open desert'.[6] Wilson, quoting a 'high authority' to the effect that 'they hovered about in an ineffective way, usually somewhat in rear of the infantry, and always moving either with great deliberation or not at all', thought that 'had they been capably led' they might have 'turned the scale in our favour'. As it was, they were never worth the heavy demands they made on the transport system.[7]

The inevitable retirement began at dawn on 9 March. The official explanation was lack of water – which only made it worse for those like Crowdy who thought it should have been easier to get forward to the Hai for water than to go back. If there was any consolation, as far as the well-informed Chalmers could see, it was that 'the arrangements for the wounded were for the first time in the campaign very good'. They were 'put in great 4-wheeled carts drawn by 6 horses . . . the ambulances from France have some idea of a bundobust. There are dozens of doctors floating around camp now and plenty of personnel.' On the 10th 'they were loading up the ships with the wounded without the rush or confusion it has hitherto been usual to have, and each ship has 2 medical officers and a complete staff whose sole job is going down in charge of a convoy of wounded'.

It is hard not to echo Edmund Candler's verdict on the battle for Dujaila. 'Nothing had been gained to balance our loss' – indeed the reverse: 'we had put up a most formidable obstacle to our next advance, heartening the Turk and demonstrating what was in our mind by the half-hearted and tentative rehearsal of an act which should have been carried out with our whole strength.' Or his later question: 'what would have happened if we had marched straight on Kut on the morning of the 8th?' Such a bold move would 'probably have thrown the Turk into confusion. For, stubborn sticker as he is, he had never shown any enterprise or initiative in attack, or organised discipline in the manipulation of a large force in the open.'[8] In combat, the British infantry were unquestionably superior (as demonstrated in a brilliant little fight by the Connaught Rangers to secure Thorny Nullah after the retreat on 10 March) and their artillery superiority was equally marked. So even though an advance south of Dujaila would have exposed the British to a flank attack – 'dead against the manual' – the Sixth Army's capacity to mount one was negligible. And could the risk have been worse than the repetition of frontal attacks? The British 'had been consistently playing into [the Turks'] hands with these attacks, and no force which could conceivably be brought up the river in time could make good the wastage involved in each new assault'.[9]

Back in camp on 11 March, Catty fumed about the 'desperately costly & ineffectual effort to relieve Kut. It ought to have been a success & it turned out almost a disaster.' The approach march had been 'excellently well carried out & well led so that at 5am we reached our post of deployment without a shot being fired or anyone knowing we were there. We had to all intents & purposes won the battle as the Turks were asleep in their camps 2–3 miles back; their trenches were empty & the redoubt only weakly held.' Then came 'the awful delay of 3 hours', which Catty found inexplicable. ('I'm told 2 hrs were wasted while the Artillery registered.') When the attack finally began the enemy had inevitably recovered from their surprise and 'poured in troops'. For Catty, it was clear that the plan had been too complicated. 'The orders issued by the Corps Cdr were too detailed & laid down exactly what every one was to do. Brigadiers' initiative was cramped.' Fraser's verdict was bleak: 'The centralised direction of operations was a hideous failure.'[10] The official historian agreed, though more guardedly, allowing that Aylmer had attributed earlier failures to the mistakes of his subordinates. For Catty, there was another villain: the tyrannous Chief of Staff. 'Such is the fear of Gorringe that no one dared stand up against him. As someone said, "Unless you have £1000 a year of your own & are a prize fighter, you can't stand up against Gorringe." Altho' any Brigade could have taken the redoubt, no one dared order it.' Crowdy judged Kemball harshly for his lack of initiative: 'he was not fitted to command the force, though he would probably have made an excellent private soldier.' But he found it hard to understand why Aylmer, 'having succeeded in concentrating six brigades unobserved against his enemy's flank, only put in half of them, and these went in in succession'. He frankly suggested that Aylmer had 'lost his nerve' when events departed from his plan. 'The ordinary fellow would probably have done the same, but one had a right to expect one's commander to be above the average.'[11]

Townshend has been criticised for his scathing comments on the relief effort, but there were many in Kut who felt the same. Major J. W. Nelson of the West Kents lamented that 'it is very bitter to know that we could have been relieved if only they had come on, and not sat down for 12 hours', bluntly charging that 'this is not the way the IEFD used to attack'.[12] Spackman wrote that 'we in the Kut trenches were wont to complain, "Townshend would have got through. Why don't they pick him up in an aeroplane and put him in command down there?"'[13] General Mellis – unusually sensitive for a senior officer – gloomily wrote to his wife, 'Aylmer has failed allright & has withdrawn to the place where he started from. He reports his casualties heavy & also that the Turks suffered very severe losses . . . It is sad to think of our poor fellows lives thrown away in a vain effort & that we could not help them.' Noting that 'Aylmer says he will try again', he added that he had 'had a talk with Townsend [*sic*] & urged him to tell Aylmer not to attempt it again until he had got up every man & gun that there is in the country and that we are prepared to starve to give him all the time it was possible. I hope he has done so & means to stick to it.' Mellis appears to have had his suspicions not only of Townshend but also of the senior medical officer who had advised on the 'bedrock' of rations below which 'we can't go'. 'I am not too sure & am going to urge Townshend to look into the matter . . . I feel we could do on less food than this & so perhaps save another week of <u>time</u>. I hate to think of our poor fellows having to attack again until they can do so in great strength.'[14]

Two months after the battle, Major Crowdy was able to go forward and inspect the Dujaila redoubt. There were 'trenches cut on both sides of the mound, really a buried city'. The defenders had dug up heaps of bricks and used them for revetting, amongst them blue glazed tiles from Babylon. The Turkish trenches were 'narrow and inconvenient, but practically invisible'. Standing on the mound, he could see Kut itself. He mused on 'the feelings of General Townshend' on the morning after the battle, 'when from the minaret he could see us retreating from the Turks, and the Turks retreating from us! It really brings home to one the great tragedy of this terrible exhibition of bad generalship which we have provided for the benefit of military historians.'[15]

10. Failure

> This last part of the siege was a bad time, hungry, sick,
> overworked. Biting flies and mosquitoes increased apace. Our
> dead stank, dead Turks stank. Never can I forget the <u>cats</u>, starved
> of course, eating dead Turks & feeding out of their skeletons.
> Diarrhoea began & fever, scurvy got worse.
> ERNEST WALKER

> The fish have left Kut. I wonder that even the birds don't fly
> away . . .
> EDWARD MOUSLEY

By the time Mellis wrote this, Aylmer was gone. His cautious
misjudgement at the opening of his great attack, followed by
an almost reckless attempt at frontal assault, had cost his corps
nearly 3,500 casualties. Edgar Bridges could not 'quite see why'
he had been pushed out: 'the plan was an excellent one and
failed because his subordinates failed him.' But he admitted
that 'he was a fearful old dodderer'.[1] How far should he be
held responsible for the decisive failure of 8 March? Whatever
Bridges thought, there can be no doubt that it was Aylmer who
selected Kemball (who had never worked with the units placed
under him) to command the key movement, and issued the
fatal 'stick to programme' order delaying the infantry advance
on Dujaila. But there seems to be some doubt whether the
plan was entirely his. The appointment of Gorringe as Chief
of Staff may (as Barker speculates) have reflected some loss of
confidence in Aylmer on the part of the new C-in-C, Sir Percy
Lake.

Lake's arrival in Mesopotamia made a difference to the
efficiency of the supply chain from Basra to the front: Buchanan
was at last given some scope for action, and plans were initiated

for a light railway from Basra to Amara. But as far as operational command went, the old arrangement persisted. Lake went up to the front briefly in late January, then returned to Basra. After the battle, Robertson fretted that 'it has always seemed to me that Lake himself ought to command at front in view of importance of operations'; instead he 'assumes part of Inspector of Communications'. Duff wrote that he could not 'understand why Lake should have sat still at Basra instead of being present personally to direct the most important phase of the operations', adding bluntly, 'it is not the troops who have failed us, but the generals in command'.[2] But though Lake left Aylmer in nominal command, he provided him with a (possibly less than welcome) minder in Gorringe, who seems to have been the brains behind both the 'reconnaissance in force' of 22 February and the Dujaila operation. Moreover, Lake interfered – perhaps fatally – in setting the timetable for the offensive which he elected not to command in person. Aylmer wanted to wait for the full deployment of the 13th Division. This, the only all-British division to go to Mesopotamia, would have created a decisive advantage. Duff, as we have seen, encouraged this. But Lake argued that the risk of flood would increase, and set a deadline of 15 March.

In the event, the weather in early March was atrocious but got much better in the latter part of the month – 'delightful weather', Chalmers recorded, with 'good grass growing all over the plain showing that it only requires water to make what appears to be desert good farming land'.[3] In fact the conditions for offensive action were now as good as could be hoped for, but instead the shattered Tigris Corps spent the time painfully regrouping under a new commander. Aylmer was replaced, inevitably, by the fire-eating Gorringe. But the painful regrouping (in which mangled regiments were brigaded in hybrid battalions such as the 'Huffs' – Hampshires and Buffs – and the 'Norsets' – Norfolks and Dorsets) showed the dangerous attenuation of the available attacking strength. For all Lake's belated efforts, too many resources remained stuck at Basra. And by the time Gorringe could think about moving forward again, the weather had turned once more. Gorringe tacitly acknowledged the logic of Candler's critique by abandoning the attempt to advance on the right bank, but only to return to the head-on assault on the left. He waited almost a month, while the river inexorably rose and the spring floods spread, narrowing the viable ground on either bank. His corps was at last reinforced with another division, the 13th, whose core were Gallipoli veterans, and whose commander, Stanley Maude, was thought 'a good man' by Leachman. Most importantly, in the eyes of many, the 13th was a British division. (Chalmers thought they looked 'quite fit but not very military in the old sense of the word'. But he allowed that 'though not well disciplined they may be able to work together'.)

The new assault on Hanna was probably the best-prepared yet, with the advantage of the first systematic air reconnaissance. Maude's operational plans were assiduously rehearsed. Shortly before the attack, he 'explained to us that all that was necessary was a bayonet rush, a mighty British cheer, and we were through to starving Townshend in Kut'. As Private Roe of the East Lancs (38th Brigade) recorded, 'we discussed the General after dismissal and came to the conclusion he was a born optimist'.[4] When the assault went in on 5 April, though, things went extraordinarily well at first. 'Only a few stray and ill-aimed shots greet us instead of the hail of lead which we expected, and the first two lines of trenches were taken with trifling loss.' In fact, the Turks had pulled back. Then war's black comedy set in. 'On meeting with no opposition our officers lost their heads, and instead of remaining for the stipulated twenty minutes in the captured Turkish trenches, flourished their revolvers and yelled "Come on boys, we've got them on the run! We won't stop until we get to Kut."' They went forward 'in what we call in army slang "columns of lumps", the grandest target an artillery or machine gun commander could wish for'. They were duly slaughtered: 'men were sent to Kingdom Come in bundles of eight by our howitzers and river monitors'.[5] The official history, unsurprisingly, told a different story, merely noting that 'a further immediate advance was rendered impossible by the fire of the British artillery, who, being unable in the dim light to distinguish the infantry signals, did not lift their fire until about 5.35 am'.

Roe blamed the regimental officers for the confusion, but Major Crowdy blamed the higher commanders, once again. 'As at Dujaila, the programme was carried right through regardless of the fact that there were no enemy at Hannah.' The half-hour artillery bombardment of the third line (timed to start three minutes after the assault began) was not suspended, even though the 13th Division was already moving on through the targeted trenches. Capturing them was an empty triumph, as Roe reflected. 'The Turks sold us another pup and withdrew all their men and guns before the fight as they knew they could not hold it without heavy loss. They preferred taking up another position at Sannaiyat and forcing us to attack again across the open.' Still, by the standards of the last three months, this counted as success. Fraser noted that 'in January, February and March we paid the penalty over and over again' for disregarding the lessons of the present war, 'but still Gorringe, Aylmer, Lake & Co would not believe'. On 5 April, at last, 'correct methods were adopted with the immediate reward of success'.[6]

But the next attacks at Falahiyeh and Sannaiyat reverted to pattern. The 7th Division was pushed on towards Falahiyeh overnight on the 5th, but it had to advance through the 13th, which was being pulled back. The inevitable confusion on a particularly dark night delayed the planned dawn assault. 'The blame for this muddle', Crowdy believed, lay at the door of the corps staff. 'There was a very complicated move' involving two divisions, 'carried out in the dark over unreconnoitred ground, known to be cut up by trenches, dugouts, and shell-holes.' Yet 'not a single officer of the corps staff was present to superintend the manoeuvre'. No attempt had been made to prepare material for crossing the Falahiyeh trenches, or to reconnoitre the routes forward. 'It seems incredible, but none the less it is a fact.' The commander of the 7th Division, Younghusband, should have stopped the attack as soon as he realised it was too late to get into position under cover of darkness, but 'he made no attempt to stop the impending massacre'. Crowdy angrily declared that this 'moral cowardice' marked all the commanders. Kemball refused even to get his brigade into open formation for the attack: as a result it was shattered, reduced from 2,500 to 693 effectives. 'The gallant, broken, and patched-up battalions of the 7th Division', detailed to lead the assault so as to spare the 13th for what was expected to be the crucial battle for Es Sinn, 'were called upon once more to illustrate the impossible, to advance in broad daylight on an entrenched position without gun preparation over a perfectly open plain.'[7]

Worse was to follow at Sannaiyat. Gorringe decided that the floods made any large-scale attempt to outflank the defenders round the Suweida marsh unviable, and did not even send a small force to attempt it. The 13th Division went forward in a frontal assault once again on 9 April. It had 650 yards of open ground to cross; when it was about two-thirds of the way there, the defenders sent up Very lights. Chalmers watched the advance from his bridge: 'I had a good view of our troops moving forward first in column and then in extended order; then long rushes and the line would disappear as it dropped flat. As they drew nearer the rushes were by two and threes and finally even one at a time would spring up and make a dash for the nearest bit of cover ahead; all the while the storm of musketry cut them down.' What followed was, as the official history admitted, 'panic . . . rendering a great part of the division temporarily impotent'.

The 13th Division lost 3,600 men at Hanna, Falahiyeh and Sannaiyat, no less than 46 per cent of its strength actually engaged. 'The field at Falahiyeh was one of the saddest sights I have ever seen,' Candler thought. 'Men who last year had been wheeling barrows, painting doors, singing in the choir, bringing round the milk, lay there in a solid square of dead in this cursed alien mud. I shall never see a man asleep in a field again without thinking of them.'[8] Crowdy was less compassionate about the failure at Sannaiyat. He believed that a 'sauve qui peut' had begun as soon as the leading troops were fired on, and that the British troops were just not good enough. It was 'very depressing – we now know that the 13th Division is a wash-out'. He would eventually change his mind, but not before another critical failure had occurred.

In response to a direct order from Lake, Gorringe now tried another advance on the right bank. It seemed obvious to many besides Lake that the Ottoman position on the left bank was too strong to carry by frontal assault, but the other bank was still promising. ('With any ordinary luck we ought to do it this time,' Crowdy hoped.) Sticking closer to the river than the previous thrust at Dujaila, the aim now was to break though the trench lines at Beit Isa and Chahela. But the weather put on an ultra-Mesopotamian show: torrential rain fell, and fierce gales shifted the marshes bodily into the British front-line trenches. The Turks added to the problem by breaking the Tigris embankments at Beit Isa and Umm al-Bahram; every day before the battle, and during it, the fighting troops had to spend hours digging and repairing flood defences. The attack was delayed for two days to allow the muddy ground to dry out. This might have been a good thing if replacement troops had been arriving in any numbers, but the river transport could still barely cope with supplying the corps. At least 5,000 replacements were available, but could not get up past Amara.

At last the assault began on 17 April, with a 'ferocious bombardment of Beit Eisa *à la Français*', as Barnett, a 3rd Division medical officer, recorded. He believed that Keary had 'refused to attack unless he had a free hand and good reconnaissance. Result – capture of whole position and small losses.' Actually, however good Keary's reconnaissance was, there was, as usual, serious confusion amongst the assaulting units as they went forward across ground still flooded to knee depth. But by rushing ahead of the artillery barrage they succeeded in seizing the front trenches while the defenders were still taking cover. 'For the first time since I was in the country did our men get into the Turks with the bayonet,' Crowdy noted. The result was a 'massacre'. Barnett believed that Keary wanted to push on immediately, but Gorringe said no. ('Obstinate mule,' he fumed.) The first objective, a series of old canals a mile behind the Beit Isa line, had been reached, and an elaborate process of replacing the 3rd Division units at the front by the 13th Division began.

The first phase was a clear success. Gorringe himself was 'pleased' with the operation, according to Fraser, 'but obviously jealous' of Keary. ('What a mean character!'⁹) But now the enemy acted untypically. During the night, Halil responded to the British seizure of Beit Isa with the most determined counter-attack yet, raking up as many as 10,000 men including the 'Constantinople Division' (the 2nd). 'This heavy counter-offensive had been quite unexpected,' according to the official history. The enemy 'had never before attempted a counter-attack with such a large force, so well organised and sustained, or carried through with such vigour and determination'. 'They came on magnificently,' Crowdy noted admiringly. Five successive Turkish assaults failed to dislodge the 8th Brigade around the 'Twin Pimples', but the 7th Brigade near Beit Isa itself suffered badly. ('Gurkhas bad – ran away – also all black doctors!' Barnett wrote.) There was official talk of an 'unauthorised order to withdraw', but Chalmers's impression was starker. 'The Brigade that broke, the 7th, seems to have lost most of their machine guns' – fifteen were lost – 'and one officer is reported to have shot 4 or 5 men running away. Incidentally he arrived at the D[ivisional] HQ and reported that he was the sole survivor of the brigade staff, which was found to be incorrect as they were holding the Turks in some trenches, even the brigadier being reduced to throwing bombs.'

The counter-attackers suffered gruesome losses, but they decisively checked the British. Though it was clear as day broke on the 18th that the Turks had fallen back from the Beit Isa position, they hung on at 'Point Z' until the evening of the 20th. The scale of the British casualties – 3rd Division was reduced to 4,347 rifles and the 13th to about 5,500 – put an end to the intended advance. Crowdy, though, was still convinced that if only Gorringe had trusted Keary, and 'had we only had some decent troops in place of the 13th Division, we could have walked into Chahela at any time' on the 18th. This was, for him, the second time that the unit the *Daily Mail* had christened the 'Iron Division' had 'let us down'. He believed that a 'magnificent opportunity' had opened up when 3rd Division saw that the Turkish attacks were weakening. Early on the 18th there were no Turks left, apart from the remnants of 35th Division. But Maude did not take the opportunity: he 'knew his men were unable to do it'. Evidence of their inadequacy was plain to see as they advanced. 'As at Falahiyeh and Sannaiyat', Crowdy witheringly alleged, 'the ground behind them was littered with rifles, spare parts of machine guns, and other oddments not required for a move to the rear.' Once again, though, the main culprit was Gorringe. He might be forgiven for lacking 'that Heaven sent spark of genius which marks the great soldier'; but he was a man of mediocre abilities who did not grasp his own limitations – 'he rates himself too high'. 'He seems incapable of allowing for what the enemy may do.'[10]

'I think – so do most – that Kut is doomed and this was our last chance,' Barnett wrote. Yet even now the way to Kut seems to have been still open, at least according to Major Catty's account of a 3rd Division operation, not mentioned in the official history. 'On the 19th strong patrols were pushed forward to the Sinn line & fired on [the retiring Turks] from the Sinn Abtar redoubt. As the Turks were evidently going the Corps Comd. ordered 3rd Div to concentrate & with Cav. Bde & 36th Bde to make a reconnaissance in force against the Dujaila.' Not only did this reconnaissance find the Dujaila redoubt unoccupied, it pushed on another six miles to the Imam al-Mansur tomb. 'It was a blazing hot day – 107 degrees by the river was the official temperature

– & no water was found en route. With their heavy full marching order the men felt the heat terribly – up to Dujaila only a few fell out but the second half of the march – done during the hottest part of the day – was disasterous [*sic*]. The road was strewn with men in the last stages of exhaustion. Approximately 600 fell out & the rest were so bad they couldn't have done anything had we been attacked.' The wells at Imam al-Mansur were dry, and apart from some chaotic attempts to fetch water from the river five miles away, the force stayed waterless all night. In the morning it marched to the river and took up a line from Magasis to the Dujaila redoubt. This remarkable movement had been carried out almost without opposition – all the problems, as Catty acidly observed, were due to 'bad bundobust'. 'What the reason for the long & exhausting march to Imam al-Mansur on 20th was I don't know. It achieved nothing & so knocked up the Division that for days after it wasn't worth a damn . . . I shan't forget that march for a long time, it's one of the worst I've ever done. As is usually the case in this country our advance was rushed & so nearly all the bundobust broke down.' Keary fulminated on 22 April that 'the latest Reuter today said "General Gorringe has <u>carried</u> the Dujaila Redoubt". . . this is the operation when I <u>walked</u> into abandoned Redoubts not firing a shot or fixing bayonets.' It had been 'much on a par with our retirement for want of water on 9 March – beaten. In that affair (like Colenso 1899)', he added, 'the troops were not beaten but the brains' – there was 'no provision for the enemy not doing what you <u>hope</u> he will do'.[11]

In spite of the remarkable position secured by 3rd Division, Gorringe threw his last effective force, 7th Division, in a do-or-die assault on Sannaiyat. The Sannaiyat position was believed by the Turks, and many others, to be virtually impregnable, all the more so since at this point high winds were driving the marsh in the no-man's-land between the British and Turkish lines southwards into the 7th Division's trenches. Gorringe seems to have thought that Halil had stripped the Sannaiyat defences to feed the great counter-attack at Beit Isa. But the forces Gorringe had left were alarmingly weak, and still few replacements were arriving. Though it had the 13th Division behind it, the 7th Division was under-strength – mustering fewer than 6,000 men. It had, as a staff officer pithily put it, been 'hammered'. Even this meagre force was reduced as the attack began on 22 April. One of the two assaulting brigades was (or claimed to be) unable to move because the flood water was too deep. It was confined to 'supporting' the other in a situation where, as Crowdy said, the only meaningful support was an attack. So the 19th Brigade staggered forward alone across the shell-pocked, semi-flooded marshland – a 'deepish quagmire' in which men sank up to their armpits. It drifted to the right to avoid the swampy ground and ran into flooded trenches without any equipment for crossing them. Men fell in, their rifles clogging with mud. In spite of the conditions, two battalions got as far as the second trench line, but a series of counter-attacks pushed them back. 'When the Turks formed up to counter-attack, only a man here and there could fire his rifle.' The turning point seems to have come when the scratch unit called up to support the 92nd Punjabis, the 'English Composite Battalion', finding the water impossibly deep, began an unauthorised retirement which the Punjabis had to follow. Then 'the whole line began to crumble backwards'.[12] A machine-gun officer of the 21st Brigade said that the men falling back were 'so demoralised that many were crying and pulling off their clothes from sheer funk'. Captain H. Davson of the 82nd Punjabis wearily wrote on 23 April, 'It is always the water that defeats us . . . I really do not see how we are to get through. The Turks are very strongly entrenched. Their positions are invisible until you come under a murderous fire.'[13]

'There will always be two contradictory views about Sannaiyat,' Candler thought. 'The general impression is that of a tragic impasse, hopeless physical odds in which the flood put the final veto on the undertaking. This is likely to be the tradition.' But an odd incident, when the Turks raised two Red Crescent flags and sent medical officers out from their third line to attend to their wounded, led some to believe that 'the back of the enemy's resistance was broken' and victory was still possible.[14] Candler reported that a supporting brigade, 'pushed in over the enemy's first and second lines while they were being held by the 19th Brigade, might have carried the third Turkish line with the bayonet'. Many of the Highlanders in the composite battalion made up of the Black Watch and the Seaforths told him they could have done it. Davson, with the Punjabis, had 'got into the Turkish two front lines', and even though they found they could not use their rifles as 'everything was under water', he thought that 'we could have stuck to what we got but when he was getting the worst of it [the Turk] asked for an armistice . . . an opportunity was lost'.[15] For Crowdy, the ease with which the first attackers got through 'shows that we could have made good, had we only been prepared to back them up properly'.

To observers on the other side of the river 'to whom the terrible havoc among the Turks was visible it was our withdrawal which seemed inexplicable'. Many found it hard to understand why, with five brigades available, only 1,800 troops in all went forward into the attack. Brigadier Arthur Lewin of the 40th Brigade – judged by many to be one of the best commanders in the force – raised a different issue. As he later wrote to the official historian, he thought that 'when the last ounce was demanded from the men' at Sannaiyat, brigadiers should have led their commands in person. This might, he believed, have tilted the balance. But though the idea was 'urgently represented to the Divisional Commander', he refused to sanction it.[16]

The fighting between 17 and 23 April struck Davson 'as a good example of a question I had in my Military History paper in my exam for promotion: "Order, counter-order, disorder. Comment on this as regards the French infantry in August 1870." Enough said!'[17] Keary himself reflected on 22 April, 'I believe the door to Kut has been opened three times by [the 3rd] Division but advantage has never been able to be taken of the chances. On the late advance I had three lines of trenches to capture and took them all as well as subsidiary lines of covering outposts &c, we finished with a grand battle of the 17–18 April when Halil Pasha threw in the whole of his strength on to my Division.' Had there been any reserve behind him 'we must have walked through into Kut and routed the Turks to Baghdad or further'. But, as he later wrote, 'I don't believe the [relief] force was ever sufficient in numbers or material for the job.'[18]

The Kut garrison was now on its last legs: 'the soles of your feet hurt if you walked or stood, the shoulders and back if you lay down, and the seat if you sat.'[19] A symbolic loss was one of the division's four brigade commanders, General Hoghton, who was taken suddenly ill in the evening of 11 April and died within a few hours – possibly from eating the weeds often used as a vegetable substitute in Kut cuisine. The floods which hampered Gorringe's attacks were the last straw for many in Kut. 'How fit I was until these wretched floods,' the habitually cheerful Mousley wrote on 14 April. 'I don't remember feeling worse.' Ten days later, 'my legs are shockingly thin, less than my arms were, and I can fold my skin round my legs'.[20] The Indian troops were especially debilitated by a long period without meat. The long saga of their resistance to eating horsemeat had gone on through February and March. Spackman noted that some sepoys committed suicide rather than eat horse. 'Poor devils I don't know how they live,' an officer of the 76th Punjabis wrote on 3 April. 'I don't wonder at them clearing off when the pangs of hunger come on extra strong, yet it is their own fault.' A week later, men were still 'most obstinate about the meat question. The Sikhs have taken to [horsemeat] but the Jhats and Mohadins absolutely refuse to have anything to do with it.' All the Indian officers had promised to eat it in front of their companies, which seems to have finally done the trick. (On the 13th, the 'whole regiment are eating meat now'.)

Was this a religious issue? Townshend's reluctance to issue a direct order to all his troops to eat horsemeat clearly stemmed from his anxiety about the fragility of morale. It showed again how British fears of provoking fanaticism could lead to exaggerated deference to Muslim sentiments. The ruling-class folk-memory of the cartridges that had sparked the great Indian 'Mutiny' lived on. The official historian pointed out that 'anyone with experience of the power and influence which caste, religion and tradition exercise in India will understand the difficulties and dangers in issuing such an order, especially if there was any chance of it not being universally obeyed'. Still, Townshend's senior brigade commanders, Mellis and Delamain, both in close touch with the Indian troops, were both in favour of issuing a direct order. They later criticised Townshend's optimistic communiqués for 'strengthening the men in their refusal to eat horseflesh', since they continually held out hope of early relief.[21]

Many regimental officers believed that the issue was one of novelty rather than principle. 'All castes were greatly prejudiced against eating horse flesh,' Phillips wrote: 'it had never been done before. The religious motive was however the one put forward until it was proved false . . . it was only in the face of actual starvation that they finally agreed to do so, but even then each regiment feared to be the one to set the example.'[22] Sandes thought that 'the Mohammedans of the smaller units refused to touch horseflesh because their co-religionists of the Indian regiments had not yet done so'. But, as he noted, Hindus had also refused the novel diet. Major Walker of the IMS recorded that even when 'the British and Mohammedans ate the horse, all Hindus (except Gurkhas) so far had refused, & GOC instead of <u>ordering</u> them to eat it issued various high flown appeals & got all sorts of Rajahs and Brahmins in India to send wireless messages promising religious absolution'. A rough calculation suggested to him that 'we could have held out for another month if the Hindus had given way from the beginning'.[23]

The only hope that remained was that extra supplies could allow them to hold out a little longer. They had already witnessed the world's first attempt to supply an army by air, beginning with the first dropping of a parcel on 31 January. But though a great variety of supplies were dropped over the following weeks – including money, drugs, machinery, newspapers, gramophone needles, fishing nets (for an attempt by Major Sandes to improve on the random dynamiting of fish) and even a granite millstone, by April it was clear that the weight of food that could be delivered this way was never going to add more than an odd day's endurance to the garrison. Sandes watched the first big sacks of flour fall on 15 April. 'The loads were slung below the fusillage [*sic*] and, when released at 6,000 feet, fell turning over and over slowly and leaving an aerial trail of flour till they plunged with dull thuds onto the plain near the Brick Kilns.' Surprisingly, 'the loads stood the shock of impact well and not much flour was lost'. On the assumption that the bigger aircraft could carry 300 pounds of flour, and that sixteen trips per day by six aircraft could deliver some 5,000 pounds altogether, the project looked feasible. But in the event, not only were there never enough aircraft, it was found that the problem of carrying flour was not so much its weight as its bulk. Crucially, also, anything like consistent accuracy was beyond the skill of the pilots, especially those of the RNAS whose seaplanes became notorious for depositing supplies in the river. (The engineer Sandes disapprovingly noted that the modifications to their wing design that would have given the pilots a downward view were 'for some reason not carried out'.[24])

Lieutenant McNeal took a less charitable view of this experiment than some later writers. He was sure that 'if the matter had been taken seriously and the work done systematically, we should have been able to hold out for some considerable time longer, as there was no scarcity of ammunition'. But once again there was a failure of organisation and command: 'the food-dropping was done in such a desultory way and started so late that it only gave us an additional two days' rations.'[25] (An interesting perspective on the airlift is provided by one of 6th Division's urgent requests – 'Kindly send by aeroplane as much carbon, foolscap and rice paper as you can spare. Our stock here is almost exhausted.'[26] Such are the necessities of modern military staffs.)

On 10 April, facing the fact that although Gorringe could of course 'in time' force his way through, he could not do it in the next week, Lake made the remarkable suggestion that Townshend should buy more time by expelling the Arab inhabitants of Kut. Townshend had more than once grumbled about his initial mistake in not evacuating them (which, as we have seen, he blamed on Cox), but now he rejected the idea as inhumane. The besiegers, fully aware of the reasons for sending them out, would be certain to use force to keep the civil population inside. Already several groups of Arabs who had tried to escape across the river had been shot down. Townshend dismissed the possibility either of herding the people out across the flooded northern trench lines, or of loading them into the thirty remaining *mahelas* and sailing them out to face the Ottoman artillery. He slightly undermined his humanitarian argument, though, by implying that, even if the Arabs could be removed, the improvement in food supply would be marginal. And the fact that the people were becoming steadily more disorderly as they grew more desperate – in the following week there would be several minor riots and stampedes as rumours of the fall of Kut multiplied – may have made him wonder whether it would in any case be physically possible to round them up and expel them.

The final act of the siege was a desperate attempt to run in 240 tons (enough to support the garrison for three weeks) by river. 'A forlorn hope', as Candler wanly noted, 'bitterly criticised: but a gallant adventure in the best manner of our ancestors.' When he heard of the plan, Chalmers wondered whether the ship chosen, the *Julnar*, was the best choice. It could only make 5 mph against the current, so would take five hours to get to Kut. Navigated by Charlie Cowley of the *Mejidieh*, there was 'just a possibility of its getting through', but he thought there would be 'more chance of success if the *Mantis* which steams 17 knots were sent. She has watertight compartments and bullet-proof sides.' There was also, he worried, 'the possibility of a wire cable having been put across the river by the Turks in the last few days'.

Sadly, it was more than a possibility. Anderson in Kut was called to HQ by the artillery commander on 23 April 'and told of a plan, which was to be kept secret, for a supreme effort to be made to get food through to us from down river'. The garrison artillery were to assist by shelling the Turkish trenches opposite the point of arrival (in line with the brick kilns) where the *Julnar* was to be unloaded before daybreak. It was too late to register the guns that day, but then the operation was postponed for twenty-four hours, and they registered ('with as few rounds as possible') on the 24th. 'About 8pm we stood to at the guns with lamps lighted on the aiming posts and waited anxiously. The officers were the only people who had definite knowledge of what was on, but the preparations of course enabled others to make a shrewd guess. After an hour or two an outburst of firing was to be heard down river and it gradually came nearer. Our feelings were tense. Then Very's lights were seen and in addition to rifle fire a gun joined in and then there was silence. We waited for a while and our hearts sank. There could be only one explanation.' Next morning they could see the *Julnar* stranded beside Magasis fort, and the 5-inch guns shelled her 'to try and prevent the Turks getting the benefit of her cargo, but she was practically beyond their limit and they were unsuccessful'.[27]

'What fools our staff are,' Barnett raged. 'For weeks before they were talking about it and every Arab knew of it and so did the Turks. Also we knew there was a cable but boat took nothing to cut it.' (The ship's chief engineer believed that the cable was for an ordinary ferry, 'not laid down with the intention of stopping the Julnar'.)[28] Barnett's verdict was stark: 'Gorringe should be shot.' Instead that fate met Cowley, who had long predicted that if he was captured by the Turks he would be executed, since they regarded him as a traitor.

'So we have failed,' Brigadier Fraser wrote bitterly in his diary. The relief efforts had cost 23,000 casualties – almost exactly the whole fighting strength of the Tigris Corps at the end of April, and twice the number of the Kut garrison itself. Who was to blame? Was anyone – or was it just the impossibility of the conditions? Problems that were inescapable, but – as some argued – aggravated by Townshend's behaviour. Or perhaps simple bad luck? Major-General Money, though he doted on his wife, ticked her off sharply when she suggested that the relief force could be exonerated for its failure. 'We none of us want "exonerating", thank you,' he snapped. (Adding, 'except perhaps the Government of India'.) 'The utmost we ever said was that the chances of success or failure were very evenly balanced . . . with a little luck we'd have done it on two occasions.' This would not do for the exasperated Fraser, who had no doubt where the fault lay: 'Kut could have been relieved by a good – or even a respectable general.' Instead the relief was commanded by a man who was 'loathed and distrusted' – and with good reason. 'The troops have been thrown away in driblets,' he fumed. 'Every principle of war has been disregarded.' Gorringe (he could not even write the name without adding 'd—n him!') and his staff had caused more vexation to their own army than the enemy's. Worst of all, they were dishonest: 'to cover the failure, the truth about our operations has been systematically concealed.'[29]

11. Surrender

This comes of negotiating with starvation at the gate.
CHARLES TOWNSHEND

Negotiating surrender was a complicated process; there were big issues at stake. After the failure of the Dujaila attempt in early March, Halil had offered to discuss terms, flatteringly assuring Townshend, 'you have heroically accomplished your military duty'. Townshend had urged Lake that the offer be taken up while he had enough food to negotiate from a position of some strength. Using a historical reference he was sure Halil would understand, he aimed to secure 'the terms granted to Masséna by the Austrians after the defence of Genoa' – that his force be 'allowed to march out through the Turkish lines with its arms, artillery and pouch ammunition and join you [Lake]'. In other words, be allowed to stay in the war. These would have been generous terms, but Lake took the view that 'the mere fact of Halil proposing to offer terms' showed that he himself was not in a strong position. The C-in-C India agreed, and London rejected the idea. Robertson thought that the Turks, under pressure from the Russians in the Caucasus and with their communications 'much congested', would find it hard to supply Baghdad. Halil's 'overtures' indicated that, 'given determined action on our part, success is assured'.[1]

By the time Gorringe accepted his final defeat on 23 April, things looked very different. Townshend gave Lake his opinion that 'short of a miracle, he will not be able to relieve me, and there are no miracles in war'. But he still hoped that Halil might be persuaded to let his force leave Kut. 'The Turks cannot feed my force', and 'they have not enough ships to take it to Baghdad.'

With grim prescience he warned that 'if it had to march, the force would all die, both from weakness and Arab bullets'. At this stage he believed that the utter exhaustion of his troops was a kind of guarantee of reasonable terms, since Halil must see that he could not cope with looking after them. He accepted, though, that 'to get Halil to agree will cost some money'. He had just been told of Kitchener's plan to offer £1 million – ostensibly to help the civilians of Kut – if Halil allowed Townshend's force to go free. This fairly naked attempt at bribery threw a lurid light on British attitudes to the Turks. Only Cox seems to have grasped that if it failed it would be deadly for British prestige. Even if it succeeded, 'the project is pretty sure to become known sooner or later and I cannot afford to be identified with it'.

Responsibility for the negotiations should logically have rested with the army commander, or at least the commander of the Tigris Corps. Townshend, whose nerves were obviously strained, repeatedly asked Lake to manage things. As early as 31 March he had held that 'as Commander of the besieged force I cannot deal with such a matter', and just before he finally met Halil on 27 April, he protested, 'I am ill in body and in mind . . . I have had my share of responsibility and I consider that you should conduct these negotiations.' Lake, equally determinedly, refused. Neither, we may assume, was keen to take responsibility for a major national humiliation. In the end, a small group of elite (but quite junior) intelligence officers, led by Aubrey Herbert and T. E. Lawrence, who had been brought over from Cairo to Mesopotamia for a quite different project, was given the task.

After rejecting the idea of negotiations in March, Kitchener had come up with a plan to weaken Halil's position further by instigating an Arab rebellion behind the Turkish lines. Military intelligence in Cairo proposed to send Herbert and Lawrence ('one of the best of our very able intelligence staff here', as the High Commissioner introduced him to Cox) with two leading Arab ex-Ottoman officers, Aziz al-Masri and Mohammed al-Faruqi, to establish contacts in Baghdad and amongst the

Euphrates tribes. But by the time Lawrence arrived at Basra on 5 April, the scheme had already been scuppered by the local authorities. 'We feel unable', wrote Lake, speaking surely with Cox's voice, 'to concur in the deputation either of Faroki or el Masri to Mesopotamia now.' They would, he said, be unable to get past the active Turkish security precautions, and in any case their political ideas were 'much too advanced to be safe pabula for the communities of occupied territories'. (A familiar argument by now.) Moreover, 'in previous attempts to utilise captured Arab officers professing to be able to influence their compatriots in the Turkish ranks, they have always eventually been found unwilling to face the practical difficulties and risks involved'.[2] On the basis of this (alleged) experience, and in spite of the extremity of the disaster now threatening, they preferred to do nothing.

Townshend met Halil early in the morning on the 27th, and came away disappointed. Halil was 'extremely nice' at first, but 'declined to hold out hopes of anything but unconditional surrender followed by captivity'. Halil artfully adopted one of his opponent's favourite methods by invoking military history. As prisoners of the Turks, the men of the 6th Division would 'certainly meet with the same reception as the troops of Osman Pasha, the hero of Plevna, had met as prisoners in Russia'.[3] But he insisted that the artillery must be surrendered. He said he would consult with Enver about the offer of money – not in itself a promising sign – but insisted that if negotiations were to continue, Townshend's force should move out of Kut into a camp provided for them. Then the cargo of supplies on the *Julnar* would be distributed. Townshend was predictably sceptical about this. Quite apart from the fact that the Turks could not possibly provide enough tents, 'I can see no use in moving out into camp from any point of view ... My sick and wounded certainly cannot be moved except in a steamer.' He suggested that his forty guns might be offered to Halil in addition to the £1 million – they would be crucial from the viewpoint of proclaiming victory – but if the troops were not to be released, they must be destroyed. Once again he asked Lake to take over negotiations 'at once, especially as I have no knowledge of international law'. The bottom line of his message, literally, was the simple sentence, 'I shall have no food in two days.'[4]

That evening, with a temporary ceasefire in force, he radioed repeating his warning about the state of his troops with added urgency. Even supposing Halil had enough steamers to take them to Baghdad (which he did not), 'you can imagine the arrival there – no proper quarters – the condition of the sick and wounded. It would be a real drama and I hope in the cause of humanity you will be firm to let us come away in our own ships to India [i.e. on parole]'. The alternative was appalling. If his troops had to go upriver 'seventy-five per cent at least would die'. He again pressed Halil for reasonable terms, but when Halil referred the question to Enver the reply was unequivocal. If Townshend would 'hand over to us everything in Kut' he would be allowed to 'go whither he will' on parole, 'with his personal effects and his sword'. If he refused this offer, Halil was to break off negotiations. As Townshend told Lake on 28 April, the offer was obviously unacceptable. But 'if the government wants to save the lives of quite forty or fifty per cent of my force', it should try offering Halil £2 million and 'an equal number to Turkish combatants', to allow them to go back to India. He thought it possible that once he had been able to announce a big victory, Enver might be more 'open to reason'. But he grumbled, understandably enough, 'this comes of negotiating with starvation at the gate', just as he had warned on 10 March. Lake told him that Herbert and Lawrence would try to talk to Halil next day (the 29th), and he would ask London about the doubling of the money available, but that Townshend had better prepare to destroy his guns, supplies and radio equipment, and try to block the river.[5]

Lawrence and Herbert, with the MEF's chief intelligence officer, Lieutenant-Colonel W. H. Beach, eventually managed to meet

Halil on 29 April. Following Enver's instructions, Halil refused to discuss any substantive issues. He confirmed that the sick and wounded men of the garrison would be exchanged for Turkish prisoners held by the British. He also asked for a temporary loan of ships to carry the rest of the garrison up to Baghdad, but Beach obviously could not agree to this. Eventually, as Herbert recorded in his diary, the Turkish general 'yawned, I thought more rudely than negligently . . . and said he had much work to do'. So 'we ended' – though as it was late they were invited to stay overnight, and were treated to what Lawrence described as 'an excellent dinner in Turkish style'. Unknown to them, Townshend had already told Halil that he would surrender unconditionally.

Next day he ordered the destruction of 6th Division's artillery and munition stores, burned his HQ flag and handed his sword and pistol over to Halil, who handed them back with the gracious (if irrelevant) insistence that 'they are as much yours as they ever were'. Halil also promised that Townshend's force would be interned somewhere with 'a good climate near the sea'.[6] Townshend, now 'the honoured guest of the Turkish nation', still believed (as he announced in his last communiqué to his troops) that he could go to Constantinople and 'get you exchanged at once'. The last message from his HQ to the Tigris Corps went out around 1 p.m.: 'To all ships and stations from Kut. Goodbye and good luck to all.'

The surrender was a crushing moment, especially for young soldiers like Private Wheeler. He wondered if perhaps regular soldiers, 'more attuned to the vicissitudes of war', might have been 'less sensitive' about it than Territorials like him. But for him, 'it was a shattering and humiliating experience, a blow to his national pride at the loss of freedom, in defence of which he had so readily taken up arms'. By coincidence, he was doing sentry duty at the same spot as he had been when the 6th Division trooped back into Kut at the start of the siege. 'What amazed me' at the time of the surrender was that 'Changing of the Guard in the normal manner took place as if nothing untoward was happening – just an hour or so before the Turks entered the town.'[7]

When he got the orders 'to destroy <u>everything</u> of military value except 25% of rifles & a little ammunition', Major Walker threw into the river 'my belt, binoculars, revolver, spare khaki clothing, & all my trophies . . . till I was left with a roll of bedding & the clothes I stood up in, my Burberry and B.W. [British Warm]'. Gunner Lee was busy destroying artillery ammunition: the caps of the shells were removed, then 'each gunner had to carry two shells to the river bank and quietly drop them in the river'. (Wooden chutes were built to run them down.) He could see 'fires burning everywhere' as stores were destroyed. Sandes was destroying all his bridging material in the RE Field Park, where he 'made a great bonfire of first-class manilla [sic] rope soaked in oil, and heaped on to it tools, timber, pontoon baulks, and everything else I could see. Columns of smoke arose in all parts of Kut.' He was surprised that 'not a shot was fired by the enemy during this process of destruction'.[8]

Lieutenant McNeal reported that when his men had heard that their guns were being offered to the Turks as an inducement to allow them to go back to India on parole, 'They said they would rather go to Turkey as prisoners of war than leave the guns that they had used for so long for the Turks to use against our own people below.' When they got the order to destroy them, 'a weight seemed to be lifted from everyone's mind'. But he admitted that the guns were utterly worn out, and regretted that so much ammunition was left to be destroyed. 'All the time during the siege we had been ordered to husband our ammunition, yet here, in my battery alone I destroyed 1,200 rounds.'[9] Could this not have been used in a final strafe of the enemy convoys passing by towards the front?

The meticulous Sandes calculated that 'our fine array of thirty-eight guns and four howitzers' destroyed in an hour or less on 29 April were worth around £100,000. The garrison's two motor launches were sunk by a six-ounce charge of dynamite each in deep water, but the *Sumana*, which had been kept operational throughout the siege by dint of extraordinary exertions and makeshift repairs, and had maintained the outpost on the right bank at Woolpress Village, was left intact. Its commander wanted 'to run the gauntlet downstream', but was peremptorily ordered to stay in Kut. Some thought that this was because the ship was 'a most valuable asset for inducing the Turks to give us transport', others that Townshend 'had retained it for his own use on a Turkish promise to allow him to go downstream to see Sir Percy Lake'. This unlikely trip never happened, and the ship (to the great chagrin of Lieutenant L. C. P. Tudway) was surrendered.[10]

At the end, Walker watched as 'the poor old battered Union Jack flying over the Serai of Kut came slowly down its flagstaff & in its place ascended a plain white flag – a hard thing to see'. Many, like Lee, naturally 'wondered how the Turks would receive us' after the surrender; they had 'already had news of the Armenian Massacres, and this left us rather in doubt'. Since, as Townshend had pointed out to Halil, the Ottoman Army could not possibly feed the 13,000 men on the 6th Division strength at the moment of surrender, the outlook was at the very least unappealing. (As Townshend ruefully reflected afterwards, the fate of surrendered armies depended absolutely on whether the enemy commander was 'a gentleman': Halil let him down.) But the reality would fulfil the most pessimistic imagination.

III: BAGHDAD

1. Policy Paralysed: Egypt v India

The fall of Kut is a serious blow and I am afraid it will be the
cause of trouble amongst the Mahomedans. They will talk
among themselves and say the hour of the British is over.
AMAR SINGH

We cannot come away and we cannot go forward.
SIR WILLIAM ROBERTSON

Townshend's surrender was a military disaster – the worst,
certainly, since the surrender at Yorktown that lost the American
colonies. (Townshend himself drew this comparison explicitly
during the siege, and Kitchener saw the issue in the same
catastrophic light.[1]) But what would be its effect? One thing all
British policy-makers had agreed on was that so heavy a blow
to British prestige would trigger a wider catastrophe in the East.
Townshend's objections to moving on Baghdad had centred on this
risk. But somehow the catastrophe did not happen. The tribes of
'Arabistan' did not rise against Britain. The Ottoman strategists
could not exploit the advantage their victory offered. One reason
may have been that Russia was at last driving the Turks back in
the Caucasus and Persia.[2] Its successes helped relieve pressure
on British forces in Egypt as well as Mesopotamia – a pressure
they felt in spite of their comfortable numerical superiority in
both theatres. The most spectacular Russian victory, the capture
of the supposedly impregnable fortress of Erzerum in February
1916, resonated loudly in Britain – not least because John Buchan
made it the climax of his thriller *Greenmantle*.

Even after Kut, the British kept the military initiative in
Mesopotamia. The decision whether to advance, consolidate,
or withdraw remained in their hands. Another way of putting

259

it would be to say that the fundamental dilemma facing the expedition remained unresolved. Days after Townshend's surrender the CIGS spelled this out: 'At present our policy in Mesopotamia is defensive and we do not attach any importance to the possession of Kut or to the occupation of Baghdad.' But for the fact that it was important to 'minimise and counteract the fall of Kut' – as well as to support the Russians – they should probably fall back to Amara or even as far as Qurna. For the time being Lake should maintain 'as forward a position as can be made secure tactically', though Robertson insisted that no forward position was worth the risk of incurring heavy loss, due either to enemy action or to 'unhealthy conditions'.[3]

This seemed reasonably clear, but privately the CIGS was less sure of the situation's strategic logic. In May, still 'turning over in my mind what is the best thing to do in Mesopotamia', he worried that 'we do not seem strong enough to get on', but 'on the other hand we should probably be making trouble for ourselves if we came back'. Three months later he was still impaled on the same dilemma: 'We cannot come away and we cannot go forward.'[4] This uncertainty was an odd contrast with Robertson's very definite general view of the war. As a leading 'Westerner' he took a dim view of the Eastern 'sideshows' in general and the Mesopotamia campaign – which he would later castigate as 'the worst that ever was run' – in particular. For a time, the Gallipoli and Mesopotamia expeditions had mutually reinforced each other's relevance, but with Gallipoli gone the point of Mesopotamia was lost. The only real exponent of an Eastern strategy within the military establishment was Kitchener himself, who always believed that a landing at Alexandretta might be strategically decisive, and even said at one point that without one the Allies would lose the war. But Kitchener's influence was waning by 1916; and in any case all military arguments about Alexandretta were trumped by one overwhelming political fact. Whatever Kitchener believed, France would not tolerate such a significant intrusion in Syria:

this was its exclusive sphere of interest. When Kitchener perished aboard the cruiser *Hampshire* en route to Russia the scheme effectively went down with him. The Mesopotamia campaign remained, as the sacked and bitter Gorringe would tell the Commission of Inquiry, 'no man's child'.[5]

Militarily, as the First Sea Lord grumbled, 'the soldier square-heads have got hold of the war solid & refuse to do anything except on the Western Front, damn it!' This meant, of course, stupendous preparations for another grinding offensive, this year to be mounted on the Somme. Political grand strategy, on the other hand, looked eastwards. At the India Office, Hirtzel greeted Robertson's April 1916 instructions with undisguised impatience. He protested that Turkey must never be seen as a mere sideshow: Britain, as a 'semi-Asiatic' power with 70 million Muslim subjects, simply could not afford to be beaten by the Turks. But so far it had been.[6] The military 'Westerner' thesis (that defeating Germany would automatically mean defeating Turkey – whereas the reverse was not the case) missed the real political point. Turkey had to be beaten, and be beaten unmistakably, if Britain's Arab policy was to work. Hirtzel could not yet persuade his minister, Austen Chamberlain, who was more inclined to accept the military priorities set by the War Office; and who merely conceded that the Turkish perspective should be 'kept in view' by the Cabinet.

Hirtzel referred to an 'Arab policy' as if Britain had one, but this was not altogether true. 'Arabia' was still a loosely defined entity, and as we have seen, the British view of the Arabs was inconsistent. In fact, the concept of the 'Middle East' itself was quite novel and malleable. Most people still thought of the Ottoman Empire as the 'Near East' and would have had some trouble saying exactly where the Near East became the 'East'. What was clear to all was that between the Suez Canal and Bombay Britain had interests that were vital to its status as a world power. But no single British agency had overall responsibility for the region. No fewer than eighteen separate individuals had

formal advisory roles on policy in various parts of it by mid-1916
– a wild proliferation even by Britain's unsystematic standards.[7]
Fortunately there were far fewer key policy lines – just two, in
effect. Less fortunately, though, the two were incompatible, if
not outright contradictory. 'We have suffered, are suffering, and
shall continue to suffer owing to the fact that political control in
Arabia is divided between India and Egypt.'

The man who wrote this in December 1916, Sir Mark Sykes,
had some claim to be the most influential of all those vying to
control Middle East policy, although his formal status was vague.
A wealthy Yorkshire baronet, MP and reserve army colonel (he
commanded a Yorkshire Territorial battalion), Sykes had already
established a national reputation as both a military expert and
an Arabist by the time the war broke out. His 1904 book *Dar
ul-Islam* (subtitled *A Journey through Ten of the Asiatic Provinces
of Turkey*) was an emotive protest against the contaminating
effect of Western power in the Arab world. (For Sykes the best
Muslims were Arabs: those in the subcontinent were some way
down the scale.) As with later ideas of a 'clash of civilisations',
for him the two worlds were absolutely incompatible. 'The most
perfect race morally may be dull and backward materially, and
vice versa.' His books created, as Elie Kedourie has said, the
'vivid impression that Eastern society is sustained by the age-old
consolatory certainties that serve to make life more decent and
merciful, and to preserve the dignity of the humblest individual. In
the East there is much cruelty and oppression, it is true, but there
are also kindly habits which take the sting out of them; whereas
in the West cruelty and oppression, which exist in equal measure,
are unredeemed by mercy, but are codified and regimented, made
monstrous and inhuman.'[8] Like many Arabists before and since,
he found Western assumptions of superiority absurd. Reflecting
on the Kurds, he insisted that 'here we Europeans must bow
to the East, for after a century of revolution and fuming, and
chattering and legislating, we are not as near true fraternity and
equality as the Kurdish Aga'.[9]

It was the very intensity of Sykes's enthusiasm that made his views influential, though it was oddly un-English. T. E. Lawrence called him 'the imaginative advocate of unconvincing world-movements', and regretted that 'he lacked patience to test his materials before choosing his style of building'. For Lawrence, Sykes's heart was in the right place, but his mind was sadly erratic. He 'would sketch out in a few dashes a new world, all out of scale, but vivid as a vision of some sides of the thing we hoped'.[10] His arguments, however, were often logically flawed to the point of incoherence. Sykes's vision of the East was a product of his Tory–Democratic hostility to the forces of middle-class progress. They had triumphed in the West, but he believed that in the East what he called Levantinism or 'Gosmopoleet' (the Orientalised versian of the 'Cosmopolite') could be defeated by the uncontaminated inner spirit of peoples such as the Arabs, the Kurds and the Armenians.[11] In a parliamentary debate shortly before the war, he suggested that the Ottoman system, whose sickness and imminent demise had so often been announced, might finally be on the brink of dissolution. But 'even supposing the Ottoman Empire fails!' he proclaimed, 'there are the seeds of native States which exist in the provinces of the Ottoman Empire at the present moment which could be made into independent States'. This belief would have profound and far-reaching consequences for Iraq and the whole Middle East.

Mark Sykes's writings made him a recognised expert on the Ottoman state, even though his attempt to write a full-scale history of the Ottoman lands petered out.[12] His researches equipped him with an information-base that he would use with skill and persistence in policy debate during the war. His expertise was already valued so much that when his battalion went to France, he went instead to the War Office as an adviser to Lord Kitchener. He was thirty-five years old. In 1915 he was given two missions which catapulted him into the centre of Britain's hesitant policy formation. In March he was put on an interdepartmental committee chaired by Sir Maurice de Bunsen of the Foreign Office, the government's first attempt to work out a Middle East policy (or as official language had it, 'to consider the nature of British desiderata' for the Ottoman territories). All its members were civil servants, apart from Sykes, who was on it as Kitchener's personal representative. He stood out in another respect as well – his confidence. The committee was baffled by the multiplicity of possible outcomes in the unexpected – and up to that point unwanted – event of defeating the Ottoman state. It came up with nine 'desiderata', and four possible frameworks for securing them – partition, zones of interest, the preservation of Ottoman independence (Britain's traditional policy), and enforced devolution within a not-quite-independent Ottoman state.

The committee eventually endorsed the last of these, proposed by Sykes as a compromise (like Kitchener, he thought partition more logical, but also much more contentious). Then Kitchener sent him forth to 'the east' to brief all the significant authorities between Egypt and India on this policy. His six-month tour in the second half of 1915 put Sykes in a unique position. He went from the Dardanelles to Cairo, and on to Aden (where he interviewed Arab prisoners of war from the Ottoman Army, as part of his pet scheme to create an Arab army), and back again briefly to Cairo before going on to India. He then went to Mesopotamia, interviewing more prisoners at Basra before going upriver to Kut just after its capture in late September. On his way back to Cairo he wrote a large-scale assessment for the War Office, detailing the inadequacy of British war propaganda in the Arab world. He had decided, unsurprisingly, that Eastern policy was suffering from the multiplicity of separate commands, and above all from the influence of India, which took a 'purely Indian' rather than an Imperial view of the Mesopotamia expedition. Britain needed a single coordinating agency; Sykes proposed the creation of an 'Islamic' or 'Arabic bureau'. This would, naturally, be in Cairo, where he had found such congenial, charismatic men as Ronald Storrs (the High Commissioner's Oriental Secretary) and Gilbert

Clayton, the Chief of Military Intelligence. (Together with the less congenial Gertrude Bell.)

Sykes was now influential enough for his proposal to be quickly approved, in January 1916. The new 'Arab Bureau', briefly known as the 'Islamic Bureau', was tasked with coordinating British political activity in the north-east of the Arabian peninsula and reporting on enemy policy there, and also coordinating British propaganda amongst non-Indian Muslims 'without clashing with the susceptibilities of Indian Muslims'. When Sykes went back to London to act as its spokesman, Professor D. G. Hogarth (with the honorary naval rank of lieutenant-commander) became the bureau's first director. 'India', as Kitchener's secretary noted, remained 'very suspicious', but Hirtzel was sympathetic and was expected to 'put it to India in such a way that I do not think we shall have any trouble from them in the future'. This would prove optimistic.

Britain made two crucial diplomatic moves in the Middle East in 1916. Unsurprisingly, they did not mesh precisely together. Both, indeed, laid powder trails of dispute into the future. The first, the 'Hussein–McMahon correspondence', is still contentious today. Its key point was the letter which the High Commissioner for Egypt, Sir Henry McMahon, sent to Sharif Hussein of Mecca in October 1915, setting out the terms on which Britain would support an Arab revolt against the Ottoman government. It was the climax of a long process that had begun early in 1914. As guardian of the holy places of Mecca and Medina, and a descendant of the Prophet, Hussein occupied a unique position in the Ottoman state. He was almost an autonomous ruler, and the Sultan's only potential rival for the caliphate, but for that very reason was suspected in Istanbul of harbouring ambitions of full independence. In 1914 he feared, with some reason, that the Ottoman government was preparing to remove him from Mecca. His son Abdallah visited Kitchener, McMahon's predecessor in Cairo, and hinted that Hussein might lead an Arab move against Turkish control. Eight months later, Kitchener – now War

Minister in London – telegraphed to Cairo, 'tell Storrs to send secret and carefully chosen messenger from me to Sharif Abdallah to ascertain whether [if Turkey took Germany's side in the war] he and his father and the Arabs of the Hejaz would be with us or against us'. The Sharif's reply was cautiously positive. When war came on, Kitchener changed the terms of the negotiation significantly: 'If Arab nation assist England in this war', he cabled to Abdallah on 31 October 1914, 'England will guarantee that no intervention takes place in Arabia and will give Arabs every assistance against external foreign aggression.'[13]

What was striking here was the phrase 'Arab nation'. The Sharif's vital importance to Britain lay in his power to neutralise the danger that the war between Britain and Turkey might be turned into a Muslim jihad. This power derived from his religious status; but Hussein could not launch a rebellion that would be seen as dividing Islam. Only as leader of a national movement to create an independent Arab state could he risk opposing the Sultan. This of course raised a major policy issue for Britain. Was Hussein a plausible ally? Did Britain really need him? Some on the British side argued that if Britain captured Constantinople it would not need his help, and if not, he would have no incentive to act. Hirtzel saw his territorial demands as too ambitious, including areas which the de Bunsen report saw as British and French zones of interest. Another India Office official argued with rare frankness that since 'we have no intention of helping him' to establish an Arab kingdom, 'we ought not to hold out even a vague hope of negotiating an agreement on this basis'.[14] At the Foreign Office the prospect of 'any really powerful Arab force' was dismissed out of hand. 'People talk of the Arabs as if they were some kind of cohesive body,' Sir Arthur Nicolson grumbled to Hardinge, whereas they were 'a heap of scattered tribes with no cohesion and no organisation. I think myself that we are trying to treat with a shadow.'

Even enthusiasts for an Arab national movement were doubtful about its potential. Although the Sharif had 'always written as spokesman of the Arab nation', Hogarth noted, he was 'not, so far as we know, supported by any organisation of Arabs nearly general enough to secure . . . the automatic acceptance of terms agreed by him. No such organisation exists at the back of any Arab whatever . . . nor can it be expected to exist.'[15] But all these doubts and objections died away when the Egyptian authorities once again flourished the nightmare of imminent jihad. The C-in-C, Sir John Maxwell, warned on 16 October 1915 that 'unless we make a definite and agreeable proposal to the Shereef at once, we may have a united Islam against us'. Three days later the High Commissioner likewise urged that unless some immediate assurance was given, the Arabs would be lost to the Allies. The only acceptable assurance would be a clear statement of support for an independent Arab authority with the borders demanded by Hussein. McMahon thought that as long as Hussein agreed to accept British advisers 'to ensure sound administration', he should be supported. But this in turn raised the problem that talk of British assistance might alarm France, all too ready, as the Foreign Secretary pointed out, to suspect that 'we were not only endeavouring to secure Arab interests, but to establish our own in Syria at expense of French'.

This objection, though, was also set aside, and Grey told McMahon that as long as the 'promised sphere of British control' was extended beyond Basra to reflect their 'special interests in Baghdad province', he could go ahead. Five days later McMahon sent the key 23 October letter to Hussein, setting out the terms by which Britain would support an independent Arab state. It contained the famous, or notorious, clause excluding from the proposed state the coastal strip 'west of the Districts of Damascus, Homs, Hama and Aleppo' which 'could not be said to be purely Arab', as well as a stronger assertion of British supremacy in Mesopotamia. In Baghdad and Basra the Arabs were to recognise that Britain's 'established position and interests necessitate special measures of administrative control in order to secure these territories from foreign aggression, to promote the welfare of the local populations and to safeguard our mutual economic interests'.

McMahon drafted the letter himself and sent it to Mecca without referring it back to London. (Although Grey had authorised him to do this, Clayton reflected admiringly that 'there is many a man who would have funked it and referred his proposed reply for approval' – knowing as any government official would that the Foreign Office instructions 'left several openings for making a scapegoat in the event of necessity'.) If he had, history might have been different. The Indian authorities were aghast at the letter. Chamberlain spluttered that 'Sir H. McMahon's "gush" seems to me to lower British prestige', and would confirm the Sharif (whom Chamberlain dismissed as a chancer) in his delusion that 'he is more important to us than we are to him'. Hardinge was frankly horrified. 'By surrendering Bussorah [Basra] vilayet to Arab Govt. of any kind we shall not only be preparing trouble for ourselves at the head of and along the southern littoral of the Gulf, but shall be giving up the main fruits of hard won victories in Mesopotamia. This will not only be abandoning enormous potential sources of revenue, but will also be resented by the Indian people . . . who look to Mesopotamia as a field for commercial expansion and emigration in return for the blood of their countrymen there shed.'[16] 'India', or at least the Viceroy, clearly still wanted annexation; this option had now been 'given away', he fumed, 'with absolutely nothing to show in return'. He was still fuming (privately) weeks later. McMahon had given France everything it wanted, but sold India out.

Hostility to the putative Arab state united the London and Delhi branches of the Indian government. While Hardinge raged, 'I devoutly hope that this proposed independent Arab state will fall to pieces, if it is ever created. Nobody could have devised any scheme more detrimental to British interests in the Middle East. It simply means misgovernment, chaos and corruption.' Hirtzel sounded, if possible, an even more portentous alarm. 'A strong Arab state might be more dangerous to Christendom than a strong Ottoman state,' he wrote in February 1916. The invocation of Christendom, oddly anachronistic in the midst of the greatest European war, revealed some deep-set preconceptions behind Western policy. 'Lord Kitchener's policy of destroying one Islamic State merely for the purpose of creating another, has always seemed to me disastrous, from the point of view no less of expediency than of civilisation.' This was heavy stuff indeed – though Hirtzel was careful to keep it within the India Office. He was consoled by the belief that since 'the Arabs have shown themselves incapable of creating or maintaining such a State', Britain's disastrous policy was 'probably sufficiently free from practical danger'. But this in itself was a real problem: 'the danger of [the policy] lies in its disingenuousness.'[17]

Even when Sharif Hussein finally announced his war against Turkey on 5 June 1916, India still refused to believe that it would produce an Arab national revolt. By that time the second of Britain's crucial Middle Eastern negotiations had been tied up. The task of clarifying 'the interests of our present Allies' – or at least the only ally whose demands could not be ignored – fell to Sykes himself. In fact, the contours of the Anglo-French agreement had been fixed some time before Sykes met the French representative, Georges-Picot. Picot had met a Foreign Office committee several times in November and December 1915, and made clear his absolute refusal to entertain any reduction in French claims to Syria. (Picot was a former French representative in Beirut, and had been picked by the Quai d'Orsay for his unshakeability on this issue: McMahon called him a 'notorious fanatic' on it.) By the time Sykes and Picot went head to head in January 1916, the idea that the former 'Turkish Arabia' would be divided into spheres of influence, alongside areas of closer British and French control or direct administration, was fixed. Sykes and Picot had the task of drawing the frontiers of France's zone of direct control in Lebanon (the 'Blue Zone') and its zone of influence in Syria ('Zone A'), and Britain's corresponding 'Red Zone' and 'Zone B' in Basra and Baghdad provinces.

The famous Sykes–Picot map was not quite an exact blueprint for the postwar settlement. On it the Blue zone, for instance, spread far into southern Anatolia, and Zone A included Mosul. The only line on Sykes and Picot's map to survive to the present day is the southern border of Syria. The areas of direct French and British administration were never created. But the broad shape of the future Middle East was clearly, and finally, laid out. Above all the 'independent Arab state' which Sharif Hussein aimed at was decisively rejected. Just what kind of semi-independence the Allies had in mind for their Arab client states was unclear. Britain and France agreed to 'recognise and protect an independent Arab state or a Confederation of Arab States'; they would have 'priority of right of enterprise and local loans' in their respective spheres, where they would 'alone supply advisers or foreign functionaries at the request of the Arab State or Confederation'.[18] The reference to a single 'Arab state' probably reflected Sykes's lingering hopes; the reality was that the two powers would make their own arrangements in their spheres of influence.

The agreement remained secret until the Bolsheviks published it after the October Revolution of 1917. It has been excoriated ever since – most bitterly by T. E. Lawrence, as a betrayal of Britain's promise of support for Arab independence. Most Arabs still see it that way. But for British policy-makers, the two commitments reflected different priorities, which could eventually be adjusted – once the war was won. Sykes himself assumed this, though as an apostle of an Arab renaissance, he saw the deal as a regrettable victory for those who had never believed in the Arabs. He went on lamenting the lack of 'a policy for the Arab race', and India's unfitness to deal with Arabs. (He charged the Government of India with treating native affairs and native government 'from a social and political standpoint as Englishmen and natives, based on a colour line and dominion, in a way which is utterly alien to Arabs'.[19])

But India too was unhappy with the Sykes–Picot agreement. It might be an improvement on the detested open-ended McMahon promise, and it secured Basra and Baghdad, but it still fell short of what was needed. Hirtzel, who had argued for the integrity of the three Iraqi provinces, deplored the cession of Mosul to France. British efforts to find a coherent policy would go on being pulled in opposite directions. To enthusiasts for 'the Arab race' like Sykes, 'Indian' policy represented an assumption that Arab independence must wait until direct British control had established the infrastructure for progress. As his friend Hogarth put it, Indian administrators believed that 'the British raj is the best form of government, and therefore to fail to impose it wherever possible is to fail in one's duty to mankind'. In late 1916 Lord Chelmsford, Hardinge's successor as Viceroy, renewed Hirtzel's argument about the moral responsibility to reclaim Mesopotamia. India did not want more responsibility, he protested, but he could not see how Iraq could realistically be 'cut away' from it. It was now, in effect, the 'Arabian frontier of the Raj'.[20]

2. Administration and Punishment

We rushed into the business with our usual disregard for a
comprehensive political scheme. The creation of an Arabia policy
should have been done at home . . . there was no one to do it, no
one who had even thought of it.
GERTRUDE BELL

Here you have empire in the egg.
EDMUND CANDLER

India's chief political officer in Mesopotamia, Percy Cox, turned
out to be no enthusiast for 'Indianisation'. So, at least, thought
Gertrude Bell, who arrived at Basra in March 1916 to represent
the Arab Bureau (with captain's rank). She was surely the most
remarkable addition to the expedition that year. She had been
sent from Cairo to try to talk Lord Hardinge, a family friend,
out of his suspicions of the Bureau. The Viceroy immediately
co-opted her as his own representative, suggesting she was
uniquely qualified to help Force D's intelligence section by
making a systematic evaluation of the Arabs of Mesopotamia.
She was undeniably unique. Wealthy (her grandfather, the
Victorian ironmaster Lowthian Bell, had become the sixth-
richest man in Britain) and formidably intelligent (she was the
first woman to take a first-class degree at Oxford), she already
had an international reputation as an Arabist and explorer.

Not just intelligent, she had always been fascinated by global
politics. But while she might, as an eight-year-old, be able to
dispute international issues with the Belgian ambassador, as
an adult such interests were bound to lead to frustration and
marginalisation in the male-dominated world of high politics.
Paradoxically, she had escaped this by plunging into the ostensibly

even more sexist world of the Arabian desert. There she went beyond being simply remarkable, and achieved a unique celebrity status – a kind of honorary desert royalty. Between 1900 and 1913 she had made a series of journeys into the deserts of Syria, as far south as Hail, and into Mesopotamia to Najaf, Baghdad and Mosul. Her classic travel book *The Desert and the Sown*, published three years after Sykes's *Dar ul-Islam*, was infused with equally big historical ideas. She believed that culture, art and religion were all 'essentially Asiatic'. 'Some day I hope the East will be strong again and develop its own civilisation, not ours,' she had written. 'Perhaps it will teach us a few things we once learnt from it and have now forgotten, to our great loss.' Islam she judged 'the greatest republic in the world' – within it there was an essential equality, 'neither class nor race'.[1]

Interestingly, in *The Desert and the Sown* she had written of Mesopotamia in far from flattering terms. She compared Baghdad unfavourably with Damascus – 'the capital of the desert', infused with the values of the bedouin, where Baghdad was dominated by 'Persian and Turkish influences'. She went further still, suggesting that 'the very soil of Mesopotamia exhaled emanations fatal to virility'. Somehow 'the ancient ghosts of Babylonian and Assyrian palace intrigue' continued to rise from their muddy graves and strangle the warrior ethos.[2] She would now have to confront these ghosts directly, though she seemed untroubled by the prospect at this point. She was more worried by the Basra climate ('a singular experience to be living always in a Turkish bath') and the problem of washing in 'a solution of Tigris mud'. But spring had its charms – 'palm gardens deep in luxuriant grass and corn, blossoming pomegranates'. She was especially charmed by Cox, and the daily tea parties on the deck of his boat in one of the palm-fringed creeks surrounding the town. More importantly, she reassured her Arab Bureau colleague T. E. Lawrence in Cairo that the chief political officer was against importing the Indian legal code. When Lawrence also arrived in Mesopotamia in April, he too found Cox unexpectedly congenial. 'Cox dissociates himself from India very clearly', he reported to Clayton, adding, 'he does not know how Cairene he is'.

But Lawrence was dismayed by much of what he found in Mesopotamia. He had set out from Cairo not to take part in the humiliating effort to bribe the Turks to release the Kut garrison, but to raise an Arab revolt behind the Ottoman front line. The 'Cairo' policy line was propelled by the belief that a significant Arab resistance movement was possible – and desirable. Resistance was thought most likely in Syria, and British contacts with dissident Arab officers in the Ottoman Army had suggested that a move on Alexandretta would trigger a widespread uprising. The arrival of Aziz al-Masri late in 1914 had been followed in September 1915 by a remarkable defector from the Ottoman lines at Gallipoli, Mohammed al-Faruqi. Another Iraqi (from Mosul), al-Faruqi claimed that there was an extensive network of Arab officers in units throughout Syria and Mesopotamia, with support among civilian leaders in both urban and rural, settled and nomadic areas. Al-Faruqi also provided detailed information about an Arab rebellion which had been planned earlier in the year in expectation of a British landing at Alexandretta, but which had been detected and broken up by the Ottoman military governor of Syria, Jemal Pasha.[3]

All this implied more substantial Arab organisation than the British had so far thought. But without a direct action such as the Alexandretta landing they could not be sure. After that plan was abandoned, British attention turned to Hussein in the Hejaz, but the prospect of Arab action in Syria and Mesopotamia – and just as important, the fear that the Arabs might give Britain up – had a strong influence on the negotiations with him. Ten days before McMahon sent his October letter, the C-in-C Egypt, Sir John Maxwell – one of the original exponents of the Alexandretta plan – told Kitchener that the issue was becoming urgent. Kitchener urged him to 'do your best to prevent any alienation of the traditional loyalty of the Arabs to England'. Contacts were kept up, and Arab dissidents played a crucial part – at least according to Lawrence – in delivering the fortress of Erzerum to the Russians. ('I put the Grand Duke Nicholas in touch with certain disaffected Arab officers in Erzeroum.') It was on the basis of these continuing contacts that Lawrence and Herbert were sent, with al-Faruqi and al-Masri, to Mesopotamia during the final effort to relieve Kut. When the project fell foul of the well-established hostility of the Indian authorities to any stimulation of Arab nationalism, Lawrence stayed on in Mesopotamia long enough not just to negotiate with Halil, but to carry out a comprehensive survey of the situation there on behalf of the Arab Bureau.

He drew up a strikingly wide-ranging report, displaying his industriousness as well as his perceptiveness. Much of it never saw the light of day – it had to be hastily edited on his return to Cairo, since Lawrence condemned the failure of the Kut relief efforts in terms too direct to be acceptable to the higher military authorities. (It got as far as Clayton, who seems to have accepted his verdict that the Kut garrison 'should have been extricated with reasonable ease' but for the incompetence of those organising the relief.[4]) Lawrence's 'Cairene' view that the Mesopotamian administration was wrong-headed was reinforced by its opposition to the idea of an Arab rebellion. His dislike of it would become sharper still: by the time he wrote *Seven Pillars of Wisdom*, he would denounce the British in Mesopotamia as 'substantially an alien force invading enemy territory, with the local people passively neutral or sullenly against them'. In 1916, though, he was slightly more positive, or more diplomatic, about the qualities of the British administrators. He does not seem to have met Wilson (significantly, perhaps). But Cox was 'delightful to work with' (even if 'entirely ignorant of the Arab Societies'), and Lawrence was confident that he could 'be brought round' to accept 'a definite declaration that we will not annex Basra'. Henry Dobbs, Cox's deputy, was 'one of the most interesting people I met'; he had strong ideas that differed from Cairo's, but would come round 'when he has learned more'. ('He suffers like all the rest', Lawrence charitably observed, 'because there is no-one out there who knows what is going on, or what the rest of the Arab world is like.') The way the administration coped with the chaos left by the departing Ottomans, especially the land question, was admirable. Dobbs and Bullard 'both understand and like the natives, took the right manner with landlords and landowners, and scored a tremendous success for the British in what was one of the most important (as it was certainly the most difficult) things we had to do'.[5]

His take on the prospects for Arab mobilisation was correspondingly less positive than it later became. In *Seven Pillars of Wisdom* he would insist that the conditions in Mesopotamia had been 'ideal for an Arab movement. The people of Nejef and Karbala, far in the rear of Halil's army, were in revolt against him. The surviving Arabs in Halil's army were, on his own confession, openly disloyal. The tribes of the Hai and Euphrates would have turned our way, had they seen signs of grace from the British.' If Britain had launched a movement based on its promises to Sharif Hussein 'enough fighting men would have joined us to harry the Turkish lines of communication between Baghdad and Kut'. A few weeks of that would have forced the Turks either 'to raise the siege and retire', or themselves suffer 'investment outside Kut nearly as stringent as the investment of Townshend within it'. But when he was there in 1916 he accepted that, with Kut lost, serious Arab action was unlikely. He made light of Cox's refusal to use Arab officers, putting it down to suspicion 'that we wish to rid Egypt of some gas-bags who are impatient there'. He told Clayton that he had 'been looking up the pan-Arab party', and found that it was 'about twelve strong' now, having 'formerly consisted of Sayed Taleb and some jackals'. At Basra there was 'no Arab sentiment . . . for us the place is negligible. This partly explains Cox's limitations.'[6] He would go on in 1917 to condemn the Arabs of Mesopotamia (along with those of Palestine and Syria) roundly for making 'no effort towards freedom for themselves', in spite of having 'every chance'.[7]

Lawrence's 1916 report did not suggest that the Arabs were waiting for a signal to join the British side, only that 'the hostility of the tribal Arabs' had been 'greatly overdrawn'. The Marsh Arabs who surrounded the British through most of the fighting up until then were a special case – 'impure savages without any code of manners or morals to restrain them'. They were not hostile to the British as such – 'they cut up our wounded and the Turkish wounded, raid our convoys and the Turkish convoys, steal our rifles and the Turkish rifles'. It was a mistake to 'make their hostility typical' of the rest – the 'real Arabs' living around them who held them in contempt. If the British took this view 'we only show up our own lack of understanding'. The 'great block of Arab irreconcilables, the tribes along the Shatt al-Hai' basically wanted only to be 'free and undisturbed'. They would 'be friendly to us only if they thought our rule so weak as to allow of general anarchy'. For the other Arabs, 'the rule is that those in front of us are hostile and those behind friendly'. They were just as hostile to the Turks: 'in truth all these people (like the 35th and 38th Divisions) do not want to fight . . . If we had played our cards better at first, I do not think there would have been even the fighting there has been.' The problem was that the British had 'entered their country like sphinxes, never saying why we came or what we meant to do'.

He did criticise the administration sharply for its social style – or lack of it. 'The local Pashas and Beys have no great one on whom they can go and call. The town notables long for a leisured and dignified vali, who would rise from the divan to meet them, would give them cigarettes and coffee, and do them little unimportant favours.' Pashas were people with influence, and 'silly though it sounds', this grievance was 'actually doing us some harm'. Britain would do well to grasp the need for traditional formal entertainment. 'Our present Headquarters in Basra is all Indian, without even an A.D.C. who can speak three words of Arabic, or a servant who could hand a cup of coffee or a cigarette to a great man in the proper form.' Interestingly, for a 'Cairene', Lawrence believed that the British should, in their second year, 'have sobered down into occupation and ownership'.

Lawrence wound up his analysis of 'local feeling' with a philosophical reflection on the process of modernisation. 'In considering Mesopotamia and the tribes, I think one should bear in mind how transient all these things are.' The British, he supposed, would not stay unless they could carry out a full irrigation scheme, and this would transform Iraqi society. 'When we regulate the rivers we also drain the lakes and swamps, and prevent marshes and floods. With these latter go the present livelihood of the marsh tribes. We will be able to starve a rebellion by shutting down a sluice, or drown it by opening them too wide. When the country is parcelled out by orderly roadways and canals, and watered by an irrigation inspector, in accordance with the bye-laws and local water regulations, the style and mode of living of the farmers there will have changed as much as their system of land tenure. The increase of land values will make the burden of great estates too heavy for any man to bear, and the sheikh and tribal organisations will have no more chance than it would have in Egypt today. In place of his present occupations of blood feud and foray, the landowner of the future will drive his motor car and gamble in margins in the pit at Basra.'[8]

For Lawrence, the main cause for optimism was Gertrude Bell. They had met in 1911 when she visited the archaeological site at Carchemish. Now the two of them 'had great talks and made vast schemes for the government of the universe', as she enthusiastically told her father. (Whether they included schemes for the government of Mesopotamia itself she did not say.) Lawrence was sure that she could 'work up the connections we require with the various Political Officers', and see that the Bureau received the information it needed. 'I think Miss Bell, by her sex and energy and lack of self-consciousness, is peculiarly likely to persuade Political Officers to send her what she asks for.' Lawrence believed that the Bureau would be so useful on the publicity side that all its activities might be welcomed in the end. But he accepted that 'the Mesopotamians' felt 'that we will use them and what they have conquered as a bribe to make our policy acceptable elsewhere'. We – Cairo – 'should go very easy' with them for the present.

In fact, Cox would go on working to limit, and perhaps eliminate, the Bureau's role in Mesopotamia. This was due not least to Sykes's behaviour. When George Lloyd, a junior Bureau member, was posted to Basra in May 1916 to assess the economic situation, he discovered that the Bureau's reputation had been undermined by the belief that Sykes's 'bitter and outspoken anti-Indian attitude was the point of view which we held in Egypt'.[9] Sykes, Arnold Wilson grumbled, had 'left us in no doubt of the views likely to prevail at home' about the future: Mesopotamia would be a protectorate at best, not, as the Indian officials still hoped, an Indian colony. Lloyd managed to repair some of the damage. Like Sykes and Aubrey Herbert, he was close to the centres of power, but Wilson felt that unlike them he approached Mesopotamian issues 'without bias', and did not offer 'dogmatic opinions' based on ignorance.[10] In 1907 he had written a report on possible commercial developments, 'The Conditions and Prospects of British Trade in Mesopotamia', which 'remained a classic in the small circle of government officials concerned with such matters'. His 1916 economic report encouraged India to send a commercial mission which became part of the infrastructure-building project now under way at Basra.

Gertrude Bell quickly became a key part of this project. Following Lawrence's advice, Clayton soon proposed that she should become the Arab Bureau's 'corresponding officer for Mesopotamia'. In May 1916 she was formally attached to the Political Department as a member of Cox's staff, and moved up from Basra to work at GHQ. But Cox took care to make clear that she was – in his view, though not hers – no longer a member of the Arab Bureau. If she wanted to communicate with Clayton and others, it would be 'incompatible with your position as a member of my staff, as also with my ideas, to write private letters at all in connection with your official duties, without first showing them to me'.[11] She agreed to this. Though she blithely went on sending reports from 'the Arab Bureau, Baghdad' right through to the end of the war, she developed a very close professional relationship with Cox. In effect she turned into his Oriental Secretary, though since Cox was assumed not to need one the term was not used until she was, eventually, formally appointed as such in 1921.

Wilson also thought well of her at first – maybe because Sykes did not. (At the time of their rivalry as desert travellers Sykes had called her a 'bitch', an 'infernal liar' and a 'silly, chattering windbag of conceited, gushing, flat-chested, man-woman, globe-trotting, rump-wagging, blethering ass!'[12]) Wilson admired – publicly at least – her 'talent and energy', the 'unwearying diligence' with which she 'indexed and cross-indexed, collated and checked, wherever possible by personal interview, every scrap of available information'. She made 'the dry bones live by virtue of her enthusiasm and the charm of her literary style'. Her office-notes were 'vivid, accurate, and withal feminine. Her sympathy with the victims of military exigencies was tempered by common sense; her righteous wrath was mingled with a sense of humour which never deserted her.'[13] As she became more closely involved in policy-making, Wilson's view would change. He would come to see her as irresponsible, indiscreet and a 'born intriguer': she to see him as overbearing, reactionary and rude.[14] (When he was knighted in 1920 she conceded that he fully deserved the honour, but wished that 'they could also endow him with the manners knights are traditionally credited with!')

For the time being, it was Wilson's sense of mission that would underpin the British role in governing Mesopotamia. He believed that Britain owed the Arabs not just liberation from Turkish rule, but an education in the virtues of good government. Though still in his mid-thirties, he was truly (as his biographer labelled him) a 'late Victorian'. He assumed instinctively that the British had

'Shadows, but never shade': palm trees by the Tigris, looking upriver from Qurna.

'Narrow and dirty and packed with Arabs': the British entering Baghdad in March 1917.

'The Turks counter-attacked so strongly . . .': Turkish infantry going forward. A Gurkha manning a Lewis gun, 1916.

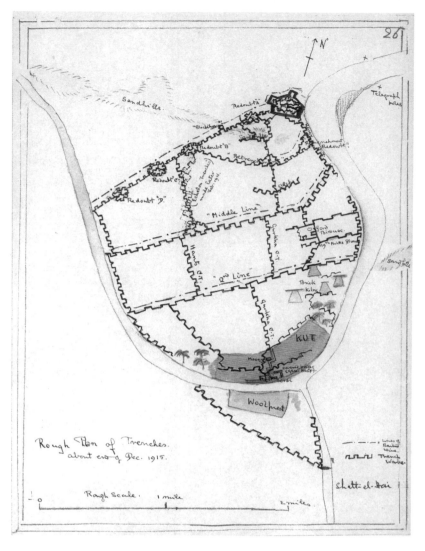

Colonel Heawood's map of the defences at Kut.

'Blood Orange': Major-General
George Gorringe.

Pasha of Baghdad? Lord Hardinge of
Penshurst.

'This comes of negotiating with starvation at the gate': after the surrender at
Kut, Charles Townshend sits on the right of his captor, Halil Pasha.

'Too much water for the army, too little for the navy': Two 'P boats' on the Tigris, each with a barge lashed on either side.

The boat bridge across the River Euphrates at Nasiriya.

'Conciliating the Arabs': Arab women selling eggs to troops on their way up the river.

'Joining those Cossacks who came to see us the other day': The Army Commander, Stanley Maude with British staff officers and Russian officers from their army in Persia.

Men of the 6th King's Own (Royal Lancaster) Regiment bathing in a creek near Basra during the summer of 1916.

Turkish troops captured at the battle of Ramadi.

Percy Cox [2] and Gertrude Bell [3] with Ibn Saud [1] and the Sheikhs of
Mohammerah [4] and Kuwait [5] during Ibn Saud's visit to Basra.

Abdallah, the 'ablest and least scrupulous' of the Hashemite princes, greeting Winston Churchill before the Cairo Conference in 1921. The Conference
agreed that Emir Faisal should be offered the throne of Iraq.

a gift for governance, and for exporting its ethos to the 'lesser breeds'. Tall and strong, he had passed out from Sandhurst with the sword of honour, and after six years with a Sikh pioneer regiment had transferred to the Indian Political Department, where he became an expert on Persia. He had been consul at Mohammerah from 1909 to 1911, and was put in charge of the international Turko-Persian Frontier Commission in 1912. At Basra, dressed in an 'old-style Indian Army tunic buttoning right up to the neck (instead of the new-fangled collar and tie), and belt with two parallel shoulder-straps (instead of the Sam Browne)', he struck a distinctive figure – 'with his flashing eyes, his beetling eyebrows, his close-cropped hair, and his biblical quotations', he reminded some of a hero of the Indian Mutiny.[15] (The image would surely not have offended him.) Behind his charismatic gaze lay a dauntingly tireless worker, shifting mountains of paper through an office festooned with encouraging Latin mottoes. Many of his subordinates found him inspiring, though many, notably St John Philby (against whom Wilson campaigned relentlessly) and even Hubert Young (whom he treated well), found him workaholic and domineering.

The biggest problem for the administration-builder was that the government had no idea what kind of administration it wanted. The result was 'weary months, and indeed years, of temporising and of expensive improvisations', Wilson wrote. 'We rushed into the business with our usual disregard for a comprehensive political scheme,' Bell lamented. 'The creation of an Arabia policy should have been done at home [but] there was no one to do it, no one who had ever thought of it, and it was left to our people in Egypt to thrash out, in face of strenuous opposition from India and London, some sort of wide scheme.' The only expectation was that the civil administration would do what the Army needed to be done. This was a lot: until late 1915, the British-controlled area was spreading, and Nixon's dream of capturing Baghdad was more of a nightmare for the administrators. (Harry St John Bridger Philby – known, inevitably, as 'Jack' – was drafted from India in November to tackle the administrative problems which would follow.) The retreat from Ctesiphon was almost a relief for them, but there was still a serious shortage of qualified staff. 'Men of very different calibres and of all ages' had to be recruited as political officers and administrators (totalling over a hundred by the end of 1917, and four times that number by 1920).[16] Drawn mainly from the army in Mesopotamia, the Indian Political Department and the civil services of India and the Sudan, they also included a notable couple of philologists, the Lorimers (she, a former Oxford don, took over editorship of the *Basra Times*). At the lower levels, quality was variable: 'not all our geese were swans.' But there were some administrative stars. Henry Dobbs, a thorough professional, had, Philby thought, 'a positive genius for unravelling the extremely complicated fiscal system of the Turks'. As Revenue Commissioner, he set about gathering 'data for revenue purposes', an instinctive British procedure that would eventually change Iraq forever. But even these stars had their limits: Dobbs suffered a near-breakdown from pressure of work and the climate in the summer of 1916, and had to be replaced by Philby.

British administrative expedients appeared merely functional, but they smuggled in an unavowed political agenda that might have been evident to anyone taking a careful look. In spite of London's strict injunction against any attempt to 'transform Basra into an Indian district', the influx of Indian officials made such a transformation almost inevitable. Because the old Ottoman legal machinery had disappeared, London's insistence on 'retention of indigenous laws and institutions' was unfeasible. In February 1915 Dobbs issued the 'Tribal Criminal and Civil Disputes Regulations', laying down judicial codes tailored to the supposedly different urban and rural societies of Mesopotamia. These were lifted almost unaltered from the colonial legal code used on the North-West Frontier. Later that year, the Senior Judicial Officer at Basra, Lieutenant-Colonel S. G. Knox – another

Indian political officer, who had been Cox's deputy resident at Bushire – issued the Iraq Occupied Territories Code. Again, this followed Indian law so closely that it could, as Philip Ireland later wrote, be seen as paving the way 'for the painless absorption of Lower Mesopotamia to India'. As Philby ploughed through the financial records of the Mesopotamia administration, he 'soon discovered that the whole system had been organised on Indian civil service lines . . . often regardless of local conditions'.[17]

Stephen Longrigg admitted that the 'honesty and inexperienced zeal' of the incoming political officers – who presented 'in almost every way the strangest of contrasts to their Turkish predecessors' – were not enough to avert 'minor trouble' with tribal communities unused to the new order. The trouble was certainly more serious than that. 'Many punitive columns ranged around Nasiriyeh to chastise those who defied the British', while 'the cramped and ill-furnished Political Offices, staffed with Indian clerks and thronged with petitioners, witnessed from morning to night the rough-and-ready disposal of land and revenue and tribal cases, criminal trials, municipal and police business, and attempts to meet the ever-increasing military demands for information, billets, labour and supplies'.[18]

Harold Dickson, newly transferred from the cavalry to the political service, found himself the sole ruler of Suk-es-Shuyukh on the Euphrates. 'I have never worked so hard in my life, trying to run the district,', he told his mother. 'I am organising the collection of revenue, the date & rice revenue, the Police department, Customs, fish & salt taxes, finally I am sole governor or "PANGANDRUM" of Suk town. I have got any sort of power & yet no power', he reported. 'Yesterday I went & called on several sheikhs who had come in, one was a very holy man who had to be placated. I am going to make use of him – get him to deal with any cases that can be dealt with by "Sheriat" or religious law, such as cases of Marriage, Divorce, Inheritance etc.. . . These are always better dealt with by religious sheikhs.'[19] Dickson followed very precisely the official recipe for reversing the Ottoman fragmentation of sheikhly authority. Within two years he could report, 'I have managed more or less to get the power into the hands of one Sheikh, in the case of each of the 22 Suq tribes' – 'every tribe has its leading Sheikh who comes to see me, and discuss his tribal questions'.[20]

The journalist Edmund Candler, touring the Euphrates area shortly after the failure of the last Kut relief operations, took an optimistic view of these local despots. 'A student of British methods could not do better', he thought, 'than pass a day in a town like Nasiriyeh a year after occupation.' Candler was there on 27 June 1916. He sketched the scene. 'In the seat of authority you will probably find a very young officer, one of the type who has been in the habit of spending his leave before the War in Persia, Arabia, or the Himalayas, picking up strange dialects and studying the ways of stranger people.' Such young captains or 'acting majors' were 'indispensable during the incubation of any new imperial brood'. Such a 'brood' was evidently incubating here: 'here', Candler vividly observed 'you have empire in the egg.' He watched one of these young officers, who had 'acquired an insight into obscure motives', and whose judgements were 'quick and summary, free of pedantry, and seldom hampered by doubts and hesitations', consider a set of cases. (Including 'Fatima', a 'black bundle' who accused her husband of confiscating her property, but whose voice clearly 'gave her shrewish temper away' – she got a week's imprisonment for contempt of court.) He concluded that the proof of the British system was its popularity, and that 'It augurs well for future relations that families should be so ready to confide their troubles to a judge who is not only very youthful, but a stranger to them in accents and mien and habits of thought.' (To say nothing of religion.) The British imperial code was, in another of Candler's arresting phrases, 'instinctive in the national character'.

But the attempt at state-building in a war zone was always likely to be flawed. For the Army, security was all that mattered, and it was quicker to intimidate the people than to win them over. Longrigg's 'many punitive columns' were far too many for the civil administration's liking. Gertrude Bell visited Nasiriyeh in June 1916, and met the local commander Major-General Harry Brooking – 'a fiery little man with a broken heart who lost his only son four months ago in France'. She was dismayed by his readiness to dispatch punitive forces whenever any kind of resistance appeared. The targeting of these blows was fairly indiscriminate; and the cultural echoes they raised were unhappy ones. 'I need not say', she wrote to her friend Valentine Chirol (the celebrated Near Eastern correspondent of *The Times*), 'that it is called "strafing". The amount of damage you can do by shelling from the water is almost negligible, and it is always followed by reprisals which get more and more people into trouble.' The result was 'an ever widening circle of unrest and hostility'. One of Brooking's soldiers, Tom Craig of the Manchester Regiment (serving with the Dorsets in the 42nd Brigade), described the operations. 'The Modus Opperandi is as follows – the artillery "strafes" the nearest village where most probably the marauders came from. Sometimes they get the wrong village which matters little! and after an hour or two's bombardment a "strafing" party of infantry, the exact numbers depends on the size of the village, go and proceed to "wipe out" all who are foolish enough to wait for us. Gurkhas, in particular, like these jobs and can be relied on to scientifically "despatch" all inhabitants mostly per the "kukri" methods, bury them and burn down the village and have everything tidied up before we arrive.'[21] When Bell was driven to remonstrate with Brooking about the strafing policy, he merely retorted (with 'half a snort and half a twinkle'), 'You've been living with the Politicals!'

Hubert Young, a fledgling 'Political' with the Euphrates Division, dodged Brooking's annoyance by saying that he was 'only seconded from my regiment, of which I believe I am still the adjutant'. ('Thank God for that,' the general replied, 'and proceeded to tell me what he thought of the Indian Political Department in general and the Chief Political Officer in particular.')

But Young's experiences with the punitive operations nicknamed 'regattas' showed that what was optimistically labelled 'the Pax Britannica in the occupied territories of Mesopotamia' left a lot to be desired.[22] The country along the Hai, between the British forces on the Euphrates and the Tigris, was occupied by 'really formidable' tribes. They had 'surrounded and badly cut up a whole Indian brigade which had sallied out on a punitive expedition in the Shatra direction' a few months before Young accompanied two infantry battalions and one of the 'fly-boats' (the river monitors of the *Fly* class) on a mission to 'chastise' Abu Risha. The village's offence was that shots had been fired from it on one of the monitors. (The British, though probably not the Arabs, were aware that these gunboats were 'by no means invulnerable': their armour was not proof even against small-arms fire at close range, and on the Euphrates they could not manoeuvre at all – they could only steam ahead or astern.) Young admitted that the chastisement operation was 'not very pleasant'. 'Grim stories were afterwards told' of it, and it was 'almost too successful for the kindly hearts of the British troops involved'.

Another, less 'successful' operation he took part in had the aim of capturing one of the principal Sa'dun leaders of the Muntafik, Ajaimi Pasha, who had fought against the British at Shaiba and Nasiriyeh. Its failure 'sadly damaged our prestige'. Even when the general 'sallied forth with practically the whole division to chastise someone or other, the Muntafiq put up a strong resistance and were not very much impressed'.[23] Harold Dickson, the political officer at Suk, who was ambushed by Arabs early in 1916, was better pleased with the GOC's reaction. Two gunboats packed with 500 troops rapidly arrived: 'resistance there was none but we blew up six large towers, and burnt some 300 houses, including grain, wheat, hay, and before coming away we cut down 300 palm trees. A goodly revenge', he savagely concluded. But he admitted that the ambush had been 'part & parcel of growing unrest among the tribes', and that the punitive force had only just 'got away in time to avoid a big attack'.[24]

The Army's pressure on the people involved not only exemplary punishment, but also forced labour. At Basra, the shortage of labourers meant that men were being 'requisitioned' in huge numbers. Before he went to Nasiriyeh, Hubert Young had been responsible for gathering a workforce to raise a huge earthwork to carry the railway from Basra to Nasiriyeh above the level of the Euphrates floods. The impact of such large-scale works on an agricultural community could be crushing, as Bell saw. They increased Britain's unpopularity, but for her there was a still more serious issue of morality. As her reaction to the word 'strafing' showed, the ascendancy of coercive military logic threatened fundamental British values: 'There is a very fine line between what we are doing here and what the Germans did in Belgium.' In fact, she thought the line was sometimes 'invisible'; punitive action could turn into atrocity, and military control might be turning into militarism. If so, the whole British project would be undermined.

3. Retooling the Army

Our army is waking up again like a huge black bear wakes up
from its long winter sleep.
HAROLD DICKSON

For the military command, the only thing that mattered was
getting supplies to the fighting front. The biggest obstacle was still
the primitive port facilities at Basra (as every new arrival there
testified, with growing incredulity as time went by and nothing
seemed to improve). But the talents of the port expert Sir George
Buchanan remained unused even after the openly obstructive
Nixon departed. Seeing conditions in Basra getting 'more and
more chaotic', Lake eventually asked Buchanan to write a
report: this, predictably, advocated a general reorganisation of
the port and transport system, including the appointment of an
experienced 'independent' (i.e. civilian) traffic superintendent to
manage the port. Still nothing was done, nothing improved, and
in Buchanan's view 'indeed matters got worse'. He decided there
was nothing for it but to go back to India himself and state his
case direct to the Viceroy and C-in-C.[1] Hardinge's successor as
Viceroy, Lord Chelmsford, duly expressed 'astonishment at all I
told him', and sent him back with a commission as a member of
the GOC Force D's staff, with entire control of the port of Basra,
as well as all river works from the Shatt-al-Arab right up to the
front line.

By the time he got back, a new Inspector-General of Communications had arrived, and things were changing at last. This was
the energetic and charismatic Major-General George MacMunn,
who had recently organised the perilous withdrawal at Gallipoli.
He was also the author of a popular illustrated book on the

288

Indian Army, and an enthusiastic proponent of the 'martial races' theory embraced by the Indian military authorities. (It was 'one of the essential differences between the East and the West', he wrote, that 'in the East only certain clans and classes can bear arms; the others have not the physical courage necessary for the warrior'.²) His arrival in mid-April soon lifted the morale of the struggling supply organisation. He went everywhere, as Wilson observed, talked to everyone, got on well with the civil administrators and – more remarkably – with India: 'the note of acrimony which was too often dominant in the endless series of demands on Simla' from GHQ in Mesopotamia was 'replaced by clearly worded and persuasive requests, punctuated by friendly acknowledgements of the difficulties under which he knew India to be labouring, and supported by cheery private letters'.³ He was one of those administrators who could get the best out of people. (An exception was the force's DAQMG, General Cowper, who grumbled that MacMunn was an empire-builder; but Cowper himself was rated 'very slow in thought and action' by the MEF's Chief of Staff. 'If I want to get a move on anything that is dealt with by his department I always go for the man below him.'⁴)

MacMunn recalled the 'melancholy sight' that greeted him on his arrival at Basra – 'twenty ocean steamers loaded with supplies and military stores lay awaiting unloading and had been so for weeks, so devoid was Basra of wharfage, port labour or port craft to handle all that was now pouring into the river'. The Commander-in-Chief had ordered three months' reserve of supplies to be built up there, but 'no one had placed before him what his order meant'; neither he nor the then Inspector-General had realised that the port facilities were hardly equal to receiving the daily requirements, let alone bringing in the tonnage needed to accumulate such a reserve.⁵

The fundamental difficulty was Basra's topography. Patches of reliably dry ground by the river were few, and often far between. Serious engineering was essential to create the sort of facilities needed, but 'no scheme of town and port planning was formulated that showed any conception of what modern transportation required ... No one', MacMunn lamented, 'seemed able to think large.' The Indian administrative system was partly to blame. 'We struck a muddy streak' of Supply and Transport Corps officers, made worse 'by an absurd audit system which sapped all their energy.' His first mission upriver was to find out what had happened to the tons of tinned milk that had been sent up to the front, about whose non-arrival General Gorringe was complaining with characteristic venom. MacMunn quickly found 'countless cases of the missing milk piled in pyramids'; it had been diverted from the troops to the hospitals on the authority of the Principal Medical Officer, whose orders had been accepted by the supply commander without question. The Quartermaster-General had no idea that the supplies had arrived. 'To keep the milk for the sick when hundreds were becoming sick for want of it' was a medical mentality MacMunn judged incomprehensible 'outside of Pekin or Nanking'.

Other problems also responded to the application of a little energy. At Amara, where many of the animals, wagons and 'oddments from brigades and divisional troops that could be spared to lessen the drain on rations' had been left, MacMunn found a militarily grim scene. 'Innumerable small parties ... were squatting under no competent control or discipline, all over a muddy plain. Tents were not properly pitched, men slept in the mud and boiled old billies uncontrolled and unhelped. The young officers, almost all temporary with no experience, had little control over their men or any idea what to do. Every sort of sickness was about, nobody shaved, nobody dressed, odd horses, mules, ordure and horse-litter lay in one unhappy confusion.' He threatened to hang the commandant from his own flagstaff if the camp was not like a Durbar when he came back in three days; and 'the curious thing about it is that it was so'. All the old colonel – capable enough but 'not man enough to assert himself' – needed was 'my *hukm* [authority] behind him'.

MacMunn, predictably, found Gorringe himself 'a little difficult'. He was 'inclined to keep steamers hanging about on the river near the troops', a practice mirroring the general tendency for all units moving along the river to keep their equipment in a couple of *mahelas*, thus tying up a mass of transport potential. MacMunn tried to explain that the net result was aggravation of the delay in bringing up supplies, but Gorringe was 'not very accessible on the subject'. MacMunn quietly took control of all the river shipping, and went on to recast the whole organisation of the transport system. A simple procedure of dividing the 'L of C' into sections (a Base Section from Fao to just above Basra; a section around Qurna and one around Amara, and an Advanced Section) made it easier to clarify who was running each part. Finding competent people to run the system was still a major problem: though MacMunn thought highly of the officer sent out by the War Office to control inland water transport, he remained 'very short of decent personnel'. The base dockyard that was so vital could not be created quickly even if the will had existed; as it was, 'no one would send us workmen or machinery'.

When Buchanan returned from Simla with his special commission as a staff officer to the Army Commander, MacMunn put him on his own staff, as Director General of Port Administration and River Conservancy. But Buchanan (whom Wilson called 'pugnacious', and even MacMunn struggled to get on with) still found himself involved in 'a continual struggle against incompetence, ignorance, and obstruction'. As late as August 1916, after Buchanan had been in control for two months, the War Office sent out a new Deputy Director of Inland Water Transport, to manage the whole fleet of river steamers. When he arrived, Buchanan handed him the report of his committee; he 'thanked me and said the reports would save him several months' work'. But he said that neither he nor the War Office knew anything about Buchanan's directorate, and he had come out to take charge of everything to do with water transport, including the management of the seaport.[6] MacMunn had his work cut out in harmonising the ambitions of these experts from the two systems which still coexisted uneasily in Mesopotamia. Gertrude Bell concluded that Buchanan was, in the end, 'not good enough for the job . . . He has a colossal estimation of himself, but Mesopotamia defeated him.'

Buchanan was sidelined into a massive dredging scheme on the Hammar Lake, where six and a half miles of channel were dredged at huge effort and cost before work was suspended. It was eventually taken up again in 1918, after Buchanan had left Mesopotamia, and completed in early 1919 'having excavated seven and a half million cubic yards'. Initially it was a tremendously impressive operation. 'The magnitude and novelty of the scheme filled the tribesmen with wonder', Wilson said, 'and the sight of the great dredgers at work inspired awe.' That a new river, 160 feet broad, 11 feet deep and 25 miles long, should have been made by the British within twelve months, for their convenience, suggested 'to their simple minds [he believed] a new and not unfruitful trend of thought'. But it was incredibly expensive, and militarily worthless.[7] Buchanan pronounced the whole scheme misguided: 'technically the work so far as it went was a success, but from every other point of view it was a melancholy failure, and a typical example of how vast sums of money can be thrown away in time of war.'

MacMunn also had a battle with the Navy for control of all the river craft, apart from the warships. ('The sailor outside his own job is a hopeless creature at running a bundobust,' he told a friend.) By late 1916 he would be able to 'deliver 800 tons a day at the front by steamer and 200 more by native craft'.[8] By then a railway line was also operating between Qurna and Amara, with another line due to cover the 140 miles to Nasiriyeh by Christmas. The first of these, a 2 ft 6 in gauge railway, had a picturesque history, beginning as the sightseeing line at the Delhi Durbar. It had been offered to Nixon when he first asked for a railway, and he had ordered it to be laid between Basra and Nasiriyeh. After several miles had been laid, and Nixon had left, Lake realised that it would be inadequate as the sole supply route for Nasiriyeh, and it was taken up again and moved to the forward area.

The final link in the communication chain, motor transport, also began to appear. It would be vital for any advance beyond Baghdad (where the Tigris was no longer navigable). But it would have even further-reaching consequences, launching a revolution in Iraqi communications that would transform the country after the war. Though no metalled roads existed yet, the potential supplies of oil were limitless. In January 1916 the first Mechanical Transport Company of the Army Service Corps arrived at Basra from Egypt, equipped with around a hundred 3-ton Crossley trucks.[9] A second followed in June, and in September an effective M.T. commander for the whole country was appointed. Developing the system was a slow process: the heavy trucks could not get up to the front until roads were built, which could hardly be done in the flood season. Most of the drivers came from India, and formed a microcosm of the Indian Army; every group not only spoke a different language but had – as Arnold Wilson pointed out – its own 'peculiarities of diet, and distinctive mentality'.[10] Discipline, always problematic in M.T. units 'where the men are scattered up and down the lines of communication and are beyond supervision for a great part of the time', was particularly hard to maintain in the empty spaces of Mesopotamia. But the force gradually acquired what MacMunn called 'a spirit of helpfulness', without 'slavish adherence to red tape'. By the end of the war it would grow to 12,000 men, with 7,000 military vehicles.

The modern world also arrived in the shape of military aviation. During the advance on Baghdad in 1915, the shortage and unreliability of aircraft had undermined vital reconnaissance, and even during the Kut relief campaign there were not enough planes to dispute air control with the Ottoman – really German – Air Force. In summer 1916 Turkish air superiority was overwhelming. Only in the autumn did it begin to be disputed, when twenty-four up-to-date machines with far more effective bomb-aiming and photo-reconnaissance equipment arrived, and a series of successful dogfights gradually gave Britain control of the air. (As well as providing some exciting entertainment for the bored men on the ground.) By September the C-in-C could report that 'on the Tigris we have got a very marked superiority in the air . . . their aeroplanes have only been up about six or seven times this month, whereas we carry out two reconnaissances daily, and the information we get is good and reliable'.[11] Out in the wilds of the Euphrates, the annihilation of distance by air travel was astonishing. When Percy Cox paid a surprise visit to Dickson's district in October, he flew back from Nasiriyeh to Basra in an hour and a half. 'Appalling and strange to think of it,' Dickson reflected, since the normal time for the journey by boat was five or six days.[12]

In time, air reconnaissance would help to overcome the limitations of military intelligence, which were mercilessly exposed in T. E. Lawrence's April 1916 report. Lawrence painted a dim picture of an intelligence system headed by a man (Colonel Beach) who, though 'very excellent', had 'never been in Turkey, or read about it, and knows no Arabic'. This might not have mattered, but for the fact that 'intelligence staff at such places as Basra, Amara, Ali Gharbi, Sheikh Saad, Nasiriya, Ahwaz, and with the Corps in the fighting line, cannot speak any of the local languages'. They were totally dependent on interpreters, with all the drawbacks they entailed. Agents were not effectively cross-questioned, and 'you get gross errors of place or number, besides confusion of technical military terms'. The officer at Amara who was 'trying very hard to work up a secret intelligence system' was stymied by his agents, who 'spent their time telling wild fictions, or denouncing their private or tribal enemies as Turcophiles'.

Lawrence noted that 'all the fighting between Sheikh Saad and Kut has been over unsurveyed country'. The only maps available were at a scale of 4 miles to the inch, showing 'almost nothing but the main stream of the Tigris'. There was a constant error of 200–300 yards, and local errors up to a mile. 'When artillery maps were first called for, the Corps produced them by enlarging the degree sheets twelve times . . . then began to fill these maps in from aeroplane photographs.' On to the 'slight enough' originals were added 'scratch productions, taken from all angles, usually without any overlap, at any time of day, and on half a dozen scales'. The drawing up was done by a staff officer who had never drawn anything in his life, had no instruments except pencil, dividers and an army protractor, and had to guess where the photographs fitted. The results lacked any topographical sense – they were 'trench diagrams only'. Finally, they were drawn by hand on a stone (of which there were only three) and printed on 'a press like a mangle which does up to three hundred a day'. The maps were 'improving steadily', but were 'still too inaccurate to be of much use, confused and difficult to read, and printed on very soft paper which tears at once in a wind'.[13]

The man responsible for these maps, Captain John Crowdy of the corps intelligence staff, was stung by these strictures. 'A fellow called Lawrence turned up,' he wrote, 'and told me that my maps made the Egyptian survey weep.' This was 'rather unkind', he thought. Crowdy had long bemoaned the difficulties faced by 'an amateur who is absolutely singlehanded and working under very adverse conditions', with hardly any equipment – not even a ruler was available when he drew his first nineteen maps – trying to copy air photographs on to fragile paper in a tent ravaged by wind. But he could console himself that, as General Maude pointed out, his maps were at least issued in time to be used in action, which the maps supplied to the Gallipoli force by the Egyptian mapmakers seldom were.[14]

Soon after Lawrence left Mesopotamia, and Crowdy left the corps staff (by the time he went to 21st Brigade as its brigade major in July, he had 'had enough of mapping to last a lifetime'), the situation began to improve at long last. Thanks to the enlargement of 30 Squadron, and the addition of a half-flight of the new Australian Flying Corps (AFC), more air reconnaissance flights could be mounted (by September the average number of plates being exposed weekly had risen to fifty-eight). By the end of October, the whole Turkish position from Sannaiyat to Shumran had been mapped on a scale of three inches to a mile. The crucial development was the introduction of the Williamson Aero camera in mid-November, dramatically improving both the quantity and quality of air photography. Mesopotamia was ideally suited to air observation, naturally. It was 'axiomatic' that 'if air reconnaissance during operations is thorough and continuous, the enemy cannot make a move of tactical importance without being observed'.[15]

The change most directly felt by the sorely tried relief force as it sat out the summer of 1916 came at the top. Robertson had often grumbled about the lack of 'a young active commander' in Mesopotamia. Now he found one. Gorringe was, if not as jaded as his troops, obviously 'strained' and 'feeling the effect of all he had gone through'. When Lake asked the senior staff for their views about him, according to MacMunn, 'we unanimously agreed that he wanted a rest'.[16] MacMunn certainly knew that the real reason was that Gorringe and Lake had fallen out spectacularly. Gorringe's objections to what Duff called Lake's 'legitimate advice' had become 'so insubordinate that the situation had to be brought to an end'.[17] His successor was the youngest of the MEF's divisional commanders, Stanley Maude – 'a stout-hearted, intelligent, pleasant-mannered man who [Robertson thought] takes a great interest in his troops', and – more crucially – 'has got his head screwed on right'.[18] Maude's ascent became vertiginous when Lake himself went shortly afterwards, Duff grumpily writing to Robertson, 'I daresay you had good reasons' for removing him. (Incredibly, Chamberlain had told Robertson early in February that 'everyone agreed that Lake is not equal to his job', yet he stayed on until July.[19])

Maude had a reputation as a 'centraliser', who kept control of every detail – not, as one staff officer put it, because he did not trust his subordinates, but rather because 'it was second nature with him to look into the details of everything. If the work was not being done to his satisfaction, he took over the personal guidance of it.' His reputation rested on his transformation of the 13th Division at the Dardanelles: he had taken it over 'just after it had been shot to pieces, and he worked it up in six months to a pitch of perfection that made it second to none'. But he remained, it seems, remarkably accessible.[20] To MacMunn the change of atmosphere was palpable – 'with Maude we soon found that we could get plenty of ideas and suggestions'. Moreover, what MacMunn called 'the human trouble' tended to disappear.

He was referring in particular to the 'religious scruples' that had led the 'rather famous Mooltani Horse' (the 15th Lancers) to refuse to march against Baghdad and the holy places of Islam during the Kut relief operations. Lake had reported on 23 February 1916 that over 400 of the 500 men of the 15th Lancers had refused to march out of Basra. This was by far the biggest mutiny of any Indian regiment during the war, and inevitably raised the spectre of the Great Mutiny yet again.[21] It capped a series of minor alarms, such as one witnessed by Chalmers during the battle of Sheikh Saad, when three Afridi sepoys of the 28th Punjabis were shot for refusing to go forward. ('They were made to dig their own graves and were permitted to lie down in them when the time came. They were finished off by Tommies as it is not advisable to get their comrades to do so.') The 'whole double company are reported bad' and a batch of twenty was taken to India to be court-martialled.

But in the case of the 15th Lancers, MacMunn heard that 'they had not been ordered to march but asked if they would like to! Phew!' he incredulously wrote (noting the similarity to the 'Curragh Mutiny' in 1914). 'Folk who do that do not deserve an army.' This mutiny clearly revealed the anxieties of the military authorities. Various signs of trouble had been seen, including 'some excitement' at the ceremony known as 'Oman manga', at which Muslim troops on their way to battle passed under the Quran and called for divine protection. There seemed to be some doubt whether the men saw it as the usual ceremony or 'whether it was intended to entail an obligation not to fight in the holy land of Iraq'. At this stage – like the commander at the Curragh – the CO took steps 'definitely to ascertain their feelings', and was rewarded with a mass refusal to march.

Minor 'mutinies' were often treated leniently, as 'disobeying a lawful command', and privately regarded as 'nothing more than the "sudden fit" which natives sometimes take'.[22] But not in this case: the regiment was disbanded on the spot. Those who had said they intended not to march were court-martialled, and handed out a variety of sentences ranging from transportation for life (3), through seven years' transportation (285) to three years' 'rigorous imprisonment' (64).[23] 'So the poor old Mooltanis were wiped off the Army List, spoilt for want of a word and a blow,' MacMunn lamented. The problem may have been slightly more serious than his instinctive Orientalism implied. But it is interesting that after Maude, who had no experience of Indian troops, took over, the earlier alarms about Muslim sentiment faded away. 'The moment the rations improved and Maude got the fighting tails up', MacMunn said, 'we heard no more of religious scruples.' (And, he added, 'even the steamers seemed to want docking less'.[24])

Certainly the troops had been in need of something. Edmund Candler painted a dismal picture of the state of Force D in the wake of the fall of Kut. He 'sampled the different kinds of heat and torment endured by that long-suffering body of troops – the moist and tropical heat of the Euphrates and the Shatt-al-Arab, the parched and desert heat of the Tigris and Karun, the heavy-laden atmosphere of Bushire. Each variety had its attendant insects, its own peculiar plague. On the Karun you might be stricken with what is commonly known as "dog-rot", the legacy of some poisonous fly. The water of the Tigris engendered colic. The Baghdad boil and the Aleppo date ... left a permanent impression of Mesopotamia burnt into you.' At Basra 'the very air seems to sweat. Strike a match and it will burn dully without a flicker as if the flame were choked.' In the desert the heat in tents and trenches felt like 'standing at the edge of a huge fire in a high wind, licked by gusts of flame'. At least this was 'fierce rather than oppressive and depressing'. The almost daily dust storms were different: 'the whole plain is in motion, the air is darkened, the heat is heavy and sullen . . . there is a uniform dead weight to support.' Lying down seemed the only option – 'but the man in the office, tent or dug-out winds a wet towel round his head and goes plugging on with his work'.[25]

Heat was crushing, but the flies were worse. 'To describe them is to hazard one's reputation for truth.' They settled in clouds on everything: like many others, Candler found himself watching bodies of troops who appeared to be wearing chain mail. 'I had walked my horse beside them some minutes before I discovered that it was the steely blue metallic mesh of flies.' At night, flies were replaced by mosquitoes and sandflies, a more insidious plague. A net fine enough to keep out sandflies was suffocating, and they 'kept one awake at night with a hose of thin acid playing on one's face'. They transmitted a virulent fever that defeated all the efforts of 'entomologists, bacteriologists, protozoologists, and learned men whose opinion was recognised as the last word in sanitation and hygiene'. (One heatstroke expert, Sir Victor Horsley, attributed all ills to alcohol consumption. 'He preached the theory that lime-juice provides the best possible protection against the sun and rendered topis and spine-pads superfluous,' Philby recorded. 'He was buried in the cemetery at Amara.'[26]) The only crumb of comfort in May 1916 was that, as an old campaigner told Candler, 'they'll die off when it gets really hot'. How hot was that? 'Oh, about 112 degrees in one's tent. Of course it goes up to anything – 130 degrees, or more.' The Mesopotamian sun, Candler reflected, 'corrodes all pride . . . the staff officer will ride abroad in his shirt-sleeves innocent of all tabs'. But certain things had to be worn at all times: sun helmets even under canvas, 'a sunguard over one's helmet, and a spine-pad, for one can get sunstroke here through the small of one's back'.[27]

The 'great discomfort and often misery of the troops', General Keary wrote in late May, was worsened by poor diet. 'No extras to be bought anywhere in the way of food, eggs, milk, fowls, vegetables etc so food is very monotonous.'[28] Weakened by short rations and grinding experience, the army was particularly vulnerable to the climate. 'Four months of reverses, the fruitless sacrifice of lives . . . did not contribute to the stiffening which body and spirit needed against the malice of the dog days. The sun when he is strong and one has no adequate defence against him is the most relentless, untiring enemy a man can have. One's skin becomes an affliction, one's blood a curse, one's tongue and throat a torture . . . '[29]

The casualty rate was staggering. 'Sickness excessive', Keary reported, 'cholera, bowel diseases of all sorts as well as jaundice and other things.' In the 82nd Punjabis in mid-July 'the rate of sickness is appalling, 18 today nearly all jaundice and scurvy. Lack of green food. We have sent 119 to hospital in 19 days.'[30] The average strength of a division in May and June 1916 was 5,000; every week 2,500 were evacuated from the casualty clearing station at Sheikh Saad. The equivalent of three divisions were invalided from Basra to India in one month. Thanks in part to sharp inequalities in rations – British troops were given one pound of fresh meat and one of potatoes or vegetables daily, Indian troops a quarter of that amount – Indian troops were particularly prone to scurvy, which caused 11,000 of them to be evacuated in the second half of 1916.[31] The unusually literate Private Roe was evacuated in April, at the climax of the relief attempts, ending up in an isolation camp at Basra. On 4 May 'a party of wounded were selected for India. As usual, my luck was out as I was away fishing at the time of the selection . . . I swore there and then that I would never indulge in Isaac [sic] Walton's favourite pastime again. The men who were on Gallipoli were selected first. My God! To think I missed India for the sake of three mudfish, the combined weight of which did not exceed ¼ lb.'[32]

Stuck at Basra, Roe was struck by the 'incredible number of "lead swingers" wallowing' there. 'They complain of heart disease today, gastritis the following day, rheumatism the day after; in fact they can invent a disease for every day of the year. If they get "well in" with the matron or in other words "dug in" behind a petticoat, the College of Surgeons could not shift them.' About 45 in every 100, he thought, 'were afflicted with "Mauseritis and shellitis"'. He penned a brilliant vignette of the contest between 'a new and fearless MO' and an experienced malingerer who had been at Basra for seven months with a series of afflictions, ending with unidentifiable 'pains in the chest'. 'Well, Brown, I consider that you have been long enough in here. I will give you a week's light duty . . . some work might do wonders with those pains.' The MO removes several more 'pillow flatteners', but 'next day Brown reports sick and produces his master card, TEETH'. Before being passed fit in England, he had been issued with a set of false teeth ('to enable him to masticate army biscuits of concrete firmness at the public expense'). He reported that he had taken them out the night before, and left them in a cup of water, which had been taken off by a jackal. 'MO sarcastically: "You don't fight Turks with your teeth. In any case, take this card across to the dentist." Brown laughs – another six months at least at the base.' As Roe reflected, jackals are audacious animals when hungry. But such audacity was not necessary: 'I have known men who were "fixed up" at home with dentures and on arrival at Basrah stated to the MO, "Sir, I was suffering from mal-de-mer in the Bay of Biscay. I was hurriedly forced to vomit over the side of the trooper. With the force of the vomiting the clasps of the dentures became loose and over the false teeth went . . . " Of course it means another set of dentures and six months at the base. The dentures that are supposed to lie on the bottom of the Bay are in his kit bag.'[33]

And of course, now the crisis was past, reinforcements flooded into the country. All the old arguments about Mesopotamia being a minor theatre seemed to have been forgotten. 'Economy was not considered, either in money or in men,' Candler wrote. 'But it was too late.' Mesopotamia, 'this cursed country', became 'a mouth which we fed lavishly with the manhood which was essential elsewhere'.[34] In mid-June Ned Roe noted that thousands of reinforcements were arriving weekly from Britain, and 'these youngsters and old men are dying like flies from heatstroke'. For every hundred soldiers who left Britain for Mesopotamia, he thought, no more than thirty reached the firing line. Aside from the problem that some were 'old crocks' and some leadswingers, there was the entirely avoidable problem caused by failure to acclimatise the drafts. The new arrivals simply disregarded all health instructions. They would gorge themselves on fruit, washed or not, and refuse to drink chlorinated water because they did not like the taste. 'They walk about at mid-day minus helmets and with only a Port Said singlet on. Results: twenty or thirty in the heat stroke station by 6pm and five or six are dead by morning.' Many of the survivors would have to be sent out of the country again. Candler itemised some of the losses, such as a draft of 139 men of the Highland Light Infantry who arrived at Basra: 28 of them reached the front. 'Perhaps the most ironic item', he noted, was a batch of 90 doctors who landed at Basra on 15 May. Within three months, 10 had died and 40 had been invalided out.[35]

Probably the most exciting military event of the tedious summer was the arrival of a Cossack contingent on a mission of no obvious military relevance, but high symbolic value. A *sotnia* of 125 cavalry, with no more than ten pack animals, had left the Kermanshah area in Persia on 8 May, and covered the 180 miles to Ali Gharbi at a rate of 24 miles a day on the march – their final day's march to the British base was 30 miles. Crossing passes over 8,000 feet high, and living off the country, their march was, as an admiring Candler said, 'a fine test of our Ally's resource, mobility and endurance'. Though they lost horses over precipices, and five horses died of thirst and exhaustion crossing the desert between the foothills and the Tigris, none of the men fell sick. 'They were a hard lot.' Arriving after nightfall, they were given a dinner and 'were singing and dancing till after one in the morning'.[36] They went on to Basra, where they were 'lavishly entertained', with caviare and champagne drawn from the big cellars of the Wonckhaus firm (one of the leading German enterprises in the Gulf, which Cox had spent years trying to hold back – its stocks had been gleefully commandeered by Wilson). Inevitably 'the proceedings were kept up till a late hour with great hilarity,' Philby recalled, reflecting how extraordinary it was that 'men who had made the strenuous march through the Persian mountains should have been able to turn out for a Basra dinner-party in full-dress Cossack uniform'.[37] After they left in early June, even General Maude, somewhat unexpectedly, fantasised about 'joining those Cossacks who came to see us the other day in their roving life about the country, travelling light and covering the ground quickly'. His more serious point was that, as he candidly added, 'We understand the science of mobility so little.'[38]

4. Captivity

We speculated on the treatment we should receive if captured.
The Turk is said to be off the civilized map . . .
EDWARD MOUSLEY

I shall be immensely surprised if more than 4,000 out of the
9,000 who were taken prisoners ever come out of Turkey alive.
H. MCNEAL

If ever there was a place which warranted the erection of a
signpost marked 'To Hell – 1,000 miles', it was this wretched
Arab village of Tikrit, and it would be well for archaeologists in
their agreeable travels to places of interest such as Nineveh . . .
to pause for one moment in memory of their fellow men, British,
Indian and Nepalese, who in 1916 passed through the country in
barbaric slavery, never again to return to their homes.
HAROLD WHEELER

Edward Mousley's estimate of his captors as 'off the civilized
map' was a common British view. But in spite of this, 'everyone
seems to think we should be done first rate', while some even
convinced themselves that the Turks 'would be so bucked at
capturing a whole army and five real live generals that we should
be offered the Sultan's Palace of Sweet Waters on the Bosphorus
and a special seraglio'.[1] Few seem to have wondered whether their
enemies might see the destruction of all the usable military stores
as a breach of contract. (Though Private Wheeler would conclude
that it 'undoubtedly was the root cause of so much malevolence',
a terrible penalty was exacted on those who had 'served their
fellow men well to the bitter end'.)[2] Turkish displeasure became
instantly apparent when the new commandant of Kut, Colonel
(Kai-Makam) Nizam Bey – 'a tall fellow wearing large pince-nez,
very stiff and erect, and of distinctly German staff-officer type'

– rode into the British lines on 29 April accompanied by Captain Shakeshaft of the 2nd Norfolks. 'Ou sont vos canons?' he demanded.[3] When Shakeshaft indicated some of the wreckage, 'the Turkish colonel exploded into very lurid French and seemed much excited'.[4]

The victorious troops followed him into Kut later that morning by way of the fort, 'and after the soldiers had piled their arms they wandered about in groups of twos and threes, looking at our gun positions and picking up anything they saw lying around'. The victors created mixed impressions. To McNeal it seemed that 'the investing force consisted chiefly of Arab irregulars, and very ragged, badly disciplined troops they were'. Sandes called them 'a very war-worn crowd of men'; compared with the British troops, 'the extraordinary variety of costume in the Turkish ranks was very noticeable'. They wore all kinds of tunics, mainly of a very coarse thick yellowish-grey material, but including a few of British khaki and German field grey. Footwear was similarly variegated, and puttees 'were of all colours and patterns, wound or coiled on in every conceivable way'. Many used their puttees as improvised footwear. The observant Sandes detailed the rest of their equipment, from the 'peculiar half helmet, half cap' called the 'Enverri', through their bulky ammunition pouches, to their Mauser-pattern rifles taking Spitzer ammunition, with long and heavy bayonets. Sandes thought that, considering their shortages of equipment, the amount of looting 'was extremely small and does credit to the discipline of the enemy'. He was unusual in this, though: many of the garrison reported widespread looting – which Ottoman officers only erratically controlled. Private Wheeler's unit was marching down to the river to embark when two of them carrying an officer's valise were 'held up at the point of the bayonet'. In this case, 'after much shouting and expostulation a Turkish officer turned up and admonished the offenders'. Other officers shot looters out of hand. But when Mousley's mess was thoroughly looted, the

Turkish officer Mousley called in to help 'pleaded with rather than ordered' the troops to stop.

McNeal thought that the kit allowance (200 lb for officers, 30 lb for men) 'seemed extraordinarily liberal'. (He later decided the reason was to permit most of it to be seized by Turkish troops.) While some officers were surprised that there was no formal surrender of swords – the divisional artillery officers were apparently ordered to keep theirs – others had certainly not expected to have to give them up. Believing it to be a military custom for officers of garrisons that surrender voluntarily after a long siege to keep their swords, Sandes was indignant that only Townshend was allowed to do so. The rest had to take theirs to the divisional staff office, where Nizam Bey 'bowed, took the sword, and shook hands with perfect courtesy'. Mousley had already handed his sword to the polite Turkish officer he found, after retrieving it from one of the soldiers. 'At this he was most moved.'[5]

The violence of the Turkish reoccupation of Kut can hardly have come as a surprise – it fitted the British propaganda of their enemy precisely – but many were still shocked by the public executions of collaborators. These were the people who had trusted in British power, and been betrayed. But whatever the British thought of the moral qualities of the Turks, most of them acknowledged that the hardships they themselves faced after the surrender were due to simple incompetence rather than deliberate policy. Sandes charitably pointed out 'in fairness to the Turks that they were hard put to it to maintain their own field army in food and ammunition with their very inadequate shipping and land transport'; and also 'perhaps they scarcely understood that British and Indian soldiers cannot exist on the food on which a Turk will thrive', much less how 'trying' the British found the heat of Mesopotamia. Still, as he added, since the fall of Kut had been expected for ten days at least, it was hard to accept that 'the Turks do not appear to have made any arrangements for feeding and sheltering our men'.

The Ottoman military authorities' inability to cope with their haul of over 13,000 prisoners (of whom 277 were British officers, and 2,592 British rank and file; 204 were Indian officers and 6,988 Indian rank and file; the rest – 3,248 – were Indian 'followers') was plain as soon as they were brought out of Kut to the Shumran bend a few miles upriver. Almost all were marched the eight miles to 'a desolate strip of land quite close to the river bank without any protection from the sun'. Most of the men 'had no tents, and were exposed to the full force of the sun, except for such slight shelter as a few could get from their blankets. Many had no blankets or kit of any sort, and no arrangements were made by the Turks to supply them with any shelter.' Sandes himself went up in a steamer with the other officers, including Shakeshaft, who had spent the day accompanying Turkish units taking over the Kut defences.

On the afternoon of the 29th, as British troops were being slowly packed on to the steamer *Basra*, 'the Turks were resting in groups on the front, or wandering in twos and threes through the streets and emergency roads of the town with a keen eye for any unguarded rifles'. The day was bright and sunny, and very hot, as the ship got under way, overhauling long columns of more unfortunate British infantry trudging through the palm groves. After passing the front-line trenches, the British officers were able to view the Turkish gun positions, 'so carefully concealed that even at such close quarters it was almost impossible to locate the guns themselves in their deep emplacements'.[6] After two hours' steaming upriver, Shakeshaft and his comrades 'disembarked in the midst of the most awful chaos imaginable', Shakeshaft wrote. Halil's idea of a camp lived down to Townshend's scepticism.

Next morning at 7 a.m. 'the Bimbashi marched in a company of infantry, well built lusty red cheeked Anatolian peasants but woefully equipped. All their uniforms were ragged & patched, & there was hardly a pair of boots amongst the lot, we felt as if we had been captured by a lot of armed tramps.' Walker, MO of the 120th Infantry, recalled that 'We & 110th piled rifles

& ammunition and handed them over – nothing more. The bimbashi was fearfully disappointed, he had expected lots of stuff, especially a telephone or several telephones. He came to me several times & demanded telephones without any success.' Walker reflected smugly, 'We had done our work of destruction with great thoroughness & the river hid everything.' The change in their lives was sudden. 'Our first day of imprisonment dragged interminably.' But it had its consolations: 'One was always listening at Kut and analysing various sounds of guns rifle and bombs, whether our own or Turks, in which section, etc; first thing we noticed after siege was over, was the relief of silence.'[7]

In the afternoon, Halil Pasha and his staff came up from Kut, accompanied by General Delamain, aboard the captured *Firefly* (renamed the *Suleiman Pak* in honour of the battle the British called Ctesiphon). Shakeshaft 'was called on to represent the case and ask Halil Pasha to send food to the troops as soon as possible'. Halil 'was extremely polite, and Kazim Bey, GOC 18th Army Corps, took down all my requests in a notebook'.[8] This was a high-level version of a procedure that would soon become depressingly familiar, though in this case there was at least some result. Several cartloads of Turkish Army biscuits were delivered that evening. These were dumped unceremoniously on the ground 'and lay there in a dusty heap until distributed by our own Supply and Transport officers'. Though many of them were mouldy and mildewed, the biscuits themselves were less of a problem than their unfamiliarity. 'Imagine an enormous slab of rock-like material, about 5 inches in diameter and ¾ inch thick . . . dark brown in colour and hard as iron.' It seems that nobody in authority on the British side knew anything about these, or could advise the starving men not to try to gnaw at them immediately, though clearly some of the wiser soldiers knew enough to soak them with river water first. That way they turned slowly into a porridge of undoubted nutritional value – this was what the Ottoman armies largely subsisted on themselves. But eaten in their hard state, they had a catastrophic effect on weakened digestive systems, and within hours men were dying of what was called 'gastro-enteritis' or 'cholerine' by the doctors. 'The silence at night was constantly broken by the agonising cries of such cases, and from a nearby tent which served the purpose of a mortuary dozens of bodies were taken away for burial.'[9] (McNeal stated that 'in one week after the surrender there were nearly 300 deaths'.)

But alongside the notorious biscuits, the prisoners received a load of 'Arab cigarettes' – twelve each, not ungenerous. The capriciousness that would become so familiar was already evident: many Ottoman troops walked amongst the prisoners selling food – some of it, possibly, rations intended for free distribution. (Sandes 'on one occasion actually caught a Turk selling our rations, and escorted him to the ration-stand, where he delivered over his stores without protest and without payment'.[10]) This was not in line with the Hague Convention, but at least those with money could improve their diet. Those without money were quickly reduced to bartering their clothing for food.

The distinction between officers and other ranks, which would soon be widened, was also already apparent. Even though the officers were sharing the same bare ground with the men, they had tents and much of their kit. ('With our camp beds and my little X-pattern table and a candle lamp', Sandes – sharing a fellow officer's single-fly 80-pound tent – was 'quite snug in our shelter'.) McNeal 'gave Rs 10 for a 1 lb tin of compressed beef, and was glad to get it'. He found that the Turks were quite willing to accept silver rupees, but not Indian notes. Shakeshaft found a Turkish post on the camp perimeter where he bought a leg of lamb, so the Norfolks had a 'good dinner (drinking the last bottle of beer, which we had kept for the relief)'. Firewood was provided free, and distributed by the British supply service. 'The Turks made no attempt to interfere in any way with the management of our camp,' Sandes wrote, 'and everything was done by our own officers and under the orders of our own generals.'

On the second day at Shumran, the 6th Division had its last shared experience. As Townshend passed by in a fast motor boat en route to Constantinople, his troops lined the riverbank – 'a most affecting sight, thousands of starved scarecrows on the beach cheering him', Walker recalled. 'I shall never forget that cheer,' Townshend wrote. 'Tears filled my eyes as I stood to attention at the salute.' Walker, though, recalled that 'he was so upset he lifted his helmet instead of saluting and rushed off'.[11] The cheering was plainly an act of defiance and self-assertion, though Russell Braddon, who for once believed Townshend's own account, found this response hard to understand. 'They cheered him then, and to this day not one of his troops can be found who does not praise him.' Even amongst the officers he could find (and not for want of trying) 'none who blame him sufficiently to condemn him'.[12]

Four days later, on 3 May, the Ottoman military authorities delivered a big shipment of food from the *Julnar*. 'This was the most cheery thing that had happened to us since Dec. 1st battle,' Walker recalled. 'We started with flour cake and a bottle of marsala, and went to a lunch of (1) turtle soup (2) cold tongue (3) sardines (4) plum pudding (5) apricots and cream assisted with some real good whisky and marsala. Our first square meal for five months . . . We were warning each other not to eat too much, poor old Hill of 110th lunched chiefly off beer and plum pudding . . . was carried off to hospital and nearly died.' The chief beneficiaries of this plenty were, of course, the British officers. Some Christmas pudding reached the ranks, and the Indian officers (who lived and ate separately from their British comrades) were permitted some food appropriate to their special diet: 'We were able to give the IOs a good lot of stores such as biscuits and cakes, they were awfully pleased.'[13]

The distribution of luxury food was immediately followed by preparations for the march into captivity. As Townshend had warned, this was always going to be grim. It was made even worse by the separation of officers from their men, and the setting of intolerable march distances for the weakened soldiers. On 6 May 'to the consternation of everyone in the Division', the Ottoman authorities announced that the officers would be taken from the men and sent up to Baghdad by boat; the men would have to march.[14] (Should Townshend have ordered his officers to remain with their troops 'even if the Turks shot them for doing so', as Braddon insisted? In light of what followed, perhaps he should. But the danger was real, and King's Regulations did not require officers to run it.) The senior officers had expected the whole force to be taken up by boat; Halil later told Mellis that he had asked Lake for enough coal to make this possible, but been refused.[15] Delamain insisted that the men could not march more than eight miles per day, and got the camp commandant to promise that this would be the maximum; but like other such commitments, this was honoured once only. (On the second day, they were pushed on for eighteen miles.) These were men for whom, at the end of the siege, 'a walk of 200 yards and most of us were played out'.[16] The efforts of medical officers like Walker to save the weakest men were defeated by Turkish medical inspection procedures. 'I picked 76 of 120th as quite unfit to march (out of 300). The inspection was a farce, I don't think the doctor meant badly but he was bullied by Tk commandant who would hardly let him put anyone back.' He ordered men to march 'with dysentery, beri-beri, scurvy, convalescent pneumonias, men shot through chest, legs, knee-joint etc. We had picked 1200 as unfit to march. Tks took 83 of them!'[17]

On 5 May 'the poor wretches of men pushed off at 3pm bereft of their officers'. 'One of the most sorrowful sights', for McNeal, 'was the parting of the officers and men who had served together for so long, and many officers broke down while saying goodbye to their units . . . A marching column was formed – six or eight abreast – with a mounted escort of Kurdish cavalry prancing about on either side.' Walker watched as 'the men marched off, about 10,000 strong and cheered their officers as they went, it was a most pathetic sight – hungry, sick, wounded, disarmed, prisoners, they kept a stiff upper lip and gave "Eyes Right" and cheered with a will'. The sequel was all too predictable. In the sober words of Harold Wheeler of the Hampshires, 'as the day wore on individuals gradually fell behind, and by late afternoon the result would be a struggling mass of humanity engulfed in clouds of dust'. Forming the tail of the British column with the Gurkhas, men of Wheeler's company who fell back 'would find themselves hopelessly mixed up with Indian troops of different castes and religion, until later when the head of the column halted they were able to regain their places'. Even a trek of no more than twelve miles 'would seem like an eternity, as with parched lips, burning brows, and aching limbs, the sick men would struggle to keep moving. Those suffering from dysentery obliged to fall out on the march, were shown no compassion whatsoever by the escort who throughout adopted a menacing attitude with cries of "Yallah, yallah, emshee, yallah" – making indiscriminate use of rifle-butt to force sick or dying men to their feet.' (A laconic diary entry is typical: 'March out 2pm 6 May, no breakfast next day. Reached Bughaila 4pm. Not a single unit had been able to keep its order . . . the last of our crowd [131 RFC and 8 AFC] did not get in till after dusk. Eighteen died on this day's march.')

Getting 'mixed up' was disastrous – the mutual support provided by units was often the difference between survival and death. The violence of the escorts – the Kurds especially – is not easy to explain. Even allowing for ignorance of international law (though the military authorities cannot have been ignorant of it), the ill-treatment of prisoners of war was certain to increase the pressures on the inadequate Ottoman medical service. (When the prisoners arrived in Baghdad, over 3,000 were admitted to hospital, according to McNeal.) The British troops were subjected to what, in a later genocidal context, would be called 'death marches'. Since there seemed no reason for the relentless and violent pressure on them – what was the hurry? – many saw it as a deliberate effort to reduce their numbers. But there may be no rational explanation of this ferocious cruelty: perhaps it simply reflected the situation in the Ottoman Army itself – observed with bemusement by the British – where the rank and file were often subject to quite arbitrary, brutal and even homicidal treatment by their officers.

The captured officers had a very different experience from their men. Arriving in Baghdad on 5 June, Walker was warmly greeted by Bimbashi Rashin Beg, who 'carried me off all round his lines, showed me the recruits at drill – I had to check their sighting and aiming drill! – introduced me to his officers and was very pleasant'. Accommodation was basic – 'We were given 3 bare stone floored rooms' – but otherwise captivity seemed surprisingly like freedom. 'After tea & a wash Martin took Baird, Burroughs & myself to the Club. We were quite at liberty, no guard or anything. The Club was really a hotel or café on the banks of the river with a nice lawn, chairs at little tables, whisky soda and <u>ice</u> . . . We stayed to dinner and had a good feed with a quart of red wine & very excellent coffee & so home to bed at 10.30. The guard at gate of barracks may have been surprised to see us roll up at this hour but they said nothing.'[18] Admittedly, not all officers had such a cheery time: McNeal (who thought that Indian Muslim officers were given much more freedom than the British) found the Turkish Cavalry Barracks, which he reached on 13 May, pretty grim. 'Some officers had smuggled their cots through from Shumran, but many had to sleep in their blankets on the stone flooring. The sanitary conditions were awful and the latrines were in a terrible state.' They were overcharged for their food by an Armenian contractor, but at least they got three meals a day (though most preferred 'to eat the stores we had brought from the boxes given us at Shumran and which our orderlies cooked for us', to the 'very dirty, and not at all palatable' Turkish cooking).

On 9 May, the senior officers 'were taken to lunch and dinner at the Hotel de France where they had real European food'. They met 'Fritz the German aviator who had bombed us in Kut', as they later told Shakeshaft. 'Said he was very affable and polite, and expressed deep regret at having bombed our hospitals.' This was followed next day by a ritual that would become familiar. The Commandant 'took all our names for the pay list'; but he 'seemed to lay more stress on one's Christian name, and father's Christian name, than surname'. Once the list was posted, Shakeshaft simply could not find himself on it – eventually opting for 'Captain Alfred Joseph' as the most likely match. Others were recorded as 'Henry Curse It Hants' (Lieutenant Henry Curtis Gallop of Hampshire), or 'John, the son of John, of London'.[19] Again, some suspected this was a way of ensuring that pay and parcels from home would fail to reach them; but it was just one amongst many cultural differences. Other problems of this kind also arose, as when the Commandant 'insisted on the Indian Officers having their meals in the same place as us'. It was 'impossible to make him see reason, so the only thing to do was to arrange with the IOs to have our meals at different times'. The deep differences of dietary culture proved durable even when all were eating the same 'bad and scanty' food.

The rank and file's problems were very different. After being herded through the streets of Baghdad – where 'angry crowds had gathered, displaying much malice and bitterness as they spat in the faces of the nearest captives' – they were taken to a 'bare piece of uncultivated land' by the railway station. (The officers found the Baghdadis rather different: McNeal found it a 'tremendous surprise' that 'though the streets were crowded with people not a word was said'.) The rank and file were without food or shelter until the US Consul sent eight sheep and 600 loaves of white bread to the camp – an action repeated every day after that. The Consul also conveyed the first cash payment, of ten shillings each, to the prisoners.

Eventually, in early August, the Ottoman authorities agreed to some prisoner exchanges with the British. Sandes complained that they always traded sick for healthy prisoners, and it is clear that the criterion for being exchanged was medical condition

– though how this was established was not always so clear. (The Turks also insisted on accepting only Turks in exchange for British prisoners, though they would accept Arabs in exchange for Indians.[20]) McNeal, who was in the first group to be exchanged, boarded the steamboat *Khalifa* on 8 August. Another group of forty British prisoners of war (not from Kut) had been brought to Baghdad from Samarra and 'told that they would go back to India with us. They were put on the boat, and half an hour afterwards the majority were taken off under the orders of a Turkish doctor, who said they were too fit to be exchanged.' In spite of this blow, 'their spirit and pluck were unbreakable, and they stood on the bank and watched us go, calling out goodbye and wishing us luck'. Wheeler recorded that when a Turkish doctor arrived at the camp, 'all those who could stand were lined up for inspection and the required number selected and ferried across the Tigris to join those released from hospital. They had barely boarded the steamer when the Turkish medical officer reappeared, demanding a further whittling-down in number.' The method of selection was 'ludicrous in the extreme – running his hand along the arm in search of muscle or fat, roughly pulling down the eyelids and closely peering into both eyes – he arrived at a decision which for many represented a death sentence'. One of Wheeler's company got away by the elementary ruse of 'placing both hands on his stomach and assuming an expression of great distress [then] he slipped away below deck, shut himself up in a water closet, being careful not to reappear until the coast was clear'.

Conditions on the boats going downstream were inevitably bad, but in the Baghdad compound they got relentlessly worse. Only 'the golden-domed minarets and mosques glistening in the sunshine and visible for miles around afforded some relief from the unsavoury surroundings where so many poor fellows died in a shocking state of neglect'. The officers were dissatisfied with their own situation at the Cavalry Barracks. On 15 May General Mellis ordered Shakeshaft (now co-opted as his ADC) to 'write a very strong letter to Halil protesting against his treatment' and the 'neglect and absolute indifference to the sufferings of our helpless men'. Next day he went into Baghdad to see Major Emin Bey, who as usual was 'most charming and really eager to help us'. Mellis kept Shakeshaft 'quite busy writing letters to those in authority' about the men's conditions. 'They were of course never answered.'

Gradually the prisoners were removed, though the march northwards did not bring any improvement in their state. 'Trainloads of British and Indian captives, standing closely packed together in open trucks, left the railway station at intervals of several days for Samara – 70 miles away.'

Travelling on 11 June Walker found the officers' train from Baghdad to Samarra 'quite comfy', and though Sandes, travelling a month earlier on the same train as Townshend, found the rail journey 'tedious and very uncomfortable' ('we rattled and bumped along, frequently stopping at uninteresting stations where there were no passengers and no towns or villages'), at least he and his companions could eat their small store of food, chat and smoke. Once again at Samarra there was 'no sign of tents or any arrangements for accommodation', and – ignoring orders to get back on the train for the night – the party (375 strong, including 88 British officers and 227 orderlies) slept on the open platform. Next day Sandes had his last sight of Townshend, being conveyed onward by carriage with his staff and a 'smart-looking Turkish officer' serving as escort and ADC.

For the rest, the next move northwards would take place on foot. The regimental officers had their baggage allowance reduced to 30 kg, and found that the provision of pack animals was 'utterly inadequate'. Delamain adamantly refused to start without more transport and a hospital cart, except 'at the point of the bayonet'; but in the end he had to go on anyway. At last, 'as the sun was sinking the head of the long column began to move off from Samarra towards the north along the wide track across the bare plain covered with coarse grass and small bushes'.

'One pressed on as in a sort of nightmare,' wrote Mousley, who was possessed by a vision of Detaille's painting 'The Dream' – 'a procession of soldier spirits marching across the sky with banners streaming, while down on the plain below, among stacks of piled rifles, men lay sleeping among the dead'. But only one kind of dream was repeatedly invoked: 'nightmare followed nightmare' on the night of 'the first great waterless march'.

'Donkey after donkey collapsed . . . an awful march after the sun got up.' Only a sudden rainstorm saved them. The men were on 'the poorest of rations, coarse dirty biscuits, a handful of flour or whole wheat with a pinch of salt'. After Baghdad, Private J. McK. Sloss wrote, 'biscuits became scarce, and they were given a ration of atta that they had to cook at the end of the day's march. It was this and the effort to gather fuel which caused a lot of sickness' – the scarcity of wood meant that the food was often only half-cooked. The ever-weakening men were treated ever more viciously by their guards. 'It was a horrible sight to see our boys driven along by rifle-butt and whip. Some were beaten until they dropped. One of our Sergeants complained to the Commandant and was given 15 lashes on the bare back.'[21] At Tikrit, thirty miles from Samarra, which put Sloss 'in mind of Biblical cities, such as one sees in art galleries', the men of the Hampshires 'were subjected to very bad treatment indeed at the hands of hostile Arabs'. They called it 'stony village' because of the 'mass of pebbles strewn around with which the Arabs stoned them on the bank of the river' where they were assembled.

At Tikrit this hostility affected the officers too, despite their easier conditions. Walker had 'a rotten time. Filthyly hot . . . Morning and evening we used to walk down to the river & see the other people, the rest of the day we lay about & slept in our room . . . We could not walk far as crowds of Arab boys & youths followed us spitting & yelling "Kafirtan [unbelievers]", also we were stoned.'

The prisoners were pushed on northwards, across 'mile after mile of desolate country until the more verdant region of Mosul was reached, and then sand-grassy waste out into the desert beyond ... During the long merciless and oft-times waterless marches, driven by the escort to the extreme limit of human endurance, only men comparatively free from any serious ailment could hope to survive.' Deliberate cruelty was added to their inevitable suffering when, before the march across a salt waste they were forced to empty their water-bottles.[22] (Yet the capricious nature of Turkish power meant that they were never systematically robbed: Sloss saved his life on the march from Mosul by selling his watch to the commandant for 2½ mejidies – the smallest Ottoman currency – with which he bought a pint of milk.[23])

What was the purpose of 'this inhuman march'? Was it, as Braddon thought, the Turks' determination 'to demonstrate their victory over the British to as many of their people as possible, and to use their prisoners as profitably as possible', that led them to despatch the surviving prisoners to the remotest regions, and set them to work building the Baghdad railway? Braddon judged the Turks to be not so much brutal as 'lazy and indifferent'. Many of the prisoners, like Mousley, felt that even in the midst of their nightmare marches, 'with proper orders much of our sorrows could have been obviated'. But if the cause was neglect, it was far from benign. When Walker got to Nisibin in mid-July, for instance, 'hearing some of our men were sick I went to see them. I found a very bad place': some hundred men were 'penned up in a series of dirty little huts without light or air or water'. This was allegedly a hospital, but the young Turkish doctor in charge 'seemed extraordinarily useless'. The men 'got no milk or medicine and were all dirty and half starved. They were not even allowed to go down to the river to wash.'[24] What was this if not systematic ill-treatment? Mousley, who had gone to the Nisibin hospital two weeks earlier to retrieve a topee from an officer who had died there, called it 'a sight that staggered the imagination'. Along the wall, 'protected by only a few scanty leaves and loose grass flung over some tatti work of branches through which the fierce sun streamed with unabated violence, I saw some human forms which no eye but one acquainted with the phenomenon of the trek could possibly recognize as British soldiery. They were wasted to wreathes of skin hanging upon a bone frame. For the most part they were stark naked except for a rag around their loins . . . their eyes were white with the death hue. One had just died and two or three corpses had just been removed, the Turkish attendant no doubt having heard of the approach of an officers' column. But the corpses had lain there for days. One saw flies which swarmed by the million going in and out of living men's open mouths.'[25]

Whatever the reason for these pitiless marches, could the suffering of the prisoners have been prevented, or even mitigated, by the British authorities? For Braddon, Townshend's pleasant progress as a kind of war hero into comfortable imprisonment on an island in the Sea of Marmara was the ultimate example of dereliction of duty. But whether Townshend could, realistically, have achieved anything by staying with his troops is harder to say. Those generals who stayed close to the forced marches – Delamain in a column of officers, and Mellis who travelled separately after recovering from illness – certainly did their best. Their prestige may not quite have equalled Townshend's, but they were treated with great respect by their captors. Mellis was tireless in harrying the Ottoman authorities. On 24 June, for instance, Shakeshaft (his ADC) recorded that they found three soldiers lying by the riverbank 'all horribly emaciated and in a dreadful state', and took them along with them to Hasan Begli, where they found twenty-four more in an equally bad way. Mellis 'sent for the Commandant and told him exactly what he thought of his behaviour'. The men were moved into a shed and given some cooked rice and meat, and Mellis insisted that all twenty-seven be sent onwards by cart: 'he would not stir until they had been moved'.[26] In his travels Mellis saved dozens of soldiers – temporarily at least – but his impact was confined to his immediate presence. (As Mousley noted, the great pity was that Mellis did not stop at Nisibin, 'the real state of the worst quarters having been withheld from him'.) Mellis fired off letter after letter, and compiled a detailed report which he sent to Enver Pasha – the reply to which was merely that such complaints could not be true. The official attitude was simply one of denial, if not obstruction. Braddon admits that when Delamain and some MOs had tried to intervene in the camp at Baghdad, 'there was little the Turks would let them do'.

Braddon also cast his charge of dereliction more widely, alleging that the C-in-C India, by forbidding the exchanged prisoners to speak publicly of the plight of those they had left behind them, 'condemned ten thousand troops to months of agony and death'.[27] Whether or not this argument convinces, Duff had no idea at this stage how bad things were. A careful report based on interviews with exchanged Kut prisoners in September 1916 showed that 'there was much difference of opinion as to the treatment British and Indian prisoners had received'. In one case, a senior officer who evidently believed that conditions were bad, refused to put forward this view because he was aware that 'a senior medical officer' completely disagreed with him. The report found that 'diametrically opposite views were strongly held by different individuals'.[28] Several other attempts seem to have been made to assess the experiences of Indian prisoners, and none produced unambiguous evidence of serious ill-treatment.

The government was certainly alert to the issue by then, but found it almost impossible to get information from the Ottoman authorities. In July 1916, Lord Robert Cecil, Undersecretary at the Foreign Office, who had been 'endeavouring for some time past to obtain from the Turks full particulars as to the welfare' of British prisoners, noted that 'we have no reason to think that the Turks are actually preventing the prisoners from writing home'. But it soon became clear that they were. Colonel Parr, imprisoned at Brussa, had written home in late June 1916 to complain that the British prisoners were only allowed to write – and receive

– four lines a week, and in fact 'we have not been allowed to send or receive letters for seven months'.[29] The restriction was said by the Turks to be a retaliation for restrictions imposed on Turkish prisoners by the British; the British said it was the other way round. The real problem, though, was – as the Foreign Secretary protested – 'the refusal of the Porte to inform Mr Philip [Hoffman Philip, the US Chargé d'Affaires at Constantinople] of the whereabouts of the force or to allow the US Consul at Baghdad to communicate with them'. The US diplomatic authorities found it virtually impossible to discover where the prisoners had been taken, though this was an elementary convention of international behaviour. (Lists of prisoners of war had been provided, as the government told parliament, by 'every hostile government except the Turkish'.) Absurdly fragmentary lists appeared from time to time; one, on 2 August 1916, reported that 'Sergeant Arthur Dykes, Pte Herbert Smith, 2nd Norfolks, and Corporal Albert Pitt, Worcester Hussars' were at Afion Kara-Hissar, while there were '23 Indians at Eskishekir'. Philip complained in November that 'communications with the interior have been strictly and jealously guarded' by the Ottoman authorities, and the lack of prompt information about conditions 'renders it so extremely difficult to meet the wants effectively'.

By that time, though, there could be no doubt that the wants were serious. Philip reported in September 1916 that letters from prisoners at Adana hospital 'all indicate that the Kut prisoners have had an extremely difficult march across the desert, very many of them have died, survivors have reached Syria or borders of Asia Minor in a pitiable condition'. In late October, military intelligence received 'information from an absolutely reliable source that men just arrived at Afion-Kara-Hissar from Kut are in an indescribably miserable condition'. Their informant suggested that only a third of the men taken at Kut were still alive, and that two-thirds of those captured in December 1915 were 'known to be dead'. Two days later, the US Embassy reported that thirty-five British prisoners had recently arrived at Konia 'in a very weak and wretched condition', and that fifteen of them had died between 18 and 27 September. Their names were listed.[30]

After arriving at Ras-el-Ain, the 'wretched village' Mousley reached on 3 July 1916 after a last grim march, the prisoners were dispersed to several widely separated places. Officers were interned at Afion Kara-Hissar, Brussa, Yozgad, Cnagri and Kastamuni (near the Black Sea). For the rank and file, 'as batch after batch left Ras-el-Ain on foot or by rail for an unknown destination, it became more and more difficult for the remnants of individual units to keep together'.[31] Most were set to work at the gaps in the Baghdad railway where the line crossed the Taurus and Amanus mountains. These were the grimmest work locations imaginable, and the conditions remained primitive – 'in temporary buildings, in some cases just skin and brushwood shelters, insufficiently fed and clothed, bullied by guards and often flogged, men toiled, collapsed and died like slaves on the track'. Others, like Private J. E. Sporle of the West Kents, were breaking stones for road-building. At Ada-Pazar 'we had to sit on heaps of snow to do our stone-breaking'.

Though parcels began to arrive from home towards the end of the year, they were routinely pilfered or simply 'lost in the post'. Medical facilities remained utterly inadequate. When Sporle was hospitalised with pneumonia in mid-1917, his bed was doused with boiling water to kill bed-bugs. 'I was then allowed to lay down in it while it was wet.' Immediately after being discharged he was given a pair of boots (two sizes too big) and sent on a twenty-mile trek. 'My comrades', as he mildly recorded, 'were surprised when they heard I had to trek this distance after being in hospital.'

Lieutenant J. G. Stilwell of the Hampshires, who had been taken prisoner during the fighting in January 1916, offered an interesting assessment of his treatment in thirty-four months of captivity. It was governed primarily by four factors – first, the state of the war; second, orders from Constantinople; third, the prisoner's rank; and finally, 'the personal inclination of individuals'. As examples, he noted that there were several reprisals for the alleged ill-treatment of Turkish prisoners in British hands, but they were given much more freedom after the failure of the German offensive in spring 1918. Enver Pasha personally 'sent us a case of bacon during the lean winter of 1917–18; while even the notoriously violent Commandant Mazlum 'would allow us to wander about at will after a show at the theatre to which he had been invited'.[32] Amongst the other ranks, who were treated far worse, there was a similar impression of capricious variation – as in the extraordinarily detailed memoirs of Sergeant Jerry Long, who went from near-starvation to employment as supervisor of a carpentry shop, and survived several attempts to escape. Like most accounts, too, Long's said nothing about the frequently aired charges of sexual abuse of prisoners.[33]

The treatment of prisoners of war by the Germans was certainly much further out of line with international law than the British then believed. Were the Turks so uniquely bad? Their use of prisoners in forced labour on the Baghdad railway was more justifiable than the (definitely illegal) German use of prisoners at the battlefront; and the conditions can hardly have been worse than those inflicted by the Russians on their German prisoners building the Murmansk railway (where 25,000 out of 70,000 died). Sick prisoners were undeniably neglected. The assurances given to the US Embassy by the Ottoman Red Crescent Society in June 1916 that there was 'an ample supply of medical stores' at Baghdad were obviously false. The Ottoman medical staff were desperately inexpert. The British officer who wrote that 'the doctors who were exchanged from Baghdad after the fall of Kut would probably have saved hundreds of lives if they had been permitted to remain', was hardly exaggerating.[34] Yet the nightmare of medical neglect afflicted Ottoman troops equally: seven times as many died of illness as died of wounds.[35] Both sides fell victim to a grossly inadequate system.

5. Inquiry

Will the public ever realise how the campaign is conducted here?
> EDWARD ROE

Only one feeling remains, gets the better of one & will not be hidden: anger, bitter anger against India! The cause of all this failure, of all the hopeless & disgraceful muddle of the campaign & its running.
> EDGAR BRIDGES

There seems to be a very strong party at home who want my blood as regards Mesopotamia.
> SIR BEAUCHAMP DUFF

Over the last century, the growing culture of official secrecy and the declining prestige of parliament have combined to bolster the natural distaste of governments for public inquiry into their actions. Asquith's government, which carried the atmosphere of Victorian liberalism into the new world of total war, was less imperturbable than its successors in its defence of incompetence. As the scale and nature of the organisational failure in Mesopotamia grew clearer, demands for investigation grew louder. In 1916 the government gave way. It was a gradual process, which began inside the official machinery. Even before the turn of the year, in late December 1915, Hardinge was becoming ever more disturbed by the steady stream of complaints about the supply system, and still more about the medical arrangements in Mesopotamia. He asked Duff to investigate the 'constant complaints as to the insufficiency of supplies'; at that stage he did not know the scale of the collapse of the medical system after the battle of Ctesiphon. But the ghastly images of the casualties arriving at Basra after their nightmare journey downriver could not be concealed, and a public outcry in Britain was certain.

Duff's first idea was to call on Lord Chelmsford, an experienced colonial governor (and the next Viceroy of India), together with the Director of Medical Services in India, Surgeon-General J. MacNeese, to conduct the inquiry. This may in a sense have been a damage limitation exercise, but Duff declared that he would 'leave no stone unturned to get at the actual facts', and seems genuinely to have believed that the fault lay outside the sphere of his own control. Chamberlain, though, who told Balfour he was 'sick as sick can be about medical mismanagement', was expecting 'a regular row here'. He admitted in parliament that there had been a 'lamentable breakdown of the hospital arrangements', and that shortages of medical supplies had been 'inexcusable'.[1] Chelmsford dodged the invitation (on the ground that he was going back to London to prepare to take up the Viceroyalty), and MacNeese only investigated the medical arrangements at Bombay and Basra. On these he returned a positive report.

Thus fortified, Duff returned to the issue in February 1916, telling Hardinge that 'everything was found all right at Basrah and from there to India, wherever, in fact, we control matters directly'. But, showing a healthy respect for public opinion, he advised that they should set up an inquiry into what had happened elsewhere in Mesopotamia 'before this is forced on us'.[2] So Sir William Vincent, a member of the Government Council of India, and Major-General A. H. Bingley, were asked to investigate. Their remit was expanded with some helpful suggestions from Lake, to include issues such as Townshend's claim that he had protested against the advance on Baghdad, and the problems of river transport. There was a hint here of a comprehensive investigation of the whole campaign, but the Vincent–Bingley inquiry was intended to focus primarily on the medical system. The decision taken in London to add a third member, E. A. Ridsdale of the Red Cross, seems to have reflected a growing uneasiness about public opinion. Chamberlain thought the addition was 'politic', but he was confident that (as he assured an anxious Robertson), '"The Commission" is not to enquire into "the Townshend business".' Indeed he added encouragingly, 'Commission is too big a word for it.' Robertson was, not surprisingly, more sceptical: 'these Commissions seldom do any good and always do some harm.'[3]

It turned out that 'Commission' was not too big a word for it. Vincent and Bingley spent eight days gathering evidence in Bombay in early March 1916, before moving to Basra in the middle of the month, and embarking on six weeks of inquiries in Mesopotamia. (Ridsdale, rather awkwardly, did not arrive until mid-April.) Their report, in mid-July, opened with a detailed military account of the campaign before turning (after seven densely printed pages of operational narrative) to the medical arrangements. These it pronounced curtly to have been 'manifestly inadequate', causing much unnecessary suffering. It concluded that the only people who were not responsible for this were the medical staff in Mesopotamia: but almost everyone else, from the top down, was to blame for the key shortages that had produced the disaster – river transport, medical personnel and hospital ships. Amidst a series of damaging criticisms, the report pointedly dissented from Sir John Nixon's telegram after the battle of Ctesiphon reporting that 'medical arrangements worked splendidly'. The deployment of 3rd and 7th Divisions to the Kut relief force without their field ambulances had brought an already overstrained system to the point of collapse. The Red Cross perspective emerged in the criticism of official attempts to limit the activity of 'charitable organisations' or to provide guidelines for possible contributions they might make when things went wrong.[4]

'Vincent–Bingley' blamed the suffering of the sick and wounded on four things: the lack of river hospital ships; the shortage of medical personnel; the shortage of river transport; and the lack of 'proper means of evacuating the wounded by land'. They hedged their bets on where the main responsibility for these shortages lay. 'On various occasions the medical arrangements might have been improved by better organisation and co-ordination, and for this defect the local officers are responsible.' But it was the authorities in India who were responsible for many of the crucial deficiencies. The Indian system, with its 'rigid economy in respect of military expenditure', had aggravated faults inherent in the Indian Army's medical organisation. More uncomfortably still, they named names: 'a grave responsibility' for avoidable suffering rested with the Senior Medical Officer of Force D, Hathaway, and with the force commander, Nixon. Hathaway had failed to 'represent with sufficient promptitude and force the needs of the services for which he was responsible', while Nixon had failed to 'appreciate the conditions which would necessarily arise if provision for the sick and wounded of his force were not made on a more liberal scale'. In India, the officer directly responsible was the DMS, but the commission held the senior Indian military authorities to be ultimately responsible.[5]

Duff was taken aback by this. He complained that the commission had 'departed from their terms of reference' in criticising 'the preparations for the campaign which were outside their purview'. He told the Viceroy that the report could not be published, because it was 'calculated to encourage the enemy and give him information of military value'. The picture it drew could be exploited by the enemy to undermine the morale of British forces.[6] But military arguments of this kind were not enough to smother the growing political pressure – not yet for a full public inquiry, but for the release of documents on the campaign to permit a public debate. One Liberal MP argued in early June 1916 that it was 'a matter of so much military and public interest' that to deny a debate would be unreasonable, and the government accepted (via the Lord President of the Council, Bonar Law) that it was 'better, on the whole, that the Papers should be published'. (Though Bonar Law added that nothing that would give information to the enemy could be released.) Lord Midleton, who (as St John Brodrick) had run both the War and India Offices at the time of Kitchener's reform of the Indian military system, renewed the call for publication later in the month, tartly suggesting that some of those responsible had 'not yet risen to the full measure of their responsibility'. Robertson naturally fended off such demands as long as possible, arguing like Duff that even if those papers that were 'most objectionable to publish' were excluded, the rest could be of use to 'an astute enemy reading between the lines'. The Committee of Imperial Defence concurred, and the Prime Minister had to invoke Bonar Law's reservation.

By now Asquith's government found itself in an awkward position, and though the Prime Minister warned against allowing 'a Debate which gave the impression to the world outside that we are in any way divided among ourselves', the Cabinet eventually accepted that an inquiry was unavoidable. Two, in fact: one for the Dardanelles and one for Mesopotamia. The model they borrowed was taken from the Special Commissions Acts of the 1880s, devised to deal with the Irish situation. It had been drawn up by Sir Edward Carson, which may not have been the best augury. After some dispute in the Commons about the suitability of the government's proposed chairman, Lord George Hamilton, a five-man Mesopotamia commission was agreed on 1 August 1916. Hamilton, the only member of the commission with real experience of Indian government, had to be strong-armed into taking the job by Lord Lansdowne with the argument that it was essential to head off a political crisis.[7] Asquith at first fended off calls for military and naval representation on it, but eventually agreed to the addition of General Sir Neville Lyttelton, Admiral Sir Cyprian Bridge and – for good measure – Commander Josiah Wedgwood, a maverick Liberal MP with service experience.

The commission's remit was remarkably wide: to inquire into 'the origin, inception and conduct of operations of war in Mesopotamia'. It opened its hearings on 21 August, taking evidence from a range of senior policy-makers (including Crewe, Chamberlain, Hardinge and Hirtzel), generals (O'Moore Creagh,

Duff, Lake, Aylmer and Gorringe), and a number of medical, political and field officers (such as George Lloyd, Captain O'Neill of the 128th Indian Field Ambulance, and Brevet-Colonel Climo of the 28th Punjabis). In all it met sixty times over ten months, and called over a hundred witnesses. Its report turned out to be another damning indictment of the decision-making process, the structure of the Indian military administration and the 'atmosphere of economy' in Indian administration generally.

For the commission, the expeditionary force was 'ill-found' from the start, because its mission fell between two directing agencies – it was ordered by London, but administered by Delhi. (Or, more accurately, by Simla – a location about whose inappropriateness the commission was scathing.) It was 'the foster-child of both Simla and Whitehall, the acknowledged child of neither'. The division of responsibilities between them was 'somewhat confused'. Although the expedition's objectives seemed initially to be set out with reasonable clarity, they were 'not so precisely limited that they could not be expanded', and the commission identified Sir Percy Cox as the source of the 'ambition' to capture Baghdad that led to such expansion. As the expeditionary force went forward, 'no full and frank exchange of opinion seems to have taken place' either about the scope of the expedition or the resources it would need. The most crucial problem, the base at Basra, should have been given 'the closest attention', but was ignored. The result was that 'makeshifts and hand-to-mouth contrivances became the order of the day'.[8]

Like Vincent and Bingley, the Mesopotamia Commission painted a grim picture of the administrative confusion that made Force D's life a misery. It heard, for instance, from the chaplain of the 7th Division that 'As soon as we arrived at Basra on January 1st it was clear that the organisation in nearly every department was very different to what the Division had been accustomed to in France. It seemed surprising that, as there was such a shortage of river transport, nothing had been done about constructing a light railway at Basra. Troops as they arrived were pushed up to the front without transport, horses or any administrative unity, and naturally there was chaos.' This chaos, the Rev. Urwin insisted, had been due not to lack of boats but to simple lack of organisation. From a higher military standpoint, the picture was as damning. Major-General Frederick Maurice, the Director of Military Operations at the War Office, told the commission that 'When the sending of the 13th Division was mooted, Sir William Robertson wished to be sure that the division could be used if it was sent.' So the WO sent a telegram to this effect, and they took Lake's reply – 'I am fully able to receive and maintain the 13th Division' – to mean that it could be used. But, Maurice pointedly added, 'As a matter of fact Sir Percy Lake did not mean that.'[9]

The commissioners unhesitatingly blamed this on grossly inadequate funding which they said resulted from two things – the defective Indian military administration, and the impact of the Indian governmental culture of economy. These two issues occupied centre stage in the commission's conclusions. Lord Kitchener's pre-war reform of the Indian military system was highlit as the root cause of the near-disaster in Mesopotamia. By centralising the top of the system while leaving the rest of it in the 'cumbrous dualism' of the old structure, Kitchener (who of course could not give evidence to the commission) had given the Commander-in-Chief an impossible role, and had created a bizarre fiction that there were 'still two people as there used to be'. The commission devoted an entire page of its conclusions to an extended quotation from the evidence of R. B. Brunyate, the Financial Secretary to the Government of India, about the practical consequences of this almost Gilbertian procedure for any efforts to make any changes in military establishments. The 'elaborate process of check and counter-check' meant that even the simplest proposal could take many weeks to determine.

The verdict was damning: 'this astounding system has only to be described to be condemned.'[10] The commissioners borrowed directly the Vincent–Bingley report's picture of the 'tendency' thus created. '(a) That there is more merit to be obtained by keeping quiet and not worrying the higher authorities than by asking for what is necessary. (b) That keeping down expenditure is more meritorious than efficiency. (c) That nothing new is likely to be sanctioned unless a corresponding saving in something else can be shown. (d) That even in small matters anything asked for will be cut down by half.'[11]

The Mesopotamia expeditionary force had initially been 'equipped as if for frontier warfare against indisciplined tribes armed only with rifles'. Even when its desperate need for war equipment became clear, there was 'little if anything in the mass of communications between the India Office, the Indian Government and the General Officer Commanding in Mesopotamia to show that the authorities either in London or Simla recognised the immense difference' between frontier war and campaigning against a modern army. Many witnesses had implied 'that the supreme Government of India did not seem adequately to recognise the immensity of the issues raised by the war, and that their response was not as whole-hearted as it might have been'. The commission agreed. The Indian government, it suggested, 'do not appear to us to have fully risen to the situation'.[12] It bolstered this judgement with a particularly nasty piece of evidence which it had, it reported, 'extracted with great difficulty' from General Cowper, the DAQMG of Force D.

'In January 1916 he, being the officer responsible for the transport, became seriously alarmed at the increasing difficulties which the shortage of transport created in the employment of troops for the relief of Kut. In consultation with General Money, Chief of the General Staff, he drafted a telegram in which they stated plainly that unless they got adequate shipping transport, and personnel to man it, Sir Percy Lake would have to abandon the idea of relieving Kut. They purposely had recourse to this language as they considered the position – to use General Cowper's words – "so frightfully serious". Sir Percy Lake carefully considered the telegram, and transmitted it after some alterations. In reply he received a personal telegram from the

Commander-in-Chief at Simla, severely rebuking him for the wording of the telegram, and the C-in-C added these words: "Please tell General Cowper that if anything of this sort occurs again, or I receive any more querulous or petulant demands for shipping, I shall at once remove him from the force, and will refuse him further employment of any kind."[13] Although Duff had claimed that his reply was 'founded on a paraphrase which distorted both the purport and language of the telegram', and that he had subsequently cancelled his censure, he was unable to supply the commission with a copy of the offending 'paraphrase'. The commissioners held that the incident was 'an extreme but characteristic illustration of the attitude of the authorities at Simla towards demands which they did not like'.

In the commission's eyes Duff was clearly the villain of the piece, though it also criticised his predecessor, O'Moore Creagh, for taking the easy option of early retirement in protest against a system he found unacceptable, rather than actively trying to change it. (He had unsuccessfully demanded modern artillery, machine guns and communications equipment to create a force capable of fighting against – for instance – Turkey.) It criticised Nixon too, as Vincent–Bingley had, though it accepted that the offensive in Mesopotamia was 'an undertaking utterly beyond the capacity' of his staff. 'To impose such a duty upon a Cavalry officer with little more than the ordinary staff of a Division was to try him altogether beyond his experience and strength.' Though his successes had led him to underestimate the full risk involved in an advance on Baghdad, the Government of India was at fault in never questioning his lack of experience in running such a campaign. 'Implicit confidence in his judgment was the basis of their communications to the Home Government.'[14]

Finally, it criticised governments. Austen Chamberlain, together with the Cabinet War Committee, bore some blame for their part in approving the advance on Baghdad. Chamberlain had, as we have seen, made his approval conditional on the best available military opinion, but the commission invoked the constitutional principle that the chief who accepts mistaken advice cannot escape ultimate responsibility. But for the commission the heaviest responsibility for the control of the Mesopotamia campaign, and the inadequacies that brought it to the brink of disaster, with so much avoidable suffering, lay with the Indian C-in-C and government. Their failure to 'minister to the wants of the forces employed in Mesopotamia' was 'persistent and continuous'. It was impossible 'to refrain from serious censure of the Indian Government for the inadequacy of their preparations' and for their lack of readiness to recognise and remedy deficiencies. 'They ought to have known,' the commission insisted, 'and with proper touch with the expedition they could have known, what were its wants and requirements.'[15]

These were, as the commission's report insisted, serious indictments. Even so, they did not go far enough for Josiah Wedgwood, who decided to submit his own 'dissentient report' instead. His fellow commissioners put a brave face on this, suggesting that the differences were mostly of emphasis rather than substance. But Wedgwood held that the commission's emphasis on the communication procedures between the Secretary of State and the Viceroy, and the effects of the Kitchener reforms, showed 'some lack of a sense of proportion'. He said it was misguided to dwell on the decision to advance on Baghdad, as the commission did, and more so to condemn Nixon and the Cabinet. In his view, 'they would have deserved as much, if not more censure had they decided against the advance', and it would be 'a bad day for our Empire when soldiers and statesmen decline all risks'. He preferred to focus on one topic above all – the failure of the Indian government (by which he meant, as he repeatedly made clear, Hardinge and Duff) to commit itself fully to the war effort. This was a far weightier charge than the commission's careful suggestion that Simla had not 'fully risen to the situation'. Wedgwood alleged that Hardinge and Duff had shown not only 'little desire to help', but even 'some desire actually to obstruct the energetic prosecution of the war'. He listed several instances of what he called the 'grudging spirit', and bolstered his contention that this was more than 'honest human error' by quoting several direct exhortations from Kitchener himself, who had written to Hardinge in September 1914, 'You hardly seem to realise the seriousness of our position on the Continent', and again, 'I do not think you yet quite realise in India what the war is going to be.'[16]

For Wedgwood, two episodes above all demonstrated the 'policy of obstruction' in India. When Kitchener offered Territorial battalions to release Indian line battalions, Duff had pronounced them 'quite unfit for frontier work', and Hardinge had said it would be 'madness to send Territorial troops to the North-West frontier' – even though, as Wedgwood noted, they had proved effective against Germans in France, and could surely have learned frontier warfare as well as any other kind. (This was no doubt true, though the cost might have been grim: Wedgwood probably underestimated the unique difficulties of trans-frontier hill fighting.[17]) And India not only refused to raise new forces of its own on the grounds that it had given up all its new rifles to the Imperial army – though as Wedgwood pointed out, Britain had not waited for the availability of rifles before raising its new armies – it maintained that it could not increase its arms manufacturing capacity.[18]

The most shameful document, for Wedgwood, was what he called the 'amazing minute' of 17 October 1915, which (as we have seen) proposed to conceal from the home government India's assembly of a reinforcing brigade because 'they will give us nothing if the least sign of willingness to find reinforcements is shown by us'. Wedgwood's take on this was venomous: 'the Indian Government "held out" while Serbia was being overrun, and while our last man was being put in at Loos.'[19] Wedgwood charged India with shirking its duty. He dismissed Hardinge's harping on the dangers that India faced: neither the external nor the internal threat matched the Viceroy's alarmist warnings. If the danger really had been serious, it would surely be 'inconceivable that the Viceroy should never have seen fit to consult his Council'. (And anyway 'there is always danger in this world: it is a question of degree'.) In any case, protecting the frontier could not justify the Indian government's attitude – 'the want of energy, the non-mobilisation of industry, the selfish financial attitude'. The bottom line was that India's duty was to save Britain from an even greater threat. As Kitchener had bluntly told Hardinge, 'if we lose it will be worse for India than any success of internal revolution or frontier attack'. An attitude that would be 'held unpatriotic in a private citizen' was worse in a public official – 'and in men in the positions occupied by Lord Hardinge and Sir Beauchamp Duff it has been a calamity for England'.[20]

The Mesopotamia Commission had been intended to avert a political crisis, but the political impact of its report was potentially catastrophic. For two months the Cabinet havered over the question of whether to publish it. Two full Cabinet meetings were consumed by it, with shorter discussions at another six. 'I regret to have to say', Curzon declaimed, 'that a more shocking exposure of official blundering and incompetence has not in my opinion been made, at any rate since the Crimean War.' Though he agreed with Robertson that publishing it in wartime was undesirable, he thought it was now unavoidable. It was eventually published on 27 June 1917 (though Robertson succeeded in excluding the supporting documents), and debated in parliament on 3 July. The most serious casualty of the storm it produced was Austen Chamberlain. He found the report 'the saddest and most appalling document that I have ever read'. What hurt most was the revelation that 'high-placed and responsible officers deliberately concealed the truth and reported falsely to my inquiries'. He was too high-minded to use this revelation to defend his own position, and decided to resign. This, as he told Lord Chelmsford, Hardinge's successor as Viceroy, was a matter of constitutional principle – ministerial responsibility, as the commission had pointed out.

At the personal level, Josiah Wedgwood later expressed grim satisfaction that his minority report had 'sent Duff drinking to his grave', and made in Hardinge 'an enemy of the everlasting variety'. At the level of national destinies, though, the consequences of Chamberlain's resignation were further-reaching. The politician who inveighed most fiercely against the conduct of the Mesopotamia campaign, Edwin Montagu, was given his job. He would become the first Secretary of State for India ever to visit the subcontinent, and launch the Montagu–Chelmsford reforms which would transform the relationship between Britain and India decisively. Hardinge and Duff were already gone from India long before the commission reported, and though Hardinge (now returned to his civil service career as Permanent Undersecretary at the Foreign Office) offered to resign – encouraged by Curzon – the Foreign Secretary refused to allow it. Bizarrely, in fact, Hardinge as a peer was able to speak in his own defence during the parliamentary debate – a highly unconventional privilege for a civil servant. The question of a possible court of inquiry lingered for a while, but the prospect of real political damage to the government was headed off, above all else by the simple fact that the situation in Mesopotamia had changed radically. By the time the commission reported, Baghdad had been captured.

6. Maude's Offensive: The Third Battle for Kut

However, here we are, and the only thing is to get at it heart and soul, for difficulties exist only to be overcome.
STANLEY MAUDE

No appreciable effect on the war would be produced even if we could later occupy Baghdad. We cannot hope to do this.
SIR WILLIAM ROBERTSON

The very mention of the name Sannaiyat freezes the blood in our veins.
EDWARD ROE

In the middle of the deadly summer of 1916, Ned Roe went back to his unit at Sheikh Saad. He was not much impressed. On the way up, ten men of his draft were evacuated to hospital even before they left Qurna. 'A good start,' he sardonically noted. The river voyage was as expected: 'terrific heat accompanied by a Sirocco-like wind makes us feel as if we were on a floating furnace.' At Sheikh Saad in mid-July the temperature was 118 degrees F in the shade, and 'on an average, within the Brigade, five funerals take place every evening'. Everyone 'seems dull and low-spirited'. Later in the month, there were daily sandstorms, and 'rations of very poor quality'. They had not been issued with long trousers, and had to wear 'shorts and putties all night and have no mosquito nets. We are eaten alive.' When another draft from England joined his battalion at the beginning of August, he reflected 'it is astonishing the number of men who are over age that are passed fit for active service. They fill the base hospitals in the various theatres of war, cost the state enormous amounts of money, and in the end are invalided as medically unfit.' The younger men were untrained – 'raw

Derbyites, and every reinforcement is alike'. They were 'rushed through a couple of months training, lack discipline, can't load their rifles properly or hit a target at 100 yards'. An old-style professional, Roe lamented the new recruits' ignorance of drill. In peacetime it had taken six months to turn out a trained soldier: could it be done in six weeks 'when everything is in a state of chaos?'[1]

Apart from the conditions, and his comrades' failings, Roe's main bugbear was the Arabs. They had 'a rather provoking habit of galloping to within rifle range of the camp and loosing off about thirty rounds' before clearing off – 'to the detriment of the tentage'. Having to stand to while bullets whizzed over your head was one thing, but more aggravating still was the Arabs' world-class skill in 'lifting rifles or blankets'. On 28 September his company lost seven rifles, despite sleeping in the open in lines of platoons with their rifles secured by the slings round their legs. 'Sentries were posted outside the laager only three yards apart. They heard and saw the Arabs several times during the night but could not fire as orders were to the contrary; neither could a sentry leave his post to charge them with the bayonet as he would most probably get knifed . . . ' The seven victims were put under close arrest and court-martialled; the battalion was punished for the loss by being made to sleep on the square in front of the officers' mess tent. After lugging their kitbags and rifles on to the square at 9 p.m. and bedding down, 'about 11.30 or midnight the officers emerge from the mess tent in a jocular mood (to draw it mild) and try to enact the role of Arab "loose wallahs" by stumbling through the sleeping lines endeavouring to abstract the men's rifles from underneath their blankets'. Even the OC indulged in this 'annoying pastime' – doubtless thinking of it as a training exercise. The rankers cynically concluded that the sentries had been ordered not to fire so as not to wake up the brigadier and the colonels.[2]

Over the torrid summer of 1916 the MEF had been belatedly and expensively made fit for purpose. Its military capacity had been transformed, but the question of what its purpose was still remained. The CIGS, as we have seen, was baffled. As autumn approached, Maude sent him a progress report. The army's foundations were being securely constructed, drafts were being pushed to the front rapidly, training was continually improving. Mounted troops were being kept back as long as possible, because they were a heavier burden on the supply system. But 'the question of mobility has been carefully prosecuted, and training of troops is being directed to that end'.[3] This was probably not so much a response to Maude's brush with the Cossacks, as to proddings from Robertson himself. (He had agreed with his friend General Sir Charles Monro, who was replacing Duff as C-in-C India, that the 'essentials' for Maude would be 'mobility, an efficient air force, and powerful artillery'.[4]) Maude took particular care to improve his bridging train, which would have a key role in any advance. He also 'devoted special attention to the question of utilising the newly arrived Stokes [trench] mortars to the best advantage'.[5] But there were still huge problems: the army was 'immobile' in October because of the 'inadequacy and insufficient organisation and distribution of transport'. Maude was 'working our land transport for all it is worth', stripping his static 'containing force' of most of its transport and using it to bring up supplies. The railway up to Es Sinn could scarcely supply the 'containing force' there, let alone allow the stockpiling needed for an offensive.

But why should there be an offensive? Strategic logic did not require one, and the conditions were as difficult as ever. As corps commander, like Gorringe before him, Maude carried out a special reconnaissance in mid-July to work out if an advance through the Suwaikiya marsh was possible; as before, 'the result was discouraging'. But Maude was offensive-minded, as he showed when he criticised the 7th Division's orders as being 'drawn up under a misconception of the policy which is to be followed. The line now held by your division is to be held offensively, not defensively.' This was explained thus – 'it has been secured as a jumping-off place for further aggressive operations as the opportunity offers'.

This attitude did not exactly fit with Robertson's views. Mesopotamia was causing him 'great concern and anxiety', he told Maude in September, 'because of the drain on our resources and the poor return promised'. Worrying over the final stages of the staggeringly costly Somme offensive (where tanks would make their first ever appearance in battle a few days later), he thought that even if enough forces could be concentrated to capture Baghdad – though 'we cannot hope to do this' – the move would have 'no appreciable effect on the war'. So he proposed a withdrawal to Amara, albeit with uncharacteristic hesitancy: it was simply that 'anything is better than continuing the present difficult, costly and objectiveless plan'.[6] Maude, who may have been stung by the charge of aimlessness, politely suggested that a limited forward movement, as far as the Hai, was feasible. Robertson could hardly accept this as an 'objective', but his proposal to withdraw was quickly rejected by the Cabinet War Committee. The net result was to leave Maude as he was, but with the instruction (issued on 30 September) that 'no fresh advance on Baghdad can at present be contemplated', and any advance should 'not be undertaken unless and until sanction for it is given'. Maude was to 'maintain as forward a position as the state of his communications will allow, and as can be made secure tactically without incurring heavy loss'. He could not expect any reinforcements.[7]

In Robertson's uncertainty about the logic of the campaign lay Maude's opportunity. Within six months of this order, his army was in Baghdad. Since an offensive was, in the view of the CIGS, strategically pointless, we may ask why one took place. The answer seems primarily psychological. Maude may have been appointed first and foremost as an organiser, but he had a strong sense of strategic vision, and an impressive capacity to instil in his force a belief in success. He certainly did not want to sit out the rest of the war in defensive positions; but more to the point, such inaction would have made it impossible to rebuild his force's morale. And the CIGS had specifically emphasised to him 'the importance of improving the <u>moral</u> of the troops'.[8] A sense of irrelevance had enveloped the army on the Tigris during the stultifying summer of 1916. However grim their experiences of the failed relief attempt, the troops felt (Candler reported) a strong desire to 'pull their weight' in the war, and 'an exhilaration in moving on' when the advance at last began.

Maude must have got some encouragement from a visit by General Monro, the new Indian C-in-C, in mid-October. Monro was the first C-in-C to visit Mesopotamia, and though he could not get to Nasiriyeh or the Karun thanks to a riding injury, he was able to take the railway up to the front at Es Sinn. This inspection, Maude's biographer thought, helped the troops to 'realise the driving power penetrating through the ramifications of the rearward services from Basra almost to the very trenches, a driving power which emanated from Maude'. The C-in-C's appearance assured them that Mesopotamia was 'no longer a Cinderella'. Maude himself thought that the soldiers at the front already looked much better – 'healthy and in good heart' – than when he had left to take up the army command at Basra in July. Monro told him that Mesopotamia 'would be reckoned in history as about the biggest expedition of its kind that England had ever sent out'.[9] The implication was that there must be some point to it.

The expedition was certainly now big. Maude's support in India and London meant that 'what he asked for he got'. This included an additional corps staff: the four divisions of the overloaded Tigris Corps were now divided between the I Indian Army Corps (3rd and 7th Divisions) under Lieutenant-General Alexander Cobbe, and the III (13th and 14th Divisions) under Lieutenant-General William Marshall. MacMunn's expansion of river transport capacity from an average of 450 tons a day in August to over 700 tons in November allowed Maude to build up 20–25 days' supply reserve (12,000 tons) at Sheikh Saad, even though the army's ration strength had grown by 50,000 men and 10,000 animals. The crucial rail link from Sheikh Saad was carried forward to Es Sinn in mid-September and to Imam al-Mansur in mid-December. Just as vital to increasing the army's offensive capacity were the Ford vans which were beginning to appear in quantity. Maude judged them 'quite tiptop', and asked for nine companies (each of 128 vans). Six of these had arrived by December. By December the British combat strength in Mesopotamia was over 100,000, and the forces on the Tigris totalled some 45,000 infantry, 3,500 cavalry and 174 field guns.

Edmund Candler, who was with the 40th Brigade for most of the three-month offensive operation, sensed a significant change. Transport at long last 'rose to the new demand'. Despite the bad weather that infallibly appeared when operations began, by adjusting loads and staging convoys some sort of mobility was achieved even when the elements 'conspired to clog all movement'. Every unit 'contributed its quota of mobility and was fed in spite of itself'. Candler ruminated on the supply issue during one of the early battles as he watched 'a convoy of 200 Ford motor vans crawling slowly through the mud on the horizon. Each contained three bundles of chopped straw for the cavalry, consumed four gallons of petrol a day, and engaged the whole-time services of an able-bodied man who might have been in the firing line.'[10] (He would ruminate, too, on the material–moral division between West and East after talking with a prisoner taken in one of the early battles, who turned out to be a Jewish lawyer from Istanbul. Speaking fluent Parisian French, and lamenting his fate in being 'thrown into this desert of savage men with the manners of children', he noticed an ammunition wagon arriving with a stack of braziers for the men in the trenches. 'You have everything,' he glumly observed.)

His commanders probably felt much the same sense of inferiority, especially since resources were being taken out of Mesopotamia rather than added. Halil Pasha's Sixth Army received very few replacements from April 1916 onwards, and in the summer the shattered 38th Division was dissolved, its units redistributed amongst the four surviving divisions.[11] Though Maude estimated Halil's strength at 20,000 infantry, it was barely half that. The Turks were well dug in, and went on elaborating their already formidable entrenchments at Sannaiyat, but their strategic position was awkward, if not perilous. On the right bank of the river, where there were only two Turkish positions, the British could move at will as far as the Hai, and even beyond Kut. The Turks' single boat bridge was vulnerable to artillery fire, and would be destroyed on 20 December. Less than a sixth of XVIII Corps' infantry battalions, and an even smaller proportion of its artillery, were available as a reserve.[12] Maude had the luxury of knowing that his enemy was virtually immobile, and certainly could not make any serious push forward from Sannaiyat. Candler was surely right to say that 'if a cadet at a military college had put up such a proposition a year or two before, he would have been rated for his ignorance of the first principles of war'.[13]

Maude's offensive plan was simple. He aimed to get his main force past Kut, and cross the river to cut off the main Turkish force east of the town. Apart from his supply problems, he might easily have bypassed the positions south of the river. He preferred to destroy them, however. This methodical approach was to cost many lives, and not only because the Turkish soldiers were still dogged defenders. First he launched a 'strong feint' against the Sannaiyat position, a manoeuvre that was open to criticism. (One senior military writer has dismissed it as 'a total waste of life'.) The unfortunate 7th Division, which had carried out the two desperate failed assaults on Sannaiyat during the Kut relief effort, had spent the following months digging and sapping in front of the Turkish defences. 'I had been sitting there the whole summer', wrote one artilleryman, 'every other day looking over and trying to see what the Turk was really up to, then having a pot with a rifle . . . so the days and months wore on.'[14] They had been working steadily for months to improve their own trench works, and 'it is only human', as Barker said, 'to imagine that if one's own position is unassailable that of the enemy is even more so'.

Sannaiyat was an immensely formidable position, which the Turks had good reason to believe impregnable. The mock attack opened on 13 December 1916 while, in the main advance, III Corps headed west towards the Hai, arriving there unopposed early on the 14th. Six bridges were quickly thrown across the river, and the light railway was brought up to Atab. Maude then ordered a crossing of the river at the Husaini bend by a cavalry brigade and an infantry brigade on 20 December. This was an odd operation. Its commander, General Crocker, heard of it only the day before, and the officer in charge of the bridging train knew nothing of it until he received the actual order. There was no technical reconnaissance – an omission made worse by the fact that the bridging train had just been issued with new wheeled transport they had not been able to test. Maude's eagerness to achieve surprise compromised the operation's chances, but its purpose was anyway obscure. Was it meant to develop into a real crossing, or was it just another demonstration? When Maude rode over to commiserate with Crocker on his failure to get across, Marshall was so astonished that he 'blurted out, "But you didn't really mean them to cross."' Maude said he had; Marshall remained unconvinced.[15] His chief of staff was more forthright: the operation was 'a shocking instance of timidity', and the withdrawal 'most humiliating'. It seems at least to have had one beneficial effect, though – it confirmed the Turks in their belief that a crossing of the river was impossible. 'None but a fool would attempt it.'[16] They would eventually suffer for this belief.

Ned Roe, who dreaded the thought of another assault on Sannaiyat, was relieved to find that the 13th Division was in the force heading for Hai. He wrote an unusually brief account of the night march, and noted that next morning, 'We gaze upon Kut for the first time.' It was 'a dilapidated looking village'. He would no doubt have been suitably amused to know that his division had been selected to lead the attack because Maude regarded 13 as his lucky number, hence also the choice of 13 December for the opening of the offensive.[17] Roe was in reserve as it began, and watched groups of Turkish prisoners coming in through the day while the Turkish artillery threw 'heavy and light "stuff" at our advancing lines'. His regiment went into the firing line in the evening, toting their newly arrived Lewis guns. (Roe airily dismissed this potent new weapon as 'something in the nature of a toy for young officers to play about with. We have no faith in it.')

The advance was promising: 'it would seem that our flank attack took the Turks completely by surprise as we have obtained a firm footing in the Muhammad Abdul Hassan loop.' But still familiar problems remained. On the night of 20 December Roe was with a stretcher party that lost its bearings trying to return from the casualty clearing station, the country being 'as flat as a billiard table with no prominent objects', wandered into the enemy lines and was 'as near shot or captured as damn it'. And water was scarce: the troops gave up eating bully beef because of the thirst it fostered, and an issue of rum on Christmas Day was a poor substitute. 'If we had a sufficiency of drinking water we would not mind.'[18] (Officers received a remarkable Christmas gift of a free ration of champagne, courtesy of Lord Curzon.[19]) Then it started to rain: an artillery driver (promoted unpaid bombardier) with 38th Brigade called it a 'monsoon . . . we lived as best we could beneath our wagons'.[20] The infantry did not even have that crude shelter: Reginald Boulton, a sergeant in the 8th Cheshires, 'slept in soaked blankets in the open air, rain beating down unmercifully. Blankets handed in every morning, rolled in bundles, sopping wet. Issued out again, two each, at night, still very wet and covered in mud from the ground and men's boots.' The nights were very cold, and the men were still in 'thin khaki, our serge not yet arrived'.[21] Roe's diary for 27–28 December read simply, 'Wallowing in mud and living on air.'

On New Year's Eve 'we are half starved and overworked. We dare not smoke owing to hunger and weakness and we know the result of making complaints . . . '[22]

They had obtained 'a footing in the Muhammad Abdul Hassan loop', but they still faced an elaborate system of defence works stretching across the Khaidiri Bend. Again the cost in blood of the attack was aggravated by Maude's refusal to delay it during the heavy rain. Once more, the British troops had to make frontal attacks on the kind of trench systems at which the Turks were so expert. (Roe was impressed to find that the Turkish trenches, when they finally got into them, were 'narrow and deep: Life Guards could stand up in them comfortably and not be exposed.') Worse, the defenders had now become more expert at mounting counter-attacks. Candler watched one early counter-attack in which the Turks 'who had been lying up in the scrub suddenly loomed out of the mist like a football crowd', and thought that another, on 11 January, was 'one of the most gallant sorties ever seen'.

It took ten days of 'very strenuous fighting' – Maude's phrase – from 9 January 1917 to eliminate this position. Roe's brigadier, O'Dowda, worried that 'numbers are dwindling fast and we shall soon be badly reduced. This digging forward against the Turks is the devil.' The night of 15 January was 'the worst – 1000 yards of trench to be dug' by 800 men under fire.[23] The defenders were finally hemmed into a small triangle of land between the end of their second-line trenches and the river; they were evacuated on the night of 18 January. The attritional warfare was aggravated by the fact that as the attackers pushed forward they were, in effect, moving into a salient where they were exposed to artillery fire from both flanks. Still, 'Our men fairly beat them at their own game, and with bomb and bayonet drove them steadily back foot by foot.' At the end they were, Maude thought, 'tremendously pleased with themselves'.[24]

Even Major Catty thought some of the operations 'very satisfactory', though as usual he detailed some less agreeable aspects of the assault. Before reaching assaulting distance 3rd Division had already suffered 400 casualties, thanks to the familiar lack of cover and the fact that 'the enemy was on the qui vive'. 'All went splendidly' on the 9th, though it was very misty and the Turkish counter-attack was helped by this. In the fighting that day, it seemed that A Company of the 59th Rifles had not 'done very well, tho exactly what happened is hard to say'. Things went well on the 10th, too, and again on the 11th 'everything seemed to be going tophole. The Turks appeared to be penned up in a small space & at midday it was reported that only a few disorganised men remained.' The clearing-up was left to a single brigade – 'a fatal mistake as the Turks during the night had ferried across a fresh Regt (43rd) & relieved the old 142nd who had only 200 men left'. The fresh troops put in a formidable counter-attack against the advance of the HLI who were driven back 'in confusion' to their starting point. 'The price was very heavy 15 Officers & 200-odd men – a high proportion of officers.' Overall the losses that day were 600, which Catty thought were heavier than the enemy's. 'A real bad show which might have been avoided.' (The official historian admitted that 'in this operation the British had been surprised by the opposition encountered'.)

Maude called for a continuous offensive, and while I Corps was pressing up to the riverbank, Marshall's III Corps was 'extending its left' into the open space west of the Hai with the object of 'ringing the Turks into the Dahra Bend'.[25] In the last week of January 'our artillery was never silent', Bombardier George Coles noted: 'the whole Turkish line from River Hai to River Tigris one sea of fire and smoke day and night. Hard to believe anyone could live through it.' On the basis of 'the way their counter-attacks have been mown down, and the number of dead that we have counted and buried', Maude was sure that enemy casualties were 'very heavy, quite out of proportion to their size'. Prisoners reported that many units had been 'practically wiped out'. By 15 February he was confident that 'things could not have gone better for us than they have done'. The bend had been cleared, a thousand Turkish prisoners had been taken, and morale was still improving. But still the enemy was not getting the message. 'They are wonderful stickers, those Turks, and there are few troops that would fight like they do.' At the front line, Ned Roe had to agree. 'We have twenty guns to the enemy's one and are full of confidence', he wrote on 5 February. Ten days later, when the battle was won, 'Although they are our enemies we cannot but admire them for the magnificent show they put up.'

Newly (and reluctantly) promoted lance-corporal, Roe found himself advancing in support of the 14th Division on 3 February, crossing the Hai and marching eight miles before relieving a brigade of the 14th. On the 5th, 'daylight reveals every shell crater and trench filled with Turkish dead. The stench is unbearable.' He may still have been sceptical about the Lewis guns (they had jammed in the mud during the Khaidiri assault), but he had no doubts about the Stokes mortars, whose 'effect is in deadly evidence here'. Yet still the enemy hung on, and counter-attacked. The mere rumour of a counter-attack caused 'absolute panic', routing a sapping party composed of Welsh pioneers and some of Roe's unit. Next day, 'We are steadily bombing the Turks out of their strong points; bloody work, and the ill-clad, bootless, emaciated Turks are putting up a desperate resistance.'[26] A symbolic moment was reached on 10 February when the Liquorice Factory – 'or what was left of it' – fell to the British. On the 14th, the 38th Brigade captured the remnant of a whole Turkish division, including three brigade commanders.[27] The prisoners were a sad lot – those taken by the Cheshires 'very dirty, hardly any equipment and very little clothing. Some had slippers tied round with string, all had beards.' Roe's unit had to give their 'very ragged' prisoners basic equipment like satchels as well as food.

Roe was, like many soldiers, an assiduous gleaner of information about the bigger plans of which he was a tiny component, often trading cigarettes for news (sometimes fictional) from the CO's cook or the adjutant's batman. But by 14 February he did not need any inside information to see the obvious: when the Turks were cleared from the right bank, 'the next operation should be the forcing of the passage of the Tigris'. If successful, this would 'place two Divisions in his rear and his lines of communication are cut. Kut must fall automatically. Mr Turk must get out and be very quick about it or he will share Townshend's fate.' Lance-Corporal Roe's view chimed with that of Maude's Chief of Staff, Major-General Money: 'If we once get a good sized force across we ought to have the Turks boiled.'[28]

Maude aimed to cross the river at the Shumran bend, but local floods delayed the move and inflicted more misery on his troops. On 16 February, the dyspeptic Sergeant Boulton of the Cheshires 'had to carry boxes of ammunition for about 2 miles in pouring rain. I had a Turk groundsheet but it was no good. Went back to trenches that we left yesterday morning. Stayed huddled together, very cold, pouring with rain, pitch dark, no coats, until 5.30am. Off again with our loads of ammunition to the dump. Had some cold tea, marched about 2 more miles, I was quite lame. Just got back in camp when we had the most terrible storm I have ever seen, flooded us all out, tents collapsed, equipment and buckets floating about everywhere.' It took all next day 'to dig trenches round tents and run water off. No sleep last night . . . '[29]

Had he known, though, he might have been grateful for the terrible weather, as those who actually had to prepare the crossing certainly were. Once again, Maude had ordered the operation at short notice – telling III Corps on 17 February to be ready to establish a force on the left bank at any time from the night of the 18th (which would have given them barely twenty-four hours to prepare). Secrecy may have been a reason for this, but a later critic doubted 'whether General Maude realised the importance of preparation' for river crossings. If so, Maude's reputation for meticulous planning needs to be adjusted. Unlike the ill-prepared 20 December operation, this one was really serious, and failure might have been disastrous. It may, ironically, have been the much-maligned weather of Mesopotamia that saved the British this time: 'those who realized the importance of preparation were not slow to take advantage of the six days which it gave them.'[30]

Maude now decided to upgrade his 'feint' or 'demonstration' at Sannaiyat into a full-scale attack, presumably to distract the enemy, though once more his motives are still obscure. Lord Carver speculates that he was perhaps 'actuated primarily by a desire to open up the river'. His decision not only cost the lives of many 7th Division troops but also undermined the tactical logic of the river crossing, which was to cut off the advanced Turkish forces. Pushing them back towards Kut would (if successful) push them out of the trap. In the event, the attack did not succeed, in spite of unprecedentedly careful planning. (The assaulting units practised on a replica of the Turkish trench system dug from air photographs, and rehearsed for three days.[31]) The attack at Sannaiyat was supposed to be synchronised with the river crossing at Shumran, but even though the crossing was delayed by flooding that attack went ahead. The rain inevitably made the situation at Sannaiyat even more difficult, but (as at the Khaidiri bend in January) Maude dismissed any idea of delaying it. In its third full-scale assault on the dreaded position, the 7th Division broke through to the second defensive line (forty yards behind the first), but was then thrown back by a series of counter-attacks, and suffered horrible losses.

At last on 22 February the bridge-building at Shumran went ahead. It was 'a momentous night' as Coles noted, but a tryingly slow process for the high command as much as for the bridging train itself – 'a very anxious time' for General Money. There were three crossing points, and each was a small epic: Edmund Candler saluted the courage these small operations required. 'They had to get enough men over in ten pontoons to seize the other bank, ferry the boats back, cross again after the alarm, and continue the passage until the whole battalion was over, then to rush the trenches and dug-outs, scupper the riflemen and machine-gun teams, and throw their thin line across the bend, while the bridge was building, before the Turks could bring up their reserves.' There was, as he said of the landing of the Gurkhas at No. 3 Ferry, 'no quick shoulder-to-shoulder rush to stimulate <u>elan</u>. Each landing was an individual piece of initiative and heroism. Judged by any standard other than mere bulk, it was as great a thing as the landing at Helles.'[32] But even with all this 'gallantry in cold blood' – Major George Wheeler won a VC for his action leading the landing at No. 2 Ferry – the crossing stalled. Footholds were established on the north bank, but the casualty rate amongst the troops rowing the pontoons was unsustainable. Before 7 a.m., 110 out of 230 of the Hampshire Regiment rowers at Ferry No. 3 had been hit. 'As one by one the rowers were killed or wounded, and the boats stranded or drifted downstream, Ferries 2 and 3 had to be abandoned.' Only one and a half companies of the two battalions had made it across, where they hung on under heavy fire.

Without the support of artillery, they might have been lost. 'It looked serious', Ralph Harrison of B Battery, 66th Brigade RFA wrote, 'as we saw this rush of black figures with their long black bayonets showing above the bund streaming down on the Gurkhas still confused from their landing in the dark.' But the batteries on the south bank 'intervened in a manner which was terrible to watch. We fired "gun fire" into this attack at ranges varying from 1,500 to 800 yards. They seemed to be literally blasted away, and the attack withered away in a moment. We were in a wonderfully powerful position . . . the Turk to reach our infantry had to cross the muzzles of these guns at point blank range.'[33]

Ferries 2 and 3 were intended as diversions, and they seem to have worked. At the main crossing point, the bridge-building operation (Ferry No. 1) went ahead without a hitch. By night-fall the pontoons had been carried to the riverbank, but as Lieutenant R. B. Woakes of Queen Victoria's Own Sappers and Miners noted, 'opposite bank looks a very long way off in this light & the river is making a lot of noise'. (It was 295 yards wide at this point, and running at five knots.) At least the Turks had 'evidently not spotted us at all'. Launching the pontoons at 5 a.m. next morning was more laborious than he expected, and once they were two-thirds of the way across, the enemy opened fire. 'Hell of a morning, bullets flying freely all the time & we were shelled continuously. Saw a lot of our pontoons drifting downstream – & one hit fair by a shell disappeared completely.' After some confusion ('empty pontoons on the opposite bank with no-one to row them back & no pontoons on this side') the pontoons were reassembled, the bridgehead troops (Gurkhas and Punjabis) ferried across, and the bridge completed by 4.30 in the afternoon. 'Turks crumped us at the bridge head all evening but failed to hit the bridge.'[34]

Roe was in the first division across the bridge, at dawn on the 24th. The previous day he had been reflecting on the information Micky Quinn from St Helens (who had joined up for the duration of the war 'or longer if it lasts') had just received in a letter – that all soldiers killed in battle went straight to heaven. Roe was not taken with this curious heterodox notion; he preferred to stay on earth, even if it meant going to hell at the end. But as his brigade crossed the bridge under enemy shellfire – over a river full of dead fish, killed by artillery shells – and as 'the pontoon rocks and sways', he reflected that 'one lucky shell and all who are on the bridge are in heaven, whether they like it or not'. They spent the rest of the day 'lying in the open under shellfire', catching all the shots that fell short of the Turks' target, the pontoon bridge. At 5 p.m. his battalion at last formed up to advance on a Turkish defensive position. The Turks 'fire a few shots and "mizzle". Battalion stand fast for the night.'[35] George Coles, the first mounted man across the bridge, was later able to see a photograph of himself making the crossing under fire – taken by Edmund Candler with a cine-camera on the far side.

As soon as the main units of III Corps got across the river, the irretrievable weakness of the Ottoman position was clear. There was not the slightest possibility of any counter-move against the extended British lines from Sannaiyat to Shumran. Halil could no longer maintain the defences at Sannaiyat, where a retreat began immediately. The Turks should have been, as Money put it, 'boiled'. Yet they pulled off another near-miraculous escape. 'They were bombing us in the trenches at eleven on the night of the 23rd, and at 7.30 on the morning of the 25th they had covered the twenty miles to Shumran.'[36] Maude sent increasingly urgent instructions to Cobbe to pin the forces opposite him and prevent them from disengaging. At midday, and again at 2.30: 'Hope you are pursuing your role vigorously, for on this much of success of our operations depends . . . You should not hesitate to attack immediately.' (He even added a history lesson in the style of Townshend – 'Remember 1814 campaign and let us not repeat mistakes of Allies then.') At 5 p.m.: 'It is essentially a time when most vigorous action is necessary to bring about decisive results.' But there was no decisive result. The ordinary soldiers were once again left to reflect, like Roe, that 'we have let the Turks slip between our fingers and that had affairs been forced on the 23rd the Kut garrison would have been captured'.

Who was to blame? Money grumbled that Cobbe 'wouldn't get a move on', and that 'the stickiness of our Cav commander let a lot of Turks escape that shouldn't have'. In fact Cobbe seems to have pushed forward – the 7th Division was in the Turkish fourth line by the evening of the 23rd when its troops were brought to a standstill by bitterly cold weather. But, unlike the cavalry, Cobbe had no way of getting across the Turkish line of retreat. The cavalry were once again the main target of criticism. 'If our Cavalry had been quicker we ought to have rounded up a great deal more,' Money thought. Maude had put the Cavalry Division under his direct orders, but it could not get on: by 5 p.m. on the 23rd it had 'made very little progress'. A couple of hours later, after getting entangled in local fighting, it turned back to the river to water its horses. Marshall's Chief of Staff tersely wrote on the 24th that the Cavalry Division 'messed about all day and lost the chance of a lifetime'.[37] Some of this could be blamed on

Maude's habit (as Money complained earlier in the month) of 'worrying the cavalry all day with orders that only reach them long after the occasion for carrying them out has passed'. Cobbe himself acidly remarked later that Maude was 'very captious' at the critical point of the battle. 'As you realise from his orders to the cavalry', he wrote to the official historian, 'he apparently assumed that there would be no opposition to speak of on the right bank and that the cavalry would get through without delay.' Cobbe claimed that he had asked to have the cavalry put under his own control, but 'got snubbed' by Money. So the cavalry 'spent the next two days moving to the west and back again to the east to water'.[38] (Indeed, nearly half the cavalry's movement during the three days of battle was taken up in marching and counter-marching to and from water.)

Candler was with the cavalry on both 24 and 25 February, hoping to take part in the 'pursuit of an army in rout across an open plain', an experience that 'every cavalryman has prayed for but not one in a thousand has known'. In the event he had 'one of the dullest days I have spent in my life'. Candler knew well enough that other soldiers tended to expect too much of the cavalry – the myth of 'riding down a mob of panic-stricken fugitives' had been squashed by modern infantry weapons. 'Even bad troops possess in the present firearm a power of resistance against which the flood will break in vain.' But if so, why maintain a whole cavalry division when supplies were at a premium? Candler like others thought it could now really have been decisive, if its leadership had been more energetic. Lack of initiative lost the advantage of mobility. When they started to worry about watering their horses, the cavalry's choice was 'to go on or go back', and he had no doubt that they should have gone on and occupied a position on the river that would have blocked the enemy's line of retreat. 'A whole cavalry division, dismounted and dug in twenty miles in rear of the tired and footsore Turkish infantry, would have left the enemy small hope of escape.'[39] But instead they went twelve miles back for water. Marshall sardonically noted the message that came from the cavalry commander on the 25th: 'that as he had not been able to water his horses all day, he was now retiring to Shumran for that purpose, and that *he had captured 3,000 sheep.*'[40]

There were extenuating factors. The Cavalry Division was a makeshift formation which had not operated as a single unit; the terrain offered little chance of screening its movements from the enemy infantry; and the need to stay near the river was a real handicap to its mobility. Maude's attempt at close control made the situation worse. For one thing, the division had a single wireless transmitter, which had to be set up every hour to comply with Maude's demand for hourly reports. Since it took some twenty minutes to set it up, and another fifteen to take it down again, the reduction in mobility was dramatic. (And particularly ironic in light of Maude's own musing about how to emulate the mobility of the Cossacks.) Even when in touch, GHQ could not fully grasp the possibilities on the ground, while the divisional HQ 'did not feel itself to be its own master', as a later staff assessment put it. Still, after making allowance for these things, the problem remains that the cavalry had got effectively into the clear on 24 February, but then wheeled west to engage the Turkish rearguard, instantly becoming immobilised in dismounted action. Any alternative would have been better than this. What seemed to have been missing was the spirit of risk-taking – the 'cavalry spirit', in fact.[41]

Marshall's infantry fought their way to Imam Mahdi and the Dahra ridge against stolid resistance; there was no rout. After that the battle petered out. Aircraft could do little more than machine-gun the retreating Turkish columns and watch the stragglers succumb to 'the attentions of the Arab tribesmen, hanging round like wolves on their trail'. Once again, it was the Navy that pushed on most effectively. For months the gunboats could not get past Sannaiyat, and had been restricted to providing auxiliary artillery there. Now they could get on again. On 24 February Nunn met Maude 'restlessly pacing up and down' at

GHQ; 'he kept saying, "I can't get a move on. So and so won't move," etc. etc.' Maude wanted the gunboats to close in on Kut, but Nunn went one better. That evening the crew of the *Mantis* landed in town and raised the flag, the second time in the campaign that the Navy had captured a defended town. (To Bombardier Coles it was 'ironical' for the Navy to take a town some 300 miles from the sea.)

Early next day the flotilla pushed on upriver; it was let through the pontoon bridge at Shumran 'amid rousing cheers from the soldiers crowding each bank'. Ned Roe was one of them, and his brigade set off in column of route in line with the gunboats. At 9 a.m. Turkish artillery opened fire on the rear monitor, hoping to block the river and 'have the other four at his mercy . . . By Christ, is she gone? No! What a close shave. We hold our breath in suspense as another salvo of "five nines" comes over.' They were drenched with spray as the shells exploded in the river, while the monitors retired and the troops wondered what would have happened if any of those heavy shells had hit their column. (Fortunately, all the 'spare stuff' dropped on the other bank.) 'Why were we allowed to come under artillery fire in column of route? . . . One lucky shot this morning and our river fleet would have "went west". We are saying all sorts of unkind things re our intelligence department.'[42]

After this small setback, the flotilla went on again – the *Tarantula*, *Mantis* and *Moth* 'passed our infantry on the bank at full steam; our cavalry watched their disappearing smoke with envy'. They fought a running battle with Turkish troops on the banks of the long loops, pushing through at top speed (16 knots), and exchanging fire at point-blank range. Though the quartermaster and the pilot were killed on the bridge of the *Mantis*, none of the boats was lost. After Sharqui, where the road ran alongside the river, they turned their guns on the retreating Turkish columns, before running up against the Ottoman flotilla in retreat. The captured monitor *Firefly*, along with three other boats, was run aground and set on fire by its crew; but it was saved. Rough-and-ready repairs would allow it to take part in the entry to Baghdad twelve days later.

The naval pursuit turned the retreating Turks into 'a disorganised rabble, no longer in column of fours', and confirmed the Navy's role 'as a kind of super-cavalry'.[43] The real cavalry at last caught up with the Turks at Aziziyeh, but could still not exploit the enemy's disorganisation. In spite of this, and though it fell short of a German-style *Vernichtungsschlacht*, the third battle of Kut was an unmistakable victory. Maude hardly exaggerated when he reported that 'the Turkish force as such has ceased to exist'. His army had taken over 7,000 prisoners, together with vast quantities of military stores and equipment. To those who had laboured and suffered through the agonies of the relief attempts – and those who had watched them from afar – Maude's achievement seemed almost marvellous. Even admitting the huge numerical and material superiority he possessed, numbers on their own are not enough, and the quality of organisation and energy he supplied was certainly out of the ordinary. Even Major-General Money, his chief of staff, reluctantly came to recognise this.

Before the offensive, Money had found Maude extremely difficult. So, he knew, did Cobbe, whom Money liked 'much the better of the two', though he admitted that 'in many ways Maude is the better soldier . . . more thorough & has more knowledge of detail'. But this was also the problem with Maude: he was a control freak. At one point in the December battles, Maude got up from a rest 'and began fussing that the firing had been going on too long & was too intense etc. He is very tiresome when he gets into one of these moods.' Next month, Money found him getting 'rather irritated when he sees that I don't get angry or excited when people don't carry out orders as they are told. He's a very unbalanced fellow at times, & goes dashing off orders to all and sundry, when if he only sat tight he'd find things would work out all right.' Money found it hard to keep his temper with him in these moods, fuming that Maude was 'a maddening fellow, never leaves anyone alone, either his staff or his subordinate commanders', who 'all hate the sight of him'. Though he conceded that 'he has ability of a sort, & is very keen', he felt he 'could not stand much more of him'. A month later Maude was still 'rather trying when there's a fight going on. He can't influence it one way or another but he is always frightfully impatient if he doesn't get reports about it every few minutes.' At last, though, just before the Shumran crossing, Money noted that Maude had 'been quite good'. He was 'certainly good at shoving people along'. ('In Lake's time I had to do all the shoving myself.'[44])

Marshall's chief of staff, Brigadier Theodore Fraser, was less easily reconciled. At the start of Maude's offensive he was grumbling, 'GHQ show no confidence, pelting us with nervous questions all day and night.' (Marshall, he added, 'bore it very quietly, but his lips tightened!') Successive operations repeatedly employed 'overwhelming force to attain a minute object'. At the end of the year he was fuming. 'What have we gained?' he asked in his diary. 'There is no strategy in this. From the start there has been no "ginger". Deliberation carried to excess, over-caution, timidity!' He thought that using cavalry to clear the right bank of the Hai had been typical of the 'ignorance of the tactical employment of the different arms' that was obvious throughout – like 'the idea that troops can move up one bank of a fordable stream without possessing themselves of both banks'. The fussy, tiresome, time-consuming interference went on all through the offensive: after the undeniably successful river crossing in late February, he was still berating the 'endless unnecessary messages from GHQ', many of them sent in cipher. He blamed all this on Money as much as Maude: 'many of the instructions and questions from the CGS have been childish.' Maude was 'a poor tactician and lacks ginger', Money was 'ignorant of war, nervous and timid'.[45]

For the troops, though, victory was sweet. 'The whole Turkish army was on the run and we were after them.' Sergeant Barber of the 13th Division artillery thought 'it was wonderful the difference in the men's feelings when they are advancing'. He had a sharp recollection of 'the gloomy way the men rode' in the retreat from Mons, and 'the surly answers one would get from the officers . . . now everyone was in the best of spirits laughing and joking'. But the fighting was still costly, and after dusk Barber found himself laying a cable to try to re-establish contact with the infantry. 'To find the battery again I put a lamp on the observation ladder and then took two men with me and started looking for the Gloucesters. We were laden with cable and scrambled up and down nullahs shouting. At last I heard a cry and we listened and finally made it out in a nullah to our right so we went over and the cries turned into screams and we ran and found a pack of jackals eating a man alive.' It was a private of the Gloucesters who had been wounded and fallen into the deep nullah, where he passed out – to be woken by the jackals tearing his flesh. After chasing the jackals off, Barber sent his men back to the battery for a stretcher; but the jackals came back, and 'it was weird to see them sitting around in a circle waiting for their prey'.[46]

7. Baghdad at Last

Let us hope that is the last infernal river we shall have to cross.
EDMUND ROE

If Maude thought of trying to press on the pursuit of the defeated
Turks, he was quickly brought up short by the inevitable fact that
his army had outrun its supplies. MacMunn persuaded him he
must call a halt for five days. Now, though, the lure of Baghdad
exerted itself again, as it had after the first capture of Kut. The
C-in-C India asked Maude whether by halting to reorganise he
was not missing an opportunity to complete 'the shattering of
the Turkish forces by an unrelenting pursuit, and giving them
time to re-form for the defence of Baghdad'. Even Robertson,
who still insisted that it would be impossible to hold the city
without Russian assistance, accepted that Maude must 'press
enemy in direction of Baghdad and so exploit your recent success
to full extent which you judge to be useful and feasible'. The
War Cabinet had 'modified' its September instructions; it was
now British policy 'to establish British influence in the Baghdad
vilayet'. Retirement was no longer either a military or political
option.[1]

Maude needed no second bidding. He believed he had 'only
the wreck of an army in front of him', and ought to be able to
get into Baghdad before the Turks could get reinforcements.[2]
He claimed he would have no difficulty in holding it. Money,
however, thought that the Turks would 'make a desperate push
to save Baghdad, or to turn us out of it if we get in there'. Lance-
Corporal Roe and his men, ever the realists, took an even more
sober view. They, after all, were the ones who were starving
because they had marched 'an agonizing eight hours through a

raging sandstorm' from 1 p.m. to 9 p.m. on 28 February only to find they had 'out-marched supplies'. One day's rations arrived on 1 March, and 'we were told to make four biscuits and a tin of "bully" between two men last us two days'. They were 'all of the opinion that General Maude can not have foreseen the extent of his victory'. At that moment the Turkish army was 'a beaten rabble pursued only by gunboats, aeroplanes and cavalry . . . We are told there is one more river to cross. If Mr Turk gets a breathing spell and digs in on the opposite bank – well – we'll have to do it all over again.'

That river was two days' march away, and they did indeed have to do it all over again. At the beginning of March, as Coles recorded, 'we were without food for 60 hours – 2 days and 3 nights . . . the mules seemed to suffer more than we did'.[3] On 3 March Roe's brigade was allowed to eat their emergency rations (if they had any left); next day 'the mules are eating each other's tails off and we are faint from hunger'. In 14th Division, after a brilliant day on 1 March when a flock of 2,000 sheep appeared outside the camp – Lieutenant Woakes's company managing to get twenty-seven – next day there were 'no rations for man or beast all day'.[4] Sergeant Boulton of the Cheshires wrote in his diary for the 2nd, 'No rations at all.' Next day, 'No dinner, just a drink of tea for tea.' Two days later, 'Absolutely done up, had no tea.'[5]

Tea or no tea, the advance began again on 5 March. By the time the army halted at 6 p.m., after a march that raised dust so thick that the troops could not see the section ahead of them, troops and animals were desperate. 'The mules make a dash for the river and the men cannot be restrained either . . . Everyone's feet are in an awful condition; soles toes and heels blood raw.' Next day, as they passed the arch at Ctesiphon with its litter of battle debris, rusty bully beef and jam tins, over seventy men of his battalion had reported sick with bad feet (and even the stoic Ned Roe admitted 'God knows they are bad'). The East Lancs' MO, of course, told them to march on, since if he hospitalised

361

every man who should be hospitalised 'we would advance on Baghdad in Red Cross vans'. Coles was on horseback but still 'done up', while 'the poor infantry weakened by hunger lined the roads in a state of collapse'. At least the Arabs had turned their attention elsewhere: at Ctesiphon Coles found a Turkish officer 'in agony and dying – cut up by marauding Arabs'. (Behind them, Maude examined the Ctesiphon defences with approval – and no doubt some relief: 'the Turks had prepared a very strong position – almost a fortress – all the work there was new and very well designed and strong.'[6])

Since they had abandoned the Salman Pak position, Maude was sure his enemy did not intend to make a stand before Baghdad. 'We hear stories of reinforcements coming from various directions', he wrote, 'but I fancy that the Turks will clear if we can only press them sufficiently.' The key question was whether they would stand on the Diyala river. The Army Commander was 'cocksure Turks won't hold Dialah', Fraser noted, but 'General Marshall thinks they will'. So did Maude's own chief of staff, General Money, and GHQ's intelligence head, Brigadier Hicks Beach. Maude simply 'scoffed' at all objections.[7]

On 7 March the 38th Brigade reached the Diyala. As Roe's East Lancs battalion followed the King's Own to the riverbank in the late afternoon to prepare to cross, things seemed quiet. The men stood talking on the riverbank – 'He's "picked him up" again, Bill,' said one. Roe 'heard some good hard swearing by the King's Own as they were manhandling the pontoons towards the river'. Discretion was thrown to the winds and conversation became general – by contrast 'the Turks never betrayed their presence even by a muffled cough'. Marshall had reconnoitred the position personally in the early afternoon, reporting that the enemy seemed to be 'in some strength' along the lower reaches, with at least seven guns. Maude issued an operation order at 6.15 p.m. declaring that the enemy had 'disclosed little strength along the Diyala' – no more than seven guns had been reported.[8] For O'Dowda the crossing 'in un-reconnoitred country' was 'a gamble' which the brigadier, unsurprisingly, did not much like.[9] Roe and his mates 'were congratulating ourselves on a bloodless victory when suddenly the right bank of the river burst into flame'. The pontoons were launched, but without artillery support the prospects were grim. 'What an awful experience it must be for those men in the pontoons, loaded with ammunition and bombs, reels of signalling wire etc, trying to cross under a converging machine gun fire.' Bombardier Coles noted that the 38th Brigade had been 'decimated by murderous machine gun fire from the north bank', and four attempts to cross by pontoon had failed, 'every man being killed'. (Officially, there were sixty-four casualties; three out of four pontoons had been lost.) It is hard to dissent from Barker's stern view that this was 'a shining example of how a river crossing should not be carried out'. With no proper reconnaissance, no alternative crossing places, no feints, and little covering fire, only the need to press on quickly could in any way justify the waste of lives here.

The Ottoman position on the Diyala was not particularly strong. Hastily prepared during 1–6 March, and some eight miles long, 'the whole front was so covered with huts, embankments, gardens and mounds that the field of gun fire was much restricted'. Many of the defenders' thirty-two field guns could not be emplaced, and the commander of the XVIII Corps decided, just before the first British assault, to hold the river only as an advanced position, and establish his main defensive line some two to four miles behind it. Indeed, the logic of the Diyala position had been disputed between the Ottoman commander, Halil Pasha, and XVIII Corps for several days as the Sixth Army regrouped. Halil had not even begun to think about how to defend Baghdad until he arrived there on 26 February, and then he came to the conclusion that it was militarily indefensible. Enver, however, ordered Halil to defend the city at all costs. After spending six days preparing a defensive position at Ctesiphon, in spite of the 'remonstrances' of his XVIII Corps commander, he abandoned it as the British advanced. His next idea was to hold the Diyala line long enough to give XIII Corps time to join him before the whole force retired on Baghdad. So Maude was right that the Diyala defence was no more than a holding operation.

Maude began with an attempt to outflank the Diyala position. First a brigade under Brigadier-General William Thomson was ferried to the right bank, then, early on 8 March, a bridge was thrown across at Bawi for the cavalry to get over. The Cavalry Division, followed by the 7th Division in the evening, were to follow Thomson's brigade (though Thomson was not told of this) up to the Shawa Khan ruins, from which it could move direct on Baghdad. But Maude's hope of a rapid advance once again evaporated: there had been no previous reconnaissance of the cavalry's route, they were issued with inaccurate maps, and the whole area was – as was already well known – intersected by a multitude of canals too deep to be crossed without ramps. ('The poor devils of men are working like blazes ramping these infernal nullahs,' Lieutenant Woakes of the 35th Brigade Sappers wrote; 'we seemed to be lost in a maze of these canals.'[10]) On top of that, the cavalry HQ staff had been reorganised just before the river crossing. 'Progress was consequently difficult and slow', and in its night march on 8–9 March the Cavalry Division 'lost direction', finding itself on the road to Qarara rather than Baghdad. Unable to find any other road, it pushed on at less than one mile per hour over the deep canals. The attempt to get round the Ottoman right failed.

The 38th Brigade made another attempt to get across the Diyala that night. The East Lancashires pushed across in four 'columns'. 'Let those in rear who hastily criticise the tardiness of forcing the passage of the river imagine or visualise, if they can, in an atmosphere of comparative safety and comfort, what it means,' chided Roe. This time, with artillery support, a hundred or so troops were landed on the opposite bank. But the rate of loss amongst the pontoons was once again crushing. Column A's pontoon reached the other side but was sunk on the way back; column B made two trips before the rowers were all hit and the pontoon sunk, then lost two more pontoons later in the night. Column C made six trips before its pontoon was sunk, while D found the bank too steep to launch its pontoon. The little force on the other side gathered in a small bend in the embankment, where it fought off a succession of attacks by the Ottoman 2/44th Regiment, which lost hundreds of men in the process. The fighting was so intense that there was no way to get ammunition to the beleaguered men of the Loyals (though even rockets were tried to carry a cable across the river).

Yet again, on 9 March drinking water was 'unobtainable', and Roe had 'seen no rations for the past two days'. On 10 March, his battalion was back 'shuffling, gliding and stealing' to the bank where they were to lead the next attempted crossing. 'If we fail, the South Lancs are to have a try, and if they fail we try again until we are all killed, so says General Maude.' This time there was plenty of artillery support; the Wiltshires crossed the river higher up against very little opposition. The first pontoon of Roe's unit got across at 4 a.m., and Roe with the medical staff at 5. By 11 a.m. a bridge had been built. The Loyals were rescued just as they ran out of ammunition. The Turkish resistance collapsed, primarily because most of their force had been transferred to counter the British move up the right bank. Roe saw a company form up in line to charge a Turkish position: 'when they see the line advancing, about one hundred Turks and two officers advance towards us with their hands up. We have taken roughly 250 prisoners, probably more. I've never seen so many Turkish dead.' Coles, praising the bridge-building under fire as 'surely an epic unparalleled in the annals of the British army', was also struck by 'thousands of dead lying everywhere'.

The crossing of the Diyala by the 'indomitable' Lancashire men was, as Arnold Wilson lamented, one of the unsung epics of the war. By 11 a.m. the leading troops of O'Dowda's brigade were facing the trenches of the second defensive line at Tel Mohammed – the last prepared position before Baghdad. By 3 p.m., while the Ottoman commanders were discussing the possibility of a counter-attack against the British forces advancing on the left bank (Halil was for it – urged on by one of his German advisers – Kâzim against), they heard that the British were outflanking the Tel Mohammed position. After more heated discussion, Halil decided on retreat at 8 p.m. By midnight the Turkish defences had been abandoned, and by 5 a.m. the last military train had left the city. The battle for Baghdad was over

The entry into Baghdad was an oddly low-key event, after the long-running drama of the Tigris battles. The journalist Edmund Candler, a less showy ancestor of John Simpson in 2003, claimed to be one of the first in. (Though he admitted that the cavalry, arriving at the city centre more directly from the left bank, were actually the first – deriving special satisfaction from capturing the intended terminus of the Berlin to Baghdad railway.) He was riding with the CO of the King's Own ahead of the 38th Brigade, marching in column of fours in the ordinary way, 'ready to deploy against a new position and with guards thrown out'. They had no idea whether they would bump into the Turks who had just withdrawn from Tel Mohammed: 'after the way they had fought for every nameless ditch between Sheikh Saad and Shumran', it was hard to believe that they 'would leave the city of the Caliphs behind without a last ambush'. Candler was chatting about something to do with the war in Europe, when the colonel of the King's Own pointed to some figures emerging through the dust haze. 'By Jove! – I believe these fellows are bringing us the keys of the Citadel.'

Lieutenant Woakes of the Sappers and Miners went in from the other side – he moved forward with his battery 'to main road which was absolutely packed with 7th Div, & we all moved forward in a wild rush to BAGDAD'. His brigade was given preference, 'so that we got ahead of everyone else & after passing IRON BRIDGE and coming out into an open maidan in sight of the walls we struck the 35th Brigade staff who had just decided to march into the town'. So he joined the 'triumphal march' through streets 'narrow and dirty and packed with

Arabs' to the bridge that the defenders had destroyed, where General Thomson gathered some boats and crossed with a force of the Buffs.

Trudging along behind the King's Own, Ned Roe could see the smoke of fires in the city by 10 a.m., but was also surprised by the absence of gunfire. A flock of storks provided the noisiest greeting they got. They halted about 2,000 yards from the city, in line with the clock tower, as the clock struck eleven. Now there were sounds of 'a row', as British troops began to take action against the looters who had come out in force as soon as the last Turkish train left at 4 a.m. Roe found his mind wandering back to his schooldays, 'when instead of doing my home lessons such as parsing Greek and Latin roots, composition and geography, I was reading all about Ali Baba and the forty thieves, Aladdin and his lamp, and the voyage of Sinbad the Sailor'. He finished the 'Thousand and One Nights' in spite of repeated canings for incomplete homework. 'Little did I dream', he inevitably reflected, 'that I would be gazing on Baghdad today.'

Colonel Wauchope of the Black Watch found himself 'lost in wonder' as he lay in the shadow of a palm, looking down the river on the brick walls and mud roofs, the mosques and minarets of the city – wonder that he had not seen a tree of any kind for fifteen months, and that a little date-seller coming towards him with hesitating steps, 'her empty basket resting on her well-shaped head', was 'the first woman I have seen or spoken to for more than a year'. Perhaps it was twilight that gave 'a feeling of mystery and beauty', as the Tigris 'seems to lose itself in the evening mists, above which the golden minarets of Kazimain still shine and glitter in the setting sun'. Was he truly in the land of reality, or lingering 'in the realm of dreams and fancies, where stand the gates of horn and ivory'?[11]

In the bright light of day, the fabled city evoked mixed reactions. The best thing about it was the sudden availability of real food: Coles, also with the 38th Brigade, 'found a grove of luscious ripe oranges' just south of the city, and once there found that fruit was plentiful and cheap. He listed with relish the 'tomatoes, dates, oranges, apricots, grapefruit, cherry plums and peaches' they could buy. On the other hand, the city was 'in the last stages of decay', as Roe put it. 'The narrow, filthy, evil-smelling streets are blocked in places by tumble-down houses and heaps of garbage. In some streets the balconies of the houses almost meet, thus shutting out the sun.' General Money curtly dismissed it as 'not much of a place to look at . . . a filthy dirty place'. Its 150,000 inhabitants were a mix of Christians, Jews and Muslims. The first priority was to halt the inevitable outburst of looting. On 13 April Woakes was ordered to find a suitable site, and construct a gallows to hang fifteen looters; one of the oddest surviving documents of the Mesopotamia war must be his meticulous scale drawing of the place of execution he built next day. A house-to-house search produced 'hundreds of rifles and other weapons', a rather modest haul. An urgent sanitation programme began, along with the cleaning of the 'indescribably dirty and verminous' larger buildings for the establishment of administrative and hospital facilities.

Baghdad, still more than Basra, heightened the sense of culture clash amongst the occupiers. Coles, who was in the city on the 11th (though the 38th Brigade was marched around to camp two miles north of the city that night) had 'an afternoon of adventure'. Inhabitants were throwing grenades from harem windows, and at one point his group burst into a 'café-chantant' with revolvers drawn. They witnessed a classic 'oriental' scene. 'About 100 Arabs were lounging on wooden settees yawning and drinking tots of mint tea whilst an Armenian girl was dancing the Salome on a platform to the music of a piano and two weird stringed instruments.' The girl 'ended the dance in a frenzy –as naked as she was born . . . the East with the lid off!' he mused.

8. Maude's Moment

> The tribes have had a taste of independence and the longer they are left to enjoy it, the more difficult it will be to control them later. At the same time they quite realise that they are incapable of developing the country even to the extent that they themselves would like to see. As the Arab proverb puts it, their brain is in their eyes.
>
> HUBERT YOUNG

> I sometimes wonder whether it is they or we whose views are worthy of the denizens of a lunatic asylum. But I feel persuaded it is they.
>
> GERTRUDE BELL

Standing with their feet at Baghdad, the British could survey the Middle East – and the world – from a new eminence. Heady possibilities seemed more real. The vision conjured up in parliament in 1916, of a future Mesopotamia with its 'irrigation works and canals all in working order under the British government . . . the banks along its rivers populated and cultivated by flourishing Indian colonies transported from the banks of the Indus',[1] entranced many in India. Others like Hirtzel could envisage 'a new dependency which will include the whole of Arabia, Egypt and the Soudan – a unilingual and unicultural area, from Sollum to the Turco-Persian frontier'.[2] The captor of the legendary city, however, was peculiarly unattuned to such political dreams. Maude, in fact, was almost a caricature of the 'unpolitical' soldier, yet it fell to him to announce a new era in the history of the Arab people.

Maude's political illiteracy was already obvious by 1917. Arnold Wilson grumbled, for instance, that he had completely failed to grasp – along with 'other questions of policy' – the significance of the visit paid to Basra in late 1916 by Ibn Saud. This was a moment of immense potential. Abdul Aziz ibn Abdur Rahman ibn Faisal al Saud was already by far the most substantial of the Arabian rulers with whom Britain had cemented 'treaty relations' in 1914 and 1915. He was emerging victorious from his long drawn-out struggle for control of southern Arabia against Ibn Rashid. He was in the process of founding the state that would become Saudi Arabia – and would eventually destroy Hussein's kingdom in the Hejaz. The land they fought for, the Najd, was territory that had never been brought under effective Ottoman rule, and even the British had hesitated to meddle there. (It was 'in the last degree undesirable that we should be drawn into Central Arabian politics', Hogarth wrote in the *Arab Bulletin* in March 1916.) British estimates of Ibn Saud's capacity varied: while Shakespear had been an ardent supporter, Hogarth judged him 'less powerful' than Rashid, and 'far less able to influence the present situation in our favour'. Gertrude Bell, on the other hand, dismissed Ibn Rashid as 'ignorant and foolish beyond belief'. Shakespear, who was killed riding with Ibn Saud at the battle of Jurrab in 1915, turned out to be right about him. Though he did not have the kind of formal religious status possessed by Sharif Hussein of Mecca and Medina, as leader of the Wahhabi movement he was a formidable force in the Islamic world, and in terms of energy and capacity he was unique.

His visit to Basra was the climax of treaty negotiations conducted by Cox over several months. He created a tremendous impression. Wilson described him with frank admiration – 'tall, dignified, and observant, he looked as big a man as he was . . . A lion in battle, a lamb in society, and an angel in council.' Meeting Cox in Kuwait, he 'played his part to perfection, receiving salutes, inspecting naval sloops, guards of honour and docks, with the intelligent nonchalance of a practised monarch'. He watched an artillery display and was shown the latest technical marvels – not just an aircraft, but even an X-ray machine at one of the base hospitals. He was 'shown the bones of his own hand under the Rontgen ray'. He 'looked at all these things with wonder', Gertrude Bell recorded; 'but the interest he displayed in the mechanism of warfare was that of a man who seeks to learn, not of one who stands confused.' She was as smitten as Wilson – not least by his 'splendid physique'. Although 'more massively built than the typical nomad sheikh', she recognised 'the characteristics of the well-bred Arab, the strongly marked aquiline profile, full-fleshed nostrils, prominent lips and long narrow chin, accentuated by a pointed beard'. He shared the 'trait almost universal among the tribes of pure Arab blood', fine hands with slender fingers, and 'in spite of his great height and breadth of shoulder he conveys the impression of an indefinable lassitude, not individual but racial, the secular weariness of an ancient and self-contained people'.[3]

All this was quite lost on Maude, who characterised him vaguely as 'a Potentate who lives some two hundred miles west from here'. Cox, Maude reported, 'has been presenting him with things like KCSI's and things like that', and was now bringing him to Basra where 'he is to have salutes fired for him (which those sort of people love), an aeroplane display, an artillery display, etc.'. Maude found himself too busy to meet him; and when Cox asked whether he could present the Emir with a jewelled sword as a gift from Maude, the general's breezy reply was, 'Certainly, as long as I don't have to pay for it!' He reflected that a jewelled sword was 'such a funny thing to be able to produce at a few minutes' notice on active service. But I suppose', he added, 'that political officers are rather like the professional ladies who make long journeys on liners, and who produce the most elaborate fancy dresses for dances on board.'[4] For Wilson, the Ibn Saud issue demonstrated something bigger than Maude's lack of political awareness: the damaging effect of Britain's mistaken decision to back the Sharifians rather than the Wahhabi leader. (If only 'our activities in Arabia had been directed from Basra instead of from Egypt', Ibn Saud's visit 'might have been the occasion for a fresh orientation of policy'.) He pointedly remarked that Ibn Saud was 'no upstart monarch, depending on British arms for security and British gold for his position' – an obvious dig at Sharif Hussein, who had proclaimed himself King of the Hejaz.[5]

Maude's political innocence led him to enter Baghdad on 11 March without ceremony (his biographer judged this a mistake – 'the Oriental believes in display'). As he steamed up the river he had been 'busy drafting proclamations, orders etc to come into effect when we get into Baghdad' – all the ordinary regulations familiar to military governors. But the proclamation that really mattered would announce Britain's 'Arab policy', and for the next week there was a flurry of political activity in London and Basra as it was drafted for him. Cox had already been told to prepare a statement, but the India Office did not think much of it. Cox merely called on 'those who have the cause of Islam and of Arab progress at heart' to help the British forces expel the Turks and 'bring the war to a speedy conclusion and to ensure their own emancipation'. His appeal was predictably minimalist, reflecting his sceptical assessment of Arab potential: people could best help by 'going about their daily avocations and assisting the British authorities to carry on normal administration'. Hirtzel took a dim view of this; it amounted to telling the Arabs 'mind your own affairs and leave us do the governing'. Something more was required at this historic moment. Britain was 'irretrievably committed to the policy of an Arab state, until, at all events, the Arab State has been tried and proved a failure'.[6]

But Hirtzel also admitted, with rare frankness, that 'before the war, Great Britain had a rather unenviable reputation for giving pledges and then receding from them owing to force of circumstances'. It was important now, he argued, 'to avoid uttering words which we may hereafter have to eat if the Arab state proves a failure'. So any British declaration must be cautious, and so must British actions. For the time being, he instructed Cox on 12 March, 'the existing administrative machinery is as far as possible to be preserved with the substitution of Arab for Turkish spirit and personnel. The façade must be Arab.' For security reasons Baghdad *vilayet* should remain under martial law, but the inhabitants should be formally invited to assume control of the civil administration with British cooperation. 'Every effort should be made to induce representative men to come forward for this purpose.'

Unsurprisingly, the man who seized the task of drafting London's policy declaration at this historic juncture was Sykes, and the proclamation he drafted was a world away from Cox's. It pulsated with romantic nationalist rhetoric – 'ebullient orientalism' as the nettled Arnold Wilson called it. Sykes laid out for the Iraqis a sweeping panorama of their history from the Mongol conquests, since when 'your palaces have fallen into ruins, your gardens have sunken in desolation, and your forefathers and yourselves have groaned in bondage'. (Wilson irritably spluttered that the proclamation's historical references were 'a travesty of the facts'.) Maude was to declare that 'it is the wish, not only of my King and his peoples, but also of the great Nations with whom he is in alliance, that you should prosper even as in the past, when your lands were fertile . . . and Baghdad was one of the wonders of the world'.

'You, the people of Baghdad, whose commercial professions and whose safety from oppression and invasion must ever be a matter of the closest concern to the British Government, are not to understand that it is the wish of the British Government to impose upon you alien institutions. It is the hope of the British Government that the aspirations of your philosophers and writers shall be realized once again. The people of Baghdad shall flourish . . . under institutions which are in consonance with their sacred laws and their racial ideals.

'Many noble Arabs have perished in the cause of Arab freedom, at the hands of those alien rulers, the Turks, who oppressed them. It is the determination of the Government of Great Britain and the great Powers allied to Great Britain, that these noble Arabs shall not have suffered in vain. It is the desire and hope of the British people and the nations in alliance with them that the

Arab race may rise once more to greatness and renown amongst the peoples of the earth and that it shall bind itself to this end in unity and concord.'

To this exalted end, Maude was 'to invite you to assume the management of your civil affairs in collaboration with the political representatives of Great Britain who accompany the British Army'. (This to be done 'through your nobles and elders and representatives'.) So 'you may unite with your kinsmen in the North, East, South and West in realizing the aspirations of your race'.

Wilson drily suggested that 'few more remarkable documents' than this proclamation 'can have received the endorsement of the British Cabinet'.[7] What the Speaker of the Commons called its 'oriental and flowery language' preserved some of the careful doublespeak of earlier declarations, but some of its points looked much more definite, and seemed to go beyond any declared British policy. There was a 'noble Arab race' whose ideals and aspirations would now at last become realities. Some form of united Arab political entity – 'North, East, South and West' – would emerge. Maude's proclamation committed Britain and its allies to that – was this really the government's intention? It is hard to be sure, even though the draft was chewed over by a formidable Cabinet committee including Lords Curzon, Milner and Hardinge as well as Austen Chamberlain. Only one of Sykes's original sentences, promising that 'the Arabs of Irak and Baghdad shall in future be a free people, enjoying their own wealth and substance under their own institutions and laws', was rejected by the India Office as too 'direct and unconditional' a promise of independence. Sykes in turn charged that Hirtzel's preferred phrase 'institutions and laws congenial to them' implied an 'Indian' kind of control: 'If we take the line of trying to rule the Arabs as we rule the Indians we shall fail . . . We shall introduce the social colour distinction and antagonize the whole Arab movement.' But his own image of the Arab–British relationship remained dangerously vague: he suggested that 'if we play our cards properly by means of "advisers" instead of "rulers" and back Arab nationalism, we shall have a permanent footing at little cost'.

It was quite clear that British policy was still hung up on conflicting ideas about the future status of Iraq. Now, at last, a step was taken to resolve the conflict. On the day that Maude's proclamation was issued in Baghdad, the Cabinet's new Mesopotamia Administration Committee held its first meeting. This was ministers' first real effort to define British interests in Mesopotamia. It had to sort out the baggage of earlier policy discussions – on whether the Foreign Office should take over responsibility (as Sykes, the MAC's secretary, urged) or whether Mesopotamia was 'the prize for which the Indian Army is fighting'. Chamberlain declared with unusual emotionalism that 'Indian blood had won' Mesopotamia for Britain. But Curzon, the MAC's chairman, was unenthusiastic. Indian immigration seemed to entail Indian political direction, and this might be all too effective for Britain's good. There was 'a serious risk that administration will be begun on Indian lines', and it might well reach such a 'pitch of efficiency that, either this efficiency will be made an argument for maintaining it after the war, or when the attempt is made to replace it with an Arab administration, chaos may supervene and our direct intervention be required'. This would be very unfortunate.[8]

The MAC managed to come up with some policy directives at the end of March 1917. The British, not the Indian, government would be responsible for Mesopotamia; though the responsible department would not be the Foreign Office but the India Office. A special administrative service would be formed for the area (including Kuwait). Basra would come under direct British administration, but Baghdad must have a local ruler under British influence. It must be 'administered as an Arab Province by indigenous agency and in accordance with existing laws and institutions as far as possible'. The employment of Indians and non-Arabic or Persian Asiatics in Basra *vilayet* was to be 'discouraged', and in Baghdad to be 'strictly discountenanced'. The Iraq legal code, which had been established (on the Indian model) in Basra, was not to be extended to Baghdad: there the local judicial system was to be maintained 'as regards both law and personnel, only substituting Arab for Turk'. All administrative arrangements 'should from the very outset strictly conform to the above principles'.[9]

These instructions, generally 'Egyptian' in line even though they fell short of Sykes's wishes, did not go down well either in India or Mesopotamia. India protested that 'any attempt to bar Indians from Mesopotamia either as immigrants or administrators' would excite 'bitter and legitimate resentment'. At Baghdad, Cox held that it would be impracticable to give Basra and Baghdad different administrative systems. The ban on Indian administrative staff would be crippling, and the idea of preserving the existing administrative machinery and merely 'substituting Arab for Turkish spirit and personnel' was dangerously illusory. There was an air of exasperation to his protest that instituting local self-government 'during the existence of martial law and while the military position at Baghdad is as it is (namely, that we are in almost daily conflict with the Arab tribes ahead of us, and we must expect severe fighting around Baghdad when the enemy has had time to recover and concentrate fresh troops against us)' was asking too much. He urged delay: a 'premature conclusion arrived at now may do irreparable damage'.[10]

This local resistance to London's policy was ominous. The ever-inventive Sykes looked for a way round it, and persuaded the War Office to instruct Maude that it was 'unsound to mark time as regards the Arab movement'. It was an opportune moment 'to exploit our Arab policy and to foster a general movement to embarrass the Turks'. Maude was to consult with Cox about 'enlisting the sympathy' of friendly Arab tribes and 'extending in a general way the scope of the whole movement'. (Sykes's sublime confidence allowed him to suggest exactly which tribes they should target – 'on the strength of a flying visit in 1915', as Wilson tartly pointed out.) But once again the local reaction was disappointing. Maude, who like most soldiers rated the fighting value of the Arabs as negligible (if not actually negative), could see no sign of any 'movement', or any utility in Arab participation. Asking whether the CIGS meant that he wanted Arabs 'employed for fighting purposes', he explained that 'hitherto I have endeavoured to keep the Arab population quiet, treating them well so long as they take no part in the operations, but repressing instantly and vigorously by force any attempt at hostility'. He added that 'when there is no fighting in their vicinity, tribesmen soon settle down, as witness peace and quiet now on our communications, but they become restless and disturbed as they are drawn into the vortex of war'.[11]

Three weeks later, he explained his position more carefully. He was in favour of employing Arabs for 'small raids against definite objectives on enemy communications when moment is opportune', but otherwise 'our policy should be to keep tribesmen quiet' and 'pay them reasonable prices for what they bring to us'. He also accepted the idea of 'developing among them some system of government' (as long, of course, as this did not interfere with military operations). But 'I am not in favour of encouraging guerrilla warfare or acts of hostility promiscuously against the Turks ... anything such as uncontrolled guerrilla warfare or raising of levies only awakens the latent fighting instinct of Arabs and unsettles the country.' The effects of irregular war 'though tiresome are negligible' for regular troops with unimpaired morale. The best that could be asked of the Arabs would be to stay quiet. (Maude reiterated that the 'primary aim should be to pacify the country and its inhabitants through dealing decisively and instantly with them if they interfere with us'.[12]) Cox, though he saw some military capacity in one or two tribes, seems to have agreed with him on the whole – if, indeed, the general ever actually consulted him on the issue.[13]

But Maude's response underlined again his refusal to look beyond the military side of things. The military view was that 'though it is our policy to represent the Arab as our ardent ally, in reality we have few genuine adherents in Mesopotamia'. Kuwait and Mohammerah, which had been 'carefully nursed' by Cox, were very different from the 'frankly hostile' tribes on the Shatt-al-Hai, the 'openly hostile' Dulaim, or even the 'sulkily obedient' Bani Lam. The military line was pithily summed up in the curt assertion that 'keeping Arabs from not being openly hostile is far more important than planning out little niceties of civil administration'.[14] As the weeks went by, such dismissive arguments began to strain even Cox's legendary patience. Though he and Maude had agreed on their response to the March policy line, he now fell out spectacularly with the stubborn general.

At one point during a visit by Ronald Storrs to Baghdad in early May, Cox 'suddenly told me that his position as High Commissioner elect, with all officials to be imposed on him by HMG, and with an omnipotent and unworkable General, would be impossible'. He would rather resign immediately.[15] A few weeks later Cox complained directly to the India Secretary. At the time Maude had taken command, he alleged, the political machinery was 'firmly established and working smoothly', helped by the fact that 'no political issues of any importance were arising'. But since the March 1917 instructions the situation had become 'unsatisfactory'. Maude's military credentials were beyond question, but he was 'purely a soldier'. Worse still, he was 'without any previous experience of the East or Orientals'. This was, for Cox, the knock-down argument. 'I find him unsympathetic and rather intolerant in regard to political questions, and unable to appreciate the important bearing of apparently simple problems of daily occurrence on larger political and even military interests.' This kind of language was rare in official communications. Cox threatened to resign unless he was 'placed in a stronger position vis-à-vis the Army Commander', or at any rate permitted to report direct 'to higher authority to keep them au fait with current questions' and larger issues.[16]

The higher authorities looked for ways out of this awkward clash. It was suggested that Cox pay a visit to the Viceroy in India: the extended trip would give him some 'much needed rest' and, it was hoped, remind Maude how much he needed his political officer. But it was becoming clear that this was not just a clash of personalities. There was friction across the whole administration: Brigadier-General C. J. Hawker, the officer Maude appointed as military governor of Baghdad, for instance, though he had experience with the Ottoman gendarmerie, knew no Arabic, and did not defer to Cox on policy. His view of his charges was predictable: 'after centuries of misrule they naturally require considerable education before they can assimilate modern ideas concerning sanitation, cruelty to animals, the necessity of giving truthful evidence, and other such matters.'[17]

The army's ever-expanding administrative structure pinched political toes. A major component was the 'Local Produce Department', set up before the advance on Baghdad to coordinate the work of the Local Produce Officers already attached to all the major military units. The aim was simple: to reduce the army's dependence on its 500-mile supply line by making maximum use of local resources. But the method was not so simple. When Hubert Young was assigned by Cox to 'assist' the newly appointed head of the LPD, Colonel Dickson, he found that the colonel had already made out a rough organisational scheme which 'included practically all the economic and commercial activities of a civil administration'. Young 'told him that Sir Percy Cox would certainly blue-pencil the whole thing if it were put up to him in that form', and that in any case it was 'unusual for a department under the control of the Director of Supply and Transport to concern itself with such matters as imports and exports, revenue, and other forms of taxation'. Dickson was clearly unconvinced.[18] The organisation – soon renamed the Department of Local Resources – expanded until it nearly equalled the size of the Political Department by the end of the war. Its task of gathering local supplies required it to deal direct with the civil population, but its actions were outside Cox's control.

When he threatened to resign, Cox conceded that he would 'no longer oppose' being made High Commissioner 'nominally' – provided that this 'did not connote any more extensive introduction of the Arab Administration than was recently agreed upon'. Cox was fighting a battle on two fronts, trying to steer between the army's contempt for the Arabs and the Cabinet's naive faith in them. (He was careful to add that the post should not bring a pay increase which would make his salary bigger than Maude's.) While the Mesopotamia Committee was considering this, Gertrude Bell privately briefed Hirtzel on just how serious the civil–military clash had become. Maude, she said, thought the whole system was wrong – 'there should be no political officers; all that is needed is Intelligence Officers directly under himself'. Almost incredibly, he based this argument on the fact that there were no political officers with the BEF in France! Maude was 'incapable of grasping' the difference between the two situations, and he was not alone amongst his fellow generals. Bell found herself despairingly wondering 'whether it is they or we whose views are worthy of the denizens of a lunatic asylum'.

She accused Maude of deliberately refusing to tell Cox of actions he was taking which had political implications. She held that his refusal to allow Cox to send a political officer to Khanikin, where Russian actions were driving the Kurds into the arms of the Turks, was truly dangerous. The military policy towards prisoners of war and deserters was 'no less disastrous'. That week (15 June) 'the height of criminal absurdity' had been reached when they exiled to Basra, in spite of Cox's protests, an Armenian doctor who had been left behind by the Turks at his own request. 'All Christians have been treated in the same way', and interned in India. Her conclusion was grim: 'that we shall ever be able to pursue a reasonable policy under Maude I don't believe.' But she was resigned to the fact that 'the WO can't be expected to remove the one successful General of the War'.[19]

Maude's blindness to the politics of his campaign was, in one sense, not unreasonable. 'It is one thing', as he complained to the C-in-C India, 'for a commander to know instinctively as he should do when a project will prejudice his military plans; it is another matter for him amid stress of war to have to justify his opinion . . . We are engaged in a vast war, and it seems to me that if we attempt to combine the general development of the country with the defeat of the enemy, we shall be attempting too much, and we shall fail.'[20] Where viable military projects could be found, Arabs were being urged to take part – he had asked the Amir of the Yezidis of Jebel Sinjar to 'harass the Turkish lines of communication between Nisibin and Mosul by attacking their railway working parties, cutting wires, capturing convoys, and every other means in his power' (and promised to reward him handsomely for such action). He would certainly try to 'get Arabs to operate against definite objectives' if the threatened enemy movement down the Euphrates should materialise. He protested that he was quite 'alive to the value of such strokes'. But there should be no false hopes about their likely results: in his experience, 'Arabs promise much and do little.' He pointed to the fact that during the fighting around Kut, 'the Arabs on the Hai – though mostly friendly to the Turks and constantly incited to action against us, caused us no inconvenience'. The bottom line for him was that the Mesopotamian Arabs were ineffective fighters – the Arabs of the Sudan were 'immeasurably superior'.[21]

Baffled by the dispute, the government decided in July to give Cox the compromise title 'Civil Commissioner'. (This would be Austen Chamberlain's last contribution to the Mesopotamia campaign before he was succeeded by Edwin Montagu. The official history, interestingly, misrendered the title as 'Chief Commissioner'.) The change was justified by the need for 'regular and frequent information' about political and economic conditions in Mesopotamia, and 'the establishment of civil institutions'. Exactly what this signified remained – no doubt intentionally – unclear. The GOC's ultimate responsibility must remain 'unimpaired'. The Civil Commissioner was to submit reports to the Secretary of State for India through the GOC; the GOC could add observations, but the Civil Commissioner's opinion was to be 'given freely and to the best of his judgment'. And Cox was offered the prospect of growing power: as 'normal conditions' were 'by degrees' re-established, and the civil staff strengthened, it would be 'desirable that a larger measure of independence should be conceded in civil affairs to the Civil Commissioner'.[22]

After all this, an ominous stand-off between political and military perspectives remained. The War Office still held that Cox was 'inclined to press a premature programme of political administration'; he did not understand that his primary duty was simply to safeguard Maude's communications by using his influence to keep the Arabs quiet and facilitate the collection of supplies.[23] Bell continued to fret at military obtuseness, for instance over the requisitioning of labour, telling Hirtzel, 'if you are faced with the prospect of a whole countryside starving & in revolt, some additional facility of transport will be bought at too dear a price'. When Hirtzel showed Gertrude Bell's letter to Lord Curzon, he responded with typical verbal pugnacity – 'it confirms my worst suspicions,' he said. 'If there is any more nonsense I will bring the whole matter before the War Cabinet and get General Maude brought to his bearings.'[24]

But the whole problem was, of course, that the government's own bearings were uncertain, and would stay that way for a long time. The day after Curzon's blustering threat, the Viceroy received the final ruling on the political question. The Mesopotamia administration should aim at only the 'minimum of administrative efficiency necessary to preserve order and meet the needs of the occupying force'. Any amendments of laws or introduction of reforms were 'to be kept within the narrowest possible limits', and 'no large or controversial questions were to be raised'. The discussions of the Mesopotamia Committee showed that Britain still had no definite political strategy. The attempt to run different structures for Basra and Baghdad, as Hubert Young noted, 'was bound to fail', at least while war was in progress. Inevitably, the Basra arrangements were extended to Baghdad, and little was heard of the representative system heralded in Maude's proclamation. Touring the country under British control in April 1917, Young saw a marked difference between urban and rural areas. The townsmen – except in Karbala and Najaf – were 'eagerly looking forward to the restoration of order'. The tribes, on the other hand, had had 'a taste of independence', and liked it. 'The longer they are left to enjoy it, the more difficult it will be to control them later,' he warned. But he was still sure that even they 'quite realise that they are incapable of developing the country, even to the extent that they themselves would like to see'. Young had no doubt that British administration would be accepted, indeed welcomed. 'As the Arab proverb puts it, their brain is in their eyes. Let them but see that a good Government will really benefit them and they will accept the discipline and the tribute without which no good Government can exist.'[25]

Young's view, that there was no alternative to British control – 'it never entered my head that Iraq was ready for independence' – was shared by all the politicals, above all of course by Arnold Wilson. For him, the instructions to preserve the existing administration and simply 'substitute Arab for Turkish spirit and personnel' were based on 'radically false premises'. (They emanated, of course, from the 'versatile' Sykes.) Neither Cox nor he could accept that they should merely aim at 'the minimum administrative efficiency necessary to preserve order'.[26] Over the next three years, under cover of the policy paralysis in London, Wilson would push on with bringing Mesopotamia up to Indian governmental standards. The result would be a personal and national disaster.

IV: MOSUL

1. Northern Exposure

It was fortunate for us that Ali Ihsan prided himself on his conduct of retirements.

SIR WILLIAM MARSHALL

Baghdad was captured because General Maude wanted action and refused to let his army vegetate in its trenches and camps. Like Nixon before him, he itched to get at the enemy; unlike Nixon, he was able to bring to bear Britain's massive military superiority over its ailing opponent. Even to the flintiest soldiers, trophies like Baghdad are irresistible proofs of success. Maude had no interest in the political implications of his offensive, but they were huge. It massively expanded the area under British control, demanding a new level of administration, and committing Britain irrevocably to the long-term future of Iraq. In military terms, ironically, his victory made little sense. The nearest the CIGS could get to a military justification for Maude's advance was the faintly convoluted argument that failure to advance might 'indirectly' be a military disadvantage – 'because of its objectionable political effect'.

The whole expedition had, of course, always been primarily political; its central objective had always been to impress the Arabs rather than to protect existing British interests like the oilfields. Arab support, or at least quiescence, was the best guarantee against any strategic threat to India. But now Baghdad was in British hands, however impressed the Arabs might be, this aggravated Britain's military difficulty. As the War Office had always said (and so had Halil Pasha), it was militarily indefensible. If the Turks cut the banks of the Tigris and Euphrates as the flood season came on, the city could be turned into 'an island surrounded by a vast lake'. It could only be made secure by advancing at least another fifty miles up the rivers that converged on it.

There were other, more positive reasons for advancing further. If the Russian army under General Baratov in Persia could keep going forward, it might be possible to trap the remnant of Halil's Sixth Army between the allied forces and eliminate it. The battered XVIII corps, hardly 5,000 strong, was falling back from Baghdad to join up with the XIII corps, which was in much better shape. With nearly 10,000 men under a resourceful commander, Ali Ihsan Bey – who would be christened 'Old Sandbag' by the British soldiers – XIII Corps had pushed the Russians back before making an orderly withdrawal towards the Diyala. On the day Baghdad fell, Ali Ihsan was nearly 200 miles away. Maude, with 45,000 troops, had a clear numerical advantage, but needed to act before the two Ottoman corps could unite. So he immediately pushed three columns upriver, towards Falluja on the Euphrates, Sumaika on the Baghdad railway near the Tigris, and Diltawa on the Khalis canal.

Any euphoria over the capture of Baghdad soon dissipated for the troops who now had to slog on again into some of the hardest fighting of the whole campaign. However overwhelming Britain's superiority over Turkey, the men on the ground still found themselves suffering from most of the same problems that had afflicted the expeditionary force since it first landed. Basra port might have been transformed into a modern facility, and the river and railway transport dramatically improved, but ration shortages went on, and the climate never changed. At least the almost unknown terrain north of Baghdad was a welcome change from the mud plains of the south. 'The river ran beneath lofty bluffs,' one infantry officer noted; 'on the left bank was a far-stretching view of low, rich country'. At Sumaika, 'the village had palms and rose bushes. We camped amid green corn; round us were storksbills, very many, and a white orchis ... A small poppy and a bright thistle set their flares of crimson and gold in the green; sowthistle and myosote freaked it with blue; a tall gladiolus made pink clusters . . . We were tasting the joy and life of springtide in happier latitudes.'

But this landscape inevitably had its other side: '"chivvy-dusters", a grass which crams the clothes and feet with maddening needles'. Sandflies and mosquitoes were outdone by large black ants that 'swarmed over us' at mealtimes: 'man after man dropped his plate and leapt into a dervish-dance, frenziedly slapping his nose and ears.'[1] The changed landscape itself was, in military terms, a mixed blessing. A 'multitude of watercourses' meant an end to the old dependence on one river, but if they increased flexibility they also hampered movement. The little hills which provided cover favoured the defender at least as much as the attacker.

Two of the columns pushed out to secure the Baghdad region were quite successful. Cobbe's column, advancing up the Tigris, fought a sharp battle to seize the Baghdad railway station at Mushahida. It involved some familiar tribulations. 'Night marches, the textbook says, may be made for several reasons,' as the commander of the 2nd Black Watch, Colonel Arthur Wauchope, wrote. 'But it does not suggest that one of these ever could be for pleasure.' This one was as difficult as any, and since British maps were so inaccurate, the suffering was wasted – at dawn the column was nowhere near the Turkish positions. When Wauchope's unit finally attacked, nearly twelve hours late, it found itself unsupported. But it pushed on at bayonet point into the town. Next day the defenders were in full retreat. This little unsung victory, as Edmund Candler reflected, 'in any other phase of the campaign would have thrilled England'.[2] Expectations had changed.

The Euphrates column did not have to fight any battles, and it carried British power deep into the Shia heartland of Falluja, Najaf and Karbala. The virtual autonomy of the Shia cities had been maintained by repeated uprisings against Ottoman rule, and the prospect of rule by a Christian power was awkward. After the British took Baghdad, Arnold Wilson disapprovingly noted the attempt of the Shia leaders in the holy cities to 'establish their position as the heads of a theocratic imperium in imperio by exchanging telegrams of congratulation with King George'. (The terms of the King's reply are worth noting: 'My earnest desire is for the well-being of Iraq and its peoples, the preservation of its Holy Places, and the restoration of its ancient prosperity.'³) They also visited Baghdad to pay their respects, and Cox treated their visit as a token of formal submission, giving them subsidies and 'a mandate to maintain order until it was possible for us to deal directly with the affairs of the two cities'. But their own view of the relationship would turn out to be rather different.

If the troops hoped that after Baghdad they were facing only the remnants of a beaten army, these hopes evaporated when the third column, under General Keary, advanced up the Diyala in the hope of trapping Ali Ihsan's corps between them and the Russians. One of Ali Ihsan's divisions had dug in on the Jebel Hamrin, a 'tangled mass of reddish sandstone, rising some 800 feet from the plain', that formed the foothills of the mountains on the Persian frontier. The omens for an assault were not good. The Turks were in a strong natural position, in three tiers of traversed fire trenches on the ridge behind the Ruz canal – 'a high-banked stream 30 feet wide, which formed a natural moat to the glacis', as Candler described it. The rocky ridge dominating the ground over which Keary advanced was a welcome aesthetic change from the plain, but in military terms it was a new difficulty. 'It was the North-West Frontier again', terrain naturally adapted to defence, calling for the hill-fighting methods familiar to the old Indian Army, but not the present one. 'It is doubtful if there was a single sepoy on Jebel Hamrin who had seen a frontier campaign.' The broken country called for special fieldcraft. 'You could not tell until the bullets came cracking over you whether you were on dead ground or exposed to fire from some projecting salient in the opposite ridge.'⁴

Moreover, Keary was advancing almost blind. The weakness of British intelligence meant that it was not until he was actually going forward into the attack that the commander of the assaulting brigade would realise just how big the Ruz canal was. Worst of all, the attackers were actually weaker than the defenders – incredibly enough, given the overall disparity of strength. Maude had somehow managed to convince himself that Keary's force was twice as strong as it was. So in his eagerness to push the Turks into the path of the advancing Russians, he peppered his column commander with increasingly urgent instructions to 'get in touch with the enemy and act vigorously so as to pin him to his ground'. After being told that 'it looks very much as if the enemy has been slipping away all night across the Diyala', and should be attacked 'vigorously', Keary ordered the assault for 24 April.[5]

As the 'vicious little shrapnel burst low over the bank' of the canal, Edmund Candler 'felt the senselessness of war' more than he had for a whole year. 'In these iris fields, I had almost forgotten we were fighting. The great objective had been grasped and left behind. None of us could have felt very warlike. A blue sky, willows, a running stream, an English spring, banks bright with charlock; buttercups, clover, veronica, pimpernel; scarlet anemones glowing through the grass; beyond the stream a plain rolling up to a scalloped ridge of rock . . . ' This was the landscape of peace. In 'the accursed dead plain' war 'had become a normal kind of hell'; but carried up into this green spot it 'seemed less a phase, more an eternal fact, than ever'.[6] The failure of reconnaissance caused delays in the canal crossing that doomed the whole operation. Keary's casualties were staggering – more than a third of the troops engaged (1,165, including 316 'missing', i.e. captured). The column was withdrawn to Baghdad.

Two days after this setback, Maude ordered Marshall to advance up the Tigris again. For the 'Old Contemptible' Ned Roe in the 13th Division, the move was almost a welcome change from Baghdad, where he had just been tricked into buying two fake bottles of Black and White whisky from an Armenian trader to celebrate St Patrick's Day.[7] (An Irishman who had been persuaded to enlist in the East Lancs thinking that it was a 'lancer' regiment, this was the story of his life.) But the march was just as hard as those before Baghdad. 'Very bad road; the heat is trying and men are falling out by the dozen,' Roe noted on the 28th. 'The worst offenders are the men who rejoined us at Baghdad after having a good spell in hospital.' They were 'hankering after a nice comfortable bed, custards and rice puddings, and a nice and sympathetic sister to take their temperature thrice daily'. Once men get a taste of such luxuries, the Mons veteran disapprovingly added, 'it is the very devil to get them to face an angry Turk'.[8]

Next day the division hit a Turkish defensive position at Duqma, on the 'marl plain' – flat, bare and very hard. ('Its surface was as smooth as a liquid which has congealed on a still night; there were stretches where you could not find an inequality that would have given bias to a marble.'[9]) Yet again the 'great dash' of the three battalions of the 39th Brigade drove the defenders into retreat, and yet again they were allowed to escape, even though divisional orders had explicitly aimed to destroy the enemy force. On the brink of cutting off the Turks' retreat, the leading brigade came to a halt, for reasons the staff could never work out.[10] Roe's own brigade was, strangely, placed in 'outposts' *behind* the 40th, and never ordered forward. Next day he saw the dead 'lying about' – it was virtually impossible to bury them in the rock-hard ground. 'They are left for the vultures and jackals.' (Though, as he remarked with an unusual bitterness a few weeks later, even when they could be buried 'no cross or mound marks the graves of the British dead on the battlefields, as a cross or mound would indicate to the Arabs that someone was buried there'. The Arabs would 'disinter a dead man for the sake of the socks he was buried with'.[11])

By this time any hope of coordinated action with the Russians was evaporating. Ned Roe got news on 8 April that the two armies had established contact at Qizil Robat. This was indeed a dramatic, seemingly historic moment. The 8th Brigade advanced to join hands with the Russians on 2 April; Candler watched as a *sotnia* of Cossacks came in 'at a walk, riding with short stirrups, toes down, heels up, leaning forward'. Wearing jack-boots and sheepskin caps, they were armed with 'curved Caucasian scimitars without handguards', as well as rifles. But 'their small horses, mostly under fourteen hands, looked thin and spent . . . there was no grain, no transport. The troopers had been reduced to two chapatties a day.' These short rations were sadly symptomatic of the Russian army that was pursuing the Ottoman army through 'country that could barely support a brigade', and which the retreating Turks were systematically laying waste as they retired. The junction between British and Russians was only a passing moment; 'the nutcrackers had closed on emptiness'. Ali Ihsan's retirement from Hamadan was notably well ordered, while the Russians did not seriously harass the retreat. The Turks had time to evacuate their wounded from Khermanshah, as well as to burn the British and Russian consulates, before abandoning the town. Once again, as Candler saw, the XIII Corps 'had extricated themselves and had not even been badly mauled'.[12]

Still trying to stop Shefket (now commanding XVIII Corps) being joined by Ali Ihsan, Maude pressed on up the Tigris. Marshall advanced on Shefket's new position on the Shatt-al-Adhaim, planning to cross the river on 11 April, but was forced into a 'most inopportune' diversion due to the earlier failure to secure the Jebel Hamrin. Maude ordered him to support the Cavalry Division, which was shadowing Ali Ihsan's advancing corps. Marshall wanted to delay the move for twenty-four hours to 'allow us to come in behind' the enemy, but Maude refused.[13] A twenty-mile overnight march on the 11th led to an encounter battle, which as Candler said had become rare in modern fighting, and was a sad verdict on British cavalry reconnaissance. Yet again the situation was saved by the spirited dash of the British infantry and artillery, beating the Turks in a race to the ridge that dominated the area by the Khalis canal.

'For the second time in a fortnight the 13th Division had, after an extraordinarily promising start, somehow failed to make good their opportunity.' To one staff officer, the top-heavy command structure had become the problem: the army, corps and divisional generals, Maude, Marshall and Cayley, 'were each endeavouring to conduct the operations'. This was the downside of modern communications.[14]

Turning back to the Adhaim, Marshall pulled off one of the most successful river crossings of the campaign by deceiving the Turks about its location. For the stoical Ned Roe in the assaulting 38th Brigade, the operation ('We are going', he laconically noted on 17 April, 'to cross the Shatt-al-Adhaim and attack the Turkish right wing at dawn.') was remarkable mainly for the issue of two days' rations. 'Think of it, two whole loaves of bread per man. Is the world coming to an end? How are we going to carry tomorrow's rations, haversack already filled to its capacity with a cardigan, socks, towel etc? We solve the difficulty by having a real "tuck in", the best we've had in Mess-pot.' After all, as he reflected, 'when fighting water is all one troubles about: food is only a secondary consideration. In any case, we may all be dead tomorrow.'[15]

Once again, though, his comrades disappointed him. As they hauled their pontoons into the river, 'some of the men soon forgot the lesson taught them on the Diyala as they imagined they were on a boating expedition on the Thames or Ribble'. Still, the defenders seemed oblivious to the threat. Not until the battalion was on the opposite bank did they 'smell a rat'. 'The attack was a complete surprise; only a few sleepy Turks manned the flanking trenches. Turkish officers were captured in bed as they languorously sipped their morning coffee.' Twenty-seven officers and over 1,200 men were captured. For once the defenders had failed to retire in time, and suffered damaging losses.

Though the weather was already getting uncomfortably hot, Maude forced two more battles on the Tigris in April. Cobbe's attack on a strong defensive position at Istabulat on the 22nd, was the fiercest-fought battle since the capture of Baghdad. Once again the attackers managed to be weaker than the defenders, but Major Catty recorded that 'prisoners told us that the Turks were done & so it seemed if 7600 let themselves be beat by 7000 in a place like Istabulat'.[16] Marshall's column, pushing on up the Adhaim, fought its way through a series of defensive positions near the foothills from which the river – and Ali Ihsan's corps – emerged. ('If operations last much longer,' Ned Roe gasped on the 26th, 'we shall all be in hospital with heatstroke.') The final battle was fought around hills labelled 'The Boot' on the right bank of the river and 'The Mound' on the other. It was as tight a struggle as Roe had experienced. 'We are promised "lacs" [*lakhs* – i.e. loads] of artillery support,' he said, but as his brigade advanced 'our artillery is giving us very little support', while 'the Turkish guns are numerous, well handled and are giving us an awful time on the exposed mounds'. Things were desperate enough for Roe's brigadier to intervene at the Mound. 'About 3pm, General O'Dowda came up to the firing line. With legs well apart, he pulled out his glasses and leisurely surveyed the Turkish position. He showed supreme indifference to bullets and shells.' Staying there an hour, O'Dowda's display of sang-froid 'renewed our courage and restored our confidence'. Even then Roe spent a 'harrowing night' anticipating a Turkish attack, but the enemy decided once more to back off – able yet again to go back at his own pace.

Roe's mild stoicism deserted him as he fumed that 'our overconfidence, or indiscretion rather, was nearly our undoing; 2,000 infantry attacking 5,000 well entrenched Turks with 37 guns to back them up, is beyond a joke'. Fortunately for him, Adhaim was to be his last battle in Mesopotamia. (Though officially none of these fights was a 'battle': Adhaim was an 'action', as were Mushahida, Jebel Hamrin and Istabulat, while the Khalis canal battle was an 'operation', and Duqma a mere 'affair'.) It was also, in a sense, the last serious military operation of the campaign. Ali Ihsan withdrew once again into the Jebel

Hamrin: Marshall wryly acknowledged that 'it was fortunate for us that Ali Ihsan prided himself on his conduct of retirements'. Had attack been 'his pet *métier*' instead, and had he thrown his numerically superior force forward while the British were blinded by the dust storm, 'I tremble to think of what might have happened.'[17]

At last, in May, both sides – 'reversing the ancient usage', as one staff officer wryly noted – went into summer quarters. It turned out to be the hottest summer in living memory. 'Most things were too hot to touch. The rim of a tumbler burnt one's hand in a tent.' The spirit of the troops, Candler thought, was high. But he was lucky enough to go to India for the hottest two months of the year. The monotony of life for those stuck in Mesopotamia was deadly, and the contrast with the life-and-death battles on the Western Front was beginning to create a sense of pointlessness. 'Every day is absolutely the same', according to Captain Baxter of the South Lancashires. 'We get up at an exceedingly early hour in the morning and wait for the Turk, who has not yet honoured us with his presence. But no matter, for we do it just the same. This is known as "standing to". Then we do a couple of hours' digging. Then breakfast, then 1½ hours' musketry and other "training". Then we attempt to live until the evening . . . a sort of mixture of life and death. In the evening, up again, and dig for 1½ hours, then dinner, then "stand to", and to bed once more.'[18]

2. Maude's End

How fortunate it is when the man dies before the name.
GERTRUDE BELL

If soldiers like Roe had known more of the wider strategic position, they would certainly have wondered why they were still struggling up the rivers of Mesopotamia. The Imperial General Staff would have preferred 'an active defensive', not offensive posture there. They wanted to throw everything they had at Germany on the Western Front. Even the old idea that Mesopotamia would make India more secure was dismissed by Arnold Wilson, since India was 'being bled white by the incessant demands of Mesopotamia for men and munitions'.[1] In any case, a British force in Persia – the South Persia Rifles – had by now secured the approaches to India. In Mesopotamia Britain now had about three men (two of them combatants) to every Turkish soldier, and outnumbered them three to one in artillery. More cavalry and motor transport arrived, 'while half a million tons of ocean shipping, innumerable river craft, and hundreds of miles of railway line and rolling stock were diverted from urgent war purposes elsewhere' (railway lines were still being torn up in India to be taken out to Mesopotamia).

The Ottoman Empire itself was on the ropes – 'its manpower reserves were spent, exorbitant inflation was strangling the economy, and starvation even stalked the capital, Istanbul.'[2] Its armies, battered by the first two years of fighting, had only been saved from collapse by the winter weather in 1916–17. In Mesopotamia, according to British estimates, the Ottoman Sixth Army now mustered about 2,200 infantry on the 'Euphrates line', 9,000 on the 'Tigris line', and 4,350 on the 'Kifri line' with a bare 1,500 more at Sulaimaniyah and Mosul.³ The only potential menace took the form of a big new 'Yilderim' army being formed, reportedly commanded by General Erich von Falkenhayn, with the intention of advancing down the Euphrates. The Yilderim Ordular Grubunu, or Lightning-bolt Army Group, was the brainchild of Enver Pasha, who planned to reinforce the Sixth Army with the newly formed Seventh (created from units returning from Galicia, Romania and Macedonia) around Mosul. After retaking Baghdad, Enver envisaged the Yilderim army renewing the advance into Persia. This was strategy on a dramatic scale, but its lack of realism dismayed other Turkish commanders when Enver announced it at a meeting in Aleppo on 24 June 1917. The troops from Europe were the last strategic reserve the Ottomans had, and Jemal Pasha in particular was anxious that they be retained as a support for his front in Syria and Palestine.⁴

British intelligence (which initially floated a figure as large as 300,000 for the Yilderim army) was probably on firmer ground in suggesting that the Germans were telling the Turks that Mesopotamia was strategically irrelevant – its fate would be determined by the peace conference, not by fighting.⁵ Falkenhayn himself wanted to use the new Yilderim army to advance towards Suez, and though he talked of a subsequent move on Baghdad, this was to keep Enver happy. Even the concentration at Aleppo stretched the creaking Ottoman communications system to the limit. The 24th Infantry Division, for instance, lost over half its strength in moving from Gallipoli to Aleppo. The great Yilderim advance towards Persia would never materialise. But the threat led Maude to order a move on Ramadi at the hottest time in a very hot summer. The temperature in the shade was 122 degrees F; in the sun 160 F. Even Maude (who was now 'introducing a strict regime of spurs and Sam Browne belts in a climate which made the latter injurious to health') hesitated, but the local commander was keen to go on. The assault on 11 July was horrendous. 'Some men lost their reason, some died of thirst, many died of heatstroke.' The main achievement of the failed attack seems to have been that, when it was renewed in the autumn, the defences had been strengthened.

By September intelligence estimates of the Yilderim army concentration had been scaled down to 100,000, but since Maude had 'only' 75,000 rifles, he was promised yet another reinforcement (the newly formed 18th Indian Division). Robertson was unsurprisingly sceptical about this, feeling it had been provoked by alarmist reports from Mesopotamia. 'I would greatly dislike you not giving your views freely and boldly,' he told Maude. But 'your official telegrams are seen by War Cabinet and others who naturally cannot always put correct military interpretation on them and are apt to become unduly anxious and therefore expect me to take action giving complete security everywhere'.[6] Still, Maude got his reinforcements, and now had 166,000 combat troops under his command – his total ration strength reached no less than a quarter of a million.

Unusually, in the autumn of 1917, Maude's subordinates – in this case the fiery Brooking – wanted to launch attacks even when the army commander hesitated. Brooking's attack at Ramadi on 28 September used a well thought-out deception plan, and a combination of much greater mobility thanks to 'our system of water supply by Ford vans', with Brooking's own 'serene optimism' when the fighting threatened once again to go wrong, led to the surrender of the entire Turkish force. Here at last was the kind of victory that had proved so elusive. It was followed next month by another push by both Cobbe and Marshall up the Tigris, towards Tikrit. Once again, though, Marshall's advance to Deli Abbas to control the Jebel Hamrin was inconclusive. 'People called it a "Reconnaissance in Force"'[7] and the Turks as usual slipped away ('an old Turkish custom which seems never to have failed to surprise us'). When Cobbe also attacked an isolated outpost at Daur on 2 November, Maude 'showed some reluctance to permit Cobbe to exploit his victory to the full and move on Tikrit'.[8]

A series of delays allowed Turkish resistance to solidify again, and the final battle for Tikrit on 5 November was surprisingly destructive. The Turks were pushed back, again at disturbingly heavy cost in British casualties. Major Clement Milward, an intelligence officer on Marshall's staff, grumbled that 'these people here do not seem to tumble to new ideas as they do in France'. He put it down to 'Indian obstructiveness'. (In spite of repeated instructions, they would not signal their location by flares for air observation, so 'the supporting brigade could not be put in through the first attack . . . and the attack came to a standstill'.) Tikrit, 'a picturesque old walled town built on a bluff', with houses standing on the edge of a sheer hundred-foot cliff above the shingly bed of the river, proved to be 'very quiet' when the Turks retreated. Few prisoners were taken, and though Tikrit had been their riverhead for months, the retreating defenders managed to remove all their stores. 'Living from hand to mouth, the Turk has a genius for spiriting stuff away,' Candler reported. 'In no place that we occupied, however rapid the operations may have been, did we find enough food to keep a brigade for half a day.'

This was, mercifully, the end of serious fighting in Mesopotamia. After this, as Candler put it, 'the Turk did not stay for much execution; the bloody, remorseless trench fighting of the last two years and a half was a thing of the past'. Just as importantly, the impetus behind the British campaign was suddenly snuffed out: General Maude, who had seemed impervious to Mesopotamia's deadly climate, went down with cholera in mid-November and died on the 21st. 'It was almost incredible to us all,' Gertrude Bell said. 'We had all been inoculated and thought no more about it.' The Army Commander, who 'saw no Arabs and scarcely ever went into town', seemed the last one likely to fall victim.[9] His death shocked the army. Letters, diaries and memoirs were filled with fulsome tributes to his military gifts (a degree short of genius, perhaps, even in the eyes of his admirers) and the noble simplicity of his character. For Arnold Wilson, 'He had become to all ranks the embodiment of victory.' Milward called him 'A great strategist, and a great master of detail – a rare combination.' On the political side Gertrude Bell, inevitably, saw it from a different angle. A tragic ending, indeed, 'and yet how fortunate it is when the man dies before the name'. Her pent-up anger, indeed, burst through the convention of politeness to the dead. General Maude 'had no knowledge of statecraft and regarded it as totally unnecessary. He was determined beyond the verge of obstinacy, a narrow intelligence confined to one channel and the more forcible for its concentration.' Had he lived, she wrote, 'there would have been a desperate tussle when administrative problems began to become more important than military'.[10] Within a few days she felt that the new commander, Sir William Marshall, despite being Maude's own nominee, was showing 'signs of being sympathetic to our side of the game', and she was soon openly delighted with the new regime. The civil–military balance would now shift decisively; the question was whether Maude had already done irreparable political damage.

Militarily, the legacy of Maude's control obsession was frustrating. His last reported words were 'Carry on'; but at what? Even though he would, if he had lived, soon have been leaving Mesopotamia for Egypt, he had briefed nobody about his plans. His death 'knocks the bottom out of this show', Milward thought – 'no one knows what he intended'. He had planned the campaign alone, 'kept his own counsel . . . took absolutely no heed of what anybody else thought'. Marshall, who protested his lack of qualification for the army command, was unlikely to imitate him. 'Poor Maude was a wonder and his place is difficult to fill,' he wrote to his brother. 'I am sorry they put me into this job as it isn't in my line at all and requires a much bigger brain than I possess.' (Sir William Robertson evidently agreed, and forced his own nominee in as Marshall's chief of staff.) Next month he told him, 'there is nothing doing here'; he had no idea what the policy in Persia was to be, and the slow progress of the Turkish railway towards Mosul – in fact it was 'practically hung up' – meant that the strategic situation was unlikely to change soon. 'I see no chance of anything big down here for some time to come.' Milward put it more pithily – 'no war here at all'.[11] Many others were 'getting fed up with Mesopotamia' – 'here we are letting our minds, such as are left of them, stagnate'. Worst of all, they felt they were 'not doing our little bit towards ending the war'. The only military activity available in February 1918 was firing off the annual musketry course. ('Though whether it is this year's course, or last year's, or even 1916's, we cannot tell.'[12]) But military frustration meant political elation. As Gertrude Bell had remarked in December 1917, 'Here War is at an end, but administration goes on apace.'

3. Strengthening the Hold

> It is clear that somehow or other we must retain predominating influence in Mesopotamia. By what means?
>
> SIR ARTHUR HIRTZEL

> The stronger the hold we are able to keep here the better the inhabitants will be pleased.
>
> GERTRUDE BELL

In 1917, the world in which the Mesopotamia campaign was grinding slowly on was changing dramatically. The Russian Revolution seemed to end the long-running rivalry between Britain and Russia in Central Asia. The Russian threat to India evaporated; but the Bolshevik seizure of power in November, the disintegration of the Russian Army during the winter, and the eventual conclusion of a separate peace with Germany, were a massive setback to the Allied war effort. The treaty of Brest-Litovsk in March 1918 threatened to open up not only the Caucasus, but the whole route eastwards though the Caspian, to German domination. Even before the war, Britain had believed that a flood of German secret agents was busily raising Muslim opposition. Two years into it, this fear had become a full-blown neurosis. John Buchan's 1916 best-seller *Greenmantle*, with its world of shadowy conspiracies, and its warning that Germany's eastern ambitions were paramount – 'she'll never give up the road to Mesopotamia till you have her by the throat and make her drop it' – simply dramatised official views.

The reinvigoration of Germany's *Drang nach Osten* was traumatic enough, but more far-reaching in its political impact was America's entry into the war in April 1917. This would have no military effect on the fighting against Turkey, but it sharply limited Britain's freedom of manoeuvre in constructing a postwar settlement. When Lord Balfour, the Foreign Secretary, went to Washington to explain Britain's war aims to President Woodrow Wilson, the problem became immediately obvious. Balfour was interviewed first by Colonel House, Wilson's confidential adviser, who told the President that the secret arrangements between the Allies for a postwar settlement were 'all bad'. The idea of spheres of influence would make the area 'a breeding ground for future war'. When House asked Balfour exactly what the influence would mean, the reply was 'hazy'. The Foreign Secretary stalled, but he was left in no doubt that an old-fashioned great-power carve-up was not going to be acceptable. When the Bolsheviks published the secret treaties later that year, the game was up.

The political atmosphere in Britain itself was becoming more hostile, with the Labour Party accusing the government of imperialistic and capitalistic aims in Mesopotamia. Allegations of this kind were likely to find a strong echo in America, and Curzon tried to counter them by restating Britain's international duty to civilisation. If the liberated regions were to be 'set on their feet again', and 'indigenous institutions are to be created amongst people who have almost lost the idea of what freedom is . . . the responsibility must be assumed by a civilised power'. The only civilised power that was 'either equipped for the task or interested in it' was Britain. If Britain gave it up, the result would be dangerous to Britain itself, and 'positively disastrous to the native peoples'.[1] But still nobody could say what sort of responsibility should be assumed. On the last day of 1917, Hirtzel warned that 'we must at least consider the possibility of a peace which will not give us the absolute political control of Mesopotamia that we should like to have'. Some new kind of arrangement must be worked out.

In the new year the Prime Minister, Lloyd George, gave a key speech to the trade unions signalling that the postwar world would be fundamentally different. The defeat of the Ottoman Empire would liberate its subject peoples. 'Arabia, Armenia,

Mesopotamia, Syria and Palestine' would, he held, be 'entitled
to a recognition of their separate national conditions.' He was
showing that Britain was ahead of the game, whose rules were
announced in President Woodrow Wilson's Fourteen Points a
few days later, on 8 January. Wilson set the principle of national
self-determination at the heart of the future international order;
but sceptics (like Hirtzel at the India Office) picked up the vital
questions that would dog the principle from the start – as they
still do. What was the self-determining unit to be? Who would
do the determining? And how? 'Is Mesopotamia to be treated as
a separate unit, and if so, what body or bodies are to exercise the
right?' What steps could Britain take 'to see that they exercise it
the right way'?

The complacent British expectation of a veiled protectorate
with an 'Arab façade' was clearly at serious risk. 'Somehow or
other we must retain predominating influence in Mesopotamia',
Hirtzel said. The question 'By what means?' was now urgent.
Mark Sykes was predictably confident that he knew how to
reconcile the position in Mesopotamia with 'the spirit of the
age'. Protectorates and spheres of influence would have to be
'consigned to the Diplomatic lumber-room' and a new mode of
international trusteeship was needed, with a fixed 25-year term,
and with American approval, which would involve an economic
open-door policy.[2] Just as predictably, Hirtzel was curtly
dismissive of 'schemes evolved from the inner consciousness of
Sykes or others without any contact with facts on the spot'. The
facts, he insisted, were 'very imperfectly known to us'. Maybe
Percy Cox's idea of a visiting commission of inquiry, which had
been thwarted by Maude, should be revived.

The idea of sending a commission had a lot to be said for
it, but it foundered on the fear that Britain's allies would see
it as staking a territorial claim. Instead, Cox was brought out
of Mesopotamia to London to brief the Cabinet's Eastern
Committee, as the Mesopotamia Administration Committee
had been renamed. For its benefit he drew up a full-scale

assessment, starting from acceptance of the fact that annexation of any part of Iraq would be 'exceedingly difficult vis-à-vis the President of the United States'. What would now be viable? Cox plumped for a very diluted version of the 'Arab façade' – a British High Commissioner aided by a council. But he thought that any arrangement which left Britain in control of foreign policy, so making the area a virtual protectorate, would do. If Allied pressure forced Britain to appoint a native ruler, Cox proposed the Naqib of Baghdad – the head of the Gilani family and the Qadiri order of dervishes, elderly and highly respected, unpolitical, and – most importantly – cooperative.

At this stage Cox showed that he was not quite as 'Cairene' as Lawrence and Bell hoped. He was well aware of Cairo's plans for the Sharifian family, but adamant that they could play no role in Iraq. In his view the Sharif was 'a figure who carries no weight in Iraq, where only the most distant interest is taken in him': he might be acceptable as the head of some loose confederation of Arab states, but no more. Just as vitally, Cox opposed any kind of plebiscite there. 'The bulk of the people [of Iraq] are not concerned with abstract theories or niceties of international principles'; indeed 90 per cent of them were 'altogether inarticulate'. If it became necessary to obtain 'public expression of feeling in favour of British control, it can be done'; but it would have to be done cautiously. He underlined this point when he met the committee two days later. But the Foreign Secretary reassuringly suggested that President Wilson did not really expect his self-determination formula to be applied outside Europe. As long as America was persuaded that the Arabs could not 'stand alone', Balfour believed, it would accept an Arab state under British protection.[3]

Hirtzel's suggestion that the facts were 'very imperfectly known' was a poor tribute to Gertrude Bell's powers of investigation and communication. She had assembled the facts and written them up for the benefit of Hirtzel and others. 'Frankly, who knows if I don't?' Her monumental project of listing all the Arab tribes had produced, amongst many other reports, *The Arab of Mesopotamia*, a set of deftly written essays which she called 'as good a plea as I can make for the Arab race'. 'I want people to listen', she told her parents. Her researches were certainly the first systematic study of Arab society in Iraq. In July 1917 she explained her research methods. Still 'busy with this huge confusion of the Euphrates tribes' which she hoped to 'reduce to order' soon, her procedure was to 'see every Sheikh when he comes in to pay his respects to Sir Percy and get all this information about his tribe direct from him'. She was becoming the pivotal figure in 'the making of a new world', a project as daunting as it was exciting to her. 'We've shouldered a gigantic task', she admitted, 'but I can't see what alternative there was . . . I want to watch it all very carefully almost from day to day, so as to be able to take what I hope may be something like a decisive hand in final disposition . . . What does anything else matter when the job is such a big one?'[4]

By early 1918 she was quite confident that the administrative system had been accepted by the people to a remarkable extent, and 'the immense energy with which agricultural development has been pushed forward has been of incalculable political value'. But the most crucial thing was to understand and use the tribal system. 'There is nothing easier to manage than tribes if you'll take advantage of tribal organization and make it the basis of administrative organization.' She was surprised to find 'how many of the Bagdad notables are tribesmen, only settled in town for the last generation or two. Some sheikh builds himself a town house, send his sons to school and starts them in a learned profession leading to Government employment. And at once they settle down into citizens.' The crucial point, though, was that 'the tribal links are unbroken'. This offered a path for nation-building. So far, the administration had recruited a few Baghdadis who had fled to their tribe in the months before the British occupation, 'and their tribal connection makes them all the more useful'. Though she admitted that there were very few 'really first-class Arab officials' as yet, Bell was confident that they were just the tip of the iceberg.

But what Bell saw as an exciting development was, in reality, a serious distortion of Iraqi society. The deliberate fostering of the power of the sheikhs was an administrative convenience which steadily eroded the traditional independence of the tribes. As Ghassan Atiyyah has shown, British policy followed that of the Turks in aiming to assert the power of government, but it differed crucially in method. 'The British adopted the Shaykh as the government's instrument, while the Turks had aimed at his destruction.'[5] As Britain's reach extended in the wake of the army, and as the need for revenue and grain grew, the demands made on sheikhs as government agents increased. Cooperative sheikhs were appointed paramount sheikhs of the tribes identified in Bell's scheme, and punishment was inflicted on other sheikhs who refused to recognise them. The paramount sheikhs became the sole official channel of communication between the people and the administration, as well as the collectors of revenue. Where land was state-owned, as much of it was between Qurna and Kut, they received generous allocations. The result was an artificial structure that replaced the traditional source of sheikhly authority, the tribesmen, by government patronage.

For the time being it worked well enough for Britain, even amongst the refractory Euphrates tribes, as long as they were within reach of British forces. The political officer at Nasiriyeh reported in 1918 that, 'It has been my endeavour during my last 3½ years in the Muntafiq to get power in each tribe in the hands of one man.' The policy had 'surpassed all expectations, and whereas one found six or seven Shaikhs in each tribe of equal standing (to say nothing of a host of pretenders) when we first occupied Nasiriyah and Suq, now we find one strong man, who gets a subsidy from the Government and knows it worth his while to play straight'.[6] Amongst the tribes of the Tigris, most directly exposed to military power, conflicts between sheikhs and their subordinates, the *sarkals*, who managed sections of the estates they acquired, led both to outbid each other in offering loyalty to the administration. One *sarkal* in the Amara division would go on, after the war, to offer to produce a petition calling for the removal of the sheikhs, with as its first clause the demand 'that there should be an English Sultan of Iraq'.[7]

It is hard to judge if Bell was right to think that the British had come a long way in establishing a popular civil administration in Basra and Baghdad by the spring of 1918. As we have seen, she was well aware that the ever-expanding military machine was making many enemies – particularly through its system of requisitioning – but she thought it had compensating positive spin-offs, notably the building of roads and railways, and the improvement of river navigation. How should the balance be weighed? Arnold Wilson noted that the Basra–Amara railroad 'took from the fields almost every able-bodied man in the Qurna district'. By April 1918 over 45,000 men had been enrolled in the Arab labour corps, and enrolment was often in effect conscription. Dragged away to work far from home, and poorly paid, they left behind a land so depopulated that large potential crop-bearing areas were deserted. The question was whether the people thought the benefits justified the burden, and it seems that for every change that was accepted as beneficial, there was another that harmed local interests.[8]

For Bell, the clearest success of the British administration lay in the spheres of law, finance and public health. Public finances were in order; after an inspection of the records by the Indian government's Controller of War Accounts, Bhupendra Mitra, the Mesopotamia administration was given wider fiscal powers. Civil courts were functioning, a public health programme developing in the cities, and there was even some educational progress. The government printing press expanded to generate the mass of forms required by the army, and the circulation of newspapers (the *Basra Times* and *Baghdad Times*) grew dramatically – acting as 'a civilising agency and the efficient handmaid of civilised government'. Sanitation in overcrowded Basra had actually been worsened at the start by the efforts to improve the military areas, but this was gradually rectified.[9] After a visit to the Baghdad Civil Hospital in January 1918, Bell enthused about how medical organisation was 'an invaluable political asset'. It was hugely popular. 'Hospitals and dispensaries are the first thing the people ask for, and they flock to them, men and women.' There was no resistance to scientific progress in this area; they 'don't hesitate to undergo operations or any treatment you please'. (And with good reason, according to Captain Carey Evans, the Municipal Doctor – 'the standard of vitality is much higher than in Europe ... people here pull through operations which he would not dare attempt at home.') When the Civil Dispensary was opened in March, 'all the notables, civil and religious' came to tea 'and talked and were pleased to see one another'.[10]

But Bell noted that public opinion remained finely balanced. Especially west of Baghdad, 'it was difficult for the tribesmen to believe that the Turks would not come back'. Resistance to British political officers was sporadic but far from uncommon. Even in Baghdad uncertainty about the Allies' long-term intentions led many to believe that 'Iraq would be handed back to Turkey in exchange for Belgium'. A flagship project designed to signal Britain's long-term presence was the rebuilding of Kut, which had been reduced to 'tottering ruins among the palm groves blasted by artillery fire, the streets choked with mud or blocked with barricades, the houses pierced by shells and rifle fire, and honeycombed by dugouts, the river front lined with trenches'. Only the minaret of the Sunni mosque had miraculously survived. The *sarai* had been destroyed. A careful rebuilding programme began, involving the straightening and widening of the wrecked streets, and the cleaning and disinfection of surviving houses. The battlefield was searched for unexploded ordnance, and bodies were properly reburied. The mosques and public buildings were restored, and a new arcaded souk on the bank of the Tigris became 'the crowning glory of Kut'. Families of those killed in the siege were eligible for grants to rebuild their houses, and

2,000 people were drawn back into the town by the middle of May 1918. The whole project produced 'a profound impression amongst the tribes'.[11] (Though the British remained unpersuaded by Kut's charms: 'particularly dirty and evil-smelling . . . it was a nice place to get away from,' said George Savage in late 1917.) In occupied Mesopotamia as a whole, health and education expenditure tripled between 1916 and 1918; but the bottom line was that the lion's share of public revenue was consumed by the pay of administrative officers and the expenses of their headquarters – over a million rupees in 1915–16, and no less than 7.6 million in 1917–18.[12]

The closest relationship between the British and the Arabs was probably the operation of the huge Local Resources Department, organising food acquisition for the now bloated expeditionary force. Lt George Savage of the North Staffordshire Regiment, who was Harvest Officer at Jerboyieh on the Euphrates, found the Arabs friendly – 'contrary to expectations'. Buying grain was simply a matter of organising weighing, packing and transport (50,000 sacks a week from the four stations of his district alone); but collecting 'tibben' or chaff for animal feed was more problematic. Getting enough Arab labour was a continual difficulty, and compulsion had to be used. 'The Arab of Mesopotamia is not fond of work', and only the lowest class would work for a wage. The small farmers, who looked down on trade, would not sell anything – though they would happily give it away. They were 'a very independent lot' and considered themselves quite equal to the British. 'They tolerate us but they don't love us,' he noted. 'The children used to stand by the river bank and curse us as we passed.'[13]

Bell remained confident that the Sunni–Shia division would not undermine the nation-building process. 'The first thing in this Shiah country', she announced, 'is that we should have a real understanding of the things that lie at the bottom of the Shiah mind.' This she proposed to do through her hobby of translating the Shia traditional books. She had a 'warm feeling of being part of it all', but was this enough? An early example of the kind of administrative problems that would emerge came with the case of the Naqib of Baghdad's water pipe. Like so much of the infrastructure of Mesopotamia, this was in chronic disrepair, causing repeated floods in the neighbourhood. But it could not be treated as a simple hydraulic device: it was 'a religious bequest and therefore must be approached with the utmost caution'. It took extended negotiations, and much 'heart searching' on the Naqib's part, before he agreed to allow its upkeep to become a municipal responsibility.

But the Naqib was unusually cooperative; not all religious questions would prove so tractable. Early in 1918, the British administration came directly up against forces that had so far remained guardedly quiet, the Shia leadership in the holy cities of Karbala and Najaf. These were the core sites of what Sunni Muslims saw as the Shia heresy: the veneration of the martyred Hussein and Ali, killed in the conflict over the succession to Muhammad in the late seventh century. (Ali, Muhammad's cousin, assassinated; his son Hussein killed in battle at Karbala.) Neither city had ever been fully reconciled to the government of the Sunni Ottomans. Both had actually rebelled against the Turks in 1916, and even though the Turks shelled the holy places in their attempt to reassert control – 'a sacrilege that will never be forgiven', the British thought – they had failed. As we have seen, the leaders reacted politely to the British capture of Baghdad. A British political officer was posted to Hilla in May 1917, but with only a small military force.

In British eyes, the Shia holy cities were 'centres of intrigue', where 'the student of Eastern lore may be initiated into the arcana of Moslem social and religious life'. In this Buchanesque world, 'Among the pious you will find suspects on the political black list, men long known in the Gulf as gun-runners, jehadists and spies, and men who come with strange, unconvincing tales, leaving suspicion behind them but no evidence for arrest.' The Najafis, the most extreme of all Shia, refused to allow Christians anywhere near the shrine of Ali. Karbala was gradually brought under British control, via a stage at which Cox recognised the authority of the dominant but unpopular local grandees of the Kammuna family. But Najaf remained fiercely independent. Four sheikhs vied for power in a form of permanent factional warfare. In 1915–16 Atiya abu Qulal, 'a powerful half-crazed ex-outlaw' and head of the Zuqurt faction (which the British of course called a 'gang'), succeeded in forming the 'Najaf interim government'. In July 1917 the British appointed Hamid Khan (a cousin of the Aga Khan) as Government Agent there, but gave him no forces. Wilson, with hindsight, thought that 'we were perhaps unduly' anxious to avoid placing garrisons there to avoid provocation. But British policy was inevitably provocative.

The holy cities had briefly enjoyed the benefits of state-free existence, including the absence of taxation. Now a whole raft of taxes – including a house tax, water tax, building tax and several other minor levies – was introduced. In late 1917 the two cities, which had shared pre-eminence in an administrative *mutasarifiya*, were separated and effectively demoted to secondary towns in the districts of Hilla and Shamiyeh. Taxation bore most heavily on the poor, and the status issue concerned the leaders. The result was a resistance movement in Najaf centring on the Political Officer's decision to allow the Aniza tribe to take grain from the city's stores. An insurgency created 'chaos' in Najaf, with riots and arson spreading to Kufa and Abu Sukhayr. A group called Jamyat al Nahadha al Islamiya (Islamic Upheaval Society) was formed. In December a set of small military garrisons and political officers were at last posted to the mid-Euphrates towns. Najaf was not included, but it was administered from Kufa. Order was restored, with the revival of the municipality, supported by a new *shabana* force, and the introduction of some urban services – paid for by redeploying money from the Oudh Bequest.

In January 1918, though, resistance to the distribution of grain to the surrounding tribes flared up again. When Aniza

were fired on as they went into Najaf to pick up supplies, two
of the city's four sheikhs accepted responsibility for the violence,
but the other two refused. Then, 'while we were debating the
punishment of Najaf' (as Candler put it), an Indian cavalry patrol
was fired on from the walls, and a sowar – 'by the irony of fate a
Shia' – was killed. Shortly afterwards some Najafis even had the
temerity to fire shots at a British aircraft. The town was punished
with a fine of 50,000 rupees, and ordered to surrender 500 rifles.
At this point its defiance was ended without more fighting, by
cutting off its water supply: fortunately its dependence on water
brought from a channel two miles outside the town made it
very vulnerable. By the end of January 500 rifles ('useless' ones,
inevitably) had been delivered and Sheikh Atiya had absconded:
his large house was confiscated in lieu of his fine.

For a few weeks order seemed to be established by a young
Assistant Political Officer, Captain W. M. Marshall, who was seen
as an administrative star in the making. ('A brilliant creature',
Gertrude Bell said.) But his very success was his undoing. The
battalion was withdrawn in early March, despite protests from
Captain Frank Balfour, Political Officer at Shamiyeh. 'Rumours
of our impending defeat and the return of the Turks began to
circulate with a persistence and wealth of detail that we had
learned by experience to be connected with external agencies.'[14]
On 19 March Marshall was killed by a group of men dressed
as *shabana*, in a disturbance which the British regarded as
premeditated. It was 'not a spontaneous exhibition of dislike of the
British Government', another political officer said, but 'conceived
some time ago'. Its leaders were 'scally wags' ('Chissab is a bull-
necked thick-headed old thing, Mazute is a cross-eyed blighter').
The local military governor, Brigadier-General G. A. F. Sanders
of the 53rd Brigade, had already noted the day before that he
might 'have to shell the town with 13-pounders tomorrow, as
insurgents seem from Political reports likely to increase'.[15]

Since this was the very action which had triggered rebellion
against the Ottoman government, the Politicals were only too

aware of how problematic it would be. Captain Balfour asked for a quick decision on whether bombardment (either by artillery or aircraft) was 'permissible in last resort'. Cox recognised the 'grave political objections to hostile action against Najaf', which was 'bound to be widely misrepresented all over the Mohammedan world'. On the other hand, 'if we fail to exact our retribution for this outrage the effect on Euphrates will be the worst'. Najaf was given another 50,000-rupee fine, and required to hand over another 1,000 rifles, together with all those guilty of the murder. A hundred people would be deported to India as prisoners of war.

For Arnold Wilson this was 'a critical moment in the history of the Civil Administration', since these terms represented 'a challenge to the fanatical elements throughout Mesopotamia'. Collective punishment was necessary; the question was how to target it. 'One can't well do what one would dearly like', the C-in-C grumbled, 'and raze the place to the ground.' The answer was not just to cut off Najaf's water supply, but to blockade the town. 'We must obviously make things pretty uncomfortable for the general population', Balfour observed, 'if there was to be any probability of their getting sufficiently screwed up to take any action against the insurgents.' If nothing could be done to support them directly, it was 'only too probable' that they would never reach that point. And there was a delicate balance: 'if the general population really begin to die in large numbers it would be extremely hard for us to continue to enforce the Blockade.' Inevitably, protests soon began. It was alleged that ordinary citizens had been subjected to machine-gun fire; this was met with the assertion that it was 'well known that our machine guns have only been used against insurgents who fire on our troops', and the petitioners 'only injure their case by making untrue statements'. The *ulema*, the city's holiest men, took a potentially more difficult line – blockading the holy city was 'calculated to bring disrespect upon the Muslim religion'.

This damage was limited by the position taken by the chief *mujtahid*, who condemned the murder of Captain Marshall, and stayed in touch with the British authorities throughout the siege. Eventually, in the second week of April, the town began to hand over the culprits, eventually giving up all 102 wanted men. By 13 April, the military had occupied the town. They found it 'indescribably dirty'; General Sanders planned to take over the entire Mishraq quarter as a military cantonment, 'demolishing all the poor and dirty houses', and placing 'a Mohammedan guard on the mosque itself'. The occupation was not easy. 'This constant watching for murderers who are never visible is hard work and entails much night duty [but] until the loyal sheikhs capture the more important proscribed persons I do not feel justified in ceasing to watch the wire fence.' Sanders set a time limit, insisting that, after the 19th, 'other measures must be taken' to deal with the 'rabbit warren' of a town. 'A systematic opening out of broad streets might bring them to reason and hasten compliance' with the British terms.[16]

Balfour asked Wilson for 'a hint how far this policy is expected to work out and how far it is to be pushed?' He was not against it, but felt that 'it may be grim'. Soon, though, he was more sanguine, reporting that 'we are making such a clean sweep of Najaf that a large number of death sentences is not necessary'. His personal estimate was that six to eight would be 'about right'.[17] In the end, eleven men were sentenced to death by the military court at Kufa. They had been charged with 'war crimes' – 'illegitimate hostilities in arms committed by individuals who are not members of the armed forces of the country'. Wilson believed that the executions (on 28 April) had 'a profound effect throughout Mesopotamia', and he claimed to have received 'more expressions of relief at the outcome of the affair than I had previously received appeals for clemency'. Harold Dickson, promoted to be Political Officer at Shattra, likewise exulted that the executions had 'done more good than anything else in the world. A tonic has been administered that won't be forgotten.'[18] Najaf submitted; but it was not the 'good-humoured submission' which British punitive action often secured amongst the desert tribes. Though the Zukurt and Shumurt factions were no longer troublesome, 'the atmosphere within, and radiating from the Shi'i shrines', Longrigg thought, 'remained sinister, obscurantist, and anti-government'.

4. Caucasian Fantasies

Lord Salisbury spoke about the danger of small-scale maps, and sometimes I could not help thinking that the Eastern Committee of the Cabinet must have provided themselves with those of a particularly small scale.

SIR WILLIAM MARSHALL

As Bolshevik Russia pulled out of the war, it opened up vistas equally alarming and elating for Britain. Conservatives invariably thought of Bolshevism as a deadly infection, and they in turn became infected with a kind of mania. Winston Churchill's obsessive desire to overthrow the Bolsheviks drove Lloyd George to distraction, but just as obsessional was the preoccupation of the Cabinet Eastern Committee – in the person of Lord Curzon – with the German threat to India. 'Bogies created by the enemy or by our own too lively imaginations', General Marshall reflected, 'are apt to become a nuisance if encouraged.' He charitably suggested that the London authorities must have had 'exact and definite information that a Turco-German move against India through Persia and Afghanistan was a concrete and dangerous fact', though he himself had only heard 'rumours, which I entirely disbelieved'.

There were some grounds for London's bogey-mongering. At the ideological level, at least, the Young Turks undoubtedly harboured dreams of a pan-Turkic union extending across the Caucasus to Central Asia.[1] Enver himself was the most committed pan-Turkist. In practical terms, though, Marshall was right to say that any significant military movement, either Turkish or German, across Persia was simply impossible. Still, a new Ottoman army (the Ninth) of some 32,000 was certainly organised to recover Batum and Kars – lost to the Russians in 1877, but restored to Turkey by the Brest-Litovsk negotiations.

This advance had Germany's blessing, though Enver's intention of pushing further on through the Caucasus to occupy the Baku oilfields definitely did not. Military intelligence thought that, 'the apparent intention of the Turks to occupy a portion of the Caucasus inhabited by Mahomedans and to exterminate the Armenian population seemed to stand a very good chance of success'. By late March 1918 the Ninth Army was approaching Batum and Kars, while another new formation, the 'Islam Army' was recruiting strongly amongst the Muslims of Azerbaijan.

British grand strategy now had two new objectives: to prevent the Germans from exploiting the oil and mineral resources in the Caucasus, and to turn Persia into an effective British ally. To achieve the first of these, the strangest command of the whole war was created. In December 1917 Major-General Lionel Dunsterville – the model for Kipling's 'Stalky' – was pulled from India to lead a force which would advance from Baghdad to the Caspian Sea port of Enzeli, and across to Baku and the capital of Georgia, Tiflis. There 'it was hoped I might be able to reorganise the revolutionary units and restore the line confronting the Turks'.[2] Dunsterville became Chief of the British Mission to the Caucasus, and also British Representative at Tiflis. Even if troops could have been spared, logistical limitations would have made it impossible to move any substantial units up to the Caspian. The idea was for Dunsterville, a fluent Russian speaker, to take a 'minute force' (in one intelligence officer's words) which could rapidly 'organise the Georgians and Armenians for resistance to the Turks'.[3] 'What was needed (in Persia and Trans-Caspia)', Robertson said, 'was to despatch to the centres of intrigue and disaffection a few Englishmen of the right type to give our version of the state of affairs, furnish them with money to pay handsomely for information and services rendered, and provide them with just sufficient escort to ensure their personal safety.'

Dunsterville was certainly given plenty of money, but in the event he did not even take the planned cadre (of 150 officers and 300 NCOs, with five armoured car squadrons). Conceived as an elite group, drawn from units in other theatres as well as Mesopotamia, it took time to assemble – the armoured car detachment, for instance, could not reach Mesopotamia before March 1918. By 27 January, Dunsterville had decided to wait no longer, and set off immediately in the hope that the rest could join him in due course. The first 'Dunsterforce' was exiguous – a mere dozen officers, with forty motor cars to carry fuel and gold, and a single armoured car for protection. Even getting these vehicles to the Caspian was not easy. They had to be manhandled across a succession of mountain ranges, through passes at altitudes of between 5,000 and 8,000 feet, in heavy snow; the road up to Hamadan was barely viable for motor vehicles even in good weather. From Hamadan there was a Russian-built road, but it was in poor shape and clogged with Russian troops on their way home. Dunsterville reached Enzeli, 650 miles from Baghdad, on 17 February. He had hoped to get to Baku in twelve days, 'before any of the various enemy plans to stop us could mature', but at Enzeli, already running late, he ran into the Bolshevik committee in charge of the town (which was in the old Russian 'sphere of influence'). Deciding that it would be impossible to take ship there, he retreated three days later – just avoiding the Red Guards sent from Baku to arrest him. He managed also to get past the independent revolutionary anti-imperialist 'Jangali' group led by Mirza Kuchik Khan – and supported by the Bolsheviks in 1920 – which had occupied the surrounding country.[4] He got back to Hamadan, 'without casualties but not without some loss of prestige', on 25 February.

Arnold Wilson acidly noted that both he and Marshall 'assumed that' London would now see that the Caucasus and Caspian areas were 'unlikely to respond to treatment on the lines originally laid down' in Dunsterville's instructions. No such revelation occurred. Dunsterville remained at Hamadan, negotiating with the only Russian military force still obeying its commander, the 1,000-strong 'Partisanski' under Colonel Bicherakov. Bicherakov held this body together by sheer force of personality, and Dunsterville found him a kindred spirit. 'Although compelled to act as a mercenary' by the circumstances, Dunsterville wrote in early April, 'he is a fine fighting soldier', and a dedicated patriot.[5] His superiors were more sceptical. In March 1918 the CIGS put Dunsterville under Marshall's orders, while specifying that he was 'to be given a free hand to raise levies and enter into arrangements with local tribes'. Henry Wilson insisted on the 'urgent importance of energetic and immediate measures to frustrate enemy penetration through North-West Persia'. He also urged action to explore the information that Russian crews might be ready to sell their gunboats. 'Control of the Caspian would be bought cheap at £100,000,' he pointed out.[6]

Some of Dunsterville's officers, cheated of their exotic Caspian adventure, wanted to leave: but London insisted they stay to organise the raising of levies. This policy proved almost too successful – the pay Dunsterville offered tempted many of the Persian police to quit and enlist in the British service, leading to 'increasing trouble' with the Persian authorities. Dunsterville disbursed copious supplies of money, much of it in food aid and medical assistance. (Marshall told him it was 'very necessary to ensure good will of inhabitants' of the districts through which British forces would be passing.[7]) The area had been picked clean by successive waves of advancing and retreating Turkish and Russian armies, and was now ravaged by famine. When Wilson went up the road from Khanikin in April, he 'saw a sight I hope I may never witness again – a whole people perishing for want of food'. In Hamadan itself, built on the site of a historic Persian capital city, a third of the population of 50,000 were starving, and 'a score or more deaths from starvation occurred daily' – a figure which would soon rise to some 200. Dunsterville's quasi-government did its best to alleviate the situation, but Britain received no credit. Instead, 'we were violently attacked for not doing more, and were held up to execration as the real cause of Persia's distress'. The depth of bitterness against Anglo-Russian intervention was obvious, and the fear that the operations of

421

forces like the 'East Persian Cordon' (along the border with Afghanistan) and Dunsterforce were part of a final dismantling of Persia would remain even after Russia's collapse.

Lord Curzon would not see this. For thirty years, as Wilson realised, he had been on a personal mission to 'infuse a new vitality into the greatest of Eastern monarchies . . . No country in the world, except his own, had exercised over him a greater fascination than Persia.' His account of his journey across the country had become a travel classic and he believed himself uniquely qualified to implement a policy of fostering a Persian revival with 'benevolent British assistance'. Sadly, he was 'perhaps temperamentally incapable of understanding that the Persian government and nation were unlikely to regard his policy in so favourable a light'.[8]

This meant that, although the British resources in Mesopotamia could not support such distant military operations, Marshall was still compelled to divert forces on missions he bluntly described as 'mad'. The problem was that even though the two core divisions of the old Tigris Corps (the 3rd and the 7th) had been sent to Palestine during the winter, he still had a big force with little obvious strategic purpose. The situation in Mesopotamia was a stalemate: 'the Turks were almost incapable of fighting for the time being, and the British lacked the transport facilities to reach them and strike a heavy blow.'[9] After advancing up the Euphrates to Hit in March 1918, Brooking virtually eliminated the 50th Division in front of him at Khan Baghdadi – taking over 5,000 prisoners at a cost of about 130 casualties. A month later III Corps took Kifri and Tuz Khurmatli, capturing 1,200 prisoners and 20 guns. These successes were still inconclusive – Milward grumbled that it was now 'always manoeuvres and walking round which leads to nothing except turning the enemy out of his position, if he is skilful'.

Tuz, in Marshall's view, was as far as his force should go. The old CIGS would no doubt have agreed with him; but Robertson had just been succeeded by Sir Henry Wilson, a less doctrinaire

'Westerner'. Though acutely aware of the perilous extension of Britain's military forces, Wilson was already casting postwar policy in global terms. (As were others, notably the increasingly influential Leo Amery – described by the Deputy CIGS as 'the most dangerous amateur strategist we have got' – who was talking in mid-1918 of securing 'that Southern British World which runs from Cape Town through Cairo, Baghdad and Calcutta to Sydney and Wellington'.[10]) He would memorably suggest later that year that 'from the left bank of the Don to India is our interest and preserve'.[11] Now he believed that 'German agents, in collusion with members of the Persian government, were preparing the ground for a general rising against us when Turkish troops appeared in Persia'. He urged Marshall to 'strike hard and immediately in the direction of Kirkuk–Sulaimaniya'; this 'would be certain to impress both the Persian government and the people of Afghanistan with a sense of British power at a critical moment'.[12]

Marshall reluctantly moved on Kirkuk on 7 May. (Arnold Wilson, who thought this his one serious misjudgement, said that if he had waited a few days, he could have exploited the belated 'admission of fallibility' in a War Office telegram which left the decision to him.) In Kirkuk he captured three damaged aircraft, a stock of ammunition, and 600 sick and wounded Turks. As usual the Ottoman forces had retreated, but this time they removed all the available grain, and slaughtered all the sheep in the area – in the lambing season. They also blew up the fourth-century Christian church, a major historical monument. Marshall was soon fed up, protesting that orders to occupy Sulaimaniyah as well were 'too much altogether'. A raid was one thing, but to maintain an occupying force 200 miles beyond the railhead was simply impossible. Shortly afterwards, he evacuated Kirkuk. The result was politically the worst of all possible outcomes. All the Kurds who had rallied to the British flag had to be evacuated to save them from Turkish revenge. The effect on British prestige was the opposite of what the CIGS had intended.

In June 1918 Curzon insisted in Cabinet that Germany's primary aim was still to strike at India, even arguing that Germany could 'afford to give up everything she has won in western parts if only this door in the East remains open'. So it was not only essential that 'neither Germany nor her allies must ever again be permitted to occupy Palestine or Mesopotamia', but Britain must 'endeavour by every means in our power to secure a friendly Persia and a loyal Afghanistan'. Sir Charles Marling, the British representative in Teheran, stepped up the pressure on the reluctant Marshall to send actual military units into Persia – a 'rotten policy', the general complained. A divide had opened up between the commander and the War Office. Henry Wilson's messages urging Marshall to action took on what the official history called 'a note almost of acerbity'.

Marshall doggedly maintained that he should keep pushing on in Mesopotamia. To create 'another seven hundred miles of communications, and most of that through a mountainous country with a mere track as a road, seemed to me to be madness'. When he 'eventually received direct orders to carry out this mad enterprise', he even considered resignation (deciding it would be unpatriotic in wartime).[13] Finally he despatched what he called a 'mobile column' (though its mobility was no better than normal), with 400 men of the Hampshire Regiment and 600 Gurkhas to join Dunsterville, and next month a further brigade of infantry (the 39th) was sent, with an artillery brigade as well. Dunsterville now had the equivalent of a division to answer the appeal for relief he received from Baku in July.

By this time Henry Wilson had changed tack more than once. On 27 May, realising that the situation in the Caucasus had 'completely changed', he instructed that Dunsterville was 'not to go there'. Whether Wilson, or indeed anyone on the British side, fully grasped how unstable the situation was, seems doubtful. Curzon's main concern was to keep Dunsterville's force in Persia; Lloyd George was against assisting the Russians to hold Baku because he thought the Turks would prove a less formidable long-term opponent there. The Foreign Office view was that 'Bolshevik power appeared to be waning, and the separatist tendencies of the various races there were becoming more marked.' Although there was some wishful thinking in this, it was accurate as far as it went in the Caucasus. Bolsheviks were in control of Baku, but it was the only city in Transcaucasia they did control, and there was a strong Menshevik and Socialist-Revolutionary presence as well. The attempt to establish a single Transcaucasian Republic broke down when Georgia declared its independence on 26 May – the occasion for Wilson's rethink – and the other two republics, Armenia and Azerbaijan, followed suit. So separatist nationalism was definitely intensifying. But Baku itself was strikingly different from the rest of Azerbaijan: it was 'a capitalist city in a feudal land . . . an island of Russian and Armenian socialist parties in a sea of Moslem nationalism'.[14]

Bolsheviks were strong there because Baku was an industrial city, which had mushroomed on the back of oil production – from barely 2,000 inhabitants at the beginning of the nineteenth century to over 200,000 in 1914. In the process its Azeri citizens had become a minority, though only just. By 1918 they were being alienated by what they saw as the anti-Muslim policies of the Baku Soviet, which was dominated by Armenians and Russians. If, as Ronald Suny suggests, 'the revolution in Baku can be seen as a struggle for the minds of the Moslem poor', it was being lost by the Soviet. Far from seeing the Turks as alien invaders to be resisted, the Azeris saw them as saviours. In the 'March Days', a Muslim insurrection against Soviet power, the Armenians had already attacked the 'Tartar' suburbs, killing thousands and driving many more out of the city. By the time Baku appealed for British help, it was under siege by substantial Muslim military forces. The so-called 'Wild Division' (or 'Savage Division', *Dikaia divisiia*, actually the Tatar cavalry regiment of the Touzemnaia [Native] Division) had arrived from Petrograd, and local Azeris were joining the Ottoman-led 'Islam division' commanded by Enver's brother, Nuri Pasha.

The Baku Soviet was split over the question of British military assistance. Until late July, it followed the Bolshevik line that it would be better for the city to fall to the Muslims than to allow the British imperialists to get a foothold in the Caucasus. On 25 July, though, a motion to ask for British help secured a majority. The Bolshevik leader Stepan Shaumian stormed out of the Soviet with his party, and the Socialist-Revolutionaries, Mensheviks and Armenian Dashnaks, accusing the Bolsheviks of desertion in face of the enemy, formed the 'Dictatorship of Tsentrokaspii'. (The Bolsheviks tried to leave the city with the Red Guards and most of the available munitions, but the Caspian fleet turned them back, and they stayed on ships in Baku harbour throughout the following fighting.) It was this coalition that Dunsterforce went to prop up.

Henry Wilson's sharp opposition to any move into the Caucasus softened as he realised that further Turkish operations in Mesopotamia were unlikely. On 28 June Marshall was ordered to review the whole situation, and make a 'greater and more sustained effort in North-West Persia'. The 'note of asperity' was evident in Wilson's remark that 'H.M. Government attach more importance to success in that sphere and to securing temporary control of the Caspian than you appear to appreciate.' Dunsterville did not seem to be keeping Marshall properly informed, Wilson suggested. 'Surely at Resht [the War Office repeatedly referred to Enzeli as Resht, presumably thanks to small-scale maps] he must be able to communicate with Bicharakoff and get details regarding the situation at Baku and Caspian shipping.' Control of that shipping, and destruction of the Baku 'pumping plant, pipeline and oil reservoirs', were now the key objectives. A naval commander for the Caspian was appointed (Commodore D. T. Norris), and in late July – almost incredibly, especially in light of Marshall's strictures about the state of the roads – a 4-inch naval gun and two 12-pounders were lugged from Baghdad up to the Caspian.[15]

Shortly afterwards, Dunsterville obligingly reported that he and Bicherakov had decided that the situation at Baku was 'more favourable than had been represented', and there was a good chance of defending it, saving the oilfields and securing the fleet by using Bicherakov's force as a nucleus. But then he pointed out that the situation at Enzeli and Baku was 'most complex'; he was not eager to disturb the delicate stand-off with the Bolshevik Red Guards at Enzeli. This brought him in his turn a rap over the knuckles from the War Office – General Dunsterville seemed 'to be drifting into a policy of inactivity'. Crucially, Wilson dropped his ban on sending a force to Baku: if circumstances allowed 'officers or a small force' to be sent, the WO 'would be glad to see it done'.[16] Dunsterville went straight to Baghdad to discuss the situation with the C-in-C, but his proposal to send a mountain battery and 500 infantry to Urmia to help Baku by diverting Turkish troops from the Caucasus was vetoed on the ground that Dunsterforce was already too dispersed.

Urmia was another grim problem in the making: there the whole population of Assyrian Christians who had retreated from the Hakkari mountains in 1915 was under siege. 'The ruin of this small nation was already imminent', as Longrigg sombrely wrote, 'and was shortly to be consummated.' The Hakkari Assyrians had taken the 'rash and fatal decision' to respond to the early Russian advance by rising against the Turks; when the Russians retreated, the Assyrians were hunted out of their homeland by every Kurdish tribe of the region. The survivors escaped eastwards to join the smaller Assyrian community at Urmia, where the final Russian collapse left them dangerously exposed: 30,000 people with 10,000 fighters. Eventually the whole community, or what was left of it, decided to break out of Urmia and seek refuge with the British – a movement which 'ended inevitably in a routed, headlong and massacre-haunted straggle by the entire community through the mountains to Sayn Qal'a', and eventually to Hamadan. They were moved into Iraq and settled in a vast refugee camp on the Diyala.

While Dunsterville was in Baghdad, the small British detachment at Resht was attacked by a force of Jangalis. He arrived back at Kazvin on 24 July to find an even more scathing War Office telegram, suggesting that his cautious attitude to the Bolsheviks was allowing the situation to 'slip from our grasp'. He was peremptorily ordered to occupy Enzeli and 'eliminate Bolshevik influence' there, and also to send a mission to Krasnovodsk. Unsurprisingly, in the light of this and his long-standing aim of supporting Bicherakov at Baku, he decided to respond to the invitation of the Dictatorship by sending a small infantry force. By the time a party of the 1st/4th Hampshires under the command of Lieutenant-Colonel C. B. Stokes of Skinner's Horse arrived at Baku, Bicherakov had left the city, and Dunsterforce's main body, the 39th Brigade, was still strung out along the road from the railhead to Kazvin. When Stokes confirmed that there was a real chance of defending the city, they pushed on, and the first elements of 39th Brigade (150 men of the 7th North Staffordshires, with the Dunsterforce Armoured Car Brigade, and various specialist officers) crossed the Caspian on 6 August. Dunsterville himself followed on the 15th, with renewed orders to eliminate Bolshevik influence in Baku and, if the worst came to the worst, to destroy the oil resources 'by force if necessary'.

The British troops found themselves in a peculiar situation. Because of a shortage of many kinds of food – cheese, for instance, was prohibitively expensive – the troops were issued with caviare, which was plentiful and cheap. (They turned their noses up at it: 'the blackberry jam was fishy and hardly fit to be eaten'.) They were puzzled by the attitude of the locals. 'They really only showed a mild interest in their own and our efforts to save the town. Right to the very last, life in Baku was as usual, the place being full of gaiety, and the boulevards crowded in the evenings with thousands of young men who should have been out in the line fighting for their very existence.'

Baku's military forces, equally charming, were a traditional soldier's nightmare. The mutual antipathy between Britain and the Bolsheviks meant that the Red Guards, probably the most effective military force, were withdrawn as soon as the British arrived, and refused the Dictatorship's invitation to take part in the defence.[17] Bicherakov's force, which was the key to all Dunsterville's plans, never returned to the city. The Dictatorship's troops were fully revolutionised: 'the Russian and Armenian troops pay more attention to politics than to saving the town.' All units were run by their revolutionary committees, and all orders had to be debated.[18] 'There was no discipline amongst these men, and frequently whole units spent a day in the town, so that there were only 20 men left on a three-mile front. At night, very few patrols ever went out, and it was possible to walk for miles along the line without being challenged by a sentry.' Nobody knew how many troops were available. When one of the British battalions liaised with the commander of the 4th Armenian Brigade, he admitted that he had never visited his line, and 'did not know the units or numbers under his command. He stated that his reserves were in a place where we knew there were no troops at all, and when told he calmly invited us to lunch and said it didn't matter, as staff in town were responsible for reserves.'[19]

The defensive line was not only dangerously porous, but also badly sited. Instead of holding the neck of the Baku peninsula at a distance which could protect the city from artillery bombardment, the defences lay close to the city, allowing the besiegers to get all the way round to the eastern side. Fortunately, they were reluctant to shell the oilfields and reservoirs; but they hardly needed to. The defensive trenches were badly sited and constructed: 'Working parties of civilians were sent up to the line at night to dig trenches and put up barbed wire entanglements, but as they smoked and talked loudly the whole time, they were probably of more value to the enemy patrols than to us.' They took a dim view of the utility of barbed wire. There seemed to be plenty of artillery in the town, and the Dictatorship had an Inspector of Artillery, but he had little interest in using it. At one point, two 6-inch howitzers were found by a Dunsterforce officer in the arsenal, and taken to the front. With his assistance the local artillerymen began to register on the besiegers' positions. 'All went well until the enemy replied, when the gun teams promptly fled into town.'

With perhaps 4,000 local troops (who tended to melt away under fire in any case) for a seventeen-mile front, the 1,000 British infantry had no hope of holding Baku. The mystery was why the besiegers did not simply walk into town through one of the many gaps in the line. In fact the Dictatorship struck first, organising a 'grand attack' – advertised in the newspapers days beforehand – which made some progress but immediately collapsed under a Muslim counter-attack. On 26 August the Islam Army put in a determined assault on the 'Dirty Volcano' (*Griasni Vulkan*), the key point of the defensive line, held by 135 men of the North Staffords. As the British had feared, the local troops did not turn up. Two artillery batteries refused to open fire at all during the battle, as the Staffords wryly recorded, 'one because the Inspector of Artillery would not give permission, the other because its leader had gone into town on business!'

On 1 September, Dunsterville told the Dictatorship that the unreliability of the Baku forces made the fall of the city inevitable, and that he would have to withdraw his force. Their response was bitter: 'you have not rendered the aid which we were entitled to expect of you.' Indeed they declared that the British, by driving off the Bolsheviks without supplying the force to replace them, had actually reduced the defensive strength of Baku. Dunsterville, for his part, remained – like all the British – baffled by the utter unreadiness of the citizens to make a serious effort to defend their city. The Dunsterforce operation had ended in fiasco, and the skilfully managed retreat in three British-controlled ships was the most impressive episode of it. But this was scant consolation to the British regiments which had sacrificed men so pointlessly. The farce would become tragedy when Baku fell on 15 September, and the irregular forces pillaged and burned it. The entire population of the Armenian suburb was massacred; estimates of the numbers killed range from 9,000 to 30,000. 'The Moslems, for the first time since 1806, were again in control of Baku.'[20]

The question remains why Dunsterville did not even try to destroy the oil plant, pipeline or reservoirs, as he had repeatedly been ordered to. Marshall's memoirs sarcastically dismiss these orders (which he rather disingenuously implies arrived at the last minute) as unrealistic. 'I had never seen Baku, but I did know that it contained some 2,000 oil-wells, each about 500 feet deep and protected by ferro-concrete and asbestos coverings.' The quantity of high explosive needed to blow them up was a question he simply 'did not enter into'. He advanced psychological as well as practical objections: however little stomach the people of Baku had shown for fighting against the Turks, he thought it hard to 'imagine that they would have looked on, with their hands in their pockets, whilst a few British troops went about blowing their means of livelihood sky-high'.[21] Whether or not this argument is convincing, the bottom line is that the mission was not adequate to carry out one of its key tasks. Dunsterville himself, 'too much of a Don Quixote' in Marshall's view, who clearly found the Baku people as likeable as they were maddening, probably never even considered attempting it.

5. Victory

Whatever form of government might ultimately be established
in Mesopotamia, it was vital to its effective continuance that it
should cover the three wilayats of Basra, Baghdad and Mosul
A. T. WILSON

In the last weeks of the war, the Young Turk government
collapsed, and Charles Townshend suddenly re-emerged on the
world stage. He had been interned on Prinkipo island in the Sea
of Marmara (where the Paris peacemakers would, incidentally,
plan to meet the Bolsheviks for negotiations in January 1919).[1]
Fretting over his isolation, his stalled career, and his grocery
bills – he had to pay his own – Townshend began to see himself
as the man best placed to arrange peace terms between Britain
and Turkey. Since his surrender he had met many of the leading
Turkish military and political figures, and his opinion of them
had become very positive. On 12 October 1918 he heard that
Izzet Pasha, a man he got on well with, had become Grand Vizier
and Minister of War. He asked for a meeting, and offered to
act as a go-between. Indeed he clearly hoped to do more, since
he had already drawn up what he thought would be acceptable
terms. (He told Izzet that Britain might still accept the integrity
of the Ottoman state, including Syria and Mesopotamia, as long
as it became a confederation – the kind of terms favoured by the
de Bunsen committee in 1915.) The new Grand Vizier seemed
delighted and, as he returned to Prinkipo, Townshend 'reflected
how strangely I had been instrumental in accomplishing by
diplomacy the object I had been unable to accomplish when sent
with a handful of men to take Baghdad'.[2] He was shipped out
on a tugboat from Smyrna to the Greek island of Mytilene, and

from there a fast Navy launch took him to Admiral Calthorpe's headquarters at Mudros on Lemnos.

Townshend's intervention did not achieve his aim of securing good terms for the Turks. Not did it, as he all too obviously hoped, save his wrecked military career. But it did allow the British government to argue that, as the first of the Allies to be approached by the enemy, Britain should (according to an earlier inter-Allied agreement) conduct the armistice negotiations alone. The exclusion of the French was deliberate – Admiral Calthorpe cabled on 20 October that 'the effect of a fleet under French command going up to Constantinople would be deplorable' – and provocative. It did not take much to rouse French suspicion that Britain was planning to exclude them from the Middle East altogether.[3] The postwar outlook was stormy.

By the summer of 1918 the Mesopotamia campaign had really ground to a halt. Britain had built up a huge military force at huge expense, but the marginality of the theatre in military terms had become clearer than ever. The successful battle at Khan Baghdadi on 26 March showed that there had been improvements in command and organisation. The lavish provision of Ford vans made it possible to create motorised infantry companies – called 'Lewis gun detachments' – of 150 riflemen with 30 machine guns in 50 vans. These, and more energetic cavalry leadership than had been shown earlier in the campaign – notably the 11th Cavalry Brigade under Brigadier Robert Cassels at Khan Baghdadi – made it possible on this occasion to capture a whole defensive force before it could retreat. But the Turks were still able to escape on other occasions, and the fundamental difficulty of supply still prohibited anything like the full exertion of the army's power. The War Office's pre-war observation that if Britain wanted to fight Turkey, it would not do it up the Euphrates, remained as true as it had always been.

The campaign of the Egyptian Expeditionary Force under General Allenby was now demonstrating a far more effective route, and Allenby's victory in September 1918 landed a blow heavy enough to raise the possibility that the Turkish leadership might look for peace terms. Suddenly the end of the war was in sight – yet Mosul was not. Marshall was peremptorily urged to push on up both the rivers to maximise Britain's advantage, but as before had to insist that supply problems made such an ambitious strategy was unfeasible. He stuck to the Tigris, where Cobbe's corps pursued the surviving Turkish units through Fat-Ha, past the Little Zab river, before finally overwhelming them at Sharqat on 28 October.

But the final act of the campaign had decisive consequences. In the early hours of 2 November, General Marshall effectively ensured that the Mosul *vilayet* would become part of Iraq. The Mudros Armistice specified that all hostilities would cease at noon on 31 October. At that moment, the leading British troops, Cassels's brigade, were at Quaiyara. By the time their commander was officially informed of the armistice in the late evening of 1 November, they had advanced to Hammam Ali. That afternoon he received a letter from the commander of the Ottoman 5th Division asking him to take them back to the point they had occupied when the armistice came into effect, but at midnight he received an order from Marshall to advance to Mosul. Leachman went straight to Mosul next day to tell the corps commander, Ali Ihsan, that Cassels was advancing and that he should retire five miles back from Mosul, leaving only enough guards to maintain order in the city. Ali Ihsan politely refused, though he indicated that he would not actually fire on British troops, and suggested that they take up positions just outside Mosul. Cassels agreed to this, but Marshall told him that he had been ordered to occupy Mosul, and that the armistice required the surrender of all garrisons in Mesopotamia. Ali Ihsan countered that his force was not a garrison but a field army, and, more importantly, that Mosul was not in Mesopotamia. The first contention was a verbal quibble, but the second went to the heart of a vital political question. Could Mosul be said to be part of Iraq?

Marshall overrode this complicated issue with soldierly simplicity by blankly refusing to listen to Ali Ihsan's objections. His army's arrival in Mosul did not settle the question altogether; after all, the Sykes–Picot agreement put the city in the French sphere, and the 'politicals' were acutely conscious that the *vilayet* was a largely Kurdish area. But Marshall's unilateral action proved ultimately irreversible. Longrigg suggested that his 'resolute attitude' was decisive in making Mosul a de facto part of Iraq: if an armistice line had been accepted that included it and its fringe of Kurdish districts in Turkish territory, 'these would form part today of Turkey and not of Iraq'.[4] Of course, as Marshall made clear to Cassels, the decision was not his: his orders from London were unambiguous.

Oil has often been said to have been the main British motive. It never figured in Marshall's instructions, however, and had only just come on to the Cabinet's horizon at the end of the war. Not until the Cabinet discussed a paper on 'The Petroleum Situation in the British Empire', prepared by Admiral Sir Edmond Slade (himself a major shareholder in APOC), at the end of July 1918, did the Cabinet Secretary, Maurice Hankey, start thinking about whether the retention of the Mesopotamia oilfields should be ranked as a 'First Class War Aim'. Slade argued that 'the Power that controls the oil lands of Persia and Mesopotamia will control the source of supply of the liquid fuel of the future'. If these sources were 'interfered with', Britain's grip on the Middle East would be weakened, and 'the effect on our position in the East would be nothing short of disastrous'.[5] The highly knowledgeable Cabinet Secretary had at this point a fairly hazy knowledge of Mesopotamia's oil resources. 'I am told there are some as far up as Mosul,' he wrote on 30 July. Strategically, the Chiefs of Staff had written Mesopotamia off as a 'dead end' since the new threat of penetration to the East through the Caucasus, Caspian and Turkestan had opened up. But Hankey now thought that the acquisition of oil-bearing territory might 'make it worthwhile to push on in Mesopotamia'. He proposed that 'before we come to discuss peace we should obtain possession of all the oil-bearing regions in Mesopotamia and Southern Persia, wherever they may be'.[6] Foreign Secretary Balfour, anticipating the American line on this, archly suggested that it would be seen as 'purely an imperialist war aim'. Hankey replied that this did not shock him, though he agreed that 'it would shock President Wilson and some of our Allies'. But he posed the question – if Mesopotamia was not to be under Turkish control, then whose? To that, he suggested, there was only one possible answer.

Britain was determined to hold on to Mesopotamia, but could still not find the political energy to work out how to do it. The meeting between Cox and the Eastern Committee in April 1918 showed how dangerously British policy was drifting in the last year of the war. Cox came away with the impression that the committee had sanctioned his policy, while the committee (like its predecessors) had actually failed to agree any clear policy line. Impending disaster in France at the time of the meeting may explain this in part. The German spring offensive had opened a month earlier and came close to breaking through and rolling up the Western Front. But even after the threat of German victory ebbed, no decisions were reached. The Cabinet's official advisers, particularly at the Foreign Office, wanted to avoid commitment to any line in advance of a general postwar settlement. When Cox's deputy, Arnold Wilson, tried to revive the idea of a special commission on Mesopotamia, the Foreign Office protested that the issues involved – not just administrative methods, but the question of political status and structure – were too complicated. Any attempt to sort them out now would simply have to be done all over again at the end of the war. So policy went on drifting, and if anything became more directionless when Cox was transferred to Teheran in September 1918 to steady the wobbly relationship between Britain and Persia and negotiate the Anglo-Persian treaty which Curzon so fervently wanted. Curzon believed that Cox was the only man who could do this, and he probably was – but whether it was worth doing is more questionable, and the price was high. The move was supposed to be temporary, but in the event he was out of Mesopotamia for two and a half years. Crucially, no successor was appointed; Wilson as Officiating Civil Commissioner was left in effective control of policy on the ground. Yet London seems not yet to have grasped how far Wilson's ideas diverged from the government's.

An investigative commission might have brought things into focus, but though the idea hovered in the background until the end of the war, the arguments for delay always triumphed. Only one attempt at a comprehensive assessment of the situation was ever made. Just after the armistice, the War Office commissioned the former Governor of the United Provinces, Sir John Hewett, to report on proposed plans for the development of irrigation and agriculture in Mesopotamia. Taking along six technical experts, he toured the country in the first three months of 1919. His report could have become the basis for a development plan, but he was only tasked to assess 'whether expenditure charged ultimately against Imperial Army funds is being duly confined to such services as are presently necessary for the prosecution of the war' – in other words, ensure that the Army was not paying for postwar reconstruction. Hewett concluded that there was no ground for the suggestion that military expenditure had been 'prompted by the desire to provide for after-peace developments'. Yet he held that the civil administration should foot the bill of £2 million – not including the cost of railways – for military works such as power plants.

Wilson, whose objection to accepting such a big debt for works which he thought were not essential for postwar needs was 'summarily, even scornfully dismissed', reacted to the Hewett investigation with a mixture of incredulity and anger. Hewett's mission underlined the confusion of agencies operating in Iraq. He was 'reporting to the Army Council', Wilson emphasised, and not the India Office, and was not asked to investigate 'broader aspects of the future administration of the country', though he was quite qualified to do so. He never discussed such issues with

Wilson; instead he bemused the Civil Commissioner by giving a lecture in Baghdad to the civil administration, many of whom were also Indian civil servants, 'in a strain so pessimistic and so frankly hostile to the terms of the Government of India Bill' (then passing through parliament) that most of his listeners believed that the Indian service was 'doomed to early extinction'. When they heard this, many of them applied to stay with the Mesopotamia administration. This was useful for Wilson, but otherwise the Hewett inquiry produced nothing. After it was published by the Stationery Office in December 1919, Hewett went on to publish *Some Impressions About Mesopotamia in 1919*, again at public expense, which Wilson found 'inexplicable'. Hewett advised that 'If Mesopotamia is to take the place it ought to in such enterprises as cotton cultivation, the manufacture of beet sugar, and sheep breeding, the impetus will have to come from the white man.'[7] Since Hewett's views ran counter to those of Churchill and the government, as well as the Chief of the General Staff, Wilson thought this demonstrated 'the extent to which the disorganization of the machinery of Government in Whitehall had proceeded'.[8]

The worrying lack of joined-up thinking could be seen in another, far more dramatic intervention from London. Just after the end of the war with Turkey, on 7 November, Britain and France issued a declaration demonstrating their commitment to the doctrine of self-determination. This document should be better known than it is. At a terse eighteen lines, it was far more concise and clear than the notorious documents so often cited as evidence of British perfidy – the Hussein–McMahon correspondence and the Sykes–Picot Agreement; and certainly much less ambiguous than the Balfour Declaration. It committed the Allies to 'the complete and definite emancipation of the peoples so long oppressed by the Turks', and the establishment of 'national governments and administrations deriving their authority from the initiative and free choice of the indigenous populations'. The words 'liberation', 'local initiative' and 'free choice' echoed down through its three short paragraphs. More than this, the Allies pledged that they would recognise 'indigenous governments . . . as soon as they are established'. Although they threw in terms intended to hedge these commitments – specifying the need for Allied 'support' and 'adequate assistance' – these were much less clear.[9] Arabs certainly did not notice them.

Sykes and Picot had been experimenting with phrases intended to say that only those Arab territories liberated by their inhabitants themselves could expect the sort of independence offered in the Hussein–McMahon negotiations. Those liberated by Allied military action would have a form of government based on consent, but under Allied supervision until they were capable of full self-government. The trouble was that the test of liberation by the inhabitants' own efforts was difficult to apply. Sykes pushed for an unmodified declaration of non-annexation, but this was impossible to sell to the French. The complicated arrangements for the administration of 'occupied' Syria were as hard to sell to the Arabs and America. The 1918 declaration, drafted by Sykes, was clearly intended to head off their suspicions. Its final wording was hammered out by the Eastern Committee on 16–17 October 1918. Curzon wanted it to mention only Syria, but Cecil pointed out that the French would never agree to this, so 'Syria and Mesopotamia' were jointly specified.

6. Self-Determination?

> The attempts which have already been made in Mesopotamia
> to arrive at any clear statement of the wishes of the people have
> only resulted in a chaos of conflicting opinions, largely influenced
> by religious propaganda.
> HUBERT YOUNG

> If Iraq-al-Jazira were really an island somewhere in mid-Pacific,
> then Colonel Wilson's constitution might do, for a time. But it is
> unfortunately in the middle of a continent.
> SIR ARTHUR HIRTZEL

By the time the Anglo-French Declaration was issued on 7 November, the war with Turkey was over. So, unlike the Balfour Declaration, and indeed the McMahon commitments, it could not be explained as a bid for support in winning the war. Its rationale is still hard to grasp. For the administrators in Iraq, it was a bombshell. It had done 'an immense amount of harm', Gertrude Bell protested: stirring up public discussion and 'a great number of windy theories'.[1] Arnold Wilson later condemned it as a 'disastrous error'. At the time, he minced his words a little more carefully: it 'bids fair to involve us in difficulties as great as Sir Henry McMahon's early assurances to the Sharif of Mecca', and 'involves us in diplomatic insincerities which we have so far successfully avoided'. This was hardly an overstatement. Some of Wilson's arguments were more doubtful, though. He held that Mesopotamia was almost entirely disconnected from 'Arabia', and that 'the Arabs of Mesopotamia will not tolerate that foreign Arabs should have any say in their affairs'. He maintained that he and his staff had been led to believe that the government favoured a Mesopotamian regime akin to Lord Cromer's veiled protectorate in Egypt; this would certainly have

440

surprised those who saw Cromer's methods as the main reason for the breakdown of Anglo-Egyptian relations, which were about to reach a terrible crisis in 1919.

Just as dubious, in the postwar context, was his dogged conviction that Britain must stay true to its civilising mission. 'I can confidently declare that the country as a whole neither expects nor desires any such sweeping scheme of independence as is adumbrated in the Anglo-French Declaration.' The average Arab, 'as opposed to the handful of amateur politicians in Baghdad', saw the future as one of 'fair dealing and material and moral progress under the aegis of Great Britain'. Arabs would learn more quickly than Indians, but still needed to catch up with them in education and experience. The Arabs accepted the British occupation, and the non-Muslim element (Jews and Christians) 'clings to it as the tardy fulfilment of the hopes of many generations'. The world at large, he believed, 'recognizes that it is our duty and our high privilege to establish an effective protectorate'. The country, which in spite of centuries of neglect was 'still the ganglion of the Middle East', must be developed. Self-determination was a dangerous illusion. 'If we allow ourselves to be diverted by political catch-words, our soldiers will have fought and died in vain and the treasure we have lavished in this country will in the eyes of the world and of peoples of the Middle East have been wasted.'[2]

Politely sidestepping Wilson's vehement manifesto, the India Secretary at last produced, in February 1919, a definition of 'our objective' in Iraq. 'A flexible constitution, giving full play to the different elements of the population, and recognizing and incorporating local peculiarities and distinctions', intended to 'provide for Arab participation as time goes on in the actual government and administration of the country'. This gradualism, and the vagueness of its timetabling, chimed with Wilson's view. But would it actually achieve the government's central objective of 'preventing Arab nationalism from being drawn into opposition to British control'? Wilson thought so. The government had asked him in late 1918 to provide 'an authoritative statement of the views held by the local populace' on (1) whether they favoured a single Arab state under British tutelage stretching from the northern boundary of the Mosul *vilayet* to the Persian Gulf; (2) if so, should 'a titular Arab head be placed over this new state?'; (3) and if so, who? The resulting report, written by Gertrude Bell (under the title 'Self-Determination in Mesopotamia'), had just been finished. It suggested that – at least until the Anglo-French Declaration – the people 'had taken it for granted that the country would remain under direct British control, and were as a whole content to accept the decision of arms'.

Bell found that 'as regards the Iraq tribes there can be no doubt that the policy of the British Administration has met with approval'. They had no interest in a pan-Arab state, preferring some kind of transitional arrangement under the universally respected Percy Cox. In the holy city of Najaf, a gathering of divines and sheikhs was 'unanimously in favour of the continuance of British protection'. But in Karbala the 'Persian priesthood' ('all born and bred in political obstruction', as Bell privately told Hirtzel) had issued a *fatwa* 'to the effect that any person who desired other than a Muhammadan Government was an infidel'; and in Khadimain the *ulema* 'threatened with excommunication and exclusion from the mosque anyone who voted for British occupation'. This rumbling of the 'less stable and more fanatical elements' in Mesopotamia reached a climax a few days later in Baghdad itself.[3] Outside these centres of agitation, though, the British remained convinced that, as in Basra, 'the Arab distrusts himself and his fellow countryman [and] feels that he needs the driving power of a non-Arab race to keep his country moving onward to prosperity'. It was 'a curious commentary on "self-determination" that the Arab seems to want it least of anybody!'[4]

Wilson and Bell still saw more or less eye to eye, and they travelled to the Paris peace conference to meet Lloyd George, Balfour and Montagu, as well as Henry Wilson. One key figure was missing, though: on 16 February 1919, Mark Sykes died in his room at the Hotel Lotti – one of the twenty million killed by the influenza that was sweeping the world in the winter of 1918–19. The sudden removal of perhaps the most powerful single influence on British policy at such a critical moment was a fateful event. In his last talk with Lloyd George, Sykes apparently admitted that his compromises with the French had been a serious error.[5] How his mind was now turning cannot even be guessed, but without him British policy was more likely than ever to lose direction. In Paris, 'experts on Western Arabia both military and civil were there in force', but apart from Bell none had any direct knowledge of Iraq or the Najd, or indeed Persia. Wilson was alarmed to find that 'the very existence of a Shia majority in Iraq was blandly denied as a figment of my imagination by one "expert" with an international reputation'. Wilson and Bell could not convince either the War Office or Foreign Office delegations that the Kurds in the Mosul area 'were numerous and likely to be troublesome', or that Ibn Saud was a power to be reckoned with, or indeed that any problems 'could not be disposed of on the lines advocated for Syria by the enthusiasts of the Arab Bureau'.[6] Wilson could see that the CIGS was worried whether enough troops could be found for the 'interregnum' in Mesopotamia, but other members of the military delegation were distinctly optimistic. They pressed Wilson 'to extend the boundaries of the future Arab state of Iraq to include not only Dair-es-Zor' – already occupied on Wilson's own initiative – but also 'the whole of the area east of the Euphrates as far north as Birejik, and including Diyarbakr, Urfa, Nisibin, and Jazirat-ibn-Umar'.

Wilson went on to London for a meeting with Curzon. The Eastern Committee endorsed his plan for the structure of Iraq – consisting of four provinces (Basra, Baghdad, Euphrates and Mosul), or five if Kurdistan was to be given 'separate status'. The country would be run by Cox as High Commissioner, and the process of political participation would begin with local councils – at both provincial and divisional level. But Wilson was gloomy; even an audience with the King, who expressed his 'confidence in the progressive spirit of the inhabitants' of Mesopotamia, did not lift his mood. He thought it 'ominous' that the Cabinet committee's written approval of his constitutional plan distinguished between 'Iraq proper' and 'the Arab province of Mosul', and obvious that, whatever Curzon said, the government's international manoeuvres took precedence over setting a clear policy line in Mesopotamia.

Though Lloyd George had already done a deal with Clemenceau at the beginning of December, detaching Mosul from the French sphere, the government went to remarkable lengths to disguise its policy on the ground – even going as far as banning the use of the Baghdad postage stamps, labelled 'Iraq in British Occupation', in Mosul. It never publicly approved Marshall's action in securing Mosul. And it temporised over Wilson's argument that Cox's immediate return to Baghdad was vital. The Lloyd George–Clemenceau deal meant that the Cabinet would 'back Faisal and the Arabs as far as we can up to the point of not alienating the French', and that point came very quickly. Early in 1919 France drew up a dossier of evidence for the 'unfriendly attitude towards French interests' of local British authorities in Mesopotamia as well as Syria. At Mosul, for instance, 'the insults put by Colonel Leachman on French-speaking natives are too numerous to relate'. French agents had been prevented from carrying out official missions; for two months, 'the British authorities obstinately refused to allow our consul at Basra to proceed to Mosul to distribute among the poor in the name of France the money sent to him for that purpose'. The British General Staff in Mesopotamia was accused of refusing to recognise French rights in Mosul, and not merely stopping anything which could 'contribute to giving the populations an accurate idea of France', but actively spreading propaganda 'to make the native populations despise and hate France'.[7] The spat blew up at summit level in Paris, with a ferocious clash in the presence of Woodrow Wilson on 20 March 1919. President

Wilson proposed a commission to investigate public opinion in Syria and Mesopotamia, but this was boycotted by France, and Lloyd George decided to follow the French line. In the end, the American commissioners, King and Crane, went to Syria, but not on to Mesopotamia.

The Versailles conference did, at long last, create a formula for the postwar political status of Mesopotamia. Britain would exercise a mandate under the auspices (and perhaps the authority, though this was less clear) of the new League of Nations. What this would mean in practice nobody knew: no concrete steps to implement the concept would be taken for at least a year, until a special League of Nations congress convened to decide the issue. So the whole political question in fact remained frozen – and the repeated demands from Baghdad for some definite declaration that could reassure the people still went unanswered. Despite the deal with the French over Mosul, the Foreign Office continued to meet all proposals connected with the future administration of Iraq with a '*non possumus* attitude'.[8]

It remains, as one historian has said, 'almost incredible' that two years should have elapsed between the Mudros armistice and the installation of Cox in Baghdad in the autumn of 1920, with 'virtual carte blanche to try to save the situation'.[9] The 'seemingly interminable wranglings and procrastinations' were fatal. While policy was on hold, an Iraqi national movement emerged which sharply curtailed Britain's options. Why was it so hard to move policy forward? In theory – or so Hirtzel thought – the essence of British policy had been fixed immediately after the capture of Baghdad. But somehow others did not grasp this. Wilson's approach still found strong support even within the India Office. When Wilson urged, after the Anglo-French Declaration, that Mesopotamia become a British protectorate, John Shuckburgh, then an Assistant Undersecretary at the India Office, thought it was 'clear that the enlightened and progressive Arab in whom the enthusiasts ask us to believe is a mere fiction as far as Mesopotamia is concerned'. Such 'progressive elements'

445

as there were consisted of Jews and Christians, not Arabs; and it would be 'a poor kind of self-determination that places such people at the mercy of an uncontrolled Arab administration'. Ten months later he still held to the Wilsonian line, asking 'how can the local population settle down when we won't tell them what we are going to do? Colonel Wilson is bound to act on the assumption that we intend to go on governing Mesopotamia. We must either govern Mesopotamia or not govern it.'[10]

This showed just how badly Britain had failed to establish a clear policy line. An exasperated Hirtzel fumed, 'I thought everyone knew that we were not going to "govern" Mesopotamia in the sense in which I understand Mr Shuckburgh to use that word.' But he could only express bafflement that even though Wilson 'has been here and seen and heard for himself', he still 'does not seem to comprehend the fact'. Three months later, Shuckburgh held to the same line, bluntly declaring that 'on the <u>merits</u> – apart from pledges and other considerations – I believe Colonel Wilson to be right'. In other words, 'the policy he advocates would conduce more to the good government and prosperity of Mesopotamia than that which we may feel ourselves bound to adopt'. Reflecting on Morley's aphorism that politics was 'the science of the second best', Shuckburgh confessed 'sympathy with Wilson's hankering after the "first best"'. Few men, he thought, 'can have worked harder for it'. Yet again Hirtzel had to hammer home the point that, even if they might sympathise with Wilson's commitment to 'efficient administration, as efficiency is understood by Anglo-Saxons', they now had to 'grasp the fact that this is not an administrative but a political question'.[11]

To reduce Wilson's sense of duty to mere administrative efficiency was to do him an injustice: it was a political, indeed ideological question for him too. 'Efficiency' stood for a particular vision of imperial authority and responsibility. It was thoughtfully examined by Gilbert Clayton – perhaps the ultimate 'Cairene' – in a letter to Gertrude Bell in mid-1919. 'I hope that the British hand in Mesopotamia will be a light one to start with, even at the cost of some efficiency, and that local national aspirations will not be too ruthlessly snubbed.' For Clayton there was a key warning: 'the lesson of the first forty years in Egypt stares us in the face.' (In March 1919 Egypt had exploded into mass rebellion against Cromer-style control.) 'I fear that catchword "British Efficiency",' he added. If Britain had 'a charter for the rule of decadent Oriental peoples', it was 'not primarily "efficiency", but "honesty and sympathy"'. Waxing still more philosophical, he told her that 'the White Man's Burden requires never failing patience and understanding with but little hope of individual achievement. The ruined civilizations of the East cannot be revived in a generation.'[12]

Clayton's recipe echoed with Bell's own: 'we should start slowly and let the people come to us for help and guidance.' But the Anglo-French declaration had dropped a bomb into that leisurely timetable. What if the people wanted more than guidance? What if they wanted self-government, and now? Edwin Montagu reflected that he would not himself 'submit to foreign administration even if it assured me "good government and prosperity"'. Montagu believed that the 'November 1918 policy' was 'the only one to succeed in the long run'. But could it be implemented by a Civil Commissioner who believed that the Cabinet had approved his own very different policy? Wilson simply went ahead with the creation of his Iraqi constitution. He never tried to disguise his belief that (as he wrote in July 1919) 'to install a real Arab government in Mesopotamia is impossible, and if we attempt it, we shall abandon the Middle East to anarchy'. Or, as he repeated in November, the immediate introduction of Arab government would produce 'the antithesis of a democratic Government'. London was equally consistent in saying that Wilson's constitution did not deliver on the undertakings given in the Anglo-French Declaration.

The Wilsonian direction of Iraqi government became ever clearer. Arabs barely figured in the central administration, while locally they were still co-opted as auxiliaries rather than raised as national forces against the Turks. In the last phase of the war, Harold Dickson was busy creating 'Muntafik Guards' to police his district, between Suk-es-Shuyukh and Shatra. In February 1918 he was recruiting steadily – he reported that since he had brought in the Indian '*silladar*' system, he had a waiting list of sixty names. 'The idea of making them deposit a sum of money in advance strangely enough appeals to them.' But the use of the Indian system spoke volumes about the underlying logic of the force. It was 'slowly worked up' in the spring, with two squadrons formed and one forming in April. With a strength of nearly 200, and a target strength of 300, Dickson declared triumphantly that he would soon have 'the first Arab Cavalry Regiment in Mesopotamia'. He was proving that 'Arabs can be turned into a decently drilled lot.' Still, the military authorities remained unsupportive: he complained repeatedly that his requests for vital kit like belts, boots, socks, bandoliers, pouches and slings, as well as rifles, were ignored. He blamed this for a distinct falling-away in recruitment: in the autumn, the Muntafik Horse stuck at 240, well short of its authorised strength of 400. He faced a struggle to convince some of the locals, 'marsh men of the wildest type, who in their own homes go about almost naked', to accept his new style of uniform, a short 'Kurta' instead of the old 'Dugla', a Cossack-style ankle-length coat: 'they not only refuse to accept the Kurta but hold it a positive disgrace and "aib" to show their legs.' Desertions were increasing, not all, he admitted, due to the influenza epidemic. There was a bigger underlying problem too. After the armistice, there was once again 'a tendency to think the Turks will return, and Iraq will be given back to them'.[13]

The stand-off between London and Baghdad was particularly damaging in the case of the Iraqi officers in Faisal's Arab Northern Army, now at Damascus. Many of the Iraqis who had joined the Arab Revolt had become significant figures, and their importance was still growing: men such as Jaafar Pasha and Nuri al-Said (who had become Faisal's right-hand man, and would later be a long-serving prime minister of Iraq). The group of officers in Syria was the nearest thing to a nationalist 'intelligentsia' that Iraq possessed. As early as January 1919 some of them requested permission to return to Iraq. The British authorities temporised, and in June, Faisal directly asked Field Marshal Allenby, now High Commissioner in Egypt, to approve this. The Foreign Office told the India Office that no further delay was possible, and the officers must be allowed to go back home. But it had to accept that each case should be vetted (for security reasons) by the Civil Commissioner. Wilson rejected all the applications. London was dismayed: Hirtzel thought that the officers were 'probably the best thing that Mesopotamia has produced yet'; many of them were 'well-educated men with western ideas'. Whatever might be thought of their pan-Arab aspirations, 'it is probably not an exaggeration to say that the success of our regime in Mesopotamia depends upon our finding a proper sphere for these men'.

These were sage words, but they had no effect. T. E. Lawrence was aghast. He told Curzon that his ambition was 'that the Arabs should be our first brown dominion, and not our last brown colony', insisting that 'the future of Mesopotamia is so immense that if it is cordially ours we can swing the whole Middle East with it'. He fumed that the officers were 'all the men in Mesopotamia who had the courage to fight for their country', but now they were 'apparently going to be driven into opposition to our administration there'. It was curious 'that men useful (indeed necessary) to Allenby in Syria should be "spreaders of undesirable propaganda" in Mesopotamia'. Hubert Young, too, protested, 'it is lamentable that those very officers with whom Colonel Lawrence, Colonel Joyce and myself lived in the closest possible touch, and who looked to the British Government as the mainstay of their revolt against the Turk, should be touring their own country in disguise [as a July 1919 Baghdad police report noted] with the object of obtaining signatures to anti-British manifestos.' Young's conclusion was indeed ominous – 'there is something very wrong somewhere'.[14]

Nobody doubted where that was. But Hirtzel still did no more than gently chide Wilson, 'As regards Arab nationalism, I think you will find yourself in pretty deep water, and to be frank I do not feel that you are going the right way to work with it', he wrote in July. 'You appear to be trying, impossibly, to stem the tide, instead of guide it into the channel that would suit you best.' He struggled to get his junior to accept the new order of things. 'You are going to have an Arab state whether you like it or not, whether Mesopotamia wants it or not.' It was 'no use to shut one's eyes to the main facts. We must adapt ourselves and our methods to the new order of ideas and find a different way of getting what we want.' A couple of months later he urged that 'we must swim with the tide which is set towards the education and not towards the government of what used to be called subject peoples. They won't have good drains of course', he sardonically added, 'but the drains of India are nothing to boast of.' Early the following year, he was still plugging away: 'I should like to put it to you – have you ever considered the possibility of having to clear out?' Public opposition to the Mesopotamia commitment was growing, and 'what we ought to have been creating in this time is some administration of Arab institutions which we can safely leave while pulling the strings ourselves ... Don't tell me that it is not what the people want, that it will reduce the administration to chaos, etc, etc, I know all that. But put it to yourself that it may be that or nothing.'[15]

For the Arab nationalists, conclusive proof of Wilson's hostility came with the case of Naji Suwaidi. Wilson had met some of the leading members of the Iraqi Ahd group – an offshoot of the original organisation, dedicated to creating a separate state in Iraq – in Damascus on his way back from London in May 1919. At that point he admitted, according to Nuri al-Said, that the lack of Arabs in the Baghdad administration was a problem, and agreed to take one or two of the Syrian officers on. Naji, a member of an important Baghdadi family, and currently the Acting Governor of Aleppo, was the first to be sent. He had graduated as a lawyer in Constantinople before the war, and held governorships under the Ottoman state before joining the Arab Revolt. When he arrived in Baghdad in June he was offered the post of Adviser to either the Judicial Secretary or the Military Governor, and took the second. He was asked to study a proposal for a new municipal council, and immediately produced a revised version – in which the council would be elected rather than appointed, and would have no British members except technical specialists, the Officer of Health and the Municipal Engineer. Within a week he decided that his scheme had no chance of acceptance, and resigned.

Once again Hirtzel lectured Wilson – 'you are going to have a lot of people whose heads will be full of absurd ideas from Syria and heaven knows where; and a room and a use must be found for them, and when you have got them in you must not let them resign.' The Foreign Office used Naji's brief appointment to demonstrate the 'desire of H.M. Government to offer Arabs of proved character and ability full scope for the exercise of their talents'. Just what had gone wrong remained uncertain. Even Gertrude Bell thought that Naji had been too impatient, and dismissed the British plans for the council 'without giving himself time to weigh them thoroughly'. Wilson produced a more damaging criticism. Naji, he suggested, had 'seen enough of the Baghdad municipality to make him realise that the duties devolving on him would be much more arduous than at Aleppo, and would involve more time and energy than he was prepared to devote to them'. The barely veiled insinuation was that British administration was far more strenuous and effective than Arab, and that Arabs like Naji were either impractical or lazy – probably both.[16]

It is obvious, in hindsight, that Wilson should have been recalled. But even though Lawrence tried to make this a condition of using his influence to persuade Faisal to compromise with the French, it seems to have been out of the question.[17] The only way forward was to get Cox back from Persia to Mesopotamia as soon as possible. Gertrude Bell fretted, 'I wish the Government would let him come back here at once. The job here is far more important than Persia.' Yet nothing was done. Although Hirtzel could see that this was 'becoming a matter of urgent necessity' in mid-1919, another whole year would pass before Cox's return. Part of the problem was that Cox refused to go back to the civil–military rivalry he had left. He insisted on being appointed High Commissioner with full powers, but military government could not be wound up until the final political settlement was reached. In any case, though, Cox remained more sympathetic to Wilson's view than London, or even Gertrude Bell, grasped. Asked for his view in November 1919, he rather blandly suggested that as far as he could see, most of the people of Mesopotamia were satisfied with the situation. Curzon grumbled that Cox was 'out of touch both with us and with Mesopotamia'. But the government seems to have been paralysed; the policy impasse went on.

7. Retrenchment

Few here are interested in Mesopotamia for its own sake. The
supreme aim now is economy.
SIR ARTHUR HIRTZEL

The end of the war left Mesopotamia in a kind of limbo. After the
Mudros armistice political initiative was stymied by the delay in
reaching a final peace settlement with Turkey. But the British public
expected all troops to be brought home immediately, a demand
reinforced by the queasy realisation of Britain's catastrophic
financial weakness. Only now did people wake up to the scale
of the commitment in a place whose magical image had been
undermined by ugly reality. Winston Churchill, the Secretary of
State for War, publicly condemned the 'vicious system' in which
'a score of mud villages, sandwiched in between a swampy river
and a blistering desert, inhabited by a few hundred half naked
families, usually starving, are now occupied . . . and are likely to
remain occupied in the future unless policy is changed, by Anglo-
Indian garrisons on a scale which in India would maintain order
in wealthy provinces of millions of people'. Less colourfully, he
told Lloyd George that he was 'immensely concerned' at the cost
of Mesopotamia, which would be at least £25 million in the
current year – far exceeding 'any return that can be secured for
many years from the province'.

The Mesopotamia garrison was indeed phenomenally expensive.
The legacy of MacMunn's great logistic system was a massive
over-provision of material throughout the command. After
the war, when Marshall was succeeded as commander-in-chief
by MacMunn himself, not much changed. (The next C-in-C,
Aylmer Haldane, described this period as 'wildly extravagant',

453

though he also charged critics with failing to grasp the issue of waging war in a country so totally lacking in the resources needed for a modern army.[1]) But in London, the traditional idea that the empire should be self-financing inevitably re-emerged. In August 1919 *The Times* started to castigate the 'squandering' of taxpayers' money in Mesopotamia – 'we read of thousands of tons of forage rotting on the wharves of Basra . . . roads made at the incredible outlay of £18,000 per mile . . . ' Lamenting that 'we ever went beyond Kurna', the newspaper predicted that because Mesopotamia had no natural defensive frontier, Britain would be forced to maintain a 'very substantial' garrison.[2] Next month it ran a series of articles by Sir George Buchanan, with (predictably) lurid headlines like 'An Orgy of Waste'.

Early in September 'the good Proemial himself began to get at me', as MacMunn put it. ('Proemial' was the War Secretary's telegraphic address.) Churchill tersely reminded the C-in-C that he had 25,000 British and 81,000 Indian troops, 18,000 local levies, with 130,000 followers and 24,000 labourers – a total of 278,000. He ordered him to reduce these immediately to the General Staff estimate of at most 16,000 British and 49,000 Indian troops. 'There can be absolutely no question of holding the present enormous forces at your disposal . . . I would remind you that under the Turks Mesopotamia not only paid its way but supplied a revenue to the central government.' Later that month he reiterated that even the reduced garrison MacMunn proposed would 'crush the province with military charges and ruin its future development'. On these terms, it would become questionable whether Britain could even hold on to the country. The C-in-C must therefore 'prepare as soon as possible a scheme for creating a special military and police instrument for maintaining internal order in Mesopotamia'. As usual, Churchill had plenty of ideas for how this should be done – 'a strong armed white police force and a small military garrison operating with light cars and motor launches carrying machine guns, in combination with aeroplanes, the whole controlling and animating a native gendarmerie'. Ramming his point home, he added, 'you will not have solved the problem unless you can devise some scheme of this kind'.[3]

MacMunn dug his heels in. 'Perhaps' by the end of 1920, he thought, but more likely not until 1921, the garrison could be reduced to one division and one cavalry brigade at Baghdad, with another mixed brigade at Mosul (as well, inevitably, as 'L of C' troops in lower Mesopotamia).[4] He complained that the task of holding Mesopotamia was 'immensely complicated by every sort of anti-British intrigue', stimulated by the postponement of the political settlement and the 'limits of the Fourteen Points'. No fewer than twenty battalions had been in action against local rebellions since June. Serious force reductions would only be possible if the railway construction programme was completed, and there was an uninterrupted line from Basra to Kirkuk. MacMunn also fended off Buchanan's allegations by taking a swipe at Buchanan's own technical competence, adding that he had 'a gift of producing intense irritation', and pointing out that people had been annoyed by his 'huge salary' of 6,000 rupees a month.

Faced with this resistance, Churchill pressed for further reductions, to at most 6 British and 25 Indian battalions, and then '4,000 white and 16,000 native troops'. At this last figure, even the War Office rebelled, the Director of Military Operations protesting that it would 'in the end prove not an economy but the reverse'. But Churchill went further still, writing in March 1920, 'my own ideas are that two or three thousand white troops and six or seven thousand native troops is all that we are likely to require'. But by this time he had – not for the first time in his life – come up with a novel idea: 'air substitution'. Churchill had a double appointment as Secretary of State for War and Air. Some exponents of air power worried that this would jeopardise the independence of the new Royal Air Force, but he took both roles seriously. He must have heard, the previous year, of Lord French's idea of using aircraft systematically to police Ireland (though it had proved impossible to implement). Soon after his appointment he asked Arnold Wilson to produce a report on the role of aircraft in Mesopotamia. Wilson's assessment was radical. After a sticky start during the war, military aviation was coming of age. Now that more sophisticated aircraft and techniques were available, they could deliver maximum effect for minimum cost. Crucially, Wilson saw them as more than an auxiliary military arm. Noting (inevitably perhaps) that 'the Government of India has not adequately appreciated the very great practical and moral value of aeroplanes', he asserted that the RAF could help the civil power to maintain order in Mesopotamia 'without the intervention of troops'. Aircraft should be able 'to do for us on land in the Middle East what the Navy have done for us in the Persian Gulf in the past'.[5]

Over the next couple of years, this would evolve into a revolutionary concept of 'air policing' which would simultaneously provide the RAF with a major imperial role (so protecting it from the jealousy of the older services), and keep the Empire viable.[6] Above all, it would resolve the question whether Britain could hold on to Mesopotamia/Iraq, where it offered an almost miraculous release from the crushing burdens of climate and communications. Churchill put this seductively as he laid out the prospect of 'a series of defended areas in which air bases could be securely established'. In these bases 'strong aerial forces could be maintained in safety and efficiency'. They could 'operate in every part of the protectorate [and] enforce control, now here, now there, without the need of maintaining long lines of communication eating up troops and money'. The RAF personnel could live in comfortable, hygienic barracks. New types of aircraft could be developed for moving small military forces to trouble spots, with specialised airborne weapons for policing purposes. These were expected to include gas bombs: as early as April 1919 Churchill approved 'the general policy of using poisonous gas against uncivilised tribes'. Unfortunately, as the Air Staff admitted, 'although considerable time and trouble was expended on research during the war, we have not yet evolved suitable and practicable gas bombs for use from aircraft'. When 31st Wing RAF called for gas bombs 'for use against recalcitrant Arabs as experiment' (an idea concurred in by the General Staff at Baghdad), they had to be told there were no such things.[7]

The Air Staff hastened to back up their minister's initiative, holding that the unique properties of the new air arm made it not just a replacement but an improvement on traditional military methods of control. 'The "long arm" of the new weapon renders it ubiquitous,' they proclaimed – or at least, it was 'practicable to keep a whole country under more or less constant surveillance'. And that surveillance had a special quality – 'from the ground every inhabitant of a village is under the impression that the occupant of an aeroplane is looking directly at *him*'. Rebellion could be nipped in the bud by prompt action, and indeed patrolling and leaflet-dropping ought to prevent 'the seeds of unrest from being sown' in the first place. If none of this worked, then 'strong and continuous action must in time compel the submission of the most recalcitrant tribes', and do so 'without the use of punitive measures by ground troops'.[8]

The airmen would not have it all their own way, however. Unsurprisingly, there was resistance from the start from those who saw air attack as indiscriminate and even inhuman, as well as from military professionals who believed that only the direct physical contact of ground forces could really do the job. Sir Henry Wilson mocked the project as 'a fantastic salad of hot air, aeroplanes and Arabs'. Harold Dickson suspected that 'it will not take long before the wily Arab gets to learn the limits of an aeroplane's power'. But the arguments for air control would be dramatically reinforced by the events of the summer of 1920.

Early that year Mesopotamia was deceptively quiet. Bertram Thomas, a Political Officer in Baghdad, recalled the 'Pleasant Sunday Afternoons' in Gertrude Bell's garden, where 'the political intelligentsia of Baghdad' gathered: 'those whose brothers for the most part were in the Sharifian camp with the Amir Faisal in

Syria'. The 'PSAs' permitted free debate about the big issues – the Sykes–Picot agreement, Zionism and the Balfour Declaration, the Anglo-French Declaration, and the Mosul question.[9] They also discussed the issue of a possible amir for Iraq – all of which increasingly angered Arnold Wilson. 'She has done a good deal of harm in Baghdad by very indiscreet discussions.'

Beyond Gertrude's garden gate, politics was inching along. Arnold Wilson set up a constitutional committee, chaired by Sir Edgar Bonham-Carter (the administration's Judicial Secretary), and tasked with 'preparing proposals for a Constitution for Iraq in accordance with the Covenant of the League of Nations and the published declarations of His Majesty's Government'. But the problem was 'insoluble', in Wilson's view. There seemed to be 'no halfway house between an unsubstantial indigenous Government, which means anarchy, or . . . effective British control'.[10] This loaded phraseology spoke volumes. Unsurprisingly, the Bonham-Carter committee concluded (in late April) that while 'a more thorough attempt should be made to ascertain the wishes of the people', the constitution 'should make it clear that the Mandatory Power possesses the necessary power to fulfil the Mandate'. Until the mandate was formalised, it would be 'impossible to elicit a frank expression of opinion'. Men of moderate views could not 'resist the pressure which the extremists can bring on them' by charging them with 'betraying their faith and race' in accepting the tutelage of a Christian power.

The committee hedged on the crucial question of whether this pressure could be overcome. It noted (with some understatement) that 'the tenets of the Shi'ah sect are a potential source of difficulty to any Government', and also that only 'the presence of a Foreigner of an alien religion' was currently unifying Shia and Sunni communities. Left to themselves, the 'difference would widen and would at an early date lead to open rupture'. Moreover, the people as a whole were 'entirely unused to free debate, and to expressing their opinions in public'. Indeed, the

Political Officer at Basra argued that Arabs were handicapped not just by inexperience, but by character. One 'trait in the Arab character that affects self-determination is that "chastity in honour which feels a stain like a wound". This keen sense of personal dignity [*sharaf*] breeds jealousy and enmity.'[11]

Bonham-Carter's committee recommended that any Iraq constitution should lay down that 'the Mandatory power has the right to insist that its advice on matters which it considers essential for the "well-being and development of the people" (to quote the Covenant of the League) be followed'.[12] This of course was the nub of the issue. While Wilson still asserted that it was the mandatory power's job 'to prescribe what form of government shall be set up', London repeatedly insisted on public consultation. (The word 'prescribe' reeked of the old imperialism.) Wilson may have been right to see this as irresponsible or deluded, but the bottom line was not political but financial. Wilson's idea of prolonged tutelage might be admirable, but it would certainly be expensive. And as Hirtzel brutally told him, few people in London were interested in Mesopotamia 'for its own sake'. 'The supreme aim now is economy, and Parliament will not sanction any expenditure except for very definite and short periods, after which an Arab state must fend for itself.'

For Bonham-Carter it was vital that the mandate should be announced as soon as possible, but in the international sphere things were still moving dangerously slowly. The mandates were supposed to be worked out at the San Remo conference, in April 1920 – nearly a year after the announcement of the concept in Article 22 of the League Convention. In the event, the San Remo meeting got no further than confirming the basic allotment of responsibility – Syria and Lebanon to France, Mesopotamia and Palestine to Britain. The arguments over oil were gradually resolved, but precise definition of the mandated areas and powers was left until the signature of the treaty with Turkey. Here things started to unravel. The Sèvres treaty, signed by the Sultan's government in August 1920, was never ratified: its punitive terms were denounced by the nascent Turkish nationalist movement led by Mustafa Kemal. Outraged by Sèvres and by British support for Greek expansionism in Anatolia, Turkey was suddenly no longer a corpse on the mortuary slab awaiting dissection. It was once again an active force. The nationalist volunteers who began guerrilla warfare against the French in Cilicia and the Greeks in Anatolia would soon grow into military forces stronger than those the great powers could find to enforce their terms. A final settlement was as far away as ever.

In any case, the mandate itself was unlikely to be the panacea that Bonham-Carter's committee hoped for. In London, there was already a gloomy realisation that, as Hubert Young put it, the word 'mandate' was generally taken as a euphemism for 'protectorate', and so 'anathema in Baghdad and Damascus'.[13] (The first Arabic word used for it was *wisaya*, meaning guardianship, which was thought very demeaning; not until later in 1920 was the word *intidab* adopted, implying choice or selection.) Even a more urgent process of definition would probably not have countered this negative perception, certainly with the assumptions operating in Baghdad. 'The attitude of the British officials', Young ruefully noted, 'was more that of administrators of a foreign population who were incapable, and would always remain incapable, of governing themselves, than of friendly advisers who started on the assumption that the Arabs were managing their own affairs', and merely made 'friendly suggestions for the improvement of their plans'.

That polite approach was what Faisal's Iraqi officers had got used to during the war. Young met Nuri al-Said in London and found that he had not even heard of Wilson's provincial and district council scheme. Young described his own experiment in council-forming at Nasiriyeh in 1916, which Nuri seemed to think sensible. If he and his friends had been asked their opinion of the plan, they would have approved, he said; 'but none of them had ever been consulted'. This conversation seems to have convinced Nuri that Britain could be trusted, but it also convinced Young that 'an immediate change was required in the spirit of our administration in Mesopotamia'. He was particularly dismayed by a survey of the administration showing that only four out of its 233 officers were over 45 years old (Wilson himself was 35), and urged Lord Curzon that 'three or four senior men of administrative experience' should immediately be sent, under a chief 'with the experience and qualifications of Sir Percy Cox'.[14]

Whether the councils really could have persuaded the Iraqi officers that something was being done towards establishing what they demanded – a 'national government' – seems doubtful. In June 1920 the first Divisional Councils met, under the supervision of senior political officers. A flavour of their proceedings can be found in the address to the Dulaim Council by its president – Lieutenant-Colonel Gerard Leachman. 'We hear murmurings beyond our borders, and evil-minded persons for their personal interest are endeavouring to stir up strife in your midst. But thank God you in this Division are not ignorant children, and the evil-workers will have no success here.' The Council duly responded, 'We the tribes of the Dulaim Division are loyal to the British Government for we have never seen anything evil in it.'[15] In London, Wilson's constitution was coolly received. There was a predictable stand-off on the Eastern Committee between Curzon, who wanted to 'put in Abdullah', Faisal's elder brother, as amir, and the India Office which wanted 'a temporary President, who might be one of the sons of the Naqib of Baghdad'. Montagu wanted sovereignty vested in the president, 'as soon as the military occupation ends'.

While waiting for that to happen, Wilson was fretting about the effect of the inflated military establishment on public opinion in Iraq. Not that he thought there were too many troops: he was alarmed by the pressure for constant reduction in the garrison, which was accelerated when MacMunn was succeeded by General Aylmer Haldane. The problem as Wilson saw it was not an excess of troops, but a vast top-heavy military administration. The army was 'growing steadily weaker', and now existed 'apparently almost entirely for the purpose of taking in its own washing'. The two divisional areas had 'large staffs, and an enormous GHQ on top'. Baghdad's streets 'are still crowded at all times of day with motor vehicles containing officers and their wives', and 'at some stations all available troops are needed for guarding the married families'. 'Any single branch of the Army contains more officers than my whole HQ.' Wilson warned that 'if the show breaks down here', this would be one of the causes. 'It makes people think we intend to maintain a predominantly military form of government', and their resentment at being 'kept out of their houses, and out of the public offices' was serious.[16]

8. Rebellion

The troops out here, for the last two months, have been fighting,
not only for this rotten country, which is not worth fighting for,
but for their very lives.

    H. S. MITCHELL

Our good name and all that the word prestige stands for have,
I fear, suffered irreparably.

    A. T. WILSON

It is an extraordinary thing that the British civil administration
should have succeeded in such a short time in alienating the
whole country to such an extent that the Arabs have laid aside
the blood feuds they have nursed for centuries and that the Suni
and Shiah tribes are working together.

    WINSTON CHURCHILL

Wilson was becoming ever more out of joint with the times, but
he did his best to get the government to grasp the nettle in Iraq.
His warnings became ever more urgent. If the government could
not face the cost of holding on to the country, with the frontiers he
argued were essential, it should 'face the alternative, and evacuate
Mesopotamia'. The military situation was deteriorating: 'Our army
is now incapable of defending the population of frontier districts
against aggression, or of maintaining order over considerable
areas.'[1] Yet even Wilson did not really grasp how dangerous the
situation had become. In 1920, things were heading towards a
decisive challenge to British power. A heavily armed society with
a deeply ingrained tradition of resistance was acquiring a political
agenda, and political leadership. The result was explosive.

    Weapons were everywhere. Immediately after the battle
of Shaiba, the men of the Muntafik tribes had fallen on the
retreating Turkish troops and carried off thousands of service

rifles, scattering their own ancient weapons as they went. The skilful and unremitting pilfering of rifles had gone on for the rest of the war. (In Wilson's sardonic words, 'in the quest for arms the Arab showed qualities of courage, cunning and perseverance which, if turned to a better cause would have insured success in any walk of life'.) The price of service rifles like Turkish Mausers and British Lee-Enfields, over £20 before the war, had fallen to a quarter that sum. In the Euphrates area, in particular, there were too many guns in too many hands, and 'ammunition had been accumulated on a scale hitherto undreamt of'. Administrators were well aware of this, and had made efforts at disarmament – notably by imposing collective fines in the form of rifles. But they jibbed at the task of total disarmament, fearing it would provoke outright rebellion. As a result the rebellion, when it finally began, was all the more serious.

This was a traditionally rebellious society, but its rebellions had so far been limited and local. In 1920, this changed. The establishment of an Arab government in Damascus by the victorious forces under the command of Prince Faisal began to reverberate across the historic 'fertile crescent'. Iraqis amongst Faisal's army grew more impatient at British failure to allow a similar political development in Baghdad. In December 1919 a force demanding independence for Iraq seized the town of Deir es-Zor on the upper Euphrates. The town should not really have been in British hands at all. The government had accepted in September that it was in Syria rather than Iraq, but this instruction had not been sent to Baghdad until late November, and then could not be decoded.[2] Wilson raged that the blunder had needlessly endangered British lives and damaged British prestige, but in any case the action at Deir was bound to reverberate in Iraq. When Wilson demanded an immediate counter-stroke to reoccupy it, the new C-in-C refused, citing London's ruling that it was 'beyond our frontier'.

Wilson was convinced that the agitation for Iraqi independence was being supported by Sharifian funds from Damascus. In fact, though, the force that seized Deir was a breakaway group from al-Ahd al-Iraqi. The Iraqi military leaders close to Faisal, like Nuri al-Said and Jaafar Askari, set their faces against anti-British agitation in 1920 in spite of their frustration with Wilson's Baghdad regime. Nuri told his friends in Baghdad that his trip to London had convinced him that 'Britain who liberated the Arab countries remains sympathetic to the Iraqi cause'. Jaafar was reported to believe that 'the pro-British Arabs are the vast majority', and most of those leading the anti-British movement were 'animated by motives of personal ambition rather than genuine patriotism'. This was exactly what the British wanted to hear, of course, but it was misleading. The growing popular movement in early 1920 was produced by a coalition of religious and tribal leaders dedicated to the removal of foreign interference.

Throughout the spring, Iraqi Muslims were becoming increasingly politicised. After a short period of quiescence, Najaf once again became a centre of resistance. The city's leaders were still antagonised by their subordination to British control, and all the inhabitants disliked the rigorous tax regime, especially in a time of economic hardship marked by high prices and scarce food. The violent suppression of the rebellion in Egypt in 1919 had sparked a lot of anti-British propaganda, and British manipulation of the Persian government was particularly objectionable to the Shia leadership with its Persian majority. (The Anglo-Persian Treaty of August 1919, which Cox had been taken from Baghdad to negotiate, confirmed their hostility to British interference.) The Russians had ostentatiously renounced their part in the notorious 1907 carve-up of Persia into British and Russian spheres of influence. Perhaps just as important, the Deir incident seemed to show that British power might be resisted. And when Faisal was proclaimed king of Syria in March 1920, a congress of al-Ahd al-Iraqi in Damascus declared Iraq independent, and Abdallah its ruler.

The death of the unusually unpolitical Shia Grand *Mujtahid* Kadum al-Yazdi in April sparked a very unusual convergence of Shia and Sunni feeling. The traditional commemorative ceremonies turned into mass political rallies, where nationalist leaders recited patriotic poetry and called for resistance to the occupation. Ramadan fell in May, and the daily religious celebrations drew large mixed Sunni–Shia audiences, almost invariably followed by nationalist speeches and poetry readings. Many of these ended with mass marches out of the mosques and through the Baghdad streets. A secret society, Haras al-Istiqlal, organised both Shia lamentations and Sunni celebrations of the Prophet's birthday (*mawlid*). The movement was seen by the Baghdad police as unprecedented in the history of Islam.[3] This kind of political ferment showed that a new political consciousness was emerging. In Najaf and Karbala printing presses were set up to distribute leaflets urging the tribes to prepare for revolt. Arab flags, whose public display had been banned by Wilson, were made in secret.[4]

When news of the San Remo conference reached Baghdad in May, many nationalist leaders began to argue that only force could secure independence. A committee of fifteen, the Mandubin ('delegated'), demanded that a national convention be immediately called to establish an Arab government. Wilson met them on 2 June, but stalled them by saying he would refer the question to the British government. His own account of the meeting shows how far nationalist thinking had now developed. He still assumed that the problem was the long delay in fixing the form of the mandate, but though the Mandubin apparently accepted his protestation that this was not his fault, they insisted that in any case 'between you and us there is a great gulf fixed'. When Wilson told them that the government would repress any disturbances, and 'begged them to realise the bloodshed that this policy must entail', they replied that it would be 'a small price to pay for independence'.

Just how far they had absorbed the global language of nationalism can be seen from their assertion that 'as between nations liberty was not given but taken', and that rebellion

– even if it failed – was the only proper way to 'advance the cause of freedom'. Wilson was confronting a phenomenon he simply could not grasp. The statements he issued in the hope of heading off the 1920 agitation were a kind of manifesto of paternalism. His attempt to create an Electoral Committee in July to prepare the way for elections to a General Assembly was too little, too late. (And even then he could not bring himself to speak of a 'national assembly'.) His complaint to his parents, 'the moment we get one party together and working on the same lines, a more extreme party is formed to intimidate them', showed that he saw the problem in Iraq as unique ('these people have little moral courage'). But it could have been said of almost any nationalist resistance movement anywhere in the world.[5]

By mid-June Gertrude Bell, who now admitted how little she really knew of the inner workings of the Shia hierarchy, was worried. 'We have had a stormy week.' Nationalist propaganda was intensifying, and there were constant meetings in mosques 'where the mental temp. rises a great deal above 113. The extremists are out for independence without a mandate', and were making great play with the twin themes of 'the Unity of Islam and the Rights of the Arab Race'. She went as far as to speak of a 'reign of terror'.[6] Worse still, perhaps, was the 'full-blown Jihad' that would follow from the declaration of al-Yazdi's successor as Grand *Mujtahid* that 'none but Moslems have any right to rule over Moslems'. Pro-British notables, like Sulayman Faidi, an associate of Sayyid Talib, saw the situation in ominous terms. 'You cannot let things go on as at present,' he urged Bell. 'The agitation is taking dangerous proportions.' He thought that 'open disturbance' was likely, not perhaps in Baghdad, but in the provinces, where all the tribes were restive. The meetings in mosques were 'abhorrent' to him; he warned that 'the combination of religion and politics is specially dangerous', as it was 'almost impossible for me or anyone else to stand up against it. Though I dislike the Mauluds [*mawlids*] intensely I find myself obliged to go to them; I dare not stay away – such pressure is brought to bear on me.' Those like him were in the same predicament. The reconciliation of Sunnis with Shias was 'most distasteful' to him: 'I should regard Shiah domination as an unthinkable disaster.'[7]

That month there was an incident at Tel Afar that seemed even more ominous than Deir es-Zor. On 3 June the British commander of the gendarmerie was shot by one of his own men, the political office was stormed, and two armoured cars which drove into the town (in defiance of standing instructions) were shot to a standstill. All their crews were killed – in all, two officers and fourteen other ranks died at the hands of the insurgents. Tel Afar was well inside the Mosul *vilayet*, and in this case, a mobile column of 150 cavalry and 500 infantry was available at Mosul: within five days the town was reoccupied. Haldane chose this moment to go on a tour of inspection in Persia, to Wilson's dismay. When he got back, Wilson told him that unless reinforcements were sent from India, 'the administration could not be carried on'. He also urged Haldane to send all the British women and children out of the country. (The families of British officials had begun to arrive in January 1920.) Haldane disliked having them there, but thought that to move them out in the heat of summer would be intolerable. He also refused to call for reinforcements – worrying no doubt about Churchill's likely reaction. He reported to the CIGS in late June that while 'the Civil Commissioner still says he is anxious regarding the situation, I am not and never have been'. ('He has not been opposed to Germans for 4½ years,' he added condescendingly.) Wilson's 'young and inexperienced underlings' were 'too ready to jump to conclusions and take counsel of their fears'.[8]

Haldane insisted on moving into summer quarters in Persia, despite Wilson's protests. He complained that continual alarms raised by the civil authorities made it 'difficult to decide as to movement of troops', and decided 'one has to follow one's own experience and judgment rather than accept political guidance'. The issue was the same everywhere – as he well knew the CIGS would agree – 'the politician always pressing for dispersion while the soldier knows he must concentrate'. His belief was that 'the situation is no worse than it was when I arrived in March. The Arab may be influenced by religious motives but is mainly out for loot and does not want to get killed. A quiet show of force is the best way to cool his ardour.' And his conclusion – 'I have no fear of a general rising' – was, surprisingly, supported by Gertrude Bell. In spite of her mid-June worries and warnings, she told him in early July that 'the bottom seems to have dropped out of the agitation'.[9] She offered this advice without telling Wilson, who was furious. (On 14 July he wrote to Cox, who was then in London, 'if you can find a job for Miss Bell at home, I think you would be well advised to do so'.)

Bell's 'private miscalculations' coincided with the start of a widespread uprising on the Euphrates. It began at Rumaitha, on 1 July, the day after the local political officer arrested a sheikh who had defaulted on an agricultural loan. The Dhawalim tribe brought their flags out – a sign that they were at war with the government – and stormed into town to rescue the sheikh. Next day they mounted a series of raids on the railway. Troops were rushed to Rumaitha, to a quite formidable total of 527, but as they assembled, tribal forces surrounded the town and began to dig trenches – showing that some at least were modifying their traditional fighting methods. A reconnaissance in force by two platoons of the 99th Infantry on 4 July was overwhelmed, and forty-three men were lost. The rest of the troops holed up in the 'political serai' and waited for relief. On the 7th, a small relief column was surrounded and forced to fall back, with the loss of forty-eight killed and 166 wounded. This was a turning point: the British setback encouraged more insurgents to mobilise. By 12 July, when the besieged force in Rumaitha reported that it was running out of food, relieving it had become a serious problem. A scratch column was assembled, with parts of four different brigades, from different divisions, but movement to a point 150 miles from Baghdad at the hottest time of the year, with a real prospect 'of the force being cut off, and having to fight its way back to Hillah' without food or water, was a daunting prospect. In the end, it advanced up the railway with a supply train – very vulnerable to attack – and only fought its way through on 20 July.

The strength of the insurgents came as a nasty surprise to the British. They were not only 'well-armed, extremely mobile, and ready to take considerable risks where loot was the reward', Haldane wrote, but also evidently 'directed by skilled brains, well versed in the power of the modern rifle, as well as in the limitations and weak points of our modern army'. These worrying developments were underlined by the fate of the 'Manchester column', sent from Hilla to Kifl on 23 July. It was brought to a halt on the Rustumia canal on the 24th through heat exhaustion, and in the evening a large insurgent force swept down on it. The column was fairly strong by the standards of traditional 'native' warfare – two squadrons of cavalry, an infantry battalion (the 2nd Manchesters), and an artillery battery – but was forced to retreat in the evening. By the time it got back to Hilla next morning it had lost 20 killed, 60 wounded, and no fewer than 318 missing. (Of these, 79 British and 81 Indians ended up as prisoners of the Arabs.) British prestige was shredded by this disaster, and over the next few weeks British control of the middle Euphrates area dissolved.[10]

Captain Bertram Thomas, tiring of Baghdad bureaucratic routine, and even of the Pleasant Sunday Afternoons, got posted to Shatra as APO just as the troubles were starting to break. On the Shatt al-Hai north of Nasiriyeh, this was an area that had 'never seen as much as a squad of British soldiers' up to this point. British authority was maintained by the political officer's personal relationship with the Sa'dun tribal leaders. Thomas had thirty *shabana*, locally recruited men who brought their own rifles and horses, and were 'put into uniform and cloaked with authority'; they acted as 'escort, messenger, gaoler, policeman and soldier', and were (fortunately for him) almost totally unpolitical, and 'capable of tremendous personal loyalty'. Shortly after he arrived at Shatra, the region was in uproar: Samawa, sixty miles west, was beleaguered, and Rumaitha and Diwaniya were being abandoned. 'Refugees, mostly women and children, came drifting in', and the atmosphere was thick with rumours of British defeats. In Shatra the tribes – dominated by Sheikh Kayyun – stayed loyal to Britain, but the surrounding area flared up in revolt. Eventually Qalat Sikr, further up the Shatt towards Kut, was abandoned, and Thomas was isolated. Throughout the middle Euphrates, 'Government had been entirely withdrawn, and the Arab tribes were delirious with success.' Though Shatra itself never rose, Thomas was ordered to leave on 27 August, and evacuated by aircraft to Nasiriyeh. Wilson ruefully reflected that although Thomas was 'personally popular amongst all classes and competent, this did not prevent growth of fanatical feeling, and only the timely arrival of an aeroplane saved his life'. The uncomfortable implication was that extricating Thomas removed the spur to revolt.[11]

An incident that was like dozens of others, except that the surviving Briton published a book about it, was the seizure of Shahraban on the Diyala route from Baghdad to Persia, in mid-August. Zetton Buchanan, the wife of the Assistant Irrigation Officer – one of the British wives not evacuated in the summer – was besieged in the Queshlah (the old Turkish barracks) with her husband, and two other British officers (the APO and the commander of the Levies). The Levies deserted, and the three British officers were killed before her eyes. She survived an alarming and fairly uncomfortable detention for a month in the home of a local sheikh before being rescued by a column under General Coningham. When she got to Baghdad she was amazed by 'the number of false reports concerning what happened'. The story that the Levies 'were loyal to the end, dying by the side of their British officers', was 'totally untrue'. The men who took these tales to Baghdad, she thought, 'were only too probably deserters, who had watched from a place of safety the storming of the Queshlah'.[12]

This was a major rebellion. For Iraqi nationalists, it became *Al-Thawra al-Iraqiya*, 'the Iraqi uprising', often rendered as 'the Iraqi revolution', the defining moment of emerging national identity. 'No episode in the history of this country has been as revered as the 1920 rebellion.'[13] Iraqi poetry, theatre and film repeatedly invoke it as the crucial factor in the country's eventual independence. Saddam Hussein's government commissioned a film – starring Oliver Reed – in which Sunni rather than Shia tribes played the leading role, and which suggested that Saddam's home town, Tikrit, had been a centre of revolt. (No rising had happened there, in fact.[14]) Yet one of the most eminent Iraqi historians called it a mere 'series of uncontrolled risings'. Few significant towns were involved: Baghdad was quiet until Wilson ordered the arrest of a number of nationalist leaders on 11 August, and several of them fled to the mid-Euphrates countryside. The key weakness of the insurgents lay in their traditional organisation. Even though a definite national rhetoric had emerged by the summer of 1920, and a body calling itself the Provisional Revolutionary Government was set up in Najaf, most tribal forces fought as they had always done, refusing to leave their own areas or to unite with others to form large units. They were inevitably picked off individually as British reinforcements came in.

Still, the rising was formidable enough to stretch the British forces to breaking point. 'Practically all the troops in this country are out in this show against the Arabs,' wrote Colonel H. S. Mitchell, with the 17th Division. 'Although we have knocked out a good number of them they have certainly had the laugh on us, as our casualties have been very heavy.' The numbers who raised the flag of revolt at some stage may have totalled 100,000, and a significant proportion of these were armed with modern weapons. Haldane said that until substantial reinforcements arrived, 'we lived on a veritable powder-mine', and 'no sooner had the revolt been crushed in one quarter than it would burst forth more intensely in another'. Communications hung by a thread – several hundred miles of the railway line had to be protected by hastily built blockhouses. Without aircraft, the situation might have been lost altogether. The troops were 'fighting not only for this rotten country', Mitchell said, 'but for their very lives, surrounded by swarms of Arabs, with all communications cut except by aeroplane-wireless'.[15]

In the same spirit as Haig during the German 1918 offensive, Wilson urged his staff to show 'the ten minutes of tenacity which Napoleon referred to as being the deciding factor in a campaign'. In mid-July he actually suggested abandoning the whole Mosul *vilayet*. By late August his despatches had a defeatist tone: the situation was still deteriorating, the failure of the army to secure any striking success was causing support to haemorrhage away. 'Even the most powerful and friendly Sheikhs are being forced into hostilities against us . . . Our good name and all that the word prestige stands for have, I fear, suffered irreparably.' Gertrude Bell's despair was even sharper: 'We are now in the middle of a full-blown jihad – we have against us the fiercest prejudices of a people in a primeval state of civilisation . . . We're near to a complete collapse of society, and there's little on which you can depend for its reconstruction. The credit of European civilisation is gone.' The India Office, with a hint of hysteria, announced that 'we are fighting in Mesopotamia for the very existence of civilisation in the Middle East'.[16]

But later British accounts stressed the limits of the rising, both geographical and ideological. Some in London even objected to the label 'rebellion'; Wilson pointed out that he had only started to use the term 'rebels' in preference to the army's politically inept term 'enemies', but promised that he would now refer to them as 'insurgents'. Many characterised the rising as no more than 'disorders' or 'disturbances'. 'Disorder at no time spread to the Kut or the Amara areas of the lower Tigris, nor, save for isolated episodes, to Baghdad: nor, in spite of agitators' efforts, to Basra.' Mosul remained untroubled 'in spite of violent trans-frontier propaganda and some formidable tribal raiding'. Southern

Kurdistan was more disturbed, and Kifri was temporarily lost, along with several outposts around Arbil. The upper Euphrates stayed quiet until 'the sordidly treacherous murder' of Colonel Gerard Leachman (as Wilson called it) at Khan Nuqta police post on 12 August triggered local risings and forced the abandonment of Hit. Leachman was the highest-profile casualty of the rebellion, and the reason for his killing remains obscure – but it was most likely revenge for his notorious rough-handling of Arabs and Kurds alike. (He had complained to a colleague, 'I can't be as strenuous with the Arabs as I need be and if I can't impress them enough they will get me.'[17])

The British admitted that the only reason why the disorders had not spread to the lower Tigris tribes was 'the continual transport of reinforcements up the river' from Basra. By now they were under few illusions about their popularity. But the insurgents' lack of unity allowed them to argue that this was not a nationalist rising. 'The differing viewpoints of Kurd, Turk, Turkoman and Arab, the irreconcilably varying objectives of the Persian Mujtahid, Iraqi nationalist, and peace-loving merchant or landlord precluded, as did the essential cleavage of town and tribe, any effective unity of effort.' The 'lack of cohesion' showed the 'parochial objectives of the sheikhs' and 'their lack of the sense of service to a common cause'.[18] Thomas insisted that in Shatra 'the spirit of nationalism did not exist, and there was no alliance between the local and neighbouring tribes for the purpose of overthrowing Government'.[19] As Haldane's reference to loot indicates, British explanations blamed 'the cause of anarchy', together with the influence of foreign agitators and propaganda. Wilson himself put Bolshevik agitation high on his list (though the file on Bolshevism in Mesopotamia ended as one of the thinnest in the whole National Archives). But his list of 'foreign influences' was quite a long one – including not just the Turks (who had sent £7,000 in gold to Karbala) but also the 'U.S. Consul and other United States citizens' who unsportingly distributed extracts from critical articles in the British press, notably *The Times*.²⁰ Another intelligence specialist drew up a remarkable chart to illustrate the vast network of 'German-Bolshevic-Asiatic Intrigue'.²¹

In time, the perspective would shift somewhat. Fifteen years on, the judicious Philip Ireland accepted that though 'the Insurrection can scarcely be called national in the strict sense of the word, it did indicate a certain national consciousness' which would 'become more clearly defined' in the next few years. Even he, though, suggested that the revolt was primarily a reaction to the efficiency of British administration: 'its thoroughness and even its probity were unfamiliar, irksome and unnecessary.' The suddenness and completeness of the change 'left the Arabs bewildered and aggrieved whereas they should have been grateful'.²² Bertram Thomas pointed out that the Ottoman taxation system had been erratic, and the strength of the Euphrates tribes, and their distance from Baghdad, meant that they were generally 'left to enjoy an almost taxless and uninterrupted existence'. What administrators saw as the best achievements of British government, such as the pacification of the Muntafik in 1918–19, could be double-edged: Thomas suggested that 'the tightening of authority was vexatious' just because it 'brought the boredom of perpetual inter-tribal peace in place of the customary incessant tumult of the land'.²³ But Harold Dickson at Hilla remained frankly baffled by the whole outbreak. 'If you ask the tribes as I have often done why they acted as they did, the answer has invariably been "We were deceived by the Ulema God curse them."' He relapsed into the view that the lure of loot – 'the predatory instinct in the hearts of the masses of Iraq' – had driven them now as it has always done.²⁴

The insurrection was eventually stifled by big reinforcements and heavy punitive measures. Haldane's garrison of 60,000 was increased to 80,000 by August, and over 100,000 by the end of September. The RAF claimed to have broken the siege of Kufa by sustained bombing – targeting the mosque where many tribesmen had taken refuge when their villages were destroyed – though the real effectiveness of air action was disputable. Wilson himself, whose optimism had helped to convert Churchill to the idea of 'air substitution', dismayed Trenchard by changing his mind about its viability.[25] But the sheer expense of the troop reinforcements would ultimately clinch the argument for air substitution. The use of air power in Iraq generated several myths, notably the widespread belief that the RAF had dropped mustard gas bombs during the rebellion. The idea was certainly present, and Haldane was keen to have the Marsh Arabs – who were hard to get at – bombed (with teargas, not mustard); but as in 1919 no such munitions were actually available. The army certainly had teargas shells, but there is no record of their being used.[26]

The recovery of Kufa and Samawa in mid-October brought major operations to an end, but irregular actions went on into the next year. Haldane flooded the countryside with punitive columns, to 'teach the insurgents the price they had to pay for throwing down the gauntlet to the British Empire'. By the end, at least 5,000 Arabs had been killed, along with 900 British and Indian troops. An astonishing number of rifles was surrendered – a total (over 63,000) actually bigger than the original estimate of guns in Iraqi hands – together with no fewer than 3 million rounds of ammunition, a remarkable figure since the army judged that the insurgents' main problem had been their shortage of ammunition.[27] The impact of the repression was severe. Even the belligerent Dickson saw that the 'surrenders' were having a perverse effect on a society already impoverished by a poor harvest and the burning of large areas of standing crops. 'The various columns in their drives to collect rifles had systematically lived off the country, sitting down and eating the reserve grain of the tribe until the rifles demanded were forthcoming.' Where military demands 'were in excess of the rifles actually possessed by the tribes, the Shaikh had to go and purchase at exorbitant rates' from other tribes.[28]

The fines struck Mrs Buchanan, naturally perhaps, as hopelessly inadequate to the scale of the offence. Her Arab captors at

Shahraban had boasted of having 'over a thousand rifles and plenty of ammunition', yet the town had only been fined 150 rifles. Four houses had been burned, one man executed and a few more imprisoned (including her host, Sheikh Majid). 'The moral effect is ruinous.' Worse in her view, however, was the attitude of the authorities to her question why she and her husband had been abandoned, and why the outpost had not been reinforced. 'Every difficulty was put in the way of my finding things out.' She concluded that 'someone had made a big blunder, and nobody was prepared to take the blame for it'.

Churchill had resisted Haldane's demand for reinforcements as long as possible ('we are at our wits' end to find a single soldier'), and was predictably horrified by the ruinous expense and destruction of the repressive campaign. Twice the annual budget – £40 million – had been consumed by 'these thankless deserts'. 'If people groused before' about the expense, Lieutenant-Colonel H. L. Scott mused at Hilla, 'what will they say now? I would not like to have to say how many million pounds' worth of Government stores have been burnt or looted.'[29] It looked as though an extra division would be needed to maintain control, but since as the CIGS said this was 'entirely beyond our powers . . . we may be forced into a difficult, dangerous and undignified withdrawal from Persia or Mosul' over the winter.

The civil administration was shaken to its roots. 'Financially the Civil Administration has been ruined', Wilson reported, 'and the country has received a setback from which it will take years to recover.' 'Two years' educational work went by the board,' the Director of Education sadly noted: schools were wrecked, stores destroyed, teachers and pupils cast adrift. Wilson's mission to create the 'first best' system of government, already on the defensive, would never recover from this blow. At the end of September, four months after he had been knighted, he was at last removed. (The decision to replace him was actually taken as early as 17 June, after Young at the Foreign Office renewed his assault on Wilson's resistance to any strategy for winning public support; he saw Wilson's 9 June telegram as 'tantamount to a resignation, and think it should be accepted as such'). 'All his work falling in ruins about his head', as Colonel Scott sympathetically remarked. Scott was 'convinced that he knew that if he was frank and told the home authorities the force required to hold the country, the Government would have refused the mandate'. Still, he might 'have just pulled through, if he had kept clear of bombing air raids and allowed good men to serve under him'.[30]

Was even the second best now possible? On 11 October, Sir Percy Cox finally returned to Baghdad with the power he demanded, as High Commissioner, to produce an exit strategy.

9. Kingdom Come

It [mandate] is a word that can be interpreted as 'colonization' or as the lightest bond of affectionate assistance which in no way touches independence.
AMIR FAISAL

The word Mandate produces much the same effect here as the word Protectorate did in Egypt.
GERTRUDE BELL

The Cabinet still had no clear idea of what to do, except to leave things to Cox. Not all ministers were convinced even of this; Churchill privately confessed that he did 'not feel any complete sense of confidence in him. His personality did not impress me, and all his recent prognostications have been falsified.'[1] Cox returned to Baghdad with the status he demanded – as 'ex officio Commander-in-Chief, the sole channel through which the GOC will communicate' with both the British and the new Arab governments.[2] He himself remained convinced that 'the maintenance of our present position in Mesopotamia' was 'a factor of enormous importance to our general interests'. He was given two sets of instructions: one addressed the familiar issue of an Arab amir, and the other the equally perennial issue of an Arab government. The High Commissioner seemed to be at liberty to construct an Arab government with or without an 'amir' – in other words, a republic might still emerge. Hogarth had argued in 1919 that 'but for our obligation to King Hussein, we might wisely promote republican institutions in both Mesopotamia and Syria', since they were best adapted to the complex diversity of their societies, and most likely to endure.

As to who might be the amir, views were changing. The respective qualifications of the two Sharifian princes, Abdallah and Faisal, had been debated ever since the Arab Revolt began. Abdallah, who had initiated the contact between Cairo and Mecca, was capable but indolent (not necessarily a disqualification, some thought). 'The ablest and least scrupulous' of the brothers, in Hogarth's opinion, he was 'intelligent enough to grasp real facts and conform to them'. Faisal, of course, had been supposedly hand-picked by Lawrence precisely for his unique combination of charisma, seriousness, and alertness to political realities. He had led the Northern Army in the Arab Revolt, captured Damascus (or at least been allowed to do so by Allenby), and attended the Versailles peace conference. He was recognised as a serious political figure – too serious, indeed, for the French, who viewed his ambitions with intense suspicion.

Cox, though, had been agnostic about Faisal as well as Abdallah. Various other candidates had been weighed up as potential amirs. Gertrude Bell had a soft spot for her friend the Naqib of Baghdad. Britain's trusty ally the Sheikh of Mohammerah put in an application, arguing that the amir must be a Shia. This produced a battery of counter-arguments: a Shia amir would 'alienate the Sunni element in Baghdad which accounts for the best educated and most advanced group in Mesopotamia'. He would 'never be accepted in the almost wholly Sunni vilayet of Mosul, for which separate government would have to be set up'. He would 'cause acute heartburnings in Syria', and 'raise throughout Iraq latent animosity between Shiah and Sunni'. (Sayyid Talib of Basra, the leading local political figure before the British invasion, was seriously pushed by Philby as a man with real weight, but dismissed by Curzon as 'undesirable' and by Bell as 'the greatest rogue unhung'.) The search went on for what Arthur Balfour called 'a King who will be content to reign but not to govern, and whose religious views are such that Sheikhs may acquiesce in his rule'.[3]

Faced with the 1920 disaster, though, Cox came off the fence. He was still against Abdallah – 'nothing I have heard in the last few months', he wrote in late July – 'has led me to modify my view as to his suitability'. Faisal was different: he was the only 'Arab potentate' who had 'any idea of the practical difficulties of running a civilised Government on Arab lines'.[4] Moreover, his personal circumstances had just changed, suddenly and dramatically. His four-month reign as King of Syria ended in late July when a French army expelled him from Damascus. After several months of uncomfortable exile at Lake Como, he was allowed to go to London, where he was received by the King on 4 December, and then began a series of political meetings under the guidance of T. E. Lawrence.

While Faisal was in Europe, Cox was engaged in setting up a provisional government, under his own 'control and supervision'. It would be 'responsible for the administrative and political guidance of the country until the general situation had returned to normal and a start could be made with the creation of national institutions'. He persuaded the venerable old Naqib of Baghdad to preside over a Council of State with eight ministers (Interior, Finance, Justice, Defence, Public Works, Education and Health, Commerce, and Religious Bequests). Probably his most urgent task was to create an Iraqi military force effective enough to allow most of the British garrison to be removed. He now saw the practical value of Faisal, whose prestige would put him 'in a position to raise a National Army quicker than any candidate from Irak'. This was a potent argument in the circumstances.

But there was a tetchy political problem. The people might well be in favour of an outsider – and indeed a Sharifian – as amir, because Hussein himself, though a Sunni, was thought to be very moderate. (Some Shia apparently believed that Hussein was secretly one of them.) But 'the majority would prefer to have the question decided for them, or at any rate that we should give them a lead'. The government, unfortunately, was acutely aware of the likely French reaction to any British move to instal Faisal in Baghdad (Curzon believed it 'would arouse a storm of indignation in France'). They would have to be 'in a position to tell the French that there was a definite desire amongst the Mesopotamians' for Faisal. This was a stand-off; Cox reiterated that the government must accept his advice, and 'the initiative as regards Faisal must come from your side'.

Once again, it was Winston Churchill who would resolve the issue. At the end of the year, Lloyd George – who had belatedly started to take an interest in the Mesopotamia problem – decided that Middle Eastern policy-making would rest with the Colonial Office, and on New Year's Day 1921 made Churchill Colonial Secretary. At last the long tussle between the India Office and the Foreign Office was ended. Churchill quickly set up a new Middle East Department, offering the headship to Hirtzel (who turned it down), and trying also to recruit Lawrence (who tried to get Churchill to promise that the wartime pledges to the Arabs would be honoured). In the end the headship went to John Shuckburgh, with Hubert Young as head of the Political and Administrative section, and Reader Bullard as Mesopotamia adviser. Young, incidentally, was unhappy with the implications of placing Arabia 'under the Colonial Office'. It would not look good internationally, he thought, and 'the chances of obtaining recognition of our special position in Arabia will be markedly lessened'.[5] Lawrence's influence on Churchill remained strong, but the only one inside the new department who definitely favoured Faisal was Young. Shuckburgh, following Hirtzel, worried about Faisal's trustworthiness, while Bullard thought that no Arab administration would survive the withdrawal of British forces. In Baghdad, Philby – the only committed republican amongst British officials – was openly against Faisal, and was eventually sacked for it.

Churchill moved cautiously at first, pressing Cox to make clear whether he favoured Faisal 'because you consider taking a long view that he is the best man', or 'as a desperate expedient in the hopes of reducing the garrison quickly'. Cox could only reply that an outsider would be better than an Iraqi amir, but that public opinion 'continues to veer in a kaleidoscopic way' on the issue. On the same day he wrote this – 22 February 1921 – Churchill met Faisal for the first time. After stalling for several weeks, Faisal was now ready to accept the crown. Churchill was supposed to secure his agreement to two conditions which his Cabinet colleagues saw as crucial: acceptance of the British mandate, and an undertaking not to intrigue against the French. But he did not, even though Faisal had already shown not only that he disliked the French, but also that (like other Arab nationalists) he disliked the term 'mandate', precisely because of the quality which the British liked about it – its imprecision. 'It is a word that can be interpreted as "colonization" or as the lightest bond of affectionate assistance which in no way touches independence.'[6]

Once Churchill did move, he moved quickly. In March he assembled his entire cast of characters for a durbar-like conference in Cairo. Even at this stage, the arguments about the candidates for rulership of Iraq had to be gone through again. Lawrence made his pitch for Faisal by arguing that the amir would have to 'counteract the claims of rival candidates, and pull together the scattered elements of a backward and half civilised country'. An 'active and inspiring personality' was needed, but Abdallah was 'lazy, and by no means dominating'. Cox stuck to his point that Faisal's military experience put him 'in the best position for raising an army quickly'. For Churchill himself, the clinching argument was the regional set of threats and promises he was threading together. 'If Faisal knew that not only his father's subsidy and the protection of the Holy Places from Wahhabi attack, but also the position of his brother in Trans-Jordan was dependent on his own good behaviour, he would be much easier to deal with.'[7] So by a stroke of the pen, almost literally, he carved a new state – Transjordan – from the mandated territory of Palestine, and handed it to Abdallah.

As Churchill made quite clear during the extended meetings of the Military Committee to analyse the security situation, the overriding argument was still economy. 'British troops, the backbone of the British Empire, were extremely costly', and should not be wasted on 'menial duties'. What was needed in Iraq was Arab levies, and though General Congreve, the C-in-C Egypt, spluttered that such forces might desert 'as soon as fighting commenced', Faisal was – in effect – hired to raise them for the Empire. He was confirmed as king in a referendum unique in the British experience – one that produced a 96 per cent 'yes' vote. As one official, who went on to work for the League of Nations, coyly observed, 'it would be difficult to ascertain whether the result of the referendum was in any way due to British pressure'.[8]

But the path had certainly been eased by the decision to deport his only serious rival, Sayyid Talib, a month before Faisal arrived in Iraq. Talib remained easily the most substantial Iraqi political figure: eager for power and ruthless in using it. One or two British officials, notably Philby, saw him as the only real basis for building a truly Iraqi state. Yes, Philby admitted, he was a murderer – but then so were 'all our best friends' like the Sheikhs of Kuwait and Mohammerah. The crucial point was that he was effective: Philby believed that he had saved Baghdad from rebellion in August 1920, and that his support – especially his standing down in favour of the Naqib – had been 'the principal factor in enabling Cox to launch the provisional Government'. He became Minister of the Interior in that government, and 'it was obvious to all of us including Cox and Gertrude Bell that the reversion of the Naqib's post was his' – he would inevitably head the government in time. As his official adviser, Philby watched the culture clash of the new hybrid administration up close. He accepted that it might 'take some time to accustom him to ordinary office and interdepartmental routine'. (Even Philby chafed at Talib's notion of office hours, arriving at 11 a.m. only to begin ordering an elaborate lunch.) In late 1920, things were 'still a little chaotic' since nearly all the official correspondence was in English, which Talib did not speak. 'It is only possible to discuss the more important cases with him, leaving the rest to be discharged as matters of routine.' But Philby held that 'it should become increasingly possible to submit and explain all matters to the Minister and leave him to issue orders'.[9]

Cox and Bell took a quite different view of the prime minister-in-waiting. The last round of the British tussle with him was suitably murky. At a dinner he gave for one of the British press correspondents in Baghdad, Sayyid Talib launched on a speech alleging that British officials were exerting unacceptable influence on the election process, and threatening to raise armed resistance. Gertrude Bell thought it 'an incitement to revolution as bad as anything said by the men who roused the country last year, and not far from a declaration of Jihad'. This might seem to be going too far, and her argument that his threats had disqualified him as a democratic politician had a whiff of hypocrisy in the circumstances. When she told Cox of the incident, and her view of its implications, he immediately took the opportunity of removing an inconvenient obstacle. To Philby's fury, Talib was arrested next day, as he left a tea party given by Lady Cox, from which Cox had carefully absented himself. He was deported for the last time. Philby fumed, 'I am afraid that Cox, with Gertrude acting the part of the serpent, deliberately stooped to an act of treachery.'

Cox showed a similar ruthlessness in taking the old Naqib out of the equation. His political fate was sealed when he was found to have been 'pursuing a strongly anti-Sharifian line behind the scenes'. Cox planned to play on the old man's infirmity, telling him that the interests of the country 'seem to require a ruler who could move about more actively among his subjects and show himself to the army'. As for the idea of a republic, still favoured by many nationalists, Cox proposed a statement that 'we hardly think that the people of Iraq have arrived at a stage of social development as would make such a solution a safe one at the present stage'.[10]

The High Commissioner insisted that 'we must now take a definite line if we are to hope for ultimate success'. Ever since the Cairo Conference he had been pressing Churchill to issue

a declaration of support for Faisal, and was obviously baffled
by the delay. Now at last it came. As Dickson recorded, 'we
politicals were given the tip that HMG would like to see Faisal
king, and we were warned that at all costs the "Mazbatas"
[meetings of local notables] must be favourable to him.' Exactly
what the costs were, he did not record. He did, though, note that
the task had been complicated by the decision of the Sharifians to
send a Marsh Arab officer, Abdul Wahid, to canvass on Faisal's
behalf. 'For Sheikhs who counted themselves "Arab" as opposed
to "Madan" [deprecatory term for March Arabs], to receive
telegrams from Abdul Wahid ordering them to come to Baghdad
to swear fealty to Faisal was a piece of insufferable impudence.'
This was a token of problems to come in establishing the new
regime.[11]

The urgent need for some viable Iraqi political authority was
underlined by an incident on the Euphrates in the early summer,
when the paramount sheikh of the Albu Khalifa was killed by
members of his own tribe. 'The murderers entered the madhif,
exchanged the customary salutations, and forthwith shot the
Shaikh and his relatives.' This assassination apparently shocked
'even the not too susceptible Marsh Arabs'. As Cox reflected,
'tribal administration is largely a game of bluff and on this
occasion the Albu Khalifa called our bluff most successfully'. No
effective response could be mounted. 'Punishment could only have
been carried out by British troops, which was not practicable, or
by Levies embarked on gunboats, and unfortunately the latter
were not available.' As a result, the public got the impression
that Britain was not supporting the new government – dangerous
since the 'anarchic traditions of the Muntafik' were still alive
throughout the area.[12]

Faisal's arrival in Iraq had to be carefully stage-managed.
Although the Naqib volunteered to oversee the Amir's reception,
the committee he set up rapidly degenerated into argument
and almost came to blows. Gertrude Bell had to take over the
arrangements for accommodation and transport (a special train

from Basra to Baghdad), and even the guard of honour. Cox then, strangely, entrusted the task of escorting Faisal to his strongest opponent, Philby, who infuriated Faisal by waxing lyrical about the claims of Ibn Saud to leadership of the Arab people, and reiterating his belief that Iraq should be a republic. But eventually, after a sticky moment as the waiting crowds in Baghdad were told that the train could not get through, Faisal was successfully established in the capital on 29 June. His coronation on 23 August 1921 seemed a British masterstroke.

Yet, by the first anniversary of his reign, Anglo-Iraqi relations were in crisis. The point of contention was the status of the mandate, but the underlying problem was that the British were still undecided about the kind of powers they wanted to exert in Iraq. Percy Cox believed he had been authorised to resolve the issue, and decided soon after the Cairo Conference that the mandate could not be made to stick. Opposition was too strong to be taken on directly. Because 'nationalism in Iraq is a plant of disappointingly sensitive and tender material', the British would have 'to bend every tendril to form and pattern a national state'. This would have to be done very gently, 'for suspicion of our motives and good faith is very near the surface'. Gertrude Bell agreed that 'we should drop the Mandate altogether and go for a treaty with the Arab state when it is constituted. It would be a magnificent move', she added, 'if we're bold enough to do it.'

Unfortunately, Cox and Bell were bolder than the authorities at home. The Colonial Office maintained that Faisal should formally acknowledge his subordination to the High Commissioner, which he adamantly refused to do. The Foreign Office was worried that the French would see any British move to set aside or supersede the mandate as undermining their own position as mandatory in Syria. So the British representative at the League of Nations in Geneva, H. A. L. Fisher, stressed in November 1921 that the proposed treaty between Britain and Iraq was 'not intended as a substitute for the mandate, which will remain the operative document' defining British 'obligations'. Cox, who had not been warned of this, was almost as shocked as Faisal. It is, as one historian says, hard to exaggerate 'the profound effect of this rift on Anglo-Iraqi relations'.[13] Faisal was now so suspicious of British motives that his enthusiasm for the treaty evaporated; negotiations bogged down, and Faisal's awkward position drove him into a series of efforts to drum up opposition to the treaty, to demonstrate that he was not (as charged by the Shia leadership, for instance) a lackey of the British.

Cox's hope that British power would sit lightly on Faisal got no response from the Colonial Office. In February 1922 Cox was still arguing that 'in view of the attitude of the British taxpayer', and hence 'the impossibility of adopting any costly policy in Iraq', it was surely 'more prudent to secure the goodwill of Iraqis' than the reverse. That meant, in effect, 'giving them what they want' as far as the mandate was concerned. Churchill, though, who grumbled soon after Faisal's coronation that the king was 'rather too prone to raise difficult constitutional and foreign questions', held that he should be never be allowed to forget 'the enormous cost and burden Iraq has been and still is to us'. 'All the time he takes our money', he brutally added, 'he will have to take our directions.' In April 1922 he reiterated the implicit threat that Britain would abandon the king: 'Faisal should be under no delusions in this matter. He will be a long time looking for a third throne.'[14]

By the end of July, the frustrated Cox was denouncing Faisal as 'crooked and insincere'. Gertrude Bell lamented that the King, so lovable, was also 'amazingly lacking in strength'. On the anniversary of the coronation, the two of them were jeered by crowds on their way to the palace to congratulate the king. The demonstrators, chanting 'down with the Mandate!', were being directed by the royal chamberlain from the palace balcony. If Faisal had not gone down with appendicitis the next day, there would have been a major crisis, and the British might well have had to depose him. Mere chance saved their policy from shipwreck. As High Commissioner, Cox was able to assume full governmental powers while the king was in hospital; he suppressed the radical parties and newspapers, banished the nationalist opposition leaders from Baghdad, and ordered the bombing of the Euphrates tribes which were threatening revolt. Finally, in October, he persuaded the Naqib to sign the treaty. But getting it ratified would still be a serious problem.

The crucial security question proved equally problematic. Cox had backed Faisal as the man most capable of raising an army, but what kind of army? The British needed an effective security force to be established as soon as possible, but they insisted that it should be organised on lines they approved. Even before Faisal arrived, the ex-Sharifian officers were pushing for a regular army. Jaafar Pasha al-Askari, the Minister of Defence in the Provisional Government, took the lead. Jaafar (who was Nuri al-Said's brother-in-law) could claim some serious military knowledge, having spent three years in a military academy in Berlin after graduating from the Baghdad Military College in 1904, and then attending the staff college at Istanbul. After joining the Arab Revolt in 1916 he had eventually become commander of the Hejaz Army. In November 1920 he drew up a report arguing – on the basis of the former Ottoman military establishment – for an army of 15,000. The British military experts broadly endorsed this total, pointing out that the Turks, who 'never wasted troops', had maintained a regular garrison of nearly 10,000 before the war, 'even at their low establishments'. They also agreed that gendarmerie-type forces would not be adequate: 'trained national land forces' were necessary. Jaafar Pasha insisted on the 'need to fill the ranks with a good class of recruit who has a certain stake in the country and who may be relied upon not to desert'. He believed that this recruitment could be achieved without conscription, by a ballot system taking 7,000 men annually. (They would serve two years with the colours, three in reserve, and then ten in the territorials.[15])

But Cox dismissed all this as far too expensive. In early 1921 a proposal to recruit an army of 6,500 in 1922–3 was reduced by the Council to 4,500. 'Defence can be purchased at too dear a price, and it would be better for Iraq to be inadequately garrisoned than to fall into bankruptcy', which would be 'inevitable' if government funds went into the army rather than 'productive expenditure'. The British stood out against any idea of a draft, much less of universal conscription. Financial arguments were important, but political issues were even more significant, on both sides of what became a long and bitter argument with the new Iraqi state. Jaafar and Nuri followed the thinking about the 'nation in arms' which had flowered in Europe after the French Revolution. The army had to represent the nation, to be a school of patriotism and an engine of modernisation. This nation-building function was even more vital in a country like Iraq than it had been in nineteenth-century France and Germany. Cox, and still more his successor Henry Dobbs, reacted to the Iraqi demand for conscription just as British people had traditionally reacted to those continental 'barrack states': compulsory military service would open the way to militarism and oppression. Dobbs held out the ghastly prospect of 'British aircraft bombing Iraq tribesmen for resistance to conscription'. The British preference for a volunteer army also rested on a belief that, whereas conscription would cement the grip of the Sunni townsmen over the countryside, the majority of those who would volunteer would be the 'virile tribal element' rather than the urban population.[16]

Having come up with the cheapest possible internal-security system, air control supported by levies, Britain was determined that Iraq should follow this line. Jaafar was aghast when he found that 'efforts are being made to constitute the present levies the nucleus of the new Army'. He insisted this could not work, repeating that they must have 'known men of property' as soldiers, not 'homeless wandering Kurds etc'. 'If you persist in enlisting this class', he warned, 'they will turn against you.' The British view was different; the Chief of the Air Staff, Hugh Trenchard, went as far as to hold that they should 'let the Arab

Army remain purely as eyewash', and concentrate on the levies. This was politically impossible, but the development of the army continued to limp along. It never became effective, yet it was much more expensive than equivalent numbers of levies. The latter, too, were a disappointment, mainly due – in the British view – to the poor quality of their Arab officers. The Inspector General lamented 'the entire lack of the power of accepting responsibility displayed by Arab officers and NCOs'. There was a 'dearth of junior Arab officers'. 'Many most injudicious selections have been made. Long service, smart, deserving soldiers have been overlooked and still remain privates, while dirty, lazy, inefficient men have been promoted.'[17]

Cox's quasi-coup impressed Faisal with British resolve sufficiently for him to work for the ratification of the treaty by the national assembly. His government took action against the Shia resistance that flared up in November 1922, with the *mujtahids* issuing *fatwas* declaring that 'participation in the elections' to the national assembly, 'or anything resembling them which will injure the future prosperity of Iraq is pronounced *haram* by the unanimous verdict of Islam'. After protracted negotiations over the winter failed, *fatwas* against participation were again issued in the spring and early summer of 1923 (supplemented by new prohibitions on assisting the government against the Turks), and in late June there were anti-government demonstrations in Khadimain and Karbala. The government then confronted the Shia leadership directly, deporting the most outspoken, Mahdi al-Khalisi, as an undesirable alien. The other leading *mujtahids* also left the country in protest.

This action only neutralised opposition in the short term. In the longer term it inevitably deepened sectarian hostilities. The British, though, went on (like Wilson) seeing the political activity of the Shia leadership as clerical 'meddling' rather than as an expression of deep-rooted Shia grievances. Even after this, the election process was still laborious: elections began on 12 July 1923, but the Constituent Assembly did not meet until 27 March

1924. And once the assembly began to meet, opposition to the treaty grew again. Dobbs reported on 2 June that he did not think there was 'the slightest chance of its being accepted'. (He believed that the government's stratagem of bringing more anti-treaty figures into the assembly, ostensibly to make it look more representative, was actually yet another of Faisal's deliberate spoiling tactics.) In fact, the treaty was at last ratified on 10 June, but the assembly added a kind of codicil stating that it would be null and void if British efforts to get Mosul incorporated in Iraq were to fail. This, by then, was the make-or-break issue for the country's future.

10. Kurdistan for the Kurds?

> It was in the cockpit of Kurdistan rather than the council-
> chambers of Europe that the future of the Middle East was being
> settled.
>
> SIR ARNOLD WILSON

> We have never succeeded in really making up our minds on this
> very difficult question of policy in Kurdistan.
>
> COLONIAL OFFICE

The Kurds were to be the biggest losers in the lottery of self-
determination after the war. Their fate pointed up one of the
great weaknesses of Wilson's concept. Although they were an
ancient and quite distinct ethnic group – some believed they were
the descendants of the Medes – the Versailles moment caught
them at a stage where they had scarcely developed the rudiments
of an organised nationalist movement. Those who had an interest
in preventing the emergence of a Kurdish national state – and
there were plenty of them – could point to the welter of tribal
rivalries as evidence of their political incapacity. 'As a race they
are not a political entity,' said Captain William Hay, political
officer at Arbil. They were 'a collection of tribes without any
cohesion', and indeed 'showing little desire for cohesion'. Even
the more sympathetic Gertrude Bell, who had fond memories of
the Kurds from her travels, tutted that while the Kurds wanted
an independent state under British protection, 'what they mean
by that neither they nor anyone else knows'. Her conclusion was
politically lethal: 'So much for Kurdish nationalism.'[1]

Yet their underlying unity was quite obvious – Captain Hay
had no trouble identifying Kurds and specifying their collective
characteristics – and 'Kurdistan' was a recognised name for the

493

region centred on the area of eastern Anatolia around Diyarbakr, Bitlis and Lake Van, and extending south-west to Kirkuk. But even their historic territory created difficulties in establishing a modern national movement. This was mountain country, and its formidable landscape conspired with tribal infighting to keep communications primitive. (So the Kurdish language, 'perhaps the most ancient tongue in western Asia', Arnold Wilson thought, had many varied local dialects.[2]) In religious terms they were also diverse – some were Christians, some Yazidis, and a few Jews – though they were overwhelmingly Sunni Muslim. Hay judged the ordinary Muslim Kurds 'by no means fanatical', and thought they treated their womenfolk 'with much more respect than do most Mohammedan races'. Their leaders, on the other hand, had become more observant (and fanatical) as Ottoman government pressure increased in the generations before the war.

A kind of national political structure began to emerge in the 1880s in the form of the Kurdish League led by Sheikh Ubaydallah of Nehri, and later nationalist groups had continued to press for administrative, linguistic and religious autonomy for the Kurdish districts.[3] Unfortunately, Sultan Abdul Hamid II fostered Kurdish consciousness by deliberately fomenting religious hostility towards the two big Christian populations of the region, the Armenians and the Assyrians. Kurds took part in the grim Armenian massacres of 1896 and 1909, though these (as Gertrude Bell wrote) 'were not comparable to the slaughter carried out in 1915 and the succeeding years'. Kurdish agency in this final programme of mass murder and expulsion left them in possession of 'the villages and lands of their dead fellow-countrymen'. By the time the British seized Mosul and came into contact with the Kurds they found 'arrayed against us a series of formidable prejudices, pan-Islamism, racial pride, cupidity, and the arrogance of the Kurdish agha, who feared the possibility of a strong European control far more than he feared the Turks'.[4]

To begin with, this was not so clear. In southern Kurdistan, the Kurdish part of Mosul *vilayet*, Kurdish hostility to the Turks was more intense than in Anatolia. Resistance focused on the most active local leader, Sheikh Mahmud Barzanji. Mahmud had taken the surrender of the Ottoman governor and garrison at the end of the war, and as the sole political authority in the Sulaimaniyah area, issued an appeal to Britain 'not to exclude Kurdistan from the list of liberated peoples'. There seemed to be the basis of a Kurdish–British understanding. Cox noted that 'the idea of Kurdish autonomy', which had taken shape in the pre-war years, 'was revived and greatly stimulated by the terms of our Baghdad Proclamation'. Shuckburgh went as far as to say that 'as far as southern Kurdistan was concerned, the people have exercised the right of "self-determination"'. For two years or so, Britain seemed to be enthusiastic for what was often referred to, rather loosely, as a 'Kurdish state'.

The strongest British enthusiast for Kurdish freedom was the first Political Officer sent to Kirkuk, Major Edward Noel. (The Kirkuk Division ran from the Lesser Zab to the Diyala, and north-east to the Persian frontier.) After visiting Sulaimaniyah, he reported that the Kurdish national movement was 'so virile that I do not see much difficulty in creating a Kurdish state under our protection, provided we take prompt and vigorous action now'.[5] He saw Mahmud as the man who could deliver the goods. On 1 December 1918, Arnold Wilson flew up to Sulaimaniyah to meet the Sheikh, who flourished a declaration signed by some forty chiefs 'as the representatives of the people of Kurdistan', asking the Civil Commissioner 'to send a representative with the necessary assistance to enable the Kurdish people under British auspices to progress peacefully on civilized lines'. They undertook 'to accept the orders and advice' of the government if it extended its assistance and protection to them.[6] Wilson approved this, though he was less happy when Mahmud went on to claim 'that he had a mandate from all the Kurds of the Mosul wilayat and many in Persia and elsewhere to represent to us their desire to form a unitary autonomous State of which he was to be the head'. Still, he accepted that 'if feasible' it would simplify the task of forming an Arab state in the rest of Mesopotamia, so 'deserved the closest consideration'.

Noel was sent, on instructions from London, to tour the western and northern Kurdish areas, 'introducing the new system of government' – resting mainly on the raising of local Kurdish levies – as he went. He got plenty of local support, thanks to the belief that Britain favoured Kurdish 'freedom'.[7] As Stephen Longrigg, the new Assistant Political Officer at Kirkuk, later said, 'the dream of "Kurdistan for the Kurds", under British patronage, seemed for a few weeks to have come true'.[8] Noel's belief in Kurdish autonomy would never falter, but Arnold Wilson professed to find it 'hard to judge how far a national movement for independence existed, and to what extent it was an artificial product of the personal ambitions of the Kurdish leaders'.[9] His loaded language showed his take on the issue, and he pounced on evidence of the Kurdish chiefs falling out over the choice of a single leader.

For Wilson, Mahmud himself was a major part of the problem. Though he authorised Noel 'to appoint Sheikh Mahmud as our representative in Suleimaniya' (he became *hukmdar* or governor of 'Kurdish Area B', between the Lesser Zab river and the Persian frontier), this owed more to the shortage of plausible rivals than to Mahmud's own qualities. 'In ignorance, but not in innocence, he was a child'; ambitious, cunning, 'given to sudden fits of passion and outbursts of cruelty which suggested that he was not always responsible for his actions'. Despite his undoubted status amongst Kurds, Wilson saw him as lacking legitimacy. His long resistance to Turkish domination, which might have counted in his favour, only proved for Wilson that he was a threat to orderly government. Soon he was 'abusing his authority', and Wilson decided to bring in Major Ely Soane, one of the very few officials who could claim familiarity with the Kurds, to replace Noel. (Noel was despatched on a tour through Kurdistan aimed, in Wilson's sceptical phrase, 'to ascertain how far the now popular heresy of self-determination could be applied to the inhabitants'.)

Soane, judged by Wilson 'one of the most remarkable men it has ever been my lot to meet', had famously travelled through Kurdistan incognito before the war – he published his remarkable account *To Mesopotamia and Kurdistan in Disguise* in 1912. Uniquely amongst British agents, he had embraced Shia Islam in 1905. 'A short and thick-set man, sharp-featured and with dark, piercing eyes, he had the power which no man in my experience has possessed in anything approaching the same degree, of dominating by sheer force of personality.'[10] He took a dim view of the administrative system Noel had set up. 'Every man who could be labelled a tribesman was placed under a tribal leader . . . Petty village headmen were unearthed as leaders of long dead tribes . . . Law was to be administered by this chief, who must recognise Shaikh Mahmud as Hukmdar.' This might be ideal for the clansman but it was 'fatal for trade, civilization and tranquillity'. Whereas Noel had 'always recognised that the right to self-government was but a right to mismanage one's own affairs', Soane was a man after Wilson's heart, insisting that local autonomy could only be allowed if it met 'civilised' standards. Under what he called the 'pseudo Kurdish state', 'the people themselves – the breath and blood of the country – were given over bound hand and foot to a clique of chiefs now empowered to bleed and depress them'.[11]

Wilson suggested that Soane had 'hitherto had no personal relations with Sheikh Mahmud', but this did not mean he had an open mind about him. 'They hated each other', in the curt view of the commander of the Kurdish levies at Sulaimaniyah, Major A. M. Daniels. Soane saw Mahmud as 'an unworthy descendant of a good man' (Sheikh Said), a despot who 'filled every post with his own relations regardless of their character or ability'.[12] Soane did, in fact, support Kurdish autonomy, but with strictly British-style government. At Mosul itself, Colonel Leachman was even more committed to direct British control. As political officer there from the armistice until the summer of 1919 he majored on punitive action – 'correcting contrary

Kurdish tribes' – rather than routine administration. (Even he admitted to his mother that he might not be 'cut out as the ideal political officer; my methods are too abrupt'.[13]) By installing men with similar outlook as assistant political officers at Arbil (Major Hay) and Keuisenjaa (Captain Rundle), Wilson showed that he saw his deal with Mahmud as a temporary compromise until British control could be effectively tightened. (Rundle, for instance, reported that he had been 'compelled' to intervene in the administration of his district to 'prevent friction or injustice'.[14]) Early in 1919 two districts, Kifri and Kirkuk, were removed from the autonomous Kurdish area.

Eventually, in May 1919, watching his authority steadily being eroded, Mahmud made a bid for effective rulership. With 500 men he took control of Sulaimaniyah on 15 May, overwhelming the half-organised levies under Daniels (who seems, ironically, to have shared Noel's rather than Wilson's view of Kurdish autonomy). 'We were not too confident about the reliability of our officers and men,' Daniels lamented. 'Everything was still very much in the melting pot, and we had not been able to enter into any regular terms of engagement with them.' The officers were mostly veterans of the Ottoman War College, 'a particularly good stamp of man, no prejudices, an uncommon amount of grit', but 'terrified that they will be placed on the same footing as Indian Officers'. The Indian Army's prejudices were well known to them. Daniels had in fact been trying to get authorisation for his levy officers to wear British uniforms; he found to his surprise that 'not only the educated classes' but also the irregulars were keen on this. 'They would have a rather higher opinion of themselves and the force they are joining if they were allowed to wear a Kitchener helmet!' Daniels reported in April. 'It is difficult to understand, but the feeling is there.' (He had designed his own uniform for them, but they were apparently 'disappointed' – finding it 'too Kurdish'.[15]) Whether through demoralisation or respect for Mahmud, the levies broke. The cavalry were the first to go; Daniels led the infantry up on to a hill outside the town in the hope of holding them together until nightfall, but 'they had seen their camp being looted, and the cavalry bolt, and many of them having relations in the town, feared the vengeance the Sheikh's men would take on them'. The force began to withdraw after dark, 'but as soon as they reached the bottom of the hill, they were surrounded . . . and threw down their arms'. The commander of the attackers solicitously made sure that Daniels was all right, before arresting him.

Mahmud's bid to create a Kurdish state was certainly not implausible. The autonomous area already had Kurdish as its official language, and possessed its own armed forces in the form of the Kurdish levies. Now Mahmud raised his own flag, issued his own postage stamps, and appointed his own 'retainers' to take control of every district (their distinctive badge was a copy of the Fourteen Points pinned to their sleeves). But he still could not control some areas, like Halabja and Panjwin, that were barely twenty miles from Sulaimaniyah. Even sympathetic historians underline his inability to stimulate a spontaneous nationalist rising in his heartland. Rivals for Kurdish primacy like the Badr Khans and Babans (long exiled to Istanbul and Baghdad), as well as local leaders, refused to recognise his claim to be 'King of Kurdistan'. Soon that claim brought down on his head the full weight of British displeasure.

Baghdad admitted that the outbreak of 'serious troubles' in Kurdistan was 'wholly unexpected locally, as Sheikh Mahmud had been steadily losing ground and was becoming personally unpopular with influential elements'. But it was certain that unless 'we at once suppress' him, 'powerful tribes will be drawn into the movement'. The movement was 'purely anarchistic', Wilson argued, and a British reoccupation of Sulaimaniyah would be popular.[16] It took a month to assemble the 18th Division for a counter-stroke, but when it advanced the issue was hardly in doubt. On 17 June, Major-General Theodore Fraser defeated Sheikh Mahmud in a mountain pass twelve miles east of Chemchemal. The 85th Burmans, 'three parts Kachin', had been hurried up by MacMunn to provide fresh legs. They bore out his martial-race theory admirably. 'At daybreak, the little men, out-"Girking" the Gurkhas, rushed in on the Sheikh and his reserve, having scaled the heights and rolled up the Kurds on the flank.' Mahmud was shot through the liver and captured, and a fast cavalry ride by the 32nd Lancers rescued the Sulaimaniyah prisoners unharmed.[17]

The next six weeks 'were spent in exacting punishment from the rebellious chiefs, small columns penetrating every mountain fastness'. Mahmud was tried in Baghdad and sentenced to death, though MacMunn – to Wilson's dismay – commuted the sentence to banishment. With him gone, the political officers set about reconstructing the administration on British lines; but still no policy direction came from London. At the end of his mission to consult the Kurds, Noel arrived at Constantinople, where the High Commissioner's political adviser worried that he might become a 'Kurdish Lawrence'. (Noel was 'a nice fellow, but he is another fanatic. He is the apostle of the Kurds. There is no-one like them, so good and noble and generous!') But if London shied away from it, Constantinople at least faced the issue of where Mesopotamia's northern frontier should be. It could not be in the plains north of Baghdad; it must be in the mountains; and since the mountains were 'essentially Kurdish . . . it becomes essential to have a Kurdish policy'.[18]

The High Commissioner sympathised with Wilson's view of the Kurds. 'There is every shade of Kurd,' he held, 'like there is every colour in the spectrum, and all history goes to show that they are mighty unreliable.' But they could not just be left alone: this was 'a big question of policy, on which an authoritative ruling must be given'. As he grumbled again to Curzon, 'all these things would be infinitely easier if one only knew what the desires of His Majesty's Government were'.[19] A month later Wilson was told by the India Secretary that, although the future of Kurdistan was still 'unsettled', it could be taken as certain that Britain's permanent responsibilities could 'in no event go beyond loose political supervision', and that 'anything in the nature of direct British administration is out of the question'. The government had been disconcerted by the Mahmud coup. Up until then, they had 'supported the policy of extending British influence to South Kurdistan because they believed that the inhabitants themselves welcomed it'; but 'it would now appear that belief was misplaced'. Wilson had suggested an extension to the Baqaba–Khanikin railway on the Diyala to Kifri and Kirkuk as 'the best means of pacifying South Kurdistan by bringing it into closer touch with Baghdad'. Montagu read this proposal as meaning that 'the inhabitants so far from welcoming British influence are so actively hostile that strategic railways are required to keep them in check'.

Wilson, naturally, rejected this view. The 'fact that order was restored by the Military Authorities within one month and that normal Civil Administration was established within three months of the rising of Sheikh Mahmud' was, for him, 'proof that the present regime is welcomed by the majority of the inhabitants'. He offered an interesting key to the situation: though the British were 'governing Southern Kurdistan not by force but by consent, no Government in these days can carry on without force behind it'. He was confident that 'after a brief taste of nationalist anarchy', the people had 'no desire to try it again'. London need not worry about the northern frontier: problems there would arise 'only if Kurdistan is left to its own devices'.[20]

Unfortunately, trouble did flare up again soon afterwards. In March the APO at Zakho, Captain Pearson, had been killed, and two months later Leachman (without consulting Wilson) installed a political officer, Captain Willey, at Amadiya, with two officers to raise a local gendarmerie force. Wilson had been against the military occupation of the valley in the first place, and when the military detachment was withdrawn he urged Leachman to remove Willey as well. Both were determined to stay, and on 14 July all three British officers were killed. Once again, major military operations by the 18th Division began – a campaign in the most hostile terrain. This was 'warfare of a type with which the Army in India has long been familiar, but wholly novel to the vast majority of troops now engaged'. We can get a vivid sense of what it was like from a report on the actions of 'Stapleton's column', whose mission was 'to kill as many armed Kurds as possible, further to punish the leaders of the rising by the destruction of their property in the implicated villages'. (But there was at last a new restriction in the rules of engagement – 'on no account were whole villages to be destroyed'.)

Colonel Scott pointed out that 'the combination of North-West Frontier conditions of country with really dense jungle, met with in Kurdistan, certainly calls for modification of the ordinary methods and principles of mountain warfare'. Movement was difficult and dangerous. Loads were lightened by halving the number of Lewis guns carried, and units experimented with having the troops carry their grenades ready fused in their haversacks, because of the 'known fear of the Kurds for this weapon'. But this proved unpopular and dangerous; after two men were killed and four wounded by a grenade explosion, the men were allowed to tie the levers down with their bootlaces. This, of course, lost the 'advantage of instant action', but in any case some disapproved of the emphasis on bombing as 'reducing the prestige of the rifle'. Picquets had to be prepared to deny ground to attackers by 'actual bayonet, and bomb and rifle attack, not fire action only'. The standard rule of 'no movement beyond picquet defences or perimeter after dark' had to be modified, 'if the danger of camps being rushed by enemy who have massed at very close range is to be avoided'. No day, as Scott said, was 'long enough to allow time for a march and also for clearing the jungle sufficiently to make the perimeter reasonably safe in the very broken country'.[21]

In guerrilla fighting, the Kurds were formidable opponents. 'Every man is mounted, and they understand North-West Frontier warfare completely.' Unlike the Arabs, 'the Kurd does no fight on horseback – he is really a mounted infantryman'. Their tactics were 'Afridi – front left alone, rear and flanks attacked'. They were 'here today and thirty miles away tomorrow'. But they had their limits. 'Of course, they have not taken a single post, and as soon as the smallest party of our people sit down they can hold off any number of Kurds.' But 'they cannot move, and someone else has to go and dig them out'. This was extremely difficult when numbers were stretched to the limit, and there was 'no striking force left'. 'It makes one very angry.'[22]

Even though they were not included in the official history, Wilson suggested that the large-scale punitive operations in southern Kurdistan should be seen as the true finale to the Mesopotamia Campaign. But they still failed to achieve complete pacification. In October 1919 Leachman's successor, J. H. H. Bill, and another British officer, Captain Scott, were killed by Kurdish irregulars on the Greater Zab near Aqra. The local gendarmerie commander had assumed that because the attackers had been reported as only 100 strong, there was no likelihood of attack; and 'being of the Zibar tribes, I did not think it was a general rising'.[23] More punitive operations followed, and the outbreak was contained. But what did it represent? As usual Wilson insisted that the attacks were unplanned and unpolitical, simply 'one of the sudden fits of anger which are typical of the Kurdish temperament'. Colonel Nalder, who succeeded Bill at Mosul, agreed about this. Nalder found the Kurds 'highly moral, in the narrower sense of the term', since, apart from one or two of the aghas, 'they appear to abstain from wine or spirits'. ('Which is lucky', he added.) But even sober, 'the Kurd seems to be possessed by an amazingly quick temper, which coupled with his natural fanaticism, produces a highly explosive mixture'.

This unruly temperament created a clash between anarchy and order. Nalder declared that 'the position of the average Kurdish Agha is incompatible with our own or any other Government'. Their lands were too small to live on, and 'their wealth depends entirely on extortion from the villages'.[24] Major W. R. Hay at Rowanduz airily assured his superiors that 'the Kurd has the mind of a schoolboy, not without the schoolboy's innate cruelty. He requires a beating one day and a sugar plum the next.' Overall, 'the Kurds may be divided into good Aghas, bad Aghas, and the people'.[25] Bad aghas were sadly all too common – every district had at least one. But the key implication was that it was possible to separate the people from the aghas. The leading British policies – establishing forces under British control to maintain order, and stimulating agricultural revival by giving funds and seed direct to the people – were clearly designed to do this. Both policies undermined the authority of the traditional rulers, and certainly played a part in provoking the repeated local rebellions – yet Britain remained committed to the political domination of those rulers. Militarily, the events of 1919 had 'proved abundantly', for Nalder, 'that we cannot administer the Kurdish mountains without the support of troops'. Air bombing had been 'splendidly carried out in circumstances of the greatest difficulty and danger', but it had 'soon lost its moral effect'.

There was another dimension to the conflict, which Wilson might minimise but could not disguise. The British attempt to settle the Assyrian refugees triggered an anti-Christian reaction: 'this just design furnished the subject-matter of the propaganda directed against us,' as he virtuously put it. This was no passing phenomenon, however. Earlier Kurdish mobilisations, like Sheikh Ubaydallah's, had been driven by the same motive – in that case, fear of the Armenians – and the formidable rebellion of Sheikh Said in eastern Anatolia in 1925 would also be a Muslim rising against the secularising Turkish republic. Military intelligence, in arguing against punitive measures in Kurdistan without 'permanent occupation', saw the problem as primarily one of 'anti-Christian disturbances'. Britain as a Christian power would (like France) inevitably be suspected of actively favouring Christian interests. This suspicion strengthened in 1919 when the Greeks, encouraged by the Allies, sent an army to Smyrna and advanced into Anatolia. 'News was spread of a massacre of Mohammedans by the Greeks. The Kurds were invited to apply the analogy of Smyrna to Diyarbekir; the English would come first and occupy the town, which would be but a prelude to the arrival of Armenian troops.'

In this volatile situation, British policy drifted for the next three years. Kurdistan was just a problem too many. 'Might it not be better to leave the Kurds to their own devices?' Montagu even wondered. Early in December 1919, Bell thought the issue was resolved: 'AT has managed the Kurds very skilfully and to our great relief they agree to come in under the Iraq state.' Their relief was partly that this supposed agreement would 'save the bother which would attend the multiplication of administrative frontiers'. But there was more to this than 'saving bother'. Though Bell believed, probably genuinely, that the Kurds' own interests would be best served by joining Iraq, the alternatives were clearly alarming. Three months later she was still urging Hirtzel that it would be 'fatal to think of an autonomous Kurdistan or a Suleimaniyah detached from Iraq'. If Britain were not to run the area, it would be better left to the Turks – 'they can't do it but they'll be better than absolutely untrammelled Kurds'.[26] On the Kurdish issue, Bell saw eye to eye with Wilson. They suggested that 'it was hard to tell how far a national movement existed and how far it was the artificial product of the personal ambitions of the Kurdish leaders, who saw in Kurdish autonomy an unequalled opportunity for furthering their own interests'.[27] Such insinuations had been common currency amongst opponents of nationalism in Europe and elsewhere for generations, and it is hard to tell how honest they were. But they would also convince Percy Cox to follow the same line when he returned to Baghdad.

In April 1920 the Cabinet had a stab at finding a clear policy line; Montagu was still in favour of 'an independent Kurdistan', but Curzon lamented that they could not find 'anyone to set up an autonomous State'.[28] Any prospect of Kurdish independence grew more illusory the longer the delay lasted, and the further the construction of the new Iraq state went. The oil resources at

Kirkuk did not figure at all in the Cabinet's discussions; but as their size became better known, they would increasingly seem vital to Iraq's viability. And despite their ethnic distinctness and their aversion to Arab rule, Kurds had their uses to the Sunni-dominated Iraq government. As Sunnis they would help offset the potentially disturbing Shia majority in Iraq. (Faisal would tell Cox that 'the excision of a large slice of Sunni districts . . . would place Shiahs in a very strong position and filled him with misgiving'.)

Most fatal to the prospect of autonomy was the fact that Kurdish opinion could not come together at this vital stage. Although Kurdistan was in turmoil like much of Mesopotamia in 1920, there was no sign of any new level of organisation. Hay blamed the trouble in his area, Rowanduz, on the 'spirit of unrest which spread upwards from the south' and acted on the wildness and ignorance of the people, who had 'grown tired of peaceful pursuits and welcomed a little excitement' – and, of course, 'the chance of loot'. He maintained that 'the mass of the people in the Arbil, Koi and Khushnao' districts, being 'an industrious race willing to pay revenue in return for the security which an honest administration assures them', were on the side of 'the Government'.[29] After he returned as High Commissioner, Cox conducted a 'plebiscite' in southern Kurdistan, but this once again was no more than a public sounding of notables, who were reluctant to defy what they took to be British policy

The drift went on into 1921. When the Middle East Department was set up, it took responsibility for 'that part of Kurdistan (known as Southern Kurdistan) which has hitherto been included in the Mosul vilayet'; but only 'pending the voluntary adherence of its inhabitants to a Kurdish state'.[30] At the Cairo Conference Churchill assembled a committee (Cox, Bell, Lawrence and Young, with Noel as 'consultative member') to discuss Kurdistan on 15 March. Though Cox (supported by Bell) argued that Kirkuk and Mosul 'formed an integral part of Iraq', the committee accepted the 'strong opinion' of Churchill's new Middle East Department (in effect, Hubert Young's view) that 'purely Kurdish areas should not be included in the Arab state of Mesopotamia'. Lawrence bluntly stated that 'the Kurds should not be placed under an Arab Government'. Britain should promote 'the principles of Kurdish unity and nationality . . . as far as possible'. The precise area involved could not be fixed until peace terms were finally arranged with Turkey, but it should be controlled by Britain via 'some form of central Kurdish Organization to which a British Adviser could be attached'. (One advantage of this was that it would 'enable us to recruit Kurdish units under British officers, and accelerate reduction of Imperial forces'.)

Churchill offered a telling take on the likely behaviour of the Iraq state: 'a Sharif whose breeding and family history probably led him to hold views on the Divine Right of Kings, might, while outwardly accepting constitutional procedure and forming a Parliament, at the same time despise democratic and constitutional methods'. If so, 'it might well be that, with the power of an Arab army behind him, he would ignore Kurdish sentiment and oppress the Kurdish minority'. His committee once again favoured keeping Kurdistan separate, and Lloyd George explicitly approved this approach.[31] But its decision was vague enough to allow Cox to go on debating the policy line. 'The impression I gained', he wrote on 20 May, 'was that Mosul and Tel Afar, and possibly Kirkuk itself, should remain within the Arab sphere, while Suleimaniya, the Kirkuk area, and the Kurdish outposts of Mosul should be permanently garrisoned by Kurdish and Assyrian levies'. He still supposed that there would be a separate Kurdish zone, and wanted to know whether Kirkuk was to be 'treated as part of Mesopotamia or as part of Kurdistan'.

But in fact he was already pressing arguments for the integration of all the Kurdish areas into Iraq. He pointed out that all the 'arteries of communication' in Kurdistan ran north, or to Mosul. There were no cross-country communications with Sulaimaniyah, and any attempt to force districts like Amadia 'to join a Kurdish unit with a centre of gravity either in Rowanduz or Suleimaniya would drive it to connect itself with the north'. He suggested that separation would not be in the economic interests of the Kurds themselves (though he also admitted that at Sulaimaniyah they were openly against Arab rule whatever the economic consequences). The ethnic mix in Kurdistan would make boundary-drawing impracticable, as well. He also argued that a stronger Iraq would be a more effective barrier to Turkey than any 'buffer state'.[32] At the same time, a group of Kurdish experts discussing the results of the opinion survey were 'unanimous' that southern Kurdistan should 'be retained as an integral part of Iraq for financial and fiscal purposes', but the High Commissioner should administer it 'direct through Kurdish and British officials, on such a basis of local autonomy as would satisfy their Home Rule ideas'. Cox urged that progress be made soon, since the exposition of the pros and cons of the issue, and the invitation to express views, had 'had a valuable effect', and this 'should not be lost'.[33]

Churchill told Cox that he had 'carried away from Cairo rather a different impression of the balance of opinion' on Kurdish policy from Cox's. He was still convinced of the value of 'a buffer state ethnologically composed of non-Arab elements and interposed between Iraq and Turkey', and he saw advantages in a weaker Iraq, which would be less able to challenge British control. His advisers, Noel and Young, saw no difficulty in drawing boundaries for a Kurdish area. He insisted again that 'we ought not to be deflected' from the policy of establishing a Kurdish buffer 'either by Arab pressure or by any other cause'. John Shuckburgh was clearly conscious that Kurdish policy was hanging in the balance, and pleaded that 'a step in the wrong direction might have disastrous results which would not be confined to Kurdistan. We are engaged in a very delicate political transaction in Mesopotamia and cannot afford to take any unnecessary risks'. When a decision was reached on Kurdish policy, it was 'most important it should be the right one'.[34]

Churchill even pressed for the release of Sheikh Mahmud, and when Cox temporised, saying that Mahmud was 'undergoing simple imprisonment' in India, tartly rebuked him – 'I do not think this will do at all.' Simple imprisonment ('what is it?' Churchill asked) seemed to be a euphemism for preventing Mahmud from having contact with the outside world; 'a great deal more trouble has got to be taken to meet wishes I express in these matters'. Cox accepted Mahmud's return under protest, and on condition of strict subordination. He held that 'our policy is more truly in the interest of Kurdish nationalism than Sheikh Mahmud's', since 'we are working with some success for a constitution, which though oligarchical in its present stage, is developing towards democracy'. Mahmud, on the other hand, was 'identified with a policy of absolutism, and is feared as a feudal baron of the worst type'.[35]

The fact that the Iraq Electoral Law of December 1920 contained no reference to the safeguards promised to the Kurds under the Treaty of Sèvres – signed only four months earlier – has been seen as proof that Britain had already abandoned any intention of safeguarding Kurdish interests.[36] But it is quite clear that Churchill and the leading officials in the Colonial Office were still committed to Kurdish autonomy long after the Cairo Conference – indeed until the fall of the Lloyd George government in October 1922. What they did not do – in sharp contrast with their policy on the Arab state – was to ensure that it was actually implemented by Baghdad. Cox and Bell were able to exploit the ambiguity of London's approach. (As late as September 1921 the Colonial Office admitted that 'we have never succeeded in really making up our minds on this very difficult question of policy in Kurdistan'.) When Faisal argued the need for the Sunni Kurds to counterbalance the Shia, Reader Bullard found it 'amusing' (since the king had previously claimed that the Shia had rebelled in 1920 because they wanted him as ruler). But he wryly suggested that 'no policy that works is really absurd!'[37] Making Iraq 'work' was a practical priority which ultimately overrode other ideas. So, while he admitted that Sulaimaniyah was opposed to incorporation in Iraq, Cox argued that Churchill must realise 'the picture would be somewhat spoilt if Sulaimaniyah alone were to be allowed to stand out'. Not only would the resulting customs barriers be 'a chronic source of difficulty', but 'Basra and other communities would want to follow suit and it would be difficult to argue with them'.[38] As the slow process of getting the Iraq national assembly elected rolled on through 1922–3, Noel lamented that he was 'up against the universal suspicion, in some cases amounting almost to a certainty, that we are determined to get the Kurds into Iraq by hook or by crook, and that the election business is all eyewash'.[39]

The Treaty of Sèvres certainly promised the formation of an autonomous Kurdish region which would have the right to petition the League of Nations for full independence after a year. (How the claim would be assessed was not clear.) This was the Foreign Office's stalling tactic, but the fierce Turkish nationalist reaction to the treaty, which was repudiated by the new Grand National Assembly under the leadership of Mustafa Kemal, meant that the delay stretched out well beyond twelve months. The National Pact adopted by the assembly in February 1920 had declared the province of Mosul to be an inalienable part of historic Turkish territory, so the chances of an agreed settlement were remote. The assembly had also promised to recognise the 'dignitaries of the Kurdish nation' as an autonomous administration. While the Greeks advanced through Anatolia, reaching the area between Eskisehir and Afion Kara-Hissar in August 1921, Britain toyed with the idea of fomenting Kurdish risings to undermine the Kemalist position. 'Every scheme for reducing the Kemalists by force of arms', the High Commissioner at Constantinople noted, 'has always included more or less vague plans for raising Kurdistan against them', and there had always been some Kurdish nationalists 'anxious to see some such plan'. (The idea was taken seriously enough to drive Cox to plead that 'a programme of Kurdish liberation be not undertaken without a full understanding by the Kurds of the extent of help we can afford them, and a clear definition of our responsibilities'.⁴⁰) But if the Kurds disliked Turkish rule, they were unlikely to applaud the spread of what looked like a new Christian imperialism. Even before Kemal's decisive victory over the Greeks outside Ankara in September 1921, the balance between a resurgent nationalist Turkey and a Britain whose army had demobilised and whose treasury was bare was shifting.

The guerrilla movement that erupted in opposition to the Greek advance spread southwards towards the French in Cilicia and eastwards towards Kurdistan, and it is not surprising that during the 1920 rebellion some in Britain considered abandoning Mosul, if not even Baghdad itself. Turkish infiltration and incitement in Kurdistan intensified during 1921. When a Kemalist battalion advanced to Rowanduz in the summer of 1921, hoping to start a revolt amongst the Surchi, the British could only respond with air action, which failed to dislodge the Turks. (The difficulties of the operation were emphasised by the RAF commander: 'Apart from the bombing of a cruel and uncivilised race, every machine that proceeded to Rowanduz had to fly more than 75 miles across one of the most terrible terrains that our force has operated over, where forced landing would mean almost certain death.') The following year, Turkish moves became more threatening: they occupied Koi and Qala Diza, while a group of rebellious tribes seized Raniya. The levies sent to retake the town in late August were routed. In the first week of September 1922 British personnel were withdrawn from Sulaimaniyah by aircraft – probably the world's first air evacuation, but a record Britain would rather not have set. Britain was reduced to bringing Sheikh Mahmud back from exile in Kuwait in mid-September as the only viable political figure in Kurdistan.

Mahmud gradually re-established his authority at Sulaimaniyah, and seems to have secured wider local support than during his first government. The Kurdish Council, the framework for Mahmud's administration, seems to have emerged

locally, though Cox claimed it as a British initiative.[41] By the
end of 1922, C. J. Edmonds, a senior official in Baghdad, was
warning that Mahmud's influence was increasing, a sign of
nationalist extremism. Cox worked persistently through 1922
to limit the extent of Mahmud's authority, and (Mahmud
alleged) deny him the aid he needed to fulfil the British demand
that he expel the Turkish force from Rowanduz. Cox also tried
unsuccessfully to revive the candidacy of a rival Kurdish leader,
Said Taha. Mahmud – whether because of Cox's obstruction is
not clear – toyed with going over to the Turkish side. At the end
of October 1922, within days of the collapse of Lloyd George's
government and Churchill's departure from the Colonial Office,
he proclaimed himself 'King of Southern Kurdistan'. Eventually
he took the fatal step of launching a second armed struggle
against British control.

In the circumstances, the RAF's eventual success in impelling
the Turkish forces to withdraw from Mosul *vilayet* stood out
as a beacon of hope for the maintenance of British influence. In
October 1922 the Turks around Aqra and Rania were driven
out by air bombardment alone. In February 1923 combined
ground–air operations, directed by one of the RAF's most
brilliant commanders, John Salmond, re-established control
of the whole area between Sulaimaniyah and Rowanduz. All
this seemed a triumphant vindication of the new theories of air
power. Both external and internal threats had been dealt with.
The last eighteen months, Salmond reported in April 1924,
had seen 'a very remarkable improvement in the respect paid
to Government, and the general condition of peace and order,
throughout the country'.[42] Outbreaks had continued, admittedly,
but they were more infrequent, localised and transient. The
final Turkish advance, by some 2,500 troops accompanied by
nationalist volunteers, in the summer of 1924, was halted by
air action alone.[43] Bombing of Turkish concentrations and
communications seems to have convinced the local tribesmen of
Britain's determination to defend Mosul.[44] Mahmud's revolt was

doomed, not least because it coincided with the long-delayed resumption of negotiations between Turkey and the Allies at Lausanne. For Bonar Law's government, there was no question of antagonising the Turks by appearing to support a Kurdish state – or even quasi-state – that might encourage Kurdish separatism within Turkey itself. Air power finally drove the King of Kurdistan out of Sulaimaniyah into the Persian hills, where 'he maintained the hunted existence of a bandit'.

'Kurdistan for the Kurds' was, painfully slowly, evaporating. The Acting High Commissioner reaffirmed in June 1923 that 'our object is to secure the closest possible association of the Kurds with Iraq consistent with our pledges to the Kurds'. But what did these really amount to? The Kurds had, he noted, 'been insistent on retention of some right of appeal for High Commissioner's intervention'; but he had 'sought as far as possible to minimise this'. When the government addressed the issue of the upcoming Iraq elections, it decided that 'the precise nature of the procedure to be adopted' in Kurdistan should be left to the High Commissioner (Cox's successor, Sir Henry Dobbs). Noel's gloomy prediction would be borne out.

11. The World Decides

The people of England have been led in Mesopotamia into a trap.
T. E. LAWRENCE

Something like a national debate on the question whether Britain should hold on to Iraq took place, belatedly, between 1920 and 1924. The press had reacted badly to the 1920 revolt, with denunciations of Britain's 'insane policy in the Middle East' beginning to appear, and *The Times* demanding an end to secrecy – alleging that operations in Kurdistan had been 'far more considerable than the public have been allowed to know'. The government was criticised for its failure to allow a public debate about Britain's commitment as mandatory power in Iraq (the change of name from Mesopotamia was identified as an attempt to avert hostility to a place of grim associations). 'The time is past when any Government could commit the nation to the acquisition of a considerable new Empire . . . without first making an exhaustive public statement of their intentions.' The *Manchester Guardian* asked why Britain needed 'all this machinery, all these forces, all these punitive expeditions, if we are establishing a political system on the basis of consent'?[1] T. E. Lawrence found a particularly galling line of attack, comparing British policy to the French, whose imperial methods the British affected to deplore. In Syria they had, he said, 'only followed in very humble fashion the example we set them in Mesopotamia'.[2]

By 1922 the cost and risk of this unloved commitment evoked general disapproval: there was a strong sense of 'imperial overstretch'. After the fall of Lloyd George in October 1922 – precipitated by his interventionist policy against Turkey – the new Conservative government under Bonar Law directly aired the possibility of abandoning either Mosul, or the whole of Iraq. The Duke of Devonshire, the new Colonial Secretary, chaired a committee to assess the issue. It heard from the Air Ministry of the strategic and political value of the air route that now operated between Cairo and Baghdad via Palestine and Transjordan. The Foreign Office laid out an unappetising set of possible outcomes, the least damaging to British prestige being the possibility that 'Turkey might be induced to sign a Treaty recognising Irak and undertaking to respect its integrity'. Unfortunately this was also the least likely outcome, the FO suggested. The most influential advice came from the Middle East Department, which stressed the historic nature of Britain's paramountcy at the head of the Persian Gulf, and warned once again how much Britain had to fear from 'a great Mohammedan combination throughout Asia directed against the West'. The Muslim world was 'in a distracted state'; Iraq was 'a key position' where 'a strong Arab state, friendly to the British Government, breaking the chain of possibly hostile influences, may be of immense importance to us in the difficult times that lie ahead'.

Then, of course, there was the oil. As the MED complained, the press and public generally assumed that Iraq was 'a mere arid desert, into whose sands millions of British money have been poured without the slightest prospect of any return'. But quite apart from the long-dreamed prospect of reviving its historic fertility under 'more enlightened administration', the oilfields offered the possibility of vast resources. So far they had not even been properly prospected, and the contention of various claimants would always be a problem, but it was surely vital 'to keep within the British sphere of influence what may prove to be one of the most important oil-fields of the future'. Whereas 'if we cut our losses now, we shall have nothing whatever to show for our heavy sacrifices of blood and treasure'. In all of this, the MED had clearly shifted its position over Kurdish autonomy in favour of buttressing the Iraq state.

The MED drew up a list of no fewer than eighteen separate occasions on which Britain had in some sense acknowledged a moral obligation to support the establishment of an Arab state, asserting that if Britain either abandoned its protégé Faisal, or even allowed 'the extent of his dominions to be seriously curtailed', it would incur 'a charge of breach of faith which would be very difficult to rebut'. Inevitably, the effect on British prestige throughout the East 'need not be enlarged on'. There was, finally, as far as Mosul was concerned, the issue of the Christian minorities. Britain had obligations to the 'Assyrians', who, after the failure of various projects, had been successfully settled (on a self-supporting basis) near the northern frontier. The Archbishop of Canterbury was 'closely interested in these people', and there could be 'no doubt what their fate would be if we abandoned them to the Turks'. (There was grim irony in this, considering their eventual fate at the hands of the Iraqis.)

Devonshire's committee eventually concluded in April 1923 that the drawbacks of withdrawal outweighed the advantages. Britain stayed in Iraq and held on to Mosul, though its status remained in limbo even after the new Turkish state finally agreed a peace treaty, at Lausanne in July 1923. In this even the vague promise of a possible Kurdish state disappeared. If there was no bilateral agreement between Britain and Turkey, Mosul's status was to be determined by the League of Nations. In fact Britain and Turkey were so far from agreement that hostilities were only narrowly avoided in October 1924 by the League drawing the provisional 'Brussels Line' along the northern frontier of the Mosul *vilayet* to separate the two sides. The League finally arbitrated Mosul's fate in July 1925, after a Commission of Inquiry had spent two months trying to assess public opinion there.

Although the fact that it had to confine its inquiry to the area south of the Brussels Line showed that any prospect of establishing a wider 'Kurdistan' had gone, its findings were interesting. It accepted that 'if the ethnic argument alone had to be taken into account, the necessary conclusion would be that an independent Kurdish state should be created'. Although Mosul city itself contained more Arabs than Kurds, and there were also significant numbers of Turks in the *vilayet*, the Kurds formed five-eighths of the *vilayet*'s population. (If the Yazidis were included, the proportion was nearer three-quarters.[3]) But the ethnic argument did not prevail. Politically, the Kurds were disunited: national feeling only manifested itself in hostility to outsiders, but not in any constructive political direction. Sulaimaniyah was different, the commission accepted: there was a national feeling there which, 'though yet young, was reasonable enough' (in that people wanted independence but recognised 'the advantages of an enlightened and intelligent trusteeship'). But it found an extra problem in the fact that none of the political boundaries under consideration were 'racial frontiers'.

The commission awarded the territory south of the Brussels Line to Iraq, but under two vital conditions. First, 'the territory must remain under the effective Mandate of the League of Nations for a period of twenty-five years'. Second, 'Regard must be paid to the desires expressed by the Kurds that officials of Kurdish race should be appointed for the administration of their country, the dispensation of justice, and teaching in schools.' Kurdish should be the official language for all these services. (Gertrude Bell had hinted at the likely fate of such measures of cultural protection when she noted that the wish that all teaching should be in Kurdish would be 'reasonable if it weren't for the fact that there aren't any Kurdish teachers and those can only be trained in Arabic for there are no Kurdish books'.) The League ratified the commission's recommendations in December 1925.

From being a majority in Kurdistan, the Kurds became a minority in Iraq. The international community had spoken, and its logic was instructive. The argument that Kurdish opinion was so divided that there was, in effect, no Kurdish opinion, implied that only those peoples with a fully developed national political organisation in 1919 could qualify for self-determination. And the argument was wrong on one key issue at least: subordination to an Arab government was universally rejected by Kurds. This had been reported so often by British officials that it is hard to see Britain's eventual stance as anything other than wilful self-deception. Kurdish identity was inconvenient. Britain had created Iraq for strategic reasons, and Iraq could only survive as a British client state if it controlled the oil resources of southern Kurdistan. The test of the 1925 settlement would be whether Britain would uphold the 'minority protection' guaranteed in it: once again, the story would end in betrayal.

Afterword

In the Book of Politics we are a people
Owners of sovereignty: yet we do not even possess wreckage we
   could call our own.
In the Book of Politics we are a people
With law and order; yet our lives are ruled by chaos.

MUHAMMAD HABIB AL-UBAIDI[1]

Britain's campaign in Mesopotamia had far-reaching consequences for the land between the rivers, and for the world.
Most of them were unintended. Britain had no definite 'exit
strategy' because its original entry strategy had been dangerously
vague. The mission given to the expeditionary force in 1914
was ambiguous. Securing and protecting the supply of oil from
southern Persia was a perfectly straightforward and realistic
aim, but it was overlaid by much more ambitious, and much
hazier, objectives. There was no real agreement about these,
even amongst British decision-makers themselves, and no single
agency had the power to shape policy. The idea that Britain
could foster an Arab breakaway from Ottoman rule was rooted
in a misreading of Arab identity, and a potent prejudice about
the faults of Turkish government. Every development of the
campaign was influenced by the crucial, but perilously imprecise,
issue of British prestige. The advance of the expeditionary force
up the two rivers was propelled not by military logic but by a
fear that even halting, let alone falling back, would destroy Arab
belief in British power. This fear eventually drove Britain into a
desperate gamble which produced the very catastrophe it was
intended to prevent.

   Given that fighting Turkey was a complete reversal of Britain's
traditional Middle Eastern policy, it is understandable that time

was needed to work out a new political strategy. But the time eventually taken was excessive, and fatally so. Even after London took direct control of the campaign in 1916, Mesopotamia as such never got to the top of the British priority list. The Middle East was obviously becoming increasingly vital to British global policy – indeed, in the postwar years, British interests in the Middle East would come to be regarded as more politically and strategically valuable than any other part of the imperial system.[2] Yet even as late as 1918 no clear policy direction had emerged.

The policy vacuum spilled over into the strange 'moment of euphoria', a kind of rush of blood to the national head, at the end of the war. Suddenly and unexpectedly, all the main players in the 'Great Game' – Russia, Germany and the Ottoman Empire – had thrown in their cards. Britain was now the only Great Power between Constantinople and Afghanistan. 'A vast middle eastern *imperium* had fallen into their laps', and briefly 'everything seemed possible'.[3] The traditional British sense of caution was overthrown by almost megalomaniac visions of Asian supremacy. But these vied with very realistic worries about the relative decline of British power since 1914. 'Torn between elation and anxiety,' as one historian has said, 'Britain behaved with unprecedented inconsistency.'[4] The inconsistency was nowhere more damaging than in Iraq.

The British campaign in Iraq was a less than convincing demonstration of military capacity. By the standards of the Western Front, the scale, and sometimes the speed, of the British advance could look wonderful. Yet the British army was never really able to exploit a numerical and material superiority that became, towards the end of the war, overwhelming. Indeed, the astonishing scale of manpower committed in Mesopotamia – totalling nearly 900,000 by the end of the war – and the even more stupendous cost of the campaign, suggests that the Turks could claim the campaign as a moral victory. Command failures were part of the reason. Edmund Candler, an embedded journalist who saw the campaign from the viewpoint of regimental officers, was so critical of the higher staffs that the War Office wanted to prevent his impressive book *The Long Road to Baghdad* from being published. It had to be 'smuggled out' of Iraq. Candler thought that the campaign had produced only 'two generals', Townshend and Maude. Even if he was right, of course, command was not the only issue. Supply and transport difficulties crippled the campaign, and were not effectively addressed for far too long. The Army had been well aware before 1914 that the obstacles to campaigning in Mesopotamia would effectively rule it out as a theatre of war. Once the decision was taken to campaign there, a massive commitment of infrastructure resources was imperative. ('Who wills the end must will the means.') But it was not made until atrocious and unnecessary suffering had been inflicted on the men of the expeditionary force. Britain's later campaigns in Iraq and Afghanistan would follow this sad example.

Even in the last stages of the war, with the Ottoman army reduced to little more than a screen, the British could not mount serious operations much further than a hundred miles north of Baghdad. The advance had been pushed too far to make military sense, and the territory conquered was already too big for Britain to control. When the prospect of seizing Baghdad was dangled before the Cabinet, the Foreign Secretary used a homely metaphor to justify the gamble: it was 'necessary to gain strength by eating <u>now</u>, even if it involved indigestion later on'. Indigestion can be uncomfortable, but is usually temporary, and seldom fatal. The outcome in Iraq was much less benign.

The campaign had started with a fatally hazy conception of its ultimate objective, and the government never managed to come up with a clear policy direction for the future of the 'liberated' territory. The sheer cost of garrisoning it, as much as the changing international environment, forced the abandonment of any idea of direct annexation. The dream of turning Mesopotamia into an Indian colony lived on for a remarkably long time, but by the end of the war it was accepted in London at least (if not in Baghdad) that the best Britain could hope for was influence behind some kind of 'Arab façade'. The new idea of a League of Nations mandate seemed to fit this idea quite neatly, and until the 1920 rebellion Britain was able to define that mysterious term in its own way. (As the French were to do in Syria.) After the *Thawra*, things were different.

Britain grasped the expedient of imposing Faisal as King of Iraq not so much out of gratitude to the prince as out of fear of Iraqi public opinion. It was already clear that anything like genuine democracy would create a Shia-dominated government unamenable to British influence, if not actually hostile to Britain. But even if Faisal was reliant on British power, this did not make him the helpless dependent imagined by Churchill at the Cairo Conference. He was strong enough to push Britain towards his own interpretation of the mandate. The recasting of the mandate as a quasi-international treaty between Britain and Iraq in 1924 was presented as a British success, and still is. Iraq's rapid progress to full independence in 1932 also looked like a success story to many. But both signalled limits to British power that would have been unthinkable even in 1919. The state that Britain contrived as Iraq was the stepchild of two distinct, and ultimately contradictory, impulses in British policy – the 'responsibility to world civilisation' and the urge to save money. Unlike France, Britain was not prepared to pay the cost of the kind of power it really wanted. But it also believed that, unlike France, it was popular enough amongst the Arabs to be able to get its way by consent rather than coercion. In this it was mistaken.

By establishing the kingdom of Iraq Britain secured its strategic interests in the short term. But it did so, as in Egypt, by fatefully distorting the country's long-term political development – and such development was the essential justification for the mandate. The 1924 Iraq constitution, as has often been said, created a political system that was, on paper, much like most Western democratic systems of the time. But in practice it worked very differently, as the British were only too well aware. The prospects of democratic politics were crippled by the 1922 *fatwa* issued by the Shia *mujtahids*, forbidding participation in elections. In 1923 there were even 'persistent rumours that the 'Ulama are considering issuing a *fatwa* against the King himself, and declare in favour of direct British rule rather than that of the Iraq Government'. It was clear that they would prefer a republic.[5]

The kingdom's ruling elite reflected the traditional social order for which romantic Tories like Mark Sykes yearned, modified by the disturbing experience of the 1920 revolt. The revolt had been overwhelmingly rural; and though British policy halted the decline of the power of tribal leaders (and effectively prevented the emergence of social classes in the modern sense) the kingdom of Iraq's governing class was overwhelmingly urban.[6] Most members of parliament were professionals – over a third were ex-army officers – while less than ten per cent had a commercial background. Nearly three-quarters of the cabinet ministers between 1920 and 1936 were from the three major cities, and only eight out of fifty-nine were tribal sheikhs. Of the eleven prime ministers, only one was from a rural area, and all but two of the others were from Baghdad. Sunnis dominated: just over a third of the population, they provided nearly three-quarters of cabinet ministers. Elections were carefully managed – by the 1930s it was not unknown for ballot boxes to be filled by the returning officers themselves – and the replacement rate of deputies was low. Skewed representation might have been off-set by a strong sense of public responsibility, but the British were reduced to helpless spectators as intrigue and corruption swamped the system.

The new Iraq kingdom was not only defective in League of Nations terms, it was distinctly more uncooperative than anything the British policy-makers could have imagined as they toyed with various forms of postwar state. There was an ironic price to be paid for imposing a Sunni-dominated system. The Shia community, the core of the rebellion which had in effect brought Faisal to power, would see themselves as the truest Iraqi patriots.

The ruling Sunni politicians could not, as Elie Kedourie remarked, afford to ignore the accusation that they had compromised with the British imperialists. 'As a result, they had to vie with the Shi'as in anti-British declarations.' (The High Commissioner's estimate of the prime minister, Jaafar al-Askari, in late 1927 was typical: to the British, 'obsequious and pathetic he will complain with tears rolling down his cheeks of his difficulties with his colleagues, their extreme views, their disloyalty. But to Iraqis he appeals for unity to defeat the intrigues of the British who are trying to enslave the country.'[7])

This was not much more than an inconvenience for Britain to begin with, but as time went on the deep current of resentment would surge up more often and more seriously. Long before the bloody destruction of the monarchy and Britain's most trusty collaborator, Nuri al-Said, in the 1958 revolution, the subordination of Iraq could only be maintained by force. Through the new system of 'air control' Britain was able to assist its favoured allies in crushing the perennial rural resistance, as well as more serious ethnic challenges to the state of Iraq. Given the extreme violence of punitive measures used by the army, it cannot be said that air control was (as its critics alleged) especially indiscriminate or inhumane. But there is a difference between war measures and those designed to establish or maintain civil peace. Air control was definitely conceived as a peacetime system, and it helped to establish a punitive ethos in government.

The Iraq Army was carefully constructed on the British model. The British Military Mission, some fifty strong, focused on the training of officer cadets and NCOs. The Royal Iraq Military College was modelled on Sandhurst. The Army was even more Sunni-dominated than the state: 58 of the 61 field officers in 1936 were Sunni, two were Christians, and just one a Shia. It remained, in line with British policy, smaller than the Iraq Levies, which recruited heavily from the Assyrians and Kurds. The question of conscription remained unresolved: it was raised during the debates of the Constituent Assembly in 1924, and in 1926 the

Iraq government established a committee to draft a military service law. Britain still refused to approve it, partly on the ground that it was 'against all our traditions', and partly because it would provoke resistance (based on memories of the 'arbitrary and brutal' Ottoman system). There were also fears that it would lead to the politicisation of the Army. The High Commissioner could not directly forbid it, but could make clear that no British forces would be used 'to suppress disturbances arising out of the policy of conscription'. There was some justification for this reluctance. When the Iraq government brought its conscription bill to parliament in 1927 (with the argument that 'a national army in every nation is its life symbol and the foundation of its independence') the Shia Minister of Education resigned in protest, and the Kurdish deputies declared that 'all the Kurds are against conscription'. Next year the leaders of the Shia tribes denounced conscription as a 'great catastrophe'.

As long as Faisal was alive, the issue was not pressed. But shortly after his death in September 1933, a new National Service Law was brought in and greeted with 'acclamation'. The Army had just been sent to crush the Assyrian demand for autonomy with the kind of violence usually witnessed only in civil wars where the survival of the state is at stake. In Mosul, triumphal arches were put up to greet the returning troops; 'some decorated with melons stained with blood and with daggers stuck into them. This delicate representation of the heads of slain Assyrians was in keeping with the prevailing sentiment in the town.' The military commander, Bakr Sidki, became a national hero, and rampant militarism followed. Within two years military education was made a compulsory part of the school curriculum, and in 1936 Bakr Sidki led the first of a succession of military coups that would culminate in 1941 with an open repudiation of the British alliance.

The performance of the Iraqi state before that did some damage to Britain's image. Britain was unquestionably committed, as was the international community, to minority protection. But Iraq resembled and indeed outdid most successor states in nationalist intolerance. The violent solution of the 'Assyrian problem' was highly embarrassing for Britain, which had authorised the settlement of the Assyrians in Iraq, and which had told the League that any special measures of protection for them might 'prevent the minorities concerned from regarding themselves, or being regarded as true citizens of their native state, in which lies the only certain hope of their future welfare'. This was true in theory, but sadly not in practice. After the massacre the British were driven to stifle any possibility of a League of Nations inquiry. The High Commissioner brutally urged that 'the orchestra at Geneva must be prevented and not merely discouraged from starting a tune the last bars of which are likely to be played solo by a British bugle'.[8]

The fate of the Kurds was to be on a larger and longer scale. Administered separately by Britain until 1924, they were consigned to Iraq by the League of Nations on condition that the mandate lasted at least twenty-five years – unless Iraq was admitted to the League before then. Barely a year later pressure was mounting for Britain to support Iraq's membership of the League in 1928. In 1927 Leo Amery, the Colonial Secretary, admitted that nobody at Geneva had dreamt of this, and that there might be accusations that 'we had acquired the Mosul frontier by a trick'.[9] Real minority rights should have been a crucial precondition for Iraq's independence. Britain induced Iraq to legislate some protection of the Kurdish language, and limited guarantees of public employment for Kurds in Kurdistan. But it had to persuade the League that Iraq was fit for admission as a member in full knowledge that the protection of Kurdish rights was fragile, if not indeed fictional.[10] The future arranged by Britain for the Kurds was not to be a happy one.

For the Jews of Baghdad, an historic community who formed a majority of the city's inhabitants in 1917, Britain's failure to preserve minority protection (which they had enjoyed for centuries under Ottoman rule) would prove catastrophic.

'Should Iraq prove herself unworthy of the confidence which had been placed in her', Britain told the League of Nations, 'the moral responsibility must rest with His Majesty's Government.'[11] It still does.

Notes

SOURCE ABBREVIATIONS

BL   British Library, London
CAB   Cabinet records [NA]
CKS   Centre for Kentish Studies
DBFP
FO   Foreign Office records [NA]
IOR   India Office Records [BL]
IWM   Imperial War Museum, London
LHCMA Liddell Hart Centre for Military Archives, King's College, London
MECA Middle East Centre Archive, St Antony's College, Oxford
NA   National Archives [Public Record Office], London
NAM   National Army Museum, London
SA   Sudan Archive, Durham University Library
WO   War Office records [NA]

NOTES

Introduction

1 John Darwin, 'An Undeclared Empire: the British in the Middle East, 1918–39', *Journal of Imperial and Commonwealth History* (1999), pp. 160–1.

PART I: BASRA

PART I: Section 1. *Into Mesopotamia*

1 F. J. Moberley, *The Campaign in Mesopotamia 1914–1918* (Official History of the Great War) [hereafter OH], vol. i, pp. 99–103.
2 William Bird diary, 26 Oct. 1914. Imperial War Museum [IWM] 88/7/1. General Force D to Chief of General Staff, India, 26 Oct. 1914. British Library [BL] India Office Records [IOR] L/MIL/5/749.
3 Keyes (Bahrain) to Knox (Bushire), 4 Nov. 1914. BL IOR L/PS/11 /86, P4923/1914.
4 Anon., *Historical Records of the 20th (Duke of Cambridge's Own) Infantry 1908–1922*, p. 7.
5 Ibid., p. 9; Bird diary, 9 Nov. 1914. IWM 88/7/1.
6 J. E. Barker, 'The Future of Asiatic Turkey', *The Nineteenth Century* (June 1916), pp. 1243–4.

7 Ely B. Soane, *To Mesopotamia and Kurdistan in Disguise*, pp. 72–3.
8 Reader Bullard, *The Camels Must Go*, pp. 78–80.
9 Hubert Young, *The Independent Arab*, pp. 26–7, 30.

PART I: Section 2. *'An unexpected stroke'*

1 War Office, 'Effect of the Baghdad Railway on our relations with Persia and on the defence of India', 16 Nov. 1914. National Archives [NA], WO 106/52.
2 Stuart A. Cohen, *British Policy in Mesopotamia 1903–1914*, p. 206.
3 MECA, Young papers; Elizabeth Monroe, *Philby of Arabia*, p. 47; H. V. F. Winstone, *Captain Shakespear*, pp. 141–4.
4 Colonial Office, Note by Middle East Department, 11 Dec. 1922. Cabinet Committee on Iraq, I.R.Q.3. NA CAB 27/206.
5 Cohen, *British Policy*, pp. 266, 320.
6 G. P. Gooch & H. Temperley (eds), *British Documents on the Origin of the War, 1898–1914*, vol. X, pt 1, pp. 465–6, q. Zeine, p. 97.
7 Peter Morris, 'Intelligence and its Interpretation: Mesopotamia 1914–1916', in C. Andrew and J. Woakes (eds), *Intelligence and International Relations*, p. 87.
8 'Plan of operations for the support of Mohammerah', NA WO 106/880.
9 OH i, p. 85.
10 Mallet to Grey, 6 Oct. 1914. NA FO 2142, q. Paul K. Davis, *Ends and Means: The British Mesopotamian Campaign and Commission*, p. 47.
11 Grey to Mallet, 23 Oct. 1914.
12 The most one-sided account in recent historical writing is in Efrem and Inari Karsh, *Empires of the Sand: The Struggle for Mastery in the Middle East 1789–1923* (London 1999), which represents the Ottoman government as bent on war, and using 'duplicity', 'lies' and 'fantastic untruth' to get there.
13 Ibid., pp. 128–9. Morris, 'Intelligence and its Interpretation', p. 84, quoting NA FO 371/2137.
14 Committee of Imperial Defence, 1906, in David French, 'The Dardanelles, Mecca and Kut: Prestige as a Factor in British Eastern Strategy, 1914–1916', *War and Society* (May 1987), p. 50.
15 'Lady Barrow talks a great deal too much and has done him a lot of harm', according to General Money, who thought him 'not a great soldier', but 'a nice old man . . . original in his ideas' and 'very much liked by his staff'. NAM 8106-61.
16 Military Secretary, India Office, minute 'The Role of India in a Turkish War', 26 Sep. 1914. Barrow MSS, BL IOR L/MIL/5/748.
17 Barrow diary, 25 Sep. 1914. BL IOR EUR. E.420/36.
18 Military Department, India Office, 'Precis of Correspondence regarding the Mesopotamian Expedition – its Genesis and Development', p. 3. BL IOR L/MIL/5.
19 Douglas Goold, 'Lord Hardinge and the Mesopotamia Expedition and Inquiry, 1914–1917', *Historical Journal* 19, 4 (1976), pp. 920–1.
20 'Precis of Correspondence', p. 6

PART I: Section 3. *Turks and Indians*

1 The word 'sepoy' was originally used by the French (cf. 'spahi'); Indian soldiers were called 'jawans' by Urdu speakers.
2 David Omissi, *The Sepoy and the Raj: The Indian Army, 1860–1940*, p. 53.
3 OH i, p. 63–6.
4 Edward J. Erickson, *Ottoman Army Effectiveness in World War I*, pp. 1ff.
5 Ahmed Emin, *Turkey in the World War*, p. 79.
6 Ulrich Trumpener, 'Turkey's War', in Strachan (ed.), *The Oxford Illustrated History of the First World War*, p. 82; Erik J. Zurcher, 'Little Mehmet in the Desert: the Ottoman Soldier's Experience', in Cecil and Liddle, *Facing Armageddon*, pp. 232–3.
7 Staff Bimbashi Mehmet Emin, 'The Turco-British Campaign in Mesopotamia and Our Mistakes', *Military Magazine* nos. 17, 18 (Aug.–Sep. 1336), translation in NA CAB 44/32, pp. 5–6.

PART I: Section 4. *Basra*

1 Diary of W. C. Spackman, 'The Waters of Babylon', 17 Nov. 1914. IWM 74/70/1.
2 Bird diary, 11, 15 Nov. 1914.
3 Spackman diary, 17 Nov. 1914.
4 Letter from a British Officer to his parents, 22 Nov. 1914. *Evening News* (London), 6 Jan. 1915.
5 Bird diary, 21 Nov. 1914.
6 E. S. Stevens, *By Tigris and Euphrates*, pp. 141–2.
7 General Force D to Sec. of State for India, 24 Nov. 1914. IO, 'Precis of Correspondence', p. 8
8 Marian Kent, 'Asiatic Turkey, 1914–1916', in F. H. Hinsley (ed.), *British Foreign Policy under Sir Edward Grey*, p. 441.
9 Sec. of State to Viceroy, 16 Dec. 1914. 'Precis of Correspondence', p. 9.
10 Viceroy to Sec. of State, 19 Dec. 1914. NA WO 106/52.
11 Private telegram from Cox, 23 Nov., in Viceroy to Sec. of State, 25 Nov. 1914. 'Precis of Correspondence', p. 10.
12 'I fear she was far from popular with the troops', in spite of her YMCA work. Coles diary, Oct. 1916. IWM 03/58/1.
13 Philip Graves, *The Life of Sir Percy Cox*, p. 156.
14 OH i, pp. 135–6.
15 Mil. Sec. IO, minute, 27 Nov. 1914. 'Persian Gulf Operations', BL IOR L/MIL/5/749.

PART I: Section 5. *'Conciliating the Arabs'*

1 Keyes to Knox, 4 Nov. 1914. BL IOR L/PS/11/86, P4923/1914.
2 Ghassan R. Atiyyah, *Iraq: 1908–1921: A Socio-Political Study*, p. 40.
3 Yitzhak Nakash, *The Shi'is of Iraq*, pp. 60–1.
4 Ajaimi al-Mansur to Abd al-Aziz ibn Saud, 11 Jan. 1917. NA FO 371/3048.
5 'A Review of the Civil Administration of Mesopotamia' by Miss G. L. Bell, Cmd 1061 (1920), p. 26.

6 Arnold T. Wilson, *Loyalties: Mesopotamia 1914–1917*, p. 12.
7 Cox to Government of India, 24 Apr. 1915. BL IOR L/PS/11/91, P1586/1915.
8 Cox to Government of India, 13 Feb. 1915. BL IOR L/PS/11/95, P2891/1915.
9 Wilson, *Loyalties*, p. 35.
10 'A Review of the Civil Administration of Mesopotamia' by Miss G. L. Bell, Cmd 1061 (1920), ch. 2.
11 Bowker, 7 Apr. 1915, IWM 99/15/1; S. H. Longrigg, *Iraq: 1900 to 1950*, p. 84.
12 Longrigg, *Iraq*, pp. 81–2.
13 Shakeshaft diary, NA CAB 45/92.
14 Maj.-Gen. Sir Alec Bishop, Memoirs, IWM 98/18/1.
15 Edward J. Thompson, *The Leicestershires Beyond Baghdad*, p. 49.
16 Graves, *Percy Cox*, p. 193.
17 Bird diary, 14 Jan. 1915.
18 Barnett diary, 24, 26 Jan., 2, 8, 16 Feb. 1916. IWM 90/37/1.
19 Kathryn Tidrick, *Heart-beguiling Araby. The English Romance with Arabia*, ch. 8.
20 Morris, 'Intelligence and its Interpretation', p. 80.
21 T. E. Lawrence, Introduction to Charles M. Doughty, *Arabia Deserta* (London 1921).
22 Toby Dodge, *Inventing Iraq: The Failure of Nation Building and a History Denied*, p. 65.
23 Martin Thomas, 'Bedouin Tribes and the Imperial Intelligence Services in Syria, Iraq and Transjordan in the 1920s', *Journal of Contemporary History* 38, 4 (2003), p. 45.
24 Samira Haj, 'The Problems of Tribalism: The Case of Nineteenth-century Iraqi History', *Social History* 16, 1 (1991).
25 *The Arab of Mesopotamia* (Basra 1916), pp. 40, 42, 93, 9.
26 Aziz al-Azmeh, 'Nationalism and the Arabs', in D. Hopwood (ed.), *Arab Nation, Arab Nationalism*, pp. 70–3.
27 Albertine Jwaideh, 'Tribalism and modern society: Iraq, a case study', in R. M. Savory (ed.), *The Cambridge History of the Middle East*, p. 164.
28 Hanna Batatu, *The Old Social Classes and the Revolutionary Movements of Iraq*, pp. 77–8.
29 Shakir Salim, *Marsh Dwellers of the Euphrates Area*, pp. 12–13.
30 [G. L. Bell], *The Arab of Mesopotamia*, p. 70.
31 Precis of Conversation with Abd El Masri on 16 Aug. 1914. NA FO 371/2140.
32 Atiyyah, *Iraq*, pp. 97–8. There were officially 15,398 male students in Iraq, but as Atiyyah notes, many were 'theoretical' enrolments.
33 Cox to Government of India, 3 Dec. 1914. NA FO 471/2479.
34 Atiyyah, *Iraq*, p. 87.
35 GOC IEF D to Foreign, Simla. Harvard University, Houghton Library bMS Eng 1252 (372), q. Jeremy Wilson, *Lawrence of Arabia*, p. 220.
36 Eliezer Tauber, *The Arab Movements in World War I*, p. 29.

37 Naval Intelligence Division, 'Iraq and the Persian Gulf', BR 524 (1944), p. 272.
38 Dickson letters, 23 Jan. 1916. MECA, Dickson MSS Box 1 file 4.

PART I: Section 6. *Qurna*

 1 V.-Adm. Wilfrid Nunn, *Tigris Gunboats*, p. 48.
 2 Wilson, *Loyalties*, p. 22.
 3 R. Popplewell, 'British Intelligence in Mesopotamia 1914–16', *Intelligence and National Security*, vol. 5 no. 2 (Apr. 1990), pp. 144–5.
 4 'The Strategic Side of I(a)', Leith-Ross MSS, NAM 8312-63-10; Popplewell, 'British Intelligence in Mesopotamia', pp. 148–50.
 5 Nunn, *Tigris Gunboats*, pp. 58–9.
 6 A. S. Cane diary, 12 Jan. 1915. IWM 76/124/1.
 7 Cane diary, 13, 21, 25 Dec. 1914. IWM 76/124/1.
 8 Spackman diary, 10, 21 Dec. 1914.
 9 Cane diary, 7 Jan. 1915.
10 OH i, p. 167.
11 Wilson, *Loyalties*, pp. 32–3.
12 Sir Percy Cox to FO, 28 Jan.; Sec. of State to Viceroy, 29 Jan.; Viceroy to Sec. of State, 30 Jan. 1915. BL IOR L/MIL/5/749.
13 OH i, pp. 183–4.
14 What is clear is that his force did not 'walk straight into an ambush', as suggested in A. J. Barker, *The Neglected War*, p. 67.
15 Viceroy to Sec. of State, and reply by Mil. Sec., 11 Mar. 1915. BL IOR L/MIL/5/750.
16 As reported e.g. by H. B. Reynardson, *Mesopotamia 1914–1915*, p. 119.

PART I: Section 7. *'Morally responsible to humanity and civilization'*

 1 According to the Official History, i, p. 196, Barrett's 'health had been failing'; Barker, *Neglected War*, p. 69, says that 'Barrett had fallen sick'; Field Marshal Lord Carver says he was 'evacuated sick' (*Turkish Front*, p. 105). Briton C. Busch, *Britain, India and the Arabs*, p. 29 has the judgement on his leadership qualities.
 2 Sec. of State to Viceroy, 10 Mar. 1915. 'Precis of correspondence', p. 21.
 3 Cox to Curzon, 27 Mar. 1915. MECA, Cox MSS file 4.
 4 Wilson to Yate, 28 Nov. 1914. Copy in BL IOR L/PS/11/88, P552/1915.
 5 Yate to Grey, 16 Feb., and Wilson to India Office, 5 Apr. 1915. BL IOR L/PS/11/88, P552/1915.
 6 War Office memo., 'Alexandretta and Mesopotamia', 16 Mar.; Admiralty memo., 17 Mar. 1915. NA CAB 42/2. David Fromkin, *A Peace to End All Peace*, pp. 140–2.
 7 War Council, 19 Mar. 1915. NA CAB 22/1.
 8 Grey to Bertie, 28 Mar. 1915. NA FO 371/2486.
 9 'The Future Settlement of Eastern Turkey in Asia and Arabistan', Note by the Secretary, Political and Secret Department, India Office, 16 Mar. 1915, p. 2. Barrow papers, BL IOR MSS EUR.E.420/12.
10 Ibid., p. 5.

11 Ibid., pp. 5–6.
12 Note by General Sir Edmund Barrow on the Defence of Mesopotamia,
16 Mar. 1915. Ibid., p. 14.
13 Comments on Sir Edmund Barrow's Note, 17 Mar. 1915. Ibid., p. 16.
14 H. H. Asquith, *Letters to Venetia Stanley* (Oxford 1982), p. 510;
an edited version was published in Earl of Oxford and Asquith,
Memories and Reflections, vol. 2 (London 1928), p. 69.
15 Viceroy to Sec. of State, 15 Mar. 1915. Ibid., p. 18.

PART I: Section 8. *'One of the decisive battles of the world'*

1 Diary/letters of Maj.-Gen. C. J. Mellis to his wife, 26 Mar., 1, 9, 15 Apr.
1915. Mellis MSS, NAM 6702-91.
2 See the thoughtful analysis in Atiyyah, *Iraq*, pp. 110–11.
3 'The losses cannot be gathered from records, but from reports of
eyewitnesses amounted to several thousands'. Mehmet Emin, 'Campaign',
pp. 16–17.
4 Bird diary, 13 Apr. 1915.
5 Mellis letters, 22 Apr. 1915.
6 Shakeshaft diary, 14 Apr. 1915. CAB 45/92.
7 Nixon despatch, 16 Apr. 1915. IOR L/MIL/5/750.
8 Narrative of action of 12–14 Apr. 1915, by Lt. C. O. Mosse.
IOR L/MIL/5/751.
9 Bird diary, 14, 15 Apr. 1915.
10 Spackman diary, p. 38.
11 According to the British official history (pp. 218–19); the Turkish official
history has a less colourful account. Edward J. Erickson, *Ordered to Die:
A History of the Ottoman Army in the First World War*, p. 110.
12 Mehmet Emin, 'Campaign', p. 18.
13 H. Birch Reynardson, *Mesopotamia 1914–1915*, pp. 179–80.
14 Lt.-Gen. Sir George MacMunn, *Behind the Scenes in Many Wars*, p. 212.
15 Atiyyah, *Iraq*, p. 111.
16 Bowker letters, 14 Apr. 1915. IWM 99/15/1.
17 Reynardson, *Mesopotamia*, p. 134.
18 Evans, *Brief Outline of the Campaign in Mesopotamia* (London 1926),
pp. 26–7.
19 Ibid., p. 6.
20 Barrow note, 3 Apr., and Crewe to Barrow [holograph], 4 Apr. 1915.
IOR L/MIL/5/750.
21 Sec. of State to Viceroy, 24 Apr. 1915. 'Brief for the Defence of the
Mesopotamia Campaign', p. 6. The published version halved the number
of references to the hot season, and toned down some of the phraseology:
instead of 'Nixon must clearly understand', for instance, it read 'I presume
he clearly understands'.
22 Cane diary, 11 June 1915. IWM 76/124/1.
23 A. R. Ubsdell diary, NAM 60-12-400; q. Lord Carver, *The National Army
Museum Book of the Turkish Front 1914–18*, p. 115.

PART I: Section 9. *Townshend's Regatta*

1 Erroll Sherson, *Townshend of Chitral and Kut*, p. 81.
2 Charles V. F. Townshend, *My Campaign in Mesopotamia*, p. 41.
3 Spackman diary, p. 45.
4 Mehmet Emin, 'Campaign', p. 24.
5 Reynardson, *Mesopotamia*, p. 144.
6 Mehmet Emin, 'Campaign', pp. 19–20.
7 Townshend, *My Campaign*, pp. 46–7.
8 Nunn, *Tigris Gunboats*, pp. 107–8.
9 Chamberlain to Hardinge, 27 May 1915. BUL AC 62/1.
10 Sec. of State to Viceroy, 23 May; Viceroy to Sec. of State, 2 June 1915.
   IOR L/MIL/5/751.
11 Reynardson, *Mesopotamia*, p. 148.
12 Townshend, *My Campaign*, pp. 63–5.
13 Reynardson, *Mesopotamia*, p. 150.
14 Nunn, *Tigris Gunboats*, p. 108.
15 Ibid., p. 117.
16 Mehmet Emin, 'Campaign', p. 21.
17 Dickson letters, n.d. (May/June 1915), MECA Dickson MSS Box 1 file 3a;
   Reynardson, *Mesopotamia*, p. 156.
18 Davis, *Ends and Means*, p. 83.

PART I: Section 10. *Up the Euphrates*

1 Mellis letters, 8, 6, 24 June 1915.
2 H. W. Fothergill Cooke letters, 4, 6 July 1915. IWM P455.
3 Bowker lettters, 7 July 1915.
4 Nunn, *Tigris Gunboats*, p. 142.
5 Evans, *Campaign in Mesopotamia*, p. 33.
6 Mellis letters, 19 July 1915.
7 Wilson, *Loyalties*, p. 61.
8 S. H. Climo to Mrs Cooke, 20 July 1915. IWM P455.
9 Nunn, *Tigris Gunboats*, pp. 146–7.
10 OH i, p. 292.
11 He swam the canal under fire.
12 Mellis letters, 1 Aug. 1915.
13 Bowker letters, 24 July 1915.
14 Nunn, *Tigris Gunboats*, p. 152.
15 Reynardson, *Mesopotamia*, p. 163.
16 A. J. Barker, *Townshend of Kut*, p. 154.

PART I: Section 11. *To Kut*

1 Townshend, *My Campaign*, p. 86.
2 Townshend to his wife, 8 Aug. 1915, q. Barker, *Townshend of Kut*,
   p. 155. Townshend to Curzon, 5 Sep. 1915. Curzon MSS, BL IOR E/6/3,
   q. Goold, 'Lord Hardinge', p. 929.
3 Buchanan, *The Tragedy of Mesopotamia*.
4 Reynardson, *Mesopotamia*, p. 193.

5 Two obsolete Farmans had arrived in May, and two Caudrons in July. The latter were barely serviceable, and one of the former was lost through engine failure at Nasiriyeh.

6 Reynardson, *Mesopotamia*, pp. 221–2.

7 Townshend, *My Campaign*, p. 97.

8 Reynardson, *Mesopotamia*, p. 206.

9 Ibid., p. 207.

10 OH i, p. 316.

11 Reynardson, *Mesopotamia*, p. 214.

12 Ibid., p. 216.

13 Wilson, *Loyalties*, p. 82.

PART II KUT

PART II: Section 1. *To Baghdad?*

1 Sir E. Barrow, 'The Mesopotamia Question in its Military Aspect', 4 Oct. 1915. BL IOR L/MIL/5 752.

2 GHQ IEF D, Memorandum on an Advance to Baghdad, 30 Aug. 1915. WO 106 893.

3 General Staff, War Office, Memo 6 Oct., and 'The Question of Occupying Baghdad', 12 Oct. 1915. BL IOR L/MIL/5/752.

4 Birmingham University Library, Austen Chamberlain MSS 46/1/16.

5 'The Chief's views on private telegram of 16 Oct. 1915 from Sec. of State', 17 Oct. 1915. NA WO 106 893.

6 Mesopotamia Commission Report, Cd 8610, 1917, p. 126.

7 Graves, *Cox*, p. 194.

8 Combined Chiefs of Staff, 'The Mesopotamian Problem', 19 Oct. 1915. NA WO 106 893.

9 Kitchener to Chamberlain, 21 Oct. 1915. OH, ii, p. 29.

10 David Gilmour, *Curzon* (London 1994), p. 477.

11 Ibid.

12 Sec. of State to Viceroy, 23 Oct. 1915. 'Precis of Correspondence', p. 38.

13 Hankey minute 22 Oct. 1915, Bodleian Library, Asquith MSS ff. 31–4.

PART II: Section 2. *To Salman Pak*

1 Copy in NA CAB 19/15, q. Goold, 'Lord Hardinge', p. 935.

2 T. A. Chalmers narrative. IWM 01/23/1.

3 Reynardson, *Mesopotamia*, pp. 228–9.

4 Mesopotamia Commission Report, App. 63.

5 Evidence of Maj.-Gen. Maitland Cowper, Mesopotamia Commission, 18 Jan. 1917. Davis, *Ends and Means*, pp. 130–1.

6 Mehmet Emin, 'The Battle of Suleiman Pak' (Military Press 1337), translation in NA CAB 44/33, pp. 6–8, 16–20.

7 'Had our cavalry charged, the enemy's cavalry and camel corps and guns must have been either destroyed or captured. However, Brig.-Gen. Roberts assured me that most unfortunately the terrain on our extreme right was absolutely impossible to charge over, and thus the enemy got away with impunity.' Townshend, *My Campaign*, p. 147.

8 W. D. Bird, *A Chapter of Misfortunes*, pp. 42–3.
9 E. W. C. Sandes, *In Kut and Captivity with the Sixth Indian Division*, pp. 56–7.
10 Shakeshaft diary, 16 Nov. 1915. NA CAB 45/92.
11 Mehmet Emin, 'Suleiman Pak', p. 32, and extract in NA AIR 1/675/21/13//892.

PART II: Section 3. *Ctesiphon*

1 Nunn, *Tigris Gunboats*, p. 172.
2 Lt. H. C. Gallup, NAM 86-11-43.
3 NAM 86-11-43.
4 Mehmet Emin, 'Suleiman Pak', pp. 72–8, 97–9.
5 Reynardson, *Mesopotamia*, p. 264.
6 Mesopotamia Commission Report, Part X, para 60.
7 Capt. J. F. W. Read, IWM 78/21/1.
8 OH ii, p. 107.
9 Nixon to Townshend, 12.15 p.m. 26 Nov. 1915. OH ii, p. 108.
10 Mehmet Emin, 'Suleiman Pak', pp. 128–31.

PART II: Section 4. *Retreat*

1 Chalmers, 28 Nov. 1916; J. McK. Sloss memoir, IWM 04/24/1.
2 Spackman diary; Sandes, *In Kut*, p. 98; Townshend, *My Campaign*, p. 194.
3 E. O. Mousley, *The Secrets of a Kuttite*, p. 15.
4 G. L. Heawood memoir, IWM 74/72/1.
5 Heawood, IWM 74/72/1.
6 Mousley, *Secrets*, p. 19.
7 Chalmers, IWM 01/23/1.
8 Sandes, *In Kut*, pp. 60–1.
9 W. D. Lee, IWM 91/25/1.
10 Sandes, *In Kut*, p. 108.
11 Chalmers, IWM 01/23/1.
12 Reynardson, *Mesopotamia*, p. 267.
13 Lee, IWM 91/25/1.
14 Spackman diary, IWM 74/70/1.
15 *A Short History of the 17th and 22nd Field Corps, 3rd Sappers and Miners, in Mesopotamia 1914–1918* (privately printed, 1932).
16 Russell Braddon, *The Siege*, pp. 115–16.
17 Townshend, *My Campaign*, p. 198.
18 Graves, *Cox*, p. 195.
19 S. de V. Julius to F. J. Moberley, 26 Sep. 1928. NA CAB 45/90. Julius, a newly promoted major at the time, clearly found this a bruising experience: 'I would rather not speak' of it. Moberley got this information too late to include it in the OH.
20 Diary of Maj. Walker, IWM 76/128/1.
21 Ibid.
22 These contain little more than a copy of a letter from Townshend to the War Office requesting that Boggis's arrears of pay be paid to his mother,

and a Christmas card from the Prinkipo grocery shop where Boggis
bought Townshend's food during his imprisonment. IWM 67/61/1.

23 Braddon, *The Siege*, p. 95. Braddon cites Lt-Col C. A. Raynor here, but
the form of the information is unspecified.
24 Staff College, Quetta 1922. 'Indoor Exercise D'. Ismay MSS,
LHC 3/2/107.
25 Duff to Robertson, 28 Mar. 1916. Robertson MSS, LHC 8/1/18.
26 Ronald Millar, *Kut: The Death of an Army*, pp. 64–6.
27 Mesopotamia Commission Report, p. 30.
28 Julius to Moberley, 26 Sep. 1928. NA CAB 45/90.
29 E. G. Barrow, 'Brief for the Defence of the Mesopotamia Campaign,'
30 June 1916. Barrow MSS, BL MSS EurE420, p. 17. He added that
hindsight confirmed that the decision, which 'gave us time to breathe',
was the 'right one at the moment'.
30 Read, IWM 78/21/1. See also the extended discussion in Sandes, *In Kut*,
pp. 143–7, reaching the same conclusion.
31 Davis, *Ends and Means*, pp. 140-2.
32 'Precis of Correspondence', p. 39.
33 Viceroy, 30 Nov. and 6 Dec. 1915. 'Precis of Correspondence', pp. 39–41.

PART II: Section 5. *Under Siege*

1 Townshend, *My Campaign*, p. 210.
2 Heawood, IWM 74/72/1.
3 Graves, *Cox*, p. 196; Wilson, *Loyalties*, p. 92.
4 H. V. F. Winstone, *Leachman: 'OC Desert'*, p. 160.
5 Sandes, *In Kut*, pp. 132–6.
6 Ibid., p. 141.
7 Ibid., pp. 148–9.
8 Mehmet Emin, 'The Siege of Kut al Amara', translated by Lt.-Col. G. O.
de R. Channer. NA CAB 44/34.
9 Emin, 'Siege of Kut', p. 9.
10 OH ii, p. 173.
11 Emin, 'Siege of Kut', pp. 11–13.
12 Townshend, *My Campaign*, pp. 232–3.
13 For example Barker, Braddon, and Wilcox.

PART II: Section 6. *To the Rescue*

1 Sec. of State to Viceroy, 20 Dec. 1915. 'Precis', p. 43.
2 Viceroy to Sec. of State, 25 Dec. 1915. Ibid., p. 44.
3 OH ii, pp. 151, 153–4.
4 Buchanan, *The Tragedy of Mesopotamia*, pp. 37–8.
5 Ibid., pp. 42–3.
6 MECA J. D. Crowdy letters, 9 Jan. 1916.
7 Mesopotamia Commission Report, Cd 8610, 1917, p. 53, para 36.
8 Anderson memoir, IWM P129.
9 OH ii, pp. 199–200.
10 Buchanan, *Tragedy of Mesopotamia*, pp. 64–5.

11 Northcote letter to his father, 10 Jan. 1916. NAM 6510-196.
12 Chalmers, IWM 01/23/1.
13 Fraser diary, 17 Jan. 1916. NA, CAB 45/96. Thorburn letters, 18 Jan. 1916. IWM 88/56/1.
14 Chalmers diary, 17 Jan. 1916, IWM 01/23/1; Northcote letter, 15 Jan. 1916. NAM 6510-196.
15 Diary of Lt.-Col. T. C. Catty, 14 Jan. 1916. NAM 7909-42.
16 Gen. Keary diary, 1 Feb. 1916. IWM Con Shelf.
17 Chalmers diary, IWM 01/23/1; MECA, Crowdy letters, 19 Jan. 1916.
18 Tigris Corps to GHQ, 16 Jan. 1916. WO 158 664.
19 Army Commander to Corps, 17 Jan. 1916. Ibid.
20 Catty diary, 22 Feb. 1916. NAM 7909-42.

PART II: Section 7. *Marking Time*

1 MECA, Crowdy diary, 29 Jan 1916; Money to his wife, q. Carver, *Turkish Front*, p. 142.
2 Wilson, *Loyalties*, pp. 112–13.
3 Carver, *Turkish Front*, p. 143, asserts that in February, 'apart from bombarding the Turkish lines at Hanna, no operations were embarked upon'.
4 The OH, however, suggested that its 'real' purpose was 'to reduce the distance his force would have to march to the attack of the Es Sinn position, which he proposed to outflank'. OH ii, p. 305.
5 Harry MacDonald diary, 25, 26 Jan., 11, 19 Feb. 1916, NAM 7705-17.
6 This rather obscure appointment (which the War Office was unaware of) is discussed further on pp. 232–3.
7 'Notes about the Surprise Attack on the Morning of the 22nd of February, 1916'. Amar Singh diary, 29 Mar. 1916. Ellinwood, *Between Two Worlds*, p. 434.
8 MECA, Crowdy letters, 25 Mar. 1916.
9 Chalmers, 28 Feb. 1916. IWM 01/23/1. More importantly, he could not ride.

PART II: Section 8. *Flood and Famine*

1 Phillips diary, 22 Feb. 1916. NA CAB 45 93. Mousley, *Secrets*, pp. 70–1.
2 Townshend, *My Campaign*, p. 283.
3 *Short History of the 17th and 22nd Field Companies*, p. 94.
4 McNeal, 'Report on the Siege of Kut-el-Amara', WO 32/5204.
5 Mousley, *Secrets*, pp. 72–3.
6 Ibid., p. 131.
7 See the terse argument in Edwin Latter, 'The Indian Army in Mesopotamia 1914–1918', Part II, *Journal of the Society for Army Historical Research* 72 (1994), p. 162.
8 Braddon, *The Siege*, pp. 122–3.
9 Norman Dixon, *On the Psychology of Military Incompetence* (London 1976), pp. 100–1. It may be noted that Dixon does not appear even to have read Townshend's own book, let alone any documentary sources.

10 Catty diary, 12 Feb. 1916. NAM 7909-42.
11 Erickson, *Ottoman Army Effectiveness*, pp. 89–92.
12 OH ii, p. 308.
13 Lee, IWM 91/25/1.
14 Wheeler to Cobb, IWM P45.
15 Diary of Maj. E. G. Dunn, NA CAB 45 94.
16 Wheeler, IWM P45
17 Anderson memoir, IWM P129, p.50.
18 Heawood memoir, IWM 74/72/1.
19 Phillips diary, 'Resumé of the Siege'. NA CAB 45 93.
20 *Short History of the 17th and 22nd Field Companies*, p. 94. 22nd
   Company had seen the mortar at Ctesiphon but neglected to destroy it.
21 IWM 91/25/1.

PART II: Section 9. *Dujaila: The Second Battle for Kut*

1 NAM 2007-03-57
2 CIGS to C-in-C Delhi, 10, 12, 17 Feb.; GOC Force D to CGS Delhi, 11
   Feb., and to C-in-C India, 12, 15 Feb. 1916. NA WO 106 905.
3 Edmund Candler, *Long Road to Baghdad*, p. 147. 'An Unsuccessful
   attempt to relieve Kut-el-Amarah', Amir Singh diary, 9 Apr. 1916.
   Ellinwood, *Between Two Worlds*, p. 436.
4 Candler, *Long Road to Baghdad*, p. 153.
5 C. D. Noyes to F. A. Smith, NAM 1967-07-44-6, q. Carver, *Turkish
   Front*, pp. 145–6.
6 Barker, *Neglected War*, p. 235.
7 Wilson, *Loyalties*, p. 117.
8 Candler, *Long Road to Baghdad*, pp. 157, 159.
9 Candler, *Long Road*, p. 160.
10 Catty diary, 11 Mar. 1916. NAM 7909-42. Fraser diary, 10 Mar. 1916.
   NA CAB 45/96.
11 MECA, Crowdy letters, 25 Mar. 1916.
12 Diary of Maj. J. W. Nelson, 10 Mar. 1916. Kent County Archive
   WKR B2/A2. Also J. W. Nelson, 'Short Diary of the Kut Siege',
   Queen's Own Gazette No. 3956.
13 IWM 74/70/1.
14 NAM 6702-91.
15 MECA, Crowdy diary-letter No. 10, 24 Jun 1916.

PART II: Section 10. *The Fall of Kut*

1 Bridges to his father, 15 Mar. 1916. NAM 2007-03-57.
2 CIGS to C-in-C India, 11 Mar. 16. NA WO 106 906. Duff to Hardinge,
   10 Mar. 1916. Hardinge papers 91/1/166. Davis, *Ends and Means*,
   p. 162.
3 Chalmers, 28 Mar. 1916. IWM 01/12/1.
4 Edward Roe, *Diary of an Old Contemptible*, p. 148.
5 Ibid., p. 153.
6 Fraser diary, 6 Apr. 1916. CAB 45/96.

7 Candler, *Long Road*, p. 180.

8 Ibid., p. 175.

9 Fraser diary, 17 Apr. 1916. CAB 45/95.

10 MECA, Crowdy diary-letter, 1 May 1916.

11 Keary to his brother, 22 Apr. 1916. IWM Con Shelf.

12 q., OH ii, p. 430.

13 MECA, Crowdy diary-letter, 1 May 1916; Davson diary, 23 Apr. 1916. IWM 82/25/1.

14 The official historian noted that this Turkish action was 'curious'. OH ii, p. 432.

15 Davson diary, 23 Apr. 1916. IWM 82/25/1.

16 A. C. Lewin to F. J. Moberley, 24 July 1921. NA CAB 45 90.

17 Davson diary, 20 Apr. 1916. IWM 82/25/1.

18 Keary to his brother, 22 Apr. and 8 July 1916. IWM Con Shelf.

19 *Short History of the 17th and 22nd Field Companies*, p. 103.

20 Mousley, *Secrets*, pp. 140, 148.

21 OH ii, p. 444.

22 Phillips diary, 'Notes on the Siege'. NA CAB 45 93.

23 Walker diary, IWM 76/128/1.

24 Sandes, *In Kut*, pp. 238–9.

25 McNeal, 'Report on the Siege of Kut-el-Amara', NA WO 32/5204.

26 GOC 6th Div to GHQ, 17 Feb. 1916. NA WO 158 655.

27 Anderson memoir, IWM P129.

28 Louis Reed, 'Report on the *Julnar*', J. Hammond, *Battle in Iraq* (London 2009), pp. 224–8.

29 Fraser diary, 28 Apr. 1916. NA CAB 45/96.

PART II: Section 11. *Surrender*

1 GOC 6th Div to GHQ, 11 Mar. 1916. NA WO 158/669. CIGS to C-in-C India, 14 Mar. 1916. NA CAB 22/13/2.

2 Army Commander to Government of India, 20 Mar. 1916. NA FO 371/2768.

3 Davis, *Ends and Means*, p. 166.

4 Townshend to Lake, 27 Apr. 1916. Wilson, *Lawrence*, p. 271.

5 Townshend to Lake, 28 Apr. 1916. Wilson, *Lawrence*, p. 273.

6 Townshend, *My Campaign*, p. 336.

7 Wheeler to Cobb, 15 Nov. 1973. IWM P42.

8 Sandes, *In Kut*, p. 254.

9 McNeal, 'Report', pp. 7–8. NA WO 32/5204.

10 Mousley, *Secrets*, pp. 152–3, 156. Mousley shared a mess with Tudway.

PART III: BAGHDAD

PART III: Section 1. *Policy Paralysed: Egypt v India*

1 GOC 6th Div to GHQ, 13 Feb. 1916. WO 158 665. Kitchener to Lake, 20 Mar. 1916. NA CAB 19/24.

2 Mesopotamia Commission, proceedings. NA CAB 19/8.

3 CIGS to C-in-C India 30 Apr. 1916. OH iii, p. 3.

4 Robertson to Duff, 18 May and 28 Aug. 1916. Robertson MSS, LHCMA 8/1/28, 47.
5 Cf J.S. Galbraith, 'No Man's Child: The Campaign in Mesopotamia, 1914–1916', *International History Review* vol. VI (1984), p. 385.
6 Busch, *Britain, India and the Arabs*, p. 119.
7 They included the C-in-C, High Commissioner, and Director of Military Intelligence in Egypt, the Director of the Arab Bureau, the British Sirdar in Sudan, the C-in-C and several political officers in Mesopotamia, the naval commander for the East Indies Station, and the Viceroy and Foreign Secretary in India as well as the Foreign Secretary and India Secretary in London.
8 Elie Kedourie, *England and the Middle East*, p. 70.
9 Sir Mark Sykes, *Dar ul-Islam* (London 1904), pp. 188–9.
10 T. E. Lawrence, *Seven Pillars of Wisdom*, p. 17.
11 There is a brilliant, chilling extended analysis of Sykes's philosophy in Kedourie, *England and the Middle East*, ch. 3.
12 Abandoned around 1909, it was eventually published in 1915 to meet the new public interest in the East, as *The Caliph's Last Heritage*. Sykes tacked some further travel writing on to his unfinished history, and rather bizarrely featured a photograph of his wife as the frontispiece.
13 Ronald Storrs, *Orientations*, pp. 173–6.
14 India Office minutes by Hirtzel and Holderness on McMahon telegram to Grey, 22 Aug. 1915. NA FO 371/2486.
15 In Cox MSS, q. Graves, *Cox*, p. 205.
16 Hardinge to Chamberlain, 7 Nov. 1915. Hardinge MSS, q. Busch, *Britain, India and the Arabs*, p. 78.
17 Busch, *Britain, India and the Arabs*, p. 92.
18 Sir Edward Grey to M. Cambon, 16 May 1916. *British Documents on Foreign Policy*, 1st series, vol. iv, p. 242.
19 M. Sykes, 'The Problem of the Near East', 20 June 1916. PRO CAB 17/175.
20 Cf the argument in James Onley, *The Arabian Frontier of the British Raj*.

PART III: Section 2. *Administration and Punishment*

1 Letters, q. Georgina Howell, *Daughter of the Desert* (London 2006), pp. 125, 127.
2 Gertrude Lowthian Bell, *The Desert and the Sown* (London 1907), p. 135.
3 There is a careful assessment of the Faruqi case in Wilson, *Lawrence*, pp. 198–202.
4 Ibid., p. 277.
5 T. E. Lawrence, 'Intelligence. IEF "D"', in Wilson, *Lawrence*, App. III, pp. 954–5.
6 Lawrence to Clayton, 9 Apr. 1916. Wilson, *Lawrence*, pp. 266–7.
7 Lawrence to his family, 12 Feb. 1917. Wilson, *Lawrence*, p. 367.
8 'Intelligence. IEF "D"', in Wilson, *Lawrence*, pp. 957–8.
9 Lloyd to Deedes, 25 May 1916. J. Charmley, *Lord Lloyd and the Decline of the British Empire* (London 1987), p. 55.

10 Wilson, *Loyalties*, p. 155.
11 Cox to Bell, 21 June 1916. Graves, *Cox*, p. 204.
12 Mark to Edith Sykes, 22 Feb. 1906. Sykes papers, q. Roger Adelson, *London and the Invention of the Middle East*, pp. 108–9.
13 Ibid., p. 158.
14 John Marlowe, *Late Victorian. The Life of Sir Arnold Talbot Wilson*, p. 111.
15 Ibid., p. 105.
16 Bullard, *The Camels Must Go*, p. 91.
17 P. W. Ireland, *Iraq: A Study in Political Development*, pp. 82–4; E. Monroe, *Philby of Arabia*, p. 49.
18 Longrigg, *Iraq*, p. 82.
19 Dickson letters, 16, 23 Sep. 1915. MECA, Dickson MSS, Box 1 file 4.
20 'Administrative Report of Suq al Shuyukh and District for Year 1916–17', 9 May 1917. Forwarded to FO 10 July 1917. NA FO 371/3059.
21 Craig memoir, IWM 05/7/1.
22 'The Pax Britannica in the Occupied Territories of Mesopotamia', *The Arab of Mesopotamia*, pp. 52–61.
23 Young, *Independent Arab*, pp. 82–96.
24 Dickson letters, 14 Jan. 1916. MECA, Dickson MSS Box 1 file 4.

PART III: Section 3. *Retooling the Army*

1 Buchanan, *Tragedy of Mesopotamia*, pp. 86–8.
2 G. F. MacMunn, *The Armies of India* (London 1911), p. 129.
3 Wilson, *Loyalties*, pp. 186–7.
4 Cowper to Moberly, 15 Apr. 1926. NA CAB 45/90. Money letters, 24 Feb. 1916. NAM 9211-19.
5 MacMunn, *Behind the Scenes in Many Wars*, pp. 219–20.
6 Buchanan, *Tragedy of Mesopotamia*, pp. 115–16.
7 Wilson, *Mesopotamia 1917–1920*, pp. 93–4.
8 MacMunn to Alexander, 'Up Tigris', 31 Dec. 1916. IWM 76/98/1.
9 OH iii, p. 21. Col. W. H. Leland, *With the M. T. in Mesopotamia* (London, 1920), noted that the trucks, though apparently standard 3-tonners, were marked 'Load not to exceed 30 cwt'.
10 Wilson, *Loyalties*, p. 201.
11 Maude to Whigham, 24 Sep. 1916, q. Andrew Syk, 'Command and the Mesopotamia Expeditionary Force, 1915–18', p. 121.
12 Dickson letters, 23 Oct. 1916. MECA, Dickson MSS, Box 1 file 4.
13 T. E. Lawrence, 'Intelligence. IEF "D"', May 1916, in Wilson, *Lawrence*, App. III, pp. 949–52.
14 MECA, Crowdy diary-letters, 13 Feb, 24 June 1916.
15 William Leith-Ross, 'Tactical Side'. NAM 8312-69-10.
16 MacMunn, *Behind the Scenes*, p. 238.
17 Duff to Robertson, 18 Aug. 1916. LHCMA, Robertson MSS 8/1/45.
18 Robertson to Duff, 11 July 1916. LHCMA Robertson MSS 8/1/40.
19 Chamberlain to Robertson, 8 Feb. 1916. LHCMA Robertson MSS 1/13/2/1.

20 The DAQMG of 13th Division, Col. Brownrigg, testified to 'how wonderfully accessible' he was. Maj.-Gen. Sir C. Callwell, *The Life of Sir Stanley Maude*, pp. 165, 230.
21 C-in-C Force D to CGS India, 23 Feb. 1916. NA WO 158/655.
22 Omissi, *The Sepoy and the Raj*, p. 139.
23 Memorandum V, 15th Lancers Case. NA WO 106/5443.
24 MacMunn, *Behind the Scenes*, pp. 230–1.
25 Candler, *Long Road to Baghdad*, i, p. 234.
26 H. St J. B. Philby, *Arabian Days*, p. 97
27 Ibid., pp. 235–8.
28 Keary letters, 22 May 1916. IWM Con Shelf.
29 Philby, *Arabian Days*, p. 285.
30 Davson diary, 19 July 1916, IWM 82/25/1.
31 Mark Harrison, 'The Fight Against Disease in the Mesopotamia Campaign', in Cecil and Liddle, *Facing Armageddon*, pp. 475, 478. The Indian troops' vulnerability to scurvy seems to have been due more to the lack of green vegetables in their diet before they arrived in Mesopotamia.
32 Roe, *Diary*, p. 173.
33 Ibid., pp. 175–6.
34 Candler, *Long Road to Baghdad*, i, p. 288.
35 Ibid., p. 290.
36 Ibid., p. 291.
37 Philby, *Arabian Days*, pp. 107–8.
38 Maude letter, 28 June 1916. Callwell, *Sir Stanley Maude*, p. 226.

PART III: Section 4. *Captivity*

 1 Mousley, *Secrets*, p. 143.
 2 H. V. Wheeler, 'The plight of "A" Company, 1/4th Battalion, Hampshire Regiment, in captivity', p. 32. IWM P42.
 3 Diary of Capt. A. J. Shakeshaft, NA CAB 45/92.
 4 Sandes, *In Kut*, pp. 256–7.
 5 McNeal, 'Turkish Treatment of British Prisoners of War', NA WO 32/5204; Mousley, *Secrets*, p. 155.
 6 Sandes, *In Kut*, p. 268.
 7 Walker memoir, pp. 65, 33. IWM 76/128/1.
 8 Shakeshaft diary, NA CAB 45/92.
 9 H. V. Wheeler, 'The plight of "A" Company, 1/4th Battalion, Hampshire Regiment, in captivity', p. 27. IWM P42.
10 Sandes, *In Kut*, p. 270.
11 Walker memoir, p. 68. IWM 76/128/1.
12 Braddon, *The Siege*, p. 262.
13 Walker memoir, p. 70. IWM 76/128/1.
14 McNeal, NA WO 32 5204.
15 Shakeshaft diary, 17 May 1916. NA CAB 45/92.
16 Sloss memoir, IWM 04/24/1.
17 Walker memoir, p. 70. IWM 76/128/1.
18 Walker memoir, pp. 80–1. IWM 76/128/1.

19 Sandes, *In Kut*, pp. 287–8.
20 Zurcher, 'Little Mehmet in the Desert', p. 232.
21 Sloss memoir, IWM 04/24/1.
22 Wheeler, IWM P42.
23 Sloss memoir, IWM 04/24/1.
24 Walker diary, 14 July 1916. IWM 76/128/1.
25 Mousley, *Secrets*, pp. 179–80.
26 Shakeshaft diary, 24 June 1916. NA CAB 45/92.
27 Braddon, *The Siege*, pp. 282–3.
28 'Information obtained from sick and wounded officers and men of the Kut Garrison', Basra, 9, 14 Sep. 1916. Transcripts of interviews with prisoners, 26 Nov. 1916. 'Interrogation of Indians who had escaped from the Turks', Kazvin, 21 Nov. 1916. NA FO 383/228.
29 Cecil to Bathurst, 21 July 1916; Col. H. O. Parr, 26 June 1916. NA FO 383/226.
30 MI1 note, 25 Oct.; US Embassy note, 27 Oct. 1916. NA FO 383/228.
31 Wheeler, Supplement, p. 32. IWM P42.
32 Stilwell, 'From the Tigris to the Mediterranean in 34 Months'. IWM 07/14/1.
33 P. W. Long, *Other Ranks of Kut* (London 1938).
34 Capt E. H. Keeling to Gen. Sir Herbert Cox, 27 Apr. 1918. NA FO 383/232.
35 Maurice Larcher, *La guerre turque dans la guerre mondiale*, p. 602.

PART III: Section 5. *Inquiry*

1 Chamberlain to Robertson, and reply, 25 Feb. 1916. Chamberlain MSS, 46/2/62-3. Goold, 'Lord Hardinge', p. 941.
2 Duff to Hardinge, 30 Dec. 1915, 22 Feb. 1916. Hardinge MSS 90/1/422, 91/1/110.
3 Chamberlain to Robertson, 7 Mar. 1916; Robertson to Chamberlain, 6 Mar. 1916. LHA, Robertson MSS 7/5/8, 1/35/14.
4 'Vincent–Bingley' Report, in Mesopotamia Commission Report, Cd 8610, 1917, Appendix 1, paras 131, 135, 164.
5 Ibid., paras 176, 177.
6 Gen. Sir Beauchamp Duff, Memorandum on the Report of the "Vincent-Bingley" Commission, ibid., Appendix 2.
7 Memo by Hamilton, 18 July 1917. Asquith MSS, 32, q. Busch, *Britain, India and the Arabs*, p. 129.
8 Mesopotamia Commission Report, Part XI, paras 1, 3, 5, 7, 9.
9 Mesopotamia Commission proceedings, NA CAB 19/8.
10 Mesopotamia Commission Report, Part XI, para. 12.
11 Ibid., para. 38.
12 Ibid., paras 38–40.
13 Ibid., para. 43.
14 Ibid., paras 36, 46, 47.
15 Ibid., Part XII, paras 8–9, 13, 19, 27.
16 Ibid., separate Report by Commander J. C. Wedgwood, paras 2, 4, 11–13.
17 Cf T. Moreman, *The Army in India*.

18 Wedgwood, Separate Report, para. 14.
19 Ibid., para. 22.
20 Ibid., paras 41–3, 45.

PART III: Section 6. *Maude's Offensive: The Third Battle for Kut*

1 Roe, *Diary*, 27, 28 June, 10–13 July , 1, 3–4, 30–31 Aug. 1916.
2 Ibid., 28, 30 Sep. 1916.
3 C-in-C Mesopotamia to CIGS, 11, 29 Sep. 1916. Robertson MSS, LHCMA 4/4/41, 96.
4 Monro to Robertson, 15 July 1916. Robertson MSS, LHCMA 8/1.
5 Callwell, *Sir Stanley Maude*, p. 231.
6 OH iii, p. 43.
7 Ibid., p. 48.
8 Ibid., p. 41.
9 Callwell, *Sir Stanley Maude*, pp. 247–8.
10 Candler, *Long Road to Baghdad*, ii, p. 23.
11 Erickson, *Ordered to Die*, p. 164.
12 GHQ Intelligence Summary, 25 Dec. 1916. NA WO 157/794.
13 Candler, *Long Road to Baghdad*, ii, p. 49.
14 'Dick' to 'Whacker', 19 Mar. 1917. IWM MISC 3395.
15 Sir William Marshall, *Memories of Four Fronts*, pp. 208–9.
16 Maj. R. H. Dewing, 'Some Aspects of Maude's Campaign in Mesopotamia. No. 1. River Crossings', *Army Quarterly* XIII, 4 (Jan. 1927), pp. 297–9.
17 Marshall, *Memories of Four Fronts*, p. 197.
18 Roe, *Diary*, 15, 16, 20, 25 Dec. 1916.
19 Nunn, *Tigris Gunboats*, p. 248.
20 G. T. Coles memoir, IWM 03/58/1.
21 R. Boulton, diary/journal, 29 Dec. 1916. IWM P109.
22 Roe, *Diary*, 6, 15, 16, 20, 25, 27–8, 29–31 Dec. 1916.
23 O'Dowda diary, 15 Jan. 1917, q. Syk, 'Command', p. 178.
24 Callwell, *Sir Stanley Maude*, p. 256.
25 Ibid., p. 257.
26 Roe, *Diary*, 3, 4, 5, 6 Feb. 1916.
27 Coles memoir, IWM 03/58/1.
28 Roe, *Diary*, 14 Feb.; Money letters, 22 Feb. 1916. NAM 8106-61.
29 Boulton diary/journal, 16, 17 Feb. 1917. IWM P109.
30 Dewing, "Some Aspects of Maude's Campaign in Mesopotamia. No. 1. River Crossings', pp. 299–300.
31 *Historical Records of the 20th Infantry*, pp. 29–30.
32 Candler, *Long Road to Baghdad*, ii, pp. 51, 54.
33 Harrison, diary, 23 Feb. 1917. IWM 74/145/1.
34 R. B. Woakes diary, 23 Feb. 1917. NAM 7408-79.
35 Roe, *Diary*, 23, 24 Feb. 1916.
36 Candler, *Long Road to Baghdad*, ii, p. 63.
37 Fraser diary, 24 Feb. 1917. NA CAB 45/97.
38 Cobbe to Moberley, 25 July 1925. NA CAB 45/90.
39 Candler, *Long Road to Baghdad*, ii, pp. 67–8.

40 Marshall, *Memories of Four Fronts*, p. 219.
41 Dewing, 'Some Aspects of Maude's Campaign in Mesopotamia. No. 2. Cavalry', *Army Quarterly* XIV, 1 (Apr. 1927), pp. 73–5.
42 Roe, *Diary*, 25 Feb. 1916.
43 Candler, *Long Road to Baghdad*, ii, p. 76.
44 Money letters, 30 Dec. 1916, 5, 8 Jan., 8, 22 Feb. 1917. NAM 8106-61.
45 Fraser diary, 13, 31 Dec. 1916, 27 Feb. 1917. NA CAB 45/96, 97.
46 G. S. Barber diary, 25 Feb. 1917. NA CAB 45/95.

PART III: Section 7. *Baghdad at Last*

1 OH iii, p. 205.
2 CIGS to General, Basra, 28 Feb. 1917. NA AIR 20/719; OH iii, pp. 201–2.
3 Coles diary/journal, 4 Mar. 1917. IWM 03/58/1.
4 R. B. Woakes diary, 1, 2 Mar. 1917. NAM 7408-79. For Woakes, the most 'awful catastrophe' was the theft of the officers' mess beer – twenty precious bottles – on the 2nd.
5 Boulton dairy, 2, 3, 5 Mar. 1917. IWM P109.
6 Callwell, *Sir Stanley Maude*, p. 272.
7 Fraser diary, 6 Mar. 1917. NA CAB 45/97. Money letter, 9 Mar. 1917. NAM 9211-19.
8 OH iii, pp. 220–1.
9 O'Dowda diary, 7 Mar. 1917. CKS WKR/B1/Z14.
10 R. B. Woakes diary, 8 Mar. 1917. NAM 7408-79.
11 [A. G. Wauchope], 'The Battle Beyond Bagdad, by a Highland Officer', *Blackwoods Magazine*, Aug. 1917, p. 254.

PART III: Section 8. *Maude's Moment*

1 Col. C.E. Yate, House of Commons, 22 Mar 1916. HC Deb 5s vol. LXXXI col.229.
2 Fisher, *Curzon and British Imperialism*, p. 51.
3 Bell, 'A Ruler of the Desert', *The Arab of Mesopotamia*, pp. 47–50.
4 Callwell, *Sir Stanley Maude*, p. 251.
5 Wilson, *Loyalties*, p. 160.
6 Hirtzel's notes, 8, 9 Mar. 1917. IOR L/P&S/10.
7 Wilson, *Loyalties*, p. 238.
8 Amar Singh diary, 29 Jan. 1916. Ellinwood, *Between Two Worlds*, p. 431. Hirtzel minute, 11 Apr. 1917. IOR L/P&S/10/666.
9 Sec. of State to Viceroy, 29 Mar. 1917. NA FO 371/3042.
10 Cox to Govt of India, 7 Apr. 1917. NA FO 371/3042; Graves, *Cox*, pp. 220–1.
11 CIGS to GOC Mesopotamia, 16 May, and reply, 1 June 1917. BL IOR L/PS/11/123, P2046/1917.
12 GOC Mesopotamia to CIGS, 24 June 1917. NA CAB 27/22.
13 Graves, *Cox*, p. 221, clearly suggests he did not: he certainly did not consult him about the telegram he sent to Robertson deprecating the idea of Arab levies.

14 'Minute by Director of Military Intelligence on Maude–Cox question',
   10 Aug. 1917. NA CAB 27/22.
15 Storrs diary, 9 May 1917. *Orientations*, pp. 254–5.
16 Cox to Sec. of State for India, 25 May 1917. Position of Chief Political
   Officer, Baghdad. Mesopotamia Administration Committee.
   NA CAB 21/60.
17 Baghdad Wilayet Administration Report, 1917. NA CO 696/1.
18 Young, *Independent Arab*, pp. 102–3.
19 Gertrude Bell to Arthur Hirtzel, 15 June 1917. Holograph in MECA,
   Cox MSS file 4.
20 GOC Mesopotamia to C-in-C India, 9 July 1917. NA CAB 27/22.
21 GOC Mesopotamia to CIGS, 3 Aug. 1917. BL IOR L/PS/11/123,
   P2046/1917.
22 Sec. of State to Viceroy, 4 July 1917. NA CAB 21/60.
23 Minute by DMI, 10 Aug. 1917. NA CAB 27/22.
24 Curzon to Hirtzel, 13 Aug. 1917. Holograph in MECA, Cox MSS file 4.
25 Diary, 21 Apr. 1917. Young, *The Independent Arab*, p. 125.
26 Wilson, *Loyalties*, p. 264.

PART IV: MOSUL

PART IV: Section 1. *Northern Exposure*

 1 Thompson, *The Leicestershires Beyond Baghdad*, pp. 27, 29, 46.
 2 Candler, *Long Road*, ii, p. 135.
 3 'A Review of the Civil Administration of Mesopotamia' by Miss G. L. Bell,
   Cmd 1061, pp. 32–3; Atiyyah, *Iraq*, pp 226–7. Wilson, *Loyalties*, p. 243.
 4 Candler, *Long Road*, ii, p. 142.
 5 This error persisted through to the middle of the battle on 25 Mar.
   OH iii, p. 282.
 6 Candler, *Long Road*, ii, p. 140.
 7 Roe diary, 17 Mar. 1917.
 8 Ibid., 27, 28 Mar. 1917.
 9 Candler, *Long Road*, ii, p. 145.
10 Alfred Burne, *Mesopotamia: The Last Phase*, pp. 27–30.
11 Roe, *Diary*, 30 Mar., 20 Apr. 1917.
12 Candler, *Long Road*, ii, pp. 147–50.
13 Marshall, *Memories of Four Fronts*, p. 235.
14 Burne, *Last Phase*, pp. 39, 43.
15 Roe diary, 17 Apr. 1917.
16 Catty diary, 28 Apr. 1917. NAM 7909-42.
17 Marshall, *Memories of Four Fronts*, p. 245.
18 Baxter letters, 17 Aug. 1917. IWM Con Shelf.

PART IV: Section 2. *Maude's End*

 1 Wilson, *Loyalties*, p. 270.
 2 Michael Reynolds, 'Buffers, not Brethren: Young Turk Military Policy
   in the First World War and the Myth of Panturanism', *Past and Present*
   No. 203 (2009), p. 145.

3 Order of battle, 20 July 1917. NA AIR 23/439
4 Erickson, *Ordered to Die*, pp. 166–8.
5 MI1, 'The Coming Campaigns in Mesopotamia, Palestine and Hejaz', 4 Aug. 1917. BL IOR L/PS/11/129, P4640, P4973/1917.
6 Robertson to Maude, 24 Sep. 1917. LHCMA Robertson MSS 4/4.
7 Baxter letters, 21 Oct. 1917. IWM Con Shelf.
8 Burne, *Last Phase*, pp. 69–70.
9 Gertrude Bell letters, 22 Nov. 1917. Lady Bell (ed.), *The Letters of Gertrude Bell*, Vol II (London 1927).
10 Elizabeth Burgoyne, *Gertrude Bell from her Personal Papers 1914–1926* (London, 1958), p. 67.
11 William to Jack Marshall, 7 Dec. 1917. LHCMA, Marshall MSS.
12 Baxter letters, 15 Jan., 22 Feb. 1918. IWM Con Shelf.

PART IV: Section 3. *Strengthening the Hold*

1 'British Policy in Mesopotamia', Memorandum by Lord Curzon, 21 Sep. 1917. NA CAB 21/61.
2 'The Position in Mesopotamia in Relation to the Spirit of the Age', 16 Jan. 1918. NA FO 800/221.
3 Cox memorandum, 22 Apr. 1918. BL IOR, L/P&S/10 4722/18/5604. Cabinet Eastern Committee minutes, 24 Apr. 1918. NA CAB 27/24.
4 *Letters of Gertrude Bell*, 11 May, 18 May 1917.
5 Atiyyah, *Iraq*, p. 235.
6 Nasiriyah Division, Reports of Administration 1918. Atiyyah, *Iraq*, p. 242.
7 Amara Division, Monthly Diary, Feb. 1919. Atiyyah, *Iraq*, p. 239.
8 Ibid., pp. 225–6.
9 Wilson, *Loyalties*, p. 289.
10 *Letters of Gertrude Bell*, 18 Jan., 6 Mar. 1918.
11 'A Review of the Civil Administration of Mesopotamia' by Miss G. L. Bell, Cmd 1061, p. 34.
12 Atiyyah, *Iraq*, p. 219.
13 Savage, *Mespots During the Great War*, p. 54.
14 A. T. Wilson, *Mesopotamia 1917–1920*, p. 74.
15 Brig.-Gen. Sanders telegram 18 Mar.; Capt. J. D. Prothero report, 19 Mar. 1918. Durham University Library, Sudan Archive, F.C.C. Balfour MSS 303/2.
16 GOC 53 Bde report, 13 Apr. 1918. BL Balfour MSS 303/2.
17 Balfour to Wilson, 21, 25 Apr. 1918. BL Balfour MSS 303/2.
18 Report, 20 June 1918. MECA, Dickson MSS, Box 2a file 1.

PART IV: Section 4. *Caucasian Fantasies*

1 But see the counter-argument in Michael Reynolds, 'Buffers, not Brethren', pp. 137–79.
2 L. C. Dunsterville, *Stalky's Reminiscences*, p. 236.
3 Michael Occleshaw, *Dances in Deep Shadows*, pp. 44–5.

4 Pezhmann Dailami, 'The Populists of Rasht: Pan-Islamism and the Role of the Central Powers', in T. Atabaki (ed.), *Iran and the First World War*, p. 137.
5 Dunsterville to Marling (Teheran), 3 Apr. 1918. NA AIR 20/662.
6 CIGS to C-in-C Baghdad, 13, 15 Mar. 1918. NA AIR 20/662.
7 Director of Military Intelligence to Dunsterville, 20 Apr.; GHQ Baghdad to Dunsterville, 26 Mar. 1918. NA AIR 20/662.
8 Wilson, *Mesopotamia*, p. 29.
9 Burne, *Last Phase*, p. 77.
10 Keith Jeffery, *The British Army and the Crisis of Empire*, p. 133.
11 Keith Jeffery, *Field Marshal Sir Henry Wilson*, p. 233.
12 WO telegram 29 Apr. 1918. OH iv, p. 159.
13 Marshall to Frederick Maurice, 2 Mar. 1918. LHCMA, Maurice papers, 3/5. Marshall, *Memories*, pp. 286–7.
14 R. G. Suny, *The Baku Commune 1917–1918*, pp. 7, 178.
15 The OH notes, with some understatement, that this was only achieved 'with considerable difficulty'.
16 WO telegram, 15 July 1918. OH iv, p. 196.
17 Suny, *Baku Commune*, p. 330.
18 Dunsterforce Intelligence Summary, Aug. 1918. NA WO 157/856.
19 *History of the 7th Battalion the Prince of Wales's North Staffordshire Regiment 1914–1919*, Whittington Barracks, Staffordshire Regt Museum.
20 Suny, *Baku Commune*, pp. 336–7.
21 Marshall, *Memories*, pp. 311–12.

PART IV: Section 5. *Victory*

1 Margaret MacMillan, *Peacemakers* (London 2002), p. 83.
2 Barker, *Townshend*, p. 216.
3 Fromkin, *A Peace to End all Peace*, pp. 369–71.
4 Longrigg, *Iraq*, p. 92.
5 'Petroleum Situation in the British Empire', 29 July 1918. NA CAB 21/119.
6 Maurice Hankey to Eric Geddes, 30 July 1918. NA CAB 21/119.
7 'Report for the Army Council on Mesopotamia by Sir John Hewett', 10 Mar. 1919. NA WO 106/55. 'Some Impressions About Mesopotamia by Sir John Hewett', 7 May 1919. NA WO 32/5224.
8 Wilson, *Mesopotamia*, pp. 169–70.
9 See e.g. T. Paris, *Britain, the Hashemites and Arab Rule*, p. 51.

PART IV: Section 6. *Self-Determination?*

1 Bell to Hirtzel, 16 Jan. 1919. MECA, Cox MSS, file 4.
2 Wilson, *Mesopotamia*, pp. 104–5.
3 'Self-Determination in Mesopotamia', Memorandum by Miss G. L. Bell, Feb. 1919. With Annex 'A', 'The Political Views of the Naqib of Baghdad'. Wilson, *Mesopotamia*, pp. 330–41.
4 Basrah Division Administration Report, 1919. NA CO 696/2.
5 George Riddell, *Lord Riddell's Intimate Diary of the Peace Conference and after* (London 1933), p. 25.

6 Wilson, *Mesopotamia*, p. 116.
7 French protests, Feb. 1919. NA WO 32/5602.
8 Wilson, *Mesopotamia*, p. 124.
9 Peter Sluglett, *Britain in Iraq, 1914–1932*, p. 25.
10 Shuckburgh minute, 9 Aug 1919, q. Sluglett, *Britain in Iraq*, pp. 36–7.
11 Sluglett, *Britain in Iraq*, pp. 26–7.
12 Clayton to Bell, 31 July 1919. MECA, Cox MSS, Box 4.
13 Dickson reports, 16 Feb., 2, 20 Apr., 20 June, 9, 15 July, Oct., Nov. 1918. MECA, Dickson MSS, Box 2a file 1.
14 Hirtzel minute, 9 July 1919, BL IOR L/P&S/10; Lawrence minute, July 1919, NA FO 608/92; Young minute, 29 Sep. 1919, NA FO 371/4750. Busch, *Britain, India*, pp. 342, 344, 361.
15 Hirtzel to Wilson, 16 July, 17 Sep. 1919, 3 Feb. 1920. Wilson MSS, BL Add. Ms. 52455.
16 PO Baghdad to IO, 28 July 1919. NA FO 371/4149. Atiyyah, *Iraq*, pp. 296–8.
17 Lawrence to Curzon, 25 Sep. 1919. *DBFP*, series I: IV, p. 422.

PART IV: Section 7. *Retrenchment*

1 Aylmer Haldane diary, quoted in Jeffery, *The British Army and the Crisis of Empire*, p. 147. Aylmer L. Haldane, *The Insurrection in Mesopotamia, 1920*, p. 65.
2 *The Times*, 14 Aug. 1919.
3 MacMunn, *Behind the Scenes*, p. 284. S/S War to GOC-in-C Mesopotamia, 9, 25 Sep. 1919, and replies. NA WO 32/5227, 3514.
4 GOC Mesopotamia, 'Note on Military Organisation in Mesopotamia and North Persia', 1 Nov. 1919. NA WO 106/55.
5 'Note of use of Air Force in Mesopotamia in its political aspects and as to its utility actual and potential in support of the Civil Government of that country', NA AIR 5/476.
6 See Charles Townshend, 'Civilization and "Frightfulness": Air Control in the Middle East between the Wars', in C. Wrigley (ed.), *Warfare, Diplomacy and Politics. Essays in Honour of A. J. P. Taylor*, pp. 142–62.
7 'Proposed use of Gas Bombs against Hostile Forces in Mesopotamia', note by Deputy Chief of the Air Staff, 11 Apr. 1919. NA AIR 2/122.
8 Air Staff Memorandum, 'On the Power of the Air Force and the Application of this Power to Police and Hold Mesopotamia', Mar. 1920. NA AIR 5/224.
9 Bertram Thomas, *Alarms and Excursions in Arabia*, p. 71.
10 Wilson to Hirtzel, 20 Mar. 1920. Marlowe, *Late Victorian*, p. 187.
11 Basrah Division Administration Report 1919. NA CO 696/2.
12 Report to Officiating Civil Commissioner, 26 Apr. 1920. NA AIR 20/527.
13 Young, *Independent Arab*, p. 290.
14 Ibid., pp. 296–8.
15 Dulaim Divisional Council, 21 June 1920. NA AIR 20/527.
16 Wilson to Hirtzel, 24 May 1920. Marlowe, *Late Victorian*, p. 201.

PART IV: Section 8. *Rebellion*

1 Wilson to Hirtzel, 9 June 1920. Marlowe, *Wilson*, p. 194.

2 Eliezer Tauber, 'The Struggle for Dayr al-Zur: The Determination of Borders between Syria and Iraq', *International Journal of Middle East Studies* 23 (1991), p. 371.

3 Abstract of Police Intelligence, Baghdad, 22 May 1920. NA FO 371/5076, q. Nakash, *Shi'is of Iraq*, p. 70.

4 Amal Vinogradov, 'The 1920 Revolt in Iraq Reconsidered: The Role of Tribes in National Politics', *International Journal of Middle East Studies* vol. 3 (1972), p. 135.

5 Wilson, *Mesopotamia*, pp. 268–9; Marlowe, *Wilson*, p. 228.

6 Bell to H. B., 14 June 1920. *Letters of Gertrude Bell*, II, p. 489.

7 'Note by Miss G. L. Bell, dated 13th June 1920, reporting conversation with Sulayman Faydhi'. Encl. in CC to IO, 14 June 1920. NA FO 371/5228.

8 Haldane to Sir Henry Wilson, 20 June 1920. K. Jeffery (ed.), *The Military Correspondence of Field Marshal Sir Henry Wilson* (London 1985), no. 124.

9 A. Haldane, *A Soldier's Saga* (Edinburgh 1948), p. 375; Marlowe, *Wilson*, p. 205.

10 Mark Jacobsen, '"Only by the Sword: British Counter-Insurgency in Iraq, 1920', *Small Wars and Insurgencies* 2 (1991), pp. 340–2.

11 Civil Commissioner to Sec. of State, 27 Aug. 1920. NA CAB 24/111. Thomas, *Alarms and Excursions*, pp. 98–111.

12 Zetton Buchanan, *In the Hands of the Arabs*, p. 236.

13 Thair Karim, 'Tribes and nationalism: tribal political culture and behaviour in Iraq 1914–20', in F. Jabar and H. Dawood (eds), *Tribes and Power* (London 2003), p. 284.

14 Fanar Haddad, 'The terrorists of today are the heroes of tomorrow: the anti-British and anti-American insurgencies in Iraqi history', *Small Wars and Insurgencies* 19, 4 (Dec. 2008), p. 458.

15 H. S. Mitchell letters, 10, 12 Aug. 1920. NAM 2006-12-60.

16 Bell to F. B., 5 Sep. 1920. *Letters*, II, pp. 497–8. IO, 'Note on the Causes of the Outbreak in Mesopotamia', 26 Aug. 1920. NA FO 371/5229.

17 Winstone, *Leachman*, p. 201.

18 Longrigg, *Iraq*, p. 123.

19 Thomas, *Alarms and Excursions*, p. 81.

20 CC to IO, 5 Aug. 1920. NA FO 371/5228.

21 'Mesopotamia. Causes of Unrest – Report No.2', by Maj. N. N. E. Bray, Oct.1920. C.P. 1990, NA CAB 24/112.

22 Ireland, *Iraq*, pp. 252, 275.

23 Thomas, *Alarms and Excursions*, p. 89.

24 Annual report for Hillah District, 1921. MECA, Dickson MSS, Box 2a file 3.

25 Air Staff Memorandum on the Air Force as an Alleged Cause of the Loss of Popularity of the Mesopotamia Civil Administration, 27 Aug. 1920. C.P. 1823, NA CAB 24/111.

26 R. M. Douglas, 'Did Britain Use Chemical Weapons in Mandatory Iraq?' *Journal of Modern History* 81 (2009), pp. 859–87.
27 'Notes on Modern Arab Warfare based on the Fighting Round Rumaitha and Diwaniyah, July–August 1920', App. IX to Haldane, *Insurrection in Mesopotamia*, pp. 332–42.
28 Annual report for Hillah district, 1921. MECA, Dickson MSS, Box 2a file 3.
29 Scott letters, 30 Aug. 1920. NA CAB 45/99.
30 Scott letters, 14 Sep. 1920. NA CAB 45/99.

PART IV: Section 9. *Kingdom Come*

1 Martin Gilbert, *Winston S. Churchill*, vol. iv (London 1975), p. 496.
2 Instructions, 12 Aug. 1920. NA WO 32/5745.
3 Political Baghdad to FO, 22 Dec., and Foreign Sec. to HC Egypt, 23 Dec. 1918. NA FO 141/444/7.
4 Memo by Cox, 31 July 1920. NA FO 141/447/7.
5 Young to Curzon, 12 Jan. 1921. NA FO 371/6342.
6 Paris, *Britain, the Hashemites and Arab Rule*, p. 135.
7 Cairo Conference Minutes, 12 Mar. 1921. Gilbert, *Churchill*, iv, p. 545.
8 J. de V. Loder, *The Truth about Mesopotamia, Palestine and Syria* (London 1923), p. 101.
9 Notes from Adviser to Minister of the Interior, end Nov. 1920. MECA, Philby MSS, 1/3/4/3.
10 Philby to Philip Graves, 26 Apr. 1939. MECA, Philby MSS, 1/3/4/3; Cox to CO, 9 June 1921. NA CO 730/2.
11 Annual report for Hillah District, 1921. MECA, Dickson MSS, Box 2a file 3.
12 Mesopotamia Intelligence Report No. 13, 15 May 1921. NA FO 371/6346.
13 Sluglett, *Britain in Iraq*, p. 74.
14 Minute by Sec. of State, Apr. 1922. NA CO 730/21/18047.
15 Memo. by Maj.-Gen. Jaafar al-Askari, 12 Nov. 1920. NA AIR 23/439.
16 Sluglett, *Britain in Iraq*, p. 144; Dodge, *Inventing Iraq*, pp. 140–3.
17 Organization of Iraq Levies, memo. by Col. Meinertzhagen, 22 Nov. 1921. NA AIR 5/295.

PART IV: Section 10. *Kurdistan for the Kurds?*

1 W. R. Hay, *Two Years in Kurdistan: Experiences of a Political Officer 1918–1920*, pp. 35–6. *Letters of Gertrude Bell*, 14 Aug. 1921.
2 C. J. Edmonds, 'Kurdish Nationalism', *Journal of Contemporary History* 6 (1971), p. 88.
3 Robert Olson, *The Emergence of Kurdish Nationalism and the Sheikh Said Rebellion 1880–1925*, ch. 1.
4 'A Review of the Civil Administration of Mesopotamia' by Miss G. L. Bell, Cmd 1061 p. 59.
5 17 Nov. 1918. NA AIR 20/512.
6 Wilson, *Mesopotamia*, p. 129.

7 Saad Eskander, 'Britain's Policy in Southern Kurdistan: The Formation and Termination of the First Kurdish Government, 1918–1919', *British Journal of Middle Eastern Studies* 27, 2 (2000), p. 143.
8 Longrigg, *Iraq 1900 to 1950*, p. 104.
9 Wilson, *Mesopotamia*, p. 133.
10 Ibid., p. 83.
11 Note by E. W. C. Noel; E. B. Soane, 'Administration Report of Sulaimaniyah Division for the Year 1919'. NA CO 730/13.
12 David McDowall, *A Modern History of the Kurds* (London 1997), p. 156.
13 Winstone, *Leachman*, pp. 202–3.
14 See 'Precis of Affairs in Southern Kurdistan during the War', Civil Commission, Baghdad 1919. NA FO 371/4192.
15 OC Kurdish Levies to PO Sulaimaniyah, 17 Apr. 1919. Daniels MSS, IWM 92/48/1.
16 Report 25 May 1919. IOR L/MIL/5/278.
17 MacMunn, *Behind the Scenes*, p. 293.
18 H. C. Constantinople to FO, 21 July 1919. NA WO 32/5226.
19 Ibid.
20 Wilson, *Mesopotamia*, pp. 143–5.
21 Lt.-Col. H. L. Scott, report on operations of Stapleton's Column, in NA AIR 1/426/15/260/1.
22 Lt.-Col. H. L. Scott letters, 5 June 1919. NA CAB 45/99.
23 Report by Assistant Commandant Gendarmes, Mosul, 4 Nov. 1919. NA AIR 1/426/15/260/1.
24 Lt.-Col. L. S. Nalder, Administration Report 1919, Mosul. MECA, Nalder MSS.
25 W. R. Hay, 'Note on Rowanduz', 26 Dec. 1919. NA FO 371/5068.
26 Bell to Cox, 6 Dec. 1919, Bell to Hirtzel, 8 Mar. 1920. MECA, Cox Mss, File 4.
27 'A Review of the Civil Administration of Mesopotamia' by Miss G. L. Bell, Cmd 1061, p. 63.
28 Interdepartmental conference, 13 Apr. 1920. NA FO 371/5068.
29 Hay, *Two Years in Kurdistan*, pp. 348–9.
30 Report of Interdepartmental Committee, 31 Jan. 1921. NA FO 371/6342.
31 Cairo Conference, Appendix 10: Kurdistan. 4th Meeting of the Political Committee. NA FO 371/6343. Lloyd George to Churchill, 22 Mar. 1921, NA FO 371/6342.
32 Cox to CO, 21 June 1921. NA FO 371/6346. Mesopotamian Intelligence Reports, 1 May, 15 May, 1 June 1921. NA CO 730/2, FO 371/6352.
33 Cox to CO, 2 June 1921. NA CO 730/2.
34 Minute by J. E. Shuckburgh (initialled by Churchill), 23 June 1921. NA CO 730/2.
35 HC Iraq to S/S Colonies, 26 Aug. 1921. NA CO 730/4.
36 McDowall, *Modern History of the Kurds*, p. 166.
37 HC Iraq to S/S Colonies, 20 Sep., and CO Minutes, 27 Sep. 1921. NA CO 730/5.
38 HC Mesopotamia to S/S Colonies, 5 June 1921. NA FO 371/6346.

39 Noel to Bourdillon, 10 Oct. 1922, q. Sluglett, *Britain in Iraq*, p. 120.
40 Rumbold to Curzon, 11 May 1921. NA FO 371/6346. Cox to CO, 21 June 1921. NA CO 730/2.
41 Saad Eskander, 'Southern Kurdistan under Britain's Mesopotamian Mandate: from Separation to Incorporation, 1920–23', *Middle Eastern Studies* 37, 2 (2001), p. 170.
42 AVM J. M. Salmond, RAF Iraq Command Report Oct. 1922–Apr. 1924. NA AIR 5/1253.
43 The Air Staff estimated that there were 7,000 men and 40 guns of the Turkish VII Corps on the border: of these 2,000 infantry and 400 cavalry, with 12 guns, operated in 'Iraq territory'. Appreciation of the Situation on the Northern Frontier of Iraq, Sep.–Oct. 1924, in CID Memo by Sec. of State for Air, 17 Oct. 1925. NA CAB 27/206.
44 David Omissi, *Air Power and Colonial Control*, p. 35.

PART IV: Section 11. *The World Decides*

1 *The Times*, 8 Nov. 1919, 15 June 1920, 31 Aug. 1922. *Manchester Guardian*, 24 June 1920. Priya Satia, *Spies in Arabia*, pp. 291–5.
2 *Observer*, 8 Aug. 1920. Wilson, *Lawrence*, p. 640.
3 MacDowall, *Modern History of the Kurds*, p. 144.

Afterword

1 Quoted in Mohammed A. Tarbush, *The Role of the Military in Politics*, p. 40.
2 John Darwin, 'An Undeclared Empire', p. 160.
3 Ibid., p. 163.
4 William Stivers, *Supremacy and Oil*, p. 25.
5 Intelligence Report No. 13, 21 June 1923. NA CO 730/40.
6 M. Farouk-Sluglett and P. Sluglett, 'The Historiography of Modern Iraq', *American Historical Review* (Dec. 1991), p. 1411.
7 NA FO 371/12660.
8 Sluglett, *Britain in Iraq*, p. 298.
9 Elie Kedourie, 'The Kingdom of Iraq: A Retrospect', in *The Chatham House Version and Other Middle Eastern Studies*, pp. 257–8.
10 Charles Tripp, *A Short History of Iraq* (2nd edn, Cambridge 2000), p. 74.
11 Elie Kedourie, 'Minorities', in *The Chatham House Version*, pp. 304, 314.

Bibliography

Adelson, Roger, *London and the Invention of the Middle East* (London 1995)
Al-Azmeh, Aziz, 'Nationalism and the Arabs', in D. Hopwood (ed.), *Arab Nation, Arab Nationalism* (London 1999)
Anon., *Historical Records of the 20th (Duke of Cambridge's Own) Infantry 1908–1922* (reprinted Uckfield, East Sussex, 2005)
Antonius, George, *The Arab Awakening* (London 1938)
Atabaki, Touraj (ed.), *Iran and the First World War* (London 2006)
Atiyyah, Ghassan R., *Iraq: 1908–1921: A Socio-Political Study* (Beirut 1973)

Barker, A. J. , *The Negelected War. Mesopotamia 1914–1918* (London 1967)
——, *Townshend of Kut: A Biography of Major-General Sir Charles Townshend* (London 1967)
Barker, J. E., 'The Future of Asiatic Turkey', *The Nineteenth Century* (June 1916)
Batatu, Hanna, *The Old Social Classes and the Revolutionary Movements of Iraq* (Princeton, NJ 1978)
Lady Bell (ed.), *The Letters of Gertrude Bell* (London 1927)
[G. L. Bell], *The Arab of Mesopotamia* (Basra 1916)
Bird, W. D., *A Chapter of Misfortunes* (London 1923)
Braddon, Russell, *The Siege* (London 1969)
Bray, N. N. E., *A Paladin of Arabia. The Biography of Lieutenant-Colonel G. E. Leachman* (London 1936)
Buchanan, Sir George, *The Tragedy of Mesopotamia* (Edinburgh 1938)
Buchanan, Zetton, *In the Hands of the Arabs* (London 1921)
Bullard, Reader, *The Camels Must Go* (London 1961)
Burne, Alfred, *Mesopotamia: The Last Phase* (Aldershot 1936)
Busch, Briton C., *Britain, India and the Arabs, 1914–1921* (Berkeley, CA 1971)

Callwell, C. E., *The Life of Sir Stanley Maude* (London 1919)
Candler, Edmund, *The Long Road to Baghdad*, 2 vols (London 1919)
Carver, Field Marshal Lord, *The National Army Museum Book of the Turkish Front* (London 2003)
Catherwood, Christopher, *Winston's Folly: Imperialism and the Creation of Iraq* (London 2004)
Cato, Conrad, *The Navy in Mesopotamia, 1914 to 1917* (London 1917)
Cecil, H. and Liddle, P. (eds), *Facing Armageddon: The First World War Experienced* (London 1996)
Clark, A. T., *To Baghdad with the British* (New York 1918)

Bibliography

Cohen, Stuart A., *British Policy in Mesopotamia 1903–1914* (London 1976)
Cox, Jafna, 'A Splendid Training Ground: The Importance to the Royal Air
Force of its Role in Iraq, 1919–32', *Journal of Imperial and Commonwealth
History* 13, 2 (1985), pp. 157–84
Crowley, Lt.-Col. P. T., 'Operational Lessons of the Mesopotamia Campaign,
1914–18', *Defence Studies* 4, 3 (Autumn 2004), pp. 335–60

Darwin, John, *Britain, Egypt and the Middle East: Imperial Policy in the
Aftermath of War 1918–1922* (London 1981)
——, 'An Undeclared Empire: The British in the Middle East 1918–39',
Journal of Imperial and Commonwealth History 27, 2 (1999), pp. 159–76
Davis, Paul K., *Ends and Means: The British Mesopotamia Campaign and
Commission* (London 1994)
Dewing, R. H., 'Some Aspects of Maude's Campaign in Mesopotamia', *Army
Quarterly* (Jan. & Apr. 1927)
Djemal Pasha, *Memories of a Turkish Statesman, 1913–1919* (London 1922)
Dodge, Toby, *Inventing Iraq: The Failure of Nation Building and a History
Denied* (London 2003)
Dunsterville, Maj.-Gen. L. C., *The Adventures of Dunsterforce* (London
1920)
——, *Stalky's Reminiscences* (London 1928)

Ellinwood, D. C., *Between Two Worlds: A Rajput Officer in the Indian Army,
1905–21* (Lanham, MD 2005)
Emin, Ahmed, *Turkey in the World War* (New Haven 1930)
Erickson, Edward J., *Ordered to Die: A History of the Ottoman Army in the
First World War* (Westport, CT 2001)
——, *Ottoman Army Effectiveness in World War I* (London 2007)
Eskander, Saad, 'Britain's Policy in Southern Kurdistan: The Formation and
Termination of the First Kurdish Government, 1918–1919', *British Journal
of Middle Eastern Studies* 27, 2 (2000)
——, 'Southern Kurdistan under Britain's Mesopotamian Mandate: from
Separation to Incorporation, 1920–23', *Middle Eastern Studies* 37, 2 (2001)

Farouk-Sluglett, M. and Sluglett, P., 'The Historiography of Modern Iraq',
American Historical Review (1991), pp. 1408–21
Fisher, John, *Curzon and British Imperialism in the Middle East 1916–19*
(London 1999)
French, David, 'The Dardanelles, Mecca and Kut: Prestige as a Factor in
British Eastern Strategy', *War and Society* 5, 1 (1987), pp. 45–61
Fromkin, David, *A Peace to End All Peace: The Fall of the Ottoman Empire
and the Creation of the Modern Middle East* (New York 1989)

Galbraith, J. S., 'No Man's Child: The Campaign in Mesopotamia, 1914–
1916', *International History Review* VI, 3 (Aug 1984), pp. 358–85
Gardner, Nicklas, 'Sepoys and the Siege of Kut-al-Amara, December 1915–
April 1916', *War in History* 11, 3 (2004), pp. 307–26

Gokay, Bulent, 'The Battle for Baku (May–September 1918): a Peculiar
  Episode in the History of the Caucasus', *Middle Eastern Studies* 34, 1 (Jan.
  1988), pp. 30–50
——, *A Clash of Empires: Turkey between Russian Bolshevism and British
  Imperialism 1918–1923* (London 1997)
Goold, Douglas, 'Lord Hardinge and the Mesopotamia Expedition and
  Inquiry, 1914–1917' *Historical Journal* 19, 4 (1976), pp. 919–45
Graves, Philip, *The Life of Sir Percy Cox* (London 1941)

Haddad, Fanar, 'The terrorists of today are the heroes of tomorrow: the anti-
  British and anti-American insurgencies in Iraqi history', *Small Wars and
  Insurgencies* 19, 4 (Dec. 2008), pp. 451–83
Haj, Samira, 'The Problems of Tribalism: The Case of Nineteenth-century
  Iraqi History', *Social History* 16 (1991): 45–58.
Haldane, Aylmer L., *The Insurrection in Mesopotamia, 1920* (Edinburgh
  1922)
Hall, L. J., *The Inland Water Transport in Mesopotamia* (London 1921)
Hammond, J. M., *Battle in Iraq: Letters and Diaries of the First World War*
  (London 2009)
Harrison, Mark , 'The Fight Against Disease in the Mesopotamia Campaign',
  in Cecil and Liddle, *Facing Armageddon*
Hay, W. R., *Two Years in Kurdistan: Experiences of a Political Officer 1918–
  1920* (London 1921)
Herbert, Aubrey, *Mons, Anzac and Kut* (London 1919)

Ireland, P. W., *Iraq: A Study in Political Development* (London 1937)

Jastrow, Morris, *War and the Baghdad Railway* (Philadelphia 1917)
Jeffery, Keith, *The British Army and the Crisis of Empire* (Manchester 1984)
——, *Field Marshal Sir Henry Wilson* (Oxford 2006)
Jones, E. H., *The Road to En-Dor* (Oxford 1921)
Jwaideh, Albertine, 'Tribalism and modern society: Iraq, a case study', in
  R. M. Savory (ed.), *The Cambridge History of the Middle East* (Cambridge
  1976)

Karsh, Efraim, 'Reactive Imperialism: Britain, the Hashemites, and the
  Creation of Modern Iraq', *Journal of Imperial and Commonwealth History*
  30, 3 (Sep. 2002), pp. 55–70
Kazemi, Farhad, 'Peasant Uprisings in Twentieth-Century Iran, Iraq and
  Turkey', in F. Kazemi and K. Waterbury (eds), *Peasants and Politics in the
  Middle East* (Miami 1991)
Kearsey, Alexander, *A Study of the Strategy and Tactics of the Mesopotamia
  Campaign, 1914–1917* (London 1934)
Kedourie, Elie, *England and the Middle East. The Destruction of the
  Ottoman Empire 1914–1921* (London 1956)
——, *The Chatham House Version and Other Middle Eastern Studies*
  (London 1970)

Bibliography

Kelidar, Abbas (ed.), *The Integration of Modern Iraq* (London 1979)
Kent, Marian, *Oil and Empire* (London 1976)
——, 'Asiatic Turkey, 1914–1916', in F. H. Hinsley (ed.), *British Foreign Policy under Sir Edward Grey* (Cambridge 1977)
—— (ed.), *The Great Powers and the End of the Ottoman Empire* (London 1984)
Khalidi, Rashid, 'The Arab Experience of the War', in Cecil and Liddle, *Facing Armageddon*

Larcher, Maurice, *La guerre turque dans la guerre mondiale* (Paris 1926)
Latter, Edwin, 'The Indian Army in Mesopotamia 1914–1918', *Journal of the Society for Army Historical Research* 72 (1994): (I) pp. 92–102, (II) pp. 160–9; (III) pp. 232–46
Lawrence, T. E., *Seven Pillars of Wisdom* (London 1935, 1954)
Loder, J. de V., *The Truth about Mesopotamia* (London 1923)
Long, P. W., *Other Ranks of Kut* (London 1938)
Longrigg, S. H., *Four Centuries of Modern Iraq* (Oxford 1925)
——, *Iraq, 1900 to 1950* (Oxford 1953)
Lukitz, Liora, *A Quest in the Middle East: Gertrude Bell and the Making of Modern Iraq* (London 2006)
Lyall, Thomas, *The Ins and Outs of Mesopotamia* (London 1923)

MacMunn, Lt.-Gen. Sir George, *Behind the Scenes in Many Wars* (London 1930)
Marlowe, John, *The Persian Gulf in the Twentieth Century* (London 1962)
——, *Late Victorian: The Life of Sir Arnold Talbot Wilson* (London 1967)
Marshall, Sir William, *Memories of Four Fronts* (London 1929)
Millar, Ronald, *Kut: The Death of an Army* (London 1969)
Millman, Brock, 'The Problem with Generals: Military Observers and the Origins of Intervention in Russia and Persia, 1917–18', *Journal of Contemporary History* 33,2 (1998), pp. 291–320
Moberley, F. J., *The Campaign in Mesopotamia 1914–1918 . (Official History of the Great War)*, 4 vols (London 1923, 1924, 1925, 1927)
Monroe, Elizabeth, *Britain's Moment in the Middle East 1914–1956* (London 1963)
——, *Philby of Arabia* (London 1973)
Moreman, T. R., *The Army in India and the Development of Frontier Warfare 1849–1947* (London 1998)
Morris, Peter, 'Intelligence and its Interpretation: Mesopotamia 1914–1916', in C. Andrew and J. Noakes (eds), *Intelligence and International Relations* (Exeter 1987)
Mousley, Edward O., *The Secrets of a Kuttite* (London 1921)
Murphy, Lt.-Col. C. C. R., *Soldiers of the Prophet* (London 1921)

Nakash, Yitzhak, *The Shi'is of Iraq* (Princeton, NJ 1994)
Nunn, Vice-Admiral Wilfrid, *Tigris Gunboats* (London 1932)

Occleshaw, Michael, *Dances in Deep Shadows: Britain's Clandestine War in Russia 1917–1920* (London 2006)

Olson, Robert, *The Emergence of Kurdish Nationalism and the Sheikh Said Rebellion, 1880–1925* (Austin, TX 1989)

Omissi, David, *Air Power and Colonial Control* (Manchester 1990)

——, *The Sepoy and the Raj* (London 1994)

Onley, James, *The Arabian Frontier of the British Raj: Merchants, Rulers and the British in the Nineteenth-century Gulf* (Oxford 2007)

Paris, Timothy, *Britain, the Hashemites and Arab Rule 1920–1925* (London 2003)

Philby, H. St J. B., *Arabian Days. An Autobiography* (London 1948)

Popplewell, Richard, 'British Intelligence in Mesopotamia 1914–16', *Intelligence and National Security* 5, 2 (1990), pp. 139–72

Renton, James, 'Changing Languages of Empire and the Orient: Britain and the Invention of the Middle East, 1917–1918', *Historical Journal* 50, 3 (2007), pp. 645–67.

Reynardson, Henry Birch, *Mesopotamia 1914–1915* (London 1919)

Reynolds, Michael, 'Buffers, not Brethren: Young Turk Military Policy in the First World War and the Myth of Panturanism', *Past and Present* No. 203 (2009), pp. 137–79

Roe, Edward, *Diary of an Old Contemptible* (Barnsley 2004)

Rothwell, V. H., 'Mesopotamia in British War Aims, 1914–1918', *Historical Journal* XIII, 2 (1970), pp. 273–94

Roy, Kaushik, 'The Construction of Regiments in the Indian Army: 1859–1913', *War in History* 8, 2 (2001), pp. 127–48

——, 'The Army in India in Mesopotamia from 1916 to 1918: Tactics, Technology and Logistics Reconsidered', in I. F. W. Beckett (ed.), *1917: Beyond the Western Front* (Boston 2009)

Salim, Shakir, *Marsh Dwellers of the Euphrates Area* (London 1962)

Sandes, E. W. C., *In Kut and Captivity with the Sixth Indian Division* (London 1920)

Satia, Priya, 'The Defense of Inhumanity: Air Control and the British Idea of Arabia', *American Historical Review* (2006), pp. 16–51

——, 'Developing Iraq: Britain, India and the Redemption of Empire and Technology in the First World War', *Past and Present* No. 197 (2007), pp. 211–55

——, *Spies in Arabia: The Great War and the Cultural Foundations of Britain's Covert Empire in the Middle East* (New York 2008)

Savage, George, *Mespots During the Great War* (Burslem 1920)

Sherson, Erroll, *Townshend of Chitral and Kut* (London 1928)

Sluglett, Peter, *Britain in Iraq, 1914–1932* (London 1976; 2nd edn 2008)

Soane, Ely B. *To Mesopotamia and Kurdistan in Disguise* (London 1912, 1926)

Stark, Freya, *Baghdad Sketches* (London 1939)

Bibliography

Stevens, E. S., *By Tigris and Euphrates* (London 1923)
Stivers, William, *Supremacy and Oil: Iraq, Turkey and the Anglo-American World Order, 1918–1930* (Ithaca, NY 1982)
Storrs, Ronald, *Orientations* (London 1937)
Suny, Roland G., *The Baku Commune 1917–1918* (Princeton 1972)
——, 'Religion, Ethnicity and Nationalism: Armenians, Turks and the End of the Ottoman Empire', in O. Bartov and P. Mack (eds), *In God's Name: Genocide and Religion in the Twentieth Century* (New York 2001).
Syk, Andrew, 'Command and the Mesopotamia Expeditionary Force, 1915–18'. D.Phil. thesis, Oxford University 2009
——, 'The 1917 Mesopotamia Commission', *Journal of the Royal United Services Institution* 154, 4 (2009), pp. 94–101

Tarbush, Mohammad A., *The Role of the Military in Politics: A Case Study of Iraq to 1941* (London 1982): 361–85
Tauber, Eliezer, 'The Struggle for Dayr al-Zur: The Determination of Borders between Syria and Iraq', *International Journal of Middle East Studies* 23 (1991)
——, *The Arab Movements in World War I* (London 1993)
Tennant, J. E., *In the Clouds Above Baghdad* (London 1920)
Thesiger, Wilfred, *The Marsh Arabs* (London 1964)
Thomas, Bertram, *Alarms and Excursions in Arabia* (London 1931)
Thomas, Martin, 'Bedouin Tribes and the Imperial Intelligence Services in Syria, Iraq and Transjordan in the 1920s', *Journal of Contemporary History* 38, 4 (2003), pp. 539–61
Thompson, Edward J., *The Leicestershires beyond Baghdad* (London 1919)
——, *These Men, Thy Friends* (London 1927)
Tidrick, Kathryn, *Heart-beguiling Araby: The English Romance with Arabia* (Cambridge 1981)
Townshend, Charles, 'Civilization and "Frightfulness": Air Control in the Middle East between the Wars', in C. Wrigley (ed.), *Warfare, Diplomacy and Politics. Essays in Honour of A. J. P. Taylor* (London 1986)
Townshend, Charles V. F., *My Campaign in Mesopotamia* (London 1920)
Trumpener, Ulrich, *Germany and the Ottoman Empire 1914–1918* (Princeton, NJ 1968)
——, 'Turkey's War', in H. Strachan (ed.), *The Oxford Illustrated History of the First World War* (Oxford 1998)

Ulrichsen, Kristian Coates, 'The British Occupation of Mesopotamia, 1914–1922', *Journal of Strategic Studies* 30, 2 (2007), pp. 349–377

Vinogradov, Amal, 'The 1920 Revolt in Iraq Reconsidered: The Role of Tribes in National Politics', *International Journal of Middle East Studies* 3 (1972), pp. 123–39

Wauchope, A. G., 'The Battle that won Samarrah', *Blackwoods Magazine* Apr. 1918, pp. 427–34

——, 'The Battle Beyond Baghdad', *Blackwoods Magazine* Aug. 1919, pp. 254–64.

——, 'The Destruction of the VIth Turkish Army', *Journal of the Royal United Services Institution* 64 (1919), pp. 437–59

Westrate, Bruce, *The Arab Bureau: British Policy in the Middle East, 1916–1920* (University Park, PA 1992)

Willcocks, William, *Sixty Years in the East* (Edinburgh 1935)

Wilcox, Ron, *Battles on the Tigris* (Barnsley 2006)

Wilson, Arnold T., *Loyalties: Mesopotamia 1914–1917* (London 1930)

——, *Mesopotamia 1917-1920: A Clash of Loyalties* (London 1931)

Wilson, Jeremy, *Lawrence of Arabia: The Authorised Biography of T. E. Lawrence* (London 1989)

Winstone, H. V. F., *Captain Shakespear: A Portrait* (London 1976)

——, *Gertrude Bell* (London 1978)

——, *Leachman: 'OC Desert'* (London 1982)

——, *The Illicit Adventure: The Story of Political and Military Intelligence in the Middle East from 1898 to 1926* (London 1982)

Wright, Quincy, 'The Government of Iraq', *American Political Science Review* 20 (1926), pp. 743–69

Yasamee, F. A. K., 'Ottoman Empire', in Keith Wilson (ed.), *Decisions for War, 1914* (London 1995)

Young, Hubert, *The Independent Arab* (London 1933)

Younghusband, G. J., *Forty Years a Soldier* (London 1923)

Zeine N. Zeine, *Arab-Turkish Relations and the Emergence of Arab Nationalism* (Beirut 1958)

Zurcher, Erik, 'Little Mehmet in the Desert: The Ottoman Soldier's Experience', in Cecil and Liddle, *Facing Armageddon*

Index

Index

GENERAL INDEX

Index

Cardew, Captain, 157, 167–8, 173, 190
Carson, Sir Edward, 328
Carter, Major, 164–5
Carver, Lord, 350
Cassels, Brigadier Robert, 433, 434–5
casualties: sight of Turkish, 32–3; after Shaiba battle, 89; at battle for Kut, 129–30, 161; at Ctesiphon, 161–6; Kut siege, 187, 190; Sheikh Saad and Wadi, 203–4; Kut relief efforts, 247–8; evacuation of sick, 300; Maude's offensive, 347, 350, 351; river crossings, 363, 365; Keary's forces, 391; Ramadi action, 398–9; Tikrit battle, 400; at Khan Baghdadi, 422; uprising (1920), 469, 476
Catty, Major T. C., 203–4, 205, 209, 210, 211, 216, 224, 229–30, 239–40, 346–7, 395
cavalry: horses, 4, 86, 353, 354–5; Indian, 24, 138, 414; reconnaissance role, 32, 61, 129, 393; Arab irregular, 59; at Ahwaz, 68; Nixon's career, 73; pursuit failures, 86, 90, 130; Townshend's forces, 99, 149, 153; reinforcements, 137; supplies for, 149, 182, 228, 342; charge against Turks, 169–70; Kut departure, 182–3; Kut relief efforts, 200, 210, 227–8; stampeded by artillery, 227; criticised as ineffective, 228, 353–5; Cossacks, 302–3; Kurdish, 311; British numbers, 342; overtaken by flotilla, 356; Maude's use of, 358; river crossings, 364; Baghdad entry, 366; reinforcements, 397; Tatar, 425; leadership, 433; recruitment of Muntafik Horse, 448; mobile column, 468; Manchester column, 470; Kurdish levies, 498–9
Cayley, General, 394
Cecil, Lord Robert, 320, 439
Chahela, 125, 237, 239

Chalmers, T. A.: skipper of *Aerial* hospital ship, 145–6; descriptions of wounded, 164, 201, 204; taking soundings, 171; opinion of Aylmer, 198; on bridge construction, 203; on casualties, 206; opinion of Gorringe, 211; on medical services, 228–9; on March weather, 233; on 13th Division, 234; on Sannaiyat, 236; on 7th Brigade, 238; on supply plan, 246; on mutiny, 297
Chamberlain, Austen: Secretary of State for India, 100; on campaign, 100–1; Hardinge's arguments, 107, 117–18; views of Nixon's strategy, 117–18, 135, 137, 192; Baghdad strategy, 137, 142; on campaign achievements, 144; War Office influence, 261; response to McMahon-Hussein correspondence, 268; on Lake, 296; Mesopotamia inquiry, 325–6, 328, 332–3, 335; resignation, 335–6; Maude's proclamation, 374; Mesopotamia Administration Committee, 375; Cox's title, 381
Chelmsford, Lord, 271, 288, 325, 335–6
Chilka, SS, 83
Chirol, Valentine, 285
Chitral, 95, 180, 197, 216
Chitty, Colonel, 86
Chosroes, King, 151
Christians: Mesopotamian communities, 6; exemption from conscription, 27; in Kut, 185; in Baghdad, 368; internment, 380; Assyrians, 427, 516; view of British occupation, 441; Kurds, 494; Kurdish disturbances, 504; in Iraq Army, 524
Churchill, Winston: Turkish battleship issue, 17; Dardanelles proposal, 18; opposition to Mesopotamia expedition, 37–8; Baghdad policy, 140–1; view of Bolsheviks, 418; Mesopotamia

policy, 438; on Mesopotamia garrison, 453, 454–6, 468; air substitution policy, 455, 476; gas policy, 456; on British administration, 463; response to uprising (1920), 477; opinion of Cox, 479; Colonial Secretary, 482; Iraqi monarchy issue, 482–3, 488, 507, 522; Middle East Department, 482, 486; Cairo Conference, 485, 506–7, 522; Kurdish policy, 507–10; departure from Colonial Office, 512
Clausewitz, 95, 124, 153
Clayton, Captain Gilbert: head of intelligence in Egypt, 56; relationship with Sykes, 264–5; on McMahon-Hussein correspondence, 268; Lawrence relationship, 274, 275, 276, 279; Bell's appointment, 279; on British administration, 446–7
Cleeve, Colonel, 86, 88
Clemenceau, Georges, 444
climate: flooding, 7, 221–2, 387–8; temperatures, 7, 67, 91, 197, 200, 298–9, 302, 337; humidity, 7; mud, 8, 30, 197; rain, 31, 200, 221, 237, 345–6, 349–50; sandstorms, 67, 337; gales, 221, 237; dust storms, 299
Climo, Lieutenant-Colonel, 111, 112, 113, 329
Cobbe, Lieutenant-General Alexander: I India Corps command, 341; battle for Kut, 353–4; Maude relationship, 357; Mushahida victory, 389; Istabulat attack, 394; advance to Tikrit, 399; pursuit of Turks, 434
Coles, Bombardier George: on attack on Turks, 347; on bridge building, 350, 365; bridge crossing, 352; on naval success, 356; on hunger, 361, 362; on casualties, 363, 365; arrival at Baghdad, 367, 368
Colonial Office, 482, 487–8, 493, 509, 512

Comet (gunboat), 104, 105, 129, 171–2
Committee of Union and Progress, 26
Congreve, General, 484
Coningham, General, 471
Constantinople, 3, 11, 16, 76, 81
Cooke, Lieutenant Fothergill, 111, 113
Cowley, Charles, 65, 246, 247
Cowper, Major-General Maitland, 194, 289, 331–2
Cox, Lady, 38–9, 485
Cox, Sir Percy: character and career, 38–9; British political representative in Gulf, 4, 38, 303; on Bahrain, 4; at Bushire, 13, 38; on territorial waters, 16; on Sheikh of Mohammerah, 19; Baghdad policy, 30, 38, 39, 56, 329; Basra proclamation, 36; advice on British occupation, 36–7; on Basra trade, 41; Ajaimi relationship, 42, 56; bribery, 44, 250; relationship with military commanders, 48; Nuri relationship, 57–8; view of Iraqi state, 58–9; Qurna surrender, 63; on Qurna position, 67; opinion of Barrett, 72; opinion of Nixon, 72, 73; Amara strategy, 74; at Suk-es-Shuyukh, 111; Kut position, 133; on Arab attitudes, 139, 276; on Kut position, 174, 181–2, 246; Lawrence relationship, 250, 273–5; Bell relationship, 272, 273, 280, 380, 469; Arab Bureau, 279; flight to Basra, 294; treaty negotiations, 370–3; on Arab tribes, 376–7; High Commissioner role, 378–80, 443, 478, 479, 488–9, 508; British administration, 379, 383; resignation threat, 380; Civil Commissioner, 381–2; Shia leaders, 390, 415; Eastern Committee briefing, 405–6, 436; Teheran transfer, 436–7; Iraq role, 442, 444,

Index

Hanna, 202, 204, 208–12, 213, 225, 234–6

Haras al-Istiqlal, 466

Hardinge, Lord, Viceroy of India: career, 21–2, 336; Mesopotamian strategy, 12, 22, 74, 109; Mesopotamian administration issue, 37, 61, 82, 268; relationship with Cox, 37, 39; Basra visit, 66, 67, 68, 72; on Indian forces, 70–1, 73; Baghdad policy, 82; Amara strategy, 93, 100–1; Nasiriyeh strategy, 107, 117–18; military relations, 122, 144; Baghdad policy, 133, 137, 141–2, 179; supply system concerns, 324; medical services concerns, 325; Arab policy, 266, 268; successor, 271, 288, 335; relationship with Bell, 272; Mesopotamia inquiry, 328, 333–5; resignation question, 336; Maude's proclamation, 374

Harrison, Ralph, 351

Hathaway, Surgeon-General, 155, 327

Hawker, Brigadier-General C. J., 379

Hay, Major William, 493, 498, 503–4, 506

health: endemic diseases in Mesopotamia, 7; sickness at Amara, 118–19; collapse while marching, 147; sickness at Basra, 198; effects of heat and insects, 298–300, 302, 337; effects of poor diet, 300; 'lead swingers', 301; waterborne sickness, 302; Turkish treatment of British prisoners, 311–12, 315; condition of feet, 361; see also medical services

Heawood, Major G. L., 169, 170, 213, 214, 221–2

Hejaz, 49, 266, 274, 370, 372, 489

Hejaz Army, 489

Herbert, Aubrey, 250, 252–3, 275, 279

Hewett, Sir John, 437–8

Hilla, 470, 475, 477

Hindu troops, 244

Hirtzel, Sir Arthur: background, 78; Gulf policy, 11, 19; oil pipeline concerns, 22; Baghdad policy, 39, 80; advice on future of Mesopotamia, 78–81, 271, 369; on Arab policy, 261, 268–9, 372, 374, 450; on Arab Bureau, 265; on Hussein's territorial demands, 266; Mesopotamia inquiry, 328; relationship with Bell, 380, 382, 406, 442, 505; Mesopotamia administration policy, 403, 404, 405, 406, 445–6, 352; on Iraq constitution, 440; on Iraqi officers, 449; on appointment of Arabs, 451; on costs of Mesopotamian policy, 453, 459; refuses Middle East Department, 482; view of Faisal, 482; Kurdish policy, 505

Hogarth, D. G., 265, 267, 271, 370, 479, 480

Hoghton, General, 127, 128, 157, 158–9, 161, 243

Hormuz, Strait of, 13

horses: artillery, 4, 214; cavalry, 4, 86, 353, 354–5; watering, 86, 353, 354, 355; stampeding, 210; slaughtered at Kut, 214; eaten, 214, 215, 243–4; wagon transport of wounded, 228; Cossack, 302, 393

Horsley, Sir Victor, 299

hospitals: Basra base, 64; Ahwaz officers', 94; boat, 146, 201; battle of Kut, 146; Kut, 163, 187, 222; ships, 164, 205, 326; milk supply, 290; bombed, 314; British prisoners in, 310, 312, 315, 318–19, 321, 322; inquiry, 325, 326; base, 337, 392; Baghdad Civil Hospital, 410

House, Colonel, 404

Huddlestone, Captain, 194

Hussein, grandson of the Prophet, 54, 412

Hussein, Sharif of Mecca: role and status, 80, 265, 370, 406; rebellion question, 265–6; territorial

settlement (1925), 517–18
Mosul (river steamer), 104
Moth (gunboat), 356
Mousley, Edward: on Townshend,
169; Ctesiphon retreat, 170; horse,
170, 214; Kut siege, 214, 232,
243; experiences as prisoner, 304,
305–6, 317–20, 322
Mubarak, Sheikh of Kuwait, xvi, 4,
14, 19, 484
Mudros Armistice, 434, 445, 453
Muhammad Abdul Hassan loop,
345, 346
Muhammad Ali, governor of Egypt,
11
Mujahidin, 43, 84, 91
mules, 4, 123, 129, 147, 170, 361
Multan, SS, 74
Muntafik: resistance, 42, 52;
leadership, 42, 51, 286, 408;
territory, 51; religion, 55;
recruitment of Muntafik Horse,
448; weapons, 463–4; uprising
(1920), 475; anarchic traditions,
475, 486
Mushahida, 389, 395
Muslim insurrection ('March Days'),
425, 425
Muslim troops in British Empire
forces, 214, 244, 297–8, 313
Mustafa Kemal, 460, 510–11
mutinies, 297–8
Mutiny, Great (1857–59), 23, 24,
111, 297
Muzaffri (stern-wheeler), 110
Muzairaa, 61

Najaf: Shia holy city, 54, 412;
pilgrimage to, 54; Shia clerics, 42,
412; autonomy, 389, 412–13; calls
to jihad, 42, 55; revolts against
Turks, 91, 276; Bell's journey, 273;
view of British control, 383, 412–
13, 416–17, 442, 465; resistance,
413–14; punishment for resistance,
414, 415–16; military occupation,
416; death sentences, 416; centre

of resistance, 465–6; Provisional
Revolutionary Government, 472
Najd, 370, 443; Amir of, *see* Ibn
Saud
Naji Suwaidi, 450–1
Nalder, Colonel, 503–4
Napoleon: sayings, 8, 145, 166, 216,
473; tactics, 96, 104, 124
Nasiriyeh: British strategy, 74, 107,
117–18, 178; advance to, 107,
109–10, 116; capture, 116–17;
Nixon's reinforcements, 192–3;
British administration, 283–7, 408,
460; railway, 292–3; air travel,
294; unrest, 470–1
Nelson, Major J. W., 230–1
Nicholas, Grand Duke, 275
Nicolson, Sir Arthur, 133, 266
Nisibin, 318, 320, 381, 443
Nixon, Sir John: personality,
121–2, 178, 179, 387; career,
73; reputation, 73, 122; on
autonomous Iraq, 59; Mesopotamia
command, 72–4, 92; orders to, 82,
92, 93; Shaiba battle, 84–5, 88;
Karun operations, 93–4; Amara
offensive, 96–7, 99–100, 103; on
Basra *vilayet* boundaries, 107;
Nasiriyeh advance, 107; Nasiriyeh
capture, 116–17; message from
King, 117; health, 119; offensive
commitment, 120; forces, 121,
138, 179, 192; advance on Kut,
120–2, 128; strategy after Kut, 133,
134–5; Baghdad advance issue,
135–8, 140–2, 179, 281; Ottoman
forces, 140, 155; river transport,
145, 195–6; railway, 292–3;
relationship with Townshend,
148–51, 155; advance on Baghdad,
150–1, 155; bridging train issues, 154;
view of troops' fitness, 154–5;
Ctesiphon battle, 157–61, 178;
Ctesiphon retreat, 165–6; HQ ship,
167; Kut position, 173, 177–8;
Braddon's account, 176; Kut relief
efforts, 180, 192–3, 199, 204; port

7